SO-BJJ-133

Issues for Debate in American Public Policy

EIGHTH EDITION

CQ PRESS

A Division of Congressional Quarterly Inc. Washington, D.C.

SELECTIONS FROM **CQ RESEARCHER**

CQ Press
1255 22nd Street, NW, Suite 400
Washington, DC 20037

Phone: 202-729-1900; toll-free, 1-866-4CQ-PRESS (1-866-427-7737)

Web: www.cqpress.com

Cover design: Kimberly Glyder
Cover photo: ©Istockphoto.com/Nancy Louie

♾ The paper used in this publication exceeds the requirements of the American National Standard for Information Sciences—Permanence of Paper for Printed Library Materials, ANSI Z39.48-1992.

Printed and bound in the United States of America

11 10 09 08 07   1 2 3 4 5

A CQ Press College Division Publication

Director	Brenda Carter
Acquisitions editor	Charisse Kiino
Marketing manager	Christopher O'Brien
Production editor	Belinda Josey
Composition	Olu Davis
Managing editor	Stephen Pazdan
Electronic production manager	Paul Pressau
Print and design manager	Margot Ziperman
Sales manager	Christopher Campbell

ISSN: 1543-3889
ISBN: 978-0-87289-464-8

Contents

Annotated Contents

The 16 *CQ Researcher* reports reprinted in this book have been reproduced essentially as they appeared when first published. In the few cases in which important new developments have since occurred, updates are provided in the overviews highlighting the principal issues examined.

EDUCATION

No Child Left Behind

More than five years have passed since President Bush signed the No Child Left Behind Act (NCLB). The controversial legislation mandates "highly qualified" teachers in every classroom and holds schools that accept federal funds accountable for raising the achievement of all students, most notably those with disabilities, those from low-income families, racial and ethnic minorities and those with limited English proficiency. Supporters call the law an evolutionary change in education policy—critics call it a revolutionary federal incursion into the historic domain of local districts and declare that it makes too many unfunded demands. Eight school districts and the nation's largest teachers' union sued the Department of Education over the law's funding provisions, and legislators in several states have introduced bills seeking exemptions from the law. Supporters, meanwhile, worry that No Child Left Behind is not being enforced stringently enough and is in danger of being diluted as Congress contemplates its renewal.

Fixing Urban Schools

African-American and Hispanic students, especially those in urban schools, lag far behind white students, who mostly attend middle-class suburban schools. Critics argue that when Congress reauthorizes the 2002 No Child Left Behind Act (NCLB), the legislative body must retarget the act to help urban schools tackle tough problems, such as encouraging the best teachers to enter and remain in high-poverty schools, rather than focusing on tests and sanctions. Some advocates propose busing students across district lines to create more socioeconomically diverse student bodies. But conservative analysts argue that busing wastes students' time and that permitting charter schools to compete with public schools will drive improvement of education for all students. Meanwhile, liberal analysts point out that successful charter programs are too costly for most schools to emulate, and that no one has yet figured out how to spread success beyond a handful of schools, public or private.

HEALTH CARE

Universal Coverage

Some 45 million Americans lacked health insurance in 2005—a number that has been climbing for two decades. Every month, about 2 million Americans become uninsured, at least temporarily, as lower-paying service jobs with minimal benefits replace union-dominated manufacturing jobs with health benefits—undercutting the nation's employer-based coverage system. Health costs—rising faster than wages or inflation—also push employers to drop coverage. Past legislative proposals for universal coverage relied heavily on government management, drawing fatal opposition from physicians and insurance companies. But now consensus may be forming around proposals that require most Americans to buy private insurance with public assistance. Republican governors in California and Massachusetts back such plans, as does former U.S. senator John Edwards, the first presidential hopeful to announce what's expected to be a slew of universal-coverage proposals in the coming 2008 election.

Rising Health Costs

Medical costs have more than doubled over the past decade, and health insurance premiums have risen nearly five times faster than wages. Americans are spending far more on health care than residents of any other industrialized country while receiving lower-quality care overall. Meanwhile, big U.S. businesses that provide health coverage to workers complain that high costs are crippling their ability to compete with companies abroad whose workers get government-subsidized care. The Bush administration is encouraging consumers to switch to consumer-directed health plans, the high copayments of which would force consumers to shop for more cost-effective care. But critics argue that individuals can do little to control costs. They argue that such plans would primarily benefit the wealthy and that society must make hard choices about which care should be paid for by public and private dollars.

SOCIAL POLICY

Stem Cell Research

President George W. Bush used his veto power for the first time on July 19, 2006, stopping a bill that would have increased federal funding for research on embryonic stem cells (ESCs). Such cells might provide cures for diseases ranging from Alzheimer's to diabetes as they are thought to have more disease-treating potential than similar cells found in adults. Their use is controversial, however, because harvesting them destroys a human embryo. The federal government supports research on several ESC cultures derived prior to 2001 from embryos created during in vitro fertilization (IVF) but not used. But the government won't pay to expand the research to other cell lines, which many scientists urge. Bush and other conservatives say morality forbids destroying additional embryos, regardless of the cells' treatment-producing potential. But ESC-research supporters argue the cells' life-saving potential outweighs qualms over destruction of IVF embryos, most of which eventually will be discarded.

Gun Violence

The shooting rampage at Virginia Tech on April 16, 2007, has raised new questions about safety on college campuses and renewed the nation's perennial debate on gun control. Virginia Tech officials face questions about whether the 32 deaths could have been prevented or limited by more effective police action at the time or by more proactive steps to deal with shooter Seung-Hui Cho's history of mental instability. Nationally, the incident has focused attention on how to reduce gun violence, which annually claims around 30,000 lives—82 lives each day, far more than twice the Virginia Tech toll. A bill to strengthen the federal background-check system for gun purchasers is gaining support on Capitol Hill, even from the powerful National Rifle Association. But some gun advocates want states to ease weapons laws. They argue that allowing more people to carry weapons will deter gun crimes and enable potential victims to protect themselves.

ENVIRONMENT

The New Environmentalism

Concern about the environment is intensifying, but new efforts to reduce pollution and save energy differ from past environmental movements. Unable to get much satisfaction from the Republican-dominated federal government, environmental activists have set their sights on businesses—trying to influence corporate behavior and even forming partnerships with companies to confront environmental challenges. A growing number of businesses—including Wal-Mart, the world's biggest retailer—are concluding that saving the environment is good for the bottom line. But some conservative critics charge that such actions actually dilute companies' primary purpose—to increase shareholder value. Meanwhile, in the absence of federal action, state and local governments are instituting policies aimed at weaning industry from fossil fuels. And some environmentalists are even rethinking nuclear power.

Energy Efficiency

In 2006 President Bush responded to escalating energy prices by suspending government purchases for the Strategic Petroleum Reserve, relaxing environmental rules for gasoline formulation and launching investigations into possible price manipulation. Soon after, Congress began debating a flurry of energy proposals, including allowing exploration in the Arctic National Wildlife Refuge, streamlining refinery regulations, expanding tax credits for hybrid vehicles and reforming fuel-economy standards for cars. With Congress polarized, the outcomes are unclear, but voter unrest over high gasoline prices might prompt the passage of some bipartisan legislation. Environmental groups are hoping for proposals focusing on promoting energy efficiency. Since the Arab oil embargo of 1973, fuel-economy standards and other energy-efficiency measures have produced energy savings throughout the economy. But market barriers prevent the adoption of many measures, and there is disagreement about how far government should go to promote them.

National Parks Under Pressure

The national parks are threatened by pollution, invasive species, climate change and encroaching development. Moreover, some observers warn that budget constraints are making the national parks and other units in the National Park Service not only more dangerous to visitors but also less satisfying and less educational. To compensate for funding shortfalls, parks are raising entrance fees, soliciting corporate donations and cutting ranger programs. Underlying the challenges is a fundamental struggle between recreational users—such as snowmobilers and jet skiers—and traditionalists who say preserving the parks' tranquility and fragile resources should always remain the paramount mission. Meanwhile, spokepersons for "gateway communities" say park officials should take the economic survival of these communities into account as they try to keep the parks meaningful for 274 million visitors a year and preserve natural values for future generations.

CIVIL LIBERTIES, CIVIL RIGHTS AND JUSTICE

Privacy in Peril

The proliferation of massive Internet-accessible databases is making corporate and government electronic snooping possible on a scale unprecedented in U.S. history. In the past year and a half Americans have been buffeted by revelations that the government is conducting warrantless spying on citizens' phone calls, that corporate directors are hiring detectives who use false identities to access private phone records and that thousands of credit-card numbers held in commercial databases have been lost or stolen. Privacy advocates warn that growing access to huge amounts of personal data—from Social Security numbers to health information—is virtually eliminating the concept of personal privacy.

Death Penalty Controversies

Critics and opponents of the death penalty are warning that capital trials and sentencing hearings are so riddled with flaws that they risk resulting in the execution of innocent persons. Supporters of capital punishment discount the warnings, emphasizing that opponents cannot cite a single person in modern times who was executed and later proven to have been innocent. The debate over erroneous convictions has increased in recent years because DNA testing now allows inmates to prove their innocence years after their convictions. Momentum on the issue appears to be with opponents, with executions on hold in nearly a dozen states and abolition receiving serious consideration. But the federal government has stepped up its pursuit of capital convictions, and several states are looking to expand the types of crime punishable by death.

BUSINESS AND THE ECONOMY

Consumer Debt

Despite an economic recovery in its sixth year, more American households are in debt now than at any point in the past 15 years, particularly the middle class. In fact, in the past several years household debt has risen faster than family income and, on average, exceeds annual income for the first time since the Federal Reserve started surveying consumer finances in the early 1980s. The explosion in debt—fueled largely by mortgage lending on residential housing that rose in value and then leveled off or declined—has some economists worrying that the next economic recession will be devastating to families who already owe so much. Others complain that state and federal governments are not protecting consumers from abusive credit card and payday-lending practices. But proponents of the expansion in consumer credit say it has helped to democratize homeownership and fuel the current economic expansion.

Controlling the Internet

Governments and corporations are increasingly concerned about political and economic threats posed by a freewheeling, global Internet. Many experts warn that the "Net" may fragment into "walled gardens" that block users' freedom to communicate and innovate. In the United States, telephone and cable companies already have won the right to block competing Internet service providers like Earthlink from using their high-speed broadband lines. Now advocates for an open Internet worry that broadband providers will use their market power to slow or block access to controversial Web sites or competing businesses like Internet telephone. These activists want Congress to require companies to treat all Internet content the same. Abroad, more nations are expanding broadband access for economic reasons, even as they crack down on citizens who access controversial material or express dissenting opinions via the Net. In the face of such turmoil, civic groups worldwide are seeking new forms of governance to keep the Internet secure and uncensored.

HOMELAND SECURITY AND FOREIGN POLICY

Rethinking Foreign Policy

President Bush has instituted several fundamental changes in U.S. foreign policy, most notably opting for unilateral action instead of multilateral initiatives and espousing a doctrine of preventive or preemptive war to ward off potential threats. Many Americans applauded the fortified U.S. policies in the immediate aftermath of the Sept. 11, 2001, terrorist attacks and in the early days of the war in Iraq. With the war now in its fourth year, however, a growing number of foreign-policy experts are saying the Bush doctrines have hurt rather than helped to advance U.S. interests around the world. They want the United States to rely more on allies and multilateral institutions, discard the preventive war doctrine and be more realistic in promoting democracy abroad. Administration supporters, however, hope the president's strategy in Iraq ultimately will bring about a military and political success that will help vindicate his policies.

Illegal Immigration

More than 10 million illegal immigrants live in the United States, and 1,400 more arrive every day. Once concentrated in a few big states like Texas and California, they are rapidly moving into nontraditional areas such as the Midwest and South. Willing to work for low wages, the migrants are creating a backlash among some residents of these states, which have seen a nearly tenfold increase in illegal immigration since 1990. While illegal immigrants only make up about 5 percent of the U.S. workforce, critics of the nation's immigration policies say illegal immigrants take Americans' jobs, threaten national security and even change the nation's culture by refusing to assimilate. But advocates for immigrants say illegal migrants fill the jobs Americans refuse to take and generally boost the economy. Proposals for increased immigration controls and a guest-worker program have divided Congress over the past year, even as massive demonstrations in cities across the country have polarized the issue among the public.

Treatment of Detainees
The Supreme Court struck down the Bush administration's system for holding and trying detainees at the U.S. Naval base at Guantánamo Bay, Cuba. The administra-tion had maintained that the Geneva Conventions did not protect alleged terrorists captured in Afghanistan and on other battlefields in the five-year-old war on terror, and critics say that policy led to the use of abusive inter-rogation methods, such as "water-boarding" and sleep deprivation. The critics, including top military lawyers, successfully argued that the United States was violating the laws of warfare. They also opposed the military com-missions the administration has proposed for conducting detainee trials. President Bush said the war on terrorism required such commissions' streamlined procedures, which deny some rights guaranteed by the Conventions. The court's decision leaves Congress with two options: require detainees to be tried under the military's existing court-martial system or create a new, legal version of the administration's commissions.

Preface

C an the United States afford universal health coverage? Is more federal action needed to encourage energy efficiency? Should states impose moratoriums on executions? These questions—and many more—are at the heart of American public policy. How can instructors best engage students with these crucial issues? We feel that students need objective, yet provocative examinations of these issues to understand how they affect citizens today and will for years to come. This annual collection aims to promote in-depth discussion, facilitate further research and help readers formulate their own positions on crucial issues. Get your students talking both inside and outside the classroom about *Issues for Debate in American Public Policy*.

This eighth edition includes sixteen up-to-date reports by *CQ Researcher*, an award-winning weekly policy brief that brings complicated issues down to earth. Each report chronicles and analyzes executive, legislative and judicial activities at all levels of government. This collection is divided into seven diverse policy areas: education; health care; social policy; the environment; civil liberties, civil rights and justice; business and the economy; and homeland security and foreign policy—to cover a range of issues found in most American government and public policy courses.

CQ RESEARCHER

CQ Researcher was founded in 1923 as *Editorial Research Reports* and was sold primarily to newspapers as a research tool. The magazine was renamed and redesigned in 1991 as *CQ Researcher*. Today, students are its primary audience. While still used by hundreds of journalists and newspapers, many of which reprint portions of the reports, *Researcher*'s main subscribers are now high school, college and public libraries. In 2002, *Researcher* won the American Bar Association's coveted Silver Gavel Award for magazine excellence for a series of nine reports on civil liberties and other legal issues.

Researcher staff writers—all highly experienced journalists—sometimes compare the experience of writing a *Researcher* report to drafting a college term paper. Indeed, there are many similarities. Each report is as long as many term papers—about 11,000 words—and is written by one person without any significant outside help. One of the key differences is that writers interview leading experts, scholars and government officials for each issue.

Like students, staff writers begin the creative process by choosing a topic. Working with the *Researcher*'s editors, the writer identifies a controversial subject that has important public policy implications. After a topic is selected, the writer embarks on one to two weeks of intense research. Newspaper and magazine articles are clipped or downloaded, books are ordered and information is gathered from a wide variety of sources, including interest groups, universities and the government. Once a writer is well informed, he or she develops a detailed outline and begins the interview process. Each report requires a minimum of 10 to 15 interviews with academics, officials, lobbyists and people working in the field. Only after all interviews are completed does the writing begin.

CHAPTER FORMAT

Each issue of *CQ Researcher*, and therefore each selection in this book, is structured in the same way. Each begins with an overview, which briefly summarizes the areas that will be explored in greater detail in the rest of the chapter. The next section, "Issues," is the core of each chapter. It chronicles important and current debates on the topic under discussion and is structured around a number of key questions, such as "Can states do more to encourage energy efficiency?" and "Has No Child Left Behind helped urban students?" These questions are usually the subject of much debate among practitioners and scholars in the field. Hence, the answers presented are never conclusive but rather detail the range of opinion on the topic.

Next, the "Background" section provides a history of the issue being examined. This retrospective covers important legislative measures, executive actions and court decisions that illustrate how current policy has evolved. Then the "Current Situation" section examines contemporary policy issues, legislation under consideration and legal action being taken. Each selection concludes with an "Outlook" section, which addresses possible regulation, court rulings and initiatives from Capitol Hill and the White House over the next five to ten years.

Each report contains features that augment the main text: two to three sidebars that examine issues related to the topic at hand, a pro versus con debate between two experts, a chronology of key dates and events and an annotated bibliography detailing major sources used by the writer.

ACKNOWLEDGMENTS

We wish to thank many people for helping to make this collection a reality. Tom Colin, managing editor of *CQ Researcher*, gave us his enthusiastic support and cooperation as we developed this eighth edition. He and his talented staff of editors and writers have amassed a first-class library of *Researcher* reports, and we are fortunate to have access to that rich cache. We also thankfully acknowledge the advice and feedback from current readers and are gratified by their satisfaction with the book.

Some readers may be learning about *CQ Researcher* for the first time. We expect that many readers will want regular access to this excellent weekly research tool. For subscription information or for a no-obligation free trial of *Researcher*, please contact CQ Press at www.cqpress.com or toll-free at 1-866-4CQ-PRESS (1-866-427-7737).

We hope that you will be pleased by the eighth edition of *Issues for Debate in American Public Policy*. We welcome your feedback and suggestions for future editions. Please direct comments to Charisse Kiino, Chief Acquisitions Editor, College Division, CQ Press, 1255 22nd Street, N.W., Suite 400, Washington, D.C. 20037, or *ckiino@cqpress.com*.

—*The Editors of CQ Press*

Contributors

Thomas J. Colin, managing editor of *CQ Researcher*, has been a magazine and newspaper journalist for more than 30 years. Before joining Congressional Quarterly in 1991, he was a reporter and editor at the *Miami Herald* and *National Geographic* and editor in chief of *Historic Preservation*. He holds a bachelor's degree in English from the College of William and Mary and in journalism from the University of Missouri.

Tom Arrandale is a freelance writer in Livingston, Montana, reporting on environmental, natural resource and wildlife issues. He is a columnist for Congressional Quarterly's *Governing* magazine, has written for *Planning Magazine*, *High Country News* and *Yellowstone Journal* and authored *The Battle for Natural Resources* (CQ Press, 1983). He serves on the Livingston Historic Preservation Commission and Board of Adjustment and regularly visits Yellowstone National Park to hike, snowshoe and photograph wildlife. He graduated from Dartmouth College with a bachelor's degree in history and from the University of Missouri with a master's degree in journalism.

Marcia Clemmitt is a veteran social-policy reporter who joined *CQ Researcher* after serving as editor in chief of *Medicine and Health*, a Washington-based industry newsletter, and staff writer for *The Scientist.* She also has been a high school math and physics teacher. She holds a bachelor's degree in arts and sciences from St. Johns College, Annapolis, and a master's degree in English from Georgetown University.

Alan Greenblatt is a staff writer for Congressional Quarterly's *Governing* magazine, and previously covered elections and military and agricultural policy for *CQ Weekly*. A recipient of the National Press Club's Sandy Hume Memorial Award for political reporting, he holds a bachelor's degree from San Francisco State University and a master's degree in English literature from the University of Virginia.

Kenneth Jost, associate editor of *CQ Researcher*, graduated from Harvard College and Georgetown University Law Center, where he is an adjunct professor. He is the author of *The Supreme Court Yearbook* and writer and editor of *The Supreme Court A to Z* (both published by CQ Press). He was a member of the *CQ Researcher* team that won the 2002 American Bar Association Silver Gavel Award.

Peter Katel is a veteran journalist who previously served as Latin America bureau chief for *Time* magazine in Mexico City, and as a Miami-based correspondent for *Newsweek* and *The Miami Herald*'s *El Nuevo Herald*. He also worked as a reporter in New Mexico for 11 years and wrote for several nongovernmental organizations, including International Social Service and the World Bank. His honors include the Interamerican Press Association's Bartolome Mitre Award. He is a graduate of the University of New Mexico with a degree in university studies.

Barbara Mantel is a freelance writer in New York City whose work has appeared in *The New York Times*, *Journal of Child and Adolescent Pyschopharmacology* and *Mamm Magazine*. She is a former correspondent and senior producer for National Public Radio and has received such journalistic honors as the National Press Club's Best Consumer Journalism Award and Lincoln University's Unity Award. She holds a bachelor's degree in history and economics from the University of Virginia and a master's degree in economics from Northwestern University.

Patrick Marshall is the reviews editor of *Federal Computer Week* and a technology columnist for the *Seattle Times*; he is based in Bainbridge Island, Wash. He holds a bachelor's degree in anthropology from the University of California, Santa Cruz, and a master's in foreign affairs from the Fletcher School of Law and Diplomacy.

Tom Price is a Washington-based freelance journalist who writes regularly for *CQ Researcher*. Previously he was a correspondent in the Cox Newspapers Washington Bureau and chief politics writer for the *Dayton Daily News* and *The Journal Herald*. His most recent book, written with former member of Congress and former ambassador Tony Hall, is *Changing the Face of Hunger: One Man's Story of How Liberals, Conservatives, Democrats, Republicans, and People of Faith Are Joining Forces to Help the Hungry, the Poor, and the Oppressed* (2006). He also is the author of two Washington guidebooks, *Washington, D.C. for Dummies* (2003), and the *Irreverent Guide to Washington, D.C* (2005). His work has appeared in *The New York Times*, *Time*, *Rolling Stone* and other periodicals. He earned a bachelor of science in journalism at Ohio University.

1

No Child Left Behind

Barbara Mantel and Alan Greenblatt

President Bush visits with students in St. Louis, Mo., on Jan. 5, 2004, the second anniversary of the No Child Left Behind Act. Bush has called the sweeping overhaul of federal education policy the start of "a new era, a new time in public education." But today the bipartisan legislation is under heavy criticism from Republicans and Democrats alike. Besides seeking exemptions from parts of the law, legislators are pressing Congress for more money to implement the act.

From *CQ Researcher,*
May 27, 2005. (Updated May 21, 2007)

P olitics indeed makes for strange bedfellows: There was President Bush standing on a Boston stage flanked by four jubilant legislators, two Republicans and two Democrats, including liberal lion Sen. Edward M. Kennedy of Massachusetts. The occasion was the signing on Jan. 8, 2002, of the No Child Left Behind Act — a sweeping, bipartisan overhaul of federal education policy.

Cheering crowds greeted Bush and the four lawmakers that day as they touted the new law on a whirlwind, 12-hour tour of three states, with the president calling the legislation the start of "a new era, a new time in public education."

Kennedy, who played a key role in negotiating the bill's passage, told Bush: "What a difference it has made this year with your leadership." [1]

The law is actually the most recent reauthorization of the Elementary and Secondary Education Act (ESEA), which since 1965 has tried to raise the academic performance of all students.

"This legislation holds out great promise for education," said G. Gage Kingsbury, director of research at the Northwest Evaluation Association, in Lake Oswego, Ore. "But it also has strong requirements and includes a host of provisions that have never been tried on this scale before." [2]

No Child Left Behind (NCLB) increases the reach of the federal government into the management of local schools and raises the stakes for schools, districts and states. It increases funding for schools serving poor students, mandates "highly qualified" teachers in every classroom and holds schools that accept federal funds accountable for raising the achievement of all students. Schools that don't meet state benchmarks two years in a row are labeled "in need of improvement" and suffer sanctions.

Few States Make the Grade on Teacher Quality

Only three states — Connecticut, Louisiana and South Carolina — received a grade of A for their efforts to improve teacher quality, according to a 2005 assessment by *Education Week*. In every state except New Mexico, more than 50 percent of secondary teachers majored in the core academic subject they teach. But only eight states had more than 75 percent of secondary school teachers who majored in their core subject.

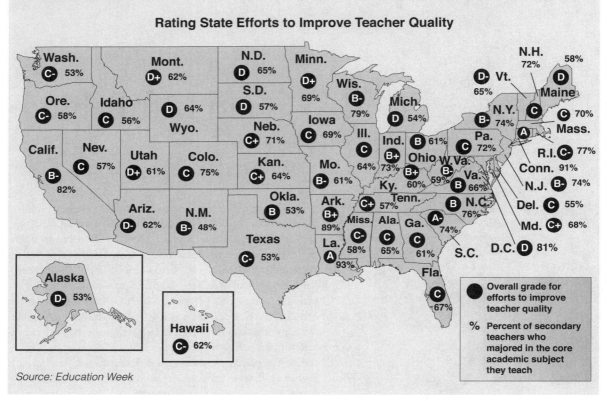

Rating State Efforts to Improve Teacher Quality

Source: *Education Week*

Most significantly, NCLB sets a deadline: By 2014 all students must be grade-level proficient in reading and math — as evidenced by their scores on annual tests in grades 3-8, and once in high school.

But more than five years after its passage, the bipartisan accord that produced the bill appears badly frayed. Kennedy now says No Child Left Behind "has been underfunded, mismanaged and poorly implemented and is becoming the most spectacular broken promise of this Republican administration and Congress. "America's children deserve better." [3]

In the states, politicians from both parties are equally unhappy, including GOP legislators from some "red states" that overwhelmingly supported Bush in last year's presidential election. "I wish they'd take the stinking money and go back to Washington," said state Rep. Steven Mascaro, R-Utah. [4]

"We have to fight back," Gov. John Baldacci, D-Maine, said. "We have to tell them we're not going to take it any more." [5]

It hasn't been just talk. In 2005, Utah's Republican governor signed legislation giving precedence to the state's education policies when they conflict with NCLB, and more than 30 states in all have introduced bills seeking release from some of the law's requirements.

Besides wanting exemptions from parts of the law, legislators are pressing Congress for more money to implement the act. Congress had appropriated $27 billion less

The ABCs of NCLB

Here are the basic provisions of the No Child Left Behind Act, which spells out its standards and requirements in more than 1,000 pages of regulations:

Standards and Testing — As in the previous version of the law, each state must adopt challenging standards for what its students should know and be able to do. Academic standards must contain coherent and rigorous content and encourage the teaching of advanced skills. States must also develop tests aligned to the standards and establish cutoff scores that classify student achievement as basic, proficient or advanced. What has changed is the amount of testing states must do. States must test children annually in grades 3-8 and once in high school. Previously, schoolchildren had to be tested only four times in grades K-12.

Public Reporting — For the first time, states must publicly report their test results, with student scores broken down into four subgroups: economically disadvantaged students; major racial and ethnic groups; students with disabilities and students with limited English proficiency. States must report each school's progress in raising student performance and the difference in teacher qualifications in high-poverty versus low-poverty schools.

Accountability — All students must reach proficiency in reading and math by 2014. States must establish annual benchmarks for their schools, with special emphasis on closing achievement gaps between different groups of students. Since 1994 states had been required to make "adequate yearly progress" (AYP) in raising achievement, but there was no firm timetable or deadline for students reaching proficiency. Now if a school does not make AYP, the state and district must develop a two-year plan to help the school improve.

Sanctions — If a school receiving Title I funds — designed to improve the performance of low-income students — does not make AYP in raising student performance for two years in a row, the state must designate it a school "in need of improvement."[1] Most states are applying this rule to all schools in a Title I district, even those that do not take Title I money. Students in these schools must be given the option of transferring out, and if a school fails to achieve its AYP for three consecutive years, it must pay for tutoring, after-school programs and summer school for those low-income students who remain. After four years, the state must restructure the school.

Teachers — For the first time, teachers must be "highly qualified," meaning they have a college degree and are licensed or certified by the state. Newly hired middle-school teachers must have a major or pass a test demonstrating their knowledge in the subjects they teach. Veteran teachers can do the same or demonstrate their competency through an alternative system developed by each state.

[1] About 55 percent of the schools in the nation's 100 largest districts were eligible for Title I funds in the 2001/2002 school year; http://nces.ed.gov/pubs2003/100_largest/table_05_1.asp.

than it authorized for the law's implementation by mid-2005. The following year, President Bush requested just $13.3 billion in funding for Title I programs — the heart of the law — out of $22.8 billion that had been authorized.

But the act's supporters say enough money is being provided, pointing out that federal funding for public education has increased by more than 30 percent since NCLB was enacted. "The education reforms contained in the No Child Left Behind Act are coupled with historic increases in K-12 funding," according to the Web site of Sen. Judd Gregg, R-N.H., who made the whirlwind trip with Bush and Kennedy three years ago.[6]

Nevertheless, in 2005 the National Education Association, the nation's largest teachers' union, sued the Department of Education on the grounds that the act is not properly funded. In addition, Connecticut also sued, estimating that NCLB will cost the state an extra $41.6 million dollars in the next few years. The atmosphere grew so disagreeable at times that Secretary of Education Margaret Spellings angrily called Connecticut officials "un-American."

Part of the states' resentment stems from the fact that Congress provides only 8 percent of total funding for public education — $536 billion in the 2004-05 school year — but since the 1960s has passed laws giving the Department of Education increasing powers over the nation's 96,000 schools.[7] The NCLB is the most far-reaching yet.

Supporters of the act say it represents an evolutionary change, while critics say it is a revolutionary incursion of the federal government into the historic domain of the states.

"I don't know any educator or parent who doesn't think our schools should be accountable," said Republican state Rep. Margaret Dayton. "The question is: To whom should they be accountable? Under No Child Left Behind our local schools are accountable to Washington, D.C., and here in Utah, we think our schools should be accountable to the parents and the communities where they are." [8]

Even supporters acknowledge that NCLB's provisions have been overwhelming for states without the administrative staff to implement the law.

In 2004, No Child Left Behind became "a significant force affecting the operations and decisions of states, school districts and schools," according to the Center on Education Policy, an independent advocate for public education. [9] For example, the law has compelled states and school districts to step up efforts to test students in more grades and put "highly qualified" teachers in every classroom. In addition, for the first time entire school districts have been labeled "in need of improvement."

However, as the law's requirements take hold, the debate about its fairness and efficacy has been escalating. Besides the debate over funding, critics argue that the law is too rigid and that too many schools — even good schools — are being told they need to improve. This has sparked widespread opposition to President's Bush's proposal to extend the law's annual testing requirements to high school students.

On the other side of the debate, many of NCLB's staunchest defenders worry that the Department of Education has become too flexible in implementing the law, citing a recent relaxation of requirements for testing disabled students and department approval of what some see as lax state plans to ensure that veteran teachers are "highly qualified."

And voices from all sides call for more guidance and technical support to localities from the Department of Education.

As the public discussion grows louder, leading up to the law's reauthorization fight in 2007, coalitions have begun to form. The American Association of School Administrators, the Children's Defense Fund, the Learning Disabilities Association of America, the National Education Association and several other groups joined together in 2004 to call for significant revisions in the law. Proponents — including the Citizens' Commission on Civil Rights, the National Alliance of Black School Educators, Just for Kids, the Education Trust and the Business Roundtable — formed their own coalition, called the Achievement Alliance, to vigorously defend the law.

As Congress begins its deliberations, the law is under attack from multiple directions. A group of 57 Republican legislators — including some of the bill's original cosponsors — introduced legislation early in 2007 that would allow any state that objects to the law's standards and testing requirements to excuse itself but continue to receive federal education aid. To answer their proposal, Kennedy several days later published an op-ed in *The Washington Post* headlined "No Retreat on School Reform." [10]

Bush, Kennedy and George Miller, the House education chairman, all vow to defend the law's main tenets during debate over its extension. But the widespread rancor NCLB has caused may mean its renewal will be delayed until the seating of the next Congress — and the election of a new president.

In the meantime, here are some of the questions parents, educators, children's advocates, lawmakers and researchers are asking:

Has No Child Left Behind raised student achievement?

The goal of the NCLB law is to ensure that by 2014 all children are at grade-level proficiency in reading and math. The law requires states to measure student achievement by testing children in grades 3-8 every year, and once in high school.

But each state determines its own academic standards, the courses taught, the standardized tests used and the cut-off scores that define a student as proficient. Thus, the rigor varies between the states, making it impossible to compare one state to another. Colorado may have reported 87 percent of its fourth-graders proficient in reading in 2003 and Massachusetts 56 percent, but no one knows what that says about the relative achievement of their students. [11]

It is possible, however, to look at student achievement within a state and ask, for example, how this year's fourth-graders compare to last year's.

With a growing number of states administering annual tests, researchers have conducted some preliminary studies. They all show that student achievement, for the most part, is improving.

Thousands of Schools Missed Progress Targets

Eleven thousand public schools — or nearly 12 percent of the nation's 96,000 public schools — failed in 2004 for the second year in a row to meet "adequate yearly progress" (AYP) targets set by the No Child Left Behind law. Such schools are labeled "in need of improvement" and must offer all students the right to transfer; after missing AYP for three consecutive years, they must offer low-income students supplemental services, like after-school tutoring. After four years, the state must restructure the school.

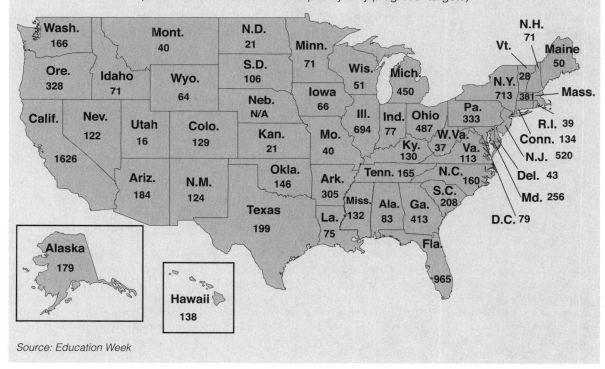

Number of Public Schools Needing Improvement
(based on failure to meet "adequate yearly progress" targets)

Source: Education Week

The Center on Education Policy surveyed states and a sampling of school districts and reported that 73 percent of states and 72 percent of districts said student achievement is improving. In addition, states and districts were more likely to say that achievement gaps between white and black students, white and Hispanic students, and English-language learners and other students were narrowing rather than widening or staying the same. [12]

Similarly, the Council of the Great City Schools, a coalition of 65 of the nation's largest urban school systems, reported that while math and reading scores in urban schools remain lower than national averages, they are rising and achievement gaps are narrowing. [13]

The Education Trust, a nonprofit advocate of school reform, also analyzed proficiency rates since No Child Left Behind took effect. It found that in most states it studied, achievement scores of elementary school students had risen, and achievement gaps had narrowed. But when the Trust looked at middle and high schools, the results were more mixed. While the majority of states in the study reported an increase in the percentage of proficient students, there was much less success in narrowing achievement gaps. [14]

Is Testing Crowding Out Art and Recess?

Testing required by the No Child Left Behind Act is taking a toll on education, says George Wood, an Ohio high school principal and director of The Forum for Education and Democracy. "School people are no fools," Wood wrote in the 2004 book *Many Children Left Behind*. "Tell them what they will be measured on, and they will try to measure up."

"Test preparation crowds out much else that parents have taken for granted in their schools," Wood said. Recess for elementary school students, nap time for kindergarteners and music and art for middle school students are some of the things being eliminated from the school day, he contends, along with reductions in class time for social studies and creative writing.

Diane Rentner, director of national programs at the Center on Education Policy, says the cutbacks haven't been too bad so far. "It's not huge, it's not a revolution yet," she says. In a March 2005 survey of school districts, the center found "a slight movement toward cutting down on other subjects to focus on reading and math," Rentner says.

More than two-thirds of districts reported that instructional time on subjects other than math and reading had been reduced minimally or not at all. However, 27 percent of the districts reported that social studies class time had been reduced somewhat or to a great extent, and close to 25 percent said instruction time in science, art and music had been reduced.

While the center's findings don't detail a revolutionary shift in class time, Rentner still calls the trend worrisome and expects that as state proficiency benchmarks rise, there may be additional pressure on schools to focus more time on reading and math. "It would be sad if there were no arts in the schools, and students didn't learn civic education," she says.

Rentner also points out another potentially troubling survey result: The poorer the school district, the more likely it was to require schools to allot a specific amount of time to math and reading. "You could jump to the next conclusion that low-income kids are receiving a less rich curriculum," Rentner says. While that might be necessary in the short term to bring kids closer to proficiency in math and reading, Rentner hopes that it doesn't have to continue.

It is this impact on low-income and minority schools that most concerns Wood. An opponent of NCLB, Wood calls for a moratorium on high-stakes testing until more research shows it to have some link to student success after leaving high school.

But Daria Hall, a policy analyst at the Education Trust, which generally supports the goals and methods of No Child Left Behind while criticizing the government's implementation of the law, says that's the wrong response. "We don't deny that focusing so much on math and reading means that other subjects might not receive the attention they deserve," says Hall. But that doesn't have to happen, she says, citing schools, many in poor districts, that have integrated math and reading instruction into their other subjects.

"So, for example, there is no need to give short shrift to social studies," she claims. "We can teach the content of social studies while at the same time covering state standards on reading." The same can be done, she says, with math and science.

But it's not something that one teacher or even one school can do alone, Hall adds. "There needs to be research from the U.S. Department of Education on how to effectively integrate standards across the curriculum," she says. "It needs to really be a systemic effort."

Delaware is a case in point. The state has made some of the largest strides in raising achievement and narrowing gaps among elementary students. For instance, the gap in Delaware between the percentage of reading-proficient white and Hispanic fifth-graders narrowed from 31 points in 2001 to less than five points in 2004, and for African-American students, the gap narrowed from 22 points to 16. [15] A 2006 study by the Education Trust found that the gap between whites and Hispanics had also narrowed. But in middle schools, achievement gaps have actually widened.

"It is a little harder to get a reform groundswell in middle schools and high schools," says Delaware's Secretary of Education Valerie Woodruff. "In math, for example, we don't have enough well-qualified teachers at the middle school level."

The fundamental question is how much of the documented improvement is a result of No Child Left Behind. Daria Hall, a policy analyst at the Education Trust, says it is a significant amount. Educators "are using the standards to develop a challenging curriculum for all students," she says. "They are using assessment results to inform their instruction in the classroom." NCLB, Hall says, gives administrators leverage to make needed changes.

Diane Stark Rentner, director of national programs at the Center on Education Policy, is hearing something different. The center did not specifically ask state and district officials if they thought the law was responsible for achievement gains. But Rentner says district officials later said they "were almost offended that No Child Left Behind would be viewed as this great catalyst of change because they felt like they had been working for years to improve student achievement."

"Our math curriculum has been completely reviewed from K-12 and in the majority of cases exceeds state standards," says Margo Sorrick, an assistant superintendent in Wheaton, Ill. For instance, the district now requires three years rather two years of math for high school graduation. "These changes have nothing to do with No Child Left Behind," says Sorrick.

But the law does shine a new light on those reforms. Now that states must report their progress in raising student achievement, the press routinely covers the release of so-called state report cards. Stiffening graduation requirements, revising the curriculum and replacing staff at the worst schools have taken on more urgency, Rentner says. "We jokingly say the news media have become the enforcer of the law," she adds.

But trying to figure out the law's exact impact is still all but impossible. Besides the difficulty of teasing out the roles of pre- and post-NCLB reforms, there are gaps in the data. Most states started testing students only about a decade ago, and many changed their tests, making before-and-after comparisons unreliable.

Several experts also warn that initial gains in achievement scores may be deceptive. Brian Stecher, a senior social scientist at the RAND Corporation, a nonprofit research organization, says that on new, high-stakes tests teachers often feel pressure to coach students in test-taking skills and to teach the material emphasized on the test. "That can allow you to get initially a relatively big gain in scores," Stecher says, "and then the increase tapers off."

That's of particular concern to states because the pace of recent improvement is not fast enough to ensure 100 percent student proficiency by 2014. "Progress needs to be accelerated," Hall says bluntly.

Are too many schools being labeled "in need of improvement?"

Holding states accountable for student achievement is central to No Child Left Behind. The law gives states a firm goal and a firm deadline, and to reach it each state must come up with annual benchmarks. In Wisconsin, for instance, 67.5 percent of a school's students had to be proficient in reading in 2005, 87 percent in 2011 and finally 100 percent in 2014. [16]

But it's not enough for a school to look at its students as a single, undifferentiated block. NCLB requires schools to divide students into subgroups — ethnic, racial, low-income, disabled and English-language learner — and each must meet the proficiency benchmarks as well.

Schools also must test at least 95 percent of students in a subgroup, meet state-determined attendance requirements and improve high school graduation rates.

Schools that meet all of these targets are deemed to have made "adequate yearly progress" (AYP). But if a school misses just one target it doesn't make AYP, and the district and state must create a two-year intervention plan. Options include reducing class size, providing extra help for disadvantaged students and increasing professional development for teachers. Local and state officials decide on the details, and the federal government provides extra funding.

Sanctions prescribed by the law, however, kick in when a school doesn't make AYP for two consecutive years. Such schools, if they take Title I funds, are labeled "in need of improvement" and must offer all students the right to transfer; after missing AYP for three consecutive years, they must offer low-income students supplemental services, like after-school tutoring. After four years, the state must restructure the school.

This system of accountability is among the most contentious elements of NCLB. While praising the overall goals of the law, the National Conference of State Legislatures called the system rigid and overly prescriptive. Too many schools, it said, are being labeled "in need of improvement," and the law, therefore, "spreads resources too thinly, over too many schools, and reduces the chances that schools that truly are in need can be helped." [17]

In 2004, 11,008 public schools — nearly 12 percent of the nation's total — were identified as needing improvement. [18] By 2006, about 1,750 schools nationwide had consistently failed to meet AYP and faced the law's ultimate sanctions, meaning they required dramatic overhauls. [19] "Essentially, all schools will fail to meet the unrealistic goal of 100 percent proficient or above," wrote testing expert Robert Linn, "and No Child Left Behind will have turned into No School Succeeding." [20]

But Kerri Briggs, acting Assistant Secretary for Elementary and Secondary Education, strongly disagrees. "We have identified schools that have beat expectations; there are several in many states," says Briggs. "We know it's possible."

Critics, however, say the accountability system has several flaws, such as not recognizing progress made by schools that start with large numbers of low-performing students. A school that significantly raises the percentage of students reading at proficiency, for example, would still not make AYP if that percentage remains below the state benchmark. Such schools "should be given credit," says Scott Young, a former senior policy specialist at the National Conference of State Legislatures.

But the law does provide a so-called safe harbor alternative for these schools: If a subgroup of students falls short of the benchmark, the school can still make AYP if the number below the proficiency level is decreased by 10 percent from the year before. But according to Linn, that's something even the best schools would have difficulty accomplishing. "Only a tiny fraction of schools meet AYP through the safe-harbor provision because it is so extreme," Linn wrote. [21]

After protests from both Republican and Democratic governors, Secretary Spellings announced in 2005 she would appoint a panel to consider allowing states to use a "growth model" to reward schools whose students make significant progress but that still miss AYP. Such a model would follow individual students as they move from grade to grade. By contrast, the current system compares the current fourth-grade class, for example, with last year's fourth-graders.

Kingsbury, at the Northwest Evaluation Association, likes the growth-model idea but says goals and timetables are needed. Otherwise, Kingsbury explains, "there is no guarantee students will end up at a high level of proficiency when they graduate."

Another frequent complaint is that the accountability system is too blunt an instrument. "The problem," says Patricia Sullivan, an education policy consultant and former director of the Center on Education Policy, "is the lack of distinction between the school that misses by a little and the school that misses by a lot." The school that misses the benchmark for one subgroup for two consecutive years is identified as needing improvement just like the school that misses the benchmark for several subgroups. Both face the same sanction: All students would have the option to transfer.

Since urban schools tend to be more diverse and have more subgroups, it is harder for them to make AYP. But the Education Trust's Hall says those who complain care more about the adults working in urban schools than the kids. "Is it fair to expect less of schools that are educating diverse student bodies?" Hall asks. "Is it fair to those students? Absolutely not."

The Department of Education has signaled its willingness to compromise, to a degree. Many districts have complained that requiring all students with disabilities to be grade-level proficient by 2014 is unfair and unrealistic. The law does allow 1 percent of all students — those with significant cognitive disabilities — to take alternative assessments. Secretary Spellings declared that another 2 percent — those with persistent academic disabilities — could take alternative tests, geared toward their abilities and not necessarily at grade level. States would have to apply to the Department of Education in order to use this option.

The reaction from educators was muted. Betty J. Sternberg, then Connecticut's education commissioner, said, "The percentages are fine. They help us. The problem may be in the details of what they are requiring us to do to have access to the flexibility." [22]

But advocates for disabled students worry that the department is backpedaling. Suzanne Fornaro, past president of the Learning Disability Association of America, is particularly concerned about students with learning disabilities: "If the changes result in lowering expectations, they might result in decreasing a student's access to the general curriculum and high-quality instruction."

Is No Child Left Behind improving the quality of teaching?

Teaching quality may be the single most important in-school factor in how well students learn. While it's difficult to know precisely what makes effective teachers, there are some common yardsticks, including mastery of their subject area. Yet government surveys show that, "One out of four secondary classes (24 percent) in core academic subjects are assigned to a teacher lacking even a college minor in the subject being taught." That figure rises to 29 percent in high-minority schools and 34 percent in high-poverty schools. [23]

NCLB required a "highly qualified" teacher in every classroom by the end of the 2005/2006 school year. Highly qualified teachers must have a bachelor's degree, be licensed or certified by the state and demonstrate that they know each subject they teach. New teachers can qualify by either passing a state test or having completed a college major in their subject area. Veteran teachers have a third option: an alternative evaluation created by each state, known by the acronym HOUSSE (high objective uniform state standard of evaluation).

Spellings pushed back that June 2006 deadline a few months before it was to take effect, giving states a one-year pass if they could demonstrate progress. A year later, only nine states had submitted plans that met all her requirements to demonstrate progress. [24]

In "Quality Counts 2005," a report by *Education Week*, researchers graded states on their efforts to improve teacher quality, looking at the amount of out-of-field teaching allowed, the quality of the state certification process and the amount and quality of professional development. Only three states got As, 14 got Bs and the rest received Cs and Ds. [25]

No Child Left Behind's ability to alter the picture may be limited, critics say. They point to the problems rural and urban schools are having recruiting and retaining skilled teachers and to many states' less-than-rigorous HOUSSE plans.

"I love my job. I know how kids learn," says Jon Runnalls, Montana's "Teacher of the Year" in 2003, "and for someone to come and say that now I'm not highly qualified, that's a slap in the face." Runnalls has taught middle school science for 31 years, but his college degree is in elementary education with an emphasis in science. According to NCLB, he'd have to go back to school, take a state test or pass the state's alternative evaluation. But Montana doesn't have a test, and its HOUSSE plan has not yet been approved by the Department of Education. It's really not a plan at all; it simply says that a veteran certified teacher is, by default, highly qualified.

Not surprisingly, Montana reports 98.8 percent of its classes are taught by highly qualified teachers.

Ten other states, like Montana, don't evaluate veteran teachers, arguing that the state certification process is a rigorous enough hurdle. But even many of the states that do have more elaborate HOUSSE plans have faced criticism.

Most states use a system in which veteran teachers accumulate points until they have enough to be considered highly qualified. "The most prevalent problem is that states offer too many options that veteran teachers can use to prove they are highly qualified — options that often have nothing to do with content knowledge," says Kate Walsh, president of the National Council on Teacher Quality. While states give points for university-level coursework, states also give them for sponsoring a school club, mentoring a new teacher and belonging to a national teacher organization. Teachers also get points for experience.

But according to Walsh, "The purpose of HOUSSE is to ensure that teachers know their content, not to count the number of years in the classroom." [26]

Even with the flexibility offered by the HOUSSE option, some schools in rural and urban areas are struggling to meet the law's requirements, although the Department of Education has given rural districts a three-year extension. After studying a rural district in Alabama that offered a $5,000 signing bonus to new teachers, researchers from the Southeast Center for Teaching Quality noted: "Central office staff told us that to ensure the bonus worked, they could only require recipients work two years. Most teachers take the bonus, serve their two years and leave." Urban districts the researchers studied struggled to find experienced teachers prepared to work with few resources and students with diverse learning and emotional needs. [27]

As a result, rural and urban schools are more likely to assign teachers to instruct in multiple subjects, often outside their field. These schools are also more reliant on teachers who have entered the profession through some alternative route, usually with little or no classroom experience. No Child Left Behind says such teachers are highly qualified if enrolled in an intensive induction and mentoring program and receiving high-quality professional development.

But Tom Blanford, an associate director for teacher quality at the National Education Association, says the quality of these programs is often poor. "We know what it takes to change classroom practice," Blanford says. "It has to do with knowledge, coaching, feedback and more knowledge, and it's a cyclical process. It's very rare that professional development meets those standards." Usually, he says, it's someone standing in front of a group of teachers lecturing them.

CHRONOLOGY

1950s-1960s *A legal challenge and federal legislation initiate an era of education reform.*

1954 In *Brown v. Board of Education*, the Supreme Court decides "separate educational facilities are inherently unequal."

1958 Congress passes National Defense Education Act in response to the Soviet launch of Sputnik.

1965 President Lyndon B. Johnson signs Elementary and Secondary Education Act (ESEA) providing funds to school districts to help disadvantaged students.

1966 Congress amends ESEA to add Title VI, establishing grants for the education of handicapped children.

1966 Sociologist James S. Coleman's "Equality of Educational Opportunity" report concludes that disadvantaged black children learn better in well-integrated classrooms, helping to launch an era of busing students to achieve racial balance in public schools. . . . Congress amends ESEA to add Title VII, called the Bilingual Education Act.

1970s-1980s *Studies criticize student achievement, and the standards movement gains momentum.*

1975 Coleman issues a new report concluding busing had failed, largely because it had prompted "white flight."

1980 U.S. Department of Education is established, ending education role of Department of Health, Education, and Welfare.

1983 National Commission on Excellence's "A Nation at Risk" report warns of a rising tide of mediocrity in education and recommends a common core curriculum nationwide.

1989 President George H.W. Bush convenes nation's governors in Charlottesville, Va., for first National Education Summit, which establishes six broad objectives to be reached by 2000. . . . National Council of Teachers of Mathematics publishes *Curriculum and Evaluation Standards for School Mathematics.*

1990s-2000s *Congress requires more standards, testing and accountability from the states.*

1994 President Bill Clinton signs the Goals 2000: Educate America Act, which adopts the goals of the first National Education Summit. The act creates the National Education

Standards and Improvement Council, with the authority to approve or reject states' academic standards. The council, however, becomes ineffective after Republicans take control of Congress during midterm elections and object to the increasing federal role in education. . . . Clinton later signs Improving America's Schools Act of 1994, requiring significantly more testing and accountability than the original ESEA.

Jan. 8, 2002 President George W. Bush signs No Child Left Behind Act, increasing funding to states while also increasing federal mandates and sanctions to an unprecedented degree. States must increase student testing, place "highly qualified" teachers in every classroom and meet state-determined annual targets for student proficiency in reading and math. By 2014, all students must be 100 percent proficient. Title I schools not meeting annual targets must offer transfers to students and provide supplemental services, like tutoring.

April 7, 2005 Secretary of Education Margaret Spellings announces her willingness to provide some flexibility to states in meeting the requirements of No Child Left Behind.

April 19, 2005 Republican-dominated Utah legislature passes a bill giving priority to state educational goals when those conflict with NCLB and ordering officials to spend as little state money as possible to comply with the federal law.

April 20, 2005 The nation's largest teachers' union and eight school districts in Michigan, Texas and Vermont sue the Department of Education, accusing the government of violating a No Child Left Behind Act provision that states cannot be forced to spend their own money to meet the law's requirements. The suit is thrown out several months later, but Connecticut has pushed forward with a similar suit of its own. Forty-five of the nation's governors agree on a common means for determining graduation rates.

2006 The Bill and Melinda Gates Foundation releases a study calling poor graduation rates "The Silent Epidemic." The Bush administration allows Tennessee and North Carolina to track advancement of individual students from year to year in reading and math, a new way to measure progress under NCLB. The administration unveils a $100 million private voucher plan that the president wants added to NCLB.

2007 A commission headed by two former governors releases a report calling for an expansion of NCLB, proposing national standards and tests and sanctions for teachers with poorly performing students. Congressional committees begin hearings on NCLB reauthorization.

Are Schools' Graduation Rates Accurate?

The No Child Left Behind Act holds schools account-able not just for student achievement but also for graduation rates. High schools must raise their grad-uation rates if they are to make adequate yearly progress. Increasing the percentage of graduates is a worthy goal, but it serves another purpose as well. The requirement is designed to prevent schools from improving achievement scores by encouraging their lowest-performing students to leave.

The system depends, of course, on accurate reporting. But researchers say that high school graduation rates reported by most states are just not believable.

The problem: States don't really know how many kids are dropping out of school.

States "consistently underestimate the number of dropouts, thereby overstating the graduation rates, some-times by very large amounts," says Jay P. Greene, a senior fellow at the Manhattan Institute for Policy Research. In a report, Greene called some states' rates "so improbably high they would be laughable if the issue were not so serious." [1]

Although a few school districts have been accused of falsify-ing dropout data, researchers don't believe deception is at the root of the problem. Rather, they say the cause is more benign: Most schools don't know what happens to students who leave. Did a student transfer to another school? Move to another state? Or really drop out? Trying to answer those questions may be a secretary or clerk who often has other responsibilities as well.

The National Governors Association has been working to convince its members to use the method of tracking all those who enter 9th grade and figure out how many of them actually graduate. A special issue of *Education Week* devoted to graduation rates in 2006 found that states tended to report graduation rates about 30 percent higher than would be the case under the individual-tracking method.

"You basically have to do detective work," says Christopher Swanson, a senior research associate at The Urban Institute's Education Policy Center. "That takes time, effort and resources that may not be available to the school." Swanson says schools don't have an incentive to distinguish dropouts from transfers if it means that the graduation rates they report will be lower as a result.

Even states with sophisticated systems to track individ-ual students over time — and there are a handful — can still report inflated graduation numbers. Texas, which reported an 84.2 percent graduation rate for its Class of 2003, counts as graduates students who have left school and either received or are working toward a General Educational Development certificate (GED). [2] No Child Left Behind prohibits the practice.

Both Swanson and Greene have developed methods for estimating how many students are actually graduating that do not rely on dropout data. Instead, they use two pieces of basic information they say are less subject to manipulation: the number of students enrolled in high school and the number of graduates. Their formulas differ, but both researchers come up with similar graduation rates that are far lower than those published by the states.

For example, South Carolina reported a high school graduation rate of 77.5 percent for the class of 2002; [3] Greene calculated the rate as 53 percent. [4] California reported a 2002 graduation rate of 87 percent; Greene put it at 67 percent. Indiana reported a graduation rate of 91 percent; Greene says it was 72 percent.

To fix the problem, Greene would like to see all states assign each student a unique identifying number for track-ing their school careers, with reasonable definitions of who is a dropout and who is a graduate and an auditing program to ensure the quality of the data.

"Starbucks knows exactly what it sells," Greene says. "Wal-Mart knows what inventory it has in every store. Schools have no idea."

Some states are developing such systems, but doing so will be time consuming and costly. In the meantime, some critics of the current reporting methods want the Department of Education to require states to estimate graduation rates using methods similar to Greene's or Swanson's. "The depart-ment's role does not end with the collection of data," the Education Trust says. "It must ensure that state calculations are accurate, complete and accessible to the public." [5]

However, federal education officials believe the responsibil-ity lies elsewhere. While the Department of Education will pro-vide technical assistance to states as they create more sophisticated systems for tracking students, it believes that the quality of the data is the states' responsibility. "Anytime there is a problem in the states, parties are always prone to point the fin-ger," says Deputy Assistant Secretary for Policy Darla Marburger. "And folks point the finger at the U.S. Department of Education. But it is not really a problem in our house."

---

[1] Jay P. Greene, "Public High School Graduation and College Readiness Rates: 1991-2002," Education Working Paper No. 8, Manhattan Institute for Policy Research, February 2005, p. 2

[2] www.tea.state.tx.us/peims/standards/wedspre/index.html?r032.

[3] Education Trust, "Telling the Whole Truth (or Not) About High School Graduation," December 2003, p. 4.

[4] Greene, *op. cit.*, Table 1.

[5] Education Trust, *op. cit.*

Gov. Jon Huntsman, R-Utah, prepares to sign a state measure on May 2, 2005, defying the No Child Left Behind Act, aided by a Provo elementary school student. In the past year and a half, more than 30 states have introduced bills that would release them from some of the law's requirements.

What rural and urban schools need to do, according to Scott Emerick, a policy associate at the Southeast Center for Teaching Quality, is use federal funds more effectively to improve working conditions, design better professional-development programs and devise sophisticated financial incentives to attract and retain teachers. But Emerick says they often don't know how, and the federal government is not providing enough guidance.

"These districts need on-the-ground assistance beyond accessing a federal Web site that tells you what other people are doing," he says.

Is No Child Left Behind adequately funded?

The funding question is so contentious it has divided former congressional supporters of the law and prompted both Republican and Democratic state lawmakers to introduce bills exempting their states from portions of the law.

The issue also has generated nearly two-dozen studies from think tanks, lobbying groups, school districts and states. Their conclusions about the adequacy of funding range from modest surpluses to shortfalls of millions, and in a few cases, even billions of dollars.

Beneath the competing claims are radically different estimates of the costs of implementing the law. Researchers can't even agree on what costs should be included, let alone their size. Adding to the problem, said a study, "is the evolving nature of the regulations, guidance and other advisories issued by the U.S. Department of Education." [28]

After reviewing the studies, the National Conference of State Legislatures concluded a shortfall is more likely and released a report in 2005 calling for change. "We would ask Congress to do one of two things," says senior policy specialist Young. "Either increase funding to levels that would allow states to meet the goals of the law or provide states waivers from having to meet requirements where there is insufficient funding."

In response, the Education Department embraced the studies projecting plenty of funds. "The perpetual cry for more money . . . simply does not comport with the facts: Since taking office, President Bush has increased education funding by . . . 33 percent," said a department press release in 2005.

To understand the debate, it is helpful to break down the costs of implementing the law into two categories: complying with the letter of the law versus bringing students to grade-level proficiency by 2014, which several states claim may be much more costly.

To comply with the letter of the law, states must establish academic standards, create assessments, monitor schools' progress, help schools needing improvement, pay for students to transfer and receive tutoring and place a highly qualified teacher in every classroom. Connecticut recently called its estimate of these costs "sobering." The state said that through fiscal 2008 it would have to spend $41.6 million of its own money to comply with the law. [29] Minnesota said its cost would be $42 million. [30]

Other states go even further. They say doing what's explicitly called for in the law will not be enough to bring 100 percent of students to proficiency in reading and math by 2014. In order to reach that goal, several states say they'll have to do much more. "It might involve after-school services and making sure children are well nourished," Young says. "Early-childhood education is a big one, essential to preventing the achievement gap from occurring."

Ohio commissioned a study that adopted an expanded notion of costs and included summer school, an extended school day and intensive in-school student intervention. The study calculated the annual cost of fully implementing NCLB at $1.5 billion; the additional federal funding that Ohio receives through the law, however, is only $44 million. [31]

The authors of the Ohio study acknowledged, "the task of assigning costs to the requirements of No Child Left Behind presents a formidable challenge." [32] Their assumptions, and the assumptions of other state studies, have come under attack.

A report in *Education Next*, a journal devoted to education reform, last spring accused the state studies of gross exaggeration. The authors, including the chairman of the Massachusetts Board of Education, contended that while there may be a shortage of money to evaluate schools and help those that need intervention, the gap can be filled by giving states more flexibility to shift existing federal money around. And it concludes, "No one — neither critics nor supporters of NCLB — really has any idea what it would cost to bring all students to proficiency by 2014, or even if it can be done at all." [33]

Accountability Works, a nonprofit research and consulting firm, goes a step further, concluding there is "little solid evidence that NCLB is insufficiently funded." In fact, the firm concluded some states might even have surpluses.

Echoing *Education Next*, Accountability Works said the reports claiming NCLB provides insufficient funding contain significant flaws. "Often, expenditures that are not required by NCLB are included in the calculations," the report said. "In other cases, such studies included expenditures that were required by prior federal law." [34]

Given the huge range of estimates and the fact that some of the repercussions of the law are just beginning to be felt, it may take years for the true costs of implementation to become clear.

But one thing is clear: State education departments are often overwhelmed. Many don't have the staff or the expertise to effectively carry out No Child Left Behind's requirements: creating data systems to monitor each school's adequate yearly progress; putting teams together to help schools in need of improvement and, as more fail, to restructure schools; and evaluating outside suppliers of tutoring services. Many states have never had to do these things, on this scale, before, and the alarm has been sounded not only by the states but also by private researchers and even the Government Accountability Office.

The Department of Education's Briggs says the federal government is helping. "We have held conferences where we have tried to bring states together to learn together."

But many states say the problem is rooted in past state budget cuts and resulting staff reductions. The extra money provided by NCLB is being used to create assessment tests or reduce class size, with little left over to hire administrative staff. That's the case in Idaho, says Allison Westfall, public information officer at the state Department of Education. "We have a very small Title I staff — we're down to five people now — who are often on the road visiting schools," she says. "So we've had to bring in people from other departments, and we're stretched really thin." And there are no plans to hire.

"This lack of capacity — not a lack of will — on the part of most states is the single, most important impediment to achieving the gains of No Child Left Behind," said Marc Tucker, president of the National Center on Education and the Economy, a research group. On average, state education departments have lost 50 percent of their employees in the past 10 years, he says, calling it "the hidden issue." [35]

BACKGROUND

Federal Reforms

On April 11, 1965, President Lyndon B. Johnson returned to the Texas school he had attended as a child to sign the nation's first comprehensive education law, the Elementary and Secondary Education Act. "As president of the United States," he declared, "I believe deeply no law I have signed or will ever sign means more to the future of America." [36]

The primary assumption in ESEA — enacted as part of Johnson's War on Poverty — was that higher-quality education would move poor students out of poverty.

With ESEA, the federal government began to address the causes of the achievement gap. In the process, the federal role in education policy — until then a strictly local affair handled by the nation's 15,000 independent school districts — grew dramatically. ESEA's signature program, Title I, initially allocated more than $1 billion a year to school districts with high concentrations of low-income students. To administer the program, federal and state education bureaucracies grew, as did the federal and state roles in local school districts.

During the next decade, minority achievement improved marginally, but dissatisfaction with public education grew faster, as did resentment over federal infringement on local education affairs. In 1981, President Ronald Reagan took office vowing to abolish the U.S. Department of Education.

"These Are the Very Weakest Programs Offered"

Arthur E. Levine, president of Teachers College, Columbia University, led a four-year assessment of the 1,200 university programs that prepare most of the nation's school principals and administrators. Released in March 2005 by Levine's Education Schools Project, the study, "Educating School Leaders," says most university-based preparation programs for administrators range in quality from "inadequate to appalling." Levine recently discussed the report with writer Barbara Mantel.

CQ: Does No Child Left Behind make the issue of how we train school leaders more urgent?

AL: No Child Left Behind demands assessment; it demands effective curricula that will move students to achievement of standards and requires that all students achieve those standards. Principals and superintendents have to lead that transformation of the schools, which requires a very different set of skills and knowledge from their predecessors.

CQ: What is your overall characterization of university-based programs that train school administrators?

AL: The quality is very weak. These are the very weakest programs offered by America's education schools. While a relatively small proportion could be described as strong, the majority vary in quality from inadequate to appalling.

CQ: Do most principals and superintendents come through these programs?

AL: I can't give you numbers on superintendents. For principals, it is 89 percent.

CQ: In what areas do these programs fall short?

AL: First of all, the curriculum for the master's degree is irrelevant to the job of being a principal, appearing to be a random grab bag of survey courses, like Research Methods, Historical and Philosophical Foundations of Education and Educational Psychology.

CQ: Your report also talks about admission standards.

AL: The standardized test scores for students in leadership programs are among the lowest of all students at graduate schools of education, and they're among the lowest in all academe. But the larger problem is that the overwhelming majority of students in these programs are in them primarily for a bump in salaries. All 50 states give salary increases for educators who take master's degrees or graduate credits. So people want quickie programs and easy degrees. There is a race to the bottom among programs as they compete for students by dumbing down the curriculum, reducing the length of the program, cutting the number of credits required to graduate and lowering expectations of student performance.

CQ: Your report also says the degrees offered don't make sense.

AL: Generally the master's degree is considered prepa-

The next year, Reagan and Secretary of Education Terrell Bell appointed the National Commission on Excellence in Education to report on the quality of public education. Eighteen months later, the commission's explosive report, "A Nation at Risk," declared, "the educational foundations of our society are presently being eroded by a rising tide of mediocrity that threatens our very future as a Nation and a people." [37]

The report focused on how poorly American students compared with students from other countries; the steady decline in science scores; a drop in SAT scores; the functional illiteracy of too many minority students; and complaints from business and military leaders about the poor quality of U.S. high school graduates.

To overcome the problems, the report called for rigorous and measurable academic standards, establishment of a minimum core curriculum, lengthening of the time

spent learning that curriculum and better teacher preparation.

"A Nation at Risk" marked the beginning of a movement for national standards and testing. Over the next decade, seven groups received federal financing to develop standards for what students should know, including the National Council of Teachers of Mathematics, the National History Standards Project and the National Standards in Foreign Language. [38]

In September 1989, President George H.W. Bush — the self-described "education president" — convened an education summit in Charlottesville, Va. Ignoring traditional Republican reluctance to actively involve Washington in education policy, Bush teamed with the president of the National Governors' Association — Democratic Gov. Bill Clinton, who had been active in education reform in his home state of Arkansas.

ration for principalship and the doctorate for a superintendency. Why does anybody need a doctorate to be a superintendent? A doctorate is a research degree. What does that have to do with running a school system?

CQ: What are some of your key recommendations?

AL: States and school boards should eliminate salary increases based on taking degrees. Or they can give people raises based on master's degrees but require that the field be germane to their work. If you're a math teacher, I can understand giving an increase in salary for taking a degree in mathematics or advanced teaching skills. Number two: close down failing programs. States can clean this up if they want to. They are in charge of the authorization of university programs and the licensure of school administrators. But I would like to see universities try first before the states step in.

CQ: How much time would you give the universities to do this?

Arthur E. Levine, president, Teachers College, Columbia University

AL: I would give universities two years to clean up their house, and then the state has an obligation to step in if they fail to do that.

CQ: What other recommendations do you have for universities?

AL: Eliminate the current master's degree and put in its place something I've been calling a master's of educational administration, which would be a two-year degree combining education and management courses, theory and practical experience. The doctor of education degree (EdD) would be eliminated. It has no integrity and no value. The PhD in education leadership should be reserved for the very tiny group of people who wish to be scholars and researchers in the field.

CQ: And your last recommendation?

AL: There is a tendency of universities to use these programs as cash cows. They encourage these programs to produce as much revenue as possible by reducing admission standards, using adjuncts and lowering academic standards for graduation in order to get enough cash to distribute to other areas. Universities need to stop doing that.

"The movement gained momentum with the 1989 education summit," wrote Andrew Rudalevige, an associate professor of political science at Dickinson College, in Carlyle, Pa. [39] Bush and the governors set broad performance goals for American schools to reach by the year 2000. It was hoped that all children would attend preschool, that 90 percent of all high school students would graduate, that all students would be proficient in core subjects, that U.S. students would be first in the world in science and math, that every adult would be literate and every school free of drugs and violence.

In 1994, President Clinton signed the Goals 2000: Educate America Act, which adopted the summit's ambitious agenda and provided federal funds to help states develop standards. The real sea change came later that year, Rudalevige wrote, when reauthorization of ESEA "signaled a nationwide commitment to standards-based reform." [40]

The law required states to develop content and performance standards, tests aligned with those standards and a system to measure a school's "adequate yearly progress" in bringing all students to academic proficiency. But there was no deadline, and it took several years for the Education Department to develop the accompanying regulations and guidelines. By 1997, only 17 states were fully complying with the law, according to Krista Kafer, a Denver-based education consultant and former senior education policy analyst at the Heritage Foundation. [41]

In January 2001, former Texas Gov. George W. Bush became president, having made education a centerpiece of his campaign. Three days after his inauguration, he proposed what became the blueprint for No Child Left Behind. Its standards-and-testing strategy wasn't new, but accountability provisions were. They significantly raised the stakes for states, local districts and schools.

The proposal called for annual testing in grades 3-8, school and state report cards showing student performance by ethnic and economic subgroups, a highly qualified teacher in every classroom and sanctions for schools not showing progress in bringing students to proficiency.

Congress finally passed NCLB after nearly a year of intense debate and political horse-trading, which included the elimination of private school vouchers, increases in funding and, significantly, addition of a provision requiring that all students reach proficiency in math and reading in 12 years.

"The political compromises written into No Child Left Behind make the regulatory process crucial," said Rudalevige. [42] That's because the law grants the secretary of Education the power to grant waivers and interpret the rules and, until the bill is reauthorized, determine the flexibility states will have to meet their goals.

Achievement Gaps

Most educators say the best thing about No Child Left Behind is its focus on minorities and low-income students.

"When you say to a school that you expect every subgroup of kids to meet standards," says Delaware Education Secretary Woodruff, "that really makes schools pay closer attention to all kids." It is now possible, for instance, to track how minority and low-income students perform on state tests at each school and to calculate the achievement gaps between them and their peers. The fundamental goal of No Child Left Behind is to close these gaps while raising the achievement of all students, which has been the goal of education reforms for decades.

But to get a sense of how students have been performing historically, researchers must look to national data, because state testing is too new.

To get that information, the U.S. Department of Education has been measuring American students' achievement levels since 1969 through its National Assessment of Educational Progress (NAEP). NAEP periodically administers what it calls a "trend assessment" to a nationally representative sample of students at ages 9, 13 and 17 and breaks down the results for white, black and Hispanic students.

The data show that black and Hispanic students have made long-term gains, thus narrowing the achievement gap. From 1971 to 1999 for example, the difference between the average reading scores of 13-year-old white and black students shrank from 39 points to 29 points.

In math, the gap plummeted 14 points — from 46 points to 32 points. [43]

However, most of the reductions in the achievement gap occurred during the 1970s and 1980s, as minorities made notable gains while white students' average achievement increased slightly or not at all. Then, in the 1990s, the gap stopped shrinking; in fact, in many cases it grew. Black and Hispanic students continued making modest gains in math and Hispanic students in reading, but those improvements no longer exceeded those of whites. [44] By 2005, according to the National Center for Education Statistics, the gaps were still not measurably different from 1992.

"When achievement goes up for all groups," the Center on Education Policy noted, "African-American and Hispanic students must improve at a faster rate than others for the gap to close." [45]

While still smaller than decades ago, the achievement gap remains quite large. For instance, the 32-point difference in math scores for black 13-year-olds and their white peers in 1999 is the equivalent of roughly three grade levels. [46]

"What, then, are the most probable explanations for the achievement gap?" asked the Center on Education Policy in a report examining minority achievement. "A complex combination of school, community and home factors appear to underlie or contribute to the gap," it answered. [47]

Just as worrying to some observers is the gap in scores between NAEP and state-level assessments. States are allowed to determine measurements for proficiency among their own students, but their results seldom track NAEP scores within their borders, suggesting they have set their own bar too low. A University of California study released in 2007 found that the gap between national and state results has grown since NCLB's passage in 10 of the 12 states studied.

For instance, Texas reported that 82 percent of its fourth graders were proficient in reading in 2006, while the federal estimate was just 29 percent. In New Jersey, the state reported that 80 percent were proficient in reading in 2006, but federal data put the number at 38 percent.

"State leaders are under enormous pressure to show that students are making progress," said Bruce Fuller, a University of California professor of education and public policy. "So they are finding inventive ways of showing higher test scores." [48]

Of course, some states maintain that their assessment systems are superior to national ones. Florida has given "A" grades to hundreds of schools found deficient under

Should annual testing be extended to high school?

YES   Bob Wise
President, Alliance for Excellent Education

Written for *CQ Researcher*, May 5, 2005

Achieving the national goal of building a better educated, more competitive work force for the 21st century requires effective tools. With two-thirds of high school students either dropping out or graduating unprepared for college, the majority of our nation's young people need more support than they are currently getting from their secondary schools and teachers. An increased number of required tests at the high school level could help to leverage the academic assistance many students require, if those tests are designed and implemented appropriately.

Last fall, President Bush set off a major debate when he proposed extending the reading and math tests required by the No Child Left Behind Act for third- through eighth-graders and in one year of high school to students in grades nine, ten and eleven. "We need to be sure that high school students are learning every year," he said.

At the Alliance for Excellent Education, we believe all children deserve an excellent education that prepares them for the economic and social challenges that follow high school. And we agree with the president that our schools must be held accountable for providing that high-quality education. Testing students during their high school years has the potential to provide needed data about their progress — as a whole, and by gender, race and ethnicity — and could allow us to better measure the effectiveness of the schools supposed to be preparing all of our young people to become productive members of American society.

But tests should help schools understand and address the needs of their students. If we are going to hold schools accountable for their students' ability to perform at high academic levels, we must also give them the resources necessary to provide the additional, targeted instruction that many teens need to become proficient in reading, writing, math and other subjects.

To be taken seriously by students, tests need to be relevant. High school tests should be aligned to the expectations of colleges and employers and provide both educators and students with a gauge to measure progress toward a successful transition to postsecondary education, technical training or rewarding jobs.

Finally, the federal government should fully cover the cost of designing and administering the exams, thus ensuring that states can adequately and effectively implement the tests they are required to give.

Tests alone won't make a difference. But as a part of a toolkit designed to improve the nation's graduation and college-readiness rates, they are worthy of our consideration.

NO   Paul Houston
Executive Director, American Association of School Administrators

Written for *CQ Researcher*, April 27, 2005

High school reform should not focus on a test but rather on what is being learned. I recently visited the Olathe, Kan., school district to learn more about a series of programs called 21st Century Schools, which have been implemented in all the high schools. These are "vocational" schools. In other words, they are focused on the future work life of students, and the programs are very rigorous and produce great results. But more important, the programs are meaningful, engaging and hands on, using the students' motivation to create a vehicle for excellence.

As I walked through Olathe Northwest High School, I saw students and teachers engaged in hard work. In one classroom, they were constructing a "battlebot," a robot that is used in gaming to battle other robots — with the last one running being the winner. The students were looking forward to taking their creation to a national competition later this year. While this sounds fun (some may say "frivolous"), what is really happening is that students are experiencing deep learning about metallurgy, structures, engines, insulation and a hundred other things I didn't understand. They were excited and knowledgeable about what they were doing — and about how much fun they were having with the learning process.

There were about a dozen students who stayed after the bell to talk with me, and every one of them plans to attend college and study engineering. There is no shortage of engineering candidates in Olathe. I asked them why they liked what they were doing, and the answer was simple. One told me he got to use what he was learning in class. "Telling me that calculus is good for me isn't very meaningful," he said. "Now I see how I can use it."

I would suggest to those who want to reform high schools that the place to start is in places like Olathe, where the school district has figured out that the best way to get students to learn more is to give them engaging, imaginative work that creates meaning for them. And we must give schools adequate resources to provide state-of-the-art opportunities for students to receive hands-on learning.

Those who are interested in reform should focus on getting schools the resources they need to do the job and then challenging them to make schools interesting and engaging places. Reform will not be achieved by mandating more testing. Education has always been about the whole child, and unless we take that into consideration, the current effort to reform high schools will be just as unsuccessful as the others that preceded it.

NCLB. That fact drew national attention when Gov. Jeb Bush, the president's brother, held a news conference in 2006 to crow about an academic study that found Florida's system superior to the federal model. [49]

CURRENT SITUATION

States Push Back

Mounting state resistance to NCLB — including its level of funding and strict achievement timetables — has led to a mini-revolution in the states.

In 2004, legislatures in 31 states introduced bills challenging aspects of the law. [50] By mid-2005, 21 states had either introduced or reintroduced legislation. [51] In Colorado, Republican state Sen. Mark Hillman proposed allowing school districts to opt out of No Child Left Behind if they forgo Title I funds; he suggested a tax increase to replace the lost federal funds. In Idaho, two Republican state senators introduced legislation demanding that predominantly rural states be exempt from the law. In Maine, Democratic state Sen. Michael Brennan sponsored a bill directing the state's attorney general to sue the federal government if federal funding is insufficient to implement No Child Left Behind.

Despite the blizzard of proposals, however, only three states actually passed legislation. The Republican-dominated Utah legislature passed a bill on April 19, 2005 — and the governor signed it on May 2 — allowing schools to ignore NCLB provisions that conflict with state education laws or require extra state money to implement. Spellings warned that Utah could lose $76 million of the $107 million it receives in federal education funding.

"I don't like to be threatened," an angry state Rep. Mascaro told *The New York Times.* [52]

Raul Gonzalez, legislative senior director at the National Council of La Raza, which advocates for Hispanic-Americans, agrees that money is tight in states still suffering from a four-year-long budget crisis. [53] "States are trying to implement this law on the cheap," Gonzalez says, "because there isn't really enough money."

For example, under the law states are allowed to test English-language learners for up to three years in their native language, but most states don't have reading tests in native languages. "We're not accurately measuring what kids can do because we're using the wrong tests," he says.

Arizona and Virginia continue to battle the federal government over rules for testing children with limited English. Utah is still fighting about qualifications for its rural teachers. The Connecticut lawsuit continues to drag on past the two-year mark. But Perry Zirkel, a professor of education and law at Lehigh University, in Bethlehem, Pa., says the states' resistance to the law is still mostly "sparks, not fire." He points out that New Mexico, Virginia and Utah are the only states to pass legislation.

"Despite all the talk," Zirkel says, "I don't think there has been sufficient momentum to convince the majority of the public that No Child Left Behind is, on a net basis, a bad law."

Moreover, a coalition of Hispanic, African-American and other educators have voiced concerns that the Utah legislature's effort to sidestep provisions of the federal law might allow minority students to fall through the cracks. [54]

Teachers' Union Sues

One day after the Utah legislature made its move, the NEA and eight school districts in Michigan, Texas and Vermont sued the Department of Education, contending it is violating an NCLB provision that says states cannot be forced to use their own money to implement the law:

"Nothing in this Act shall be construed to authorize an officer or employee of the Federal Government to mandate, direct, or control a State, local education agency, or school's curriculum, program of instruction, or allocation of State or local resources, or mandate a State or any subdivision thereof to spend any funds or incur any costs not paid for under this Act."

"We don't disagree when the Department of Education says federal funding has increased," explained NEA spokesman Dan Kaufman. "We just don't believe that the funding has been enough for the types of really strict, comprehensive things that it requires states to do." The teachers' union wanted to see Congress appropriate the full amount it authorized when passing the bill. At that point, it was $27 billion short.

"We . . . look forward to the day when the NEA will join us in helping children who need our help the most in classrooms, instead of spending its time and members' money in courtrooms," the Department of Education said in response. [55]

The lawsuit was filed in the U.S. District Court for the Eastern District of Michigan, which has jurisdiction over one of the school districts joining the suit. The suit asks the court to declare that states and school districts do not have to spend their own funds to comply with NCLB and that failure to comply for that reason will not result in a cutoff of federal education funds.

A federal judge acted quickly to dismiss the suit, finding that Congress had not intended to pay for all of the costs imposed by NCLB. "If Congress meant to prohibit 'unfunded mandates' in the NCLB, it would have phrased [the law] to say so clearly and unambiguously," he wrote in his decision. [56]

"The courts' view is that if you have problems with this law, then go lobby Congress to change it," Lehigh's Zirkel says. In fact, the lawsuit may actually have been an indirect way to lobby Congress, he adds, and it may be effective because it's so public.

War of Words

Zirkel says Connecticut's decision to sue may also be an indirect attempt at lobbying Congress. In early April 2005, Connecticut Attorney General Richard Blumenthal announced he would sue the Department of Education on grounds that the federal government's approach to the law is "illegal and unconstitutional." [57] Connecticut's argument is essentially the same as the teachers' union's, but the state — which has a direct stake in the outcome — has better legal standing, Zirkel says. Blumenthal has estimated the annual testing required by the law would create an additional financial burden for the state, which now tests students every other year.

While a few school districts have sued the government over the law, Connecticut was the first state to do so. A federal judge in 2006 dismissed much of Connecticut's case but allowed the state to go forward with its claim that Washington treated it unfairly in negotiations over how to carry out the law. [58] As of mid-2007, that portion of the case had not been settled.

Meanwhile, the state's dispute with the Education Department had become very public. "We've got better things to spend our money on," former Connecticut Education Commissioner Sternberg said in explaining her opposition to annual testing. "We won't learn anything new about our schools by giving these extra tests." [59]

But Secretary Spellings clearly was not willing to compromise on annual testing, consistently calling it one of the "bright lines" of NCLB. She and Sternberg engaged in a war of words, with Spellings calling the law's opponents "un-American" and Sternberg demanding an apology.

Spellings also accused Connecticut of tolerating one of the nation's largest achievement gaps between white and black students. Sternberg has said the huge gap was due to the extraordinary performance of white students in Connecticut's affluent suburbs.

Reform Unlikely?

If the NEA's lawsuit and Connecticut's threat to sue are indirect ways of lobbying Congress, their timing may be off.

Jeffrey Henig, a professor of political science and education at Columbia University's Teachers College, says some constituents in prosperous suburban school districts are beginning to grumble as well-regarded schools fail to make "adequate yearly progress" because one or two subgroups of students miss proficiency targets.

"But I don't think it has really gelled into clear, focused pressure on Congress to reform the law," Henig says, adding that the situation could change if more schools fall into that category.

Moderate Democrats are committed to the law's focus on raising achievement levels for minority, low-income and disabled students, he says, and they fear that any reworking could result in easing the pressure on states to shrink the achievement gap. And a core group of Republicans is committed to the law's tough accountability provisions. Both groups, Henig says, would prefer "to hold to the legislation and to placate any dissatisfied groups through the regulatory process."

The Department of Education has already amended the law's regulations, guidelines and enforcement. For instance, in 2003 and 2004 it allowed English-language learners to be tested in native languages for their first three years, gave rural districts more time to place highly qualified teachers in classrooms and allowed some flexibility on testing participation rates.

In 2005, Spellings — then just three months into her new job as secretary — told states they could apply to test a greater portion of disabled students using alternative assessments. In addition, Spellings said she would grant states flexibility in other areas if they could show they were making real progress in closing achievement gaps and meeting proficiency targets.

But Young, formerly of the National Conference of State Legislatures, says states are trying to decipher what she means. "There is no indication of what that flexibility would include," he says, "and there is no indication of how states would be judged by these indicators."

So far, Spellings is holding firm on annual testing, but she did grant North Dakota a waiver temporarily allowing new elementary school teachers to be rated highly qualified without taking a state test. She also offered all states more time to meet the requirement for placing "highly qualified" teachers in all classrooms.

"The Department of Education is really feeling the heat and is trying to compromise," says educational consultant Scott Joftus, former policy director at the Alliance for Excellent Education.

The department also has allowed some states to lower the cutoff point for proficiency on their student assessment tests and to use averaging and other statistical methods to make it easier for schools to make adequate yearly progress. Young calls it gaming the system and expects it to continue unless Congress reforms No Child Left Behind.

OUTLOOK

As Congress prepares to extend the law, which it is scheduled to do in 2007, it will have to contend with critics from both the left and right. Prepared to engage in that battle is an unusual bipartisan coalition made up of President Bush, Secretary Spellings, Sen. Edward M. Kennedy and Sen. George Miller, the chairman of the House Education Committee. All have proposed various changes, but none will accept a retreat from the basic promise contained in the title of the law, that all children — even or especially those in populations that have traditionally been badly served — are entitled to a measurably decent education.

"When Republicans and Democrats take a look at this bill, I strongly urge them not to weaken the bill, not to backslide, not to say accountability isn't that important," Bush said at an April 2007 appearance at a Harlem charter school. [60]

The continuing controversy over the bill's approach and cost mean that the Bush administration's hopes of extending its tenets into high school or even college are probably dead letters for now. Kennedy and Miller support maintaining standards in lower grades and are focused on improving teacher quality and boosting spending.

Even the law's critics concede that it has focused attention and resources on groups of children who often had been neglected, including minority populations in urban districts and low-achieving students in the suburbs. But few students have been well served by the law's sanctions.

Only tiny fractions of eligible students have transferred out of so-called failing schools — less than 1 percent. Nationwide, only 18 percent of students have received free tutoring as they have become eligible for it. [61]

Meanwhile, the law's central goal — making sure that all students test as proficient by 2014 — is under increasing attack as being unrealistic and unobtainable. "There is a zero chance that we will ever reach a 100 percent target," said Robert L. Linn, codirector of the National Center for Research on Evaluation, Standards and Student Testing at UCLA. "But because the title of the law is so brilliant, politicians are afraid to change this completely unrealistic standard. They don't want to be accused of leaving some children behind." [62]

Under Spellings, the Bush Education Department has grown more flexible about allowing states leeway in meeting various goals under the law. But the underlying law remains something the administration wants to expand rather than from which to retreat. Spellings has joked that it's like Ivory soap: "It's 99.9 percent pure or something." [63]

Few lawmakers share that assessment. The National Conference of State Legislatures and the American Association of School Administrators have called for full federal funding to meet the law's requirements. The National Governors Association wants states to have much more authority in determining how to carry out the law's mandates.

Given the continuing controversy about the law and the criticism it generates among teachers unions, states, the education establishment and conservative lawmakers, most prognosticators say that the law's extension will be a tough sell. Many predict that Congress will fail to enact new legislation, leaving the job to a new Congress — and new president — in 2009.

But regardless of the short-term outcome, and despite its political problems, No Child Left Behind capped a fundamental shift in American education toward greater accountability and a move to place the blame for poor performance not on students themselves but on educators. That is a course that no new version of the law is likely to undo anytime soon.

NOTES

1. Dana Milbank, "With Fanfare, Bush Signs Education Bill," *The Washington Post*, Jan. 9, 2002.

2. Northwest Evaluation Association, "The Impact of the No Child Left Behind Act on Student Achievement and Growth: 2005 Edition," April 2005, p. 2.

3. http://kennedy.senate.gov/index_high.html.

4. Sam Dillon, "Utah Vote Rejects Parts of U.S. Education Law," *The New York Times*, April 20, 2005.

5. "Governor worried about costs of Bush education reform law," The Associated Press State & Local Wire, April 26, 2005.

6. http://gregg.senate.gov/forms/myths.pdf.

7. www.ed.gov/nclb/overview/intro/guide/guide_pg 11.html#spending.

8. National Public Radio, "Talk of the Nation," May 3, 2005.

9. Center on Education Policy, "From the Capital to the Classroom: Year 3 of the No Child Left Behind Act," March 2005, p. v.

10. Edward M. Kennedy, "No Retreat on School Reform," *The Washington Post*, March 26, 2007, p. A15.

11. *Ibid.*, p. 4.

12. *Ibid.*, p. 1.

13. Council of the Great City Schools, "Beating the Odds: A City-By-City Analysis of Student Performance and Achievement Gaps on State Assessments," March 2004, pp. iv-vi.

14. The Education Trust, "Stalled in Secondary: A Look at Student Achievement Since the No Child Left Behind Act," January 2005, p. 1.

15. University of Delaware Education Research and Development Center, "Awareness To Action Revisited: Tracking the Achievement Gap in Delaware Schools, State of Delaware Report," March 2005, p. 2.

16. www.dpi.state.wi.us/dpi/esea/pdf/wiaw.pdf.

17. National Conference of State Legislatures, "Task Force on No Child Left Behind: Final Report," February 2005, p. vii.

18. http://edcounts.edweek.org.

19. Stephanie Banchero, "Pupils Still Far Behind Despite Law," *Chicago Tribune*, Jan. 7, 2007, p. 1.

20. Center for the Study of Evaluation, "Test-based Educational Accountability in the Era of No Child Left Behind," April 2005, p. 19.

21. *Ibid.*, p. 14.

22. Susan Saulny, "U.S. Provides Rules to States for Testing Special Pupils," *The New York Times*, May 11, 2005, p. A17.

23. The data are from 2000, the most recent available. See The Education Trust, "All Talk, No Action: Putting an End to Out-of-Field Teaching," August 2002, p. 4.

24. Michael Alison Chandler, "For Teachers, Being 'Highly Qualified' Is a Subjective Matter," *The Washington Post*, Jan. 13, 2007, p. A1.

25. Education Week Research Center, "Quality Counts 2005," January 2005, p. 92. www.edweek.org/rc/index.html.

26. National Council on Teacher Quality, "Searching the Attic," December 2004, p. 12.

27. Southeast Center for Teaching Quality, "Unfulfilled Promise: Ensuring High Quality Teachers for Our Nation's Students," August 2004, pp. 8-9.

28. Augenblick, Palaich and Associates, Inc. "Costing Out No Child Left Behind: A Nationwide Survey of Costing Efforts," April 2004, p. 1.

29. Connecticut State Department of Education, "Cost of Implementing the Federal No Child Left Behind Act in Connecticut," March 2, 2005, p. iii.

30. Center on Education Policy, *op. cit.*

31. Ohio Department of Education, "Projected Costs of Implementing The Federal 'No Child Left Behind Act' in Ohio," December 2003, p. vi.

32. *Ibid.*

33. James Peyser and Robert Castrell, "Exploring the Costs of Accountability," *Education Next*, spring 2004, p. 24.

34. Accountability Works, "NCLB Under a Microscope," January 2004, p. 2.

35. Joetta L. Sack, "State Agencies Juggle NCLB Work, Staffing Woes," *Education Week*, May 11, 2005, p. 25.

36. www.lbjlib.utexas.edu/johnson/archives.hom/speeches.hom/650411.asp.

37. www.ed.gov/pubs/NatAtRisk/risk.html.

38. For background, see Kathy Koch, "National Education Standards," *CQ Researcher*, May 14, 1999, pp. 401-424, and Charles S. Clark, "Education Standards," *CQ Researcher*, March 11, 1994, pp. 217-240.

39. www.educationnext.org/20034/62.html.

40. *Ibid.*

41. Heritage Foundation, "No Child Left Behind: Where Do We Go From Here?" 2004, p. 2.

42. www.educationnext.org/20034/62.html.

43. National Center for Education Statistics, "Trends in Academic Progress: Three Decades of Student Performance," 2000, p. 39.

44. *Ibid.*, p. 33.

45. Center on Education Policy, "It takes more than testing: Closing the Achievement Gap," 2001, p. 2.

46. *Ibid.*, p. 1.

47. *Ibid.*, p. 3.

48. "Study Shows More Discrepancies between State, National Assessments of Student Proficiency," *The Washington Post*, April 16, 2007, p. B2.

49. Sam Dillon, "As 2 Bushes Try to Fix Schools, the Tools Differ," *The New York Times*, Sept. 28, 2006, p. A1.

50. National Conference of State Legislatures, "No Child Left Behind Quick Facts: 2005," April 2005.

51. www.nea.org/lawsuit/stateres.html.

52. Dillon, *op. cit.*

53. For background, see William Triplett, "State Budget Crisis," *CQ Researcher*, Oct. 3, 2003, pp. 821-844.

54. Dillon, *op. cit.*

55. U.S. Department of Education, "Statement by Press Secretary on NEA's Action Regarding NCLB," April 20, 2005, p. B1.

56. Kavan Peterson, "Schools Lose Round in NCLB Challenge," Stateline.org, Nov. 30, 2005.

57. Sam Dillon, "Connecticut to Sue U.S. Over Cost of School Testing Law," *The New York Times*, April 6, 2005.

58. Sam Dillon, "Connecticut Lawsuit Is Cut Back," *The New York Times*, Sept. 28, 2006, p. A18.

59. Michael Dobbs, "Conn. Stands in Defiance on Enforcing 'No Child,' " *The Washington Post*, May 8, 2005, p. A10.

60. Jim Rutenberg, "Bush Presses Schools Plan During Trip to New York," *The New York Times*, April 25, 2007, p. A20.

61. Banchero, *op. cit.*

62. Amit R. Paley, "'No Child' Target Is Called Out of Reach," *The Washington Post*, March 14, 2007, p. A1.

63. Paul Leavitt, "Education Chief Says Law Close to Perfect," *USA Today*, Aug. 31, 2006, p. 4A.

BIBLIOGRAPHY

Books

Meier, Deborah, and George Wood, eds., *Many Children Left Behind: How the No Child Left Behind Act Is Damaging Our Children and Our Schools*, Beacon Press, 2004.
Meier, the founder of several New York City public schools, and Wood, a high school principal and the founder of The Forum for Education and Democracy, and other authors argue that the law is harming the ability of schools to serve poor and minority children.

Peterson, Paul E., and Martin R. West, eds., *No Child Left Behind: The Politics and Practice of School Accountability*, Brookings Institution Press, 2003.
Peterson, director of the Program on Education Policy and Governance at Harvard, and West, a research fellow in the program, have collected essays that examine the forces that gave shape to the law and its likely consequences.

Rakoczy, Kenneth Leo, *No Child Left Behind: No Parent Left in the Dark*, Edu-Smart.com Publishing, 2003.
A veteran public school teacher offers this guide to parents for becoming involved in their children's education and making the most out of parent-teacher conferences in light of the new law.

Wright, Peter W. D., Pamela Darr Wright and Suzanne Whitney Heath, *Wrightslaw: No Child Left Behind*, Harbor House Law Press, 2003.
The authors, who run a Web site about educational law

and advocacy, explain the No Child Left Behind Act for parents and teachers.

Articles

Dillon, Sam, "New Secretary Showing Flexibility on 'No Child' Law," *The New York Times*, Feb. 14, 2005, p. A18.
Education Secretary Margaret Spellings has shown a willingness to work with state and local officials on No Child Left Behind, saying school districts need not always allow students in low-performing schools to transfer to better ones if it caused overcrowding.

Dillon, Sam, "Battle Over Renewing Landmark Education Law," *The New York Times*, April 7, 2006, p. A10.
Laying out the battlelines over reauthorization, with the law's original supporters remaining firm but opponents believing they have a chance to gut a law they have never liked.

Friel, Brian, "A Test for Tutoring," *The National Journal*, April 16, 2005.
Friel examines the controversy surrounding some of the outside tutoring firms providing supplemental services to students under provisions of No Child Left Behind.

Hendrie, Caroline, "NCLB Cases Face Hurdles in the Courts," *Education Week*, May 4, 2005.
Hendrie describes the hurdles facing the National Education Association's lawsuit against the Department of Education.

Ripley, Amanda, and Sonja Steptoe, "Inside the Revolt Over Bush's School Rules," *Time*, May 9, 2005.
The authors examine efforts by states to seek release from aspects of No Child Left Behind and the teachers' union's lawsuit against the federal government.

Thornburgh, Nathan, "Dropout Nation," *Time*, April 17, 2006, p. 30.
The high school dropout rate is higher than generally acknowledged, with researchers saying that one in three public high school students — and 50 percent of African-Americans and Hispanics — will fail to receive a diploma.

Tucker, Marc S., and Thomas Toch, "Hire Ed: the secret to making Bush's school reform law work? More bureaucrats," *Washington Monthly*, March 1, 2004.

The authors discuss staffing shortages at state departments of education that are slowing implementation of No Child Left Behind.

Weisman, Jonathan, and Amit R. Paley, "Dozens in GOP Turn Against Bush's Prized 'No Child' Act," *The Washington Post*, March 15, 2007, p. A1.
More than 50 Republican members of Congress support legislation that would severely undercut NCLB by allowing states to opt out of its testing mandates.

Reports and Studies

Center on Education Policy, *From the Capital to the Classroom: Year 3 of the No Child Left Behind Act*, March 2005.
The center examines the implementation of No Child Left Behind at the federal, state and local levels and points out positive and negative signs for the future.

Citizens' Commission on Civil Rights, *Choosing Better Schools: A Report on Student Transfers Under the No Child Left Behind Act*, May 2004.
The commission describes the early efforts to implement the school-choice provision of No Child Left Behind, calling compliance minimal.

National Conference of State Legislatures, *Task Force on No Child Left Behind: Final Report*, February 2005.
The panel questions the constitutionality of No Child Left Behind and calls it rigid, overly prescriptive and in need of serious revision.

Northwest Evaluation Association, *The Impact of No Child Left Behind Act on Student Achievement and Growth: 2005 Edition*, April 2005.
The association reports the percentage of proficient students is rising on state tests but also notes the disparity between the achievement growth of white and minority students.

Southeast Center for Teaching Quality, Unfulfilled Promise: Ensuring High Quality Teachers for Our Nation's Students, August 2004.
The center finds that rural and urban schools don't have the skills and training to recruit and retain highly qualified teachers and offers recommendations for change.

For More Information

Achieve, Inc., 1775 I St., N.W., Suite 410, Washington, DC 20006; (202) 419-1540; www.achieve.org. A bipartisan, nonprofit organization created by the nation's governors and business leaders that helps states improve academic performance.

Alliance for Excellent Education, 1201 Connecticut Ave., N.W., Suite 901, Washington, DC; (202) 828-0828; www.all4ed.org. Works to assure that at-risk middle and high school students graduate prepared for college and success in life.

Center on Education Policy, 1001 Connecticut Ave., N.W., Suite 522, Washington, DC 20036; (202) 822-8065; www.cep-dc.org. Helps Americans understand the role of public education in a democracy and the need to improve academic quality.

Council of the Great City Schools, 1301 Pennsylvania Ave., N.W., Suite 702, Washington, DC 20004; (202) 393-2427; www.cgcs.org. A coalition of 65 of the nation's largest urban public school systems advocating improved K-12 education.

Editorial Projects in Education, 6935 Arlington Rd., Suite 100, Bethesda, MD 20814-5233; www.edweek.org. A nonprofit organization that publishes *Education Week*, *Teacher Magazine*, edweek.org and *Agent K-12*.

Education Commission of the States, 700 Broadway, Suite 1200, Denver, CO 80203-3460; (303) 299-3600; www.ecs.org. Studies current and emerging education issues.

The Education Trust, 1250 H St., N.W., Suite 700, Washington, DC 20005; (202) 293-1217; www2.edtrust.org/edtrust. An independent nonprofit organization working to improve the academic achievement of all students.

National Conference of State Legislatures, 7700 East First Pl., Denver, CO 80230; (303) 364-7700; www.ncsl.org. A bipartisan organization serving the states and territories.

Northwest Evaluation Association, 5885 Southwest Meadows Rd., Suite 200, Lake Oswego, OR 97035; (503) 624-1951; www.nwea.org. A national nonprofit organization dedicated to helping all children learn.

Southeast Center for Teaching Quality, 976 Airport Rd., Suite 250, Chapel Hill, NC 27514; (919) 951-0200; www.teachingquality.org. A regional association dedicated to assuring all children have access to high-quality education.

U.S. Department of Education, www.ed.gov/nclb/landing.jhtml?src=pb. Describes the provisions of the No Child Left Behind law.

Wrightslaw, www.wrightslaw.com. Provides information about effective advocacy for children with disabilities, including "Wrightslaw: No Child Left Behind."

2

Fixing Urban Schools

Marcia Clemmitt

Philadelphia police officers guard West Philadelphia High School on March 12, 2007, where a teacher was attacked by three students three days earlier. Experts suggest that a "behavior gap" between black and white students parallels the academic achievement gap between high- and low-performing students.

"I didn't go to school much in elementary, and they saw me as a bad girl" who skipped class, says Jeanette, a Houston high-school student who dropped out several times but is struggling to get a diploma. After her parents divorced when she was in grade school, she fell into a pattern typical of urban students, repeatedly "switching schools," sometimes living with her mother, sometimes her father and sometimes with an aunt who "didn't make us go to school" at all. [1]

In middle school, Jeanette began taking drugs but later got involved in sports, which motivated her to try, sometimes successfully, to keep up her grades and stay off drugs. Some teachers have tried hard to help her, but like many troubled urban kids, she pulls back. "If I need help . . . I don't say anything. . . . They have to ask me." Still, Jeanette is determined to avoid the fate of her parents, who dropped out of school when they had her. At the time, her mother was only 13. "I don't want to live like them. I want to have a better life," she says.

Jeanette typifies the daunting challenge that urban schools face in promoting academic achievement among children whose lives have been disordered and impoverished.

Most middle-class families with children have moved to the suburbs, leaving urban schools today overwhelmingly populated by low-income, African-American and Hispanic students. "Nationally, about 50 percent of all black and Latino students attend schools in which 75 percent or more of the students are low-income, as measured by eligibility for free and reduced-price lunch," according to the Center for Civil Rights at the University of North Carolina. Only 5 percent of white students attend such high-poverty schools. [2] (*See graph, p. 30.*)

From *CQ Researcher*, April 27, 2007.

Minority Districts Often Get Less Funding

In 28 states, school districts with high-minority enrollments received less per-pupil funding (shown as a negative number, top map) than districts with low-minority levels. For example, in Illinois, the highest-minority districts received an average of $1,223 less per student than the lowest-minority districts. In 21 states, the highest-minority districts received more per pupil (shown as a positive number, bottom map), than the districts with the lowest-minority enrollments. For example, in Georgia, the highest-poverty districts received $566 per student more than the lowest-poverty districts.

Minority Funding Gaps by State, 2004

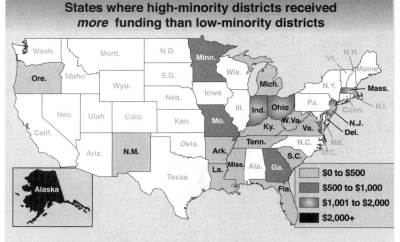

States where high-minority districts received *less* funding than low-minority districts

- -$2,000+
- -$1,001 to -$2,000
- -$500 to -$1,000
- -$1 to -$500

States where high-minority districts received *more* funding than low-minority districts

- $0 to $500
- $500 to $1,000
- $1,001 to $2,000
- $2,000+

Note: Hawaii is not shown because data are not available.

Source: Funding Gaps 2006, The Education Trust, 2006

These schools, mostly urban, aren't making the grade, even in the context of lagging achievement in American schools overall.

Although states show significant variations, nationwide "71 percent of eighth-graders are not reading at grade level," and the percentage shoots up to between 80 and 90 percent for students of color, says former Gov. Bob Wise, D-W.Va., now president of the Alliance for Excellent Education, a broad-based coalition that advocates for academically stronger high schools.

Furthermore, of the approximately 15,000 U.S. high schools, 2,000 — mostly in cities — account for half of the nation's school dropouts, says Wise.

When President George W. Bush joined Massachusetts Sen. Edward M. Kennedy and other congressional Democrats to enact the No Child Left Behind Act (NCLB) in 2002, a key aim was requiring states to report achievement scores for all student groups. That ensured that lagging scores of low-income and minority students wouldn't be masked by having only state or district overall average scores reported. [3]

This year, Congress is expected to provide funding to keep the law in operation, but there's considerable disagreement about where federal education law should go next, and lawmakers may wait until next year to consider revisions (see p. 43).

NCLB's test-score reporting requirements "make it more possible to look at whether schools are doing well just for more affluent students or for poor students" as well, and that's valuable, says Jeffrey Henig, professor of political science and education at Columbia University's Teachers College.

But some supporters, including President Bush, say the NCLB has done more than just improve data-gathering, arguing that the law itself has pushed achievement upward. "Fourth-graders are reading better. They've made more progress in five years than in the previous 28 years combined," he said on March 2. [4]

Many education analysts disagree with that rosy assessment. The small improvement in fourth-grade reading and mathematics scores is part of a long-term trend, which began years before NCLB was even enacted, said Harvard University Professor of Education Daniel M. Koretz. "There's not any evidence that shows anything has changed" since NCLB, he said. [5]

And for urban schools, the post-NCLB picture is especially grim.

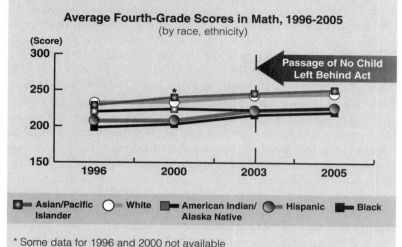

All Racial/Ethnic Groups Improved on Test

Fourth-graders in all racial and ethnic groups began modestly improving in math on the National Assessment for Educational Progress several years before passage of the No Child Left Behind Act.

Average Fourth-Grade Scores in Math, 1996-2005
(by race, ethnicity)

Passage of No Child Left Behind Act

Legend: Asian/Pacific Islander — White — American Indian/Alaska Native — Hispanic — Black

* Some data for 1996 and 2000 not available

Source: U.S. Department of Education, National Center for Education Statistics

Of the non-achieving schools in New York state, for example, 90 percent are in cities and 80 percent in the state's five biggest cities, says David Hursh, an associate professor of teaching and curriculum at the University of Rochester's Margaret Warner Graduate School of Education.

The gap between average reading scores of black and white fourth-graders narrowed by only one point on the 500-point National Assessment of Educational Progress test (NAEP) between 2002 and 2005, and the narrowing appears to be part of a long-term trend, since it narrowed by three points between 1998 and 2005. Between 2002 and 2005, the reading-score gap between white and black eighth-graders actually widened, from 25 points to 28 points. [6]

The continuing severe achievement gap, newly highlighted by NCLB's data-reporting requirements, leaves lawmakers and educators scratching their heads about what to do next.

Some analysts say lagging achievement in urban schools demonstrates that poor families in poor communities require much more intense interventions than middle-class students, including better teachers and longer school days as well as improved health care, nutrition and parenting education.

A public school enrolling mainly middle-class white students has a one-in-four chance of producing good test scores, across years and in different subject matter, according to Douglas N. Harris, assistant professor of education policy at the University of Wisconsin, Madison. A school with a predominantly low-income minority population has a 1-in-300 chance of doing so. [7]

Experts blame the poor outcome on the fact that urban schools, like all schools, are staffed and organized to provide substantial extra help to only 15 percent of students and curriculum enrichment to another 15, while "the students in the middle are supposed to take care of themselves," says Robert Balfanz, associate research scientist at the Johns Hopkins University Center on the Social Organization of Schools and associate director of the Talent Development High School program, a reform initiative in 33 schools nationwide. The formula for extra help fits most suburban schools, "but in urban schools 50 to 60 percent, and sometimes up to 80 percent, of the kids are "high-needs," defined as

English-as-a-second-language students, special-education students or students below grade level or with severe attendance problems.

"We're not set up to respond when that many kids need one-on-one tutoring, monitoring of their attendance on a daily basis, [or] people calling up to say, 'Glad you came today,' " Balfanz says.

One of the biggest problems is the kind of "student mobility" experienced by Jeanette, the Houston dropout.

"Homelessness is much underreported," says James F. Lytle, a professor at the University of Pennsylvania and former school superintendent in Trenton, N.J. "Statistics are based on who's in shelters and on the streets. But 20 to 30 percent of our kids were living in 'serial households' on a day-to-day basis," or moving about from parents to grandparents to relatives to friends — not living in the same house all the time.

Inner-city schools have a 40 to 50 percent student-mobility rate, which means up to half the students change schools at least once a year because of parents losing or changing jobs, evictions and other factors, says Columbia University's Henig. That disrupts students' ability to keep up with work and build relationships with the adults in a school.

In addition, city students miss school for a wide range of reasons, including high asthma rates; lack of school buses, forcing kids to get to school on their own, often through unsafe neighborhoods; and family responsibilities, like caring for younger siblings.

"Imagine the teacher's dilemma in a classroom where the population is different every day," says Balfanz.

But some conservative analysts argue that a large proportion of high-needs students is still no reason for schools to fail.

"Schools frequently cite social problems like poverty . . . and bad parenting as excuses for their own poor performance," said Jay P. Greene, a senior fellow at the Manhattan Institute, a conservative think tank. "This argument that schools are helpless in the face of social problems is not supported by hard evidence. . . . The truth is that certain schools do a strikingly better job than others," including public, private and charter schools. [8]

Some educators say one solution for low-quality urban schools is establishing publicly funded "charter" schools and awarding vouchers for private-school tuition. [9] When choice is expanded, "urban public schools that once had a captive clientele must improve the education

they provide or else students . . . will go elsewhere," said Greene. [10]

But others argue that lessons from successful urban schools, including charters, demonstrate that raising low-income students' achievement requires resources and staff commitment that may be tough for the nation to muster.

"Teachers in high-poverty urban schools are as much as 50 percent more likely to . . . leave than those in low-poverty schools," in part because of the intensity of the work, according to researchers at the University of California, Santa Cruz. [11]

A second-grade teacher fluent in Spanish who reported working 10 hours a day, six days a week said she'd probably stop teaching when she had children: "It's too time-consuming and energy-draining," she said. [12]

"None of the teachers in our sample could conceive of being a successful urban teacher without an extraordinary — perhaps unsustainable — commitment to the work," the researchers commented. [13]

Not just schools but communities must help in the effort to improve students' performance.

"There ought to be a parade through the heart of town" every time a student achieves an academic goal, says Hugh B. Price, a fellow at the Brookings Institution, a liberal think tank. "We need to wrap and cloak kids in this message of achievement." That's how the military successfully trains soldiers, Price says. "They will praise anything that's good."

Schools and communities also have a role in helping parents better equip their children for school, says Mayor Douglas H Palmer of Trenton, N.J., president of the National Conference of Democratic Mayors. "You don't have to be rich to talk to your child, help her build vocabulary and learn to reason and negotiate," as psychologists recommend, he says. "We can help parents with these skills."

As educators and lawmakers debate the next steps to improving urban schools, here are some of the questions being asked:

Has the No Child Left Behind law helped urban students?

NCLB was intended to improve overall academic achievement and raise achievement for minority and low-income students, in particular, mainly by requiring more student testing, getting schools to report test data separately for student groups including minorities and the poor and requiring schools to employ better-qualified teachers.

The law, scheduled for reauthorization this year, gets praise for focusing attention on the so-called achievement gap between minority and low-income students and their middle-class counterparts. But critics say the legislation doesn't do enough to assure that low-performing urban schools get the excellent teachers they need.

Student achievement also has improved slightly under the law, some advocates point out. "Is NCLB really paying off? The answer is yes," U.S. Chamber of Commerce Senior Vice President Arthur J. Rothkopf told a joint House-Senate committee hearing on March 13. While current testing data is still "abysmal," it nevertheless "represents improvement from where this nation was" before the law.

The law has benefited urban schools by raising reading scores for African-American and Hispanic fourth- and eighth-graders and math scores for African-American and Hispanic fourth-graders to "all-time highs." Achievement gaps in reading and math between white fourth-graders and African-American and Hispanic fourth-graders also have diminished since NCLB, he noted. [14]

NCLB's data-reporting requirements have "lifted the carpet" to reveal two previously unrecognized facts about American education — "the continuing under-performance of the whole system and the achievement gap" for low-income and minority students, says Daniel A. Domenech, senior vice president and top urban-education adviser for publisher McGraw-Hill Education and former superintendent of Virginia's vast Fairfax County Public Schools. [15]

And while some critics complain that NCLB gave the federal government too much say over education — traditionally a state and local matter — "there needs to be a strong federal role for these kids" in low-income urban schools "because they have been left behind," says Gary

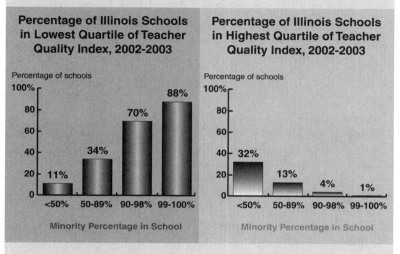

Minority Enrollment and Teacher Quality

In Illinois, 88 percent of the schools that were virtually 100 percent minority ranked in the lowest quartile of the state's Teacher Quality Index (graph at left). By comparison, only 1 percent of the all-minority schools ranked in the highest quartile (right). High-quality teachers have more experience, better educations and stronger academic skills. Similar patterns are found in most other states.

Percentage of Illinois Schools in Lowest Quartile of Teacher Quality Index, 2002-2003

Percentage of schools

- 11% (<50%)
- 34% (50-89%)
- 70% (90-98%)
- 88% (99-100%)

Minority Percentage in School

Percentage of Illinois Schools in Highest Quartile of Teacher Quality Index, 2002-2003

Percentage of schools

- 32% (<50%)
- 13% (50-89%)
- 4% (90-98%)
- 1% (99-100%)

Minority Percentage in School

Source: "Teaching Inequality: How Poor and Minority Students Are Shortchanged on Teacher Quality," The Education Trust, June 2006

Ratner, a public-interest lawyer who is founding executive director of the advocacy group Citizens for Effective Schools. "States and localities have not stepped up."

Now NCLB "has got the country's attention," and when Congress reauthorizes the law, "the federal role can be redirected to focus on Title I schools" — those serving a large proportion of disadvantaged students — "and do more of the things that professional educators support," Ratner says.

NCLB's requirement that every school "have very qualified teachers is good," says Gary Orfield, a professor of social policy at the Harvard Graduate School of Education and director of The Civil Rights Project.

But critics argue that NCLB doesn't put muscle behind the high-quality teacher requirement and sets unrealistic goals and timetables for school progress.

NCLB actually "incentivizes teachers to leave failing schools," the last thing lawmakers intended, says Jennifer King-Rice, an economist who is associate professor of edu-

Blacks, Hispanics Attend High-Poverty Schools

Black and Hispanic students are more likely to be concentrated in high-poverty schools than white students. Forty-seven percent of black and 51 percent of Hispanic fourth-graders were in the highest-poverty schools in 2003 vs. 5 percent of white fourth-graders. By contrast, only 6 percent of black and Hispanic fourth-graders were in the lowest-poverty schools compared with 29 percent of the whites.

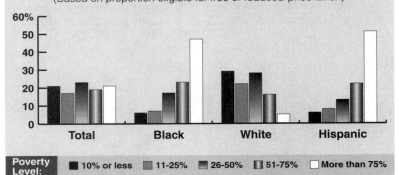

Percentage of Fourth-graders in High-poverty Schools
(Based on proportion eligible for free or reduced-price lunch)

Poverty Level: ■ 10% or less ■ 11-25% ■ 26-50% ■ 51-75% □ More than 75%

Source: "The Condition of Education 2004 in Brief" National Center for Education, June 2004

cation policy at the University of Maryland, College Park. "Teachers say, 'I can't produce the AYP [average yearly progress] results' " the law calls for in low-performing schools with few resources and, frustrated, go elsewhere, she says. Nevertheless, it's still unclear whether and how the government can enforce the qualified-teacher rule. (*See graphs, p. 29.*)

The law provides no additional funding to help schools meet the teacher-quality goal, said Richard J. Murnane, professor of education and society at the Harvard Graduate School of Education. "Teaching in these schools is extremely difficult work," and "very few school districts provide extra pay or other inducements to attract talented teachers to these schools. [16]

"As a result, all too often these schools are left with the teachers other schools don't want," he continued. "And the teachers who do have options exercise seniority rights to leave . . . as soon as they can." [17]

The achievement targets set by NCLB are panned by many. The main goal schools must meet is moving kids over a standardized-testing threshold from "basic" or "below basic" understanding of reading and math to a "proficient" level or above. But focusing on that narrow goal as the key measure by which schools are judged created bad incentives to game the system, many analysts say.

Rather than concentrating on raising overall achievement or trying to give the most help to students who score lowest, many schools concentrate "on students who are on the bubble" — those who need to raise their scores by only a few points to move into the "proficient" range — and "forget the others," says Patrick McQuillan, an associate professor of education at Boston College's Lynch School of Education. Schools that succeed at pushing the scores of "bubble" students up by a few points are deemed successful, according to current NCLB standards, even if they leave the neediest students even farther behind, he says.

The law's pronouncement that 100 percent of U.S. students will test at the "proficient" level is simply unrealistic, some critics say.

"We've never fully funded education in the United States," and achievement continues to lag far below the "proficient" level, especially for low-income students, says Domenech. So "let's not kid around and say that by 2014" all students will be academically proficient, he says. "That's like saying, 'I'm going to push you out the window, and I know you can fly.' "

Furthermore, NCLB's focus on a handful of standardized tests as the sole measures of children's progress puts teachers in an ethical bind that "definitely lowers their morale," says Marshalita Sims Peterson, an associate professor of education at Atlanta's Spelman College, an historically black school for women.

Teachers in training are taught that students are individuals with a wide variety of learning styles, and that no single assessment can define a student, says Peterson. The NCLB's excessive focus on a single measurement of achievement "leaves the teacher in an awful position" she says. "You need to keep the job, but when you are actually completing that form" stating the single score "for a third-grader, you're asking, 'Is that all there is to this child?' "

Should governments make schools more racially and economically diverse?

Today, most African-American and Latino students attend urban schools with a high concentration of low-income students and very few white classmates.

Some advocates argue that the country has back-tracked to an era of separate but unequal schools and say government programs aimed at creating more racially and socioeconomically diverse schools are good tools for narrowing the achievement gap. Opponents of government interference with children's attendance at neighborhood schools argue that with residential neighborhoods increasingly segregated by race and income, school integration is unrealistic, and that governments should focus instead on improving achievement in urban schools. [18]

"The effort to get the right racial balance is misguided" and represents a kind of "liberal racism — a belief that black children need to be in school with white children to learn," says Stephan Thernstrom, a history professor at Harvard University and a fellow at the conservative Manhattan Institute.

If integration "can be managed naturally, that's fine, but there is no clear correlation that can be drawn from data" showing it's important for closing the achievement gap, Thernstrom says. He rejects as incomplete and flawed studies that suggest integration does make a big difference. Furthermore, "if you need a white majority to learn," learning will soon be impossible in America, since Hispanic, Asian and African-American populations are growing faster than the current white majority, he notes.

Racial concentration is not the same as segregation and doesn't stand in the way of achievement, said his wife, Manhattan Institute Senior Fellow Abigail Thernstrom. School districts are powerless to change housing demographics, making it highly unlikely that racial concentration of students ever could be ended, she said. [19]

Some school districts are attempting to integrate lower-income and higher-income students, rather than integrating schools based on race. But Abigail Thernstrom argued that giving children a longer commute to schools outside their neighborhoods, for any reason, simply wastes time better spent in the classroom. "Busing doesn't raise the level of achievement," she told

C-SPAN. "Now they're going to start busing on the basis of social class. And I have a very simple view of that. Stop moving the kids around and teach them." [20]

Meanwhile, some charter schools — such as the Knowledge Is Power Program (KIPP), begun in Houston — are making great strides in reducing the urban achievement gap, and for the most part those schools are not racially integrated, wrote *New York Times Magazine* features editor Paul Tough last year.

Most of the 70 schools that make up the three charter networks he observed have "only one or two white children enrolled, or none at all," he noted. Leaders of the networks, all of them white, actually intend to educate their students separately from middle-class students, according to Tough. However, unlike those who've argued that schools can be "separate but equal," the successful high-intensity charter schools aim for "separate but better." Their founders argue that "students who enter middle school significantly behind grade level don't need the same good education that most American middle-class students receive; they need a better education," he said. [21]

But many advocates argue that data show a proven way to improve education for thousands of low-income students rather than for the handful that attend the highly successful charter schools is integration of minority and poor students with middle-class children.

School desegregation by race "has clear academic benefits," wrote R. Scott Baker, an associate professor of education at Wake Forest University. Data from Charlotte, N.C., show that the longer both black and white students spent in desegregated elementary schools, the higher their standardized test scores in middle and high school. Research also suggests that "where school desegregation plans are fully and completely implemented," local housing also becomes more integrated. [22]

In the 1960s and '70s some federal courts mandated programs to help urban minority families move to middle-class white suburbs. Long-term data from those cases show that children who moved did better than those who stayed behind, according to Howell S. Baum, a professor of urban studies and planning at the University of Maryland. In St. Louis, 50 percent of the black students who moved to the suburbs graduated from high school, compared to 26 percent of those who remained in the high-minority, low-income urban schools. [23]

Many policy analysts agree that segregating low-income children in some public schools "perpetuates failure," wrote the Century Foundation's Task Force on the Common School. Nevertheless, there is an "equally durable political consensus that nothing much can be done about it." The panel argued that this must change: "Eliminating the harmful effects of concentrated school poverty is the single most important step that can be taken for improving education in the United States." [24]

"Dozens of studies" dating back to the 1960s "find that low-income children have . . . larger achievement gains over time when they attend middle-class schools," said the panel. [25]

"The tragedy right now is that places that were once forced to [integrate their schools] now aren't allowed to," says Orfield of The Civil Rights Project. "That will be seen as a cosmic blunder" for white Americans as well, he said. "We're not preparing ourselves for the multiracial society and world" of the 21st century.

Are teachers prepared to teach successfully in urban classrooms?

Urban schools have high teacher turnover, low test scores and many reported discipline problems. Furthermore, most of America's teaching force still consists of white, middle-class women, while urban schoolchildren are low-income minorities, creating a culture gap that may be hard to bridge.

Consequently, some analysts argue that today's teachers aren't prepared to teach successfully in urban classrooms for a variety of reasons, from discipline to second-language issues. Others, however, point to sterling examples of teachers and schools that do succeed and argue that the real problem is teachers not following good examples.

Fifth-grade teacher Rafe Esquith, at the Hobart Elementary School in central Los Angeles, routinely coaches his urban Korean and Central American-immigrant students to top standardized-test scores. Furthermore, his classes produce Shakespearean plays so impressive they've been invited to perform with Britain's Royal Shakespeare Company, said Abigail Thernstrom. [26]

But despite Esquith's success, "nobody copies him," even in his own school, said Thernstrom. "I went to the fifth-grade [classroom] next door [to Esquith's] one day," and "it was perfectly clear nothing was going on." When Thernstrom suggested the teacher might copy Esquith's methods — which include beginning class as early as 6 a.m. and working with students at his home on weekends — he remarked that "it's an enormous amount of work." [27]

Today, around the country, "we do have shining examples" of schools that succeed at urban education, says Timothy Knowles, executive director of the University of Chicago's Center for Urban School Improvement and a former deputy school superintendent in Boston.

Ratner, of Citizens for Effective Schools, agrees. "I spent time in an elementary school in Chicago a few years ago where all the teachers were teaching reading," even at the upper grades, equipping students with the vocabulary and comprehension skills needed for future academic work, he says. "They had a good principal, and they were showing that it can be done."

But while successful urban schools and classrooms are out there, many education analysts say the know-how and resources needed to spread that success to millions of students are sorely lacking.

Some individual schools are closing the achievement gap for needy students, but "very few, if any" entire school districts have had equivalent success, says Knowles.

Charter schools also haven't seen their successes spread as widely as many hoped.

Out of Ohio's "300-plus charter schools," for example, "some . . . are indeed excellent, but too many are appalling," wrote analysts Terry Ryan and Quentin Suffran of the conservative Thomas B. Fordham Foundation in a recent report. [28]

There are reasons for that, said Mark Simon, director of the Center for Teacher Leadership at Johns Hopkins University, in Baltimore. "Teaching lower-class kids well is tougher than teaching middle-class kids." Furthermore, "it is surprising how little we know about teaching practices that cause students to succeed, particularly in high-poverty schools." [29]

"You have poverty in many districts, but in urban schools you have a concentration of it" that makes teaching successfully there much harder than in middle-class suburbs, says Timothy Shanahan, professor of urban education at the University of Illinois at Chicago and president of the International Reading Association. Schools are traditionally set up to deal with 15 to 20 percent of a student body having very high needs, says Shanahan. But urban schools usually have 50 percent or more of their students needing special attention of some kind, "and that's a huge burden on the teachers," he says.

"Literally, we have 5-year-olds who come into the Chicago school system not knowing their own names," he says. "I know local neighborhoods with gang problems, where the kids are up all night. Their mothers are hiding them under the bed to protect them from shootings in the street. Then teachers can't keep them awake in class."

The nation's rapidly growing Hispanic population is heavily concentrated in urban schools. That new phenomenon presents another tough obstacle for the urban teaching force, because "older teachers know nothing about working with non-native English speakers," says McQuillan of Boston College.

Not just language but race complicates urban-school teaching. As many as 81 percent of all teacher-education students are white women. [30]

"Those most often entering teaching continue to be white, monolingual, middle-class women," wrote Jocelyn A. Glazier, assistant professor of education at the University of North Carolina at Chapel Hill. [31]

Many teachers, especially white women, shy away from making tough demands on African-American students, according to a survey of urban community leaders by Wanda J. Blanchett, associate professor of urban special education at the University of Wisconsin, Milwaukee. "Especially with African-American males, you hear the teachers say, 'Oh, he is such a nice kid.' But . . . this irks me when teachers baby their students to death instead of pushing. . . . I get that a lot when you have white teachers who have never worked with black students from the urban environment." [32]

Many entering education students at Indiana University-Purdue University, in Indianapolis, balked at the school's fieldwork and student-teaching venues, which were in urban schools, wrote Professor Christine H. Leland and Professor Emeritus Jerome C. Harste. "They saw our program's urban focus as an obstacle to their career goals" of teaching in schools like the suburban ones most had attended. [33]

Some viewed urban students as an alien race they didn't want to learn to know. "Students rarely felt the need to interrogate their underlying assumption that poor people deserve the problems they have" or "spent any time talking or thinking about issues such as poverty or racism," Leland and Harste wrote. After student teaching, however, some students changed their plans and applied to become urban teachers. [34]

Race is a taboo subject in America, which some analysts say compounds urban teachers' difficulties. Many teacher-preparation programs center on an effort not to see or at least not to acknowledge race differences, according to Glazier. But "by claiming not to notice [race], the teacher is saying that she is dismissing one of the most salient features of a child's identity." [35]

"Many teachers believe that if they recognize a student's race or discuss issues of ethnicity in their classroom, they might be labeled as insensitive and racist," wrote Central Michigan University graduate student in education Dreyon Wynn and Associate Dean Dianne L. H. Mark. But white teachers' deliberate color-blindness ignores students "unique culture, beliefs, perceptions, [and] values," blocking both learning and helpful student-teacher relationships, Mark and Wynn argue. [36]

BACKGROUND

Educating the Poor

American education has long struggled with providing equal education for the poor, racial minorities and non-English-speaking immigrants. Until recently, however, even people who never made it through high school could usually find a good job. A new, global, technical economy may be changing that.

In the earliest years in the United States, schooling wasn't widespread. A farm-based economy made extensive education unnecessary for most people. In 1805, more than 90 percent of Americans had completed a fifth-grade education or less, and education for richer people was often conducted by private tutors. [37]

State legislatures were just beginning to debate whether to establish free tax-funded schools for all children. [38] Nevertheless, even in those early days, some religious and other charitable groups considered it a moral duty to educate the poor. In New York City, for example, the Association of Women Friends for the Relief of the Poor opened a charity school in 1801. By 1823 the group was providing free elementary education for 750 children, with some public assistance. Similar charity schools sprang up in most other major cities.

But as all states began establishing public education systems — between the late 18th and the mid-19th century — questions over equality in education arose, first for black students and later for immigrants. "When public

CHRONOLOGY

1950s-1960s *Concerns grow over student achievement and racially segregated schools.*

1954 Supreme Court rules in *Brown v. Board of Education* that separate schools are inherently unequal.

1965 Title I of the new Elementary and Secondary Education Act (ESEA) targets the largest pool of federal education assistance to help schools serving disadvantaged students.

1966 Sociologist James S. Coleman's "Equality of Educational Opportunity" report concludes that disadvantaged African-American students do better in integrated classrooms.

1969 National Assessment of Educational Progress (NAEP) tests launched but report statewide average scores only, allowing states to mask lagging achievement among poor and minority students.

1970s-1980s *Latinos are becoming most segregated minority in U.S. schools. "Magnet schools" are established. School integration efforts gradually end.*

1973 Supreme Court rules in *San Antonio Independent School District v. Rodriguez* the Constitution does not guarantee equal education for all children. . . . In *Keyes v. School District No. 1*, the court bans city policies that segregate Denver schools.

1990s-2000s *Steady gains in African-American students' test scores over the past two decades begin to taper off by decade's end. . . . Poverty concentrates in cities. . . . Governors lead efforts to raise education standards.*

1990 New Jersey Supreme Court rules in *Abbott v. Burke* the state must provide more funding for poor schools than for richer ones.

1991 Minnesota enacts first charter-school law.

1994 In reauthorizing ESEA, Congress requires states receiving Title I funding for disadvantaged students to hold them to the same academic standards as all students.

1995 Knowledge Is Power Program charter schools launched in Houston and New York City. . . . Boston creates Pilot School program to research ideas for urban-school improvement.

1999 Florida establishes first statewide school-voucher program.

2000 Countywide, income-based school integration launched in Raleigh, N.C.

2002 Cambridge, Mass., schools begin integration based on income.

2002 No Child Left Behind Act (NCLB) requires states to report student test scores "disaggregated" by race, income and gender to avoid masking the failing scores of some groups. . . . U.S. Supreme Court rules in favor of Ohio's school-voucher program, which allows public funding for tuition at Cleveland parochial schools. . . . State takes over Philadelphia's bankrupt school system, allows private companies to run some schools.

2005 Hoping to halt isolation of the lowest-income students in inner-city schools, Omaha, Neb., tries but fails to annex neighboring suburban districts.

2006 Department of Education admits that few students in failing city schools receive the free tutoring NCLB promised and that no states have met the 2006 deadline for having qualified teachers in all classrooms. . . . Government Accountability Office finds that nearly one-third of public schools, most in low-income and minority communities, need major repairs.

2007 Gov. Deval L. Patrick, D-Mass., puts up $6.5 million to help schools lengthen their hours. . . . Democratic Mayor Adrian Fenty, of Washington, D.C., is the latest of several mayors to take control of schools. . . . New York City Schools Chancellor Joel Klein says he will fire principals of schools with lagging test scores. . . . Teachers' unions slam report calling for all high-school seniors to be proficient in reading and math by 2014. . . . Houston school district calls for state to replace NCLB-related standardized periodic testing on math and reading with traditional end-of-course subject-matter exams.

schools opened in Boston in the late 18th century, black children were neither barred nor segregated," wrote Derrick Bell, a visiting professor at the New York University School of Law. "But by 1790, racial insults and mistreatment had driven out all but three or four black children." [39]

Later, some black families joined with white liberals to form black-only schools in Massachusetts and in other states. But complaints about poor conditions and poor teaching in those schools led others to sue for integrated education.

Even in the early 19th century, some courts were bothered by race-based inequities in education, said Bell. A federal court struck down a Kentucky law directing that school taxes collected from white people would maintain white schools, and taxes from blacks would operate black schools. "Given the great disparities in taxable resources" this would result in an inferior education for black children, the court said. [40]

Around the 1820s, waves of non-English immigration began, raising new controversies over educating poor children of sometimes-despised ethnicities.

Before 1820, most U.S. immigrants were English, and a few were Dutch. But between 1820 and 1840 Irish immigrants became the first in a long parade of newcomers judged inferior by the predominantly English population. A rising tide of immigration in the late 19th and early 20th centuries included many non-English-speakers — Italians, Germans, Chinese, Russians, Poles and many others — who posed new challenges for schools and were looked down on by many citizens.

The new immigrants generally clustered in cities, the economic engines of the time, and overcrowded city schools were charged with integrating them into American life. Critics charged that the urban schools used rigid instruction and harsh discipline to control classrooms bursting with 60 or more children, many of whom spoke no English.

Two Tracks

In the economy of the early 20th century, however, there remained little need for most students to learn more than basic reading and writing, so the failure of poor urban schools to produce many graduates wasn't seen as a problem.

In current debates over U.S. education, "people aren't looking at education historically" and therefore expect American schools to do things they were never designed to do, says Ratner of Citizens for Effective Schools.

"We consciously decided to have a two-track system," he says. In the early 20th century, education experts generally agreed that "in the industrial age there are lots of immigrants and poor people, and most are going to work on the assembly line, so how about if we create an academic track and a general/ vocational track" mostly for the poor?

The school system that we have "was never set up to educate all students to the levels of proficiency now being asked for," Ratner says.

"I graduated exactly 40 years ago, and then about half the kids — 52 percent — were graduating," says Wise of the Alliance for Excellent Education. "And the non-graduates could still get good jobs."

But today "the fastest-growing sectors of the economy require two years of post high-school training," says Daniel J. Cardinali, president of Communities In Schools, a dropout-prevention group that helps school districts bring services like tutoring and health care to needy students.

Calls in the 1990s for higher academic standards by groups like The Business Roundtable brought widespread attention to the problems of low student achievement, especially in low-income schools.

Today few question the premise that all students should attain higher levels of literacy, mathematical problem-solving and critical thinking. Many who work in schools argue that simply setting higher standards isn't nearly enough, however, especially for urban schools where most students already are behind grade level.

As standards rise, for example, "ninth-graders are increasingly placed in introductory algebra classes . . . despite skill gaps in fundamental arithmetic," wrote Balfanz and Ruth Curran Neild, research scientists at the Johns Hopkins University Center on the Social Organization of Schools.

But few resources exist to help kids catch up, "nor are there many curriculum materials that specifically target the spotty skills of urban ninth-graders," the Johns Hopkins researchers said. And when students reading behind grade level enter middle and high school, their "secondary-certified English teachers" — educated to teach high-school-level literature and composition — "are generally unprepared" to diagnose reading problems or to teach the comprehension strategies and background vocabulary they need. Science and history teachers are even less prepared to help, Balfanz and Neild said. [41]

Dropouts' Problems Often Begin Early

Clear warning signs appear, such as skipping class

With the baby-boom generation on the verge of retirement, sustaining the American workforce and economy depends on having a cadre of new young workers to replace them, says former Gov. Bob Wise, D-W.Va., now president of the Alliance for Excellent Education. But with jobs in the fastest-growing economic sectors now requiring at least a high-school diploma and, often, two years or more of post-high-school training, coming up with an adequately trained new workforce won't be easy, Wise says.

The annual graduation rate has risen from a little over 50 percent per year in the late 1960s to 73.9 percent in 2003. If it's to rise higher, however, the improvement must come among poor and minority students, mostly in urban schools, who are far less likely than others to earn diplomas. [1]

For example, while about two-thirds of all students who enter ninth grade graduate four years later, on-time graduation rates for minority and low-income students, especially males, are much lower. In 2001, for example, only about 50 percent of African-American students and 51 percent of Latino students graduated on time, compared to 75 percent of white students and 77 percent of Asian and Pacific Islanders. [2]

Students with family incomes in the lowest 20 percent dropped out of school at six times the average rate of wealthier students. [3]

In about a sixth of American high schools, the freshman class routinely shrinks by 40 percent or more by the time students reach senior year. For the most part, those schools serve low-income and minority students. Nearly half of African-American students, 40 percent of Latino students and 11 percent of white students attend high schools where graduation is not the norm. A high school with a majority of students who are racial or ethnic minorities is five times more likely to promote only 50 percent or fewer freshmen to senior status within four years than a school with a white majority. [4]

Meanwhile, the earning power of dropouts has been dropping for three decades. For example, the earnings of male dropouts fell by 35 percent between 1971 and 2002, measured in 2002 dollars. Three-quarters of state prison inmates and 59 percent of federal inmates are dropouts. In 2001, only 55 percent of young adult dropouts were employed. Even the death rate is 2.5 times higher for people without a high-school education than for people with 13 years or more of schooling. [5]

But if the consequences are known, the cures may be harder to pinpoint.

Many educators say dropping out starts early. "Disengagement doesn't start in the ninth grade. It starts in fifth," says James F. Lytle, a University of Pennsylvania professor and former superintendent of the Trenton, N.J., public schools. For on-track students in middle-class schools, "middle school has the most interesting, exciting stuff in class" — science experiments, readings about interesting people in history and studies "of how the world works" — he says.

But once students are judged to be reading behind grade level, as happens with many urban fifth-graders, middle schools turn to "dumbed-down remedial work" that's below students' real intellectual level and leaves them bored and dispirited, Lytle says. It doesn't have to be that way, he says. "But I wish that educational courseware was farther

Retooling the school system to support higher standards may seem daunting, but "a quick walk through history" shows that it wouldn't be the first time the United States has made heroic efforts on education, says Wise. For example, "after World War II, you had soldiers coming home in need of better skills, and you had the GI Bill" to help them continue their educations.

Then "in the civil rights era we said, 'We believe that every child should be able to enter school,' and that happened," Wise says. "Now we're saying that every child should graduate."

For a time, the civil rights era seemed to be accelerating growing academic parity in learning, at least between black and white students. Following World War II, standardized test scores for black students began moving closer to white students' scores. The years from the 1960s to the '80s saw fully half of the black-white academic achievement gap eliminated, says The Civil Rights Project's Orfield.

down the road" of providing ways to combine skills teaching with subject matter that is at students' actual age level.

"Kids disengage early," says Lalitha Vasudevan, an assistant professor at Columbia University's Teachers College who works in an education program for young African-American males who've been diverted from jail and are mostly dropouts. "Often, early on, they've had teachers say things to them that they interpret as, 'You don't really care that I'm here,'" she says.

Dropping out "is not a decision that is made on a single morning," says a report from the Bill & Melinda Gates Foundation. In an extensive survey of dropouts, researchers found that "there are clear warning signs for at least one-to-three years" before students drop out, such as frequently missing school, skipping class, being held back a grade or frequently transferring among schools. [6]

Some key factors cited by the dropouts in the Gates study: Schools don't respond actively when students skip class and don't provide an orderly and safe environment. "In middle school, you have to go to your next class or they are going to get you," said a young male dropout from Philadelphia. "In high school, if you don't go to class, there isn't anybody who is going to get you. You just do your own thing." [7]

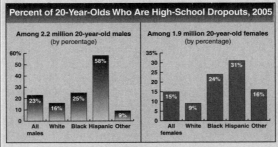

Majority of Dropouts Are Hispanic, Black

More than 50 percent of 20-year-old male high-school dropouts are Hispanic or African-American (graph at left). By comparison, 55 percent of the females are black or Hispanic (graph at right).

Percent of 20-Year-Olds Who Are High-School Dropouts, 2005

Among 2.2 million 20-year-old males (by percentage)

All males	White	Black	Hispanic	Other
23%	16%	25%	58%	9%

Among 1.9 million 20-year-old females (by percentage)

All females	White	Black	Hispanic	Other
15%	9%	24%	31%	16%

Source: "The Costs and Benefits of an Excellent Education for All of America's Children," Teachers College, Columbia University, January 2007

Lytle says cities could also establish post-dropout academies, like the Dropout Recovery High School he started in Trenton, which helped increase that city's graduation numbers.

"Rather than defining the whole problem as stopping dropouts, we can also reach out to those who already have," he says. "There are a slew of people around" who are out of school and would like to go back, from teenage mothers caring for their children to 60-year-olds, he says. "They need a school that is built around their lives. I simply don't understand why urban districts haven't been more imaginative" about this.

---

[1] Nancy Martin and Samuel Halperin, *Whatever It Takes: How Twelve Communities are Reconnecting Out-of-School Youth*, American Youth Policy Forum, www.aypf.org/publications/WhateverItTakes/WITfull.pdf.

[2] *Ibid.*

[3] *Ibid.*

[4] Robert Balfanz and Nettie Legters, "Locating the Dropout Crisis," Center for Social Organization of Schools, Johns Hopkins University, June 2004.

[5] Martin and Halperin, *op. cit.*

[6] John M. Bridgeland, John J. DiIulio, Jr. and Karen Burke Morison, *The Silent Epidemic: Perspectives of High School Dropouts*, Bill & Melinda Gates Foundation, March 2006.

[7] Quoted in *ibid.*

In the late '80s, however, the progress of African-American students in closing the gap stalled, and between 1988 and 1994, average test scores for black students actually began falling. [42]

Minority Schools

U.S. schools briefly became more integrated after the civil rights battles of the 1950s and '60s, but shifting housing patterns have caused the concentration of poor, minority and non-English-speaking students in urban schools to rise for the past 25 years.

"One thing that's not fully understood is that, through a long historical process, we've concentrated our most needy students in a small subset of schools and districts" in rural and, mostly, urban areas, vastly increasing the burden those schools face in raising academic achievement, says Balfanz.

In its landmark 1954 *Brown v. Board of Education* ruling, the Supreme Court declared it illegal to inten-

The "Behavior Gap" Between Black and White Students

Many educators blame a system that's middle-class and white-centered

Data from around the country indicate that black students, especially males, are cited much more often for disciplinary infractions than whites. The resulting "behavior gap" parallels the much-talked-about academic achievement gap.

Many analysts blame the phenomenon in part on a "culture clash" between black students, many poor, and an education system that's white-centered and middle-class. But there's little agreement about exactly what the gap means and what to do about it.

"You find the gap in all schools," including wealthy ones, says Clara G. Muschkin, a researcher at the Duke University Center for Child and Family Policy. Nevertheless, some evidence suggests there may also be a behavior gap between richer and poorer students, which accounts for just under a third of the black-white gap, Muschkin says.

In North Carolina schools, the racial gap "is persistent at all the grades" but is widest in seventh grade, says Muschkin. About 30 percent of black seventh-graders and 14 percent of whites have at least one disciplinary infraction reported during the school year.

African-American male students have the highest rates of suspensions and expulsions in most metropolitan areas around the country, according to Denise L. Collier, a doctoral candidate in education at California State University, Los Angeles. In New York, for example, where African-American males are 18 percent of the student population, they account for 39 percent of school suspensions and 50 percent of expulsions. In Los Angeles, black males make up 6 percent of the population but account for 18 percent of suspensions and 15 percent of expulsions. [1]

Some educators say that many urban African-American students don't learn at home the kinds of communication behaviors that are the norm for the middle class, and that this lack of background accounts for much of the gap.

"Americans of a certain background learn . . . early on and employ . . . instinctively" techniques like sitting up straight, asking questions and tracking a speaker with their eyes in order to take in information, said David Levin, a founder of the Knowledge Is Power Program (KIPP) charter schools, which serve mainly black and Hispanic students in several cities. [2]

When students in one Levin class were asked to "give us the normal school look," they responded by staring off into space and slouching, recounted *New York Times Magazine* editor Paul Tough in an article last year on successful urban charter schools. "Middle-class Americans know intuitively that 'good behavior' is mostly a game with established rules; the KIPP students seemed to be experiencing the pleasure of being let in on a joke," Tough observed. [3]

Behavior like a proper in-school work ethic has to be taught "in the same way we have to teach adding fractions with unlike denominators," said Dacia Toll, founder of the Amistad Academy charter school in New Haven, Conn. "But once children have got the work ethic and the commitment to others and to education down, it's actually pretty easy to teach them."

The academic gap that puts many black students in remedial instruction as they move through school may worsen the problem, says Robert Balfanz, associate research scientist at the Johns Hopkins University Center on the Social Organization of Schools. "In traditional remedial instruction, I assume you know nothing, so I teach the

---

tionally segregate schools by race. [43] In 1964, Congress passed the Civil Rights Act, outlawing discrimination in any institution that received federal funds, including schools. [44] As a result, more schools accommodated lower-income students along with middle-class students, white students and students from other ethnic groups.

The civil rights era lasted a scant 20 years, however, and housing patterns and new waves of immigration

soon led to concentrations of poor and minority students in many urban school districts again.

As early as 1974, the Supreme Court effectively set limits on how far racial integration of students could go. The court ruled in *Milliken v. Bradley* that the remedy to racial segregation in Detroit could not include moving children to schools in the surrounding suburbs. [45]

times table" and basic reading skills like letter sounds, he says. "But the majority of kids behind can actually read at a basic level. What they're missing is comprehension skill, vocabulary. So they get bored and frustrated."

Middle-class education majors student-teaching in urban schools found that using books about topics their students personally had encountered — including homelessness, racism and poverty — decreased discipline problems, even though the teachers initially resisted the books as inappropriate for children, according to Professor Christine H. Leland and Professor Emeritus Jerome C. Harste of Indiana University-Purdue University, Indianapolis. Once the student teachers broached the tough subject matter, they began reporting "fewer discipline problems . . . the children listened carefully and engaged in thoughtful discussions when they perceived that the issues being discussed were worth their attention." [4]

Many African-American student discipline problems involve "defiance" issues such as acting threatening or making excessive noise rather than activities like drug use or leaving the classroom without permission, according to University of Virginia Assistant Professor Anne Gregory. [5]

Seventy-five percent of African-American disciplinary referrals were for "defiance" behaviors in a study Gregory cites, many more than for other ethnic groups. That may suggest that teachers judge African-American students' behavior more "subjectively" than that of other students, Gregory says. Based on their past feelings of being restricted and excluded, some African-American students may be more likely to act out when they perceive that teachers are being unfair, Gregory suggests.

"If I was this little Caucasian boy or this preppy girl, she wouldn't talk with me that way. I am like the opposite. I am this little thug . . . I mean, she don't know," one student in Gregory's study said of a teacher perceived to be unfair. [6]

Avoiding excessive discipline battles in urban schools requires a seemingly contradictory set of characteristics that not everyone can muster, said Franita Ware, a professor of education at Spelman College, a historically black school for women in Atlanta. Teachers who succeed tend to be "warm demanders," those whom "students believed . . . did not lower their standards" but also "were willing to help them." [7]

"Sometimes I mean-talk them in varying degrees of severity," one teacher told Ware. But "sometimes you have to go back and say, 'What was really going on with you when I yelled at you? I'm just so sorry.' " [8]

Often the adult is the provocateur in the behavior situation, even if they don't realize it, such as when a student finds the nurse's office door locked at 3:02 and starts pounding on it, says James F. Lytle, a professor at the University of Pennsylvania and former school superintendent in Trenton, N.J.

"A lot of it is just the way you talk to people — respect," Lytle says. "Many are so accustomed to being denigrated. The kids have so little that the protection of one's ego is very important."

---

[1] Denise L. Collier, "Sally Can Skip But Jerome Can't Stomp: Perceptions, Practice, and School Punishment (Preliminary Results)," paper presented at the American Educational Research Association annual meeting, San Francisco, Calif., April 2006.

[2] Quoted in Paul Tough, "What It Takes To Make a Student," *New York Times Magazine*, Nov. 26, 2006, p. 51.

[3] *Ibid.*

[4] Christine H. Leland and Jerome C. Harste, "Doing What We Want to Become: Preparing New Urban Teachers," *Urban Education*, January 2005, p. 67.

[5] Anne Gregory, "Justice and Care: Teacher Practices To Narrow the Racial Discipline Gap," paper presented at the American Educational Research Association annual conference, San Francisco, Calif., April 2006.

[6] Quoted in *ibid.*

[7] Franita Ware, "Warm Demander Pedagogy: Culturally Responsive Teaching that Supports A Culture of Achievement for African-American Students," *Urban Education*, July 2006, p. 427.

[8] Quoted in *ibid.*

Then, in the 1980s, federal efforts to desegregate schools effectively ended. During the presidency of Ronald Reagan (1981-1988), the U.S. Justice Department backed off forcing states to comply with desegregation mandates. Two Supreme Court decisions in the early 1990s effectively declared the goal of black-white school integration had been addressed, as the court ruled that school districts could be excused from court-ordered bus-

ing if they had made good-faith efforts to integrate, even if they had not fully complied with court orders. [46]

At the same time, however, Hispanic students were becoming a new minority that concentrated in schools with bigger academic challenges than others, such as teaching English-language learners.

The segregation of Latino students soared during the civil rights era. In 1973, in *Keyes v. School District No. 1*,

AP Photo/Mike Derer

Edwin Bradley listens to his fifth-grade daughter Antoinette read at the South Street School library in Newark, N.J. One of the poorest in the state, the school district has been encouraged under a new program to support parental involvement in an attempt to improve student performance.

the Supreme Court outlawed policies in Denver that had the effect of segregating Hispanic and African-American children into separate schools. In ensuing years, however, this somewhat complex ruling was only spottily enforced, according to civil rights advocates. [47]

Today Latinos "are America's most segregated minority group," said Orfield. "The average Latino student goes to a school that is less than 30 percent white, has a majority of poor children and an "increasing concentration" of students who don't speak English. [48]

Poor in School

Until around the 1970s, children of all races and classes attended urban schools, and their average achievement levels didn't draw the same alarmed attention as today. Urban sprawl and white flight from cities over the past three decades have not only increased the number of urban schools with high minority populations but also increased the concentration of urban poverty as well, increasing the burden on urban schools.

"Sprawl is a product of suburban pulls and urban pushes," said the University of Maryland's Baum. "Families move to the suburbs for good housing, open space. They leave cities to avoid bad schools, threats to safety . . . contact with other races and poor public services." [49]

Furthermore, minority children are more concentrated in urban areas than the general population, largely because white families with children move to suburbs while childless whites are more likely to remain in the city, said Baum. Nationally, in nearly all school districts with more than 25,000 students, interracial contact has declined since 1986. [50]

Even more than ethnic minorities, poor people have concentrated in cities, says Balfanz. Over the past 20 years, even in periods when overall poverty has dropped, "the cities have gotten poorer and the concentration of poverty there deeper."

Between 1960 and 1987, the national poverty rate for people in central cities rose from 13.4 percent to 15.7 percent. At the same time, the poverty rate for rural residents fell by one-half and for suburban residents by one-third. By 1991, 43 percent of people with incomes below the federal poverty line lived in central cities. [51]

"The nation's student population is two-thirds middle class (not eligible for federally subsidized lunches), yet one-quarter of American schools have a majority of students from low-income households," according to The Century Foundation. [52]

Among the burdens urban schools bear are poverty-related learning deficiencies children bring to school with them, regulations and economic barriers that limit urban-school resources, and a historical role as job providers in inner cities.

A large body of research shows that many low-income parents interact with their children in ways that hinder them in school, wrote Tough last year in *The New York Times Magazine*. For example, professional parents speak to their young children about two-and-a-half more times in an hour than poor parents do and encourage them verbally about six times more often than they discourage them; low-income parents discourage their children about three times as often as they encourage them, he said.

Unlike poor parents, middle-class parents also encourage their children to question, challenge and negotiate. In short, "in countless ways, the manner in which [poor children] are raised puts them at a disadvantage" in a school culture, Tough noted. [53]

For a variety of reasons, urban schools also have a much harder time keeping good teachers. "Many thousands — perhaps millions — of urban students don't have permanent, highly qualified teachers, ones with the skill to communicate important stuff to kids," says Kitty Kelly-Epstein,

Would raising teacher pay help struggling schools?

YES   Patty Myers
Technology coordinator, Great Falls (Montana) Public Schools

From testimony on behalf of the National Education Association before U.S. Senate Committee on Finance, March 20, 2007

Ensuring a highly qualified teacher in every classroom is critical to closing achievement gaps and maximizing student learning. No single factor will make a bigger difference in helping students reach high academic standards. . . .

Unfortunately, difficulty in attracting quality teachers and high turnover rates severely hamper the ability to maintain a high-quality learning environment. Approximately one-third of the nation's new teachers leave the profession during their first three years, and almost one-half leave during their first five years. And turnover in low-income schools is almost one-third higher than the rate in all schools.

The teaching profession has an average national starting salary of $30,377. Meanwhile, computer programmers start at an average of $43,635, public accounting professionals at $44,668 and registered nurses at $45,570.

Annual pay for teachers has fallen sharply over the past 60 years in relation to the annual pay of other workers with college degrees. The average earnings of workers with at least four years of college are now over 50 percent higher than the average earnings of a teacher. Congress should reward states that set a reasonable minimum starting salary for teachers and a living wage for support professionals working in school districts. NEA recommends that all teachers in America enter the classroom earning at least $40,000 annually.

NEA also supports advancing teacher quality at the highest-poverty schools by providing $10,000 federal salary supplements to National Board Certified Teachers. Congress also should fund grants to help teachers in high-poverty schools pay the fees and access professional supports to become certified.

Often schools with the greatest needs and, consequently, the most challenging working conditions have the most difficulty retaining talented teachers. . . . Many hard-to-staff schools are high-poverty inner-city school or rural schools that, as a consequence of their location in economically depressed or isolated districts, offer comparatively low salaries and lack [the] amenities with which other districts attract teachers.

NEA strongly supports federal legislation with financial incentives for teaching in high-poverty schools, such as the Teacher Tax Credit Act introduced in the 109th Congress. The bill would provide a non-refundable tax credit to educators who work at schools that are fully eligible for federal Title I funds for disadvantaged students and would help hard-to-staff schools retain the quality teachers they need to succeed.

NO   Jay P. Greene
Senior Fellow, Manhattan Institute

Posted on the Web, 2006

The common assertion that teachers are severely underpaid is so omnipresent that many Americans simply accept it as gospel. But the facts tell a different story.

The average teacher's salary does seem modest at first glance: about $44,600 in 2002 for all teachers. But when we compare it to what workers of similar skill levels in similar professions are paid, we find that teachers are not shortchanged.

People often fail to account for the relatively low number of hours that teachers work. Teachers work only about nine months per year. During the summer they can either work at other jobs or use the time off however else they wish. Either way, it's as much a form of compensation as a paycheck.

The most recent data indicate that teachers average 7.3 working hours per day, and that they work 180 days per year, or about 1,314 hours. Americans in normal 9-to-5 professions who take two weeks of vacation and another 10 paid holidays put in 1,928 hours. This means the average teacher's base salary is equivalent to a full-time salary of $65,440.

In 2002, elementary-school teachers averaged $30.75 per hour and high-school teachers $31.01 — about the same as architects, civil engineers and computer-systems analysts. Even demanding, education-intensive professions like dentistry and nuclear engineering didn't make much more per hour.

Some argue that it's unfair to calculate teacher pay on an hourly basis because teachers perform a large amount of work at home — grading papers on the weekend, for instance. But people in other professions also do off-site work.

Many assume that teachers spend almost all of the school day teaching. But in reality, the average subject-matter teacher taught fewer than 3.9 hours per day in 2000. This leaves plenty of time for grading and planning lessons.

It is well documented that the people drawn into teaching these days tend to be those who have performed least well in college. If teachers are paid about as well as employees in many other good professions, why aren't more high performers taking it up?

One suspects that high-performing graduates tend to stay away because the rigid seniority-based structure doesn't allow them to rise faster and earn more money through better performance or by voluntarily putting in longer hours. In any case, it's clear that the primary obstacle to attracting better teachers isn't simply raising pay.

The Knowledge Is Power Program (KIPP) charter school in the Bronx, N.Y., boasts the highest test scores in the area. Although most KIPP schools are not racially integrated, they are reducing achievement gaps between black and white students.

a professor of education at the Fielding Graduate University in Santa Barbara, Calif. In California, at least, state rules force some urban school districts to rely on temporary teachers because not enough applicants have required certifications, she says. "There never has been a time when low-income schools were fully staffed," she says.

With joblessness high in cities, especially for minority applicants, it's also "not uncommon" for school districts to be the major job source in the area, according to Johns Hopkins University Associate Professor of Education Elaine M. Stotko and colleagues. In a tradition that dates back to patronage systems in the early 20th century, urban politicians often interfere with schools' hiring the best managerial and teaching candidates by pressuring them to hand out jobs "as political favors." [54]

The Supreme Court is due to rule by the end of June in two race-based integration cases. With a new conservative majority, the court is widely expected to rule in favor of the white parents who are seeking to end race-based school integration in Seattle and Louisville, Ky. Decisions against the school districts could end many similar programs around the country, many of which were court-ordered in the past. [55]

But some school districts still worry that schools with high concentrations of minority and poor students harm achievement. Over the past several years, a few districts, including Raleigh, N.C., and Cambridge, Mass., have experimented with integrating students by socioeconomic

status. In 2000, for example, the school board in Wake County, N.C., which includes Raleigh and its suburbs, replaced its racial integration system with the goal that no school should have 40 percent of students eligible for free or reduced-price lunch. [56]

Raleigh's effort was simpler politically than most, because the school district contains both the area's low-poverty and high-poverty schools. If the higher-income suburbs had been outside the district, political push-back would have made the program a tougher sell.

Some early Raleigh results look promising. On the state's 2005 High School End of Course exams, 63.8 percent of the low-income students passed, as did 64.3 percent of its African-American seniors, compared to pass rates in the high-40 and low 50-percent range for the state's other urban districts. [57]

CURRENT SITUATION

Congress Divided

The No Child Left Behind Act (NCLB), enacted in 2002, is intended to push American schools to raise achievement for all students, including low-income and minority children. As such, it represents one more step down a road that Congress embarked on in its 1994 reauthorization of the Elementary and Secondary Education Act — exerting federal influence to ensure that all students meet higher academic standards.

With NCLB up for reauthorization, Congress is struggling to figure out its next steps, with little apparent agreement on the horizon. With the press of other business, and strong disagreements in Congress about the education law, it's not clear that it will be reauthorized this year. The new congressional Democratic majority has already begun to hold hearings, however.

U.S. businesses have become increasingly involved in education policy, and many business leaders are urging Congress to continue and strengthen federal efforts to raise academic standards and provide incentives for states and localities to extensively retool their school systems to improve student achievement.

"Unless we transform the American high school, we will limit economic opportunities for millions of Americans," declared Microsoft Chairman Bill Gates at a Senate Health, Education, Labor and Pensions Committee hearing on March 7. [58]

Meanwhile, a group of conservative congressional Republicans has introduced legislation that would replace most of the NCLB achievement and reporting requirements that determine funding with block-grant funding that states could get whether they met NCLB standards or not. The measure would restore states and localities to their traditional role as prime overseers of schools, said Rep. Peter Hoekstra, R-Mich., who sponsored the legislation. "President Bush and I just see education fundamentally differently," he said. "The president believes in empowering bureaucrats in Washington, and I don't." [59]

But many congressional Democrats argue that a strengthened federal hand in education is warranted, partly because NCLB data now clearly reveals that the state-run systems of old have left so many poor and minority children disastrously behind.

Rep. George Miller, D-Calif., and Sen. Kennedy, key supporters of NCLB and chairs of the House and Senate committees that govern it, have both held pre-authorization hearings this year. Both say they're committed to increasing resources for struggling schools in a new bill, especially by supporting the hiring and training of more and better teachers.

"We know the law has flaws, but we also know that with common-sense changes and adequate resources, we can improve it by building on what we've learned," said Kennedy in a statement.

Retooling NCLB?

Education analysts have no shortage of changes to suggest.

President Bush is looking at "tinkering" with NCLB in a reauthorization, but Democrats are "interested in something broader," says Cardinali of Communities in Schools. "The [current] law is too fixated on academics," he says. After 30 years of experience helping students get additional services they need like tutoring and health care, "we've learned that student services are a critical component," he says.

"The brutal truth is that there is only one institution in America where you can get to kids in a thoughtful way — the school," he says. "Let's make that the center" where parents and children can get needs met that are critical for learning readiness. "Are we trying to make public education something it's not? No. It's a holistic view" of what it takes to educate a child.

One gap the University of Chicago's Knowles would like to see rectified: In NCLB's reporting requirements "the unit of analysis is the kid, the school and the district, and there's a stunning absence there if we really believe that instruction is at the heart of learning." Research indicates, he says, that individual classroom teachers may be the strongest in-school influence on student achievement.

However, "Democrats' strong ties to labor" helped keep teacher accountability out of the bill, he says.

In addition, "higher ed has been given pretty much a free pass," Knowles says. A future bill should focus attention on which education schools are producing the best-quality teachers.

Low-achieving schools shouldn't be punished, but given the tools to do better, says Knowles. Supports like teacher development and well-integrated extra services like social worker, closely targeted on high-need schools, are a "precondition" for improvement, he says.

Another key: additional flexibility for leaders of low-achieving schools to hire and fire and set policy and schedules. Principals say, "Yeah, you give me the hiring and firing of teachers and I'll give you the better results," and they're correct, says Knowles.

Reporting data for accountability isn't the problem. It's the very narrowly focused reporting requirement, many analysts say.

"Replace the overreliance on standardized testing with multiple measures," such as attendance figures and accurate dropout rates, says the University of Rochester's Hursh.

The federal government should also support strong, unbiased research on what improves instruction, especially in the middle- and high-school years, which are federally funded at a tiny fraction of the level of elementary schools and colleges, says Wise of the Alliance for Excellent Education. "No state or local district has the money for this," he says.

OUTLOOK

Agreeing to Disagree

There's growing agreement that schools should be educating all students to a higher standard. However, there's still disagreement about how much and what kind of help schools would need to do it.

An ideal outcome would be for institutions that are the most lasting presence in cities, such as business groups like the Chamber of Commerce, local hospitals and colleges to take ownership of urban education to drive change, says Balfanz of Johns Hopkins. A movement in that direction may be beginning, he says. "For awhile, there were mainly rhetorical reports," but today groups like the Chamber of Commerce are producing more potentially useful policy work, he says.

"The climate is shifting" toward the conclusion that everyone needs a diploma, says Balfanz. "You can't even find an employer who says, 'I'll hire people who aren't high-school graduates.' " So when students drop out, "it just feeds the next generation of poverty," he says.

There's currently an opportunity to revise NCLB in a way that helps low-achieving schools, says the University of Chicago's Knowles. Nevertheless, "people have already formed hard opinions," and debate could turn solely partisan, he says.

Lawmakers must aim for a delicate balance on federal initiatives, says Columbia's Henig. Federal interventions must aim at "making local processes work," since local on-the-ground actions are ultimately what make or break schools, he says.

The University of Pennsylvania's Lytle fears that privatization may be on the verge of overwhelming education, with potentially disastrous consequences for low-income families.

"I think the K-12 education business is in the process of deconstructing," he says. "The middle class is looking outside the schools" to private tutoring companies and Internet learning for academics. "More and more, for them, schools are amounting to expensive child care." Some states are aggressively pioneering "virtual" online charter schools and charters granted to home-schoolers, he says.

"The cost side and the efficacy side of education are on a collision course, and I think Congress will end up endorsing fairly radical experimentation" with vouchers, for example, Lytle says. "They'll say, 'There's no evidence that reducing class size or other expensive measures helps, so let's let American ingenuity work. Where does that leave urban kids? Out of luck," Lytle says. "You've got to be pretty sophisticated to make market forces work for you."

But "there's been progress in the last decade with whole-school reform," says Balfanz. "The big question now is how we [change] whole school districts. "It's a big job but within human capacity," he says.

NOTES

1. Quoted in Judy Radigan, "Reframing Dropouts: The Complexity of Urban Life Intersects with Current School Policy," paper presented at the Texas Dropout Conference, Houston, Oct. 6, 2006.

2. "The Socioeconomic Composition of the Public Schools: A Crucial Consideration in Student Assignment Policy," University of North Carolina Center for Civil Rights, Jan. 7, 2005, www.law.unc.edu/PDFs/charlottereport.pdf.

3. For background, see Barbara Mantel, "No Child Left Behind," *CQ Researcher*, May 7, 2005, pp. 469-492.

4. Quoted in David J. Hoff and Kathleen Kennedy Manzo, "Bush Claims About NCLB Questioned," *Education Week*, March 9, 2007, www.edweek.org.

5. Quoted in *ibid.*

6. "The Nation's Report Card: Reading 2005," U.S. Department of Education Institute of Education Sciences, www.nationsreportcard.gov.

7. Douglas N. Harris, "Ending the Blame Game on Educational Inequity: A Study of 'High-Flying' Schools and NCLB," Education Policy Studies Laboratory, Arizona State University, March 2006.

8. Jay P. Greene, "Education Myths," The American Enterprise Online, American Enterprise Institute, August 2006.

9. For background, see Charles S. Clark, "Charter Schools," *CQ Researcher*, Dec. 20, 2002, pp. 1033-1056; Kenneth Jost, "School Vouchers Showdown," *CQ Researcher*, Feb. 15, 2002, pp. 121-144.

10. Greene, *op. cit.*

11. Brad Olsen and Lauren Anderson, "Courses of Action: A Qualitative Investigation Into Urban Teacher Retention and Career Development," *Urban Education*, January 2007, p. 5.

12. Quoted in *ibid.*, p. 14.

13. *Ibid.*

14. Arthur J. Rothkopf, "Elementary and Secondary Education Act Reauthorization: Improving NCLB To Close the Achievement Gap," testimony before the Senate Committee on Health, Education, Labor, and Pensions and the House Committee on Education and Labor, March 13, 2007.

15. For background, see Kenneth Jost, "Testing in Schools," *CQ Researcher*, April 20, 2001, pp. 321-344.

16. Richard J. Murnane, "Improving the Education of Children Living in Poverty," unpublished paper, Jan. 25, 2007.

17. *Ibid.*

18. For background, see Kenneth Jost, "School Desegregation," *CQ Researcher*, April 23, 2004, pp. 345-372.

19. Quoted in "Center on Race and Social Problems Commemorates *Brown v. Board of Education*," University of Pittsburgh School of Social Work, May 7, 2004.

20. Quoted in Brian Lamb, "No Excuses: Closing the Racial Gap in Learning," transcript, "Booknotes," C-SPAN, Feb. 1, 2004.

21. Paul Tough, "What It Takes To Make a Student," *The New York Times Magazine*, Nov. 26, 2006, p. 70.

22. R. Scott Baker, "School Resegregation: Must the South Turn Back?" *Journal of Southern History*, November 2006, p. 993.

23. Howell S. Baum, "Smart Growth and School Reform: What If We Talked About Race and Took Community Seriously?" *Journal of the American Planning Association*, winter 2004, p. 14.

24. "Divided We Fail: Coming Together Through Public School Choice," Task Force on the Common School, The Century Foundation Press, 2002, p. 3.

25. *Ibid.*, p. 13.

26. Quoted in Lamb, *op. cit.*

27. *Ibid.*

28. Terry Ryan and Quentin Suffren, "Charter School Lessons from Ohio," *The Education Gadfly*, Thomas B. Fordham Foundation, March 15, 2007, www.edexcellence.net.

29. Mark Simon, "What Teachers Know," *Poverty & Race*, September/October 2004, www.prrac.org.

30. Dreyon Wynn and Dianne L. H. Mark, "Book Review: Educating Teachers for Diversity: Seeing With a Cultural Eye," *Urban Education*, May 2005, p. 350.

31. Jocelyn A. Glazier, "Moving Closer to Speaking the Unspeakable: White Teachers Talking About Race," *Teacher Education Quarterly*, winter 2003.

32. Wanda J. Blanchett, "Urban School Failure and Disproportionality in a Post-*Brown* Era," *Remedial and Special Education*, April 2005, p. 70.

33. Christine H. Leland and Jerome C. Harste, "Doing What We Want to Become: Preparing New Urban Teachers," *Urban Education*, January 2005, p. 60.

34. *Ibid.*, p. 62.

35. Glazier, *op. cit.*

36. Wynn and Mark, *op. cit.*

37. For background, see Wayne J. Urban and Jennings L. Wagoner, *American Education: A History* (2003); Stanley William Rothstein, *Schooling the Poor: A Social Inquiry Into the American Educational Experience* (1994).

38. For background, see Kathy Koch, "Reforming School Funding," *CQ Researcher*, Dec. 10, 1999, pp. 1041-1064.

39. Derrick Bell, *Silent Covenants:* Brown v. Board of Education *and the Unfulfilled Hopes for Racial Reform* (2004), p. 88.

40. *Ibid.*, p. 91.

41. Ruth Curran Neild and Robert Balfanz, "An Extreme Degree of Difficulty: The Educational Demographics of Urban Neighborhood High Schools," *Journal of Education for Students Placed at Risk*, spring 2006, p. 135.

42. V. W. Ipka, "At Risk Children in Resegregated Schools; An Analysis of the Achievement Gap," *Journal of Instructional Psychology*, December 2003, p. 294.

43. The case is *Brown v. Board of Education of Topeka*, 347 U.S. 483 (1954).

44. For background, see Jost, "School Desegregation," *op. cit.*; Gary Orfield and John T. Yun, "Resegregation in American Schools," The Civil Rights Project, Harvard University, June 1999, www.civilrightsproject.harvard.edu/research/deseg/reseg_schools99.php.

45. The case is *Milliken v. Bradley*, 418 U.S. 717 (1974).

46. Ipka, *op. cit.* The cases are *Board of Education of Oklahoma City v. Dowell*, 498 U.S. 237 (1991) and *Freeman v. Pitts*, 498 U.S. 1081 (1992).

47. Gary Orfield and Chungmei Lee, "Racial Transformation and the Changing Nature of Segregation," The Civil Rights Project, Harvard University, January 2006, www.civilrightsproject.harvard.edu.; *Keyes v. School District No. 1*, Denver, Colorado, 413 U.S. 189 (1973).

48. Gary Orfield and Susan E. Eaton, "Back to Segregation," *The Nation*, March 3, 2003, p. 5.

49. Baum, *op. cit.*

50. *Ibid.*

51. Neild and Balfanz, *op. cit.*, p. 126.

52. "Divided We Fail," *op. cit.*, p. 17.

53. Tough, *op. cit.*

54. Elaine M. Stotko, Rochelle Ingram and Mary Ellen Beaty-O'Ferrall, "Promising Strategies for Attracting and Retaining Successful Urban Teachers," *Urban Education*, January 2007, p. 36.

55. Patrick Mattimore, "Will Court Put Integration on Hold?" *San Francisco Examiner*, Dec. 8, 2006, www.exaaminer.com. The cases — argued on Dec. 4, 2006 — are *Meredith v. Jefferson County Board of Education*, 05-915; and *Parents Involved in Community Schools v. Seattle School District No. 1*, 05-908.

56. Richard Kahlenberg, "Helping Children Move from Bad Schools to Good Ones," The Century Foundation, 2006, www.tcf.org/list.asp?type=PB&pubid=565.

57. *Ibid.*

58. Quoted in Michael Sandler, "Minding Their Business," *CQ Weekly*, April 2, 2007, p. 952.

59. Quoted in Jonathan Weisman and Amit R. Paley, "Dozens in GOP Turn Against Bush's Prized 'No Child' Act," *The Washington Post*, March 15, 2007, p. A1.

BIBLIOGRAPHY

Books

Kozol, Jonathan, *The Shame of the Nation: The Restoration of Apartheid Schooling in America*, Three Rivers Press, 2006.

A longtime education writer and activist reports on his five-year journey to closely observe 60 schools in 11 states. He describes almost entirely resegregated urban schools with dilapidated buildings, dirty classrooms and a dearth of up-to-date textbooks.

Rothstein, Richard, *Class and Schools: Using Social, Economic, and Education Reform to Close the Black-White Achievement Gap*, Economic Policy Institute, 2004.

A research associate at a think tank concerned with low- and middle-income workers and families argues that raising the achievement of urban students requires public policies that address students' multiple social and economic needs.

Thernstrom, Abigail, and Stephan Thernstrom, *No Excuses: Closing the Racial Gap in Learning*, Simon & Schuster, 2004.

A husband and wife who are senior fellows at the conservative Manhattan Institute for Public Policy Research argue that charter schools and the No Child Left Behind Act's focus on holding schools accountable for poor student achievement can close the achievement gap for urban students.

Articles

Boo, Katherine, "Expectations," *The New Yorker*, Jan. 15, 2007, p. 44.

A reform-minded superintendent closes Denver's lowest-achieving high school, hoping its students will accept the offer to enroll in any other city school, including some with mainly online classes. Mostly Latinos from the city's poorest families, the displaced students struggle with losing their old school, which has provided many with a sense of community, and with new choices that confront them, as well as the ever-present choice of dropping out.

Moore, Martha T., "More Mayors Are Moving To Take Over School System," *USA Today*, March 21, 2007, p. A1.

Albuquerque's mayor is among those who believe they could run schools better than their local school boards.

Saulny, Susan, "Few Students Seek Free Tutoring or Transfers From Failing Schools," *The New York Times*, April 6, 2006, p. 20.

The No Child Left Behind Act promises free tutoring for many students in low-achieving schools, but few of those students' families know about the option or have been able to enroll their children in good-quality tutoring programs.

Tough, Paul, "What It Takes To Make a Student," *The New York Times Magazine,* **Nov. 26, 2006, p. 44.**
A handful of charter schools are making strides against the achievement gap. But largely because low-income and minority students arrive at school with smaller vocabularies and far less knowledge about how to communicate with adults and behave in a learning situation, the work requires extra-long school hours and intense teacher commitment.

Reports and Studies

Beating the Odds: An Analysis of Student Performance and Achievement Gaps on State Assessments: Results from the 2005-2006 School Year, **Council of the Great City Schools, April 2007.**
A group representing 67 of the country's largest urban school districts examines in detail the recent performance of urban students on state tests.

Bridgeland, John M., John J. DiIulio, Jr., and Karen Burke Morison, *The Silent Epidemic: Perspectives of High School Dropouts,* **Bill & Melinda Gates Foundation, March 2006.**
Nearly half of high-school dropouts say they left school partly because they were bored. A third of the students left because they needed to work, and more than a fifth said they left to care for a family member.

Divided We Fail: Coming Together Through Public School Choice, Task Force on the Common School, **The Century Foundation, 2002.**
Basing its discussion on the idea that race- and class-segregated schools have proven a failure, a nonpartisan think tank explores the possibility of encouraging cross-district integration of low-income and middle-income students by methods like establishing high-quality magnet schools in cities.

Engaging Schools: Fostering High School Students' Motivation to Learn, Committee on Increasing High School Students' Engagement and Motivation to Learn, **National Research Council, 2003.**
A national expert panel examines methods for re-engaging urban high-school students who have lost their motivation to learn, a problem they say is widespread but solvable.

Levin, Henry, Clive Belfield, Peter Muennig and Cecilia Rouse, "The Costs and Benefits of an Excellent Education for All of America's Children," Teachers College, Columbia University, January 2007; www.cbcse.org/media/download_gallery/Leeds_Report _Final_Jan2007.pdf.
A team of economists concludes that measures to cut the number of school dropouts would pay for themselves with higher tax revenues and lower government spending.

For More Information

Achieve, Inc., 1775 I St., N.W., Suite 410, Washington, DC 20006; (202) 419-1540; www.achieve.org. An independent bipartisan group formed by governors and business leaders to promote higher academic standards.

Alliance for Excellent Education, 1201 Connecticut Ave., N.W., Suite 901, Washington, DC 20036; (202) 828-0828; www.all4ed.org. A nonprofit research and advocacy group seeking policies to help at-risk high-school students.

The Center for Education Reform, 1001 Connecticut Ave., N.W., Suite 204, Washington, DC 20036; (202) 822-9000; www.edreform.com. A nonprofit advocacy group that promotes school choice in cities.

The Century Foundation, 41 E. 70th St., New York, NY 10021; (212) 535-4441; www.tcf.org. Supports research on income inequality and urban policy.

Citizens for Effective Schools, 8209 Hamilton Spring Ct., Bethesda, MD 20817; (301) 469-8000; www.citizenseffectiveschools.org. An advocacy group that seeks policy changes to minimize the achievement gap for low-income and minority students.

Council of the Great City Schools, 1301 Pennsylvania Ave., N.W., Suite 702, Washington, DC 20004; (202) 393-2427; www.cgcs.org. A coalition of 67 urban school systems dedicated to improving urban schools.

Education Next, Hoover Institution, Stanford University; www.educationnext.org. A quarterly journal on education reform published by a conservative think tank.

The Education Trust, 1250 H St., N.W., Suite 700, Washington, DC 20005; (202) 293-1217; www2.edtrust.org. Dedicated to closing the achievement gap in learning and college preparation for low-income and minority students.

National Center for Education Statistics, 1990 K St., N.W., Washington, DC 20006; (202) 502-7300; http://nces.ed.gov. A Department of Education agency that provides statistics and analysis on U.S. schools, student attendance and achievement.

3

Universal Coverage

Marcia Clemmitt

Many working Americans, like Daniel and Mindy Shea, of Cincinnati, are un- or under-insured. Young workers are hit especially hard: In 2004, a third of Americans ages 19-24 were uninsured. Only 61 percent of Americans under age 65 obtain health insurance through their employers. As health costs rise and incomes sag, more and more companies are dropping coverage, especially restaurants and small businesses.

From *CQ Researcher*, March 30, 2007.

When Emily, a 24-year-old graduate student, discovered a lump on her thigh, her doctor told her to get an MRI to find out whether it was cancerous. But Emily's student-insurance policy didn't cover the $2,000 procedure, so she skipped it. [1]

Several weeks later, during outpatient surgery to remove the lump, Emily's surgeon found a rare, invasive cancer underneath the benign lump — with only a 20 to 40 percent survival rate. The skipped MRI could have detected the cancer much sooner, improving her chances for recovery.

Emily pieced together payment for her treatment from her school insurance, two state public-aid programs and a monthly payment plan that ate up more than 40 percent of her take-home income. But a year later she learned that annual health premiums for all students at her school would rise by 19 percent because a few, like her, had racked up high expenses. The price hike led many more students to skip purchasing the coverage altogether.

Advocates say such stories are a good reason why Congress should enact a universal health-insurance program. While Congress has been expanding public health insurance programs covering the very poor — especially children and their mothers — students and lower-income workers increasingly are losing coverage or are finding, like Emily, that they can't afford adequate coverage.

Today, 45 million Americans — about 15.3 percent of the population — lack health insurance, usually due to job loss, student status, early retirement or because they have entry-level jobs or work in a service industry or a small business. Only about 40 percent of businesses employing low-wage or part-time workers offer health

Cost of Premiums Rising Rapidly

The average annual cost of family health coverage has risen more than 50 percent since 2001, to $11,500, and is expected to exceed $18,000 in the next five years. Most of the cost is borne by the employer.

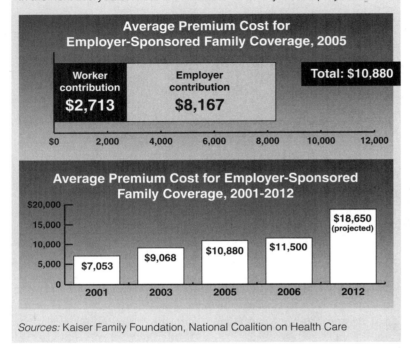

Average Premium Cost for Employer-Sponsored Family Coverage, 2005

Worker contribution	Employer contribution	Total: $10,880
$2,713	$8,167	

$0   2,000   4,000   6,000   8,000   10,000   12,000

Average Premium Cost for Employer-Sponsored Family Coverage, 2001-2012

$20,000 —
15,000 —
10,000 —
5,000 —
0 —

2001	2003	2005	2006	2012
$7,053	$9,068	$10,880	$11,500	$18,650 (projected)

Sources: Kaiser Family Foundation, National Coalition on Health Care

dramatically, health insurance costs will overtake profits by 2008."[6]

"If there's one thing that can bankrupt America, it's health care," warns U.S. Comptroller General David Walker, chief of the Government Accountability Office, Congress' nonpartisan auditing arm. And in response to those who say the United States can "grow" its way out of uninsurance by creating more and better jobs with coverage benefits, he states flatly: "Anybody that tells you we are going to grow our way out of this . . . probably isn't very proficient at math."[7]

While the public often pictures the uninsured as being unemployed, the fact is that most un- and under-insured Americans have jobs. Only 61 percent of Americans under age 65 obtain health insurance through their employers — down from 69 percent in 2000. And as health costs rise and incomes sag, more and more companies are dropping coverage, especially very small businesses. Because insurers raise premium prices for high-cost

benefits, and at $11,480 a year, the average family's health-insurance premium now costs more than a minimum-wage worker makes in a year. Young workers are hit especially hard: In 2004, more than a third of Americans between the ages of 19 and 24 were uninsured.[2] And in the construction and service industries, only 80 percent of the managers have health coverage.[3]

And the situation is only expected to get worse. U.S. health spending is expected to double by 2015 — to more than $12,300 per person.[4] As health-care costs skyrocket, so does the cost of health insurance, whether purchased by individuals or by employers. Between 2000 and 2006, health premiums for employer-sponsored insurance jumped 87 percent, far outpacing inflation's 18 percent overall increase.[5]

"Health insurance expenses are the fastest-growing cost component for employers," according to the National Coalition on Health Care. "Unless something changes

groups — as happened with Emily's grad-school coverage — small companies whose employees get seriously ill or injured or pregnant often find themselves priced out of coverage altogether.

Now some states are trying to create new sources of affordable coverage. Massachusetts is launching a universal-coverage plan in 2007 that has bipartisan support, and Republican California Gov. Arnold Schwarzenegger hopes to enact a similar measure. At the federal level, no new initiatives are expected this year — except for a probable expansion of children's coverage — but many expect universal coverage to be a major theme in the 2008 presidential election.

America's creeping lack of health coverage constitutes a crisis for the uninsured, even as the skyrocketing cost of health care makes it inevitable that even more people will be uninsured in the future. If health premiums continue rising at their current rate, about 56 million Americans are predicted to be uninsured by 2013 — 11 million more than today, according to a University of California at San Diego study. [8] The increase will cause 4,500 additional unnecessary deaths per year and $16 billion to $32 billion in lost economic productivity and other "human capital," the study says. [9]

The leading public myth about the uninsured is that "people without health insurance get the medical care they need," said Arthur Kellerman, chairman of Emory University's Department of Emergency Medicine and co-chairman of an Institute of Medicine (IOM) panel that has called for universal coverage by 2010. [10]

In fact, the uninsured seldom receive appropriate care at the appropriate time, said Kellerman. "The uninsured are less likely to see a doctor or be able to identify a regular source of medical care and are less likely to receive preventive services," he said. [11] And uninsured children admitted to a hospital due to an injury are twice as likely to die and 46 percent less likely to receive rehabilitation after hospitalization, according to a recent study by the consumer advocacy group Families USA. [12]

The growing number of uninsured Americans also pushes up the cost of publicly subsidized health insurance like Medicare, the panel said. Working-age uninsured patients with uncontrolled diabetes or high blood pressure eventually enter the health system sicker than they would have been had they been insured. [13] And about 20 percent of those with schizophrenia and bipolar disorder are uninsured and end up in jail or prison when their untreated conditions trigger illegal behavior, said the panel. [14]

Adding to the problem, manufacturing and unionized jobs were the mainstay of job-based coverage, but their numbers have been dropping for 20 years. "I suspect you're going to see wholesale withdrawal of employer-sponsored health care" for anyone earning less than twice federal poverty-level wages, said National Governors Association Executive Director Ray Scheppach. [15]

Americans Without Health Insurance

In 25 states, between 14 percent and 19 percent of the adults ages 18-64 did not have health insurance in 2005. States with high levels of uninsured residents typically have minimal state and employer insurance coverage.

Percentage of People Ages 18-64 Without Insurance, 2005

- 23% and over
- 19-22.9%
- 14-18.9%
- Under 14%

Source: Kaiser Family Foundation, statehealthfacts.org, 2005

"Economic security, jobs, health care and retirement security — those are all now one and the same issue," says Henry Simmons, president of the National Coalition on Health Care, which includes employers, unions and academic and other groups advocating universal coverage.

Pension investment funds have recently realized that skyrocketing health-care costs could bankrupt Americans' future if they are not checked, says Simmons. Since Medicare covers only some of the health services needed by retirees, virtually all elderly people who can afford it also purchase private supplemental insurance to fill the gaps. But pension-fund investors are finding no investments that grow fast enough to allow retirees' savings income to keep up with the anticipated soaring cost of future Medicare and supplemental-coverage premiums.

While no one expects significant action from Congress until after the 2008 presidential election, federal policymakers increasingly acknowledge a need for action. Consensus appears to be growing for some type of hybrid universal coverage that combines public and private insurance.

Universal Coverage Faces Financial Obstacles

Reducing health-care costs is the big challenge

Now that Americans appear to be reaching some consensus on the need for universal health coverage, major hidden obstacles — all involving money — must be overcome. Among those thorny financial issues are questions over who is going to pay for the coverage, how can affordable access be ensured for all and how can overall health-care costs be reduced.

Perhaps the most controversial issue is who will pay for the coverage. In 2005, employers paid 75 percent of workers' health-premium costs — about $500 billion compared to the approximately $170 billion that workers paid. [1] That's "most of the money outside the government that's spent on health care," says Stanley Dorn, a senior research associate at the liberal Urban Institute. To work, any universal-coverage plan will have to either continue to use those employer contributions or come up with a suitable replacement for them.

That's why many universal-coverage proposals ask employers for financial contributions. But making those contributions both fair and adequate is difficult, mainly because businesses vary so widely in what they pay today: Many contribute nothing, but others pay hundreds of millions of dollars each year.

Dorn says policymakers may want to consider asking all employers to pay a set amount into a general pool but vary the amount by companies' line of business and their geographical location. That way, companies that compete with one another would share the same burden.

Lawmakers also must figure out how to ensure affordable access to all. Many Republican proposals for expanding coverage rely on tax subsidies to help more people buy individual health policies. Because such coverage wouldn't be tied to a job, it would be "portable," so employees who switch or lose jobs would not be without insurance.

But buying individual health insurance can be far more expensive than purchasing through an employer because insurers don't "pool" risks the way they do for workers under employer-based policies. So individual purchasers pay based on their family's health status and age, which makes it the most expensive way to buy health insurance. Moreover, insurers won't even sell coverage to some people because the companies themselves consider it unaffordable.

"The words 'kinda crummy' come to mind when I think of the individual market," said former Maryland Insurance Commissioner Steve Larsen, now a private attorney. For example, a case of mononucleosis and a chronic condition like hay fever is enough for some insurers to deem a potential buyer unaffordable. "And if you have any type of serious mental illness, forget it," he said. [2] A study by the Georgetown University Institute for Health Care Research and Policy found that a 62-year-old overweight moderate smoker with controlled high blood pressure was deemed an unaffordable risk 55 percent of the times he sought individual health coverage. [3]

Buying an individual policy is more affordable for the young and healthy, says health-care consultant Robert

"In the past the debate got bogged down because different groups wanted their first-priority proposal only," says Ron Pollack, founding executive director of Families USA. "One group would say, 'Coverage must be financed through public programs,' while another would say, 'There should be no government action in the marketplace,' And since everyone's second-favorite program was the status quo, nothing happened."

But that decades-old logjam may be breaking up, as advocates on all sides of the issue creep closer to one another in their proposals. "The very grand visions on both sides" — a single-payer government system or relying on individuals saving money for their own care via

Health Savings Accounts (HSAs) — "are both completely impossible in our political system," says Yale University Professor of Political Science Jacob Hacker.

Even President George W. Bush, a longtime proponent of individually purchased HSAs, softened that stance in his most recent proposal. Bush's fiscal 2008 budget plan would offer similar tax breaks to those buying all kinds of health insurance, not just HSAs, either as individuals or through employers.

Paul Ginsburg, president of the nonpartisan research group Center for Studying Health System Change, says critics rightly point out that Bush's tax break doesn't target lower-income people who are most in danger of losing

Laszewski. His 20-something son found an individual health policy for $150 a month several years ago, but "if he was 58 years old, his premium would have been $1,500," he says. "If you're going to do universal health care, you can't age-rate premiums or bar people based on pre-existing conditions."

No matter how widely risk is shared, however, behind the high cost of insurance lurks the ever-rising cost of health care. "The 10,000-pound elephant in the room is cost," says Laszewski.

Health-care costs have been growing faster than the entire economy or any other sector in it for the past 45 years, says Gail Wilensky, a senior fellow at the nonprofit health-education foundation Project HOPE and former head of Medicaid and Medicare. "They can't go on doing it for the next 30 years" without crippling other parts of the economy, she says.

U.S. health-care costs are the world's highest because of insurers' high administrative and marketing costs and because American doctors and medical suppliers enjoy higher profits and salaries than their counterparts in other industrialized countries. [4]

In today's fragmented insurance system, insurers' efforts to attract the healthiest, cheapest customers add extra overall costs, point out Paul Menzel, a philosophy professor at Pacific Lutheran University in Tacoma, Wash., and Donald W. Light, professor of comparative health care at the University of Pennsylvania. [5] For example, they wrote, a Seattle survey found that 2,277 people were covered by 755 different policies linked to 189 different health-care plans.

"The $420 billion (31 percent!) paid [annually] for managing, marketing and profiting from the current frag-mented system could be drastically cut" if insurers had to take all comers rather than carefully jiggering their policies, premiums and marketing strategies to attract only the healthiest, least expensive buyers, they said.

A key is to cut spending on care by "learning more about what works for whom," says Wilensky. But getting that information requires investment, she says.

In addition to cutting excess services, says Laszewski, making coverage affordable will ultimately mean sacrificing some of the health-care industry's high profits and salaries. International comparisons show that other countries spend less on health care while delivering the same amount or even more services to patients.

Americans don't understand that controlling cost is crucial to sustaining the health system, let alone expanding coverage, says Laszewski. "I'll bet you if you told consumers that if they lost their jobs, replacing their insurance would cost $15,000 or $16,000 a year, they'd understand that," he says.

---

[1] Aaron Catlin, Cathy Cowan, Stephen Heffler and Benjamin Washington, "National Health Spending in 2005: The Slowdown Continues," *Health Affairs*, January/February 2007, p. 148.

[2] Quoted in "Reinsurance for Individual Market Pricks Up Many Ears," *Medicine & Health*, "Perspectives," Oct. 28, 2002.

[3] "Hay Fever? Bum Knee? Buying Individual Coverage May Be Dicey," *Medicine & Health*, June 25, 2001.

[4] For background, see Marcia Clemmitt, "Rising Health Costs," *CQ Researcher*, April 7, 2006, pp. 289-312.

[5] Paul Menzel and Donald W. Light, "A Conservative Case for Universal Access to Health Care," *The Hastings Center Report*, July 1, 2006, p. 36.

coverage. Nevertheless, "eventually, the Democrats may see that the president has given them something — a revenue source" to help pay for expanding coverage, he says.

So far, every Democrat who has announced he or she will run for president has declared a commitment to universal coverage, tying the issue to the country's overall economic health, but only former Sen. John Edwards, D-N.C., has announced a specific coverage plan. "The U.S. auto industry is struggling, in part because of the rising cost of health care that this administration has done nothing to address," newly announced Democratic candidate Sen. Barack Obama, D-Ill., said last November. "I have long proposed that the government make a deal with the Big Three automakers that will pay for a portion of their retiree health costs if they agree to invest those savings in fuel-efficient technologies." Health-care costs account for approximately $1,000 of the cost of each car produced by the America's largest automakers — more than they spend on steel. [16]

Among Republican presidential candidates, former Massachusetts Gov. Mitt Romney last year backed legislation intended to achieve universal coverage in his state, and former House Speaker Newt Gingrich, who has not yet thrown his hat into the presidential ring, also has called for systemic reforms in the health-care system.

Private Insurance Coverage Dropped

The percentage of people with private health insurance dropped by 8 percentage points from 1987 to 2005 (right). At the same time, the percentage of people insured by either government or private insurance dropped 3 percentage points (left). As people lost private coverage, government picked up the slack to keep as many people insured as possible.

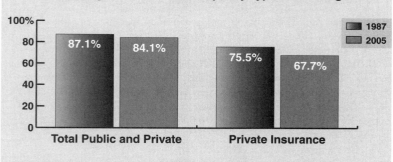

Percentage of Uninsured People by Type of Coverage

Source: U.S. Census Bureau, "Historical Health Insurance Tables"

While a consensus may be developing on the need for some kind of universal coverage, many contentious debates remain. For example, both the right and the left have criticized the California and Massachusetts plans for requiring individuals to buy health insurance, just as drivers are required to carry automobile insurance.

Nevertheless, many believe the country is on the verge of a focused, national debate on universal coverage. "In 2008, universal coverage will be up there with Iraq as top election issues," says Pollack.

As policymakers gear up for that debate, here are some of the questions being asked:

Can America afford universal health coverage?

Critics of universal-insurance proposals have long argued that while expanding coverage is desirable, covering everyone would simply cost too much. [17] Universal-coverage advocates, however, argue that current administrative expenses are high partly because the United States has a piecemeal system with many uninsured.

"It is impossible to get everybody covered," former Senate Majority Leader Bill Frist, R-Tenn., a transplant surgeon, said in 2004. [18] State efforts have shown that universal coverage is not financially feasible, he said.

For example, his home state of Tennessee managed to cover about 93 percent of residents — a national high — by having Medicaid cover both the uninsured and the uninsurable. But "in attempting to do this the state is going bankrupt," he said, "and there is a major effort to backtrack." [19]

Universal-coverage plans generally are "unrealistic," said former Health and Human Services Secretary Tommy G. Thompson. I just don't think it's in the cards. . . . "I don't think that administratively or legislatively it's feasible." [20]

While few politicians today will say America cannot afford universal coverage, both sides agree that the costs will be high. A study by the liberal Urban Institute says that in 2004 universal coverage would have added about $48 billion to the $125 billion the nation spent on health care for uninsured people — most of which was paid out of pocket by the uninsured or was delivered without compensation by doctors and hospitals. [21] A proposed universal-coverage plan for Maryland would raise that state's health spending by some $2.5 billion per year, while a Minnesota proposal to cover the state's 383,000 uninsured is projected to cost an estimated $663-$852 million in new annual funding. [22]

Most proposals for universal coverage call for increased government spending. And finding those dollars will be tough, given that the federal budget and many state budgets are facing substantial deficits. [23]

"The public sector has fewer resources" now compared to when the issue was debated previously, says Ginsburg, of the Center for Studying Health System Change. A lack of willingness or ability to commit new revenue has doomed at least one state plan, he adds. When Maine launched a universal-coverage initiative in 2003, the state "put almost no money in and got almost nothing out," he says.

The Democratic presidential hopefuls who have called for universal coverage "will be desperate for revenues when they put out their plans," says Robert Blendon, professor of health policy and management at the Harvard School of Public Health. "Money is going to be hard to come by. We've got defense costs that are very, very high."

A 2006 Massachusetts law requiring every resident to purchase subsidized coverage — unless that coverage is "unaffordable" — is already running into an affordability crisis, said Jonathan Gruber, a professor of economics at the Massachusetts Institute of Technology. [24] The state has said it would subsidize only those who earn up to three times the federal poverty level (about $30,000 for an individual and $60,000 for a family of four), said Gruber. But "at three times poverty, health insurance is still expensive. . . . It's not feasible to have someone spend 20, 30 or 40 percent of income on health insurance." [25]

While some say universal coverage is too expensive for America, many economists point out that industrialized nations with universal coverage spend less per capita on health care than the United States. In 2004, for instance, the United States spent $6,102 per capita on health care while Australia spent $3,120; Denmark, $2,881; Germany, $3,043; Luxembourg, $5,089; Sweden, $2,825 and Switzerland, $4,077. [26]

Not only are Americans paying more for health care than those in any other industrialized country, but they are getting lower-quality care — by some measurements — than consumers in countries with universal coverage. While new drugs and technology have improved longevity and quality of life for many Americans, the United States is ranked 37th by the World Health Organization in overall quality of care, based on adult and infant mortality rates. The United States also ranks 24th among industrialized nations in life expectancy. [27]

Those stark realities, coupled with the fact that U.S. health-care costs are spiraling out of control, lead a growing number of analysts to argue that the United States can't afford not to have universal coverage.

"I've always believed universal coverage would carry significant costs and would bring daunting . . . economic challenges," said Harold Pollack, associate professor at the University of Chicago School of Social Service Administration. [28] But recently, he says, he has decided "there is no alternative" to pushing forward with universal insurance. "The current system is no longer able to accomplish important things we expect from our health care." [29]

Former Gov. John Kitzhaber, D-Ore. — an emergency-room physician who now heads the Oregon-based

Wages Lagged Behind Increases in Premiums

Workers' wages rose less than 3 percent from 2004 to 2005 while health-insurance premiums jumped 9 percent.

Comparing Increases in Health Insurance Premiums and Workers' Earnings, 2004-2005

Sources: Alliance for Health Reform; Kaiser Family Foundation and Health Research and Educational Trust, 2005

Archimedes Project, a health-reform initiative — agrees. Economic growth depends on good health for all, he said. Good health "is the first rung on the ladder of opportunity . . . the cornerstone of a democratic society, allowing people to . . . be productive and to take advantage of the opportunities of upward mobility." [30]

Others argue that having more than 15 percent of the population uninsured means that all Americans pay more for health care. "The uninsured are one of the inefficiencies" driving health costs into the unaffordable range, says Robert Greenstein, executive director of the liberal Center on Budget and Policy Priorities.

"Reining in health-care cost growth" — which soared by 7 percent last year alone — is a prerequisite for universal coverage, says Robert Laszewski, an independent health-care consultant and a former health-insurance executive. Health-insurance premiums grow even faster than costs, and neither government subsidies nor the incomes of lower-wage working people can keep up with the current growth rate for long, he says.

If coverage expansion were accompanied by efforts to rein in spending and improve care, "there's absolutely no doubt that you can have universal coverage without substantially raised costs," says Simmons, president of the National Coalition on Health Care. "Every other country does it" already, he says.

Universal coverage is needed to "get a [health-care] market that works," he adds. "You can't fix the issue of cost" — which affects everyone, insured and uninsured — "without universal coverage," he says. Absent a universal-coverage requirement, "what markets do is avoid risk," such as when insurance companies develop marketing and risk-assessment procedures to avoid selling policies to sick people. "It's an open-and-shut case that universal coverage is cheaper and better" than the status quo.

Getting everyone covered and specifying uniform benefit packages would create a huge, immediate, one-time financial saving, Simmons says. "Automatically, you're talking about hundreds of billions of dollars" in savings that "every other nation has already captured," partly accounting for lower costs abroad.

Should Americans depend on states to expand coverage?

In recent years, states have been far more active than the federal government in expanding health coverage. Massachusetts and Vermont passed universal-coverage laws in 2006, and Illinois created a program to cover all children. Other proposals are being discussed in state legislatures this spring. [31]

States' uninsured populations vary widely around the country, so they are the natural venue for expanding coverage, say some analysts. "All states face different challenges in reducing the number of uninsured residents," so "imposing a one-size-fits-all program" at the federal level "will not work," said Arthur Garson, dean of the University of Virginia School of Medicine. [32]

With no national consensus emerging on how to cover the uninsured, encouraging state action is the only way forward, said Stuart M. Butler, vice president for domestic and economic policy at the conservative Heritage Foundation. "Successful welfare reform started in the states," and coverage could be expanded by removing federal roadblocks and offering federal incentives to states "to try proposals currently bottled up in Congress." [33]

In California over the past year, the Republican governor, Democratic legislators and top executives from the state's largest private insurer all proposed universal-coverage plans, though none has yet been enacted. The California-based Kaiser Foundation Health Plan offered a plan that would provide "near-universal coverage" within two years to California's 5 million uninsured — who represent a whopping 10 percent of all uninsured Americans. "Despite the greater dimensions of the problem in California, we believe that a state-based solution is possible," wrote Kaiser executives. [34]

While federal laws restrict states' ability to expand Medicaid and set rules for employer-sponsored coverage, that hasn't stopped some states from expanding coverage, says Stanley Dorn, a senior research associate at the liberal Urban Institute. In the early 1990s, for example, Minnesota and Washington state both "implemented coverage systems that succeeded brilliantly," he says.

Regardless of whether they succeed completely, state initiatives provide models and impetus for future national efforts, say many analysts. "The state action provides great momentum," says Dorn.

"States are hugely important," says Hacker at Yale University. "When two Republican governors" — Romney and Schwarzenegger — "break with the national party to propose universal coverage, that's a huge boost," he says.

Ginsburg, of the Center for Studying Health System Change, says the 2006 Massachusetts law has been a catalyst — "the answer to political gridlock." It is supported by both Republicans, who've traditionally been skeptical of universal coverage, and liberal Democrats who favor a single-payer system, he says.

The flurry of major state proposals shows the nation is ready for change, he says, even though "the federal government has been dysfunctional on domestic issues for many years." He predicts "a few more states" will expand coverage soon, but many states are limited in what they can accomplish.

All states can't emulate the Massachusetts model, said James J. Mongan, chief executive of the New England-based hospital and physician network Partners HealthCare, because Massachusetts is very different from most other states. [35]

"We started with half the problem solved," said Mongan, a former congressional health aide who also worked in the Carter administration. Only about 10 percent of Massachusetts residents were uninsured, compared to uninsurance rates in other states of 25 percent and higher. And the state was already spending more than $500 million annually to compensate hospitals for treating the uninsured. [36]

"Federal action ultimately [will] be essential," said Shoshanna Sofaer, professor of health policy at Baruch College in New York City and a member of the IOM insurance panel. States don't have the steady financing or the legal flexibility to expand coverage to all of their residents. One roadblock, she said, is the federal Employee Retirement Income Security Act (ERISA), which limits states' power to control insurance. [37]

"The best thing states can do is set up role models," says Brandeis University Professor of Health Policy Stuart Altman. "You can't design true national health insurance state by state, because you'd get past a few states, then stop."

While states' efforts are important, says the National Coalition on Health Care's Simmons, "we don't think that any single state, no matter how large," can accomplish universal coverage of its residents "without major federal policy changes." Many governors agree and acted on their own only because they're frustrated with a lack of federal action, he says.

Furthermore, even if all states achieved universal coverage, the result would be a cost-increasing nightmare — the last thing the health system needs, says Simmons. "If you think we have administrative complexity now, imagine 50 individual state programs."

Should individuals be required to buy health insurance?

At the turn of the new century, few people were advocating that all Americans be required to buy health insurance, but in recent years such voices have grown louder. With interest growing in a system that subsidizes the cost of private coverage, advocates say unless everyone participates no functioning insurance market can develop. Insurance is designed to even out annual health costs for everyone by having everyone pay similar amounts into an overall pool each year, whether they are healthy in that particular year or facing an unexpected sickness or injury.

But opponents on the left say mandating insurance is unfair to lower-income families who can't afford even heavily subsidized private insurance. And conservative critics say a requirement to purchase is undue government intrusion into private life.

"You can talk until you're blue in the face about risk pools and actuarial tables and all the green-eyeshade reasons that the health insurers need everyone to participate

in order to write affordable policies. I understand all that, and I basically don't care," wrote lawyer and policy blogger David Kravitz about Massachusetts' new buying requirement. "It is fundamentally wrong to force people to buy an expensive product in the private market, simply as a condition of existing in this state," he wrote on the Blue Mass Group policy blog. [38]

Monitoring who is obeying the requirement and determining subsidy sizes creates "one more aspect of citizens' lives" that government would monitor, complains Michael D. Tanner, director of health and welfare studies at the libertarian Cato Institute. A mandate would also be extremely difficult to enforce, he says.

"An individual mandate crosses an important line: accepting the principle that it is the government's responsibility to ensure that every American has health insurance," said Tanner. "In doing so, it opens the door to widespread regulation of the health-care industry and political interference in personal health-care decisions. The result will be a slow but steady spiral downward toward a government-run national health-care system." [39]

Advocates of a mandate argue that if government can require automobile insurance to ensure that costs are paid when drivers cause accidents, then health insurance shouldn't be any different, notes Tanner. But economists say there are some key differences between the two kinds of coverage. For example, few people will drive more recklessly just because they have auto insurance. But the prevalence of generous health insurance has been shown to encourage patients to seek — and doctors to prescribe — more and sometimes unnecessary or unduly expensive treatments. [40]

Nevertheless, policymakers from both parties increasingly consider mandating health insurance "an essential accommodation to limited public resources," explains Ginsburg of the Center for Studying Health System Change. In 2004, for instance, then-Senate Majority Leader Frist said "higher-income Americans have a societal and a personal responsibility to cover in some way themselves and their children." [41] If those who can afford coverage don't enroll, the government should enroll them automatically in a high-deductible insurance plan that covers catastrophic expenses and obtain the payment for the premiums at tax time, Frist said. And the mandate should apply to the "very, very rich" initially, then expand over time, he said. [42]

Requiring everyone to buy coverage ensures that those with lower medical needs will pay premiums alongside

CHRONOLOGY

1880s-1920s *Most European countries adopt compulsory health insurance.*

1895 German physicist William Roentgen discovers the X-ray, ushering in the age of modern medicine and rising health-care costs.

1920 Public commissions in California, New Jersey, Ohio and New York recommend universal state health coverage.

1926 The private Committee on the Cost of Medical Care (CCMC) endorses developing private health insurance; American Medical Association (AMA) opposes the idea.

1929 The first hospital prepayment insurance plan is launched for school teachers in Dallas, Texas.

1930s-1940s *Private hospital prepayment insurance spreads around the country, as hospitals worry they'll go under when poor patients don't pay. Congress and legislatures in at least eight states debate but don't enact compulsory health insurance.*

1935 Attempts to include health coverage in the new Social Security Act are unsuccessful.

1943 The first measure calling for compulsory national health insurance is introduced in Congress. . . . National War Labor Board declares employer contributions to insurance income-tax free, enabling companies to offer health insurance to attract workers.

1950s-1960s *Health spending and consumption rise rapidly, and workplace-based health insurance spreads. Medicare and Medicaid are enacted for the poor and elderly.*

1970s-1980s *Worries grow about health care becoming unaffordable. Presidents Nixon and Carter propose universal health coverage and health-care price controls. Cost controls reduce federal spending on Medicare, but doctors and hospitals shift their costs to employers.*

1990s *Federal government expands Medicaid and enacts a new children's health program, but employers begin dropping health benefits. Washington lawmakers shy away from large-scale coverage expansion after President Clinton's ambitious attempt to enact universal coverage fails.*

Sept. 22, 1993 Clinton unveils sweeping plan to reform U.S. health-care system.

Sept. 26, 1994 After a year of fierce debate, Senate leaders declare Clinton's bill dead.

1996 Congress enacts Health Insurance Portability and Accountability Act to make employer-provided coverage transferable between jobs and more accessible to the self-employed.

1997 Congress enacts State Children's Health Insurance Program (SCHIP) to help states cover children from low-income families.

2000s *As health costs and the ranks of the uninsured rise, Congress mulls new tax deductions and credits to help consumers buy coverage; interest grows in compulsory insurance.*

2002 Congress enacts Health Care Tax Credit, available to whose who lose their jobs due to foreign competition.

2006 Massachusetts enacts universal-coverage plan requiring all residents to buy health insurance. . . . Vermont enacts voluntary coverage plan with subsidized insurance and medical cost trimming. . . . Maryland plan to force large employers to supply coverage or pay into a state insurance pool is struck down in federal court.

2007 President Bush proposes replacing the tax break received by those with employer-based coverage with a tax deduction available to everyone. . . . Gov. Arnold Schwarzenegger, R-Calif., proposes universal, state-subsidized health insurance. . . . Advocates press Congress to expand SCHIP to more children and parents.

those with expensive illnesses, analysts point out. "If the government says an insurance company must take whoever comes their way, they couldn't predict risk and might go broke" if only sicker people enrolled, says Marian R. Mulkey, senior program officer at the California Healthcare Foundation, which funds health-care research. A mandate like the one Schwarzenegger proposes "relieves this concern of insurers, who are businesses and must be on solid financial footing to offer benefits."

The Medicare drug benefit works similarly, says health-care consultant Laszewski. Medicare doesn't require seniors to enroll but strongly encourages it by imposing a financial penalty on those who wait to sign up, he says.

The drug benefit "created a huge pool of people from age 65 to 95," he explains. "And you allowed people in at the same rates no matter what their age or pre-existing condition, so long as they signed up as soon as they became eligible."

The proof of that approach is in the pudding, he says. Private insurers have "flooded the market with plans," and people are not faced with steeply escalating premiums as they age or their health worsens, he says.

BACKGROUND

America vs. Europe

From the beginning, America differed sharply from other industrialized nations in its approach to health insurance. While Europe turned to social insurance, in which all residents pay into a common fund that provides population-wide benefits, American physicians resisted, fearing such an approach would encourage government influence over the practice of medicine. [43]

The development of the American workplace-based insurance system echoed "themes that distinguish the more general history of the United States," wrote Rosemary A. Stevens, University of Pennsylvania professor emeritus of the history of science. Social insurance was trumped by "the commitment to private solutions to public needs" and "the belief in local initiatives wherever possible." [44]

As the 19th century ended, Europeans leaned more toward "social democracy" — the belief the free market cannot supply certain human necessities, such as a minimum income to purchase food, clothing, housing and access to health services. Governments were seen as necessary to guarantee those needs, explains Thomas

Bodenheimer, adjunct professor of community medicine at the University of California, San Francisco. [45]

In the late 1800s a conservative German government enacted the first social-insurance programs in hopes of heading off a wholesale movement toward more radical socialism with government ownership of industries. Supported by mandatory contributions from all citizens, the first programs paid out when people lost their livelihood through unemployment, disability or retirement. In 1883, Germany added health care to its social-insurance offerings, though with a twist. Unlike other programs, health insurance was run by privately operated "sickness funds." Social insurance, including for health care, soon became the European norm.

In the United States, lawmakers debated social insurance for decades and ultimately used it for a few programs. But health insurance remained a voluntary purchase, managed by private companies.

American liberals argued that social insurance for health would unite the entire population into a single risk pool and serve everyone's long-term interest, according to Bodenheimer. Though younger people would pay for older people, and healthy people for sick people, this would even out in the end, progressives argued, since the young will one day be old and the healthy injured or sick. [46]

But conservatives answered that it's unfair to force young people to subsidize health care for older, sicker neighbors and that people will spend more prudently on medical care if they buy their own.

Sickness Insurance

The private market for what we call health insurance today — policies that pay medical bills — grew slowly, mainly because health costs were low, even in the early 20th century. Before 1920, there were virtually no antibiotics and few effective drugs, and X-rays had been discovered only in 1895. Most of the financial burden from illness was due to lost wages, so insurers sold income-protection "sickness" or "accident" insurance.

The first such policy was sold in 1850 by the Massachusetts-based Franklin Health Assurance Company. For a 15-cent premium, the policy paid $200 if its holder was injured in a railway or steamboat accident. [47]

Some employers offered sickness insurance as a worker benefit. In 1910, the catalog store Montgomery Ward and Co. established a group insurance plan to pay half of an ill or injured employee's salary. [48] In 1918, the

Looking Into the Future of Health Coverage

New proposals offer new approaches

With the number of uninsured Americans creeping inexorably upward, universal coverage is likely to become a hot political issue in the 2008 presidential campaign. While former Sen. John Edwards, D-N.C., is the only candidate to have offered a specific plan so far, the state and federal plans being considered contain some new wrinkles that might help policymakers reach a compromise on how to expand coverage.

Massachusetts — A 2006 state law requires all residents to buy insurance, beginning this year, or pay a penalty. Massachusetts will subsidize premiums for those earning under 300 percent of poverty level (about $60,000 for a family of four) and waive the coverage requirement if no "affordable" policies are available.

Coverage will be sold through a state-operated market, the Massachusetts Health Insurance Connector, and the state is negotiating with insurers to get affordable premiums for comprehensive policies, something that's proven to be more of an uphill struggle than lawmakers imagined.

"Massachusetts decided consciously not to grapple with rising health-care costs and decided to do it later," says Paul Ginsburg, president of the Center for Studying Health System Change, a nonpartisan research group. "Now they're having a problem with the bids coming in higher than expected."

That decision may have doomed the plan, says Robert Laszewski, a consultant and former insurance executive. Annual health-insurance premiums for the average Massachusetts family had already reached $15,000 a few years ago — higher than the current national family average of $12,000 — in part because of the state's high-cost academic medical centers and plethora of physicians, he points out. "Yet the Massachusetts legislature came up with $200 a month" — $2,400 a year — "as a reasonable premium for their plan," he laments. "The chances that the law will ever be implemented are slim."

California — In January, Gov. Arnold Schwarzenegger unveiled a universal-coverage plan that also would require all residents to buy a minimal level of coverage. Public programs would be expanded to cover the lowest-income Californians, and subsidies would help others buy private insurance.

Insurers would offer policies to all comers, at state-approved rates. Employers with 10 or more workers would pay at least 4 percent of payroll for health insurance or pay that amount into a state pool. To trim costs, insurers would be required to spend at least 85 percent of every premium dollar on patient care.

To entice more hospitals and doctors to participate in California's subsidized Medi-Cal program, the state would increase payments to participating providers. This would also eliminate what Schwarzenegger calls the "hidden tax" — low public-program payments and uncompensated care for uninsured people that providers now pass along as higher prices to paying patients. The Medi-Cal pay boost would be funded by a tax on non-participant doctors and hospitals.

Some employers are skeptical of the plan, which must be approved by the California legislature. The plan would help companies that already provide health benefits because it would force their competitors to ante up for health care also, said Scott Hauge, president of the advocacy group Small Business California. But that could be perceived as unfair by some companies with young workers, whose "invincibility-of-youth syndrome" means they'd prefer cash to health benefits they believe they don't need, he said. [1]

Insurers are expected to balk at being forced to spend 85 percent of premiums on patient care, says Laszewski. "Wellpoint, California's biggest [for-profit] insurer, puts 80 cents on the dollar toward care, holding on to a full 20 cents for profits and administration," he says. Nevertheless,

---

Dallas, Texas, school system established sickness insurance to protect teachers against impoverishment during the great influenza epidemic. [49]

The mining, railway, and lumber industries led the way in establishing insurance plans more similar to modern HMOs (health maintenance organizations), paying medical costs. Their workers faced serious health risks and labored in remote locations where traditional care wasn't available. So companies established clinics that prepaid doctors fixed monthly fees to provide care.

Nevertheless, between 1910 and 1920, near the end of the so-called Progressive Era in American politics,

"everybody knows that it can be done for less. In Medicare, 95 cents on every dollar goes to patient care."

President George W. Bush — The president wants to replace the current unlimited government subsidy for employer-sponsored health coverage with a flat standard deduction available to everyone who buys at least catastrophic health coverage on their own or through an employer. Federal funds would be available for states to improve their markets for individual health policies, where people would shop for non-workplace coverage.

Economists praise Bush for proposing to replace the government's current subsidy for health insurance — the exclusion from taxable wages of employer-sponsored coverage — with more widely available assistance. But some critics on both the left and right agree the proposal doesn't target the people most in need of subsidies and doesn't help create enough affordable coverage for them to buy.

"Replacing the current tax treatment with a new standard deduction is a big step in the right direction," said Heritage Foundation Vice President Stuart M. Butler and Senior Policy Analyst Nina Owcharenko. Nevertheless, "an even better step would be to replace it with a tax credit," which would help lower-income families who are least likely to have insurance, they said. Unlike tax credits, which benefit everyone equally, Bush's proposed deduction has a much higher dollar value for higher-income people. [2]

Former Sen. John Edwards, D-N.C., is the first presidential candidate to propose a detailed universal health-care plan.

The Edwards plan — The presidential candidate also proposes an individual mandate, but the requirement would only kick in once new, affordable coverage options are available and employers are either contributing to a general pool or helping their own workers buy coverage through new, regional nonprofit purchasing pools known as "health markets." The federal government would help states or groups of states set up such health markets, which would offer a choice of competing health policies. Unlike most current proposals, the health markets would offer all buyers — in addition to private coverage — a public-insurance plan modeled on Medicare.

"Let's have real competition between public and private systems," says Yale University Professor of Political Science Jacob Hacker, who consulted with Edwards on the proposal. "If you put a level playing field between the public and private sectors" — as in the health markets — the public programs "might turn out to be cheaper. If that happens over time, people would vote with their feet," he says.

[1] Renuka Rayasam, "Schwarzenegger Health Plan Raises Doubts." *U.S. News & World Report*, Jan. 10, 2007, www.usnews.com/usnews/biztech/smallbizscene/070110/schwarzenegger_health_plan_rai.htm.

[2] Stuart M. Butler and Nina Owcharenko, "Making Health Care Affordable: Bush's Bold Health Tax Reform Plan," *WebMemo No. 1316*, Heritage Foundation, Jan. 22, 2007.

"government-sponsored health insurance seemed a practical possibility in the United States," according to the University of Pennsylvania's Stevens. In 1920, expert panels in four large states — California, New Jersey, Ohio and New York — recommended universal state-sponsored health insurance. [50]

However, doctors, hospitals and insurance companies feared if universal coverage was adopted they would lose control and cash. The chairman of Ohio's commission complained about "the confusion into which the public mind had been thrown by the misleading, malicious and false statements emanating

Stakeholder Groups May Balk at Changes

They fear paying more, losing coverage

As costs and the ranks of the uninsured soar, there's plenty not to like about the current health-care system. Nevertheless, many longtime stakeholders fear change. As has often happened in the past, insurance companies, health providers, employers and those with expansive work-based health coverage all may balk at the changes universal coverage may bring.

"You often see interest groups wearing a cloak of ideology," saying they oppose a reform plan on economic or philosophical grounds when they're really protecting their money, says Stanley Dorn, a senior research associate at the liberal Urban Institute.

For example, he says, during the bitter debate over President Bill Clinton's universal-coverage plan in the early 1990s, "you had companies that didn't provide insurance to their workers and knew they could lose money" if the proposal succeeded. "But they didn't talk about that. They talked about how evil it would be for the government to take over the health system."

Various employer groups are likely to weigh in on both sides of the debate. Those who offer health coverage as a benefit today are more likely to embrace the change, although they may still be hesitant to endorse all universal-coverage proposals, says Paul Ginsburg, president of the Center for Studying Health System Change, a nonpartisan research group. "They'd like to get out of the business of coverage long term, but the issue has always been whether they'd end up paying more in taxes" for a new universal coverage system than they spend now to provide benefits, he says.

Large, unionized employers like U.S. automakers initially supported the Clinton plan in 1993, said Walter Mahan, former vice president for public policy of DaimlerChrysler Corp. [1] Employers who didn't offer health benefits strongly opposed the Clinton plan, which, like many universal-coverage plans today, asked all businesses to chip in, including those that didn't offer health benefits before.

Caught somewhat off guard by ferocious opposition from businesses that didn't offer coverage — like restaurants and soda manufacturers — architects of the Clinton plan reduced the payments required from companies that had not previously offered coverage and hiked the amount asked from employers who offered coverage. Complaining of unfairness, unionized employers then pulled their support, said Mahan. The bad news for the new crop of

from an interested and active commercial insurance opposition." [51]

Soon, popular support for government-sponsored insurance dropped to a low level again, as financial worry receded in the 1920s economic boom. In the overall prosperity of that decade, the medical system flourished, and hospitals built new wings in the mood of general optimism.

By 1929, however, more than a third of hospital beds were empty, and many hospitals struggled to pay off the loans that had funded expansion. Baylor University Hospital in Dallas, for example, had $1.5 million in overdue loan payments for construction and was behind in other bills. "Baylor was just 30 days ahead of the sheriff," said one observer. [52] Baylor's crisis led to health insurance as we know it today.

In search of cash, Baylor made common cause with local employers. In late 1929, the Dallas school system set up a hospital-service prepayment plan that operated alongside its sick-benefit fund. For a monthly premium of 50 cents, teachers would get free hospitalization for 21 days and a one-third discount on additional days. Benefits became effective on Dec. 20, 1929, less than two months after the stock market crash. [53]

A few days later, elementary-school teacher Alma Dickson slipped on an icy sidewalk and broke her ankle. [54] Hospitalized with a cast, Dickson became the first patient in the first prepaid hospitalization plan, the forerunner of today's Blue Cross system. [55]

By 1935, 19 such plans had been created in 13 states, as hospitals struggled to stay afloat during the Great Depression. [56]

But many influential physicians argued that "prepayment" threatened professional independence. Recommendations that the nation adopt insurance to protect people against the rising cost of care amounted to "socialism and communism — inciting to revolu-

reformers: More and more companies have been dropping coverage since then, so the constituency of businesses not offering coverage "is stronger now," he said. [2]

Insurers may have the biggest stake in the current system. Most analysts say proposals that would abolish private insurance in favor of a government-run universal plan modeled on Medicare are politically impossible today. However, most reform plans would force insurers to cover potentially sicker beneficiaries than most do today and would tighten rules for selling and marketing insurance policies.

Many insurers mistrust changes because the current employer-based system works well for them by weeding out the sickest populations, said former Rep. William Thomas, R-Calif., who chaired the House Ways and Means Committee. Employed people "have to get up every morning, go to work and carry out difficult and complex tasks." They're essentially prescreened to be, on average, healthier than the general population and thus easier to cover and still earn profits, he said. [3]

Insurers also distrust government-run "insurance exchanges" in many universal-coverage plans that would establish standard benefit packages, ensure affordability and replace insurers' marketing with government-scrutinized plan descriptions. Insurers have "traditionally hated" government limits on their marketing, says Dorn.

Finally, virtually all economists say any health system reform must include cost cutting, including reining in salaries and profits of doctors, hospitals and drug manufacturers. Some proposals ask providers to put money in up front to support coverage proposals. Providers always push back against such steps.

For example, when Democratic Maine Gov. John Baldacci unveiled a universal-coverage program in 2003, he included a tax on insurance premiums along with both voluntary and mandatory price caps on many health services, without which the governor said the program could not survive. Maine's hospitals said they couldn't survive having prices capped.

"That cannot happen . . . without irreparably harming Maine's hospitals," said Warren Kessler, a consultant and former head of the Maine General Medical Center in Augusta. [4]

Finally, those who currently have good coverage are sensitive to any proposal that might make their own insurance worse or cost more. Interest groups like insurers and doctors who oppose any new plan "just have to play on the public's fear of losing what they now have," says Dorn.

---

[1] "Universal Coverage: It Can't Happen Here . . . Or Can It?" *Medicine & Health Perspectives*, March 31, 2003.

[2] Quoted in *ibid.*

[3] Quoted in "Thomas Takes Aim Again at Tax-Favored Employer Coverage," *Medicine & Health*, Feb. 16, 2004.

[4] Quoted in "Baldacci Says Everyone Must Give a Little to Fund Care," *Medicine & Health*, May 12, 2003.

---

tion," wrote Morris Fishbein, editor of the *Journal of the American Medical Association.* [57]

Workplace Plans

During the 1930s, as businesses folded and millions sank into poverty, the United States made its largest-ever foray in social insurance.

Developed by Democratic President Franklin D. Roosevelt and enacted in 1935, Social Security is a mandatory, universal system that provides income support for retirees, severely disabled people, widows and under-age bereaved children. During the debate over passage, activists argued for including health insurance, but the administration declined, in part because it feared the contentious health issue might doom the whole plan. [58]

Later, members of Congress made unsuccessful attempts to extend social-insurance to health in 1943, 1945, 1947, 1949 and 1957. Nevertheless, by 1966, 81 percent of Americans had hospitalization insurance — mostly offered through their workplaces and often as a result of labor union demands — compared to only 9 percent in 1940. [59]

Unlike today, from 1940 to 1966 large unionized companies dominated the economy. Offered as a worker benefit, employer-sponsored health plans successfully pooled the risk and contributions of many employees in order to keep individuals' costs low and uniform, even in years when they had accidents or illness. And, since the sickest people are unlikely to be employed, relying on workplace-based plans allowed private insurers to more easily predict and control costs.

As the primary source of Americans' health insurance, the still union-dominated U.S. auto industry has evolved over the years into "a social-insurance system that sells cars to finance itself," said Princeton University economics Professor Uwe Reinhardt. [60]

But even in the early days, employer-provided insurance had limits. Many retired people, very low-income families and the disabled never had workplace-based insurance and were too poor to buy individual policies, for which they would be charged premiums based on health status.

After several years of debate, Congress in 1965 enacted a new compulsory, universal insurance plan — the Medicare program — to provide health coverage for elderly and some disabled people and Medicaid to provide health care for the poorest mothers with children, elderly and the disabled.

Coverage Declines

With Medicare and Medicaid in place, most Americans had access to health care.

Nevertheless, health spending was rising sharply, and Presidents Richard M. Nixon and Jimmy Carter both proposed reforms to keep care affordable, including universal coverage. Neither plan gained traction, however.

Gradually, the higher costs and the changed nature of American business began to erode the work-based insurance system.

"Forty years ago, the largest private employer was AT&T, a regulated monopoly with guaranteed profits," wrote Stanford University Professor Emeritus Victor Fuchs and Ezekiel Emanuel, chairman of clinical bioethics at the National Institutes of Health. "If health-insurance premiums rose, they could easily be passed on to telephone subscribers." [61]

That changed, however, as union membership began declining in the 1980s, and manufacturing jobs began migrating overseas and U.S. companies had to compete with foreign competitors that don't offer health benefits. More and more Americans ended up working in the largely non-unionized service industry, which offered few benefits.

"Today, the largest private employer is Wal-Mart, which despite its size faces intense competition daily from a host of other retail outlets," Fuchs and Emanuel wrote. "When they offer health insurance, it must come out of their workers' wages; for minimum-wage employees, this is not possible." [62]

Over the past two decades, employer-sponsored coverage has gradually waned, along with the number of insured Americans. Government programs have grown and picked up some of the slack, however.

In 1987, fully 87.1 percent of Americans were insured, with 75.7 percent insured through private,

mostly employer-sponsored, coverage. By 1999, the percentage of insured Americans had dropped to 85.5.percent, 71.8 percent through private coverage. In 2005, the overall percentage had dropped to 84.1 percent — 67.7 percent with private insurance. [63] (*See graph, p. 54.*)

In the face of declining coverage, proposals to expand coverage have been advanced repeatedly by the White House, members of Congress, state and local governments and others. Only some small-scale efforts have gone anywhere, however.

In 1994, Tennessee used federal Medicaid dollars and state funding to create TennCare. State officials hoped money-saving HMOs could provide coverage to many lower-income people and sicker Tennesseans, who were ineligible for Medicaid and couldn't afford insurance on their own.

For a few years, the program saved money and enrolled 500,000 residents who would otherwise have been uninsured. But the federal government had agreed to contribute funding for only 1.5 million people, and when enrollment exceeded that cap, TennCare refused to accept new applicants and struggled financially. For the past several years, TennCare has fought to survive, plagued by charges of poor care at its HMOs and disputes with the federal government over funds.

Clinton Plan

The highest-profile recent effort to enact a universal health care plan was President Bill Clinton's ambitious proposal to restructure the nation's health care system, unveiled on Sept. 22, 1993. His Health Security Act was proposed at a time when the uninsured ranks had swelled to 40 million, and polls showed that up to two-thirds of Americans favored tax-financed national health insurance. [64] Yet, within a year Senate Democrats had pronounced the plan dead, the victim of bruising attacks by business, insurers and medical providers. [65]

Five days after his inauguration, Clinton announced that first lady Hillary Rodham Clinton would chair a health-care task force made up of Cabinet members and White House staffers. It held hearings for a year and produced a plan to attain universal coverage mainly through expanded private coverage. It aimed to offer people a choice of affordable coverage while maintaining the existing private insurance industry and holding down health-cost growth.

To do that, the Clinton panel proposed creating regional government-managed insurance markets to

Should Congress enact President Bush's tax proposal for expanding health coverage?

YES
Stuart M. Butler, Vice President
Nina Owcharenko, Senior Policy Analyst
The Heritage Foundation

From the foundation's Web site, January 2007

President Bush's proposal to reform the tax treatment of health care takes a bold step toward fixing America's health system by widening the availability of affordable and "portable" health plans and by defusing some of the pressure that currently leads to higher health costs.

Although some Americans would have more of their compensation subject to taxes, this proposal is no more a tax increase than limiting or ending tax deductions to move toward a flatter tax system. It would remove distortions and inequities and make tax relief for health insurance more widely available.

While the proposal can be improved in ways that would further reduce uninsurance, it is a big step toward sound tax and health policy. It would treat all Americans equally by ending the tax discrimination against families who buy their own health insurance, either because they do not have insurance offered by employers or because they prefer other coverage.

Ending that discrimination would have the added advantage of stimulating wider choice and greater competition in health coverage, which will help moderate the growth in costs. It would also make it easier for families to keep their chosen plan from job to job, reducing the loss of coverage that often accompanies job changes.

The president's proposal could be improved. While replacing the tax treatment with a new standard deduction is a big step in the right direction, an even better step would be to replace it with a tax credit more like the current child tax credit — at least for those buying health coverage outside their place of work. A tax credit would especially help lower-income families. With a deduction, many families would still be unable to afford basic coverage, but a credit set at a flat dollar amount or a high percentage of premium costs would make coverage more affordable.

A tax credit could be grafted onto the president's current proposal and would strengthen it considerably.

By taking this step, Congress can help make the tax treatment of health care more equitable and efficient, help more Americans choose the coverage they want and retain it from job to job and begin to reduce the tax-break-induced pressure that is a factor in rising health costs.

NO
Karen Davis
President, The Commonwealth Fund

From the fund's Web site, January 2007

While it is encouraging that President Bush made health care a theme of the State of the Union address, his proposal to offer tax deductions to those who buy health insurance would do little to cover the nation's 45 million uninsured.

Under the president's proposal, Americans with employer-provided health insurance would have the employer contribution counted as taxable income. But anyone with health coverage — whether provided by an employer or purchased individually — would have the first $7,500 of income excluded from income and payroll taxes or, in the case of families, the first $15,000 of income.

Those purchasing coverage in the individual market would get a new tax break, as would those whose employer contribution currently is less than the new standard deduction for health insurance.

The proposal would increase taxes on workers whose employers contribute more to health insurance than the premium "cap" allows, such as those that serve a large number of older workers. The administration estimates this change would translate into a tax increase for about 20 percent of employees. However, this could rise to more than half of employees by 2013, if increases in health-insurance premiums continue to outpace general inflation. In addition, the president proposes diverting federal funds from public hospitals to state programs for the uninsured.

Although the plan would offer subsidies to people looking to buy insurance on the private market, it would fail to assist most of the uninsured. Insurance premiums would still be unaffordable for Americans with modest or low incomes. And the tax increase for employees would likely lead to the erosion of employer-sponsored health insurance over time.

The proposal wouldn't do anything to make individual coverage available or affordable for those with modest incomes or health problems. The Commonwealth Fund found that one-fifth of people who had sought coverage in the individual health-insurance market in the last three years were denied coverage because of health problems or were charged a higher premium. The proposal, unlike plans in California and Massachusetts, does not require insurers to cover everyone.

Nor would the proposal likely help the currently uninsured. More than 55 percent of the uninsured have such low incomes that they pay no taxes, while another 40 percent are in the 10-to-15-percent tax bracket and would not benefit substantially from the tax deductions.

negotiate health-care and premium prices and insurance-benefit packages and to oversee insurance marketing. It also called for annual caps on health-coverage cost increases, and a requirement that all employers contribute to the cost of coverage.

But opposition soon grew from businesses that believed they had more to lose than to gain from change. Employers who didn't offer coverage balked at proposed fees to help finance the plan. Insurers objected to regulations aimed at keeping them from skimming off healthy customers. After 10 months of strenuous campaigns by opponents, public approval had dropped to a lukewarm 40 percent. [66] (*See sidebar, p. 62.*)

Former first lady Clinton — now the Democratic senator from New York who is running for president — has assured voters she still believes in universal health coverage, but she has not yet announced a specific plan. "I think she's learned her lesson" and likely will propose something "not quite as big and ambitious" this time, says Brandeis' Altman.

For the next decade the dramatic failure of the Clinton plan frightened lawmakers away from the issue, while conservative lawmakers said the booming 1990s economy would enable the United States to "grow its way" out of uninsurance by creating more and better jobs with coverage benefits.

But that did not turn out to be the case. From 1997 to 2001, the economy boomed and jobs were created, but rates of employer-sponsored health insurance did not rise. The late '90s experience "tells us that relying on economic growth alone to reduce the number of uninsured won't work," said Ginsburg at the Center for Studying Health System Change. [67]

Since Clinton's efforts, Congress enacted two coverage expansions. The State Children's Health Insurance Program (SCHIP) was enacted in 1997. The Clinton administration and a bipartisan group of lawmakers led by Sens. Edward M. Kennedy, D-Mass., and Orrin G. Hatch, R-Utah, gave states federal matching funds to expand coverage for children in low-income families. Today, SCHIP operates in all states, making nearly all otherwise uninsured children with family incomes up to twice the poverty level eligible for public coverage.

With Republicans dominating the White House and Congress, most recent debate over coverage has focused on tax incentives to help Americans buy insurance. Criticized by lawmakers of both parties for offering too-small tax breaks in its early proposals, the Bush administration has gradually expanded its plan each year but has seen none enacted.

The only federal health-coverage expansion enacted in this decade was a tax credit to assist workers unemployed due to competition from international trade, enacted in 2002 after a long contentious delay. But the credit has reached only 10 to 20 percent of those eligible for it, says the Urban Institute's Dorn, which he calls a "tragic" outcome for states like North Carolina, where it was intended to help people facing "the largest layoff in the state's history — the closing of the textile mills."

The program failed to catch on because its premiums are too high, he says. "It's not realistic to ask people to pay 35 percent of premiums when they're not working" when working people pay only 15 to 25 percent of theirs, he says. In addition, the tax credit in most states could only be used for individual policies, whose premiums generally are based on age and health status. "Even with a 65 percent subsidy, people were facing an unaffordable $1,000 a month premium."

Over the past decade, some congressional Republicans also have proposed allowing business and professional groups to offer association health plans (AHPs), which would enable small businesses and the self-employed to band together to buy health insurance free from the state regulations that apply to individual and small-group insurance plans, which AHP advocates say unduly drive up coverage costs for small business.

In the 1970s Congress waived state insurance regulation for large employers to encourage them to provide coverage for workers. But today both Democratic and some Republican lawmakers staunchly oppose allowing AHPs the same freedom. AHP opponents argue that it is too easy for such loosely formed groups to skim off workers most likely to be healthy and low-cost, which would raise premium costs even higher for those left behind.

Meanwhile, outside of legislative chambers advocates increasingly have been calling for universal coverage. In 2004, a three-year-long Institute of Medicine study declared that eroding coverage poses such a threat that the federal government must launch a "firm and explicit" plan to achieve universal coverage by 2010. [68]

Many analysts agree that universal coverage has been stalled not because of a lack of knowledge of how to accomplish it but because lawmakers lack the will to demand sacrifices. (*See sidebar, p. 52.*)

There are "at least four ways" to get universal coverage, says Simmons of the National Coalition on Health Care. "This problem is solvable. It does not require atomic science."

CURRENT SITUATION

Interest Grows

A few states are moving forward with universal-coverage plans, but little action is expected on Capitol Hill this year. Meanwhile, all Democratic contenders for the 2008 presidential nomination have advocated universal coverage, although only former Sen. Edwards has offered a specific plan so far. (*See sidebar, p. 60.*)

While few expect federal action until after the next president takes office in 2009, many Washington hands think the tide finally may be turning.

"One big difference between now and several years ago is that there is a loss of faith in employer-provided coverage as capable of covering everyone, including from unions and key business groups" who have been its strongest supporters, says Yale's Hacker.

Coalitions of interest groups have come together in 2007 to announce support for universal coverage. In January, the Health Coverage Coalition for the Uninsured (HCCU) advocated a phased-in approach to universal coverage, beginning with an expansion of SCHIP and creation of tax credits for families with incomes up to about $60,000, and then creating similar programs for childless adults. [69]

The coalition includes groups that have traditionally sparred over health care, including Families USA, the retiree organization AARP, the American Medical Association, the American Hospital Association and the health-insurance lobby America's Health Insurance Plans. "Organizations that have never spoken to one another in a friendly manner are now talking about this, and that has transformed the debate," says Pollack of Families USA.

Others aren't convinced. The HCCU's "rhetoric was wonderful," says Altman of Brandeis. "But the result shows how little they actually agree on."

But Pollack says the coalition's proposal is a "sequential" plan that will follow expansion of the children's program — expected to be enacted this year — with a move to universal coverage after that.

In February the Service Employees International Union joined with Wal-Mart, an employer whose limited health benefits have been sharply criticized by the union, to form the Better Health Care Together group, calling for "quality, affordable" universal health care by 2012. The group plans a national summit this spring to rally support but has not announced a proposal, saying only that it supports joint public and private-sector efforts. [70]

But Dana Rezaie, a Wal-Mart shelf stocker in Fridley, Minn., says, "anybody can say they support something. They need to show they really do." After six years at the store, the widowed mother of three says she can't afford Wal-Mart's health plan. [71]

Congress is reviewing President Bush's fiscal 2008 budget, which proposes a new version of his tax-based coverage-expansion proposals. Bush would ditch the current tax break Americans receive for employer-sponsored coverage and replace it with a more general tax break that would apply both to employer coverage and to insurance purchased individually.

The plan gets points from Greenstein at the Center on Budget and Policy Priorities for tackling the unfairness of the current tax treatment of insurance, which penalizes those who purchase insurance on their own. But the plan "has an Achilles' heel," Greenstein says, since it doesn't encourage pooling sicker and healthier people to spread costs and skews its tax benefits toward higher-income people.

Nevertheless, Pollack does not expect "a serious productive debate on universal coverage" in 2007, with a presidential campaign heating up. However, he does expect Congress to reauthorize — and possibly expand — the 10-year-old SCHIP program "before the end of the calendar year."

The Bush budget recommends funding SCHIP leanly, by not offering federal assistance, for example, to the 14 states anticipating shortfalls in their 2007 SCHIP budgets. But both political parties strongly support SCHIP and are likely to ride to the rescue. Sen. Gordon Smith, R-Ore., has called for doubling the federal cigarette tax to pay for the aid. [72]

State Steps

As health insurance gains momentum as a public issue, many states are flirting with expanding coverage, and three are struggling to get universal coverage off the ground.

Massachusetts was first out of the gate, enacting a plan in 2006 that will require residents to buy health insurance, often with government assistance. A state-operated clearinghouse — the Health Insurance Connector — will help consumers comparison-shop for affordable coverage. So far, however, the state is struggling to define benefit packages that insurers can sell at "affordable" prices.

Meanwhile, the California legislature is considering Gov. Schwarzenegger's proposal to require individuals to buy coverage. The plan would be funded with contributions from multiple sources, including government, individuals, employers, insurers and health-care providers.

Vermont's new Catamount Health program will focus first on promoting information technology and other reforms to shave administrative costs and an evidence-based standard of care "community by community," says Emory University's Thorpe, who consulted on the program. Then the state will turn to expanding coverage.

In Texas, where more than 25 percent of the population is uninsured, Republican Gov. Rick Perry is looking for revenue sources to subsidize more coverage. In February he proposed selling off the state lottery and putting part of the proceeds in an endowment fund to expand insurance coverage. [73]

Last year, Rhode Island began requiring insurers to develop "wellness benefit" policies to help individuals and small businesses afford at least basic coverage. [74]

OUTLOOK

Health Politics

Consensus has been building around proposals that link public subsidies to private coverage. But it remains an open question whether Congress will finally enact a universal-coverage plan, which undoubtedly would shift some resources and benefits away from currently insured people and health providers.

Some interest groups that helped bring down the Clinton plan have softened their stance, says Ginsburg at the Center for Studying Health System Change. In Massachusetts, he points out, insurers have accepted the new state-run insurance marketplace, even though in the past they would have preferred to send out their own people to market policies and avoid head-to-head consumer comparisons of plans. But insurers realize that their long-time bread and butter — employer-sponsored

coverage — "has topped out," Ginsburg says, so they anticipate no growth unless they embrace government-sponsored expansions.

"There's [been] a dramatic change in national political attitudes," says Simmons of the National Coalition on Health Care. One "truly remarkable thing is that every Democratic and some Republican candidates now say we have to achieve universal coverage."

But others say the country may still not be ready to make the concessions needed.

"It's not clear to me that life has changed very much," says Altman of Brandeis. Forces that have resisted change in the past "are stronger today," and "you have very weak leadership" from the White House and Congress.

Endorsement by Democratic presidential hopefuls doesn't necessarily mean much, says Harvard's Blendon. "Democratic primary voters disproportionately care about this," he says. But different priorities will prevail in the general election. "The biggest thing on everyone's mind is casualties in Iraq."

Furthermore, Americans generally "do not want an alternative health system," he continues. "They want to fix the one they have."

Unfortunately for politicians, the simplest, catchiest sound bite on health reform involves covering the uninsured, but that doesn't "play politically," says Blendon. While people do want everyone to have access to health care, "what they want most is cheaper premiums for themselves."

NOTES

1. Jay Himmelstein, "Bleeding-Edge Benefits," *Health Affairs*, November/December 2006, p. 1656.

2. Jeffrey A. Rhoades, "The Uninsured in America, 2004: Estimates for the U.S. Civilian Noninstitutionalized Population Under Age 65," *Medical Expenditure Panel Survey Statistical Brief #83*, June 2005, Agency for Healthcare Research and Quality.

3. Diane Rowland, executive vice president, Henry J. Kaiser Foundation, "Health Care: Squeezing the Middle Class With More Costs and Less Coverage," testimony before House Ways and Means Committee, Jan. 31, 2007; for background, see Keith Epstein, "Covering the Uninsured," *CQ Researcher*, June 14, 2002, pp. 521-544.

4. Christine Borger, *et al.*, "Health Spending Projections Through 2015: Changes on the Horizon," *Health Affairs* Web site, Feb. 22, 2006.

5. Rowland testimony, *op. cit.*

6. "Facts on Health Care Costs," National Coalition on Health Care, www.nchc.org.

7. Quoted in Steven Taub and David Cook, "Health Care Can Bankrupt America," CFO.com, March 6, 2007, For background, see Michael E. Chernew, Richard A. Hirth and David M. Cutler, "Increased Spending on Health Care: How Much Can the United States Afford?" *Health Affairs*, July/August 2003.

8. Todd Gilmer and Richard Kronick, "It's the Premiums, Stupid: Projections of the Uninsured Through 2013," *Health Affairs*, April 5, 2005, www.healthaffairs.org.

9. *Ibid.*

10. "Coverage Matters: Insurance and Health Care," statement of Arthur L. Kellerman, co-chairman, Consequences of Uninsurance Committee, Institute of Medicine, www7.nationalacademies.org/ocga/testimony/Uninsured_and_Affordable_Health_Care_Coverage.asp.

11. Quoted in "IOM Uninsured Report Cites Rising Costs, Attacks Myths." *Medicine & Health*, Oct. 15, 2001.

12. "The Great Divide: When Kids Get Sick, Insurance Matters," Families USA, March 1, 2007, www.familiesusa.org/assets/pdfs/the-great-divide.pdf.

13. "Expanding Coverage Is Worth It for All, IOM Panel Insists," *Medicine & Health*, June 30, 2003.

14. *Ibid.* For background, see Marcia Clemmitt, "Prison Health Care," *CQ Researcher*, Jan. 5, 2007, pp. 1-24.

15. Quoted in "States Scramble for Ways to Cover Working Uninsured," *Medicine & Health*, "Perspectives," Feb. 8, 2005.

16. Barack Obama, "Obama Statement on President's Meeting with Big Three Automakers," press release, Nov. 14, 2006, http://obama.senate.gov.

17. For background, see Marcia Clemmitt, "Rising Health Costs," *CQ Researcher*, April 7, 2006, pp. 289-312.

18. Quoted in "Frist: 100 Percent Coverage Impossible, 93 Percent Not Working So Well Either," *Medicine & Health*, Feb. 9, 2004.

19. Quoted in *ibid.*

20. Quoted in "Who Should Pay for Health Care?" PBS Newshour Extra online, Jan. 19, 2004, www.pbs.org/newshour/extra/features/jan-june04/uninsured_1-19.html.

21. Jack Hadley and John Holahan, "The Cost of Care for the Uninsured: What Do We Spend, Who Pays, and What Would Full Coverage Add to Medical Spending?" The Kaiser Commission on Medicaid and the Uninsured, May 10, 2004, p. 5.

22. "Maryland Universal Coverage Plan Estimated to Cost $2.5 Billion," *Healthcare News*, News-Medical.Net, Feb. 21, 2007, www.news-medical.net; also see "How Much Would It Cost to Cover the Uninsured In Minnesota? Preliminary Estimates," Minnesota Department of Health, Health Economics program, July 2006.

23. For background, see Marcia Clemmitt, "Budget Deficit," *CQ Researcher*, Dec. 9, 2005, p. 1029-105.

24. "Universal Coverage Rx: Tax-Code Changes, Money, Insurance Pools and a Mandates," interview with Jonathan Gruber, "On My Mind: Conversations with Economists," University of Michigan Economic Research Initiative on the Uninsured, www.umich.edu.

25. *Ibid.*

26. "Health Expenditure," Organization for Economic Cooperation and Development, www.oecd.org/document/16/0,2340,en_2649_37407_2085200_1_1_1_37407,00.html; also see Rhoades, *op. cit.*

27. See Clemmitt, "Rising Health Costs," *op. cit.*

28. "Pushed to the Edge: The Added Burdens Vulnerable Populations Face When Uninsured," interview with Harold Pollack, "On My Mind: Conversations With Economists," University of Michigan Economic Research Initiative on the Uninsured, www.umich.edu.

29. *Ibid.*

30. John Kitzhaber, "Why Start With the Health Care Crisis?" The Archimedes Movement, www.JoinAM.org.

31. "Access to Healthcare and the Uninsured," National Conference of States Legislatures, www.ncsl.org/programs/health/h-prmary.htm.

32. "Arthur Garson, "Help States Cover the Uninsured," *Roanoke Times*, May 26, 2006.

33. Stuart M. Butler, "The Voinovich-Bingaman Bill: Letting the States Take the Lead in Extending Health Insurance," *Web Memo No. 1128*, The Heritage Foundation, June 15, 2006.

34. George C. Halvorson, Francis J. Crosson and Steve Zatkin, "A Proposal to Cover the Uninsured in California," *Health Affairs*, Dec. 12, 2006, www.healthaffairs.org.

35. Quoted in Christopher Rowland, "Mass. Health Plan Seems Unlikely to Be U.S. Model," *The Boston Globe*, April 14, 2006.

36. *Ibid.*

37. Quoted in "IOM Panel Demands Universal Coverage by 2010," *Medicine & Health*, "Perspectives," Jan. 19, 2004.

38. David Kravitz, "The Individual Mandate Still Sucks," Blue Mass Group, Jan. 30, 2007, www.bluemassgroup.com.

39. Michael D. Tanner, "Individual Mandates for Health Insurance: Slippery Slope to National Health Care," *Policy Analysis No. 565*, Cato Institute, April 5, 2006, www.cato.org.

40. "Problems of Risk and Uncertainty," The Economics of Health Care, Office of Health Economics, p. 26, www.oheschools.org/ohech3pg3.html.

41. Quoted in "Frist: Limit Tax Exclusion for Employer-Based Coverage," *Medicine & Health*, July 19, 2004.

42. *Ibid.*

43. For background, see Anne-Emmanuel Birn, Theodore M. Brown, Elizabeth Fee and Walter J. Lear, "Struggles for National Health Reform in the United States," *American Journal of Public Health*, January 2003, p. 86; Laura A. Scofea, "The Development and Growth of Employer-Provided Health Insurance," *Monthly Labor Review*, March 1994, p. 3; Thomas Bodenheimer, "The Political Divide in Health Care: A Liberal Perspective," *Health Affairs*, November/December 2005, p. 1426.

44. Rosemary Stevens, foreword to Robert Cunningham III and Robert M. Cunningham, Jr., *The Blues: A History of the Blue Cross and Blue Shield System* (1997), p. vii.

45. Bodenheimer, *op. cit.*, p. 1426.

46. *Ibid.*, p. 1432.

47. Scofea, *op. cit.*, p. 3.

48. *Ibid.*

49. Cunningham and Cunningham, *op. cit.*, p. 5.

50. Stevens, *op. cit.*, p. vii.

51. Quoted in Scofea, *op. cit.*

52. Quoted in Cunningham and Cunningham, *op. cit.*, p. 4.

53. *Ibid.*, p. 6.

54. "Dallas School Teachers, 1928," Rootsweb.com; http://freepages.history.rootsweb.com/~jwheat/teachersdal28.html.

55. Cunningham and Cunningham, *op. cit.*, p. 6. For background, see also "Sickness insurance and group hospitalization," *Editorial Research Reports*, July 9, 1934, from *CQ Researcher Plus Archive*, http://library.cqpress.com.

56. Scofea, *op. cit.*

57. Quoted in Cunningham and Cunningham, *op. cit.*, p. 18.

58. For background, see "Federal Assistance to the Aged," Nov. 12, 1934, in *Editorial Research Reports*, available from *CQ Researcher Plus Archive*, http://library.cqpress.com.

59. Cunningham and Cunningham, *op. cit.*

60. Quoted in Danny Hakim, 'Health Costs Soaring, Automakers Are to Begin Labor Talks," *The New York Times*, July 14, 2003, p. C1.

61. Victor R. Fuchs and Ezekiel J. Emanuel, "Health Care Reform: Why? What? When?" *Health Affairs*, November/December 2005, p. 1400.

62. *Ibid.* For background, see Brian Hansen, "Big-Box Stores," *CQ Researcher*, Sept. 10, 2004, pp. 733-756.

63. "Historical Health Insurance Tables," U.S. Census Bureau, www.census.gov.

64. Bridget Harrison, "A Historical Survey of National Health Movements and Public Opinion in the United States," *Journal of the American Medical Association*, March 5, 2003, p. 1163.

65. For background, see "Health-Care Debate Takes Off," *1993 CQ Almanac*, pp. 335-347, and "Clinton's Health Care Plan Laid to Rest," *1994 CQ Almanac*, pp. 319-353.

66. Harrison, *op. cit.*

67. "Rising Tide of Late '90s Lifted Few Uninsured Boats," *Medicine & Health*, Aug. 6, 2002.

68. "IOM Panel Demands Universal Coverage by 2010," *op. cit.*

69. "Unprecedented Alliance of Health Care Leaders Announces Historic Agreement," Health Coverage Coalition for the Uninsured, press release, Jan. 18, 2007, www.coalitionfortheuninsured.org.

70. Dan Caterinicchia, "Rivals Want Health Care for All," *Columbus Dispatch* [Ohio], Feb. 8, 2007.

71. Quoted in *ibid.*

72. Alex Wayne, "War Supplemental To Include Money for Children's Health Insurance Program" *Congressional Quarterly Healthbeat*, Feb. 27, 2007.

73. Quoted in The Associated Press, "Texas Governor Has Funding Idea: Sell the Lottery," *The Washington Post*, Feb. 7, 2007, p. A7.

74. "Rhode Island: Making Affordable, Quality-Focused Health Coverage Available to Small Businesses," *States in Action: A Bimonthly Look at Innovations in Health Policy*, The Commonwealth Fund, January/February 2007.

BIBLIOGRAPHY

Books

Derickson, Alan, *Health Security for All: Dreams of Universal Health Care in America*, Johns Hopkins University Press, 2005.
A professor of history at Pennsylvania State University examines the ideas and advocates behind the numerous 20th-century proposals for universal health care in the United States.

Funigello, Philip J., *Chronic Politics: Health Care Security from FDR to George W. Bush*, University Press of Kansas, 2005.
A professor emeritus of history at the College of William and Mary describes the politics behind a half-century of failed attempts at major health reform.

Gordon, Colin, *Dead on Arrival: The Politics of Health Care in Twentieth-Century America*, Princeton University Press, 2003.
A professor of history at the University of Iowa explains how numerous private interests — from physicians desiring autonomy to employers seeking to cement employer-employee relationships — have helped halt development of universal health coverage in America.

Mayes, Rick, *Universal Coverage: The Elusive Quest for National Health Insurance*, University of Michigan Press, 2005.
An assistant professor of public policy at Virginia's University of Richmond explains how politics and earlier policy choices regarding the U.S. health system shape the range of possibilities available for future reforms.

Richmond, Julius B., and Rashi Fein, *The Health Care Mess: How We Got Into It and What It Will Take to Get Out*, Harvard University Press, 2005.
Two Harvard Medical School professors recount the history of American medicine and trends in financing health care and conclude that the United States could afford universal health coverage.

Swartz, Katherine, *Reinsuring Health: Why More Middle-Class People Are Uninsured and What Government Can Do*, Russell Sage Foundation, 2006.
A professor of health policy and economics at the Harvard School of Public Health argues that more people could buy insurance and coverage would be cheaper if the federal government offered insurance companies financial protection for the highest-cost illnesses.

Articles

Appleby, Julie, "Health Coverage Reform Follows State-by-State Path," *USA Today*, April 5, 2006.
States take different approaches to expanding health coverage as worry over lack of insurance grows.

Gladwell, Malcolm, "The Moral Hazard Myth," *The New Yorker*, Aug. 29, 2005.
Some fear that large-scale expansion of health coverage would encourage patients to rack up higher amounts of useless health-care spending.

Holt, Matthew, "Policy: Why Is Fixing American Health Care So Difficult?" The Health Care Blog, Oct. 16, 2006; www.thehealthcareblog.com/the_ health_care_blog/2006/10/abc_news_why_is.html# comment-2418315.
An independent health-care consultant — along with blog comments by analysts, businesspeople and members of the public — describes and discusses the interest-group politics that shape the universal-coverage debate.

Holt, Matthew, "Risky Business: Bush's Health Care Plan," Spot-On Blog, Jan. 25, 2007; www.spot-on.com/archives/holt/2007/01/bush_tax_deductions _and_the_lo.html.
An independent health-care consultant explains the concept of risk-pooling for insurance and the current tax break already enjoyed by workers with employer-sponsored coverage.

Reports and Studies

Burton, Alice, Isabel Friedenzoh and Enrique Martinez-Vidal, "State Strategies to Expand Health Insurance Coverage: Trends and Lessons for Policymakers," The Commonwealth Fund, January 2007.
Analysts summarize recent state initiatives to extend health coverage to more adults and children.

"Covering America: Real Remedies for the Uninsured," Vols. 1 and 2, Economic and Social Research Institute, June 2001 and November 2002.
Economists assembled by a non-partisan think tank analyze multiple proposals for achieving universal coverage.

Haase, Leif Wellington, *A New Deal for Health: How to Cover Everyone and Get Medical Costs Under Control,* The Century Foundation, April 2005.
A health analyst for the nonprofit group outlines cost, quality and coverage issues that the group says make it necessary for the United States to switch to universal coverage.

"Insuring America's Health: Principles and Recommendations," Institute of Medicine Committee on the Consequences of Uninsurance, National Academies Press, 2004.
In its sixth and final report, an expert panel urges federal lawmakers to create a plan for insuring the entire population by 2010.

For More Information

Alliance for Health Reform, 1444 I St., N.W., Suite 910, Washington, DC 20005; (202) 789-2300; www.all-health.org. Nonpartisan, nonprofit group that disseminates information about policy options for expanding coverage.

Economic Research Institute on the Uninsured, www.umich.edu/~eriu. Researchers at the University of Michigan who conduct economic analyses of the hows and whys of uninsurance and coverage-expansion proposals.

Families USA, 1201 New York Ave., N.W., Suite 1100, Washington, DC 20005; (202) 628-3030; www.familiesusa.org. A nonprofit group that advocates for large-scale expansion of affordable health coverage.

The Health Care Blog, www.thehealthcareblog.com. Blog published by health-care consultant Matthew Holt; analyzes coverage proposals and other insurance issues.

Heritage Foundation, 214 Massachusetts Ave., N.E., Washington, DC 20002-4999; (202) 546-4400; www.heritage.org. Conservative think tank that supports state-organized purchasing groups for health care.

Kaiser Family Foundation, 1330 G St., N.W., Washington, DC 20005; (202) 347-5270; www.kff.org. Nonprofit private foundation that collects data and conducts research on the uninsured.

National Coalition on Health Care, 1200 G St., N.W., Suite 750, Washington, DC 20005; (202) 638-7151; www.nchc.org. Nonprofit, nonpartisan group that supports universal coverage; made up of labor, business and consumer groups, insurers and health providers' associations.

Physicians for a National Health Program, 29 E. Madison, Suite 602, Chicago, IL 60602; (312) 782-6006; www.pnhp.org. Nonprofit group that advocates for single-payer national health insurance.

4

Rising Health Costs

Marcia Clemmitt

University of Miami janitor Zoila Garcia faces expensive surgery for a blood clot in her leg but has no insurance and can't afford the $4,000 operation. Rising costs have made health care too expensive for tens of millions of Americans, including many with health coverage. In the last five years, insurance premiums jumped 73 percent, but wages rose only 15 percent.

From *CQ Researcher*, April 7, 2006.

Z oila Garcia, who works the 10 p.m. to 6 a.m. shift as a janitor at the University of Miami, recently developed a blood clot in her calf that needs surgery. But her job doesn't offer health insurance, and she can't afford the $4,000 procedure.

"Where do you get that money?" making only $6.70 an hour, she asks. [1]

Other Americans are in similar predicaments. Jeannie Brewer's job as a contract physician at the Alta Bates-Summit Medical Center in Oakland, Calif., doesn't provide health insurance either. So Brewer — who has suffered from depression, multiple sclerosis and back problems and has two diabetic daughters — has been paying $15,000 to $20,000 a year in medical bills out of her own pocket in recent years. Finally, in June 2005, she filed for personal bankruptcy, "after having liquidated every single asset I ever had." [2]

Economists estimate more than $2 trillion will be spent in the United States on medical care this year — about $6,830 per person — which amounts to 16 percent of the nation's gross domestic product (GDP). [3] That's far more than any other industrialized country: In 2002, the most recent year for which international comparisons are available, Americans spent an average of $5,267 per person on health care, compared to $3,446 in Switzerland and $3,093 in Norway, the next biggest per-capita spenders. [4]

Furthermore, U.S. government actuaries predict that U.S. health spending will double by 2015 — to more than $12,300 per person — and account for 20 percent of the nation's GDP. [5]

Relentlessly rising U.S. health-care costs have made health insurance too expensive for many employers to offer and health care itself too costly for tens of millions of Americans, from the 46 million

Health Costs to Top $4 Trillion

Health spending is expected to rise to more than $4 trillion by 2015 (top graph), or one-fifth of the nation's projected $20 trillion gross domestic product (middle). At the same time, health expenditures are projected to rise to more than $12,000 per person (bottom).

U.S. Health Expenditures
(1993-2015)

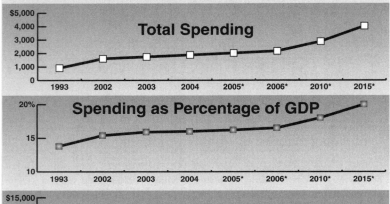

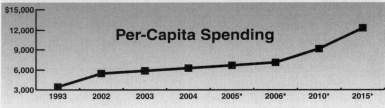

* Projected

Source: Christine Borger, *et al.*, "Health Spending Projections Through 2015: Changes On The Horizon," *Health Affairs*, published online Feb. 22, 2006.

percentage of workers' compensation is now provided through health-care benefits instead of higher wages.

"Most employees don't realize how much their employer is actually spending to provide them with health care," says Baicker. A family health-insurance policy now costs nearly $11,000 a year — more than a full-time, minimum-wage worker earns. [8]

With such high costs, it's not surprising that fewer employers — especially small companies — are offering health insurance, said Altman. In the last five years, 266,000 companies have stopped offering it. As a result, only 60 percent of Americans receive health insurance through their employers today, down from 69 percent in 2000. And the trend "is mostly affecting lower-wage workers, who are the folks who really take it on the chin," said Altman.

Public-sector employers are under even more pressure, often caught between the "rock" of expensive health insurance and the "hard place" of budget cutbacks. Health-insurance costs have risen to a level where they are "seriously impacting school resources," Paul Burrow, an Iowa public school teacher who chairs the State Employees Benefits Association Board, told the Senate Health Appropriations Subcommittee. For example, teachers in Oskaloosa last year effectively took no increase in salary to enable the district to pay for a 19-percent increase in premiums, he added, and in at least two Iowa districts the cost of family coverage "already equals the salary of a beginning teacher." [9]

The number of Americans without health insurance — mostly lower-wage workers — has steadily risen over the past 30 years, according to a study by two professors at the University of California, San Diego. [10] They attribute the phenomenon almost entirely to the fact that per-capita health-care spending has increased far more

who are uninsured to low- and middle-income workers with insurance. In the last five years, insurance premiums jumped 73 percent, but wages rose only 15 percent, according to Drew Altman, president of the nonprofit Kaiser Family Foundation, which tracks health-care issues. During the same period, workers' annual payroll deductions for health insurance went up $1,100, on average. [6] Health coverage alone "is eating up about a quarter of the increase in workers' earnings," Altman said. [7] Moreover, says Katherine Baicker, an associate professor of public policy at the University of California, Los Angeles, and a member of President Bush's Council of Economic Advisors, much of the apparent stagnation in wage growth can be attributed to the fact that a greater

rapidly than income. At the current rate of growth, they predict, the number of uninsured Americans will reach 56 million by 2013, or 27.8 percent of the working-age population. [11] High health-care costs discourage the uninsured from getting needed treatment. A 2003 national survey found that 82 percent of insured people suffering from one of 15 serious symptoms had talked to a health professional about their symptoms, but only 37 percent of the uninsured with similar symptoms consulted a health professional. [12]

Rising costs also affect public hospitals, community-health and mental-health clinics and Medicaid — which covers poor children, their mothers and the disabled. As a result such tax-supported health programs gobble up ever-bigger bites from state budgets, says former Oregon Gov. John Kitzhaber, an emergency physician and organizer of the Archimedes Project, a campaign to encourage states to undertake large-scale health reform.

"Since 2003, Medicaid has exceeded the cost of primary and secondary education as the largest item in many state budgets," says Kitzhaber. Out-of-control health costs are "undermining our ability to invest in our public school system, which offers the best opportunity of success" for American children.

Worse, the nation's highest-in-the-world health spending isn't necessarily buying the highest-quality health care. (*See chart, this page.*) While new drugs and medical technology have improved longevity and quality of life for many Americans, the United States is ranked 37th by the World Health

U.S. Spends More, Gets Less Health Coverage

The United States spends far more for health care than 29 other countries but has fewer doctors per 1,000 population than most of them. The U.S. ranks last in the percentage of its population that is eligible for government-mandated hospitalization insurance.

Spending on Health Care by the U.S. and Other Industrialized Countries, 2002

Country	Per-capita ($U.S.*)	Percent of GDP	Doctors per 1,000 population	% of Population eligible for mandated hospitalization insurance#
Australia**	$2,504	9.1%	2.5	100.0%
Austria	2,220	7.7	3.3	99.0
Belgium	2,515	9.1	3.9	99.0
Canada	2,931	9.6	2.1	100.0
Czech Republic	1,118	7.4	3.5	100.0
Denmark	2,583	8.8	3.3	100.0
Finland	1,943	7.3	3.1	100.0
France	2,736	9.7	3.3	99.5
Germany	2,817	10.9	3.3	92.2
Greece	1,814	9.5	4.5**	100.0
Hungary	1,079	7.8	3.2	99.0
Iceland	2,807	9.9	3.6	100.0
Ireland	2,367	7.3	2.4	100.0
Italy	2,166	8.5	4.4	100.0
Japan**	2,077	7.8	2.0	100.0
South Korea	996	5.1	1.5	100.0
Luxembourg	3,065	6.2	2.6	100.0
Mexico	553	6.1	1.5	68.5
Netherlands	2,643	9.1	3.1	74.1
New Zealand	1,857	8.5	2.1	100.0
Norway	3,083	9.6	3.0**	100.0
Poland	654	6.1	2.3	na
Portugal	1,702	9.3	3.2**	100.0
Slovak Republic	698	5.7	3.6	na
Spain	1,646	7.6	2.9	99.3
Sweden	2,517	9.2	3.0	100.0
Switzerland	3,446	11.2	3.6	99.5
Turkey	446+	6.6+	1.3	55.1++
United Kingdom	2,160	7.7	2.1	100.0
United States	**5,267**	**14.6**	**2.4****	**46.0**

* Represents purchasing power parity.
** 2001
+ 2000
++ 1990
# Based on data available as of 1997
Source: Organization for Economic Cooperation and Development, 2004

Slicing the Big Pie

Taxes fund nearly half of all U.S. health spending (left graph). Hospitals get the biggest share of health-care dollars while drugs get only 12 percent (right graph).

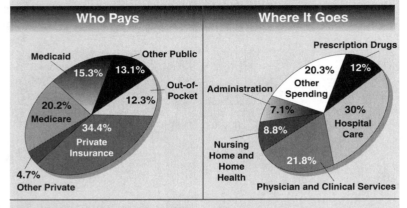

Projected 2006 Health-Care Spending

Who Pays

Medicaid 15.3%
Other Public 13.1%
Out-of-Pocket 12.3%
Medicare 20.2%
Private Insurance 34.4%
Other Private 4.7%

Where It Goes

Prescription Drugs 12%
Other Spending 20.3%
Administration 7.1%
Nursing Home and Home Health 8.8%
Physician and Clinical Services 21.8%
Hospital Care 30%

Source: Centers for Medicare and Medicaid Services

But because of the substantial subsidies and the commitment to insure everyone, Swiss cantons — similar to U.S. states — strictly control insurers' price negotiations. [14] The Swiss end up spending about two-thirds as much as Americans on health, while covering the entire population. [15]

Besides spending more overall, Americans pay the highest health-care prices, according to Gerard Anderson, a professor of health policy and management at Johns Hopkins University. For example, in 2002 the average cost for a day in a U.S. hospital was $2,434, compared to $870 in Canada. [16]

Efforts to control costs have had limited, temporary success. In the mid-1990s, for example, managed-care insurance plans successfully pressured doctors and hospitals to lower prices and limit some services, but after a public backlash spending began to rise again.

The Bush administration has suggested controlling health costs by encouraging the establishment of so-called consumer-directed health plans (CDHPs) — insurance coverage that requires individuals to pay larger-than-normal portions of their health-care costs out of pocket.

Spending more of their own money on health care — rather than relying on comprehensive insurance coverage — will motivate patients "to find out more about what health care costs and what they're getting for their money," said Gail Wilensky, a senior fellow at the non-profit research organization Project HOPE. [17]

But economists say eventually the United States will have to take much tougher action. "The situation has become genuinely nasty," according to Henry Aaron, an economist at the liberal/centrist Brookings Institution. "Costs are rising fast, just as budgets, public and private, are tightening." [18] One option is to follow other industrialized nations in limiting what kind of care is provided, such as paying only for cost-effective treatments, he says, acknowledging that "rationing" would be unpopular and hard to introduce to the decentralized U.S. system.

Organization (WHO) in providing overall quality care, based on adult and infant mortality rates, says economist Len Nichols, director of the health-policy program at the progressive New America Foundation think tank. The United States also ranks 24th among industrialized nations in life expectancy.

Other recent studies have also shown that high spending does not necessarily ensure high-quality care. For instance, in states where the spending is highest for Medicare — the federally subsidized health insurance program for the elderly and disabled — the quality of care is lower than in states that spend less, according to a study at Dartmouth College. [13] (*See graph, p. 86.*)

Many economists say America spends more than any other country on health care because, unlike all other industrialized countries, it does not provide universal health-care insurance. Countries that ensure all citizens a basic level of health care end up spending less because they have a strong motivation to hold costs down by limiting which treatments are subsidized and/or aggressively negotiating lower prices.

In Switzerland, for example, every resident is required to buy private health insurance, with the government picking up part of the tab for lower-income residents.

"If we do not ration, we are going to be spending a very great deal of money on health-care services, an increasing, absolute amount of which is not going to be worth what it costs society to provide," Aaron says.

As economists, lawmakers and consumers wrestle with rising costs, here are some of the major questions being debated:

Will cutting costs harm Americans' health?

Much of the higher health spending in the past few decades has gone toward new drugs, surgical techniques and high-tech diagnostic devices, many of which have helped people live longer, healthier lives. And emphasizing cost control could jeopardize progress in the search for new cures, say some economists. But others argue that European nations — and many lower-spending U.S. states — score as high or higher than high-spending U.S. regions on many health measures, indicating that health can be improved while cutting spending.

Opponents of cost controls, like Duke University economist Henry Grabowski, note that American pharmaceutical companies now lead the world in introducing important new drugs, thanks largely to high drug prices. Between 1993 and 2003, he points out, U.S. companies introduced 48 percent of the world's innovative drugs, 52 percent of all biotech drugs and 55 percent of all "orphan" drugs that treat rare diseases.

That success depends on continued strong financing, says Grabowski, who conducted a study partially funded by drugmaker AstraZeneca. For example, development of new drugs would drop off if Congress imposed price controls on Medicare's new prescription-drug benefit, he says.

Likewise, medical-technology discoveries have been a major driver of higher costs, but imposing cost controls on technology could impede medical innovation, according to a landmark 2001 study by Harvard economist David Cutler and physician Mark McClellan, a former Stanford economist who now heads the Medicare and Medicaid programs. They analyzed spending growth between the 1950s and 1999 and improvements in longevity and quality of life for five medical conditions and found that higher spending had bought health improvements that far exceeded the cost for heart attacks, low-birth weight babies, depression and cataracts. For breast cancer, however, the benefits were roughly equivalent to the higher costs. They concluded

that the quality-adjusted price of medical care is actually falling — not rising. [19]

Meanwhile, cost controls have made health care less accessible for Europeans and Canadians, according to George Halvorson, CEO of Kaiser Permanente, a nationwide health-care delivery organization, and George Isham, medical director of HealthPartners, a Minnesota-based health maintenance organization (HMO). "In most countries with government-run health systems, a great many specialized services are in very short supply . . . because the government doesn't have the money for more," they argued. [20]

For example, the average British patient had to wait more than 29 weeks to get elective surgery in 2000, according to Halvorson and Isham. "This 'rationing' keeps British costs at about half of U.S. costs," they concluded, but the British system "isn't anywhere near as responsive to patient needs."

However, some physicians say, Americans often pay for services that are not health- or life-enhancing. "My mother is 88 and very frail," said physician and former Gov. Kitzhaber. After a physical exam showed signs of a possible tumor, the normal procedure would have involved an endoscopy, a colonoscopy and "a whole lot of things that she had no desire to have done," he said. The doctor recommended re-checking her blood work in a few weeks to see how she was doing, but Kitzhaber asked him, "Why continue to check the blood work on an 88-year-old woman who has decided she doesn't want a bunch of treatment? You're not going to change the outcome." [21]

Evidence clearly shows that much of today's higher health-care spending does not improve health and may even harm it, according to Dartmouth Medical School Professor of Medicine Elliott Fisher. Medicare spending varies widely across the United States, and an extensive analysis shows that "higher spending is associated with lower quality, worse access to care and no gain in satisfaction," he said. In fact, higher spending "is associated with a small increase in the risk of death." [22]

According to a Medicare study at Dartmouth, patients in high-spending states showed no significant difference on nine out of 26 quality measures and, in fact, did worse on 15. Those in higher-spending states, for instance, were less likely to obtain mammograms at recommended intervals, annual eye exams for diabetics and beta-blocking drugs after heart attacks. The

Elderly Won't Cause Health-Cost Tsunami

In coming decades, the elderly in the United States and other industrialized nations not only will be older than today's seniors, but there will be more of them. While that certainly will mean higher health spending, many economists say the biggest growth in health-care costs will be caused by new technologies, not the growing elderly population.

In fact, the United States won't experience the same huge senior demographic wave as many other countries for nearly 20 years, said Johns Hopkins University economist Gerard Anderson. For example, in 2000, the over-65 crowd comprised only 12.5 percent of the U.S. population, compared to 17.1 percent in Japan and 15.2 percent in Germany. The American over-65 population is not projected to hit 16.6 percent until 2020. [1]

After analyzing two decades of national spending data, Brandeis University economists concluded that 72 percent of future health-spending growth will be caused by expensive new technology and higher prices. Only 18 percent of the higher spending will be due to population growth and only 10 percent to an aging population. [2]

As Princeton University economist Uwe Reinhardt described it, the economic impact of the additional elderly on health-care costs "isn't a tsunami, but a little ripple." Evidence for that conclusion comes from countries like Germany and France, whose demographics already mirror what the United States will look like in two decades, Reinhardt said. [3]

Aging has had less impact than many expected because health-care costs, while highest in the last year of life, aren't the same for every patient, said Harvard University economist David Cutler. As lifespans lengthen and death rates decline, a smaller share of the elderly will be in their expensive last year at any given time, he explained. In addition, more people will die in their 80s or 90s, rather than earlier, and studies show that end-of-life costs generally decline for very old people, in part because their families and doctors make different choices about their care. [4]

Cost pressures due to aging are expected to ease over time for two reasons, according to economists at the Organization for Economic Cooperation and Development (OECD), a group of 30 industrialized democracies, including the United States. First, increases in longevity "are assumed to translate into additional years of good health," which should help hold down medical cost increases. Second, because medical costs are highest in the last months of life, increased longevity will cut costs for every age cohort of the elderly. As people live longer, more and more individuals will " 'exit' an age group by moving into an older group" rather than " 'exit' by dying," thus lowering the group's average costs. [5]

Medicare data demonstrate the lower cost of end-of-life care for much older people, according to the late Norman Levinsky, a professor of medicine at Boston University Medical School. In a study of 1996 Medicare spending for patients in their last year of life, Levinsky and his colleagues calculated per-

researchers hypothesize that in lower-spending areas a patient is more likely to depend on a single general practitioner who ensures that cost-effective, preventive procedures are prescribed. In high-spending areas, on the other hand, patients visit specialists more than twice as often as in lower-spending areas, but specialists are more expensive and don't usually coordinate overall care.

According to some economists, using cost controls to reverse the American trend of favoring specialty care over primary care — provided by internists, general practitioners and pediatricians — could reap huge cost savings while promoting better health. The U.S. physician mix consists of about one-third generalists and two-thirds specialists, unlike countries such as Australia and Canada, where generalists make up about half of all doctors. [23]

An American is three times more likely to see a specialist than a British patient. [24] And U.S. specialists earn more than generalists. The median annual income for anesthesiologists, for example, was $321,686 in 2004, compared to $156,010 for family-practice doctors. [25] U.S. specialists also earn more than their counterparts abroad.

However, studies show that having more specialists in a region does not improve care. Adding one additional primary-care physician per 10,000 population produces a 6 percent drop in mortality from all causes and a 3 percent drop in infant mortality, according to Barbara Starfield, a professor of health policy at the Johns Hopkins Bloomberg School of Public Health. But having an above-average number of neonatologists — infant specialists — does not decrease the infant death rate in a

patient costs averaged $35,300 in Massachusetts and $27,800 in California for patients 65 to 74. But costs dropped to $22,000 in Massachusetts and $21,600 in California for dying patients 85 or older. [6]

However, future generations could throw a monkey wrench into this benign scenario if they turn out to be less healthy than anticipated, according to Dana Goldman, director of health economics at the RAND Corporation, a Santa Monica, Calif., research organization. "The past few decades have witnessed alarming increases in obesity and diabetes among the young," and "disability rates for the young have risen within all demographic and economic groups," Goldman said. That could mean future cohorts of the elderly would be more costly to treat. [7]

But while the aging population may not substantially drive up health costs overall in the United States, it could still alter the health-care payment landscape dramatically, moving more and more private-sector spending into the public Medicare and Medicaid programs, according to Cutler.

The aging of the nation's population will account for only 10 percent of future health-care spending increases, according to Brandeis economists.

Meanwhile, under current laws, the general tax revenues that help fund Medicare will grow to only 3.8 percent of GDP by 2050. Thus, to meet costs, Medicare spending would have to be cut by more than half from its projected level. "No one has a way to do that," Cutler said. [8]

[1] Gerard F. Anderson and Peter Scott Hussey, "Population Aging: A Comparison Among Industrialized Countries," *Health Affairs*, May/June 2000.

[2] Quoted in "Hospital Forum Airs Predictions on Health-Care Future," *Medicine & Health Perspectives*, May 5, 2003.

[3] Quoted in *ibid.*

[4] David M. Cutler, "The Potential for Cost Savings in Medicare's Future," *Health Affairs* Web site, Sept. 26, 2005; www.healthaffairs.org.

[5] "Projecting OECD Health and Long-Term Care Expenditures: What Are the Main Drivers?" Organization for Economic Cooperation and Development, Economics Department Working Paper No. 477, www.oecd.org/eco, February 2006.

[6] Norman G. Levinsky, *et al.*, "Influence of Age on Medicare Expenditures and Medical Care in the Last Year of Life," *Journal of the American Medical Association*, Sept. 19, 2001, p. 1349.

[7] Dana P. Goldman, *et al.*, "Consequences of Health Trends and Medical Innovation for the Future Elderly," *Health Affairs* Web site, Sept. 25, 2005; www.healthaffairs.org.

[8] Cutler, *op. cit.*

region, she says, nor does having more specialists increase the number of people whose cancer is diagnosed at earlier, more treatable stages. [26]

Deciding what care to pay for based on evidence of what works could substantially cut costs without harming health, argues Karen Davis, president of the Commonwealth Fund, which supports international research on health care and insurance. [27] Many studies now demonstrate techniques that preserve care quality while lowering costs, she said, such as having advanced-practice nurses visit frail, elderly patients. They could detect serious conditions early, cutting those patients' annual health costs by 36 percent. In another study a hospital decreased average maternity costs from $1,622 to $1,480 per person by encouraging obstetricians not to induce labor until at least the 39th week of pregnancy. [28]

Davis challenged the "typical assumption" that other countries are "rationing effective care" and "have long waiting lists." While U.S. patients do wait shorter times for surgery, she pointed out, sick Americans wait longer to see a doctor than patients in other countries, and more Americans rely on emergency rooms for primary care.

Would health care be cheaper if everyone were insured?

As the cost of health care becomes further and further out of reach for uninsured Americans, U.S. lawmakers face policy and ethical dilemmas. [29] On one hand, it would cost a whopping $48 billion a year, according to

Health Insurance Premiums Fluctuated

Annual growth in the cost of health-insurance premiums fluctuated dramatically over the last two decades, dipping precipitously in the early 1990s after Congress began discussing universal health insurance. At the same time, inflation and earnings remained relatively flat. In the mid-1990s, a backlash against managed-care restrictions designed to cut costs caused premium growth rates to rise again. Although the rate of premium growth turned downward in 2003, experts doubt it will drop to 1996 levels.

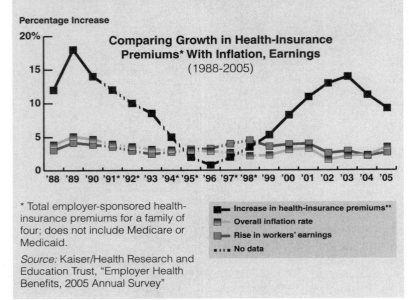

Percentage Increase

Comparing Growth in Health-Insurance Premiums* With Inflation, Earnings (1988-2005)

* Total employer-sponsored health-insurance premiums for a family of four; does not include Medicare or Medicaid.

Source: Kaiser/Health Research and Education Trust, "Employer Health Benefits, 2005 Annual Survey"

■— Increase in health-insurance premiums**
■ Overall inflation rate
■ Rise in workers' earnings
▪▪▪▪ No data

one estimate, to extend health-insurance coverage to the nation's 46 million uninsured. [30] But some economists argue that much of those costs would be offset by other economic gains and that covering only a small number of the uninsured — such as more mothers with young children — could cost even more than universal coverage.

If all uninsured Americans had health coverage, the average annual cost of the care they receive now would rise by 39 percent — from $2,034 per person to $2,836 — or $802 per person, according to Jack Hadley and John Holahan, economists at the liberal-leaning Urban Institute. [31]

"From a purely selfish economic perspective . . . leaving the uninsured in their current predicament turns out to be cheaper than stepping up to underwrite with added taxes a move to universal coverage," said Princeton University Professor of economics Uwe Reinhardt.

While Congress wants to take small steps to help at least some people get more coverage — such as enabling small businesses to pool administrative costs to save money on insurance — Senate Majority Leader Bill Frist, R-Tenn., a cardiologist, said it would be "impossible to get to 100 percent" coverage. His own home state of Tennessee has been "going bankrupt" trying to achieve universal coverage, he said. [32]

Furthermore, offering everyone the same level of comprehensive health insurance enjoyed by most Americans would increase demand for services — and thus overall spending — because insurance itself drives up costs, says Brookings' Aaron. "By shielding patients from all or most of the cost of care, insurance encourages patients to demand all care, however small the benefit and however high the cost of producing it." [33]

Nevertheless, Hadley and Holahan argue, covering everyone could be cheaper than covering only a few, small additional groups, because if everyone were covered, programs that specifically fund uninsured care could be dismantled and tens of billions of dollars redirected to subsidizing universal coverage. [34]

Currently, uninsured patients receive about $125 billion worth of care annually and pay only about 26 percent of the cost. Public and private programs that serve the uninsured — such as community health centers and special payments to hospitals serving large numbers of the uninsured — pick up some of the tab while hospitals provide the rest, passing some of the costs on to other patients. [35]

Moreover, an expert government panel has estimated that covering the uninsured would create $65 billion to $130 billion worth of improved health and productivity annually, more than enough to make the cost of coverage worthwhile. [36]

The uninsured often foster ineffective, excessive spending because they wait until their health condition reaches a critical stage and end up in the emergency room — instead of getting more cost-effective preventive care in a physician's office, said Kitzhaber. He related the penny-wise-but-pound-foolish case of Douglas Schmidt, an Oregon man who suffered from a seizure disorder. In February 2003, to balance the budget in a recession, the Oregon legislature discontinued prescription-drug coverage for the medically needy, he said. Without his anti-seizure medication, Schmidt went into a sustained grand mal seizure, suffered serious brain damage and ended up on a ventilator in intensive care for months. Schmidt died in November 2003 after life support was withdrawn.

Schmidt's anti-seizure medication would have cost $14 a day, Kitzhaber said, while his intensive care cost $7,500 a day — more than $1.1 million — "all of which was simply billed back to the state." [37]

Every country with universal coverage spends less on health care than the United States because their governments have an incentive to hold down costs, say some economists. They do that by paying only for treatments shown to be effective and negotiating price cuts from suppliers and health providers.

"Countries with national health systems . . . often [have] historically low levels of spending," said Julian Le Grand, a professor of social policy at the London School of Economics. The United Kingdom, for instance, spends about half as much of its GDP on health care as the United States. (*See chart, p. 75.*) [38]

Does the U.S. health-care industry charge too much?

Some economists say U.S. health spending is the highest in the world because the American health-care industry charges higher prices for the same services and enjoys larger profits than its counterparts in other countries. Moreover, those higher prices and profits do not necessarily buy more or better-quality health care, they argue.

Opponents of that view contend that higher U.S. profits often underwrite necessary but underfunded services — such as uninsured care and research and development — and that income disparity between U.S. jobs in general is much wider than in other countries.

Johns Hopkins' Anderson says that despite their higher spending Americans are not getting their money's worth. Studies show that U.S. patients get less health care than residents of many other industrialized countries, he said, citing statistics showing that in 2000 the United States had fewer physicians per 1,000 people;

A fourth-grader in Cicero, Ill., gets a free checkup at Loyola University's Pediatric Mobile Health Unit, which serves needy children in the Midwest. Some economists say using fewer specialists and more primary-care doctors — such as internists and pediatricians — could save money while promoting better health.

fewer doctor visits per capita and fewer hospital admissions per 1,000 people than the median for industrialized countries belonging to the 30-member Organization for Economic Cooperation and Development (OECD).

In an earlier study Americans were found to pay 40 percent more per capita than the Germans for four diseases — diabetes, gall stones, breast cancer and lung cancer — but got 15 percent fewer services. Many OECD countries also have more high-tech imaging devices — such as MRIs (magnetic resonance imaging) and CT (computerized tomography) scanners — per capita than the United States. Less care but higher overall costs means U.S. prices are significantly higher, Anderson explains. [39]

For example, U.S. physicians' incomes are much higher, according to an analysis by Princeton's Reinhardt. In 1996 — the last year for which international comparisons are available — the average American physician's income was $199,000, compared to the OECD median of $70,324. [40]

And U.S. providers are determined to keep their incomes high, even when Medicare and private insurers strive to keep prices down, said the Commonwealth Fund's Davis. "[P]hysicians respond to reduced fees by

C H R O N O L O G Y

1920s-1950s *Health costs increase, and U.S. reformers press for social insurance covering all citizens. Large industries begin offering health coverage to workers.*

1932 Committee on the Cost of Medical Care details the growing difficulties families face in paying for care.

1948 President Harry S Truman's National Health Insurance initiative fails after the American Medical Association criticizes it, and some congressional Republicans compare it to communism.

1960s-1970s *Medical science advances, costs rise and the U.S. government provides health coverage for poor mothers with young children, the disabled and the elderly. President Richard M. Nixon and Congress offer grants to develop health maintenance organizations (HMOs) to control costs.*

1960 U.S. health spending totals $28 billion, or 5.2 percent of gross domestic product (GDP).

1965 President Lyndon B. Johnson signs Medicare and Medicaid programs into law.

1971 President Nixon imposes wage-and-price controls on medical services.

1980s *New rules reduce Medicare spending, but as payments fall hospitals charge private insurers more.*

1980 Health spending tops $255 billion, or 9.1 percent of GDP.

1983 Medicare begins reimbursing hospitals for overall treatment of illnesses rather than for individual services.

1990s *Health-spending growth slows as employers embrace managed care, and President Bill Clinton promises health-system reforms. By mid-decade, Clinton's plan is stalled, consumers lash back against managed care and spending rises again.*

1993 First lady Hillary Rodham Clinton leads an effort to reform the health-care system by compromising between government price controls and competition among private health plans.

1997 A presidential commission urges Congress to protect patients from potentially harmful managed-care cost controls. . . . Congress cuts Medicare and Medicaid.

1999 An Institute of Medicine panel casts doubt on the quality of U.S. health care, finding that tens of thousands of patients die and hundreds of thousands are injured each year from medical errors. . . . Backlash from medical providers leads Congress to undo the 1997 Medicare payment cuts.

2000s *Congress enacts tax breaks for consumer-directed health plans (CDHPs) and health safety accounts (HSAs). States and the federal government begin studying the cost-effectiveness of medical treatments.*

2000 Health spending totals $1.4 trillion, or 13.8 percent of GDP.

2001 Oregon uses research on drug effectiveness to determine how much Medicaid will pay for them.

2003 Congress enacts tax breaks for HSAs and a research program to compare treatment costs and effectiveness.

2004 Dartmouth University analysts find that Medicare patients get worse care in states where spending is higher.

2005 Health insurer Aetna discloses what it pays physicians in Cincinnati.

2006 Health spending totals $2.2 trillion — 16.5 percent of GDP. . . . President Bush proposes greatly expanded tax breaks for HSAs. . . . White House asks insurers and employers to pressure providers to reveal their prices and quality ratings.

2011 First baby boomers are eligible for Medicare, increasing the proportion of subsidized health spending.

2015 Health spending projected to rise to more than $4 trillion — 20 percent of GDP.

working longer hours, seeing more patients, having patients come back more frequently and performing more billable procedures," she told the Senate Health Appropriations Subcommittee. [41]

For example, she said, when Congress enacted Medicare cuts in 1997, average physician incomes dropped over the next few years; in response, doctors began performing more services. Between 2000 and 2001, the number of doctor visits by Medicare beneficiaries increased by 4.3 percent, while use of some lab tests grew 22 percent and brain MRIs increased 15 percent.

"It is hard to believe that Medicare beneficiaries suddenly demanded 15 percent more brain MRIs," said Davis. More plausibly, she said, doctors simply took it upon themselves to schedule more patients for the non-invasive, high-paying, diagnostic procedures — at least partly in order to boost revenues.

Reinhardt points out that there is a wider disparity between American doctors' incomes and other U.S. workers' salaries than there is in other OECD countries. In 1996, for instance, U.S. doctors' average income was about 5.5 times the average U.S. worker's salary. By comparison, German doctors earned 3.4 times the average worker's income, Australians, 2.2 times and Swedes, 1.5 times. [42]

But economists say it is not surprising that U.S. providers are high earners, given other features of the U.S. economy. The income disparity for all U.S. occupations is far wider than in other OECD countries, Reinhardt said, so the disparity between American doctors' incomes and the average worker is well in line with salary differences between other top U.S. professionals and other workers. The incomes of skilled health workers "are determined partly with reference to the incomes that equally able and skilled professionals can earn elsewhere in the economy," he said.

Moreover, the higher American physicians' incomes may be justifiable because medical education leaves U.S. doctors with substantial debt, unlike in OECD countries where governments often subsidize medical students, according to Reinhardt. In 2004, more than 80 percent of U.S med-school graduates were in debt. [43]

Physicians also earn high incomes because they face long, irregular working hours; more than one-third of full-time physicians and surgeons worked 60 hours or more a week in 2004, according to the U.S. Bureau of Labor Statistics. [44]

And while many segments of the U.S. health system are overpaid, others are woefully underfunded. The behavioral and psychiatric units of the Children's Hospital and Research Center in Oakland, Calif., suffered deficits "in excess of $2 million" over the past two years, according to that hospital's May 2005 Web posting. "Most insurance providers now pay us only half or less of what it actually costs to provide these services." [45]

"Many inner-city hospitals caring for large numbers of uninsured patients continue to struggle financially," said the Center for Studying Health System Change. For example, in northern New Jersey, suburban hospitals have expanded into new buildings while "hospitals in declining urban areas . . . have struggled" just to keep existing facilities upgraded. And in Miami, the county hospital system "is facing significant deficits stemming in part from charity-care needs growing faster than . . . funding from a dedicated half-penny sales tax." [46]

BACKGROUND

High Tech, High Cost

In the early 20th century, medicine began to morph from a hands-on, low-tech profession — with matching low pay — to the high-tech, expensive health system we know today. [47]

But University of Pennsylvania medical historian Rosemary Stevens warns that it's easy to be beguiled by tales of kindly 19th-century physicians who made house calls and accepted chickens for payment from farmers. "We over-romanticize the past," she told the Public Broadcasting Service. "Doctors went to bedsides to give cheer because they often couldn't do anything else." [48]

Over the last half-century, however, medicine has had "a very, very different potential," dominated by drugs and technology with the potential to prevent and cure disease. "Antibiotics only came into general use in the 1940s," Stevens pointed out.

But the higher cost of the new and more effective drugs and technologies posed a public-policy conundrum and ethical dilemma: Who, if anyone, should be ensured access to care, and at whose expense? By the end of the 1990s, all of the OECD countries except Mexico, Turkey and the United States had answered that question by instituting some version of universal or near-universal coverage. [49]

Over the past 40 years, health spending worldwide has consistently risen faster than national incomes. Finland,

Should the Rich Pay More for Health Care?

As an emergency physician and public official, John Kitzhaber viewed health-care delivery two ways. As a doctor, he was trained to "use every resource on the person in front of me, regardless" of how few resources that may leave for others, he says. But as Oregon's governor (1995 to 2003), he realized, "you can't practice medicine one person at a time. You can't make a healthy system that way."

Unfortunately, "We've created a system where we lavish unlimited resources on one person at a time, but we give little thought to the big-picture consequences of those person-by-person decisions," says Kitzhaber, who founded and runs The Archimedes Movement, a campaign to encourage states to undertake large-scale health reform.

Some economists now say rising costs are creating a health-care dilemma that may force Americans to debate fundamental principles about rights to care. A growing number of workers cannot afford health insurance and end up paying much higher prices than insured people for the same care.

"Our health-care system is in real trouble, but we are not even discussing the fundamental cause" — a "mismatch between demand and the available supply," said Humphrey Taylor, chairman of the Harris Poll. The key question is "whether health care is, or should be, more a common good (i.e., an entitlement) or more a private economic good, where you get what you are willing and able to pay for. We should debate that." [1]

To some, providing basic health-care resources to everyone is a self-evident ethical principle. "There are 10,000 technical issues involved with health-system reform, but one fundamentally moral question: Who shall be allowed to sit at our health-care table of plenty?" asks economist Len Nichols, who directs the health-policy program at the progressive New America Foundation think tank. "Many scriptural traditions and much humanistic philosophy admonish full communities to feed the hungry. . . . For us to deny [health care] because of cost is tantamount to denying food to the starving poor." [2]

But David Kelley argues that entitling all citizens to receive health care unfairly imposes government control on taxpayers and on physicians and other care providers. "If health care is a right, then government is responsible for seeing that everyone has access to it, just as the right to property means that government must protect us against theft," says Kelley, founder and senior fellow of the Objectivist Center, a think tank that espouses limited government and laissez-faire capitalism. "A political system that tries to implement a right to health care will necessarily involve forced transfers of wealth to pay for programs, loss of freedom for health-care providers, higher prices and more restricted access by all consumers." [3]

The range of opinion is so broad that the country probably can't come to a single conclusion about how to allocate health resources, said Gail Wilensky, a senior fellow at Project HOPE, a nonprofit research organization, and a former head of the Medicare and Medicaid programs. "Should ethical issues be a part of national health policy?" Wilensky asks. She does not believe they will be, because the United States has a heterogeneous population that is very different ethnically, religiously and racially. "It would be very difficult for us to have a single, uniform policy with regard to rationing of health care." [4]

With regard to a sense of responsibility, she continues, "we are clearer for some populations. Most people would agree that the poor . . . will need some or a lot of help [to finance] their own health care." Even within that basic consensus, however, there is disagreement over who is considered poor, she added.

The Bush administration is promoting expansion of consumer-directed health plans (CDHPs), which require consumers to pay more for health care than in traditional insurance coverage and are designed to encourage consumers to shop for the most cost-effective treatments. Encouraging more cost-conscious buying is basically sound, says Uwe Reinhardt, professor of economics at Princeton University, but current proposals put disproportionate demands on lower-income people, he says.

CDHPs generally require owners to spend $4,000-$6,000 a year out of pocket. "To a waitress and a husband with $40,000 or less family income, $4,000 is a huge hit," says Reinhardt. But for a two-lawyer household with an annual income in the $200,000 range, a $4,000 deductible "is nothing. It's a skiing trip."

Ireland, New Zealand and the United Kingdom have been the most successful — and the United States the least successful — at keeping health spending from greatly outpacing national income growth. [50] By 1960, U.S. annual spending on health care was already 50 percent higher per capita than in any other OECD country, and it continued to rise, growing an average of 2.4 percentage points faster than gross domestic product between 1960 and 2000. [51]

A more ethical and effective approach would be to increase CDHP deductibles on a sliding scale, based on income, Reinhardt suggests, with a family earning $200,000 obligated for $20,000-$30,000 — five times the deductible paid by a family that earns one-fifth their income. "This should be the debate," he says.

Similarly, tax breaks proposed by the Bush administration for consumers who use CDHPs also favor the well-off, who get proportionally higher tax deductions than the poor, says Stuart Butler, vice president of domestic and economic policy studies at the conservative Heritage Foundation, "It's very badly targeted. I would have liked to see the administration moving more in the direction of a tax-credit approach" that would target lower-income people only.

Under the existing system, the poor end up paying more for all health services than the rich. Low-income people and individuals without insurance face so-called discriminatory pricing when they purchase health services. That's because pharmacies, hospitals and other health providers offer volume discounts to insurers and large government-subsidized programs like Medicare and Medicaid. But the uninsured or self-insured don't get those discounts and often are billed at highly inflated list prices. Conservative advocates worry that CDHP-insured people may face similar price discrimination for services they pay for out of pocket.

"Typically, a hospital will charge uninsured patients three, four, five or even 10 times as much as what an insured patient pays for the same procedures or services," according to K. B. Forbes, head of Consejo de Latinos

Former Gov. John Kitzhaber, D-Ore., an emergency physician, urges states to undertake large-scale health reform.

Unidos, an advocacy group based in East Los Angeles. [5] In Fort Myers, Fla., for example, an uninsured man who broke his leg paid $15,100 for a procedure that would have cost an insurer around $5,500, Forbes says, and an uninsured woman was charged $7,271 for a cesarean section that would have cost an insurer around $3,600.

The Consejo group focuses its efforts on the Hispanic community, in part because Hispanics are least likely to have health insurance. In 2004, 34.3 percent of non-elderly Hispanics were uninsured, compared to 29.1 percent of American Indians/Alaska Natives, 21.2 percent of non-Hispanic blacks and 13.2 percent of non-Hispanic whites. [6]

High charges for uninsured people are "economic discrimination that impacts minorities," Forbes said. "We have a responsibility to protect their rights and livelihood." [7]

---

[1] Humphrey J. F. Taylor, "The Health Care Debate We Are Not having Now," EyeNet, American Academy of Ophthalmology, March 2003.

[2] Len M. Nichols, "Outline of the New America Vision for a 21st-Century Health-Care System," *Issue Brief #1*, New America Foundation Health Policy Program, January 2006.

[3] David Kelley, "Is There a Right to Health Care?" www.objectivist-center.org.

[4] Gail Wilensky, interview, "Healthcare Crisis: Who's at Risk" www.pbs.org.

[5] K. B. Forbes, "Unconscionable," http://hospitalpricing.com, Oct. 27, 2003.

[6] *The Uninsured: A Primer*, Kaiser Commission on Medicaid and the Uninsured, January 2006.

[7] Quoted in "Latino Advocacy Group Calls on Hospitals to Invoke Six-Month National Moratorium on Lawsuits Against Uninsured Patients," *Hispanic Business*, www.hispanicbusiness.com.

During the 1990s, spending growth slowed because employers had turned to cost-conscious managed-care insurers for employees' coverage, and health providers reined in cost increases in hope of warding off the large-scale health-system reform sought by President Bill Clinton. By 1996, however, Clinton's reform effort — led by first lady Hillary Rodham Clinton — had spectacularly failed, doctors and patients were lashing back

Medicare Spending Varies Widely

Federal health-care spending for the elderly varies widely, largely because patients in some cities see more doctors and specialists than in other cities. In Miami, for instance, Medicare spends more than twice as much on the average beneficiary as in Rapid City. Numerous studies show, however, that patients are healthier in cities where expenditures are lower, in part because seeing a lot of specialists does not result in coordinated, preventive care.

Medicare Spending in Selected Cities
(2003)

Amount Spent Per Enrollee

City	Amount
Miami	$11,351
Los Angeles	9,752
Philadelphia	8,344
Boston	7,900
Chicago	7,740
Jackson, Miss.	6,768
Anchorage, Alaska	6,430
Phoenix, Ariz.	6,363
Raleigh, N.C.	6,168
Davenport, Iowa	5,302
Minneapolis	5,212
Rapid City, S.D.	5,122
*National Average	6,611

Source: Dartmouth Atlas of Health Care database, http://cecsweb.dartmouth.edu/release1/datatools/bench_s1.php

he explains, rises for three main reasons:

- Some diseases, such as diabetes, are more common;
- Doctors have begun treating some chronic conditions like high blood pressure, high cholesterol and depression at earlier stages; and
- Many new drugs and technologies have been invented.

Medical innovation is a major cost driver, Thorpe said. For example, spending per newborn infant increased fivefold between 1987 and 2002, due almost entirely to new technology.

Meanwhile, the U.S. health system has its own unique cost generators, which helps explain why U.S. spending is the highest in the world. To begin with, the non-centralized American system has steep administrative costs. Between 1970 and 1998, for example, the number of people holding administrative jobs — such as claims processors, billing clerks and business managers — in U.S. health care swelled 24-fold, according to David Himmelstein and Steffie Woolhandler, associate professors of medicine at Harvard Medical School, who advocate a single-payer health system in which the federal government would provide insurance to everyone. During the same period, the number of doctors and other clinical workers grew only two-and-a-half-fold. [53] By 1999, the administrative costs of insurers, employers and health providers amounted to about 24 percent of total health spending, Himmelstein and Woolhandler estimate, compared with Canada, for example, which spends only about half as many of its health dollars on administrative paperwork. [54]

Meanwhile, U.S. prices for goods and services also have risen higher than elsewhere, largely because hundreds of individual insurers, employers and government programs each buy care on their own, enabling doctors, hospitals and drug companies to charge higher prices

against managed-care restrictions, and spending began rising again.

Sticker Shock

When it comes to predicting how high a nation's health-care spending will rise, John Poisal, an actuary for the federal Centers for Medicare and Medicaid Services, says that, in essence, "income drives the bus." As personal and national incomes rise, he explains, people worldwide spend increasing amounts on health care.

As medicine develops new treatments and technologies and serves ever more consumers, spending is pushed higher, not always for good clinical reasons, according to Kenneth Thorpe, chairman of the Department of Health Policy and Management at Emory University's Rollins School of Public Health in Atlanta. [52] Health spending,

than those in countries with single-payer government systems or government oversight of insurers' prices. [55]

Technology also enters the U.S. system more easily and disperses more quickly than in other industrialized countries. In Germany, for example, only about 20 percent of new technologies are approved for payment after careful costs/benefit analysis by health providers and government officials, said Anne Haas, senior officer for health policy at AOK Bundesverband, the largest government-approved and regulated company among those managing Germany's cradle-to-grave social-insurance system. [56]

In the United States, on the other hand, not only do doctors and hospitals increase usage of new technologies unchecked, but only a handful of poorly funded U.S. organizations analyze clinical technology before insurers pay for it, said Robert Laszewski, North American chairman of the Global Medical Forum, a nonprofit group that studies cost issues. The U.S. health system "may be the biggest supply-side economy in the universe" with "an unfettered ability to simultaneously create both supply and cost," Laszewski said. [57]

John Wennberg, director of Dartmouth Medical Schools' Center for Clinical Evaluative Services and a pioneer in studying how medical costs vary regionally, says that "ignorance and silence" surround the question: How much care is the right amount?

"For example, how frequently should a doctor schedule office visits with a patient chronically ill with diabetes? Every three months? Every six months? The fact is, nobody knows or has supported research to find out," he says.

Cost-Control Battles

In the mid-20th century — as health-care spending began its steep upward climb — U.S. policymakers started looking for ways to keep care affordable.

"The puzzle over what to do about the high costs of health care — who pays for it and are we getting what we pay for — has confounded every administration since Truman's 60 years ago," said Risa Lavizzo-Mourey, president of the Robert Wood Johnson Foundation, a major source of funding for health-policy research. "Richard Nixon is the first president I can remember who warned us of a 'crisis' in [health] costs." Nixon called for a new system "that makes high-quality health care available to every American in a dignified manner and at a price he can afford." [58]

President George W. Bush calls for the use of consumer-directed health plans (CDHPs) in a policy address in February at the headquarters of Wendys International, in Dublin, Ohio. Bush says CDHPs will encourage consumers to "shop around until you get the best treatment for the best price."

Getty Images/Jim Watson

In 1971, Nixon ordered wage-and-price controls for health care, along with other parts of the economy, in hope of reining in inflation and stemming the crisis in health-care affordability. "I was brought into the White house in 1971 and was told by . . . the president that if [health spending] reached 8 percent of GDP . . . the American way would deteriorate," said Stuart Altman, former deputy director of Nixon's Cost-of-Living Council and now a professor of health policy at Brandeis University. [59]

While the controls held costs down somewhat, they sparked passionate resistance by businesses and health providers. The administration ended the program in 1974.

Over the years, some insurers have tried "bundling" medical charges — paying for the entire treatment of an injury or illness rather than allowing providers to charge easily inflatable prices for individual goods and services like the notorious $10 aspirin appearing on many a hospital bill.

In an effort to encourage a market-based program combining bundling with preventive health care, Nixon pushed Congress to provide funds to encourage development of enough health-maintenance organizations (HMOs) to enroll about 40 million people by 1976. [60]

By 1973, Congress had handed out some $7 million in HMO planning grants. But the initiative drew fire from the American Medical Association (AMA), the nation's largest physicians' organization, which resisted having doctors abandon their individual practices to work as employees on HMO staffs.

Many liberal commentators also denounced Nixon's plan, arguing that the country needed universal national health coverage rather than limited, market-based expansion of HMOs. Ultimately, the Watergate scandal forced Nixon's resignation from office in 1974, ending his ambitious — though mostly ill-fated — efforts to control health costs.

Through the 1970s and '80s, health spending continued to soar. Medicare costs, for example, grew an average of 19 percent annually from 1979 to 1982. [61] In response, Medicare began to develop charge-bundling programs for various health sectors — an effort that continues today. In 1983, Medicare introduced its first such "prospective payment system" (PPS) — the Diagnosis-Related-Group (DRG) system — in which hospitals are paid a set amount for a patient's entire stay, based on the diagnosis.

The DRG-PPS system helped hold down Medicare hospital costs and was eventually copied by many private insurers and overseas governments. But in the late 1980s, with providers earning less from Medicare, they got tougher in price negotiations with private insurers, causing workers' insurance premiums and overall spending to soar again.

In response, employers turned again to Nixon's HMO idea. In the late 1980s and early '90s, more and more companies adopted managed-care coverage for their workers and scored some cost-control victories as their HMOs bargained aggressively with providers. In addition, Clinton entered office in 1992 promising large-scale health reform, and the prospect of a government-regulated system scared some health organizations into voluntarily slowing cost increases.

By 1996, however, Congress had blocked the Clinton plan, and doctors had made common cause with patients to oppose HMO restrictions. With Congress threatening to enact a Patients' Bill of Rights that would ban managed care from imposing certain cost-control measures — such as limiting which doctors a patient could see — insurers and employers backed off aggressive cost controls, and spending rose anew. [62]

Although the PPS approach had worked in the Medicare program, providers began using other methods to obtain higher payments — many that probably didn't improve patient care. For example, when Medicare began paying more for catheterization — the insertion of a thin tube into the artery to take measurements such as blood pressure inside the heart — in heart-attack victims, "you can imagine what happened to catheterization rates," says White House adviser Baicker.

CURRENT SITUATION

Savvier Shopping

In 2006, health spending continues to climb with no slowdown in sight. The Medicare PPS still functions, and some managed-care cost-containment practices remain in place, such as emphasizing preventive care and carefully managing drug utilization by high-cost patients. But the 21st century has seen only one new idea for keeping costs down: President Bush's consumer-directed health plans.

CDHPs are insurance plans in which individuals pay larger-than-usual health costs out of their own pockets, often aided by health savings accounts (HSAs), to which employers may contribute. In 2003 at the president's urging, Congress made HSA contributions by employers and individuals tax deductible, much like today's flexible-spending accounts. However, unlike flexible-spending accounts, unspent balances in HSAs roll over from year to year, and workers can take their HSAs with them when they change jobs.

This year, in hope of expanding CDHPs' reach, the administration has proposed major additional tax breaks, particularly aimed at the self-employed and those who do not buy health coverage through their jobs. Under the plan, HSA owners would get a tax credit — in addition to the existing tax deductibility — and an additional deduction for premiums paid for HSA-related health coverage. Higher-income taxpayers would get bigger tax breaks in absolute dollars, since higher-income people generally claim higher deductibles (the amount paid out of pocket before coverage kicks in).

The hope is that CDHPs would encourage workers to "shop around until you get the best treatment for the best price," said President Bush in a February speech at the Dublin, Ohio, headquarters of the Wendy's restaurant chain. HSAs provide tax-favored savings from which workers may pay for health care, Bush explained. "When you inject this type of thinking in the system, price starts to matter. You begin to say, well, maybe there's a better way to do this, and a more cost-effective way." [63]

Should the government do more to lower Medicare drug costs?

YES Dean Baker
Co-Director, Center for Economic and Policy Research

From "The Excess Cost of the Medicare Drug Benefit," Institute for America's Future, February 2006

The waste and inefficiency built into the 2003 Medicare Modernization Act (MMA) will add more than $800 billion to the cost of prescription drugs to the government and beneficiaries over its first decade, compared to a drug bill designed to maximize efficiency.

Congress deliberately structured the bill to ensure that multiple private insurance companies would provide the benefit rather than Medicare. This design substantially increased the cost of the program for seniors and the disabled, leaving many with large drug expenses. The structure designed by Congress also made the program more costly for the federal government and state governments.

The waste built into the MMA is easy to show. . . . The Congressional Budget Office (CBO) projected that the marketing and the profits of the insurance industry would add $38 billion to the cost of the MMA over the first eight years, due to the fact that Medicare is not allowed to use its bargaining power to gain discounts from the industry.

Virtually every other country in the industrialized world imposes some constraint on drug prices, either through formal price controls or negotiated prices. Consumers in these countries pay, on average, between 35 and 55 percent less than consumers in the United States. The [negotiated] discounts obtained by the Veterans Administration were even larger.

If Medicare was allowed to use its bargaining power to negotiate prices . . . it could almost certainly obtain discounts that are at least as large as the highest discounts obtained in other countries, since it would be by far the biggest drug buyer in the world. If Medicare could negotiate the same schedule of prices as Australia (the lowest-cost country), the savings over the first eight years of the drug benefit would be almost $560 billion.

The combined savings from having Medicare negotiate prices directly with the industry and from having Medicare directly offer the benefit instead of private insurers would be more than $600 billion . . . from 2006 to 2013. These savings are so large it would be possible to fully pay for all drugs for Medicare beneficiaries, with no premiums, deductibles or copayments. Alternatively, it would be possible to have a modest schedule of copayments, comparable to those in most private health-insurance plans, and save federal and state governments more than $100 billion compared to the spending projected in the MMA.

NO Center for Health Policy Studies

From the Heritage Foundation Web site, www.heritage.org, Nov. 5, 2005

While price controls guaranteeing cheap prescription drugs for everyone may sound appealing, the consequences of imposing price controls would harm seniors and all Americans.

Commerce Department researchers recently examined the prescription-drug markets in member countries of the Organization for Economic Cooperation and Development (OECD) and determined that these "governments have relied heavily on government fiat rather than competition to set prices, lowering drug spending through price controls applied to new and old drugs alike." The study found that price controls in OECD countries caused a $6 billion to $8 billion annual reduction in funding for drug research and development worldwide.

The impact of price controls would vary with the degree to which the controls were set below market prices. According to a recent study published by the National Bureau of Economic Research, a 40-45-percent cut in pharmaceutical prices "would have a significant impact on the incentives for private firms to invest in research and development." The study estimated that under such price controls, the number of compounds moving from the laboratory into human trials would decrease by 50-60 percent.

Because of the uncertainties involved, fewer compounds moving into clinical trials directly translates into fewer new products — the effects of which wouldn't be fully felt for several decades because of the long development cycle. Moreover, because of the spillover effects of [research and development], less activity today reduces the possibilities for new opportunities in the future.

Not only would price controls add to the delay in the development of drugs and eliminate new drugs, they would also delay the introduction of new drugs into the market. The Boston Consulting Group found that the more interference in the market in a given country, the longer it took approved drugs to reach the marketplace.

With the passage of the Medicare Modernization Act in 2003, the government dramatically increased its activity in the prescription-drug market. Not surprisingly, as cost estimates for benefits soar, some in Congress are looking toward price regulation as a way to hold expenses down. . . . [L]egislation has been proposed that would allow the federal government to "negotiate" the prices of drugs covered by the benefit. "Negotiate," however, is misleading. What the term really means is price controls.

No politician, over the course of 4,000 years of experience, has yet devised a humane system of price controls that spares consumers from the risks of shortages and declines in quality.

So far, no one knows how many people have set up HSAs. However, the insurance-industry group America's Health Insurance Plans estimates that as of January 2006, 3.2 million people were enrolled in the high-deductible CDHP insurance that HSA owners must purchase to qualify for tax breaks. That's up from 438,000 enrollees in September 2004. [64]

If new tax incentives are enacted that attract more people into CDHPs, there's a good chance patients could exercise their purchasing clout to get more value for their health dollars, says Baicker.

However, critics argue that even widespread adoption of HSAs won't do much to slow spending, since the highest-spending patients are very sick and incur their expenses far beyond the level of CDHP deductibles. But Baicker says that — counting both the deductible and patient copayments for things like doctors'-office visits and prescriptions — about 50 percent of all health spending is "in the cost-sensitive range," or enough to make a real difference if patients start demanding value for their dollars.

But Baicker agrees with administration critics who say CDHP enrollees can't really make cost-sensitive purchases today because, she says, "they don't have the information needed" to compare the cost and quality of health providers.

Price Transparency

Bush has recently been meeting privately with large employers and insurers, urging them to undertake voluntary initiatives to publish cost and quality information, says Roy Ramthum, a senior adviser at the Treasury Department. To "get people more used to caring about price," the White House also will ask Medicare, the Federal Employee Health Benefit Plan and the Department of Defense's TriCare insurance to begin telling enrollees the prices of treatments, even though most of their members don't face high out-of-pocket expenses, Ramthum says.

Aetna insurance already has launched a transparency program, making available online the prices it has negotiated with Cincinnati-area doctors for various medical procedures, says Ramthum. [65] Similar efforts are in the development pipeline at other large insurers and employers, and four bills were introduced last year in Congress to require disclosure. But no committee or floor debates have been scheduled so far on these measures.

It's no wonder hearings have not been scheduled, given the continuing opposition by health providers like hospitals and doctors to disclosing price and quality information. Meanwhile, Bush is pressing forward. But publicly accessible price and quality transparency "has been promised for 20 years," says Princeton's Reinhardt. Yet, so far, almost no comparative information is available to the public, he says. "I can just see the [American Hospital Association] going nuts over the very idea of forcing that much competition. Providers don't like this. They are powerful, and they will fight you every step of the way." [66]

For evidence of congressional reluctance to even produce cost-benefit information — let alone publish it — one need look no further than the Effective Health Care program authorized by Congress in 2003 as part of Medicare prescription-drug legislation. It authorized $50 million a year for research on what treatments give the best value for the dollar, but Congress — at the suggestion of the White House — only provided $15 million for each of the program's first two fiscal years, and there is no indication the funding will rise. [67] That is less than one-thousandth of 1 percent of total spending in the $2-trillion U.S. health-care system.

Even this modest program has aroused opposition among health providers. For example, drug and medical-device companies also have complained recently that they want more input into whatever research is funded. [68]

Even if more consumer information were available, accelerated expansion of CDHPs is unlikely for the present, because Congress probably will not act on Bush's proposal this year, say congressional health leaders. No suitable tax legislation is scheduled to come out of the Senate that could include Bush's proposals, said Senate Finance Committee Chairman Charles Grassley, R-Iowa, on March 7. "Without that, I don't see how you move things like this." Furthermore, said Grassley, "before we add more tax subsidies, we first should look to see if we can make the incentives we have today work better." [69]

Employers and states also have a role in helping trim costs, most analysts agree. However, large health-care purchasers are not exactly "sitting there with lots of big weapons they haven't deployed yet to attack this problem," said the Kaiser foundation's Altman. They are already managing chronic diseases like diabetes, switching patients to generic drugs and similar actions.

For example, in Pennsylvania a new state program has begun sending "unsales" representatives to doctors' offices to convince them to prescribe drugs based on clinical evidence rather than sales pitches from brand-name pharmaceutical companies and to use cheaper generic drugs where appropriate. The Pennsylvania Department of Aging hopes the project can help bring down spending while improving care. "We're trying to go directly to the physicians . . . and have a dialogue . . . about prescribing practices that we think should be corrected," said Thomas Snedden, who heads the drug-assistance program. [70]

On April 4, Massachusetts enacted an ambitious, bipartisan plan to require — and heavily subsidize — all state residents to buy health coverage. With insurance reforms to cut costs, the law aims to cover 95 percent of uninsured people in the state in three years. [71]

Over the years, however, funding shortfalls, health-provider opposition and disagreement about program goals have characterized many such programs. In Indianapolis, for instance, four different employer coalitions have tried since 1996 to spur local health providers to adopt quality and transparency programs, according to analysts at the Center for Studying Health System Change. But none "has had a sustained impact" — in part because the employers haven't been able to agree about what type of data should be released. [72]

OUTLOOK

Higher and Higher

Many economists and lawmakers confess they are fresh out of new ideas for slowing health spending. Nevertheless, in the next few decades, the United States must slam the brakes on rising health costs or begin slashing spending in other areas in order to afford health care.

Until now, rising health costs have seemed relatively affordable — at least for middle- and upper-income people — because prices have been rising from a relatively low base in the 1960s, says Michael Chernew, a professor of health management and policy at the University of Michigan. Today, however, with health spending already consuming more than 16 percent of GDP, rapid growth in health costs quickly translates into something the country almost certainly cannot afford, he says.

Even if the growth of health spending could be slowed through the year 2075 to a rate just one percentage point faster than GDP — about half as fast as it's grown historically — the United States still would spend a little more

than half of its cumulative annual income increases on health. That's steep, but not completely unaffordable, since nearly half of each year's income growth would still be left over to spend on other priorities. [73]

But if health spending continues to grow two percentage points faster than GDP each year — the historical average — big trouble looms quickly, Chernew explains. Under the 2 percentage-point scenario, 44.9 percent of the increase in per-capita income between 1999 and 2010 goes to health care. Then, from 2010-2050, health care eats up 87.8 percent of income growth. "You get to use only a little over 10 percent of your new raise for anything" else, Chernew says. Then from 2050-2075, things would get even worse: 165.6 percent of the increase in GDP would go to health care. "In other words, spending on everything but health care would actually drop" year to year, even though incomes kept going up, he explains.

If that happened, the United States would have to resort to some kind of health-care rationing, even though the U.S. health-care system currently has no idea how to use clinical evidence to parcel out health care rationally, says Aaron of the Brookings Institution. "We need to acquire a great deal of knowledge," he continues. The nation will face choices that "will strain the democratic fabric" of society, because of the "emotional content and economic stakes involved."

On the bright side, says Chernew, the question is how to cut future growth in health spending, not how to give up current spending levels. "The prospect isn't as scary as some may think," he says. "Things will still get better, just less better than they otherwise might."

Despite arguments that physicians and insurance companies make too much money, "this isn't a villain situation," says Jack Meyer, president of the nonpartisan Economic and Social Research Institute. "Is it a problem that a neurosurgeon earns $500,000 a year?" he asks, pointing out that Yankee third-baseman Alex Rodriguez earns $25 million a year — "50 times what the neurosurgeon is making."

Rather than searching for a villain, Meyer says, we must acknowledge, "we have met the enemy and he is us." Americans expect unlimited health care with little financial pain, he says. Generous insurance benefits enjoyed by well-insured people drive up premium costs for everyone, and many workers expect to retire early, even though Medicare would be easier to sustain if the eligibility age were nudged up by a few years.

For the hard answers, "we have to look in the mirror," says Meyer. "Americans don't like being told to wait, let alone being told, 'No.' "

NOTES

1. Quoted in Ana Menendez, "While Shalala Lives in Luxury, Janitors Struggle," *The Miami Herald*, March 1, 2006.

2. "Coping Without Health Insurance," transcript, "Newshour With Jim Lehrer," www.pbs.org, Nov. 28, 2005.

3. Stephen Heffler, *et al.*, "U.S. Health Spending Projections for 2004-2014," *Health Affairs* Web site, Feb. 23, 2005. Gross national product is roughly equivalent to the nation's total spending.

4. Gerard F. Anderson, *et al.*, "Health Spending in the United States and the Rest of the Industrialized World," *Health Affairs*, July/August 2005.

5. Christine Borger, *et al.*, "Health Spending Projections Through 2015: Changes on the Horizon," *Health Affairs* Web site, Feb. 22, 2006.

6. Employer Benefits Survey, 2005, The Kaiser Family Foundation and Health Research and Educational Trust, September 2005, p. 7.

7. "2005 Annual Employer Health Benefits Survey, transcript," www.kaisernetwork.org, Sept. 14, 2005.

8. Employer Benefits Survey, 2005, *op. cit.*

9. Paul Burrow, testimony before Senate Appropriations Subcommittee on Labor, Health and Education, May 14, 2003.

10. Richard Kronick and Todd Gilmer, "Explaining the Decline in Health Insurance Coverage, 1979-1995," *Health Affairs*, March/April 1999.

11. Todd Gilmer and Richard Kronick, "It's the Premiums, Stupid: Projections of the Uninsured Through 2013," *Health Affairs* Web site, April 5, 2005.

12. Jack Hadley and Peter J. Cunningham, "Perception, Reality, and Health Insurance," *Issue Brief No. 100*, Center for Studying Health System Change, October 2005.

13. Katherine Baicker and Amitabh Chandra, "Medicare Spending, the Physician Workforce, and Beneficiaries' Quality of Care," *Health Affairs* Web site, April 7, 2004.

14. For background, see Jim Landers, "Swiss Health-Care System Might Serve as Model for U.S.," *Dallas Morning News*, Feb. 20, 2006.

15. *Ibid.*

16. Anderson, *et al.*, *op. cit.* Data are for 2002, the latest year for which international comparisons are available.

17. Quoted in "President Participates in Panel Discussion on Health-Care Initiatives," transcript, www.whitehouse.gov, Feb. 16, 2006.

18. Henry G. Aaron, "The Unsurprising Surprise of Renewed Health-Care Cost Inflation," *Health Affairs* Web site, Jan. 23, 2002. For background, see "Setting Limits on Medical Care," *Editorial Research Reports*, Nov. 23, 1990, available at *CQ Researcher Plus Archive*, CQ Electronic Library, http://library.cqpress.com.

19. David M. Cutler and Mark McClellan, "Is Technological Change in Medicine Worth It?" *Health Affairs*, September/October 2001.

20. George C. Halvorson and George J. Isham, *Epidemic of Care* (2003), p. 48.

21. John Kitzhaber, transcript, Citizens' Health-Care Working Group, Public Meeting, Portland, Ore., Sept. 23, 2005.

22. "Supply, Prices — Not Quality — Push Spending Upward," *Perspectives, Medicine & Health*, June 23, 2003.

23. Medicare Payment Advisory Commission, "Report to the Congress: Medicare Payment Policy," March 2006, p. 15. For background, see Bob Adams, "Primary Care," *CQ Researcher*, March 17, 1995, pp. 217-240.

24. Barbara Starfield, *et al.*, "The Effects of Specialist Supply on Populations; Health: Assessing the Evidence," *Health Affairs* Web site, March 15, 2005.

25. "Physician Compensation and Production Report, 2005," Medical Group Management Association.

26. Starfield, *op. cit.*

27. Karen Davis, "Taking a Walk on the Supply Side: 10 Steps to Control Health-Care Costs," The Commonwealth Fund, April 2005, www.cmwf.org.

28. *Ibid.*

29. Keith Epstein, "Covering the Uninsured," *CQ Researcher*, June 14, 2002, pp. 521-544.

30. Jack Hadley and John Holahan, "The Cost of Care for the Uninsured: What Do We Spend, Who Pays, and What Would Full Coverage Add to Medical Spending?" *Issue Update*, Kaiser Commission on Medicaid and the Uninsured, May 2004.

31. *Ibid.*

32. "Frist: 100 Percent Coverage Impossible. 93 Percent Not Working So Well Either," *Medicine & Health*, Feb. 9, 2004.

33. Henry J. Aaron, William B. Schwartz and Melissa Cox, *Can We Say No: The Challenge of Rationing Health Care* (2005), p. 2.

34. Hadley and Holahan, *op. cit.*

35. *Ibid.*

36. Institute of Medicine Committee on the Consequences of Uninsurance, *Hidden Costs, Value Lost*, National Academies Press, 2003.

37. Kitzhaber, transcript, *op. cit.*

38. Julian Le Grand, "Methods of Cost Containment: Some Lessons from Europe," paper delivered at the International Health Economics Association, San Francisco, June 2003.

39. Gerard F. Anderson, *et al.*, "It's the Prices, Stupid: Why the United States is so Different From Other Countries," *Health Affairs*, May/June 2003.

40. Uwe E. Reinhardt, Peter S. Hussey and Gerard F. Anderson, "U.S. Health-Care Spending in an International Context," *Health Affairs*, May/June 2004.

41. Karen Davis, "American Health Care: Why So Costly?" testimony before Senate Appropriations Subcommittee on Labor, Health, and Education, June 11, 2003.

42. Reinhardt, Hussey and Anderson, *op. cit.*

43. "Physicians and Surgeons," *Occupational Outlook Handbook, 2006-07 Edition*, U.S. Department of Labor, Bureau of Labor Statistics.

44. *Ibid.*

45. For background, see Adriel Bettelheim, "Hospitals' Financial Woes," *CQ Researcher*, Aug. 13, 1999, pp. 689-704.

46. Insurance Update: May 4, 2005, Children's Hospitals and Research Center, Oakland, www.childrenshospitaloakland.org.

47. For background, see Aaron, Schwartz and Cox, *op. cit.*

48. Rosemary A. Stevens, interview, PBS, "Healthcare Crisis," www.pbs.org, 2000.

49. Gerard F. Anderson and Jean-Pierre Poullier, "Health Spending, Access, and Outcomes: Trends in Industrialized Countries," *Health Affairs*, May/June 1999.

50. Anderson and Poullier, *op. cit.*

51. *Ibid.*, Reinhardt, Hussey and Anderson, *op. cit.*

52. Kenneth E. Thorpe, "The Rise in Health-Care Spending and What to Do About It," *Health Affairs*, November/December 2005.

53. David Himmelstein and Steffie Woolhandler, *Bleeding the Patient: The Consequences of Corporate Healthcare* (2001).

54. Steffie Woolhandler, Terry Campbell and David Himmelstein, "Costs of Health-Care Administration in the United States and Canada," *New England Journal of Medicine*, Aug. 21, 2003, p. 768.

55. Reinhardt, Hussey and Anderson, *op. cit.*

56. Quoted in "Analysts Want to Buy Value, but Public May Not Be Ready," *Medicine & Health Perspectives*, Dec. 13, 2004.

57. *Ibid.*

58. Risa Lavizzo-Mourey, "The State of the Union's Health Care," www.rwjf.org, January 2006.

59. Quoted in "The 12th Princeton Conference — How Will the States Pay for Health Care?" transcript, May 20, 2005, www.kaisernetwork.org.

60. For background, see Sarah Glazer, "Managed Care," *CQ Researcher*, April 12, 1996, pp. 313-336; and Adriel Bettelheim, "Managing Managed Care," *CQ Researcher*, April 16, 1999, pp. 305-328.

61. Judith Mistichelli, "Diagnosis Related Groups (DRGs) and the Prospective Payment System: Forecasting Social Implications," *Cope Note 4*, National Reference Center for Bioethics Literature, http://bioethics.georgetown.edu.

62. For background, see Kenneth Jost, "Patients' Rights," *CQ Researcher*, Feb. 5, 1998, pp. 97-120.

63. George W. Bush, "President Discusses Health Care," address delivered Feb. 15, 2006, www.whitehouse.gov.

64. John Reichard, "Ignagni: 'Young Immortals' Aren't Dominating HSA Enrollment," *CQ Healthbeat*, March 9, 2005.

65. For background, see Vanessa Fuhrmans, "Insurer Reveals What Doctors Really Charge," *The Wall Street Journal*, Aug. 18, 2005.

66. Uwe E. Reinhardt, "A Primer for Journalists on Reforming American Healthcare: Proposals in the Presidential Campaign," unpublished paper, September 2004.

67. John Reichard, "First Finding of Landmark Program to Get Better Value for Medicare: Drugs as Good as Surgery for GERD," *CQ Healthbeat*, Dec. 14, 2005.

68. John Reichard, "Big Lobbies Angling to Reshape Landmark Research Program," *CQ Healthbeat*, Jan. 11, 2006.

69. John Reichard, "No HSA Markup This Year," *CQ Healthbeat*, March 8, 2006.

70. Scott Hensley, "Harvard Professor Helps Team in Pennsylvania Publicize Alternatives to Pricey Pills," *The Wall Street Journal*, March 13, 2006, p. A1.

71. William C. Symonds, "In Massachusetts, Health Care for All?" *Business Week Online*, April 4, 2006.

72. "What's Driving Spending? More Stuff, No Brakes," *Perspectives, Medicine & Health*, Sept. 22, 2003.

73. Michael E. Chernew, Richard A. Hirth and David M. Cutler, "Increased Spending on Health Care: How Much Can the United States Afford?" *Health Affairs*, July/August 2003.

BIBLIOGRAPHY

Books

Aaron, Henry J., William B. Schwartz and Melissa Cox, *Can We Say No: The Challenge of Rationing Health Care*, Brookings Institutions Press, 2005.
Brookings economists argue that rising health-care costs will force the U.S. to follow Great Britain in imposing top-down decisions about who can have what health care.

Cutler, David M., *Your Money or Your Life: Strong Medicine for America's Health Care System*, Oxford University Press, 2004.
A Harvard University economics professor finds that while expensive medical advances of the past half-century have improved health overall, substantial amounts of low-value care also have been provided.

Gingrich, Newt, *Saving Lives and Saving Money*, The Alexis de Tocqueville Institution, 2003.
A former Republican speaker of the House outlines a plan for cutting health costs and improving quality by promoting preventive care and investing in information systems to help consumers become better health-care buyers.

Halvorson, George C., and George J. Isham, *Epidemic of Care*, Jossey-Bass, 2003.
The CEO and the medical director of two leading managed-care organizations examine policy alternatives and new medical practices that might reduce rising health costs.

Articles

Appleby, Julie, and Sharon Silke-Carty, "Ailing GM Looks to Scale Back Generous Health Benefits," *USA Today*, June 23, 2005.
Rising health-care costs are a significant contributor to the financial woes of the large U.S. automaker.

Mullan, Fitzhugh, "Wrestling with Variations: An Interview with Jack Wennberg," *Health Affairs* Web exclusive, Oct. 7, 2004, www.healthaffairs.org.
A former chief of the federal Bureau of Health Professions discusses medical-cost and practice variations with the Dartmouth Medical School professor who pioneered the study of regional variations in health spending.

Reports and Studies

"2005 Employer Benefits Survey," Kaiser Family Foundation and Health Research and Education Trust, 2005.
This annual national survey of employers details current trends in health-care coverage and spending.

Doty, Michelle M., Jennifer N. Edwards and Alyssa L. Holmgren, "Seeing Red: Americans Driven Into Debt by Medical Bills," The Commonwealth Fund, August 2005.
Analysts estimate that about two-in-five American adults have trouble paying medical bills, based on a biennial insurance survey conducted by the nonprofit fund.

Hadley, Jack, and Peter J. Cunningham, "Perception, Reality, and Health Insurance," Center for Studying Health System Change, October 2005.
Economists describe how health status and patterns of seeking health care vary between the insured and the uninsured, based on a multiyear, national survey.

Hadley, Jack, and John Holahan, "The Cost of Care for the Uninsured: What Do We Spend, Who Pays, and What Would Full Coverage Add to Medical Spending?" The Kaiser Commission on Medicaid and the Uninsured, May 2004.
Economists from the liberal-leaning Urban Institute explain how the uninsured population affects American health-care financing overall.

"Health Status, Health Insurance, Health Services Utilization: 2001," Household Economic Studies, U.S. Census Bureau, February 2006.
The latest Census Bureau survey describes the health status and health-service-usage patterns of different economic and demographic groups.

"Hidden Costs, Value Lost: Uninsurance in America," Institute of Medicine Committee on the Consequences of Uninsurance, National Academy Press, 2003.
An expert panel analyzes recent research on the financial, health and productivity burdens of having substantial numbers of people uninsured.

Lesser, Cara S., Paul B. Ginsburg and Laurie E. Felland, "Initial Findings From HSC's 2005 Site Visits: Stage Set for Growing Health-Care Cost and Access Problems," Center for Studying Health System Change, August 2005.
Economists who have tracked the health-care systems in 12 U.S. cities for a decade report that many hospitals and physician-owned clinics are increasing their capacity, a trend expected to push costs higher.

Tu, Ha T., "Rising Health Costs, Medical Debt and Chronic Conditions," Center for Studying Health System Change, September 2004.
About 57 million working-age Americans have chronic illnesses, and more than one-in-five has trouble paying medical bills, according to a national survey.

For More Information

Alliance for Health Reform, 1444 Eye St., N.W., Suite 910, Washington, DC 20005-6573; (202) 789-2300; www.allhealth.org. A nonpartisan, nonprofit group that disseminates information about ways to improve access to affordable health care.

California Healthcare Foundation, 476 Ninth St., Oakland, CA 94607; (510) 238-1040; www.chcf.org. An independent philanthropy that commissions and disseminates research on the way health care is delivered and financed in California.

Center for Studying Health System Change, 600 Maryland Ave., S.W. #550, Washington, DC 20024; (202) 484-5261; www.hschange.com. A nonpartisan policy-research group that chronicles long-term trends in American health care through a multi-year, in-depth survey of 12 cities.

Citizens' Health Care Working Group, www.citizenshealthcare.gov. Established by Congress in 2003, the 14-member panel is holding nationwide public hearings on health-care reform and will recommend to Congress how to extend affordable care to all.

Commonwealth Fund, One East 75th St., New York, NY 10021; (212) 606-3800; www.cmwf.org. A private foundation that funds independent research on health-care cost, access and quality in the United States and abroad.

Consejo de Latinos Unidos, 820 South Indiana St., East Los Angeles, CA 90023; (800) 474-7576; www.consejohelp.org. A nonprofit advocacy group that informs and assists uninsured Latinos and others on how to fight high hospital charges.

Council for Affordable Health Insurance, 127 S. Peyton St., Suite 210, Alexandria, VA 22314; (703) 836-6200; www.cahi.org. This advocacy organization made up of insurers that sell individual, small-group and consumer-directed health plans disseminates market-oriented proposals for improving access to affordable care.

Heritage Foundation, 214 Massachusetts Ave., N.E., Washington DC 20002-4999; (202) 546-4400; www.heritage.org. A conservative think tank that analyzes health-care-policy proposals from a free-market perspective.

Kaiser Family Foundation, 1330 G St., N.W., Washington, DC 20005; (202) 347-5270; www.kff.org. A nonprofit private foundation that conducts and disseminates research on national health-care issues including access, quality and cost.

National Business Group on Health, 50 F St., N.W., Suite 600, Washington, DC 20001; (202) 628-9320; www.wbgh.org. A national organization of more than 200 large employers and companies that provides information on health-care cost and quality issues.

National Coalition on Health Care, 1200 G St., N.W., Suite 750, Washington, DC 20005; (202) 638-7151; www.nchc.org. A nonprofit, nonpartisan group that advocates for improved access to affordable coverage and improved health-care quality. Its 100 members include associations of insurers, labor organizations, businesses, consumer groups and health providers.

New America Foundation, 1630 Connecticut Ave., N.W., 7th Floor, Washington, DC 20009; (202) 986-2700; www.newamerica.net. A nonpartisan, nonprofit research and information group seeking public-policy options to ensure affordable, portable health coverage and high-quality care for all.

5

Stem Cell Research

Marcia Clemmitt

President Bush holds a "snowflake" baby during a July 19 ceremony for children born from unused frozen embryos that were given up for "adoption" by the couples who created them. Bush said he vetoed a bill calling for expanded funding for stem cell research because it would have supported "the taking of innocent human life in the hope of finding medical benefits for others." A majority of Americans say the potential benefits of such research outweigh the concerns.

Getty Images/Mark Wilson

From *CQ Researcher*, September 1, 2006.

For the first time in his five-and-a-half years in office, President George W. Bush used his veto power on July 19, rejecting a bill Congress sent him on the grounds that it trespassed "a moral boundary that our decent society needs to respect." [1]

The Stem Cell Research Enhancement Act would have expanded federal funding for research on so-called embryonic stem cells (ESCs), which are derived from human embryos left over from in vitro fertilization (IVF) treatments. [2]

In August 2001, eight months after he first took office, Bush had restricted federal funding to ESC lines that had already been harvested from the embryos, despite biologists' insistence that ESC research is vital to understanding how humans develop and to curing or treating devastating degenerative illnesses like juvenile diabetes and Parkinson's disease.

But the use of donated frozen embryos — called blastocysts — for research outrages many conservative Christians. They say the embryos, which must be destroyed to harvest ESCs, have the same moral status as adult humans and must not be used in research to which they, obviously, cannot consent.

Bush explained his veto at a White House event highlighting a group of so-called snowflake kids, children born from unused IVF embryos that were given up for "adoption" by the couples that created them. The bill would have supported "the taking of innocent human life in the hope of finding medical benefits for others," Bush said. [3]

Named by the California-based Nightlight Christian Adoptions agency to highlight the uniqueness of each frozen embryo, the snowflake children also visited members of Congress this summer.

"Yesterday, Hannah Strege, the first known snowflake embryo adop-

Support for Research Is Growing

Fifty-six percent of Americans believe the potential benefits of embryonic stem cell research outweigh concerns about the destruction of human embryos involved in the research, up from 43 percent in 2002. At the same time, the percentage who said they didn't know about the issue dropped by 7 percentage points, reflecting the growing interest and awareness in stem cell research.

Attitudes About Embryonic Stem Cell Research

It is more important to . . .			
	March 2002	August 2004	December 2004
Conduct research	43%	52%	56%
Protect embryos	38	34	32
Don't know	19	14	12

Source: The Pew Research Center For The People & The Press, May 23, 2005; survey results are based on telephone interviews with a nationwide sample of 2,000 adults age 18 and older.

tion, told a small group of us, 'Don't kill the embryos, we are kids and we want to grow up, too,' " Rep. Chris Smith, R-N.J., said as he urged his colleagues to uphold Bush's veto. "How come a 7-year-old gets it and we don't?" [4]

According to California's Rand Corporation, 400,000 frozen blastocysts have been stored since the late 1970s, and the couples who created them are no longer likely to use them. [5]

Thus, say ESC-research supporters, conducting life-saving medical research on ESCs harvested from the embryos is justified because the blastocysts are otherwise slated for eventual destruction.

Anti-abortion members of Congress disagree. "This last week, the 108th baby was born through . . . Operation Snowflake," said Sen. Tom Coburn, R-Okla., so suggesting that research or destruction are the only options is "a false choice." [6]

This summer, the House, which passed the vetoed legislation by a 238-194 margin in 2005, failed to muster the two-thirds majority vote needed to override the presidential veto.

The story did not end there, however. For one thing, some states are now putting up their own money to fund in-state ESC research. In November 2004, for example,

California voters agreed to a $3-billion state investment in ESC research over 10 years. And on July 20, 2006, the day after Bush vetoed the federal funding expansion, California Gov. Arnold Schwarzenegger (R) added $150 million from state general funds to the ESC pot. (*See chart, p. 102.*)

Other states — including New Jersey, Wisconsin, New York and Illinois — also are actively building ESC research capacity.

Stem cell research is also moving forward abroad. In July, the European Union voted to allow EU funds to be used for ESC research. And along with Japan, Israel, Australia, Canada and several European nations, the burgeoning high-tech economies of Singapore, Taiwan, China and South Korea are quickly jumping into the game.

"Asia has never dominated [any field in] cutting-edge biology," said Chunhua Zhao, director of Beijing's National Center for Stem Cell Research. "This could be our chance." [7]

State and national governments are drawn to ESCs both by medical promise and as a way to bolster their economies through biotech-industry development. ESCs — which can be used to form any of the more than 220 cell types in the human body — hold secrets to how life develops as well as the tantalizing promise of treatments that could change the face of medicine.

The ultimate in medical research would be "a disease in a dish," where degenerating cells themselves could be observed and treatments tested as a condition like Parkinson's develops, says Christopher Scott, executive director of the Program in Stem Cells and Society at Stanford University's Center for Biomedical Ethics.

"The ultimate treatment is to put somebody back to normal," says Alan Leshner, CEO of the American Association for the Advancement of Science (AAAS). In "any disease or injury where tissue is being depleted, or has been damaged or removed, you would like to put a bridge there and make it grow back." ESCs may work as such bridges, Leshner says.

Many scientists say current federal funding restrictions, along with the limited number of ESC lines available, are slowing development of important science and may also put the United States at risk of losing its premiere position in biomedical research.

As a result, only a few U.S. labs can conduct significant ESC studies, and such isolated efforts aren't enough to tackle the huge and highly significant field, cell biologists say.

"I'm a tenured professor at Harvard, where I have a president who backs my freedom of inquiry — and puts money behind it," said Douglas Melton, co-director of the Harvard Stem Cell Institute. "If I'd been at a [less well-funded] state college, it would have been a different story. . . . The bottom line here is that it's unlikely that one person or one lab will solve a problem as big as degenerative disease," he said. [8]

"It takes a community . . . to solve a big problem. If you were trying to solve cancer at [only] two places, no one would think that was enough," Melton said.

Some scientists also argue that scientists and private companies are more likely to bypass ethical, financial and scientific standards for gain without the National Institutes of Health (NIH) acting as a central arbiter of the research agenda.

For example, *Science* magazine reported last month on a private clinic, the Preventive Medicine Center, in Rotterdam, Netherlands, which advertises $23,000 treatments that the clinic claims can create "often spectacular" improvements for patients with incurable neurological diseases like Parkinson's and multiple sclerosis. [9]

Such reports suggest that without a strong federal infrastructure in the United States stem cell science could become a kind of medical Wild West, with doctors touting "cures" that aren't backed up by evidence, said stem cell pioneer Irving Weissman of Stanford University. Some clinics are "preying on desperate patients. . . . It's a horrible disservice" and may tarnish the field's reputation. [10]

Many Nations Permit ESC Research

More than 30 nations have explicit policies permitting at least some research into embryonic stem cells (ESCs).

Research Policies on Embryonic Stem Cells (ESC)
(As of mid-2006)

Permissive or Flexible Policy

Australia, Belgium, Brazil, Canada, China, Czech Republic, Denmark, Estonia, Finland, France, Greece, Hong Kong, Hungary, Iceland, India, Iran, Israel, Japan, Latvia, Netherlands, New Zealand, Russia, Singapore, Slovenia, South Africa, South Korea, Spain, Sweden, Switzerland, Taiwan, Thailand, United Kingdom

Tightly Restricted

Germany, Italy, United States

Banned

Austria, Ireland, Lithuania, Norway, Poland

Sources: Minnesota Biomedical and Bioscience Network, Aug. 28, 2006; The Century Foundation, 2006

But opponents argue that NIH has no business funding ESC research. As soon as an egg is fertilized, the resulting embryo deserves the full respect that's accorded to a child or adult, putting ESC research off-limits for an ethical society, they contend.

"Personally, I would not consent to having my body's resources exploited and my life ended in order to provide benefits to other people's bodies and lives," said David Gushee, professor of moral philosophy at the "Christ-centered" Union University in Jackson, Tenn. "At least, I would want to have the opportunity to make such a decision for myself [but] embryos . . . are not able to speak up for themselves." [11]

The argument that most frozen IVF embryos are slated to die anyway doesn't hold water, according to Gushee. "People on death row are going to die anyway. So why not experiment on them, even if those experiments involve killing them? After all, we might as well get some good use out of them. The same thing could be said for, say, millions of people with terminal illnesses, or in nursing homes in their very last days." [12]

Most opponents of ESC research take pains to say that they're not opposed to stem cell research generally. In fact, most tout what they say are treatment advances attained not with ESCs but through research on so-called adult stem cells (ASCs), which are found in infants' umbilical cord blood as well as throughout the bodies of all humans beyond the blastocyst stage.

The FDA has approved nine treatments developed using adult stem cells. But ASC supporters claim more than 60 treatments have proven effective although only small, unverified trials have been conducted using the treatments. "Adult stem cells have been shown to be safe. Adult stem cells have been shown to treat a whole host of conditions," said Rep. Dave Weldon, R-Fla. [13]

Meanwhile, public and congressional opinion continues to shift, apparently toward a more favorable view of ESC research, some analysts say.

"Even though President Bush was adamant about vetoing the bill, the fact that so many members of his party were willing to vote for it speaks volumes," says Joanne Carney, director of the AAAS' Center for Science, Technology and Congress. "I don't think you can take lightly" the fact that congressional support has grown, even among Republicans.

Sean Tipton, president of the Coalition for the Advancement of Medical Research and public-affairs administrator at the American Society for Reproductive Medicine, agrees that public sentiment is shifting in favor of ESC research.

Radio talk-show appearances to discuss ESC research in July 2006 and in August 2001 "were very, very different experiences," Tipton says. "People are understanding it more and are much more favorably disposed." In 2001, many listeners who called in vented anger about the research, but this year "we didn't get one hostile call" on Wisconsin Public Radio, Tipton says. "As bad as it got was, 'We wish we didn't have to destroy the embryos.' "

As scientists push for expanded funding for stem cell research and opponents cite their ethical concerns, here are some of the questions being discussed:

Is conducting medical research on unused embryos from fertility clinics immoral?

In the past year, Congress has debated whether the federal government should fund ESC research with excess IVF embryos.

Backers argue that the research is justified because of the potential for finding cures for diseases like diabetes and sickle-cell anemia. But several religious groups, including Catholics and some evangelical Christians,

consider the blastocysts to have the same status as fully developed human beings and oppose the research on those grounds. Other denominations support ESC research. (*See sidebar, p. 103.*)

Embryos should be protected because they are "that which we all once were," said Kevin T. Fitzgerald, a Jesuit priest who is a bioethicist and professor of oncology at Georgetown University Medical School. [14]

Over the years, conservative lawmakers increasingly have expanded legal protections to earlier stages of human development, including a fertilized egg, or zygote. To many conservative Christians, that protection is a point of religious faith. "The fact that Jesus became a human being at the moment of conception reinforces that all stages of human life have inherent value," said Nancy Jones, an associate professor of pathology at Wake Forest University School of Medicine. [15]

Indeed, according to Gilbert Meilander, a professor of Christian ethics at Indiana's Valparaiso University and a member of President Bush's Council on Bioethics, advances in medicine are putting mankind in danger of forgetting potentially higher values. "So great is our modern concern to overcome suffering, we may almost forget that there are perspectives" — such as Stoic philosophy and some Christian theologies — "that put other principles first, Meilander said. [16]

Using embryos that can't consent to research is equivalent to forcibly drafting any other human being to be an experimental research subject, he said. A military draft is sometimes needed "to save our society," he said. But "the fact that we do not ordinarily conscript" experimental subjects indicates that, however much we value research, we do not think of it as an "obligation" equivalent to national defense. [17]

"The vulnerability that ought to concern us most is not our own vulnerability to illness and suffering but, rather, the vulnerability of those whose very helplessness might make them seem all too readily available to us . . . in our never-ending struggle to make progress," Meilander said. [18]

Some argue that it's inappropriate to use tax dollars to fund research that a significant number of taxpayers oppose. "I believe it is morally wrong to take the tax dollars of millions of pro-life Americans, who believe that life is sacred, and use it to fund the destruction of human embryos for research," said Rep. Mike Pence, R-Ind., who voted to sustain Bush's veto. [19]

In July, a *USA Today*/Gallup poll found that 36 percent of Americans approved of Bush's veto of the ESC funding bill, and 61 percent said that he vetoed the legislation because of his personal moral beliefs, not politics. [20]

Supporters of expanding ESC funding dispute the idea that a blastocyst — even one that is not implanted in a woman's uterus — has the same ethical status as a further-developed human.

"An embryo in a dish is more like a set of instructions or blueprint for a house," said Arthur Caplan, professor of medical ethics at the University of Pennsylvania. "It can't build the house. For the cells to develop into a human being requires an interactive process in the uterus between the embryo and the mother." [21]

"If you were to leave that fertilized blastocyst in the petri dish and provide it with nutrients and go away for a trip to the beach, you won't come back and find your son or daughter in the petri dish," said Gary Pettett, a neonatologist at the Center for Practical Bioethics in Kansas City, Mo. "It will reach a stage where it will simply die." [22]

In 1994, a National Institutes of Health panel deemed ESC research permissible "because, although embryos deserve respect, they are not morally equivalent to human beings," according to policy analysts Jonathan Moreno and Sam Berger of the progressive Center for American Progress. [23]

The panel's conclusion: Rather than being an all-or-nothing proposition, full human status accrues to an embryo over time, as it develops more qualities that distinguish humans. "Arguing that . . . a collection of cells in a petri dish are morally equivalent to a living person or even a developing fetus, fails to recognize the emergent character of human life and personhood," Moreno and Berger say. [24]

Evidence exists that most people view early-stage embryos in at least slightly different terms, says Philip Nickel, an assistant professor of philosophy at the University of California at Irvine. For example, while it's well known that "many embryos are shed naturally, in very early abortions and miscarriages," no one makes an effort to save or grieve for them, as frequently happens with later-stage fetuses. This shows that "people do view embryos as somewhat different from people, even though they may not realize it," he says.

"Different religions take different views on it," says the AAAS' Leshner. "But what has happened recently is that

Senate Majority Leader Bill Frist, R-Tenn., left, supports the Stem Cell Research Enhancement Act (HR 810) while Sen. Sam Brownback, R-Kan., opposes it. Three years ago, Brownback proposed criminalizing embryonic stem cell research.

people have realized that there are some 400,000" unused IVF embryos, many of which "will be discarded anyway.

"People have said, 'Wouldn't a better use be to take for research the ones that we aren't going to implant?' " he says. "I would rather save lives and not worry about angels on the head of a pin."

ESC research crosses a "particular ethical line" that "looms large only for a narrow segment of the population," *The New York Times* editorialized last year. "It is not deemed all that critical by most Americans or by most religious perspectives." Bush's determination to ban funding is "based on strong religious beliefs on the part of some conservative Christians." But, while "such convictions deserve respect . . . it is wrong to impose them on this pluralistic nation." [25]

"What we have before us is an opportunity to move forward on stem cell research with very strict ethical guidelines" by bringing it under the umbrella of federally funded research, said Sen. Richard Durbin, D-Ill. "We have a choice: Will we take these thousands of stem cells [and discard them] as waste and surplus . . . or use them in a laboratory to give a 12-year-old girl suffering from juvenile diabetes a chance for a normal, happy life?" [26]

Does research on adult stem cells hold as much promise as embryonic stem cell research?

Lawmakers who support Bush's veto argue that research on adult stem cells is not only the moral approach but

States, Foundations Provide Research Funding

A growing number of foundations and states are providing funding for research on human embryonic stem cells (ESCs) in response to President Bush's July 19 veto of stem cell funding legislation.

Non-Federal Funders of ESC Research

State commitments		Upcoming ballot issues	
California	$3 billion over 10 years	Florida	2008
Connecticut	$100 million over 10 years	Missouri	2006
Illinois	$15 million	New Jersey	2006
Maryland	$15 million this year, to start	New York	2006
New Jersey	$5 million		
Wisconsin	$5 million to attract companies		

Private Donations That Include Support for ESC Research

Donor	Amount	Recipient
Mayor Michael Bloomberg	$100 million	Johns Hopkins University
Starr Foundation	$50 million	Rockefeller U., Cornell U., Sloan Kettering Cancer Center
Broad Foundation	$25 million	U. of Southern California
Ray and Dagmar Dolby	$16 million	U. of California, San Francisco
Sue and William Goss	$10 million	U. of California, Irvine
Stowers Medical Institute	$10 million	Kevin Eggan, Chad Cowan, Harvard University
Leon D. Black	$10 million	Mount Sinai School of Medicine
Private individuals	Nearly $40 million	Harvard Stem Cell Institute

Source: The Century Foundation, 2006; Science, July 28, 2006

also the more scientifically fruitful. ESC-research backers, however, say that most scientists believe that research on all kinds of stem cells is required.

ASCs "hold more promise for helping patients with diseases and injuries" than ESCs, said David Prentice, a senior fellow at the conservative Family Research Council and a former professor of life sciences at Indiana State University. "Their normal function is repair, and we're seeing more and more examples of their utility." [27]

According to Sen. Sam Brownback, R-Kan., "There are 72 clinical human trials using adult cord [blood stem cell] research," while ESC research has not reached the clinical trial stage. "Here is a gentleman I hosted at a hearing about Parkinson's disease," Brownback said, holding up a photograph. He had "adult stem cells put back in his . . . brain. . . . He was Parkinson's-free for five years. We had trouble getting him in to testify. He was out doing African safaris and things." [28]

Indeed, said Brownback, the 70th peer-reviewed study showing the medical effectiveness of ASCs was published in June. "I want you to see where we're seeing successes without bioethical questions," he said, pointing to an 18-year-old spinal-injury patient who said that feeling was restored to her hip after an ASC transplant. [29]

"During the past 30 years, there have been more than 50 clinical applications in humans of adult stem cells, primarily from blood and bone marrow," said Andrew Lustig, a professor of religion at Davidson College in North Carolina. "In addition, recent animal studies and several human clinical trials have achieved promising results in repairing damaged organs and in 'tweaking' specific types of adult stem cells into other sorts of tissue." [30]

But many scientists say that ESC opponents overstate the achievements of ASCs.

Some ASC-based treatments have been developed, but the cells remain very difficult to work with, says Scott of Stanford's Program in Stem Cells and Society. ASCs "have a bunch of problems," including being hard to keep alive in the lab, he says.

After ASCs are removed from a patient's body, they often must be propagated in tissue culture for long periods of time before transplantation back into the patient. That's "impractical from a clinical standpoint and can lead to potentially damaging changes" in the cells, said Mehmet C. Oz, a professor of surgery at Columbia University. Harvesting ASCs may "often require damage to the host organ, which is awkward if they are to be used clinically for regeneration of the same organ!" [31]

Religious Views Vary on Stem Cell Research

Polls indicate that a majority of Americans favor embryonic stem cell (ESC) research. However, 29 percent of Americans said they either "somewhat" or "strongly" oppose it, and 57 percent of the opponents based their opposition on religious principles, according to a 2005 poll by the pro-ESC research group Research America. [1] The following sampling reflects the wide range of religious views on the morality of ESC research:

Religious Groups That Generally Approve of ESC Research

- **United Methodist Church** — At its 2004 general conference, the church, of which President George W. Bush is a member, approved ESC research using excess embryos from in vitro fertilization (IVF). "Given the reality that most, if not all, these excess embryos will be discarded, we believe that it is morally tolerable to use existing embryos for stem cell research purposes. This position is a matter of weighing the danger of further eroding the respect due to potential life against the possible, therapeutic benefits that are hoped for from such research." [2]

- **Committee on Jewish Law and Standards of the United Synagogue of Conservative Judaism** — The committee in 2003 "overwhelmingly" approved ESC research. Research on cells from excess frozen IVF embryos slated for discard is permissible "for research into creating cures for a number of human ailments," and the synagogue should "publicly advocate" for use of the cells "in all appropriate ways," the group said. [3]

- **General Convention of the Episcopal Church** — A task force to the 2003 convention concluded that making research use of embryos that would otherwise be discarded is "in keeping with our call to heal the afflicted." [4]

- **Islam** — Among Muslims as among Christians, beliefs vary. Some Islamic groups and scholars support ESC research. For example, IVF is permissible in Islam as long as the embryo is implanted into the mother whose egg was used to create it, not a surrogate mother, wrote Muzammil Siddiqi, past president of the Islamic

Society of North America. And, while an embryo outside the womb "has the potential to grow into a human being, it is not yet a human being," according to Muslim law, Siddiqi wrote. That being the case, "there is nothing wrong in doing this research, especially if the research has a potential to cure diseases," if the embryo used would otherwise simply be wasted. [5]

Religious Groups Opposed to ESC Research

- **Christian Coalition of America** — The conservative grass-roots political group calls ESC studies "unethical research resulting in the killing of human embryos." [6]

- **U.S. Conference of Catholic Bishops** — It called the Clinton administration's 2000 decision to fund ESC research at the National Institutes of Health both immoral and illegal. It also criticized President George W. Bush's 2001 partial funding of ESC research on cell lines already in existence, calling it an "accommodation" of the "morally unacceptable" act of killing IVF embryos to obtain the cells. [7]

- **Southern Baptist Convention** — At its 2005 annual meeting, the convention declared that ESC research "currently requires the destruction of human embryos," and "it is never morally acceptable to prey on some humans to benefit others." [8]

---

[1] "Taking Our Pulse: The PARADE/Research! America Health Poll," Charlton Research Company, 2005.

[2] "Religions Have Sound Moral Reasons to Favor Expanded Funding for Embryonic Stem Cell Research," Religious Coalition for Reproductive Choice, www.rcrc.org/news/views/stemcells.cfm.

[3] "Stem Cell Research and Education," United Synagogue of Conservative Judaism, 2003, www.uscj.org.

[4] "Stem Cell Research: Religious Groups Weigh In," beliefnet, www.belief.net.

[5] Muzammil Siddiqi, "An Islamic Perspective on Stem Cell Research," Islam101, www.islam101.com.

[6] "Christian Coalition Urges Senate to Delay Embryonic Stem Cell Vote," press release, Christian Coalition of America, Aug. 22, 2005, www.cc.org.

[7] "Stem Cell Research: Religious Groups Weigh In," op. cit.

[8] Resolution No. 2: On Stem Cell Research, Southern Baptist Convention, Annual Meeting 2005, www.sbannualmeeting.net.

While most ASC advocates claim 65 or more proven ASC-derived treatments, the U.S. Food and Drug Administration has approved ASC treatments for only nine conditions, including anemia, according to Shane Smith of the Children's Neurobiological Solutions Foundation in Santa Barbara, Calif., William Neaves of the Stowers Institute for Medical Research in Kansas City, Mo., and Steven Teitelbaum, a professor of pathology and immunology at Washington University in St. Louis. [32]

Most ASC-related treatments "remain unproven and await validation," while some, "such as those for Parkinson's or spinal-cord injury, are simply untenable," wrote Smith, Neaves and Teitelbaum. They noted that a list of 60-plus therapies assembled by Prentice is not based on peer-reviewed scientific studies but on "various case reports, a meeting abstract, a newspaper article and anecdotal testimony before a congressional committee." [33]

"We really are limited in our ability to use adult cells," says William Brinkley, dean of the graduate school of biomedical sciences at Baylor College of Medicine in Houston. "People tend to overinterpret" very small-scale clinical results on ASCs, says Brinkley. "The tendency is to say, 'We think there's lots of potential.' But there's not much data." Data from most of the small trials cited by ASC supporters has never been verified by other labs.

Since ASC research began long before ESC studies and has had more funding, comparisons of the two aren't meaningful, according to Stanford's Scott. "ASC and ESC are on different time lines," Scott says. "ASC understanding has a 20-year history, beginning from bone marrow, and, as a result, science knows more about ASCs. ESCs only became part of the science in 1998."

"And in that time," he adds, "we've been doing it with one hand tied behind our back" because of federal funding restrictions. "That makes it kind of hard to compare them competitively."

Research on both cell types is necessary because ASC and ESC research "inform each other extensively," says Melton, of the Harvard Stem Cell Institute. As a result, "the adult vs. embryonic distinction is not something that scientists think about very much."

"From a biologist's point of view, you can't separate them," Scott agrees. "What you discover today about adipose tissue" — fat, in which some versatile stem cells have been found — "may tell you something tomorrow about ESCs."

For example, scientists hope to learn enough about how ESCs turn into ASCs to be able to manipulate ASCs into regaining the potential they once had to produce any kind of tissue. In fact, a paper in the Aug. 25 issue of *Cell*, the bible of cell biology, claims that scientists at Japan's Kyoto University have accomplished just such a feat with mouse ASCs. [34]

The prospect excites scientists "since it reveals a roadmap by which ESCs might be obtained . . . without having to obtain them from embryos," said John Lough, a stem cell researcher at the Medical College of Wisconsin. "Ethical dilemmas would largely be defused," and cell-based treatments could be freely pursued. [35]

But finding the right genetic pathways to trigger an ASC-to-ESC conversion requires research on ESCs, not just ASCs, says Scott. "So if you can't work with embryonic cells, then you'll never get to the point where you don't need them."

The bottom line for many scientists is that only ESCs — called pluripotent because they are capable of developing into every type of body cell — offer a research window into the "earliest story of human development." In other words, only pluripotent cells can explain how an undifferentiated clump of cells develops into a complex organism, says Terry Devitt, a University of Wisconsin science writer who specializes in stem cells.

"When the history is written in 100 years, probably the most important upshot" of ESC research "will be what we learn about the very earliest stages of human development," Devitt says. "If you understand that, it may be possible to understand what happens when things go wrong and perhaps develop prevention strategies. That would be a much better way" to treat disease than techniques like cellular transplants.

Are Bush administration policies on ESC research crippling U.S. biomedical research?

Opponents of the Bush administration's limited ESC funding argue that the resulting lack of a federal infrastructure to support the research may cause long-term damage to American biomedicine. But ESC opponents argue that limiting the research ensures that science is used for ethical purposes only.

Far from crippling American biomedical research, Bush's veto strengthens the enterprise by maintaining its ethical core, said the Family Research Council's Prentice. "It's important to continue to hold the ethical line that no human life, at any age, should be used as raw material or be under the threat of government-sanctioned destruction," Prentice said. "My colleagues and I are pro-science, and that's why we want to see the ethical science flourish." [36]

Despite federal restrictions, ESC research thrives in the United States, said Rep. Roger Wicker, R-Miss. "Embryonic stem cell research is legal in America, and nothing in the administration's current policy affects that legality; 400 [ESC] lines are currently" used for studies "in the private sector and by the federal government." [37]

"It is false to suggest that medical breakthroughs come only through government research," said Wicker. "Private researchers discovered penicillin and the polio vaccine" and "conducted the first kidney and lung transplants . . . without federal dollars." [38]

The United States currently leads the world in ESC research, said Rep. Cliff Stearns, R-Fla. "A recent [issue of] *Nature* states that U.S. scientists contributed 46 percent of all stem cell publications since 1998. Germany comes in second, representing 10 percent of studies, and the remaining 44 percent derive from between 16 other countries." [39]

Even those who hope to expand federal funding note that current state efforts — undertaken to compensate for federal restrictions — are providing more ESC funds than NIH probably could, even without the Bush restrictions.

"The day after the veto, California put in $150 million," says Tipton of the American Society for Reproductive Medicine. "So in some ways it turned out to be a good thing."

And while the formerly large U.S. lead in ESC research publications is slipping, the situation is "not, Oh my God! The sky is falling!" says Harvard's Melton. "It's not the case that scientists are all calling their travel agents" to relocate in countries more hospitable to ESC research, he said.

Nevertheless, while the number of stem cell papers "is ever rising, the U.S. proportion is steadily declining," Melton says. "That's definitely a trend."

ESC papers with U.S. authors held "relatively constant at approximately 40 percent from 1999 to 2002," but "dropped to 30 percent in 2003 and remained at this lower level in 2004," according to a September 2005 study by Princeton University doctoral candidate Aaron Levine. [40]

And while the unprecedented rise in state biomedical funding — virtually all to support ESC research — is "better than nothing," there are "very good reasons" why research should remain a federal responsibility, says Tipton.

NIH "understands grant review," and there's widespread confidence that its funding generally goes to scientists best suited for the job, Tipton says. "With the states doing it, this little sliver of money will go to the best scientist in Illinois, for example. But what if the best scientist for that study is actually in Texas?"

Federal funding rules prohibit the use of federally subsidized equipment or employees in research on non-federally-approved cell lines. And Harvard, for example, "already has spent hundreds of thousands of dollars on lawyers and accountants" to make sure its records clearly demonstrate the university is abiding by that rule, says Melton.

One university lab even "has police tape down the middle to remind students and staff not to mingle equipment," says Stanford's Scott. Stanford itself is building an off-campus lab for non-federal funding. "That's really inefficient," he says.

State-by-state funding is raising new, time-consuming questions, since the new laws aren't necessarily clear, Melton says. For example, "we have already had confusing conversations with California" about whether California-funded personnel and lab materials can participate in research outside the state, at Harvard.

Clarity about how the overall stem cell research portfolio is progressing also will wane, says Tipton. "With NIH, everything goes in a peer-reviewed journal, and there's access to the list of who's doing what." But private foundations and companies funding research "have different incentives" for announcing findings or a new study, he says. For example, a foundation may tout a study in order to increase donations or a company may tout one "because it will help their stock price."

"What worries me most is the generational brain drain," says Tipton. "The lifeblood of an academic career is NIH funding. It leads to scientific status." If students find they can't get that funding to study ESCs, "they'll choose another field, where you don't have to fight all this."

If younger American scientists desert the ESC field, the United States could lose its technological edge in biomedicine to other countries, says Daniel Perry, executive director of the Alliance for Aging Research.

C H R O N O L O G Y

1980s-1990s *Scientists deepen their understanding of embryonic and adult stem cells as political and public anxiety grows over medical research involving embryos and fetuses. In vitro fertilization (IVF) is launched in the United States as an unregulated business.*

1981 Researchers isolate mouse embryonic stem cells (ESCs). . . . The first IVF clinics open in the United States.

1995 Primate ESCs from rhesus macaque monkeys are isolated. . . . Congress passes the Dickey amendment, banning federal funds for research involving creation or destruction of human embryos.

1996 U.S. IVF birth rate reaches 20,000.

1997 Dolly the sheep is cloned by scientists at the Roslin Institute in Edinburgh, Scotland.

1998 Scientists at the University of Wisconsin and Johns Hopkins University isolate human ESCs for the first time. . . . American scientist Richard Seed announces plans to open a human-cloning clinic, but his effort fails.

1999 President Bill Clinton's National Bioethics Advisory Commission recommends that federally funded scientists be allowed to extract cells for ESC research from embryos left over from IVF treatments but not create embryos expressly for research.

2000s *Stem cell research moves ahead around the world. Federal funding of ESC research is limited in the United States.*

2000 Actor Michael J. Fox, who has Parkinson's disease, pleads for more U.S. funding of ESC research in a column in *The New York Times.* . . . Clinton administration announces that the National Institutes of Health (NIH) will not fund scientists to derive ESC cultures from embryos but will fund research on ESCs harvested with non-federal funds. . . . An expert panel advises the British government to allow cloning for research into medical treatments but not reproduction.

2001 Pro-life groups sue the U.S. government to stop ESC research funding. . . . Pope John Paul II and the conservative Christian group Focus on the Family condemn ESC research, but the United Church of Christ supports federal ESC funding. . . . After putting NIH funding for ESC research on hold, newly elected President George W. Bush announces that the federal government will fund studies only on ESC lines that already exist. Eventually, most of the 60-to-70 lines the administration says exist are found to be unavailable or unsuitable for research. . . . About 40,000 IVF babies are born in the United States.

2002 Former first lady Nancy Reagan supports ESC research, which she says might provide a cure for Alzheimer's disease. Her husband, former President Ronald Reagan, suffered from the disease.

2003 Analysts at the Rand Corporation report that as of 2002 about 400,000 unused embryos had been frozen and stored at U.S. IVF clinics since the late 1970s.

2004 New Jersey and California launch state ESC-research initiatives. . . . The world's first publicly funded stem cell "bank" for researchers opens in Britain. . . . South Korean scientists announce they cloned a human but admit a year later that the claim was based on faked data.

2005 House of Representatives passes legislation expanding federally funded ESC research to include cell lines newly derived from donated, leftover IVF embryos. . . . Connecticut, Illinois, New Jersey and Maryland join the list of states funding ESC research.

2006 Congress passes legislation to expand federal ESC-research funding, but President Bush vetoes the bill. . . . The Nightlight Christian Adoption agency says more than 100 babies have been born from leftover IVF embryos "adopted" by other couples. . . . California Gov. Arnold Schwarzenegger (R) pledges an additional $150 million for ESC research in the state. . . . The European Union votes to allow EU general research funds to pay for ESC studies. . . . Biologists claim to have developed a technique for establishing colonies of human embryonic stem cells from an early human embryo without destroying it. But critics immediately question the new method, reported by California-based Advanced Cell Technology on Aug. 23.

Will that matter? "Does it matter that we lost the semiconductor and computer industries to Japan, and now we buy their [electronics]?" he asks. Today, countries including Australia, France, Israel, and Singapore "are seeing a chance to steal a march on the United States for bragging rights and attracting venture capital" to ESC research, Perry says.

BACKGROUND

Cell Search

As much as a hundred years ago, doctors knew there was something special about bone marrow — the blood-making tissue found in the center of large bones. Physicians attempted to cure patients with anemia and leukemia by feeding them bone marrow. [41] The marrow-by-mouth treatment didn't work, but the physicians were onto something big: stem cells. [42]

Stem cells are very basic cells in humans and animals that when needed can renew themselves indefinitely and repeatedly produce at least one kind of highly specialized cell, such as a muscle, skin, blood, brain or intestinal cell.

Such regeneration occurs most vividly when a salamander grows a torn-off tail or a deer drops its antlers and grows a full new rack. But regeneration routinely occurs in humans, too, at least in some organs. For example, skin cells regenerate skin that has been wounded, and the human liver regenerates itself after part of it has been removed by surgery.

Of the two kinds of stem cells — embryonic and adult — ESCs are the more versatile, capable of becoming any of the more than 200 types of tissue that make up a human body.

A human's development begins with a single cell, or zygote, which forms after an egg is fertilized by a sperm. After about five days, the zygote develops into a ball of around 150 cells, called a blastocyst, a very early-stage embryo. So far as we know today, pluripotent cells are found only in the center of the blastocyst.

After ESCs differentiate into the many cell types that make up the fetus, most lose the power to become different kinds of cells. However, because cell systems like blood and skin need to be regenerated repeatedly, some cells with limited regenerating power — ASCs — remain. Found in all humans and animals that are past the blastocyst stage, ASCs come in many varieties and exist in organs throughout the body, such as the skin and liver. Current science indicates that each ASC can develop into only a limited number of cell types.

More than 50 years ago, in the earliest therapeutic use of stem cells, scientists injected bone marrow into the bloodstreams of mice to cure them of blood-depleting illnesses like radiation sickness. At the time, no one knew that ASCs in the injected marrow created new blood. Instead, it was widely believed that some chemical in the marrow must spur blood to renew itself. A series of experiments during the 1950s eventually revealed the existence of hematopoietic — blood-making — ASCs in marrow.

Since then, knowledge of stem cells has advanced slowly, despite intense scientific interest.

According to Sean Morrison, associate professor of cell biology at the University of Michigan, scientists seek to find, grow and study ESCs and ASCs in tissue cultures for three main purposes:

- To determine if transplanted stem cells might replace cells damaged or destroyed by physical injury, such as to the spinal cord, and diseases, such as diabetes and Parkinson's.
- To gain insight into the way bodies develop and the ways in which development can go wrong when diseases such as cancer strike.
- To explore whether stem cell cultures of cells that bear the genetic stamp of certain diseases might be grown in the lab, where scientists could use them to test potential new treatments. [43]

Basic research on stem cells provides "the first window into the very earliest story of human development," says Wisconsin's Devitt.

Although news headlines occasionally tout stem cell advances as if major, new cures were on the doorstep, stem cell science actually is in its early infancy. Until very recently, the study of ASCs, for example, "was in the bird-watching phase," says Stanford's Scott. "If you could spot stem cells, it was a big deal, like a birdwatcher yelling, 'Hey, I saw a yellow flycatcher!'"

Scientists probably don't have anything like a full catalog of the body's ASCs. "They're damnably hard to find in the body" because they're scattered about among other cells, and "there aren't very many" in any one place, says Scott.

The result: Scientists have known of ASCs' existence for decades, "but we still know very little about them," says Baylor's Brinkley.

The Research Breakthrough That Wasn't

South Korean biologist Woo Suk Hwang became a sensation in the biotech world when he reported dramatic breakthroughs in stem cell research. But the hero had crashed to Earth by New Year's 2006, when a South Korean scientific panel declared that Hwang had falsified his data.

In a 2004 paper in the respected journal *Science*, Hwang reported producing the first stem cell line from a cloned human embryo. Then, in 2005, he reported the creation of 11 patient-specific human stem cell lines. Such lines are among the Holy Grails of stem cell science because — if and when stem cell therapies are developed — patient-specific cells could be transplanted into a patient's body to regenerate tissue without rejection by the immune system. Hwang claimed that his 11 lines matched patients with spinal-cord injury, diabetes and an immune-system disorder. [1]

But the triumph for South Korea's fledgling biotech efforts soon began unraveling. On June 1, a young scientist anonymously reported to investigative journalists at Seoul's Munhwa Broadcasting Corp. (MBC) that there were problems with Hwang's research, ranging from coercion of junior female scientists to donate eggs to the project to actual faking of data. [2]

Eventually, MBC reported the fraud allegations about Hwang, who was enjoying almost rock-star status. The report triggered a public outcry against MBC as well as a full-scale investigation by Seoul National University. On Dec. 29, 2005, university investigators announced they had found no evidence in Hwang's lab that any of the 11 cloned cell lines even existed. [3]

The finding sent shock waves through the international scientific community as well as through South Korea. In its rush to report Hwang's exciting firsts, had *Science* — published by the American Association for the Advancement of Science — and the peer reviewers who OK'd the paper overlooked evidence of fraud? Editor-in-chief Donald Kennedy insisted that the answer is no. "Peer review cannot detect [fraud] if it is artfully done." [4]

Nevertheless, a desire to rush hot, new discoveries into print before other scientists have a chance to reproduce them in their own labs contributed to the mess, said Katrina Kelner, *Science's* deputy managing editor for life sciences. "A culture that wanted to see things reproduced before making a big deal out of them would probably be a healthier culture." [5]

In its eagerness to become a stem cell powerhouse, the South Korean government and academic community skipped safeguards that might have kept a hot-dogging scientist like Hwang in check, said some analysts.

"For the Korean government, Hwang was sort of the shortcut [to the] biotech revolution," said University of Vienna stem cell expert Herbert Gottweis. "There was this desire to move ahead rapidly, and Hwang was supposed to be the person to pull this cart." [6]

High expectations created reluctance to rein in a scientist who promised results, said Jang Sung Ik, editor of *Environment and Life*, a Korean journal. "The government is

As for ESCs, stem cells from a mouse blastocyst were first isolated and grown in the laboratory in 1981. Primate ESCs from rhesus monkeys were isolated in 1995. In 1998, scientists at the University of Wisconsin and Johns Hopkins University both isolated and grew human ESCs.

Today, science is learning ever more about ESCs and ASCs, with constant surprises along the way. For example, while ASCs in bone marrow were long believed capable of creating only new blood cells, "it now looks as if some cells in bone marrow may be able to make different" tissues, says Stephen Emerson, a professor of stem cell medicine and transplant immunology at the University of Pennsylvania. In fact, "most everywhere in the body" a few stem cells may lurk that are not as "tissue limited" as previously thought, he says.

ASCs also are playing a major role in unraveling the mysteries of cancer. For years, biologists puzzled over a "bizarre situation" — cancer frequently returned, even when doctors thought a therapy had destroyed all the cancerous cells, Emerson says.

Then biologists discovered that in any cancerous outbreak a handful of cancer cells pump out a particular protein that fights off chemotherapy treatments — and that the same protein pump exists in stem cells. "We now know that cancer is a disease of tissue-specific" — adult — "stem cells," says Emerson. "And it means we need to change our whole way of treatment."

most responsible," he said. "It gave people an impression that Hwang's technology was a goose that lays golden eggs." [7]

Stem cell scientists worry the Hwang debacle might further taint the image of their field among the public and lawmakers.

"It has to raise, in the public's mind, the question as to whether there's legitimacy to this kind of science," said Douglas Melton, director of the Stem Cell Institute at Harvard University. "Fortunately, stem cell research is not dependent on one discovery," and Hwang's claimed work was a technical accomplishment only, not a paradigm-changing scientific finding. [8]

"I'd like to tell you I suspected something; I didn't," said Melton, when asked whether he had been skeptical. "When his papers were published, I read them carefully. I was impressed by the speed and the efficiency with which he'd cloned a human embryo. We hadn't done those experiments ourselves. So I didn't know how difficult it would be. . . . I met Dr. Hwang . . . several times. He didn't seem nutty, squirrelly or deceptive or anything like that," Melton said. [9]

Hwang was fired from his job and in May 2006 was indicted for fraud, embezzlement and bioethics-law violations. [10] But his supporters in the public were reluctant to

Getty Images/Chung Sung-Jun

South Korean stem cell scientist Woo Suk Hwang.

give up. On week-ends throughout the spring, pro-Hwang rallies in downtown Seoul drew crowds numbering in the thousands. One man protested the university's fraud allegations against Hwang by burning himself to death. [11]

[1] Woo Suk Hwang, *et al.*, "Evidence of Pluripotent Human Embryonic Stem Cell Line Derived from a Cloned Blastocyst," *Science*, March 12, 2004, p. 1669, retracted Jan. 12, 2006; Woo Suk Hwang, *et al.*, "Patient-Specific Embryonic Stem Cells Derived from Human SCNT Blastocysts," *Science*, June 17, 2005, p. 1777, retracted Jan. 12, 2006.

[2] Sei Chong and Dennis Normile, "How Young Korean Researchers Helped Unearth a Scandal," *Science*, Jan. 6, 2006, p. 22.

[3] *Ibid.*

[4] Quoted in Jennifer Couzin, "And How the Problems Eluded Peer Reviewers and Editors," *Science*, Jan. 6, 2006, p. 23.

[5] Quoted in *ibid.*

[6] Quoted in Choe Sang-Hun, "Lesson in South Korea: Stem Cells Aren't Cars or Chips," *International Herald Tribune*, Jan. 11, 2006.

[7] Quoted in *ibid.*

[8] Quoted in Claudia Dreifus, "At Harvard's Stem Cell Center, the Barriers Run Deep and Wide," *The New York Times*, Jan. 24, 2006.

[9] *Ibid.*

[10] Lee Hyo-sik, "Hwang Woo-suk Indicted for Fraud," *The Korea Times*, May 12, 2006, http://times.hankooki.com.

[11] "Hwang Love Persists," *Science*, April 14, 2006.

Fetal Attraction

The potential of stem cells to unravel medical mysteries has long fascinated scientists, but it didn't catch the attention of policymakers and the public until 1998, when researchers first isolated human ESCs.

The excitement wasn't just about the biological advance, however. Lawmakers became involved because of where the ESCs came from. James Thomson, of the University of Wisconsin, isolated his ESCs from a blastocyst — an approximately six-day-old embryo — left over from an in vitro fertilization procedure.

Obtaining ESCs from donated, frozen, leftover embryos might not have raised much opposition if scientists had not also been exploring cloning technologies.

Cloning is the process of creating a genetically identical copy of an existing organism by removing the nucleus of an egg cell and replacing it with a cell, such as a skin cell, from the organism to be duplicated. [44]

If it turns out that ESCs can provide actual tissues that can be transplanted to repair diseased or injured organs, a cloned human embryo could supply ESCs that would be an exact genetic match for the patient. ESCs from the clone would make the treatment work because, unlike ESCs from another donor, they would not be rejected by the patient's immune system.

But implementing such cures would require cloning embryos for the sole purpose of destroying them. That led conservative Christians to oppose embryonic stem

Couples Reluctant to Abandon Their Frozen Embryos

A majority of Americans favor conducting embryonic stem cell (ESC) research on cells harvested from donated, unused frozen embryos at in vitro fertilization (IVF) clinics.

But the question becomes more pressing for the couples whose unused embryos are being stored in IVF clinic freezers. Meanwhile, some ethicists argue that the virtually unregulated IVF business in the United States raises at least as many moral dilemmas as ESC research.

In 2003, analysts at the Rand Corp., a California think tank, estimated that as of 2002 nearly 400,000 IVF embryos — or blastocysts, fertilized eggs that have developed for six or fewer days — had been stored in IVF clinic freezers around the country. [1]

The IVF process often produces more embryos than a couple can use, and in the United States deciding what to do with the extra embryos is up to the couples who produced them. And with greater use of IVF technologies, the number of frozen embryos seems destined to grow. In 2003, for example, 123,000 IVF procedures were performed in the United States to help some of the estimated one-in-seven couples who have difficulty conceiving. [2]

Options for couples with unused frozen embryos include donating them to help other infertile couples have children; making them available for biomedical research, mainly for harvesting ESCs; or designating that they be discarded. But, according to the Rand analysts, most couples simply do nothing.

Of the 400,000 embryos frozen over two-plus decades, 88.2 percent were being held for family building, while 2.8

percent — 11,000 — were designated for research, 2.3 percent had been donated for other patients' fertility treatments and 2.2 percent designated to be discarded. About 4.5 percent of the embryos were being retained in storage because clinics had lost track of the couples or because death, divorce or abandonment had made it unclear who controlled the embryos. [3]

The produce-and-hold strategy most couples adopt for their embryos typifies a general, largely unspoken unease about these tiny byproducts of the IVF process, some analysts say.

Some ESC-research opponents argue that U.S. IVF clinics should more tightly control the number of embryos produced. European IVF clinics create fewer excess embryos, a pattern U.S. IVF doctors should follow, Sen. Tom Coburn, R-Okla., suggested in July. "We create about four times as many" embryos for fertility procedures "as the rest of the world," which is "overdoing" it, he said. [4]

In general, however, both anti-abortion and pro-choice forces keep mum on the subject of IVF.

IVF remains unregulated and, largely, undiscussed even by those most closely involved in it because it "touches two fatal third rails" in American life and politics, says Arthur Caplan, a professor of medical ethics at the University of Pennsylvania.

Pro-abortion people leave IVF alone because they don't want to interfere with their top principle — reproductive choice — says Caplan. Meanwhile, pro-life people are eager to promote family life and so are also reluctant to say "stop making embryos" or to "acknowledge that embryos die all the time for the purpose of making babies," Caplan says.

cell studies as soon as the first human ESCs were isolated. Other critics also voiced concern that women might be coerced into donating the millions of human eggs that might be demanded for clone creation, if stem cell-based therapies proved to be effective.

Debate over ESC research takes place as a growing number of state and federal laws declare that "independent personhood" exists at earlier and earlier stages of development.

At least 36 state laws criminalize fetal homicide, and in at least 15 states fetal-homicide laws "apply to the ear-

liest stages of pregnancy" — immediately after fertilization — according to the National Conference of State Legislatures. [45]

In Alabama, for example, legislation that took effect on July 1, 2006, designates full victim rights to "an unborn child in utero at any stage of development, regardless of viability," according to the National Right to Life Committee. [46]

In response to worries that scientists might clone human embryos for research purposes, Congress in 1996 passed the so-called Dickey Amendment, banning the

As the years wear on and more frozen embryos accumulate in IVF clinics, however, unease about their fate grows among fertility patients and clinic operators.

"I created these things, I feel a sense of responsibility for them," an IVF patient told *Mother Jones* magazine. "Describing herself as staunchly pro-choice, this patient found that she could not rest until she located a person — actually, two people — willing to bring her excess embryos to term," the magazine reports. [5]

In fact, "ambivalence" and "personal connection" seem to be the best descriptions of fertility patients' feelings toward the embryos they created. For instance, in one study, seven-out-of-eight couples who at the beginning of the IVF process planned to donate their embryos for research ultimately decided they would rather use them themselves or designate them to be thawed and destroyed. In the same study, "nearly all" the couples who initially planned to donate their embryos for use by another infertile couple later decided not to do so.

On the other hand, more than half the couples who originally said they'd discard their unused embryos also changed their minds, deciding instead to donate or use them. In total, 71 percent of couples changed their original decisions about how to handle the excess blastocysts. [6]

Several studies abroad suggest that giving up one's own genetically related embryos for use by other infertile couples is one of the hardest decisions.

In Denmark, where embryos may be stored for a couple's own use for only two years, 60 percent of surveyed couples with frozen embryos said they would donate them for research, but only 29 percent were willing to donate them to other infertile couples. [7]

In an Australian study, 18.8 percent of couples chose to discard their embryos, compared to only 5.9 percent who donated them to other couples. [8]

Unlike in most other countries, IVF is unregulated in the United States, and embryos can be stored indefinitely, sharpening the dilemma about what to do with them for clinic operators as well as patients.

Clinics are afraid to dispose of embryos on their own, even when they've been unable to contact the parents for years. "Nobody does it," said Alan DeCherney, a reproductive endocrinologist at the National Institutes of Health. [9]

"I have thousands of embryos from patients who have been through this program for . . . 10-, 12-plus years, changing addresses, never called back, never paid storage fees — you can't track them down," said Vicken Sahakian of the Pacific Fertility Center in Los Angeles. His "biggest nightmare" — trying to retire but being unable to sell his practice because "People do not want to inherit embryos. . . . I have embryos that have been here since 1992." [10]

---

[1] "How Many Frozen Human Embryos Are Available for Research," Research Brief, *RAND Law and Health*, 2003. The Rand estimate is the most current and most widely accepted.

[2] Liza Mundy, "Souls on Ice," *Mother Jones*, July/August 2006, pp. 39-45.

[3] *Ibid.*

[4] *Congressional Record*, Senate, July 17, 2006, p. S7583.

[5] Mundy, *op. cit.*

[6] *Ibid.*

[7] S. Bangboll, A. Pinborg, C. Yding Anderson, and A. Nyboe Andersen, "Patients' Attitudes Towards Donation of Surplus Cryopreserved Embryos for Treatment or Research," *Human Reproduction*, Aug. 13, 2004, http://humrep.oxfordjournals.org.

[8] Neroli Darlington and Phillip Matson, "The Fate of Cryopreserved Human Embryos Approaching Their Legal Limit of Storage," *Human Reproduction*, September 1999, http://humrep.oxforjournals.org.

[9] Quoted in Mundy, *op. cit.*

[10] Quoted in *ibid.*

---

use of federal funds for research involving creation or destruction of human embryos. [47]

Following the 1998 breakthrough that allowed scientists to grow stem cell cultures — derived from early-stage embryos — in the lab, the Clinton administration, backed by the science community, wanted NIH to fund ESC research.

In 1999, the U.S. Department of Health and Human Services (HHS) declared that, while the Dickey Amendment prohibited spending federal dollars to harvest ESCs from embryos, federally funded research could be conducted on cell lines that had been derived with other funds.

Limited Cell Lines

When President Bush took office in January 2001, the NIH had just begun to establish a research portfolio for ESCs, based on the 1999 HHS ruling, but the new president's conservative Christian base vehemently opposed that effort. Under heavy pressure from both sides of the ESC divide — and with federal funding on hold until a decision was announced — Bush eventually unveiled a plan that didn't fully satisfy either group.

The Rev. Flip Benham, director of the anti-abortion group Operation Save America (formerly Operation Rescue) leads protesters on Capitol Hill against President George W. Bush's 2001 decision to allow some stem cell research, although he restricted federal funding to ESC lines that had already been harvested from the embryos.

On Aug. 9, 2001, Bush announced that NIH would begin funding ESC research, but only on stem cell lines that had been harvested and established before that date. After a quick international survey, the administration announced that about 66 lines worldwide met that criterion.

In the past five years, NIH has funded about $90 million in ESC research, a tiny segment of the agency's full research portfolio. [48] In fiscal 2003, for example, NIH spent less than one-tenth of 1 percent of its research budget on ESC studies — $25 million out of a total of around $28 billion. [49]

Part of the reason for the limited federal support is that, in the end, only about 20 ESC lines were available, not the 60-to-70 that the administration had estimated.

In addition, even some of those presidentially approved lines didn't pass muster with many researchers, says Harvard's Melton.

Nevertheless, "anyone who says that the presidential lines are useless is wrong," Melton says. "They are useful because they allow people to begin." Melton's lab is producing its own non-presidentially approved ESC lines, of which "a couple of thousand" batches have been sent out to scientists around the world, he says.

The administration's count was wrong because it "just asked people all over the world if they had" previously derived ESC lines, "and people said yes, even if they were just starting, or just intending" to grow the cultures, "even if they hadn't unthawed the embryos yet," Melton says. Many small players, such as biotech companies and labs in developing countries like India, promised lines "so they could say they were suppliers."

As a result, many of the presidentially approved lines have no descriptive information published in peer-reviewed journals, says Melton. "Do [the cells] have enough chromosomes? We don't know." Scientists are reluctant to pursue research on cell cultures "when they don't know what they are and whether they're good. And the way in which these were collected means we don't know that."

Action by States

With most scientists agreeing with Melton that "there will always be more stem cell lines needed," some states have jumped into the ESC fray, announcing they'll fund in-state research on their own.

In May 2004, then-Gov. James McGreevey, D-N.J., was the first to respond, committing $9.5 million to create a new stem cell institute.

Then, in November, California voters approved a ballot proposition dedicating $3 billion in funding over 10 years to build and support an infrastructure for ESC studies. Other states, including Connecticut, Illinois, Massachusetts, New York, Maryland, Washington and Wisconsin, also have launched or are considering initiatives. [50]

States with strong traditions in academic medicine or with burgeoning biotech sectors are most likely to jump in. "Some states hope to benefit economically by encouraging the development of the stem cell equivalent of Silicon Valley within their borders," says Princeton's Levine.

The state efforts, if they persist, likely will direct more funding toward ESCs than NIH could, even if federal funding were not restricted. However, analysts say that supporting research involves more than funneling in dollars.

With state funding, "a lot of science will get done, but it won't be coordinated as well," says Leshner of AAAS. For example, "you won't have standard ethical regulations." And while the state approach is "very clever," it's still untried and involves "reproducing an infrastructure that we would prefer not to reproduce."

State money will be helpful, but NIH is a better venue for the research, says Perry, of the Alliance for Aging Research. "We would want this to be done with

Does embryonic stem cell research amount to murder?

YES

Sen. Sam Brownback, R-Kan.

Excerpted from the *Congressional Record*, June 29, 2006

The differences over embryonic stem cells come down to the basic view of the youngest of human life. I view human life as sacred at all of its stages and all of its places. Period. It is unique. It is beautiful, it is a child of the living God. It deserves our respect and protection under law at the very earliest stages of life.

We can try to divide it under law. We can say it is property at this stage of life; it is not worth living at that stage. All of those, I think, are false distinctions. Life is sacred, period, because it is human. That is the point of view from which I think a lot of Americans come.

In our jurisprudence system, they are either a person or a piece of property.

What is the youngest of human life? Is it person or property?

We have had this debate before in this country. We have looked at it; we have drawn distinctions. At points in time, even in our Constitution, we have said a person was only three-fifths of a person, and yet we knew at that time: How can you be three-fifths of a person? That didn't stand the test of time and reason then, and it doesn't stand the test in this country now.

Some will say that the youngest of human life is property and at some point in development it becomes a person. Yet in our jurisprudence system, we don't recognize the transition that goes from property to personhood, and if, so, where would you draw that line? When would it happen?

The biology is quite clear on this point. If you start out a person, you end up a person. If you start out a human being, you don't become a plant. If you start out a human being, you don't become a desk. If you start out a human, you end up a human.

The biology on this is clear. If you are a human embryo and you are given nurture, you end up, by anybody's definition, a full-scale human being.

At one time, we have all started out as an embryo. Whether you are Sam Brownback or anybody else in this room, we all started out being a human embryo. If you destroy us at the earliest stage, you never end up with us at this stage.

NO

Sen. Byron Dorgan, D-N.D.

Excerpted from the *Congressional Record*, July 10, 2006

It has been just over one year now since the U.S. House of Representatives passed legislation called the Stem Cell Research Enhancement Act, with very broad bipartisan support.

Those of us in the Senate and those across this country who have lost loved ones to some dread disease — Alzheimer's, Parkinson's, heart disease, diabetes — understand that the urgency to do the research to find the cures for these diseases really must be pre-eminent. So many in this country are very concerned that we move forward on stem cell research and try to find ways to unlock the mysteries of juvenile diabetes, ALS [amyotrophic lateral sclerosis], Parkinson's, Alzheimer's and so many more.

There are now more than 1 million people living among us who were born as a result of in vitro fertilization. At IVF clinics, more eggs are fertilized than are actually implanted and used. There are roughly 400,000 embryos that are now cryogenically frozen at these clinics. Somewhere between 8,000 and 10,000 each year are simply discarded.

Those who say that the use of those embryos for research is the equivalent of murder, I believe also probably say the same of the discarding of embryos that are not going to be used — that it represents 8,000 or 10,000 murders a year.

I don't believe that. Those embryos can never and will never become a human being, unless implanted into a uterus.

The question is: Can we use these embryos to create stem cell lines to try to find cures to dread diseases?

I believe that we ought to proceed with thoughtful, ethical guidelines on stem cell research. I understand that is a controversial position for some. In fact, in the last campaign for office for me, my opponent ran a television advertisement. In it was a fellow who was sitting around a campfire with some children. One of the children said: Tell us a scary story.

And the campfire leader said: Well, there is a man named Dorgan who has a plan to put embryos inside the womb of a mother and grow them for body parts to be harvested later.

I am mindful that there should be solid ethical guidelines for the research. But I don't believe this is about harvesting body parts. This is about giving life. This is about giving hope. It is about giving life, providing opportunity for those who are suffering from dread diseases.

informed consent" — by embryo donors and clinical-trial patients — "and without financial incentives" that might taint reporting of results, he says. "NIH has the reputation for assuring that."

Anti-ESC groups have their own reasons for criticizing the state efforts.

California Gov. Arnold Schwarzenegger "is supposed to be a Republican, so I don't understand his thinking here," said Dana Cody, executive director of the Life Legal Defense Foundation. The millions in research funds that Schwarzenegger has promised are "coming out of the taxpayers' pocket for something that is questionable at best."

Besides state dollars, private donations also support ESC research at a handful of elite institutions, including Cornell University, the University of California and Mount Sinai School of Medicine in New York. Nearly $40 million in individual private grants back ESC research at Harvard's Stem Cell Institute. [51]

In one of the newest developments, some scientists and ethicists think they see a way out of the dilemma that pits potentially life-saving research against destruction of blastocysts: developing methods of obtaining ESCs without destroying embryos.

Interest is high in potential alternative methods to derive ESCs, but no method has yet been proven in the lab. Last year, the President's Council on Bioethics published a white paper outlining four ways that ESC-like cells might be derived without destroying embryos. One possibility involves deriving cells from blastocysts that are found to be "organismically dead," because they've lost the capacity for the integrated, continued cell division and differentiation needed to produce a viable fetus. [52]

Another suggested method — altered nuclear transfer, or ANT — would be a twist on cloning. An unfertilized egg cell would be implanted with DNA that lacks a few of the elements needed to develop into a full organism.

But analysts who object to ESC research are generally skeptical that alternate methods would withstand their ethical objections either.

ANT, for example, would deliberately create an embryo that develops normally to a certain point but which scientists would deliberately prevent "from developing fully." Deliberately creating such a stunted embryo is itself an unallowable act, said Assistant Professor of Theology Jose Granados of Catholic University and Malcolm Byrnes, a biochemistry professor at Howard University College of Medicine. [53]

On Aug. 23, 2006, the Massachusetts biotech company Advanced Cell Technologies announced that it had created an ESC line from only one cell removed from an embryo, a process that the company argues would bypass ethical objections because it allows the original embryos to survive. The method hasn't yet been verified by another lab, however. And some ESC opponents argue that it may not pass their ethics test because it is possible that the single removed cell could itself develop into a complete human being, making non-consensual research on the cell immoral. [54]

CURRENT SITUATION

Shift in Congress

Many members of Congress, including Republicans, have warmed up to federally funded ESC research, perhaps in response to appeals from groups such as the Christopher Reeve Foundation, which advocates for research on spinal injury, and juvenile diabetes and Parkinson's disease groups.

"There's been a very slow, deliberate change in the House and the Senate," says Stanford's Scott. "Three years ago, Sen. Brownback proposed criminalizing the research, and that bill won big in the House and got 47 votes in the Senate," Scott says.

By May 2005, however, Congress had passed legislation to expand federal funding to include research on any ESCs that were derived from donated, leftover IVF embryos. The Stem Cell Research Enhancement Act of 2005 (HR 810), sponsored by Reps. Michael Castle, R-Del., and Diane DeGette, D-Colo., passed on nearly "the same vote as the Brownback bill, but in the opposite direction," Scott says.

The change "is a good example of how public discourse has moved the debate," says Caplan of the University of Pennsylvania. "Even to a conservative Congress, the groups that have really mattered are the patient groups. They backed off the pro-life forces."

After the House passed HR 810, Senate Majority Leader Bill Frist, R-Tenn., promised to bring the bill to a vote in the Senate. But after trying to craft a more limited measure, Frist, who had previously opposed federal funding, unexpectedly announced in July 2005 that he supported the bill.

"I personally believe human life begins at conception," said Frist, a heart-lung transplant surgeon who is considering a run for the presidency in 2008. "But it isn't just about faith; it's a matter of science." [55]

In late June 2006, Frist introduced HR 810 and two other stem cell bills for Senate consideration.

Congressional Republican leaders intended to pass and send to Bush all three bills: HR 810 and two others — one supporting research into methods of obtaining ESCs without destroying embryos and one outlawing "fetal farms," where human embryos would be created for the purpose of harvesting tissue for transplant.

The idea was to give the president a "safe haven" to signal his support for research by signing the stem cell alternative bill, says Carney, of the AAAS Center for Science, Technology and Congress. Then, Bush could maintain his pro-life credentials by vetoing the funding-expansion bill and signing the bill outlawing fetal farming.

The Senate quickly passed all three bills. But the leadership plan went awry when the House failed to pass the alternative-methods bill. So in the end, Bush was only able to sign the bill outlawing fetal farming and veto the funding-expansion measure.

With ESC research growing in popularity among voters, GOP House leaders facing a potentially tough election this November scheduled a vote on overriding Bush's veto, but it came 51 votes short of passage, and the funding restrictions stand.

Supporters of the legislation to expand funding of ESC research argue that President Bush is denying hope to people with degenerative diseases like Parkinson's and juvenile diabetes. Bush is "putting himself in the company of people . . . who told Galileo it was heresy to claim that the Earth revolved around the sun," said Sen. Tom Harkin, D-Iowa. [56]

Cell Cultures

While the United States and a few other countries deny federal funding to most ESC research, many other nations support it, although not without controversy.

In 1997, the Council of Europe adopted a Convention on Biomedicine and Human Rights, allowing ESC research but banning procedures such as the creation of embryos for research purposes. By 2006, 32 of the Council's 46 members had signed the treaty. [57]

Individual nations have taken a variety of stances toward ESCs. Austria, Ireland, Lithuania and Poland have banned the research outright. But many countries, including Australia, Brazil, Canada, Denmark, Finland, France and Spain allow research using unused IVF embryos.

After contentious debate, the European Union (EU) on July 24 agreed to allow money from EU's general research budget to fund ESC research on unused IVF embryos. Several predominantly Catholic countries, including Malta, Lithuania, Poland and Slovakia, had loudly opposed the plan. It won the day, however, when Italy, Slovenia and Germany agreed to support the proposal after first opposing it. [58]

Germany has particular qualms about ESC research, based on its history of Nazi genetic experiments conducted on non-consenting subjects. "The protection of human dignity, the right to life, needs to be properly entrenched," said Germany's research minister, Annette Schavan. "There should be no financial incentives for the destruction and killing of embryos." [59]

Countries that support ESC studies argued that scientific progress demands the research. "It is morally unacceptable to withhold these advances from patients, because it offers potentially tremendous advantages to European citizens," said British science minister David Sainsbury. [60]

Since most research in Europe is paid for by individual countries, however, and not by the EU, it's not clear that the EU funding will do much to drive the research forward.

Meanwhile, many Asian nations, including traditional scientific powerhouse Japan and newcomers like South Korea, Singapore, Taiwan and China, are pushing ESC studies. China, for example, has about 30 stem cell research teams, and the number continues to grow. [61]

Unlike in the United States and Europe, research regulations are looser in some Asian countries, such as China. And some U.S. scientists are noticing: A growing number of foreign-trained Chinese scientists are leaving U.S. and European jobs to work in China. [62]

"Most major teams" in Chinese ESC research now have U.S.- or European-trained scientists in senior roles, said Sheng Hui Zhen, an ESC researcher at Shanghai Second Medical University. Sheng, who spent 11 years at NIH before going to Shanghai in 1999, leads a 50-person team hoping to create human ESCs by inserting the nuclei from human skin cells into rabbit eggs. [63]

That research program would be banned in many countries, including the United States, because it raises the specter of creating chimera — human-animal hybrids. But Sheng said the project's aim is only to create human ESCs without the need to create and destroy human embryos.

"My Chinese lab does not have everything my NIH lab had," said Sheng. "But here I can work on this important problem, and there I couldn't." [64]

OUTLOOK

Long Road Ahead

Stem cells are a political issue and could figure in November's mid-term elections.

"I've heard from candidates for sheriff, quite literally, who say that they're interested and that, 'It'll do well for me politically if I can be associated with it,'" says Tipton of the Coalition for the Advancement of Medical Research.

Nevertheless, with other hot issues like the Iraq war predominating, stem cell research "won't play a major role across the board in the next election," says the University of Pennsylvania's Caplan. "But in parts of the country where biotech is part of the economy" — such as Missouri and Wisconsin — "or places where being pro- or anti-science counts, like Massachusetts, Connecticut and Florida, it will be an issue."

Despite occasional newspaper-headline hype suggesting that patient-specific stem cell treatments or "organ farming" are right around the corner, stem cell science is in its infancy, with such developments decades down the road, biologists say.

There will be "major advances over the next few years" stemming from our new understanding that ASCs are the root of cancers, says Emerson of the University of Pennsylvania.

When it comes to ASC-based therapies for other conditions, however, "it's very early. Bone-marrow stem cells are the only ones that have worked" so far, he says.

If ESC research restrictions are removed, biologists say that studies would profit from having as many lines as possible available. As long as creation of those lines depends on donation of unused IVF embryos, however, the number would be limited. For example, about 11,000 unused IVF blastocysts have been designated as available for research by the couples who created them, but only about 275 ESC lines, at most, could be created from those embryos, given the trickiness of the process.

Today, we still don't know many basic facts about ESCs, says Emerson. For example, "we don't yet know how to make single tissues" out of ESC cultures but can only coax a culture to develop into several different kinds of cells, perhaps with one type predominating.

Nevertheless, "I'm optimistic that, within a decade, if you call me up and say, 'I need toenail cells, heart cells, I can give them to you," says Harvard's Melton. "But not today."

The bottom line: "We're years away from going into human clinical trials of ESC-based therapies," says Melton.

The first practical application to emerge from ESC research will be far less glamorous-sounding, say cell researchers. ESC cultures will provide a new way to conduct so-called "high throughput" drug screening — quick, accurate testing of many new drug candidates on the exact cells that the drugs are intended to affect, something that's not possible today.

When scientists learn to securely direct development of a cell culture, they can develop a "disease in a dish" — a cell culture that, for example, includes only the brain cells that become defective when Parkinson's disease prevents a patient from producing required amounts of dopamine, says Melton.

Such disease-in-a-dish cultures will bypass much of the animal testing and clinical testing in humans that's done on drugs today, thus eliminating risk to those research subjects and targeting the trial more precisely on the exact cells that drug developers hope to treat.

"These would be drugs that would slow the generation of defective cells," not the tissue-based total cures that are sometimes hyped, but they are still very important drugs, says Melton.

NOTES

1. Susan Ferrechio and Elizabeth B. Crowley, "Bush Cites 'Decent Society' in Vetoing Bill Broadly Supported by Congress," *CQ Today*, July 19, 2006.

2. For background, see Adriel Bettelheim, "Embryo Research," *CQ Researcher*, Dec. 17, 1999, pp. 1065-1088.

3. Quoted in *ibid*.

4. *Congressional Record*, House, July 19, 2006, p. H5444.

5. "How Many Frozen Human Embryos Are Available for Research?" Research Brief, *RAND Law and Health*, 2003.

6. *Congressional Record*, Senate, July 17, 2006, p. S7583.

7. Quoted in Dennis Normile and Charles C. Mann, "Asia Jockeys for Stem Cell Lead," *Science*, Feb. 4, 2005, p. 660.

8. Quoted in Claudia Dreifus, "At Harvard's Stem Cell Center, the Barriers Run Deep and Wide," *The New York Times*, Jan. 24, 2006.

9. Martin Enserink, "Selling the Stem Cell Dream," *Science*, July 14, 2006, p. 160.

10. Quoted in *ibid.*

11. David P. Gushee, "The Stem Cell Veto," The Center for Bioethics and Dignity, July 20, 2006, www.cbhd.org.

12. *Ibid.*

13. *Congressional Record*, House, July 13, 2006, p. H5218.

14. "An Interview with Kevin T. Fitzgerald," *Student Pugwash USA*, www.spusa.org.

15. Nancy L. Jones, "The Stem Cell Debate: Are Parthenogenic Human Embryos a Solution?" Center for Bioethics and Human Dignity, June 2, 2003, www.cbhd.org.

16. Gilbert Meilander, "Bioethics and Human Nature: Exploring Some Background Issues," Pew Forum on Religion and Public Life, Dec. 7, 2004, http://pewforum.org.

17. *Ibid.*

18. *Ibid.*

19. Quoted in "Pence Applauds Bush Veto, Votes to Sustain," press release, office of Rep. Mike Pence, July 19, 2006, http://mikepence.house.gov.

20. *USA Today*/Gallup national poll of 1,005 adults, July 21-23, 2006, www.pollingreport.com.

21. Quoted in Patricia Schudy, "An Embryo by Any Other Name: The Battle Over Stem Cell Research Begins With Language," *National Catholic Reporter*, Aug. 26, 2005.

22. Quoted in *ibid.*

23. Jonathan Moreno and Sam Berger, "Taking Stem Cells Seriously," *American Journal of Bioethics*, May-June 2006, http://ajobonline.com.

24. *Ibid.*

25. "The President's Stem Cell Theology," editorial, *The New York Times*, May 26, 2005.

26. *Congressional Record*, Senate, July 18, 2006, p. S7654.

27. Quoted in "Ethical Alternatives Q & A" *National Review Online*, July 19, 2006, http://article.nationalreview.com.

28. *Congressional Record*, Senate, July 17, 2006, pp. S7592, S5793.

29. Quoted in John Reichard, "Stem Cell Wars: Of Mice and Men," *CQ Healthbeat*, June 20, 2006.

30. Andrew Lustig, "Cloning for Dollars: Morality and the Market for Stem Cells," *Commonweal*, June 17, 2005.

31. Mehmet C. Oz, "Demystifying Stem Cells," *Saturday Evening Post*, November-December 2004.

32. Shane Smith, William Neaves and Steven Teitelbaum, "Adult Stem Cell Treatments for Diseases?" letter to the editor, *Science*, July 28, 2006, p. 439.

33. *Ibid.*

34. Kazutoshi Takahashi and Shinya Yamanaka, "Induction of Pluripotent Stem Cells from Mouse Embryonic and Adult Fibroblast Cultures by Defined Factors," *Cell*, Aug. 25, 2006, p. 1.

35. "Stem Cell Work Could Heal Ethical Rift," *Milwaukee Journal Sentinel*, Aug. 11, 2006, www.jsonline.com.

36. "Ethical Alternatives Q & A," *op. cit.*

37. *Congressional Record*, July 19, 2006, *op. cit.*, H5437.

38. *Ibid.*

39. *Ibid.*, p. H5448.

40. Aaron Levine, "Trends in the Geographic Distribution of Human Embryonic Stem-Research," *Politics and the Life Sciences*, Sept. 14, 2005, p. 41.

41. "History of Marrow and Blood Cell Transplants," National Marrow Donor Program, www.marrow.org/NMDP/history_of_transplants.html.

42. For background, see Ann B. Parson, *The Proteus Effect: Stem Cells and Their Promise* (2006) and "Stem Cell Information," National Institutes of Health, http://stemcells.nih.gov.

43. Sean J. Morrison, written testimony, Ad Hoc Congressional Hearing on Stem Cell Research, May 16, 2005, www.lifesciences.umich.edu/research/featured/sjmtestimony.pdf.

44. For background, see Brian Hansen, "Cloning Debate," *CQ Researcher*, Oct. 22, 2004, pp. 877-900.

45. "Fetal Homicide," National Conference of State Legislatures, June 2006, www.ncsl.org/programs/health/fethom.htm.

46. "State Homicide Laws That Recognize Unborn Victims," National Right to Life Committee, June 16, 2006, www.nrlc.org.

47. For background, see "Stem Cells and Public Policy," Century Foundation, 2006.

48. Jodi Rudoren, "Stem Cell Work Gets States' Aid After Bush Veto," *The New York Times*, July 25, 2006.

49. "Fact Sheet on Embryonic Stem Cell Research," U.S. Department of Health and Human Services, July 14, 2004.

50. Aaron Levine, "The Rise of State-Sponsored Stem Cell Research in the United States," unpublished paper, 2006. The author is a doctoral student at Princeton University.

51. "States, Foundations Lead the Way After Bush Vetoes Stem Cell Bill," *Science*, July 28, 2006, p. 420.

52. Bonnie Steinbrook, "Alternative Sources of Stem Cells," *The Hastings Center Report*, winter 2005, p. 24.

53. John Reichard, "Split Among Abortion Rights Foes Over Santorum-Specter Stem Cell Bill?" *CQ Healthbeat*, June 19, 2006.

54. Gareth Cook, "Stem Cell Method Preserves Embryo," *The Boston Globe*, Aug. 24, 2006.

55. Quoted in Kate Schuler, "Senate Deal Clears Way for Debate on Three Stem Cell Measures," *CQ Weekly*, July 10, 2006, p. 1904.

56. "Statement of Senator Tom Harkin on the President's Veto of HR 810," press release, July 19, 2006, http://harkin.senate.gov.

57. For background, see "Stem Cells and Public Policy," *op. cit.*

58. For background, see Dan Bilefsky, "EU to Fund Stem Cells," *International Herald Tribune*, July 25, 2006.

59. Quoted in *ibid.*

60. Quoted in *ibid.*

61. Normile and Mann, *op. cit.*

62. *Ibid.*

63. Quoted in *ibid.*

64. *Ibid.*

BIBLIOGRAPHY

Books

Parson, Ann B., *Proteus Effect: Stem Cells and Their Promise for Medicine*, Joseph Henry Press, 2006.
A journalist recounts the scientific history that led to current discoveries about stem cells, beginning with 18th-century natural philosophy and giving full accounts of the 20th- and 21st-century experiments leading to the current view of stem cells' potential for producing medical treatments.

Ruse, Michael, and A. Christopher Pynes, eds., *The Stem Cell Controversy: Debating the Issues*, Prometheus Books, 2006.
Philosophy professors at Florida State and Western Illinois universities assemble essays by biologists, doctors, theologians and others that lay out the main ethical, scientific and public-policy issues at stake in the stem cell debate.

Scott, Christopher Thomas, *Stem Cell Now: From the Experiment That Shook the World to the New Politics of Life*, Pi Press, 2005.
A biologist who is executive director of Stanford University's Program in Stem Cells and Society explains the history and possibilities of stem cell research and the political and ethical controversies that surround it.

Articles

Arnold, Wayne, "Science Haven in Singapore," *The New York Times*, Aug. 17, 2006, p. C1.
In hopes of becoming a biotech powerhouse, Singapore is luring U.S. stem cell researchers to its new labs.

Cook, Gareth, "Stem-cell Method Preserves Embryo," *The Boston Globe*, Aug. 24, 2006, p. A1.
A Massachusetts biotech company says it can grow embryonic stem cell cultures without destroying embryos.

Fitzpatrick, William, "Surplus Embryos, Nonreproductive Cloning, and the Intend/Foresee Distinction," *The Hastings Center Report*, May 2003, p. 29.
An assistant professor of philosophy at Virginia Tech University outlines the ethical issues that distinguish embryo creation and destruction in the course of in vitro fertilization procedures from embryo creation and destruction related to stem cell and cloning research.

Kolata, Gina, "Embryonic Cells, No Embryo Needed: Hunting for Ways Out of an Impasse," *The New York Times*, Oct. 11, 2005, p. F1.
Scientists and ethicists seek methods to produce embryonic stem cell lines without transgressing the moral boundaries of conservative Christian opponents.

Vergano, Dan, "U.S. Stem Cell Researchers Sense a Chill," *USA Today*, July 26, 2006, p. 8D.
With federal funding for embryonic stem cell research severely restricted in the United States, biologists say that promising studies have been put on indefinite hold.

Reports and Studies

"Ethical Issues in Human Stem Cell Research," National Bioethics Advisory Commission, September 1999.
A panel appointed to advise the Clinton administration lays out the background and arguments that led it to recommend federal funding of research on embryonic stem cells.

"Guidelines for Human Embryonic Stem Cell Research," Institute of Medicine Board on Health Sciences Policy, The National Academies Press, 2005.
An expert panel describes current U.S. regulations pertaining to stem cell research and recommends regulatory steps for governments and research institutions that would facilitate future research while protecting the rights of humans involved in studies, such as egg donors.

"Monitoring Stem Cell Research," President's Council on Bioethics, January 2004.
A panel appointed to advise the Bush administration examines the history and potential of stem cell research and its moral and social significance.

Parens, Erik, and Lori P. Knowles, "Reprogenetics and Public Policy," The Hastings Center, 2003.
The report examines ethical issues connected with the largely unregulated proliferation of reproductive technologies and research involving use and storage of embryos outside a uterus, including stem cell research and technologies such as pre-implantation diagnosis to weed out embryos at risk for genetically based diseases in in vitro fertilization procedures.

Simpson, John M., "Affordability, Accessibility and Accountability in California Stem Cell Research," The Foundation for Taxpayer and Consumer Rights, January 2006.
California's taxpayer-supported stem cell research initiative raises questions about who should have patents to, profit from and have access to whatever medical therapies the initiative ultimately develops.

"Stem Cells and Public Policy," The Century Foundation, 2006.
The progressive public-policy foundation offers a primer on stem cell science and current events and controversies, including a summary of stem cell regulation and funding systems in the United States and abroad.

For More Information

Alliance for Aging Research, 2021 K St., N.W., Suite 305, Washington, DC 20006; (202) 293-2856; www.agingresearch.org. Promotes research into the aging process, including medical research on stem cells.

American Society for Cell Biology, 8120 Woodmont Ave., Suite 750, Bethesda, MD 20814-2762; (301) 347-9300; www.ascb.org. Provides information and education about stem cell science.

American Society for Reproductive Medicine, 1209 Montgomery Highway, Birmingham, AL 35216-2809; (205) 978-5000; www.asrm.org. Provides information on issues including in vitro fertilization and stem cell science.

Bedford Stem Cell Research Foundation, P.O. Box 1028, Bedford, MA 01730; (617) 623-5670; www.bedfordresearch.org. Conducts biomedical research in fields that supporters believe are insufficiently supported by the federal government, such as stem cells.

California Institute for Regenerative Medicine, www.cirm.ca.gov. A new California state agency that will make grants and provide loans for stem cell research.

Center for Bioethics and Human Dignity, 2065 Half Day Road, Bannockburn, IL 60015; (847) 317-8180; www.cbhd.org. Provides information and education about Christian perspectives on biomedical issues including stem cells.

Center for Genetics and Society, 436 14th St., Suite 700, Oakland, CA 94612, (510) 625-0819; http://genetics-and-society.org/. Advocates for the responsible use of new biomedical knowledge and technologies, opposing applications that members believe would objectify human beings.

Christopher Reeve Foundation, 636 Morris Turnpike Suite 3A, Short Hills, NJ 07078; (800) 225-0292; www.christopherreeve.org. Advocates for stem cell research and other efforts to cure spinal-cord injuries.

Coalition for the Advancement of Medical Research, 2021 K St., N.W., Suite 305, Washington, DC 20006; (202) 725-0339; www.stemcellfunding.org. Advocacy group that promotes stem cell research.

Genetics Policy Institute, 701 8th St., N.W., Suite 400, Washington, DC 20001; (888) 238-1423; www.genpol.org. Advocates for public policies to promote responsible use of therapeutic cloning and stem cell science.

Geron Corp., 230 Constitution Dr., Menlo Park, CA 94025; (650) 473-7700; www.geron.com. Holds patents on embryonic stem cell research findings and hopes to commercialize therapies for cancer and degenerative conditions based on them.

Institute for Ethics and Emerging Technologies, Williams 229B, Trinity College, 300 Summit St., Hartford, CT 06106; (860) 297-2376; http://ieet.org/. Supports the examination by philosophers and ethicists of the social implications of new technologies such as stem cell therapies.

International Society for Stem Cell Research, 60 Revere Dr., Suite 500, Northbrook, IL 60062; (847) 509-1944; www.isscr.org. Provides information to the public and to doctors and scientists on stem cell research and its applications.

National Institutes of Health, Stem Cell Information, 9000 Rockville Pike, Bethesda, MD 20892; e-mail: stemcell@mail.nih.gov; http://stemcells.nih.gov/. The federal government's central information bank on stem cells and federal stem cell policy and research funding.

President's Council on Bioethics, 1425 New York Ave., N.W., Suite C100, Washington, DC 20005; (202) 296-4669; www.bioethics.gov. Advises the Bush administration on bioethical issues including stem cells.

6

Gun Violence

Kenneth Jost

The chilling video made by gunman Seung-Hui Cho is broadcast at a bar near the Virginia Tech campus on April 18. Cho mailed the profanity-laced tape to NBC News during a lull in his rampage — the worst mass shooting in U.S. history. The massacre renewed the perennial debate in the United States over gun control and raised new questions about safety on college campuses.

From *CQ Researcher*,
May 25, 2007.

Seung-Hui Cho was a faceless e-mail address when he ordered a .22-caliber Walther P-22 pistol for $267 from Wisconsin gun dealer Eric Thompson via the Internet on Feb. 2. The Virginia Tech senior drew no special attention when he picked the weapon up a week later from JND Pawnbrokers, near the spacious Blacksburg campus in southwest Virginia.

Cho was hardly more memorable a month later when he traveled in person to Roanoke Firearms about 35 miles away and made a $571 credit-card purchase of a 9 mm Glock 19 pistol and 50 rounds of ammunition. "A clean-cut college kid," said John Markell, the store's owner, quoting the after-the-fact description from the clerk who handled the March 13 transaction.

Twice, the Korean-born Cho presented the necessary identification — his Virginia driver's license, checkbook and immigration card — to complete the federal background check required for handgun purchasers. Twice, computers took only moments to display the needed authorization: PROCEED.

Nothing particularly distinguished Cho's transactions from any of the other estimated 2 million handgun purchases in the United States each year. Thompson in Wisconsin and the gun dealers in Virginia had no reason to know or even suspect that Cho was an extremely troubled young man whose bizarre and sometimes aggressive behavior had disturbed his parents, schoolmates and teachers for years.

Two years earlier, in fact, a state judge in Virginia had ordered Cho to receive outpatient psychiatric treatment after finding him to be "an imminent danger to himself" because of mental illness. Had they known that history, people at both stores said afterward, they would not have sold Cho the guns.

Most States Allow Concealed Weapons

Forty states have so-called right-to-carry laws allowing citizens to carry concealed firearms in public. In 36 of the states, "shall issue" laws require the issuance of permits for gun owners who meet standard criteria (top map). Only two states — Illinois and Wisconsin — and Washington, D.C., prohibit carrying altogether (bottom map).

Right-to-Carry Laws by State, 2006

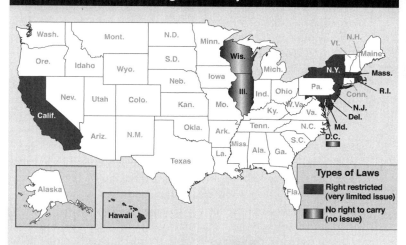

Source: Right to Carry Laws 2006, National Rifle Association Institute for Legislative Action, www.nraila.org

But they did. And so, on the morning of April 16, Cho used the weapons to kill 32 people on the Virginia Tech campus before taking his own life with a final shot to the head. The death toll — along with the 29 others wounded — marked Cho's intricately plotted, alienation-driven rampage as the worst mass school shooting in U.S. history. [1] (*See chart, p. 124.*) *

The massacre left the 26,000-student state university in a state of shock and brought forth outpourings of sympathy from officials and private citizens around the world. Hardly any time had passed, however, before the tragedy renewed the perennial debate in the United States over the rules for buying, selling and possessing firearms and the penalties for misusing them. [2]

The debate remains volatile in a country with what experts say is probably the highest rate of civilian gun ownership in the world and also the highest rate of gun-related injuries and deaths among major industrialized nations. Americans own what has been variously estimated as 200 million to 250 million firearms, around one-third of them handguns. Surveys indicate that more than 40 percent of all U.S. households own at least one firearm. [3]

Meanwhile, the number of gun-related deaths in the United States has been around 30,000 per year for

---

* The deadliest school attack ever in U.S. history appears to have been the dynamiting of a school in Bath, Mich., on May 18, 1927, by a school board member upset about a property tax increase. The death toll was put at around 40 children and several adults, including the bomber, Andrew Kehoe. (See Ryan Grim, "1927 School Attack More Deadly," *The Politico*, April 18, 2007, p. 6.)

more than two decades, according to the federal Centers for Disease Control and Prevention. For 2004 — the most recent year available — the number included 11,624 homicides and 16,750 suicides. [4] (*See chart, p. 126.*)

Gun advocates — including the powerful, 3-million-member National Rifle Association (NRA) — defend what they view as an individual constitutional right to use firearms in hunting, sport shooting and self-defense. They argue that gun owners and dealers are already subject to a web of federal, state and local firearm laws and regulations. The key to reducing gun violence, they say, lies with tougher penalties against criminals who use guns instead of more restrictions on gun owners.

"We have adequate gun laws on the books," says Andrew Arulanandam, the NRA's director of public affairs. "If a crime occurs, those criminals need to be prosecuted to the fullest extent of the law. The question becomes how do you make something that is already illegal more illegal."

Gun control advocates, including the influential Brady Campaign to Prevent Gun Violence, counter by depicting the widespread availability of handguns as a primary factor in the high rate of gun-related injuries and deaths. * They call for strengthening enforcement of existing federal laws barring possession of firearms by certain criminals, drug users and people with mental illness. They also favor restrictions on certain specific types of weapons or ammunition and generally oppose laws favored by gun groups easing the rules for the carrying of concealed weapons. (*See maps, p. 122.*)

---

* The Brady Campaign and the affiliated Brady Center to Prevent Gun Violence, formerly Handgun Control and the Center to Prevent Handgun Violence, were renamed in 2001 to honor former White House press secretary James Brady and his wife Sarah. James Brady was partially paralyzed in the 1981 assassination attempt on President Ronald Reagan; Sarah Brady heads the campaign and the center.

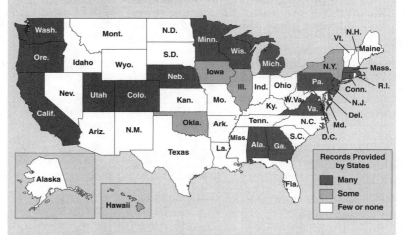

Background Checks Lack Mental Health Records

Out of 78 million background checks, only 2,608 people have been denied permission to purchase a gun on the basis of a mental health disqualification since the National Instant Criminal Background Check System began operation in December 1998. The pro-gun control group Third Way credits 22 states with providing records of mental health adjudications for use in gun background checks; the other 28 are said to provide few or no records for the purpose.

Source: Third Way, "Missing Records: Holes in Background Check System Allow Illegal Buyers to Get Guns," May 14, 2007; www.third-way.com

"We have weak, almost nonexistent gun laws in this country," says Paul Helmke, president of the Brady Campaign and its affiliated education arm, the Brady Center to Prevent Gun Violence. "And we're seeing almost the natural result of having weak, nonexistent gun laws with the Virginia Tech shootings and the 32 murders [in the United States] that happen every day."

The post-Virginia Tech debate features familiar arguments over the effectiveness of the landmark Gun Control Act of 1968 and the National Instant Criminal Background Check System, established in 1998 to enable gun dealers to enforce the act's prohibitions on gun ownership by criminals and others. But Cho's history of mental illness highlights an issue given less attention in the past: the conflicting federal and state definitions used to disqualify people with a history of mental illness from owning a gun.

Mental health groups, however, caution against viewing mental illness as an indicator of potential violence.

Virginia Tech Is Deadliest School Shooting

Last month's rampage by student Seung-Hui Cho at Virginia Tech is the deadliest school shooting in U.S. history. With 33 deaths, including Cho, the toll was more than twice the number killed at Columbine High School in 1999 or at the University of Texas in 1966.

Major Shootings at American Schools Since 1966

Date	Location	Dead and Wounded	Killer(s)
Aug. 1, 1966	University of Texas, Austin	14 dead (including gunman), 31 wounded	Student Charles J. Whitman
July 12, 1976	California State University, Fullerton, Calif.	7 dead, 2 wounded	University custodian Edward C. Allaway
Jan. 1, 1989	Cleveland Elementary School, Stockton, Calif.	6 dead (including gunman), 30 wounded	Stockton resident Patrick Purdy
Nov. 1, 1991	University of Iowa, Iowa City	6 dead (including gunman), 1 wounded	Physics graduate student Gang Lu
Feb. 2, 1996	Frontier Junior High School, Moses Lake, Wash.	3 dead	Student Barry Loukaitis
Aug. 15, 1996	San Diego State University, San Diego, Calif.	3 dead	Graduate student Frederick M. Davidson
Dec. 1, 1997	Heath High School, West Paducah, Ky.	3 dead, 5 wounded	Student Michael Carneal
March 24, 1998	Westside Middle School, Jonesboro, Ark.	4 dead, 11 wounded	Students Andrew Golden and Mitchell Johnson
April 20, 1999	Columbine High School, Littleton, Colo.	15 dead (including gunmen), 23 wounded	Students Eric Harris and Dylan Klebold
Aug. 10, 1999	North Valley Jewish Community Center Pre-School, Granada Hills, Calif.	5 dead	White supremacist Buford O. Furrow Jr.
Jan. 16, 2002	Appalachian School of Law, Grundy, Va.	3 dead, 3 wounded	Student Peter Odighizuwa
Oct. 28, 2002	University of Arizona College of Nursing, Tucson, Ariz.	4 dead (including gunman)	Student Robert Flores
March 21, 2005	Red Lake High School, Red Lake Indian Reservation, Minn.	10 killed (including gunman), 7 wounded	Student Jeffrey Weise
Sept. 2, 2006	Shepherd University, Shepherdstown, W.Va.	3 dead (including gunman)	Douglas Pennington, parent of two students
Oct. 2, 2006	West Nickel Mines School, Nickel Mines, Pa.	6 dead (including gunman), 6 wounded	Truck driver Charles Carl Roberts IV
April 16, 2007	Virginia Tech University, Blacksburg, Va.	33 dead (including gunman), 29 wounded	Student Seung-Hui Cho

Sources: "No Gun Left Behind: The Gun Lobby's Campaign to Push Guns Into Colleges and Schools," Brady Center to Prevent Gun Violence, May 2007; "The long history of deadly shootings at US schools," Agence France-Presse, April 16, 2007; Lauren Smith, "Major Shootings on American College Campuses," The Chronicle of Higher Education, April 27, 2007

Honberg, director of policy and legal affairs for the National Alliance on Mental Illness. "That's not borne out for the majority of people with mental illness."

The Blacksburg massacre is also giving new and urgent attention to questions of safety and security on the nation's college campuses. Some gun advocacy groups see Cho's ability to carry out the shootings, including the nine-minute rampage inside a classroom building, as an argument for lifting the ban on guns imposed by most schools, including Virginia Tech.

"The latest school shooting demands an immediate end to the gun-free-zone law, which leaves the nation's schools at the mercy of madmen," said Larry Pratt, executive director of Gun Owners of America, in a statement released on the day of the massacre. "It is irresponsibly dangerous to tell citizens that they may not have guns at schools."

Campus law enforcement officials, along with other police groups as well as gun control supporters, disagree. "The only folks who should have firearms on a campus are those people who are sworn and authorized to protect and are duly trained to do that," says Steven Healy, director of public safety at Princeton University and president of the International Association of Campus Law Enforcement Administrators.

Congress is considering legislation previously introduced to give states financial incentives to improve their reporting to the background-check system in hopes of

"It's very easy and very tempting when something as horrible as Virginia Tech occurs to assume that mental illness correlates with a propensity for violence," says Ron plugging gaps in enforcement of the federal restrictions on gun possession. But the political climate is widely viewed as unfavorable for any broader measures. "In the very short run, I don't expect we'll do anything seriously," says David Hemenway, a professor at the Harvard School of Public Health and longtime gun control advocate.

Meanwhile, gun advocacy groups are hoping to preserve a major victory in the courts: a federal appeals court on March 9 struck down Washington's strict local law banning possession of handguns even in private homes. In a 2-1 decision, the U.S. Court of Appeals for the District of Columbia Circuit ruled that the 1976 measure violates the Second Amendment's guarantee of a right to bear arms.

The ruling contradicts the view long held but recently being reconsidered that the Bill of Rights provision protects state militias but does not establish an individual's right to own firearms. Washington Mayor Adrian Fenty is weighing whether to try rewriting the ordinance or to ask the Supreme Court to review the decision. (*See sidebar, p. 132.*)

With the Virginia Tech shootings still very much a scar on the national psyche, here are some of the major gun policy questions being considered:

Denver area high school students Rhianna Cheek (left), Mandi Annibel (center) and Rachel Roof (right) comfort one another during a candlelight vigil in Denver's Civic Center Park on April 21, 1999. The vigil honored the victims of the massacre at Columbine High School in Littleton, Colo., the previous day. Students Eric Harris and Dylan Klebold shot and killed 12 schoolmates and one teacher during a four-hour rampage and then turned their guns on themselves.

Should schools adopt additional security measures to try to prevent mass shootings?

Virginia Tech officials learned of a shooting in the West Ambler Johnston dormitory at around 7:15 a.m. on April 16, but postponed sending a campuswide e-mail about the incident for nearly two hours. University President Charles Steger later explained the initial suspect was wrongly thought to be a spurned boyfriend who had already left campus. But Steger also said a campuswide e-mail would have missed any students or faculty who were not online.

At Princeton University, administrators would have had other options, according to Healy of the campus law enforcement group. The emergency notification system for the New Jersey campus reaches students, faculty and staff up to eight different ways, using land lines, cell phones, e-mail and text messaging.

A "robust" notification system is needed, Healy explains, because e-mail is almost passé among Generation Next. "We've been slow to recognize that young people use text messaging" more than e-mail, he says. The system — useful in any emergency — is "not inexpensive," Healy says, "but it's not over-the-top expensive." And, yes, he adds, "It's definitely worth it."

"Redundant" emergency communication systems like Princeton's are among the recommendations the campus law enforcement group had listed for schools to consider before the Virginia Tech massacre. The agenda includes such common-sense steps as developing emergency-management plans not only for "active shooter" situations but also for various other potential hazards, coordinating with other local police agencies and actually practicing planned emergency responses.

"It's one thing to have a plan on paper," says Healy, who headed police departments at Syracuse University and Wellesley College before coming to Princeton in 2003. "It's another thing to play it out." [5]

Opposing groups in the gun policy debate agree campus security needs more attention, but they leave the particulars to others. "There's a universal agreement that we have a problem with gun violence in schools," says NRA spokesman Arulanandam. "If you look at the reality today, we protect our assets in our banks, we protect our airports, we protect special events more than we protect our children in our schools."

The NRA favors "a national dialogue" among experts and interested parties to figure out what needs to be

Annual U.S. Gun Deaths Near 30,000

Annually, there are roughly 30,000 U.S. gun deaths. The total number of firearm deaths in the United States decreased by around 12 percent from 1981 to 2004; a decrease in crime in the late 1990s may have been a factor.

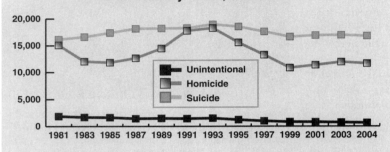

Gun Deaths by Intent, 1981-2004 *

* Does not include deaths by legal intervention or those with undetermined intent

Note: Comparisons over time are difficult because of a change in the reporting methodology.

Source: Web-Based Injury Statistics Query and Reporting System, Centers for Disease Control and Prevention

done, Arulanandam says. But he stops short of a step now called for by many gun advocates: allowing possession of guns on college campuses. "We're not advocating a policy change," he says.

For his part, the Brady Center's Helmke seconds the various suggestions for improving campus police training and planning. "Colleges try to do the right thing," he says. "We've learned from Virginia Tech there are things you can do better." But Helmke also points to what gun control supporters say is the need for stronger laws. "Colleges can't do it on their own," he says.

"The elephant in the room is the guns," says Harvard's Hemenway. "It's hard for any individual college to change that."

One gun policy expert, however, finds the rush to rethink campus security after Virginia Tech an overreaction. "Campuses are the safest places in America," says Gary Kleck, a professor at Florida State University's College of Criminology and Criminal Justice. "Serious violence on campus is the exception to the rule."

Kleck, a centrist on gun control issues best known for research depicting defensive gun use as generally safe and effective, points to the use of alcohol as a more serious cause of campus violence. He finds no fault with steps such as improving emergency communication systems but cautions against looking for proof of their effectiveness. "If the problem it's intended to address is virtually nonexistent, it would be impossible to find out whether it is effective," he says.

Healy sees no overreaction in the post-Virginia Tech policy debates. "It's obviously heightened the sense of urgency," he says. But he cautions against expecting a guarantee against another Virginia Tech in the future.

"These types of situations can happen any time, anywhere," says Healy. "One hundred percent safety is a fallacy for all of us — not just colleges and universities, but for general society."

Should it be harder for someone with a history of mental illness to obtain a gun?

In December 2005, midway through his sophomore year, Seung-Hui Cho was referred to a mental health clinic by Virginia Tech police after he had threatened suicide following two female students' complaints he was harassing them. In a hearing held Dec. 14 after an overnight evaluation, special judge Paul Barnett found Cho to be "an imminent danger to himself" and ordered outpatient treatment. [6]

The judicial finding arguably disqualified Cho from buying a handgun under federal law. Virginia authorities, however, never fed that information into the federal background-check system. Why not? Unlike the federal law, Virginia's corresponding law specifically requires commitment to a mental hospital to block an applicant from purchasing a firearm. [7]

The information gap that might have blocked or at least delayed Cho from buying the guns he used in his rampage is not unique to Virginia. In fact, the pro-gun control group Third Way rates Virginia among the best in reporting mental health information to the FBI's instant-check system. Overall, the group reports, only 22 states provide mental health records to the system — "rendering this provision of the law useless in most states." [8]

Legislation to improve the background-check system — reintroduced in Congress after Virginia Tech — has the backing not only of gun control groups but also of the NRA, the most powerful of the gun advocacy groups. "Someone who's dangerous to himself or others because of mental illness shouldn't get a gun," says the Brady Center's Helmke. "That's what the law says."

"We've been on record for decades that records of those adjudicated as mentally defective and deemed to be a danger to others or to themselves should be part of the national instant-check system and not be allowed to own a firearm," says NRA spokesman Arulanandam. "The mental health lobby and the medical lobby are the impediments — they are against release of the records."

The rival Gun Owners of America, however, opposes any strengthening of a background-check system that it calls both ineffective and intrusive. "All the background checks in the world will not stop bad guys from getting firearms," the group's Web site declares.

Mental health groups are raising more specific concerns about the legislation. They warn that more extensive reporting of people with a history of mental illness will expose them to discrimination and prejudice and possibly deter some people from seeking treatment altogether. "We have real grave concerns about people with mental illness being a population that's singled out," says Honberg, at the National Alliance on Mental Illness.

"Even if someone was severely disabled 30 years ago, we have plenty of examples of people who have gone on to recover and are living independently and are working and are upstanding citizens," Honberg adds. "Do we want to include all those people in the database?"

The Gun Control Act of 1968 prohibits possession of a firearm by anyone "adjudicated as a mental defective" or who has been committed to any mental institution. The law defines a "mental defective" as a person who "is a danger to himself or others" or "lacks the mental capacity to contract or manage his own affairs" as a result of "marked subnormal intelligence" or "mental illness." The regulations broadly define adjudication to include "a determination by a court, board, commission or other lawful authority." [9]

The statutory phrase "mental defective" is both outmoded and stigmatizing, Honberg says. "It's a term no

AP Photo

Charles J. Whitman, 24, a student at the University of Texas, shot and killed 13 people and wounded 31 others on Aug. 1, 1966, from the school's 27-story tower using an arsenal of three pistols and four rifles. Two police officers eventually broke into the barricaded observation deck and shot the former Eagle Scout and Marine.

one has used for 30 to 40 years," he says. The regulatory provisions, he adds, are "vague and potentially overbroad."

The bills pending in Congress leave the definitions unchanged. Honberg suggests the mental health provisions should be amended to include "some durational limitation" as well as a process for someone to petition for removal from the list. More broadly, he worries about possible abuses from a more rigorously maintained list.

"We're concerned that the very agency charged with managing these records, the FBI, maintains a whole lot of other lists," Honberg says. "We're talking about a population that is oftentimes victimized by breaches of confidentiality and prejudice."

Gun Owners of America seconds those concerns. "What type of record are we talking about sucking in?" asks Mike Hammond, a legal and legislative adviser to the group.

The Brady Center's Helmke counters that states are being asked only for court records. "It's not checking hospital records or doctors' records," he says. "This shouldn't be something that discourages people from getting help for problems."

In Virginia, meanwhile, Democratic Gov. Tim Kaine has moved to tighten the state's law on access to guns for people with histories of mental illness. On April 30, he ordered state agencies "to consider any involuntary treatment order . . . whether inpatient or outpatient" as disqualifying an applicant from buying a gun. [10]

Should laws limiting the carrying of concealed weapons be relaxed?

When a disgruntled student at Appalachian School of Law in southwestern Virginia went on a deadly shooting rampage in January 2002, two students — one current and one former police officer — dashed to their cars to get their own guns. As gun advocates tell the story, former police officer Mikael Gross and sheriff's deputy Tracy Bridges brandished their weapons at the shooter, who dropped his gun and was then subdued with the help of two other, unarmed students. *

No one confronted Cho, however, during the shootings in the West Ambler Johnston dormitory or the nine-minute rampage inside Norris Hall. One reason, gun advocates say, is Virginia Tech's ban on private possession of firearms on campus — a proscription Gross and Bridges apparently disregarded at the Appalachian law school.

"If there were more responsible, armed people on campuses, mass murder would be harder," writes Glenn Reynolds, a law professor at the University of Tennessee and author of the conservative blog InstaPundit. [11]

Gun advocates point to the Appalachian law school incident as one among many examples showing "defensive gun use" is both more common and more effective in protecting lives and property than widely assumed or acknowledged by gun control supporters. They favor easing laws on carrying concealed weapons and repealing "gun-free zone" laws that prohibit carrying a weapon in specific places, such as campuses.

Police organizations and gun control advocates disagree. They depict defensive gun use as rare and risky and widespread carrying of weapons as an invitation to more gun violence. And they specifically dispute any suggestion that an armed student or teacher might have been able to prevent or limit Cho's rampage at Virginia Tech.

"Every time I play that out, I come up with worse results," says Healy of the campus police group. "When you have untrained people with obviously someone who was extremely mentally ill and several [police] agencies responding simultaneously, it's a recipe for disaster."

"What we're wishing for is that John Wayne or James Bond had been sitting in the classroom," says the Brady Center's Helmke, who as mayor of Ft. Wayne, Ind., directed the city's police department before his present position. "In the real world, it doesn't work that way."

The use of guns in self-defense has been an especially contentious piece of the gun policy debate since the early 1990s, when Florida State's Kleck produced research that is now used to estimate as many as 2.5 million defensive uses of guns per year in the United States. Seven years later, economist John Lott, then at the University of Chicago, coauthored a study claiming that states with laws making it easier to carry concealed handguns had lower overall crime rates than those without such laws.

Expanded later into books, both studies drew fire immediately from gun control organizations on policy grounds and from like-minded academics, who have exhaustively documented what they regard as patent flaws in the statistical methods used. [12] Whatever the validity of the studies, they both became useful ammunition for gun advocates in resisting additional gun measures and, in particular, in easing laws allowing qualified citizens to carry concealed weapons.

With eased carry laws on the books today in 40 states, gun advocates continue to endorse them and urge the rest of the states to follow suit. "Law-abiding people have the right to defend themselves," says the NRA's Arulanandam. "The sad reality is that just because you're

---

* Three people were killed and three others wounded in the incident. Gross' and Bridges' use of a weapon in subduing the shooter, Peter Odighizuwa, went unmentioned in most news stories. Odighizuwa pleaded guilty to capital murder and other counts in February 2004 and received six life prison sentences.

outside your home, you're not immune from crime. Crime can happen to anyone, anywhere."

Gun control supporters, on the other hand, oppose what they call the "radical liberalization" of concealed carry laws pushed by gun advocates. "An armed society is an at-risk society," a Brady Center position paper declares. The paper cautions that people "underestimate" the difficulty of successfully using a gun for self-defense and also warns that the availability of weapons allows minor arguments to escalate into "deadly gun play."

Lott, now a visiting professor at the State University of New York, Binghamton, and Kleck continue to defend their studies and their policy conclusions. Lott, for example, strongly argues against laws creating gun-free zones. "You unintentionally make it safer for the criminal because there's less for them to worry about," he says.

Kleck insists that despite contrary examples cited by gun control opponents, people using guns in self-defense rarely injure themselves and typically succeed in preventing injury or loss of property at the criminal's hands. Interestingly, Kleck rejects Lott's conclusion that concealed-carry laws lower overall crime rates and points to studies showing that only a small fraction of people ever actually carry weapons. But Kleck says he still favors those laws on self-defense grounds.

Harvard's Hemenway, however, insists that guns represent a greater risk than a potential benefit for public safety. "There's strong evidence that where there are more guns generally, there are lots, lots, lots more gun problems," he says.

As for guns on campus, Hemenway professes horror. "I would expect it would rarely do much good, and it has enormous potential for harm," he says. "The notion of allowing drunk frat boys to go around campus armed, that would be scary for me."

BACKGROUND

"Gun Culture"

Guns have been an important but controversial part of American life since Colonial times. The citizen soldier of the Revolutionary era and the rifle-carrying frontiersman of the Western expansion are mythic figures of U.S. history. But so too are the machine-gun-wielding gangsters of the early 20th century and the heat-packing street thugs of the urban underclass at the century's end.

Concern about gun crimes led to new, stricter gun control laws beginning in the early 20th century and culminated in the law that Congress passed in 1968 after the decade's wrenching assassinations of national leaders, including President John F. Kennedy. [13]

The historian Richard Hofstadter famously gave a name to Americans' attachment to firearms with an article in 1970 entitled "America as a Gun Culture." [14] Political scientist Robert Spitzer at the State University of New York, Cortland, notes in his overview of the gun debates that even gun control proponents acknowledge the special role of firearms in U.S. history. [15] Still, the exact extent of gun ownership and gun use through history is hotly disputed.

In the most dramatic dispute, historian Michael Bellesiles won wide attention and acclaim in 2000 for his book, *Arming America*, minimizing the role of private ownership of guns before the Civil War, but he had to resign from a professorship at Emory University amid accusations of questionable scholarship. After dropping a previous reference to Bellesiles' work in his most recent edition, Spitzer nevertheless reiterates two widely shared generalizations that citizen militias played a lesser role in the Revolutionary War and armed frontiersmen a lesser role in westward expansion than gun advocates contend or popular literature and media depict. [16]

Gun laws also date from Colonial times in America and from the early days of newly established frontier towns in the 19th century, according to historian Alexander DeConde. [17] The modern era, however, dates from the enactment of a strict New York law in 1911 that state Sen. Timothy Sullivan proposed after the heavily publicized shooting of New York City's mayor in 1910. The Sullivan law — still on the books — prohibits owning or carrying a concealable weapon except with a permit, issued for two years and only on a showing of "proper cause."

Two decades later — with the so-called gangster era still near its height — Congress passed the first major federal gun laws, but both laws emerged weaker than proposed because of opposition from, among others, the NRA. The National Firearms Act of 1934 required registration of and a prohibitive tax on sawed-off shotguns and machine guns, but handguns were dropped from the original version. The Federal Firearms Act of 1938 required federal licensing of firearms manufacturers and dealers and prohibited sales to criminals, but prosecutions were made virtually impossible by a requirement to prove a knowing violation.

CHRONOLOGY

Before 1960 *"Gun culture" is influential in the United States; first federal gun laws are passed.*

1911 New York's "Sullivan law" requires state-issued license to possess a handgun.

1934, 1938 National Firearms Act sets high tax on machine guns, sawed-off shotguns; handguns exempted. . . . Federal Firearms Act requires licenses for gun manufacturers, dealers; ban on gun sales to criminals proves unenforceable.

1939 Supreme Court upholds National Firearms Act; ruling appears to limit Second Amendment.

1960s-1970s *Violent crime, political assassinations trigger new gun law.*

1966 University of Texas student kills 13, wounds 31 others in sniper shootings from tower on Austin campus; police charge observation deck and shoot killer.

1968 After Martin Luther King, Robert F. Kennedy assassinations Congress enacts Gun Control Act, barring interstate firearms sales or sale of guns to criminals, "mental defectives" or others.

1970s National Rifle Association stiffens opposition as anti-gun groups form to get stricter gun laws.

1980s-1990s *Gun advocates, gun control supporters swap victories.*

1981 White House press secretary Jim Brady is left partially paralyzed during assassination attempt on President Ronald Reagan; Brady and wife Sarah become prominent gun control advocates.

1986 Reagan signs Firearm Owners Protection Act, legalizing interstate sale of rifles, shotguns; eases other 1968 restrictions.

1989 Drifter Patrick Purdy uses AK-47 to kill five, wound 30 in Stockton, Calif., schoolyard before killing himself; incident spurs President George H. W. Bush to ban some assault rifles.

1993 Democratic-controlled Congress passes Brady Handgun Violence Prevention Act, signed by President Bill Clinton; establishes five-day waiting period for buying guns to allow background checks; instant check system to be established within five years.

1994 Congress bans assault weapons for 10 years. Republicans win control of Congress in November, dooming further gun control measures.

1995, 1997 Supreme Court Justices Clarence Thomas, Antonin Scalia endorse individual rights view of Second Amendment.

1999 Columbine High School massacre spurs new school security and anti-bullying measures.

2000-Present *Gun debate dormant, renewed by Virginia Tech massacre.*

2000 Gun control viewed by some as a liability for Democrat Al Gore in presidential campaign; some in party de-emphasize issue.

2002 Disgruntled student Peter Odighizuwa kills three, wounds three at Appalachian School of Law in Grundy, Va.; two police officer-students use their guns to help subdue him. . . . Bush administration tells Supreme Court Second Amendment protects individual right to firearms.

2004 Republican-controlled Congress allows assault weapon ban to expire.

2005 High-school student Jeffrey Weise kills nine, wounds seven at school on Red Lake Indian Reservation in Minnesota.

2006 Democrats win control of House, Senate; muting of gun control issue viewed by some as factor.

2007 Federal appeals court strikes down District of Columbia handgun ban (March 9); gun control advocates leery of appealing. . . . Student Seung-Hui Cho kills 32 at Virginia Tech before killing himself; university officials' actions questioned, defended; Congress urged to tighten background check system; gun advocates want to lift campus gun bans, but administrators, law enforcement disagree.

Another two decades later, a public concerned with rising crime, especially among juveniles, began to voice support for stricter gun laws. [18] The calls for federal action intensified in the 1960s, driven in part by the rising crime rate but more significantly by the seeming epidemic of assassinations beginning with Lee Harvey Oswald's use of a mail-order rifle to kill President John F. Kennedy in 1963. As Kennedy's successor, President Lyndon B. Johnson capitalized on the shock over the killing and his own considerable legislative skills to gain congressional approval of a long list of domestic policy initiatives. But his support of a broad gun control bill failed to move lawmakers until two more assassinations in 1968: civil rights leader Martin Luther King Jr. on April 4 and Sen. Robert F. Kennedy, D-N.Y., on June 5 — the evening of his victory in California's Democratic presidential primary.

In successive messages to Congress in June 1968, Johnson called first for banning the out-of-state sale of rifles, shotguns and ammunition and then, more broadly, for national registration of all firearms and federal licensing of all gun owners. Polls registered strong public support for gun control. [19] Two weeks after Robert Kennedy's death, a Harris poll found 81 percent of Americans favored gun registration. But an effective grass-roots lobbying campaign by the NRA helped doom the licensing and registration provisions.

As enacted, the Gun Control Act of 1968 banned the interstate shipment of firearms or ammunition to individuals and prohibited the sale of guns to convicted felons, fugitives, drug addicts, the mentally ill or minors. It also strengthened licensing and record-keeping requirements for gun dealers and collectors. As Spitzer notes, the measure was "the most sweeping federal gun regulation" in U.S. history but also "very modest" in scope. As a result, he writes, the law's actual impact was "minimal." Nevertheless, gun advocates "immediately set to work to erode the act, if not overturn it entirely." [20]

Gun Debates

With the passage of the 1968 law, gun control debates became if anything more polarized and more volatile. Gun control proponents continued to call for stricter regulation, while pro-gun groups and individual gun owners intensified efforts to block new restrictions and relax existing laws. Over time, Republicans hardened their position against additional gun controls. Through the 1990s,

Democrats supported some gun control measures, but some in the party began downplaying the issue after 2000 as many strategists came to view it as a handicap in presidential campaigns and some congressional races.

In the early 1980s, the opposing lobbies swapped largely symbolic victories. Morton Grove, Ill., banned handguns in 1981. Kennesaw, Ga., responded a year later by requiring all households to own a gun. The Kennesaw ordinance was later amended to be discretionary, and Morton Grove's has been largely unenforced. After its ban was upheld in court, however, gun advocates responded by seeking and winning passage of laws in many states that pre-empted local firearms regulations — leaving the issue with state legislatures, where gun groups had greater clout. Gun control supporters countered with ballot measures that voters in some states approved.

At the federal level, gun control opponents achieved a signal victory in 1986 with passage of a law that neutralized some of the major provisions of the 1968 law. Culminating a six-year fight, the Firearms Owners Protection Act permitted the interstate sale of rifles and shotguns — but not handguns — if legal in the buyer's and seller's states. It also allowed gun dealers to sell at gun shows and made it easier for individuals to sell weapons on an occasional basis. It also specifically prohibited any comprehensive system of firearms registration or centralized record-keeping on gun dealers. Despite opposition from some Democrats — and from police groups — the bill was approved by lopsided margins in both the Senate and the House and signed into law by President Ronald Reagan on May 19, 1986.

Gun control supporters responded by focusing on two major proposals — a national waiting period for handgun purchases and a ban on so-called assault weapons — which both became law early in the Clinton administration. The Brady bill won passage by substantial margins in late 1993 in the House and then in the Senate; President Bill Clinton signed it into law on Nov. 30, 1993. The bill's major provisions — a five-day waiting period to be replaced by an instant background-check system within five years — were backed up by federal funding to help states improve the computerization of criminal records. The instant-check system went into effect in 1998 even though gun control groups called for extending the five-day waiting period because of uneven state reporting of information needed to make the instant-check effective.

The Case of the Overturned Gun Ban

Will Washington's mayor appeal or rewrite law?

Gun rights advocates won a major victory in March when a federal appeals court struck down the District of Columbia's strict handgun ban by recognizing an individual right to keep and bear arms under the Second Amendment.

Now, gun rights advocates are in the unusual position of urging Mayor Adrian Fenty to appeal the ruling to the Supreme Court. They hope the high court will definitively approve a broad view of the Second Amendment that the justices and most state and federal courts have rejected until now.

Meanwhile, gun control groups worry about the prospects of an appeal to the Supreme Court. And Fenty apparently plans to take his time in deciding whether to ask the justices to review the ruling or ask the D.C. City Council to rewrite the law in the light of the appeals court's decision.

"It's a little early to say which way we're going to go," Fenty told a May 8 news conference. "We will weigh everything." [1]

The meaning of the Second Amendment — part of the Bill of Rights adopted in 1791 two years after ratification of the Constitution — has been a major dispute between gun rights and gun control groups at least since the 1960s. The amendment states: "A well regulated militia, being necessary to the security of a free state, the right of the people to keep and bear arms, shall not be infringed." [2]

Through history, the amendment has generally been interpreted to protect a "collective right" for states to organize and control militias, but not to bestow an individual right to own or possess firearms. The Supreme Court appeared to uphold that view in a somewhat cryptic 1939 decision, *United States v. Miller.* [3]

In its 2-1 ruling rejecting the D.C. handgun ban, the U.S. Circuit Court of Appeals for the District of Columbia reasoned that the amendment could not effectively protect state militias unless it also guaranteed an individual right to keep and bear arms. "Preserving an individual right was the best way to ensure that the militia could serve when called," Judge Laurence H. Silberman wrote.

The appeals court's March 9 ruling in *Parker v. District of Columbia* marked the first time a federal court had used the Second Amendment to strike down a gun regulation. [4] In the only previous appellate decision endorsing the individual view of the amendment, the Fifth U.S. Circuit Court of Appeals in New Orleans agreed in 2001 that the Second Amendment protects the individual right to bear arms, but it nevertheless upheld a federal prosecution of a Texas physician for carrying a pistol — even though he was under a court protective order. [5] Ten other federal appeals courts and 10 state courts have ruled the amendment does not create an individual right to bear arms.

In his opinion, Silberman said the Second Amendment permits "reasonable regulations" of firearms. But the District's nearly total ban on registration of handguns went too far, he said, because pistols are "the most preferred firearm" for self-defense in the home. The ruling also struck down a requirement that any handguns in a home be kept disassembled and trigger-locked and an interpretation of the District's ban on carrying a weapon that prevents moving a gun within a home.

The District's lawyers asked the full appeals court to rehear the case, but the judges rejected the request by a 6-4 vote. With Fenty equivocating about the District's next

The push for an assault weapons ban moved to the forefront after an anger-venting drifter used an assault rifle in the Stockton, Calif., schoolyard massacre in 1989. President George H. W. Bush earned the enmity of gun groups by banning imports of certain assault rifles. Clinton expanded the scope of Bush's regulatory ban in 1993 and meanwhile pushed Congress for a broader, legislative prohibition. In its final form, the ban outlawed for 10 years

sale and possession of 19 specified types of weapons and others with some similar characteristics. The bill won strong approval in the House and cleared the Senate after half-a-dozen Republicans provided the needed margin to thwart a filibuster. Clinton signed it on Sept. 13, 1994.

The two measures represented the peak of gun control supporters' influence. Broader gun controls became politically impossible after Republicans gained control of

step, lawyers for the plaintiffs are urging him to appeal to the Supreme Court.

"We would like the entire nation to benefit from our efforts," says Alan Gura, an Alexandria, Va., lawyer representing the six D.C. residents challenging the handgun ban. "We believe that this is a wonderful case with which to redeem Second Amendment rights for all Americans."

Gun control advocates, however, openly worry that the broad D.C. ban will be hard to defend. "Why is this the one we're going to be taking up to the Supremes?" asks Paul Helmke, president of the Brady Campaign to Prevent Gun Violence. [6]

The District has until Aug. 7 to ask the Supreme Court to hear the case. Two justices — Antonin Scalia and Clarence Thomas — are on record as endorsing the individual rights view of the Second Amendment. In addition, Justice Samuel A. Alito Jr. voted in dissent in a 1996 case to strike down the federal ban on machine guns while he was a judge on the Third U.S. Circuit Court of Appeals. In addition, the Bush administration is on record since 2002 as endorsing the individual-rights view. [7]

Washington, D.C., Mayor Adrian Fenty (left) and Assistant Chief of Police Winston Robinson voice disappointment with federal appeals court ruling on March 9, 2007, striking down the District of Columbia's strictest-in-the-nation handgun ban. The ruling rejected previous doctrine that the Second Amendment only protects states' rights to organize and control militias.

AP Photo/Jacquelyn Martin

"There's certainly a risk at the Supreme Court" for gun control advocates, says Carl Bogus, a professor at Roger Williams University School of Law in Cranston, R.I.

[1] Quoted in Carol D. Leonnig, "Gun Ban Ruling Puts Fenty on the Spot," *The Washington Post*, May 17, 2007, p. B1. Some other background drawn from story. See also, by same reporter, "Full Court Will Not Review Ruling," *ibid.*, May 9, 2007, p. B4; Gary Emerling, "Court Denies D.C.'s Gun Appeal," *The Washington Times*, May 9, 2007, p. A1.

[2] For opposing views of the Second Amendment, see Stephen P. Halbrook, *That Every Man Be Armed: The Evolution of a Constitutional Right* (2d. ed.), 1994; Carl T. Bogus (ed.), *The Second Amendment in Law and History: Historians and Constitutional Scholars on the Right to Bear Arms* (2000).

[3] The citation is 307 U.S. 174 (1939).

[4] *Parker v. District of Columbia*, 04-7401 (CA-DC March 9, 2007)http://pacer.cadc.uscourts.gov/docs/common/opinions/200703/04-7041a.pdf. All documents in the case are on a site maintained by Alan Gura, lawyer for the plaintiffs: www.gura-possessky.com/ parker.htm.

[5] The Fifth Circuit's decision is *United States v. Emerson*, 270 F.3d 203 (CA 5 2001). For a compilation of other cases, see Robert J. Spitzer, *The Politics of Gun Control* (4th ed.), 2007, pp. 34-35 and accompanying notes.

[6] Quoted in Leonnig, *op. cit.*, May 17, 2007.

[7] See *Printz v. United States*, 521 U.S. 898 (1995) (Thomas, J., concurring); Antonin Scalia, *A Matter of Interpretation: Federal Courts and the Law* (1997), pp. 136-137 n. 13; *United States v. Rybar*, 103 F.3d 273 (3d Cir. 1996) (Alito, J., dissenting). For the government's position, see Linda Greenhouse, "U.S., in a Shift, Tells Justices Citizens Have a Right to Guns," *The New York Times*, May 8, 2002, p. A1.

both houses of Congress in the 1994 election. The Columbine High School shooting in 1999 spurred Senate approval of a package of restrictions, but the measure failed in the House. Five years later, with Republicans still controlling both houses, Congress allowed the assault weapons ban to expire.

Some Democratic strategists, meanwhile, were blaming the gun control issue for President George W.

Bush's narrow victories over gun control supporters Vice President Al Gore in 2000 and Sen. John F. Kerry in 2004. Many analysts disputed the argument, but it gained credence in 2006 when Democrats regained control of the Senate, thanks in part to the election of gun-owning Democrats in two Republican-leaning states: Jon Tester in Montana and Jim Webb in Virginia.

Mayor Bloomberg's Gun Control Tactics Draw Fire

NRA says he's harassing 'law-abiding Americans'

All New York City Mayor Michael Bloomberg wants to do is get illegal guns off the streets. Crime control, not gun control, Bloomberg declares.

But the National Rifle Association (NRA) says Bloomberg is harassing gun dealers and trying to disarm law-abiding Americans. "A national gun-control vigilante," the NRA magazine, *America's 1st Freedom*, calls him in its April 2007 issue. [1]

Bloomberg, a moderate Republican, is drawing fire from the NRA and other gun advocates for a variety of tactics he insists are aimed only at enforcing existing and largely non-controversial gun regulations.

The second-term chief executive of the nation's largest city is sending undercover agents to conduct sting operations against out-of-state gun dealers to detect illegal gun sales. He is winning court settlements against some of the dealers but also drawing scorn from the NRA and resentment from officials in some of the states.

Bloomberg is also spearheading Mayors Against Illegal Guns, a coalition of more than 200 city chief executives that he helped start — and personally bankrolled — in fall 2006. The coalition is concentrating now on urging Congress to repeal a law that prevents the federal Bureau of Alcohol, Tobacco, Firearms and Explosives (BATFE) from sharing gun-trace data with local police. [2]

NRA officials deride both Bloomberg and the mayors' coalition. "He's become the poster boy for gun bans in America," says Wayne LaPierre, the NRA's chief executive officer, explaining the article in the group's magazine. When the mayors' coalition was forming, NRA spokesman Andrew Arulanandam said, the effort was misdirected.

"If the mayors were serious about reducing crime," he declared, "they would work with city prosecutors to enforce gun laws as opposed to having press conferences." [3]

Bloomberg blames illegally sold guns for much of the crime in New York City. He had city lawyers sue a total of 27 out-of-state dealers in May and December 2006, charging them with violating federal law by selling guns to "straw purchasers." In a straw purchase, a qualified gun purchaser fills out the paperwork for the federal background check and buys the gun for someone who would not be qualified to buy a gun. [4]

By March, 12 of the sued dealers had agreed to settlements that include monitoring of their operations, videotaping of transactions and training of store personnel. But the use of out-of-state undercover teams raised the ire of the

Guns and Schools

Gun policy debates in the United States since the 1960s have played out against the backdrop of recurrent fatal shootings at schools. Although school shootings have claimed relatively few lives in comparison to the total number of gun-related deaths, several of the incidents produced a pervasive sense of shock that added urgency to the gun debates. The Virginia Tech massacre, however, shook the nation profoundly and put gun policy back at the top of the national agenda after a period of relatively little action.

At least 30 major school shootings and massacres have occurred since the first — and also one of the deadliest — of the modern-era episodes: Charles Whitman's sniper shooting from the 27-story tower at the University of Texas in Austin on Aug. 1, 1966. [21]

Whitman, a UT student, killed 13 people and wounded 31 others, using an arsenal of three pistols and four rifles.

The lunch-hour massacre extended over 96 minutes until two Austin police officers broke into the barricaded observation deck and shot the former Eagle Scout and Marine. President Johnson responded to the tragedy by calling for stricter gun policies, but Congress did not act until after Rev. King and Sen. Kennedy were assassinated two years later. The tower sniper episode is credited, however, with prompting police departments to form SWAT ("specialized weapons and tactics") teams to handle such high-risk situations.

Three decades later, a rash of smaller-scale incidents over a period of several years presented what was in some respects a more troubling phenomenon: fatal

Virginia General Assembly, which passed a law in summer 2006 aimed at prohibiting the practice. [5]

Arulanandam says gun dealers violating the law should be prosecuted, but enforcement should be handled by the BATFE and "not the private police force of a billionaire politician." (Bloomberg amassed a fortune as head of a financial-information service before his election as New York's mayor in 2001.)

The mayors' issue in Congress stems from an appropriations rider sponsored by Rep. Todd Tiahrt, R-Kan., that limits the BATFE from sharing gun-trace data with local law enforcement unless related to a specific criminal case or investigation. Tiahrt says the amendment safeguards sensitive information that, if released, could jeopardize a criminal case. Bloomberg, however, says the limitation hampers local enforcement. And gun control groups say the amendment is principally aimed at protecting gun dealers and manufacturers from lawsuits. [6]

Tiahrt first added his amendment, which is supported by the NRA, to the BATFE funding measure in 2003. The NRA has been one of Tiahrt's major contributors since his first election to Congress in 1994. Today, Arulanandam says the amendment ensures that gun-trace information is used only for law enforcement purposes. "Politicians, special-interest groups and the media shouldn't have access to that information," he says.

But Bloomberg says the restriction handcuffs police departments. "Right now, federal law prevents our police officers from looking at all the data on guns used in crimes in our region," Bloomberg wrote in an op-ed article in *Newsweek* the week after the Virginia Tech massacre. "That means we can't easily identify crooked dealers and illegal trafficking patterns." [7]

Ten police organizations, including the International Association of Chiefs of Police, support repealing Tiahrt's amendment. But the Fraternal Order of Police, the largest police group, says repealing the amendment "could compromise the safety of law enforcement officers and the integrity of law enforcement investigations." [8]

[1] See Michael Bloomberg, "The Changing Gun Debate," *Newsweek*, April 30, 2007, p. 47; James O. E. Norell, "Tentacles," *America's 1st Freedom*, April 2007.

[2] www.mayorsagainstillegalguns.org.

[3] LaPierre quoted in Diane Cardwell, "N.R.A. Covers Bloomberg, and Results Aren't Pretty," *The New York Times*, April 15, 2007, sec. 1., p. 31; Arulanandam quoted in F. N. D'Alessio, "Bloomberg, Daley Lead Mayors in Coalition Against Gun Violence," Associated Press, Oct. 26, 2006.

[4] See Damien Cave, "6 Gun Dealers Will Allow City New Oversight," *The New York Times*, Dec. 8, 2006, p. A1.

[5] Associated Press, "Virginia Warns Bloomberg on New Gun Law," May 11, 2007.

[6] See Sam Hananel, "Lawmakers Ask Feds to Share Data on Guns," Associated Press, May 2, 2007. Some other background drawn from story.

[7] Bloomberg, *op. cit.*

[8] From a memo to the FOP executive board and other leaders from National President Chuck Canterbury, May 17, 2007; www.fop.net/servlet/display/news_article?id=441&XSL=xsl_pages%2fpublic_news_individual.xsl&nocache=12192484.

shootings at public schools by teenage or even pre-teenage students. In the deadliest of those incidents, two students at Columbine High School, near Littleton, Colo., killed 12 students and wounded 23 others on April 20, 1999, before committing suicide. Eric Harris and Dylan Klebold had plotted the massacre for a year as retaliation for what they saw as bullying and harassment from classmates. They used two sawed-off shotguns, a rifle and a semiautomatic pistol in a rampage that extended over more than four hours before the shooting stopped — allowing police to enter the school and find the bodies of Harris and Klebold and their victims.

Combined with earlier school shootings, Columbine spurred school districts around the country to institute new safety measures, including the use of metal detectors and security guards, as well as zero-tolerance policies for any student behavior deemed as even potentially violent. Many experts also called for stronger action by principals and teachers to prevent bullying or harassment of students by other classmates. [22] In Congress, lawmakers fashioned a post-Columbine bill that, among other things, increased penalties for providing guns to juveniles and prohibited importation of high-capacity ammunition clips. The Senate narrowly approved the measure, but gun control opponents voted it down in the House.

Cho's actions in the Virginia Tech massacre combined features of the University of Texas and Columbine shootings. Estranged from and resentful of his classmates, Cho specifically referred to Harris and Klebold as "martyrs" in the chilling videotape he mailed to NBC

Columbine killers Eric Harris, left, and Dylan Klebold, are shown at Columbine High School in a video they made for a school project before their rampage. They had plotted the massacre for a year in retaliation for what they saw as bullying and harassment from classmates.

News between the dormitory shootings and the classroom rampage two hours later. Like them, Cho apparently plotted the shootings over a long period — at least since the purchase of his first weapon two months earlier. At Norris Hall, Cho mimicked Whitman by sealing the building from the inside using chains and padlocks. And like Whitman — but unlike Harris and Klebold — Cho appears to have fired randomly.

Virginia Tech officials came under criticism almost immediately for failing to take quicker action to notify students and teachers about the shootings or to order a campus-wide "lockdown" — as had been done eight months earlier during a hunt for an escaped jail inmate. As Cho's history of disturbed behavior emerged, administrators also faced questions about whether other steps could have been taken to direct him to mental health treatment.

The day after the shootings, Gov. Kaine said he would create an independent commission to study the incident and recommend any steps to take. But Kaine said any gun policy debate was premature. "I think for people who want to take this after just 24 hours and make it into their political hobbyhorse to ride, I've got nothing but loathing for them," Kaine said. "They can take that elsewhere." [23]

CURRENT SITUATION

Making Campuses Safer

College campuses are relatively safe places, according to higher-education officials, but the Virginia Tech massacre is driving stepped-up efforts to make them safer.

Administrators at campuses around the country are putting new security measures in place while continuing to work on professionalizing campus police forces. Meanwhile, mental health experts are emphasizing the need to identify and provide treatment for students under stress and to address the legal and ethical issues of breaching confidentiality if a patient poses a risk of dangerous or violent behavior.

Just one week after the Virginia Tech shootings, the head of a university presidents' group told the Senate Homeland Security and Government Affairs Committee of steps undertaken by half-a-dozen universities "to prepare for the unthinkable and the unforeseen." [24]

Several of the measures cited by David Ward, president of the American Council on Education, seemed to directly address issues raised by Cho's rampage and Virginia Tech's response. Rice University and the University of Iowa, for example, are both installing improved campus communication systems, Ward told the committee. Johns Hopkins University is installing "smart" surveillance cameras linked to computers that can alert campus and local police of any suspicious situations. And the University of Minnesota has electronic access devices at 101 of its 270 buildings that can selectively lock and unlock doors and send emergency e-mail and phone messages.

Along with Ward, other witnesses called for colleges to have plans for dealing with any emergency or disaster. Healy of the campus law enforcement group and Irwin Redlener, director of the National Center for Disaster Preparedness at Columbia University's School of Public Health, both outlined steps for the federal government, such as establishing preparedness standards and studying ways to better identify students who are potential threats. Healy called for federal, state or local funding for campus police forces.

Colleges face problematic issues in dealing with students with mental health problems in part because of legal and ethical requirements of patient confidentiality. Two federal laws in particular limit sharing of informa-

Should guns be allowed on college campuses?

YES   **Larry Pratt**
Executive Director, Gun Owners of America

Written for *CQ Researcher*, May 2007

Gun-free school zones have proven to be a dangerous delusion that has resulted in people being forced to be victims.

The only people guaranteed to be safe in gun-free zones are criminals. They can count on the law-abiding being disarmed. In reality, gun-free zones are nothing more than criminal safe zones.

Criminals have proven that they not only disrespect laws, they are willing and able to break them. The island nation of Great Britain has banned guns. In 1997 they confiscated virtually all legal guns. Yet today, the police there estimate that England has twice the number of guns in the country — illegally. The press in Manchester refer to their city as "Gunchester."

Stricter gun control laws than those in the United States have not protected Canada, Scotland and Germany from mass murderers striking schools.

The solution is to empower the most responsible people in America to be intermixed with potential victims so that they might have the opportunity to be the first responders to head off attacks such as the one at Virginia Tech. We have enough people licensed to carry concealed firearms that we can now say with certainty that these are the folks who commit the fewest crimes in our society.

Concealed-weapons carriers commit even fewer violent crimes than do police.

Yet our federal and state laws (with a few exceptions such as Utah and Arizona) prohibit these potential Good Samaritans from being armed on our college campuses. One concealed-carry permit holder is a graduate student at Virginia Tech. After a murder at the edge of the campus last August, he wrote a letter to the editor of the local paper, confessing that he had not been carrying his gun on campus because he did not want to jeopardize his graduate career should he get caught. But afterwards, he noted, he considered the fact that had he been killed, that also would have jeopardized his graduate career.

We have seen that armed civilians, students and staff alike have been able to get their guns and stop campus killers in the past — such as in Pearl, Miss., (1997) and Grundy, Va., (2002). But in those cases, the heroes had to run to their cars and get their guns and run back to the scene of the crime to stop the killer, losing valuable time.

Armed self-defense works. Disarmament kills.

NO   **Paul Helmke**
President, Brady Campaign to Prevent Gun Violence

Written for *CQ Researcher*, May 2007

College campuses will not be safer if we give everyone a gun and encourage the crossfire. Schools should be sanctuaries where students can grow and learn in an environment free from the risks of gunfire. The fact that such sanctuaries have been invaded by dangerous individuals with guns is a reason to strengthen state and federal laws designed to keep guns away from people like the shooter at Virginia Tech, not to weaken policies that tightly restrict firearms on campus. A thorough Brady background check would have stopped the purchase of the guns used in that massacre. This is a far more effective way to reduce the risks of gun violence on college campuses, and one that carries no downsides.

Despite the horrific massacre at Virginia Tech, college and university campuses are much safer than the communities that surround them. College students are almost 20 percent less likely than non-students of the same age to experience violence, and 93 percent of the violence against students occurs off campus.

If students and teachers start carrying guns on campus, we can anticipate the increased dangers and risks that will follow: greater potential for student-on-student and student-on-faculty violence, and more lethal results when such violence occurs; an increased risk of suicide attempts ending in fatalities; and gun thefts and subsequent harm to people on and off campus.

The college-age years — 18 to 24 — are the most volatile years in most people's lives. These are the peak years for binge drinking and drug use, mental health challenges and suicide risks — and commission of violent gun crimes, including homicides. Two studies have confirmed that college gun owners are more likely than the average student to engage in binge drinking, need an alcoholic drink first thing in the morning, use cocaine or crack, be arrested for a DUI, vandalize property, be injured in an alcohol-related fight and get in trouble with police. Binge-drinking, drug-using students are dangerous enough; let's not give them guns.

The Virginia Tech shooter was a 23-year-old college student who the Commonwealth of Virginia thought was a lawful firearms purchaser. Allowing guns on college campuses would not only have armed him more easily, but other potentially dangerous individuals as well.

Adding more guns to a home, a state or a country leads to more gun violence, not less. The same lesson holds true for schools, too.

President Bill Clinton and James Brady, former press secretary to President Ronald Reagan, attend a ceremony commemorating the seventh anniversary of the Brady law. After he was wounded in a 1981 assassination attempt on Reagan, Brady and his wife, Sarah, helped pass the landmark gun-control legislation, which Clinton signed into law on Nov. 30, 1993.

tion about students with mental health problems. The Family and Educational Rights and Privacy Act generally prevents universities from disclosing student records, including any mental health counseling or treatment, to anyone — including the student's family. Separately, the Health Insurance Portability and Accountability Act prevents a health-care facility from communicating with an educational institution about any treatment it may have provided to a student.

Cho's family has indicated they were aware of his emotional difficulties from an early age, but it is not clear what information his parents had regarding his behavioral problems at Virginia Tech or the mental health proceeding in December 2005 when he was ordered to get outpatient psychological treatment. Virginia Tech mental health officials have declined to discuss Cho's case because of privacy laws, but it appears unlikely that the school was informed of the order. In any event, *Washington Post* reporters concluded three weeks after the shootings, neither the court nor the school followed up on the order. [25]

Russ Federman, director of counseling and psychological services at the University of Virginia, told the Senate committee a survey of university counseling centers indicated that about 9 percent of enrolled students sought psychological help in 2006, but a separate survey indicated a much larger incidence of emotional prob-

lems. The survey by the American College Health Association indicated that nearly half of students surveyed — 44 out of 100 — reported feeling so depressed it was difficult to function, 18 out of 100 reported a serious depressive disorder and 9 out of 100 had seriously considered suicide within the previous year.

Most psychological problems pose no special risk of violence, Federman said. But he said universities "need to be able to communicate with one another, and sometimes with parents, when student threat of harm reaches a threshold where the university community is no longer safe."

Federman believes the educational privacy law does allow discretion to breach patient confidentiality when necessary. But Redlener and Ward both urged the senators to revise the law to provide more discretion. "I think we got a positive response from Congress . . . on putting some flexibility into the law," Ward says.

Meanwhile, elected state officials are responding to Virginia Tech in various ways, according to *The Chronicle of Higher Education.* [26] Maine lawmakers are studying whether the state's colleges have appropriate authority to regulate firearms on campuses. By contrast, Gov. Rick Perry, R-Texas, and some Republican legislators are considering a possible repeal of the state law banning possession of firearms on campus. In at least two states — Florida and Wisconsin — governors are following Virginia's example in creating special panels to examine campus-security issues.

Improving Gun Checks

Gun control supporters are renewing efforts to strengthen the federal background-check system for gun purchases in the wake of the Virginia Tech massacre, but they acknowledge they have little chance of winning congressional passage of any other measures.

The information gaps in the National Instant Criminal Background Check System have been recognized by the government and advocacy groups on both sides of the gun policy debate for years. But they are now a primary focus of the post-Virginia Tech debate because of Cho's ability to purchase two pistols after a favorable background check despite a disqualifying prior adjudication of dangerousness due to mental illness.

Testifying before a House subcommittee on May 10, Brady Campaign President Helmke said the background check cleared Cho to buy the weapons because of "lethal loopholes" in the system. Virginia law did not count Cho's earlier diagnosis as disqualifying even though federal law did. Effective background checks "would have stopped the sale," Helmke told the House Oversight and Reform Domestic Policy Subcommittee. [27]

A ranking Justice Department official told the panel that both the FBI and the Bureau of Alcohol, Tobacco and Firearms have made "continuing efforts" to encourage states to correct what she called "the limited submission . . . of disqualifying mental health records." But Rachel Brand, assistant attorney general for legal policy, said some states have privacy laws prohibiting the furnishing of the information, and others lack the resources to do a better job.

National Alliance for Mental Illness lobbyist Honberg, however, called for narrowing the definitions used in the law before addressing states' failure to comply with reporting requirements. Honberg said the term "mental defective" used in the law is "vague and outmoded" and the use of involuntary commitment as a disqualification too broad. In addition, he said, the law should be amended to give persons with mental illness a procedure to be removed from the disqualified list and to limit the information provided to a person's name and address without specifying the reason for being on the list.

The NRA supports improving the background-check system, but a second, smaller gun group opposes moves to tighten the screening process. "It wasn't a good idea in theory," says Gun Owners of America consultant Hammond. "It's been used by people who don't like firearms to try to do away with firearms."

Legislation introduced in Congress would provide up to $350 million to states to improve their reporting of mental health and other records to the federal background-check system. The bill is sponsored in the House by Rep. Carolyn McCarthy, a New York Democrat whose husband was killed in 1993 by a gunman on the Long Island Rail Road. The chief Senate sponsor is another New York Democrat, Sen. Charles E. Schumer.

The bills seek to close another major gap in the background-check system by requiring states to automate criminal-justice records. Brand told the subcommittee that about half the arrest records in the interstate database scanned by the background-check system are missing dispositions. The missing information causes background checks to be delayed, often for more than three days, she said. An application not acted on after three days is approved by default.

In a new report, the pro-gun control group Third Way also points to large gaps in the background-check system despite some improvements since a comparable report in 2002. The number of mental health disqualifications in the federal database has increased from about 90,000 then to 234,628 today, the report says. But that number accounts for less than 10 percent of the 2.6 million such records that the Government Accountability Office estimates should be in the system. [28]

The report estimates that one-fourth of felony convictions are not available in the database. But it credits states with improved reporting of domestic violence misdemeanor convictions and restraining orders since Congress amended the law in 1996 to add those to the list of disqualifications for possessing or buying a firearm.

Support for the McCarthy-Schumer legislation is seen as building on Capitol Hill, but Third Way's vice president for policy Jim Kessler says the bill could languish if Congress does not move quickly. "There's a will to do something," says Kessler, a former Schumer aide. "But you have to strike while the iron's hot because when momentum fades, complacency takes over."

In his testimony, Helmke also called for requiring background checks for gun sales by private individuals, not just by licensed gun dealers as under current law. That change would close what gun control groups called the "gun show loophole" that allows buyers at those events to circumvent the background check. Helmke also called for restoring a ban on assault weapons such as Uzis and AK-47s. Kessler says he doubts that Congress will act on either of those issues.

The Bush administration has not taken a position on the McCarthy-Schumer legislation. But the administration has proposed a measure to give the attorney general discretion to deny gun sales to suspected terrorists. Sen. Frank Lautenberg, D-N.J., is sponsoring the administration proposal in the Senate.

OUTLOOK

"Our Minds Still Reel"

Congratulations mixed with condolences, smiles with tears, as Virginia Tech prepared to graduate some 4,800 students on the weekend of May 11-12 — less than four weeks after one of the school's own carried out the deadliest shooting by an individual in U.S. history.

"Today is a special day, a time of celebration," university President Steger told the crowd of 30,000 assembled in the school's Lane Stadium. But the celebration was necessarily "subdued," he added, in recognition of the "great tragedy" of April 16. "Our minds still reel from the violence," he said. [29]

Even as the nation reeled from the news of the massacre, however, gun violence continued elsewhere across the country. The day after Cho's rampage, New York City police said a 20-year-old man with a history of mental disturbance shot and killed his mother, her companion and her companion's health-care aide in what *The New York Times* account described as "a quiet Queens neighborhood." Three days later, a NASA worker apparently fearful of being fired barricaded himself inside a Johnson Space Center building in Houston and shot one of two hostages before killing himself. [30]

In an ironic symmetry, the Brady Campaign's Helmke notes that the death toll in Blacksburg — 32 not counting Cho — equals the daily average of gun homicides in the United States. "That's a Virginia Tech massacre every day in our streets and in our homes," Helmke says.

To stem the violence, gun control supporters call for stronger laws — by which they mean more thoroughgoing enforcement of existing restrictions on owning or possessing firearms, prohibitions on specific types of weapons or ammunition and mandatory safety features on firearms, especially handguns. Virginia Tech "points out to people how poorly enforced our laws are," Helmke says. "It points out to people how easy it is to get a gun."

The NRA and other gun groups also call for stronger laws, but they want stiffer penalties for people who commit crimes using guns. "Any substantive measure aimed at decreasing crime ought to have the vital component of the criminal, and stiffer penalty for the criminal, as the major part of it," says NRA spokesman Arulanandam.

The Virginia Tech massacre may change the climate on college and university campuses in ways comparable to the heightened emphasis on security in the United States after the Sept. 11 terrorist attacks in 2001. College campuses are not like airports, but security precautions are likely to increase. Virginia Tech graduates, for example, were asked to wear their academic gowns open and to pass through metal detectors.

"There will be more meetings between police chiefs and the [campus] operating officer. There will be more meetings about dorm safety," says American Council on Education President Ward. "There will be greater consciousness of the need to be aware of this potentiality."

"It would be an absolute shame if we weren't better prepared a year from now," says Princeton's Healy. "If this situation does not prompt people to action, I don't know what will."

Mental health advocates hope that Virginia Tech will also bring about increased attention to — and increased funding for — mental health services. "For us, the thing that the Virginia Tech tragedy teaches us the most is that we have in most parts of the country, including that part of Virginia, no mental health system," says the National Alliance on Mental Illness' Honberg. "As a result, people who need treatment tend to fall between the cracks. And that's what happened to [Cho]."

Opposing advocates and experts, however, doubt that Virginia Tech will fundamentally change the broader debate over gun policy. "The gun rights/gun control debate has prevailed for decades," says Arulanandam, "and it will likely prevail for another year or three years or five years — and possibly longer."

"Congress has not shown the political will to do anything," says Helmke. "When the immediate incident fades, it's a lot easier for elected officials to do nothing, especially when they're concerned about the perceived power of the gun rights advocates."

Reminders of the massacre were all around on the Virginia Tech campus, however, during commencement weekend. [31] Stone markers on the drill field bore the names of Cho's victims; nearby, on Cho's unmarked memorial, a printed sheet bore the biblical injunction: "You shalt not kill." Cho's name went unmentioned during the ceremonies. But his 27 student victims were awarded posthumous degrees.

"It is our sacred duty to mourn those who lost their lives so suddenly and tragically and to help their friends and their families through these most difficult of times," keynote speaker Gen. John Abizaid, former commander of the U.S. Central Command, told the audience.

Many of the graduates had already adopted the message. Written on their mortarboards for all to see was the motto unofficially adopted on campus since April 16: "We will prevail."

NOTES

1. Accounts of Cho's gun purchases drawn from Brigid Schulte, "Kaine May Seek More Data for Gun Sales," *The Washington Post*, April 25, 2007, p. 1A; Laurence Hammack, "Gun Sale Policy in Va. Broke Down, Lawyer Says," *Roanoke Times*, April 21, 2007, p. 5; Thomas Frank and Chris Colston, "Despite questions about mental state, Cho could buy gun," *USA Today*, April 19, 2007, p. 10A. For an early comprehensive account of Cho's mental state, see N. R. Kleinfield, "Before Deadly Rage, a Lifetime Consumed by a Troubling Silence," *The New York Times*, April 22, 2007, sec. 1., p. 1.

2. For background, see these *CQ Researcher* reports: Bob Adams, "Gun Control Debate," Nov. 12, 2004, pp. 949-972; Kenneth Jost, "Gun Control Standoff," Dec. 19, 1997, pp. 1105-1128; Richard L. Worsnop, "Gun Control," June 10, 1994, pp. 505-528.

3. A study completed in 1997 estimated 192 million privately owned firearms, including 65 million handguns. See "Guns in America: National Survey on Private Ownership and Use of Firearms, National Institute of Justice, May 1997, cited in Robert J. Spitzer, *The Politics of Gun Control* (4th ed.), 2007, p. 6. Jim Kessler, vice president for policy of the progressive, pro-gun control group Third Way, estimates current ownership at 250 million based on approximately 8 million background checks for new purchases per year with some reduction for lost or destroyed weapons; he says other estimates are lower. As for household ownership, in one recent poll 50 percent of those responding said they or someone in their household owned a gun; the account noted that previous polls had indicated household ownership rates of 42 percent to 48 percent. See Dana Blanton, "FOX News Poll: Would Tougher Gun Laws Have Helped Stop Virginia Tech Rampage?" April 22, 2007; www.foxnews.com/story/0,2933,267085,00.html.

4. See "Web-Based Injury Statistics Query and Reporting System," Centers for Disease Control and Prevention; www.cdc.gov/ncipc/wisqars.

5. The group's Campus Preparedness Resource Center can be found at www.iaclea.org/visitors/wmdcpt/cprc/aboutcprc.cfm.

6. See Brigid Schulte and Chris L. Jenkins, "Cho Didn't Get Court-Ordered Treatment," *The Washington Post*, May 7, 2007, p. A1.

7. See Schulte, April 25, 2007, *op. cit.*; Michael Luo, "U.S. Law Barred Sale of Weapons to Campus Killer," *The New York Times*, April 21, 2007, p. A1.

8. Third Way, "Missing Records: Holes in Background Check System Allow Illegal Buyers to Get Guns," May 14, 2007; www.third-way.com.

9. The statutory provision is 18 U.S.C. section 922(d)(4); the regulations can be found at 27 CFR 555.11.

10. Tim Craig, "Ban on Sale of Guns to Mentally Ill Expanded," *The Washington Post*, May 1, 2007, p. B1.

11. Glenn Reynolds, "Armed college students mean fewer victims," *Rocky Mountain News* (Denver, Colo.), April 21, 2007, p. 28.

12. See Gary Kleck, *Targeting Guns: Firearms and Their Control* (1997); John R. Lott Jr., *More Guns, Less Crime: Misunderstanding Crime and Gun Control Law* (1998). For a summary of the critiques, see Spitzer, *op. cit.*, pp. 57-68.

13. Background drawn in part from *ibid.*

14. Richard Hofstadter, "America as a Gun Culture," *American Heritage*, October 1970, pp. 85ff.

15. See Spitzer, *op. cit.*

16. *Ibid.*, pp. 7-12. Bellesiles' book, *Arming America: The Origins of a National Gun Culture*, originally published by Vintage, was reissued by Soft Skull Press after Vintage discontinued publication in 2003. Bellesiles resigned from the Emory professorship at the end of 2002 after an academic panel concluded he had been guilty of "unprofessional and misleading work" — an accusation that Bellesiles denied. See "Author of Gun Report Quits After Panel Faults Research," The Associated Press, Oct. 27, 2002.

17. See Alexander DeConde, *Gun Violence in America: The Struggle for Control* (2000). DeConde is professor of history emeritus, University of California-Santa Barbara.

18. See "Firearms Control," *Editorial Research Reports*, Nov. 11, 1959, at *CQ Researcher Plus Archive*, CQ Electronic Library, http://library.cqpress.com.

19. See *Congressional Quarterly, Congress and the Nation, Vol. II*, 1965-1968, pp. 328-330.

20. Spitzer, *op. cit.*, p. 125.

21. See Agence France-Presse, "The long history of deadly shootings at U.S. schools," April 16, 2007. For additional background, see Kathy Koch, "School Violence," *CQ Researcher*, Oct. 9, 1998, pp. 881-904; and Kathy Koch, "Zero Tolerance for School Violence," *CQ Researcher*, March 10, 2000, pp. 185-208.

22. For background, see John Greenya, "Bullying," *CQ Researcher*, Feb. 4, 2005, pp. 101-124, and Sarah Glazer, "Boys' Emotional Needs," *CQ Researcher*, June 18, 1999, pp. 521-544.

23. See Carlos Santos and Rex Bowman, "Independent Panel to Study Actions Taken at Va. Tech," *Richmond Times-Dispatch*, April 18, 2007.

24. For coverage, see Adam Schreck, "Senate Hearing Focuses on Campus Safety," *Los Angeles Times*, April 24, 2007, p. A16; Michael Luo, "Senators Discuss Preventing College Attacks," *The New York Times*, April 24, 2007, p. A17.

25. Schulte and Jenkins, *op. cit.*

26. See Sara Hebel, "States Review Campus-Safety Policies," *The Chronicle of Higher Education*, May 11, 2007.

27. For coverage, see Peter Hardin, "Closing Firearm Loopholes Explored," *Richmond Times Dispatch*, May 11, 2007, p. A7; Dale Eisman, "Gun-Control Group: Cho Exposed Loophole," *The Virginian-Pilot* (Norfolk), May 11, 2007, p. A15.

28. Third Way, "Missing Records: Holes in Background Check System Allow Illegal Buyers to Get Guns," May 2007; www.third-way.com.

29. Accounts drawn from Rex Bowman, "Mourning Continues on Graduation Day," *Richmond Times Dispatch*, May 12, 2007, p. A1.

30. Cara Buckley and Thomas J. Lueck, "Queens Man Kills Mother and 2 Others, Then Himself," *The New York Times*, April 18, 2007, p. B1; Peggy O'Hare, Paige Hewitt, Mark Carreau and Bill Murphy, "JCS Shooter Lived in Fear of Losing Job," *The Houston Chronicle*, April 22, 2007, p. A1.

31. Some details from Greg Esposito, Christina Rogers and Anna Mallory, "The Promise of Tomorrow," *Roanoke Times*, May 12, 2007, Virginia Tech Commencement: p. 1; Joe Kennedy, "Emotions Run Gamut on Day of Joy Sorrow," *ibid.*, p. 2.

BIBLIOGRAPHY

Books

Bogus, Carl T. (ed.), *The Second Amendment in Law and History: Historians and Constitutional Scholars on the Right to Bear Arms*, **New Press, 2000.**
Ten contributors carefully examine the history and current meaning of the Second Amendment from a variety of perspectives — all concluding that it affirms the states' rights to organize a militia but not an individual right to possession of firearms. Bogus, a professor at Roger Williams University School of Law, provides an insightful overview of "the history and politics of Second Amendment scholarship" to open the book. Includes detailed chapter notes.

Halbrook, Stephen P., *That Every Man Be Armed: The Evolution of a Constitutional Right* (2d ed.), **Independent Institute, 1994.**
The longtime gun rights advocate traces what he calls "the deep history" of "the right of the citizen to keep arms" from Greek and Roman times through the American Revolution and subsequent U.S. history. Includes case index, detailed notes.

Hemenway, David, *Private Guns, Public Health*, **University of Michigan Press, 2004.**
A professor of health policy at Harvard's School of Public Health — and a gun control advocate — argues that gun violence and gun-related injuries are a major public health problem that calls for gun safety measures and nationwide licensing and registration of guns. Includes tables, appendixes, 46-page bibliography; an afterword is included in a paperbound edition issued in 2006.

Kleck, Gary, and Don B. Kates, *Armed: New Perspective on Gun Control*, **Prometheus, 2001.**

Two longtime critics of restrictive gun measures argue in eight separate chapters that academic scholarship and news coverage are slanted in favor of gun control, that defensive gun use is more common and more effective than gun control proponents contend and that the Second Amendment protects a personal right to possess firearms. Includes detailed chapter notes. Kleck, a professor of criminology at Florida State University, is author of the earlier book, *Targeting Guns: Firearms and Gun Control* (Aldine de Gruyter, 1997). Kates, a retired professor of constitutional law, is affiliated with Pacific Research Institute, a free-market think tank in San Francisco.

Lott, John R. Jr., *The Bias Against Guns: Why Almost Everything You've Heard About Gun Control Is Wrong*, Regnery, 2003.
An economist reargues with updated statistics his earlier thesis that states with higher gun ownership have lower crime rates overall and contends that news organizations and the government minimize the benefits of defensive gun use because of a bias against firearms. Lott is now a visiting professor at the State University of New York, Binghamton. His earlier book is *More Guns, Less Crime: Understanding Crime and Gun Control Laws* (2d ed.), University of Chicago Press, 2000.

Spitzer, Robert J., *The Politics of Gun Control* (4th ed.), CQ Press, 2007 (forthcoming).
A professor of political science at the State University of New York, Cortland, discusses the history of gun use and gun controls in the United States and the current political environment on the issue, along with a proposed "new framework" for gun policy. Includes detailed chapter notes.

Virginia Tech Massacre: News Coverage

National, regional and local news media covered the Virginia Tech massacre intensively from the day of the shootings (April 16, 2007) through the university's graduation ceremonies four weeks later (May 11-12, 2007).

The Roanoke (Va.) *Times* has PDFs of the special print sections for the week after the tragedy on its Web site (www.roanoke.com); the site also includes subsequent stories and a four-page graduation section.

The Richmond (Va.) *Times-Dispatch* and two other Media General news organizations — the *Lynchburg* (Va.) *News & Advance* and NewsChannel 10 in Roanoke — have a comprehensive Web site "Tragedy in Blacksburg" that includes the *Times-Dispatch's* four-page, same-day extra edition along with photos, slide shows, audio and video and profiles of each of the 32 people killed (http://media.mgnetwork.com/imd/VT Shooting/index.htm).

The New York Times and *The Washington Post* provided comprehensive coverage, much of which was used in preparing this report. In addition to stories specifically footnoted in the text, one vivid reconstruction of the shootings is David Maraniss, "That Was the Desk I Chose to Die Under," *The Washington Post*, April 19, 2007.

Time and *Newsweek* both published comprehensive packages on April 30, 2007. In addition to stories recounting the shootings, each of the magazines had articles exploring the causes of mass killings: Sharon Begley, "The Anatomy of Violence," *Newsweek*, pp. 40-46; Jeffrey Kluger, "Why They Kill," *Time*, pp. 54-59.

For More Information

Brady Center to Prevent Gun Violence, 1225 I St., N.W., Suite 1100, Washington, DC 20005; (202) 289-7319; www.bradycenter.org. Nonpartisan, grass-roots organization dedicated to ending gun violence without banning all guns.

Coalition to Stop Gun Violence, 1023 15th St., N.W., Suite 301, Washington, DC 20005; (202) 408-0061; www.csgv.org. Coalition of 45 national organizations — including religious organizations, child welfare advocates and public health professionals — pushing a progressive agenda to reduce firearm death and injury.

Gun Owners of America, 8001 Forbes Place, Suite 102, Springfield, VA 22151; (703) 321-8585; www.gunowners.org. Nonprofit lobbying organization defending Second Amendment rights of gun owners.

International Association of Campus Law Enforcement Administrators, 342 N. Main St., West Hartford, CT 06117-2507; (860) 586-7517; www.iaclea.org. Advances public safety for educational institutions through educational resources, advocacy and professional development.

National Alliance on Mental Illness, Colonial Place Three, 2107 Wilson Blvd., Suite 300, Arlington, VA 22201-3042; (703) 524-7600; www.nami.org. Grass-roots organization seeking to eradicate mental illness and improve the lives of those affected.

National Center for Disaster Preparedness, Mailman School of Public Health, Columbia University, 722 W. 168th St., 10th Floor, New York, NY 10032; (212) 342-5161; www.ncdp.mailman.columbia.edu. Academically based, interdisciplinary program focusing on the nation's capacity to prevent and respond to terrorism and other major disasters.

National Rifle Association, 11250 Waples Mill Rd., Fairfax, VA 22030; (800) 672-3888; www.nra.org. Promotes the safety, education and responsibility of gun ownership.

Second Amendment Foundation, 12500 N.E. 10th Place, Bellevue, WA 98005; (425) 454-7012; www.saf.org. Educational and legal policy center dedicated to promoting a better understanding about our Constitutional heritage to privately own and possess firearms.

Third Way, 2000 L St., N.W., Suite 702, Washington, DC 20036-4915; (202) 775-3768; www.third-way.com. Nonprofit, nonpartisan policy center for progressives incorporating as one initiative the former organization Americans for Gun Safety.

7

The New Environmentalism

Tom Price

Huge windows reduce energy bills at the experimental Wal-Mart Super Store that opened in Aurora, Colo., in November 2005. The eco-friendly store uses recycled materials for construction and solar and wind power to supplement standard power sources. Wal-Mart and many other businesses are jumping on the conservation bandwagon, joining environmental groups they once fought with.

From *CQ Researcher,*
December 1, 2006.

A cross the globe, evidence abounds of a rising concern for protecting the planet.

But the new concern about the environment is not your father's environmental movement. Corporate executives, investors, conservative Christians, labor unions and others not traditionally associated with the cause have joined the intensifying campaign to save the Earth. There's even a handful of environmentalists who are promoting nuclear power.

- Environmental Defense, a leading advocacy group, hires a director of corporate partnerships and begins helping businesses "go green." Among the many fruits of these collaborations: fuel-efficient hybrid FedEx delivery trucks, reusable UPS shipping envelopes and measures to cut greenhouse-gas emissions at DuPont facilities that saved the company $325 million in one year. [1]
- The National Association of Evangelicals — known for conservative politics — proclaims a "sacred responsibility to steward the Earth," urging governments to "encourage fuel efficiency, reduce pollution, encourage sustainable use of natural resources and provide for the proper care of wildlife and their natural habitats." [2]
- British chemist and environmentalist James Lovelock — famous for arguing that Earth acts as a self-sustaining organism — says building more nuclear power plants is "the only green solution" to the threat of global warming. [3]

In the burgeoning, new environmental movement, a growing number of people are perceiving threats to the environment, busi-

145

Public Support for Environment Is Up

Support for the environment is up after taking a big dip beginning in 2000. Pro-environment respondents outnumbered pro-economy respondents by 17 percentage points in 2005 and 15 points this year.

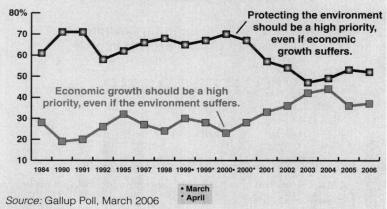

Percentages of Americans who agree with the following statements:

Protecting the environment should be a high priority, even if economic growth suffers.

Economic growth should be a high priority, even if the environment suffers.

• March
* April

Source: Gallup Poll, March 2006

nesses are jumping on the conservation bandwagon and environmentalists are joining hands with groups they once crossed swords with.

"We're seeing the environmental movement getting deeper and broader at the same time," says Rainforest Action Network Executive Director Michael Brune. "We're seeing an increase in straight-up, old-school, traditional grassroots activists wanting to get involved. We're also seeing genuine interest from the business community, evangelicals, labor and other non-traditional allies."

In the words of Oklahoma State University sociology Professor Riley Dunlap, who has studied public opinion about the environment for 40 years and is the Gallup Organization's environmental scholar, "These local government initiatives, state initiatives, corporate initiatives represent a different kind of environmentalism."

The broadening consensus has been spurred mainly by concerns that global warming poses a real and potentially catastrophic threat to life on Earth but that a conservative federal government refuses to act.

"There's undoubtedly a buzz about global warming that wasn't there a year ago," says David Yarnold, executive vice president of Environmental Defense. "The sense

of urgency has grown. And the more people learn about climate change, the more they want to know what they can do."

In a July poll by the Pew Research Center, 70 percent of Americans said there is "solid evidence" for global warming, and 74 percent said it constitutes a serious or somewhat serious problem. In a measure of public confusion about the topic and what should be done, however, 59 percent who believed in global warming thought human activity is the cause, while 30 percent blamed natural climate patterns. [4]

In another poll last January, Pew found that nearly 60 percent of Americans wanted the federal government to make energy and the environment top priorities, the highest percentage since 2001. [5] A Harris Poll last year found three-quarters of Americans feel "protecting the environment is so important that requirements and standards cannot be too high, and continuing environmental improvements must be made regardless of cost." [6]

Despite pubic support, "there's been an appalling vacuum of leadership coming from within the [Washington] Beltway — on both sides of the aisle," Brune says. "The current administration and [Republican-controlled] Congress can't be accused of being environmental leaders, but even most Democrats haven't been stepping up and showing an appropriate level of response to the environmental threats we face."

In the absence of action in Washington, he adds, "You're seeing a lot of others trying to show leadership."

Although environmentalists were heartened by the Democratic capture of Congress in the November 2006 elections, they're not expecting revolutionary changes in federal policies. President George W. Bush has two more years in office, Democrats hold only a slim majority in the Senate and not all Democrats are environmentalists. For instance, Rep. John D. Dingell, D-Mich. — the presumptive chair of the Energy and Commerce Committee, whose district includes Detroit — has opposed raising automobile gas-mileage requirements.

The most that U.S. Greenpeace Executive Director John Passacantando expects out of the Democrats are "some baby steps." So environmentalists aren't about to change the strategy they've developed since Republicans seized control of Congress in 1994: influencing corporations and state and local governments.

Environmental Defense presents itself to businesses essentially as a consulting firm, offering advice on how they can increase profits by adopting green business practices. The more aggressive Rainforest Action Network (RAN) also enters partnerships — but usually only after businesses succumb to public protests.

"We're not as confrontational as some other groups," says Gwen Ruta, Environmental Defense's corporate partnership director. "We've had pretty good success in going to companies in the spirit of cooperation and saying, 'This is what we want to do.' "

RAN usually stages public demonstrations to "get on the radar screen," says Ilyse Hogue, who manages the organization's campaign to promote green banking, or socially responsible investing. Once a bank agrees to work with her organization, she says, "the intellectual capital at these institutions is so vast that it's fun to participate in the dialogue. These are very bright people who just never really looked at these issues."

Investors also are pressuring companies to adopt green business practices, using tactics such as proposing policy resolutions at shareholders' meetings or investing only in corporations with positive environmental records. How-to guides to shareholder activism have been published both by Friends of the Earth and a partnership of the As You Sow Foundation and Rockefeller Philanthropy Advisors. [7]

"Not to engage the private sector is to miss a huge opportunity to have a positive impact on global warming," says Rockefeller Senior Vice President Doug Bauer.

Some investors band together to increase their clout. Through the Carbon Disclosure Project, for instance, major global investors each year ask about 2,000 companies — including the world's largest 500 — to reveal their impact on greenhouse-gas emissions. In 2006, 225 investors with $31.5 trillion in assets made the request — up from 143 investors the year before. Nearly three-quarters of the largest 500 companies responded this year, up from just under 50 percent in 2005. [8]

The project aims to spur companies to reduce emissions after they've compiled the information needed for

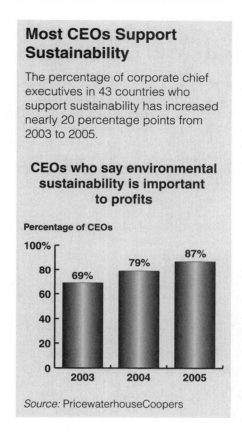

Most CEOs Support Sustainability

The percentage of corporate chief executives in 43 countries who support sustainability has increased nearly 20 percentage points from 2003 to 2005.

CEOs who say environmental sustainability is important to profits

Percentage of CEOs

- 2003: 69%
- 2004: 79%
- 2005: 87%

Source: PricewaterhouseCoopers

the report. Wal-Mart's experience indicates that's happening. In preparing its report, Wal-Mart discovered that refrigerants used in its grocery stores caused more of the company's "greenhouse-gas footprint" than its truck fleet did. Wal-Mart said it is acting on that discovery. (*See sidebar, p. 148.*)

Complaining that the federal government is not acting effectively, cities and states are adopting their own environmental-protection programs — forcing nationwide companies to cope with a patchwork of environmental regulations.

Nearly half the states are requiring that power plants use at least some renewable fuels, and California just mandated cuts in motor vehicles' carbon dioxide emissions. If that law withstands the auto industry's challenges, other states are prepared to act. Meanwhile, just as they did in striving to reduce acid rain, Northeastern states are establishing a consortium to set limits on greenhouse-gas emissions, distribute emission allowances to plants and permit cleaner plants to sell their allowances

Wal-Mart Sets Ambitious "Green" Goals

Wal-Mart, the world's largest retailer, wants to be the greenest as well. President and Chief Executive Officer Lee Scott laid out the corporation's ambitious long-term goals a year ago: to use only renewable energy, to create no waste and to sell products that "sustain our resources and environment."

He also established specific short-term goals:

- increase truck fuel efficiency by 25 percent in three years and 100 percent in 10;
- cut store energy consumption by 30 percent and reduce facility greenhouse-gas emissions by 20 percent in seven years;
- reduce solid waste at stores by 25 percent in three years;
- establish a program within 18 months that gives preference to suppliers that "aggressively" reduce their greenhouse-gas emissions, and
- increase sales of organic food and other environmentally friendly products.

"Environmental problems are *our* problems," Scott told employees at the company's Bentonville, Ark., headquarters. Solving them is good for humanity, he said, and it's good for business. [1]

During 2005, Wal-Mart opened two experimental stores — in McKinney, Texas, and Aurora, Colo. — to test green technology.

Highly efficient light-emitting diodes — or LEDs — illuminate exterior signs and interior display cases. Heating systems burn cooking oil and motor oil from the stores' restaurants and auto repair shops. Heat is recovered from refrigerators and freezers, and solar collectors and wind turbines supply electricity. Doors were installed on refrigerated cases that usually are left open, and their lights brighten and dim as shoppers open and close the doors. The restrooms have water-conserving sinks, and the men's rooms use waterless urinals. Countertops are made with recycled glass and concrete.

Outside, drought-tolerant vegetation cuts the water needed for irrigation. Food waste is composted and sold. Roads are paved with recycled materials, and concrete is mixed with fly ash from burned coal and slag from steel production. [2]

Some of the innovations were immediate hits, the company reported in a one-year review, while others "still need to be refined." Some of the earliest successes — the lighting, landscaping, sinks and urinals — will begin showing up in other Wal-Marts in 2007. The company hopes the other innovations will prove themselves over the next two years.

"Due to our size and scope, we are uniquely positioned to have great success and impact in the world, perhaps like no company before us," Scott said.

Seemingly small changes, when Wal-Mart makes them, can save millions of dollars.

Because its truck fleet travels a billion miles a year, for instance, raising fuel efficiency by just one mile per gallon would save the company more than $52 million annually at current fuel prices, Scott said. Meeting his goal of doubling efficiency by 2015 would jump that savings to $310 million.

If the company could sell one compact fluorescent light bulb to each of the 100-plus million shoppers who walk into Wal-Mart stores every week, those customers' electric bills would drop a collective $3 billion. If the company succeeds in encouraging green practices by its 60,000 suppliers and 1.3 million employees, environmental benefits will ripple around the world. [3]

Known primarily for its low prices, Wal-Mart confronts a stiff challenge in selling green products that often cost more than their non-green counterparts.

to dirtier facilities. Western states are crafting a similar agreement. [9]

Gov. Arnold Schwarzenegger, R-Calif., reached across the Atlantic to explore global-warming strategies with British Prime Minister Tony Blair. Former President Bill Clinton is discussing emission-reduction efforts with leaders of the world's 22 largest cities. [10]

Labor unions — which in the past clashed with environmentalists — have joined the new movement through the Apollo Alliance for Good Jobs and Clean Energy. [11]

Named for the project that put man on the moon, the alliance promotes both jobs and the environment through government incentives for high-mileage autos, clean and efficient manufacturing, green buildings, renewable energy, public transportation and hydrogen-fuel technology. [12]

Environmentalism has become such a popular topic that it turned former Vice President Al Gore into a best-selling author and movie star while inspiring a real movie star — Leonardo DiCaprio — to try to take environmentalism to television. Gore's book about the threat of

"We've seen that if a green product costs the same, it's a runaway success," Vice President Andrew Ruben says. "If it costs a little more, it can be successful. Above that, we've got to do things in a smarter way" to try to bring the price down. The company's goal is to price organic products no more than 10 percent above their conventional counterparts.

Environmentalists and organic-farming advocates give Wal-Mart's plan mixed reactions.

The company has consulted with the World Wildlife Federation, the Natural Resources Defense Council, Greenpeace and other environmental organizations. Environmental Defense, another Wal-Mart advisor, opened a Bentonville office so it could dispatch a representative to corporate headquarters at a moment's call.

Describing Wal-Mart's impact on the U.S. economy as "almost beyond calculation," Environmental Defense Executive Vice President David Yarnold said he and his colleagues "really believe that Wal-Mart can create a race to the top for environmental benefits." [4]

The Sierra Club refused to work with Wal-Mart because of concern about its labor policies, but Executive Director Carl Pope said Wal-Mart managers "deserve the chance to show that their business model is compatible with high standards, not just low prices." [5]

Nu Wexler, a spokesman for Wal-Mart Watch — which was created to challenge the company's business practices — said his organization is "encouraged by Wal-Mart's new environmental initiatives because they could, if implemented, change the way American businesses approach environmental sustainability." [6]

The Cornucopia Institute, an advocate for small organic farms, attacked the company for purchasing from "industrial-scale factory farms" and from China. Pressure to cut prices could destroy family farms and reduce some of the environmental benefits of organic farming, said Mark Kastel, Cornucopia's senior farm-policy analyst.

"Food shipped around the world — burning fossil fuels and undercutting our domestic farmers — does not meet the consumer's traditional definition of what is truly organic," Kastel said. [7]

Ronnie Cummins, national director of the Organic Consumers Association, questioned the authenticity of organic food grown in China, where "organic standards are dubious, and farm-labor exploitation is the norm." [8]

Wal-Mart replied that it would not compromise organic standards. [9] In addition, a spokesman said, "whenever possible, as with all fresh merchandise, we try to purchase fresh organic products from local suppliers for distribution to stores in their areas. This is good for the surrounding communities and helps to generate savings on distribution costs that we can pass on to our customers." [10]

---

[1] Lee Scott, presentation to Wal-Mart employees, Bentonville, Ark., Oct. 24, 2005; www.walmartstores.com/Files/21st%20Century%20Leadership.pdf.

[2] "Experimental Wal-Mart Stores One Year Later," Wal-Mart; www.walmartfacts.com/FactSheets/11132006_Experimental_Stores.pdf.

[3] Marc Gunther, "The Green Machine," *Fortune*, Aug. 7, 2006. p. 42. Michael Barbaro, "Wal-Mart Effort on Health and Environment Is Seen," *The New York Times*, June 22, 2006, p. 2.

[4] "Environmental Defense Will Add Staff Position in Bentonville, Arkansas," Environmental Defense, July 12, 2006; www.environmentaldefense.org/pressrelease.cfm?ContentID=5322.

[5] Abigail Goldman, "Wal-Mart goes 'green,'" *Los Angeles Times*, Nov. 13, 2006.

[6] *Ibid.*

[7] Mark Kastel, "Wal-Mart Declares War on Organic Farmers, the Cornucopia Institute, Sept. 28, 2006; www.cornucopia.org/WalMart_News_Release.pdf.

[8] Ronnie Cummins, "Open Letter to Wal-Mart," the Organic Consumers Association, July 4, 2006; www.organicconsumers.org/2006/article_1009.cfm.

[9] Tom Daykin, "Wal-Mart threatens farmers, report says," *The Milwaukee Journal Sentinel*, Sept. 28, 2006.

[10] Mya Frazier, "Critics' latest beef with Wal-Mart is . . . organics?" *Advertising Age*, Oct. 16, 2006, p. 47.

---

global warming, An Inconvenient Truth, made *The New York Times* best-seller list, and his movie of the same name was a surprise box-office hit. DiCaprio is teaming up with "Survivor" producer Craig Piligian to create a "reality" television show in which a down-and-out American town gets re-made into a healthy green community. DiCaprio and Piligian are shopping the concept, tentatively titled "E-topia," to networks and sponsors. Instead of just upgrading a wardrobe or a room, as other such shows do, "E-topia" will "take an American town that has been destroyed and bring it back to its former glory and then some," Piligian said. "This town will be reborn as the prototype for the future." [13]

As activists and business executives confront environmental challenges, here are some of the questions they're trying to answer:

Is going "green" good for the corporate bottom line?

A growing number of companies are adopting environmental-protection policies they say are good for business.

Rainforest Action Network, Global Exchange, Ruckus Society

The Rainforest Action Network's Jumpstart Ford campaign urges Ford and other corporations to reduce their dependence on oil. The campaign claims Ford has the worst fleetwide fuel efficiency and the highest average vehicle greenhouse-gas emissions of major U.S. automakers.

Some conservative critics contend, however, that such actions actually dilute companies' primary — some say only — purpose: to increase shareholder value.

Corporate executives say they implement green practices for a variety of reasons: to attract more customers, cut costs, drive up the value of their companies' stock, recruit and retain high-quality employees and assure their companies' long-term health.

"Increasingly, suppliers and customers are demanding greater devotion to the environment," says Douglas Pinkham, president of the Public Affairs Council, the professional association for public affairs officers.

Employees prefer environmentally friendly corporations because "nobody wants to work for a company that's known as an environmental pirate."

But companies are not going green "just because it helps their reputation," Pinkham adds. "Companies are saying we can make a buck by being environmentally sustainable."

And that goes beyond short-term profit-and-loss calculations, says business consultant Margery Kraus. "I heard an executive comment once that you can't have a successful business in a failed world," explains Kraus, head of APCO Worldwide, an international consulting firm. "I think that says it all." (*See "At Issue," p. 161.*)

According to Oklahoma State's Dunlap, American businesses are beginning to practice "what people in Europe call ecological modernization."

"You don't hear much talk about business vs. environment there," Dunlap explains. "They've adopted the approach that what's good for the environment is good for the economy, and I think we're seeing America kind of struggling to do the same.

"In the old days, it was easy to blame industry for 'greenwashing,'" or trying to appear more environmentally active than they really are. "But I'm increasingly convinced that we're seeing industries realize they have to integrate environmental concerns into their bottom line if they're to be successful."

A 2005 PricewaterhouseCoopers survey of chief executives in 43 countries found 87 percent saying environmental sustainability is important to company profits. That represented a rapid rise from 79 percent in 2004 and 69 percent in 2003. [14] (*See graph, p. 147.*)

Cost-saving is the most obvious benefit of greening a business. As Wal-Mart Chief Executive Lee Scott put it, when a company doesn't recycle, "We pay twice — once to get it, once to have it taken away." [15]

Wal-Mart expects to save $2.4 million a year by shrinking packaging for one private-label toy line, $26 million by cutting delivery-truck idle time and $28 million by recycling plastic in its stores. For really big savings, the giant retailer plans to reduce its stores' energy use by 30 percent and cut its trucks' fuel consumption by 25 percent in three years and 50 percent within 10 years. [16]

DuPont has already saved more than $3 billion by cutting energy use by 7 percent. [17] FedEx is deploying hybrid trucks that reduce fuel costs by more than a third. [18] PNC Financial Services Group is building green bank branches that use 45 percent less energy than standard structures. [19]

General Electric is betting billions that environmentalism sells as well as saves. In mid-2005, the global conglomerate launched its "Ecomagination" initiative to develop products and services that address environmental challenges. GE Chairman and CEO Jeff Immelt announced the company will produce improved technology in solar energy, hybrid locomotives, fuel cells, low-emission aircraft engines, light and strong materials, efficient lighting and water purification.

GE will invest $1.5 billion in research and development in those technologies by 2010 — up from $700 million in 2004 — "and we plan to make money doing it," Immelt said. Moreover, the company intends to double its revenues in those areas, from $10 billion in 2004 to at least $20 billion in 2010 and substantially more later. [20]

Potlatch Corp. Public Affairs Vice President Mark Benson isn't as precise about his forest-products company's future earnings, but he agrees it makes sense to prepare for a green marketplace. Potlatch seeks to distinguish itself from competitors by complying with all of the American Forest and Paper Association's environmental guidelines and then earning certification from the environmental movement's Forest Stewardship Council as well. As a result, Benson says, "we've positioned ourselves so, if that [green] market takes off, we're going to be there to serve it."

Retailers are discovering that "dedication to the environment makes them more attractive to consumers — especially if they're trying to appeal to an upscale audience," Pinkham says. Potlatch's policies also may make it more attractive to green investors, a group that is growing in numbers and influence, Benson says.

Assets devoted to so-called socially responsible investing (SRI) — of which green investing is a part — have grown slightly faster than other kinds of investing over the last decade, according to the Social Investment Forum, the SRI industry's trade association. SRI investments now represent 9.4 percent of all professionally managed assets tracked in Nelson Information's *Directory of Investment Managers.* [21]

Among SRI investors, 37 percent consider companies' environmental records when making investment decisions, the forum reported. Many also attempt to influence corporate environmental policy by introducing resolutions at shareholders' meetings.

Investors are proposing a growing number of resolutions, according to a report from the As You Sow Foundation and Rockefeller Philanthropy Advisors. Investors' proposals have addressed the environment more than any other issue in recent years, the report said, and the number of environmental resolutions proposed has increased faster than most other topics. [22]

But not everyone is bullish on green business.

Jerry Taylor, a senior fellow at the libertarian Cato Institute, suggests that talk of consumers' and companies' concern about the environment is overblown. "Public demands have always been for bigger and bigger and bigger homes," he notes. "How do you square that with the rise of environmentalism? And if consumers are looking at more fuel-efficient cars, I think that has more to do with the price of gas than anything else." If gas prices drop, Americans might go right back to their big SUVs, he says.

Businesses may find conservation economical now, he adds, but if energy prices drop, companies might find it less expensive to use more energy than to buy energy-efficient equipment, he says. Competition could force companies to enlarge packaging to catch consumers' eyes, he says, even if that uses more materials.

While executives contend they adopt green policies to boost the bottom line, Competitive Enterprise Institute President Fred Smith Jr. charged the policies usually are intended "to appease [a business's] critics, to apologize for past mistakes, to bribe its opponents."

"The modern firm solves one — but only one — of the major problems of mankind: the creation of wealth," Smith said. "That wealth then allows individuals in their various roles the opportunity to protect values they care about." [23]

Is more federal action needed to encourage energy efficiency?

Almost everyone agrees Americans would be better off if they used energy more efficiently. Even those who don't fear global warming see benefits in reducing U.S. dependence on energy sources from unstable regions of the world, such as the Middle East. Most also agree that only federal action could spur significant gains in efficiency.

But there is disagreement over whether the desire for efficiency warrants government intervention and which measures would be most effective. Most environmental organizations advocate government mandates. Many businesses prefer incentives for voluntary action.

"We cannot solve these issues without the active participation of the federal government," says the Rainforest Action Network's Brune.

"There is no substitute for having clear national goals," Sierra Club spokesman Eric Antebi agrees. "It's great to have over 300 mayors doing their part. It's critical that states are taking the lead. But there are still too many gaps."

"There are some places where voluntary business actions will offer the greatest opportunities," says Denis Hayes, president and CEO of the Bullitt Foundation, and one of the key organizers of the first Earth Day. "But it's nice to have a regulatory basement beneath which you're not allowed to sink."

U.S. energy consumption is like a giant ocean liner that can't change direction quickly, says Americans for Balanced Energy Choices Executive Director Joe Lucas. "We don't want draconian measures," says Lucas, whose advocacy group is funded by coal producers and consumers. "Don't force the ocean liner to do a U-turn immediately."

The federal government should continue to fund efforts to develop technologies that burn coal more efficiently and with fewer emissions, he says. And the government should offer incentives for farmers and foresters to adopt practices that absorb more greenhouse gases from the atmosphere.

Similarly, the auto industry opposes higher fuel-efficiency standards but favors tax breaks for those who buy fuel-efficient cars. "Competition among the automakers will drive this process far better and with fewer disruptions to the marketplace than any regulations that can be adopted," said Frederick Webber, president and CEO of the Alliance of Automobile Manufacturers. [24]

American businesses and individuals have become much more energy efficient since the emergence of the modern environmental movement and the 1973 Arab oil embargo. Today coal emits 70 percent less pollution per unit of energy produced than it did 30 years ago, Lucas says. Compared with the growth in gross domestic product, the United States puts a declining amount of greenhouse gases into the air, he adds.

America's new cars and light trucks average about 24 miles per gallon now, up from 15 in 1975. The typical refrigerator uses less than half as much electricity as its counterpart in 1972. [25]

Population growth, economic expansion and consumer tastes, however, have driven total energy consumption up by a third since 1973, and it is expected to jump another 30 percent by 2025. [26] Americans burned 75 percent more coal in 2005 than in 1980, and the coal industry says consumption will increase more than 30 percent over the next two decades. [27]

This doesn't surprise Joel Schwartz, a visiting fellow at the American Enterprise Institute (AEI), who doubts the need for, or effectiveness of, government regulations. "When you make things more efficiently," he explains, "you free up resources to make something else. Pound for pound, cars are more energy efficient now. Because of consumer demand, the efficiency benefits have gone into creating bigger cars that get about the same fuel economy."

If the United States did import less oil, Schwartz adds, "it would get used somewhere else. Developing countries would use that energy."

Nevertheless, environmentalists want the federal government to impose tougher restrictions on the use of fossil fuels. Cars began getting better gas mileage after federal corporate average fuel economy (CAFE) standards were enacted in 1975, they note. But the standard for passenger cars has not been raised since 1990, and the average fuel efficiency of cars and light trucks has actually declined since 1987. Over the last two decades, the auto industry has focused technology on getting heavier vehicles to run faster, and the growing American population has driven more miles.

The Union of Concerned Scientists wants CAFE standards increased to more than 40 miles per gallon (mpg) by 2015 and 55 mpg by 2025. Boosting mileage standards would not require U.S. auto companies to reinvent the wheel, the organization contends. For instance, Ford could apply existing technology to boost the Explorer SUV's fuel efficiency to 36 miles per gallon from 21. [28]

Environmental organizations also want restrictions on greenhouse-gas emissions, which are not regulated because they are not legally classified as pollutants under the Clean Air Act. [29] One often-advocated plan would assign every company an emissions allowance and let those that emit less sell their excess allowance to others. This so-called "cap-and-trade" scheme has been used successfully to reduce the sulfur emissions that cause acid rain.

Sens. John R. McCain, R-Ariz., and Joseph I. Lieberman, D-Conn., introduced legislation to do that in early 2005, and Maryland Republican Rep. Wayne T. Gilchrest did the same in the House. Neither bill got out of committee.

Recently some conservatives, concerned about U.S. reliance on imported oil, have suggested raising taxes on fossil fuels. "That's the way to get consumption down," said Alan Greenspan, former chairman of the Federal Reserve Board. "It's a national-security issue." Joining him have been such prominent conservative economists as Gregory Mankiw, former chairman of President Bush's Council of Economic Advisors, and Andrew Samwick, the council's former chief economist. [30]

While he doesn't agree that it's needed, Schwartz says a tax would be the most effective way to curb fossil-fuel use, as long as it were combined with other tax cuts so it didn't depress the economy.

Can the industrial world switch from fossil fuels to other forms of energy?

Environmentalists argue the only way to stop global warming is to stop burning fossil fuels. But switching from coal and oil is no easy task, and alternative energy sources have their own drawbacks — including damage to the environment.

"No energy source is perfect," says David Hamilton, director of the Sierra Club's global warming and energy program, using words echoed by Lucas, the coal-industry advocate.

For Hamilton, that means accepting the shortcomings of alternative fuels in the near term while conducting the research and development needed to make them work over the long haul. For Lucas, it means environmentalists have to accept that fossil fuels will be the world's primary energy source for the foreseeable future.

Eliminating coal and oil is "a pipe dream," that could occur only in "science-fiction land," Lucas says. "For the next 30 to 50 to 100 years, folks are going to have little choice but to use coal."

Currently, nearly 80 percent of the world's energy comes from burning fossil fuels. [31] In the United States, it's 86 percent. [32] Coal produces 52 percent of the electricity consumed in the United States, [33] and oil powers nearly all U.S. transportation. [34]

The coal producers and their customers project that America will continue to get a majority of its electricity from coal in 2025. They also say they will steadily reduce coal emissions during that time and will begin building "ultra-low-emissions plants" in the decade following 2025. Those plants could eliminate more than 99 percent of sulfur, nitrogen oxide and particulate emissions,

along with 95 percent of mercury, they say. They also aim to be able to capture and sequester carbon dioxide, fossil fuels' primary contributor to global warming. [35]

The Rainforest Action Network's Brune acknowledges that "we have massive amounts of coal in the United States and around the world. If we want to extract every bit of fossil fuel, we could go for a couple hundred more years. But the planet wouldn't be able to survive."

Industry has not proven that it can capture and sequester greenhouse gases on a commercial scale, he says, and coal mining itself does terrible damage to the environment.

Even if factories could capture greenhouse gases in the future, Hamilton says, "scientists say we need to actually reduce emissions now, not just get on a path to reducing emissions in 10 years."

That would require a variety of methods for conserving and switching to alternative sources of energy, environmentalists say. "There is no silver bullet," Sierra Club spokesman Antebi says. "I heard someone say that you need silver buckshot.

"We're going to need to make our cars go further on a gallon of gas," he continued. "We're going to need solar and wind power and biofuels. We're going to need to design our buildings to operate more efficiently. We're going to need to clean up our power plants and use new technologies to reduce their impact on global warming."

Wind power has been the fastest-growing U.S. source of energy, jumping by 160 percent from 2000 to 2005. But it accounts for less than two-tenths of a percent of American energy consumption. [36] And it is not without its problems.

Jesse Ausubel, director of Rockefeller University's human-environment program, terms wind one of environmentalism's "false gods." To replace a typical, traditional power plant, he said, a windmill farm would have to cover 300 square miles. Other environmentalists oppose windmill farms because they endanger birds and can clutter the landscape. [37]

Similarly, U.S. use of ethanol — a fuel made from corn and other plants — increased by 145 percent from 2000 to 2005. Like wind power, however, it supplies a tiny fraction of America's energy — about a third of a percent. [38] Spurred by government incentives, annual ethanol production may more than double from 4.5 billion gallons now to more than 10 billion by 2010. [39] But that still would represent less than 1 percent of U.S.

C H R O N O L O G Y

1870-1900 *Environmentalists organize, and Congress begins to act.*

1870 Congress passes law to protect Alaska wildlife.

1872 Yellowstone becomes world's first national park.

1891 Congress empowers president to create national forests.

1900-1969 *Teddy Roosevelt leads crusade to protect the environment. Modern environmental movement is born.*

1901 President Theodore Roosevelt makes conservation a priority.

1906 Congress passes Antiquities Act; Roosevelt creates the first national monuments — Devil's Tower in Wyoming and Petrified Forest in Arizona.

1916 National Park Service created.

1962 Writer and biologist Rachel Carson warns of the dangers of pesticides in her landmark book *Silent Spring*.

1970-1979 *Modern environmental movement soars into prominence; Congress responds with landmark laws.*

1970 Some 20 million Americans celebrate first Earth Day. . . . Clean Air Act passed. . . . Environmental Protection Agency created.

1972 Clean Water Act passed; DDT is banned.

1973 Endangered Species Act passed.

1974 Safe Water Drinking Act enacted.

1975 Fuel-economy and tailpipe-emission standards are established.

1980-1987 *Environmental activism slows, but Congress passes significant legislation, and international agreements target global environmental challenges.*

1980 Superfund created to clean hazardous-waste sites. . . . Landmark Alaska Lands legislation sets aside more than 100 million acres, doubling U.S. parks and refuge acreage.

1987 Two-dozen nations agree to phase out chlorofluorocarbons, which damage Earth's ozone layer.

1990-1999 *Climate change becomes top global environmental issue.*

1992 U.N. convention calls for greenhouse-gas reductions.

1994 Republican takeover of Congress diminishes environmentalists' power in federal government.

1995 Attack on acid rain launched.

1997 Kyoto Protocol mandates greenhouse-gas reductions; U.S. fails to ratify.

2000-2006 *Republican control of Congress and White House further weakens environmentalists' voice. Environmentalists increase efforts to influence business. More businesses go "green."*

2000 Republican George W. Bush wins White House; GOP holds Congress. . . . Thirty-five institutional investors with several trillion dollars in assets launch Carbon Disclosure Project to pressure corporations to address global warming.

2001 Vermont Sen. James Jeffords, an environmentalist, leaves Republican Party mid-year, giving Democrats control of Senate.

2002 GOP regains control of Senate.

2006 Environmentalists celebrate Democratic capture of Congress but don't expect great success while Bush occupies White House and Senate is nearly evenly divided. . . . Carbon Disclosure Project grows to 225 investors with $31.5 trillion in assets. . . . Tyson Foods warns meat prices to rise because ethanol production is driving up cost of corn.

energy sources, and ethanol, too, carries environmental baggage. (*See sidebar, p. 156.*)

Despite problems posed by some alternative-energy sources, Hamilton says, "we're going to need almost every tool in the shed for a while.

"Scientists are saying we won't have the luxury to go back and stop global warming if we reach some of these biological tipping points," he continues. "We need to solve this problem now, and if we do we will then have the opportunity to make technological improvements later.

"You can always take the wind turbines down because some people think they're ugly. You can't take the carbon dioxide out of the air — it stays there for 200 years."

Many environmentalists place hope in solar energy, even though it currently produces less than a tenth of a percent of U.S. power. A handful of environmentalists are calling for more use of nuclear power. A growing number of environmental organizations are acknowledging that nuclear shouldn't be rejected out of hand. But most argue that nuclear's downsides will not be overcome in the foreseeable future.

Pro-nuclear environmentalists, such as British scientist Lovelock, contend it offers the only realistic alternative to fossil fuels. Other alternatives are "largely gestures," Lovelock said. "If it makes people feel good to shove up a windmill or put a solar panel on their roof, great, do it. It'll help a little bit, but it's no answer at all to the problem." [40]

Bruce Babbitt — Clinton administration Interior secretary and one-time head of the League of Conservation Voters — described nuclear power as "the lesser [evil] of the only two alternatives that are on the table right now. One is to fry this planet with continuing use and burning of fossil fuels, and the other is to try to make nuclear power work." [41]

Environmentalists can't "just say 'no way, no how,'" Environmental Defense's Yarnold says. "That's one reason some people look at a caricature of environmentalists and say, 'There they go again.'"

But he also says the nuclear industry must answer tough questions about reactor safety, waste disposal and weapons proliferation before new plants should be opened.

The industry might be able to address some concerns about safety, the Bullitt Foundation's Hayes says, "but the one I can't think of any way to make progress on is nuclear proliferation. I'm pretty terrified of a world in which 60 countries have nuclear stockpiles, and if they all have nuclear power I can't think of any way to avoid that."

BACKGROUND

Early Warnings

American environmentalists can trace their roots to distinguished writers — and some obscure bureaucrats — of the mid-19th century. [42]

Students still read Henry David Thoreau's *Walden* (published in 1854) and his other paeans to nature. In 1857, after the discovery of the California redwoods, poet James Russell Lowell proposed establishing a society for the protection of trees.

But even earlier, the U.S. commissioner of patents warned in 1849 about "the folly and shortsightedness" of wasting timber and slaughtering buffalo. Other commissioners of patents and of agriculture issued similar warnings about environmental destruction throughout the 1850s and '60s.

Congress had gotten the message by 1864, when it gave Yosemite Valley to California to establish a state park. Eight years later, it made Yellowstone the world's first national park.

During the 1870s, Congress passed legislation to protect fur-bearing animals in Alaska, fisheries in the Atlantic Ocean and Eastern lakes and trees on government lands. Environmental organizations also began to sink roots. Botanists and horticulturalists created the American Forestry Association (now known as American Forests), and New Englanders founded the Appalachian Mountain Club.

The 1890s also proved to be "green." Congress established Sequoia and General Grant (now part of Kings Canyon) national parks, and brought Yosemite back under federal control. Congress also gave the president power to create national forests, and President Benjamin Harrison issued a proclamation that created the first national wildlife refuge, in Alaska. In the private sector, John Muir and some friends on the West Coast founded the Sierra Club to preserve wilderness. Back East, creation of the Massachusetts Audubon Society touched off the Audubon movement, which led to the National Association of Audubon Societies in 1905.

President Theodore Roosevelt (1901-1909), an avid outdoorsman, doubled the acreage in national parks and established 53 wildlife sanctuaries. Following congressional passage of the American Antiquities Act in 1906, Roosevelt created the first national monuments —

The Promise — and Problems — of Ethanol

For environmentalists, ethanol wields a double-edged sword. It replaces oil-based fuels, reducing emissions of greenhouse gases and other pollutants. But it poses its own threats.

Tyson Foods, the world's largest meat processor, recently underscored one ethanol worry — that increased production of ethanol, almost all from corn, will drive up the price of that widely used grain. Rising corn prices will lead to higher chicken, beef and pork prices in 2007, the company announced in November.

"The American consumer is making a choice here," Tyson President and CEO Richard Bond said. "This is either corn for feed or corn for fuel. That's what's causing this." [1]

Critics also worry that devoting more land to expanded corn production could damage the environment by increasing harmful runoff of pesticides and fertilizers and by discouraging the preservation of land for conservation reserves, wetlands, wildlife preserves and wilderness. [2] According to Friends of the Earth, corn requires nearly six times more fertilizer and pesticide than most crops. [3]

Ethanol enjoys substantial government subsidies, in no small part because of farm-state lawmakers whose constituents grow corn. Ethanol production consumed about 14 percent of U.S.-grown corn in 2005 and was projected to run as high as 19 percent this year. America's entire corn crop would supply just 3.7 percent of the energy demanded by the U.S. transportation sector, however, researchers at the Polytechnic University of New York estimated. [4]

Corn ethanol contains less energy than gasoline, so an ethanol-fueled vehicle gets lower fuel efficiency. *Consumer Reports* magazine compared gasoline with an ethanol fuel burned in a Chevy Tahoe sport utility vehicle, a so-called "flexible fuel" model that can run on gasoline or a mixture of up to 85 percent ethanol and 15 percent gas. The ethanol blend delivered 27 percent lower gas mileage. [5]

According to a team of researchers from the University of California at Berkeley, corn ethanol can make a real, but relatively small, contribution to reducing greenhouse-gas emissions. They compared the energy in the ethanol with the fossil fuels used to make it — powering farm machinery and production equipment, for instance. The ethanol contained 20 percent more energy than was used to make it, and it reduced greenhouse-gas emissions by 13 percent. [6]

Most modern cars can run on a 10 percent ethanol blend, and about a third of U.S. motor fuel uses that mixture to reduce pollution. But only about 5 million of America's 230 million passenger vehicles can run on 85-percent ethanol, called E85, and many of them are gas-guzzlers like the Tahoe. [7] The United States had 70 percent more E85-dispensing service stations in August than it did at the beginning of last year, but that's still just 850 of 169,000 stations nationwide. [8]

Ethanol proponents hope other crops will prove to be more efficient energy sources.

Ethanol from sugarcane has eight times the energy of corn ethanol. [9] It delivers 40 percent of Brazil's automobile fuel, costs less than half as much as gasoline there and helps to generate electricity as well. [10] But the United States doesn't have much land suitable for the crop. In addition, federal laws keep sugar prices artificially high and restrict imports of cheaper sugar from overseas. [11]

Entrepreneurs and scientists are trying to produce ethanol from more economical plant matter, such as farm waste, municipal trash, grass, leaves and wood. Corn ethanol is made from the corn's starch. Ethanol also can be made — with greater difficulty — from cellulose, which is the main component of plant-cell walls.

Devil's Tower in Wyoming and Petrified Forest in Arizona. The early-20th century also spawned Western opposition to federal environmental-protection activities, notably when Western business and government representatives met at the Denver Public Lands Convention and demanded that federal lands be turned over to the states.

While most early 20th-century environmentalism focused on preserving pristine nature, public officials also began to take note of a growing side effect of urbaniza-tion — pollution of waters near big cities. Congress responded in 1910 by passing legislation that restricted dumping refuse into Lake Michigan in or near Chicago.

In something of a harbinger of current partnerships between environmental organizations and businesses, conservationists and sportsmen found allies within railroads and travel agencies. Together, they promoted creation of a federal bureau to look after the national parks. Congress responded in 1916 by establishing the National Park Service.

Not only can cellulosic ethanol be made from more materials, it also can reduce greenhouse-gas emissions by 67 to 89 percent, according to the U.S. Energy Department's Argonne National Laboratory. [12]

The economies of tropical and subtropical countries, with year-round growing seasons, could benefit from the growing demand for sugarcane ethanol. "The risk," Earth Policy Institute President Lester Brown warned, "is that economic pressures to clear land for expanding sugarcane production . . . in the Brazilian cerrado and Amazon basin . . . will pose a major threat to plant and animal diversity." [13]

The Rainforest Action Network is "very concerned about biofuel's impact on rain forests," Network Executive Director Michael Brune says. Ethanol can contribute to reducing fossil-fuel consumption, he says, but only as part of a comprehensive approach that includes more efficient motor-vehicle engines and clean generation of electricity.

"If we replaced gas-guzzling internal-combustion engines with a similar engine that uses biofuel, we'll just be replacing one problem with another," Brune says. "If we use more advanced auto technology and 'green' the electricity grid, then the impact of an appropriate use of biofuels would be revolutionary."

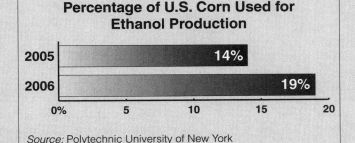

More Corn Used for Ethanol

Nearly 20 percent of the corn grown in the United States this year — a five-percentage-point increase over 2005 — was used for ethanol production. If the nation's entire corn crop were used for ethanol, it would supply just 3.7 percent of the energy needed for transportation alone.

Percentage of U.S. Corn Used for Ethanol Production

2005	14%
2006	19%

0%   5   10   15   20

Source: Polytechnic University of New York

[1] Marcus Kabel, "Tyson Foods Sees Higher Meat Prices," The Associated Press, Nov. 13, 2006.

[2] Brad Knickerbocker, "Why the Next Congress Will Be 'Greener,' But Only by a Few Shades," *The Christian Science Monitor,* Nov. 15, 2006, p. 2.

[3] Mike Nixon, "Skepticism Rides along with Gasoline Ethanol Requirement," *St. Louis Daily Record,* July 15, 2006.

[4] Adriel Bettelheim, "Biofuels Boom," *CQ Researcher,* Sept. 29, 2006, pp. 793-816.

[5] "The Ethanol Myth," *Consumer Reports,* October 2006, p. 15.

[6] Elizabeth Douglass, "Report Challenges Claims about Ethanol," *Los Angeles Times,* Jan. 27, 2006, p. C2.

[7] Elizabeth Douglass, "A Future Without Oil?" *Los Angeles Times,* April 16, 2006, p. C1; "Annual Vehicle Distance Traveled in Miles and Related Data 2004," Federal Highway Administration, www.fhwa.dot.gov/policy/ohim/hs04/htm/vm1.htm.

[8] Alexei Barrionuevo, "An Alternative Fuel Is Scarce, Even in the Farm Belt," *The New York Times,* Aug. 31, 2006, p. C1.

[9] Jerry Taylor and Peter Van Doren, "California's Global Warming Dodge," *The Arizona Republic,* May 7, 2006.

[10] Marla Dickerson, "Homegrown Fuel Supply Helps Brazil Breathe Easy," *Los Angeles Times,* June 15, 2005, p. 1.

[11] "Sugar's sweet deal," *Sarasota Herald-Tribune,* Aug. 15, 2006, p. A10.

[12] Barbara McClellan, "Biofuel Crossroads," *Ward's Auto World,* Nov. 1, 2006, p. 30.

[13] Lester R. Brown, "Rescuing a Planet Under Stress," *The Futurist,* July 1, 2006, p. 18.

Three years later, supporters of the parks founded the National Parks Association (which was renamed the National Parks and Conservation Association in 1970). The organization sought to build public backing for the parks through educational activities and by encouraging Americans to visit.

The roaring '20s became better known for environmental exploitation than environmental protection, as Congress opened federal lands to mining and drilling for small fees, authorized federal hydroelectric projects and set the U.S. Army Corps of Engineers to dredging and damming inland waters.

In the 1930s, the Great Depression was worsened when poor agricultural practices contributed to massive dust storms that turned formerly bountiful farmland on the Plains into the Dust Bowl. In efforts to fight the Depression, President Franklin D. Roosevelt's New Deal policies created the Civilian Conservation Corps, through which unemployed workers planted trees, built roads, erected fire towers and carried out other public works.

The Kumeyaay wind farm on the Campo Indian Reservation serves 30,000 customers in San Diego. Wind power is the fastest-growing U.S. source of energy but accounts for less than two-tenths of a percent of American energy consumption. Replacing a typical, traditional power plant with wind power would require a 300-square-mile wind farm, according to one expert.

The environmental costs of industrialization commanded increasing attention during the 1930s, '40s and '50s. Offshore oil drilling began. Smog episodes in St. Louis led to the nation's first smoke-control ordinance. Los Angeles established the first air-pollution control bureau. California adopted the first automobile-emissions standards. Congress passed laws — that would be strengthened after the '60s — to address water and air pollution.

The political and counter-culture ferment of the 1960s spurred interest in environmentalism that emphasized personal responsibility. This manifested itself in movements to encourage recycling, organic gardening and farming, cooperatives and purchases of "green" products.

Mimicking the violent political activists of the era, a few organizations and individuals began engaging in "ecoterrorism," destroying property that they viewed as encroaching on nature and setting booby traps to threaten loggers. Their legacy included trials and guilty pleas this year from alleged members of the Earth Liberation Front and Animal Liberation Front who were charged with firebombing ranger stations, corrals, lumber mill offices, ski resorts, slaughterhouse and federal plant-inspection facilities throughout the West between 1996 and 2001. [43]

Era of Activism

Taking an entirely different tack, biologist Rachel Carson wrote *Silent Spring*, highlighting the dangers posed by DDT and other pesticides and foreshadowing the coming era of massive environmental activism.

That era was kicked off by the first Earth Day, on April 22, 1970. The event was conceived by Democratic Sen. Gaylord Nelson of Wisconsin as a way to "shake up the political establishment and force this issue onto the national agenda." [44] He modeled it after the teach-ins that built opposition to the Vietnam War on college campuses, and it succeeded beyond his wildest dreams.

An estimated 20 million Americans — including 10 million students from 2,000 colleges and 1,000 high schools — participated in a wide variety of activities throughout the country. There were marches, rallies, songfests, mock funerals for the internal-combustion engine, mock trials of polluters, trash pickup drives, protests against aircraft noise and polluting companies. New York City closed Fifth Avenue for Earth Day events. Congress shut down because so many members were out participating. Earth Day speakers ranged from famed anthropologist Margaret Mead to liberal Sen. Edward M. Kennedy, D-Mass., to conservative Sen. Barry Goldwater, R-Ariz., to Nixon administration Cabinet officers. [45]

At the same time, according to organizer Hayes, Attorney General John R. Mitchell ordered the FBI to investigate the organizers of Earth Day. [46] In addition, a Georgia gubernatorial candidate called Earth Day a communist plot because it was held on Russian revolutionary Vladimir Lenin's birthday, and the Daughters of the American Revolution denounced it as "subversive." [47]

But lawmakers heard loud and clear that Earth Day was above all an expression of national will. Later in 1970, Congress passed the Clean Air Act, and President Richard M. Nixon established the Environmental Protection Agency. These were followed in subsequent years by a flood of landmark laws, including the Clean Water Act, the Endangered Species Act, the Marine Mammal Protection Act, the Safe Drinking Water Act, the Toxic Substances Control Act, the Resource Conservation and Recovery Act to regulate hazardous waste, fuel-economy standards, tailpipe-emission and lead-paint restrictions, bans on DDT, the phasing out of leaded gasoline, PCBs and ozone-destroying chlorofluorocarbons and a U.S.-Canada agreement to clean up the polluted Great Lakes.

The '70s also witnessed the birth of Green political parties, which eventually wielded significant influence in Europe but not in the United States. While the first Green parties were organized in New Zealand and Australia, the first Green Party candidate won election to a national legislature in Switzerland, in 1979. Green parties contributed to some of the movements that overthrew communist regimes in former Soviet-bloc countries. The German Green Party joined the governing coalition in 1998, and its leader served as foreign minister. Greens also have been mayors of Dublin, Rome and other major European cities.

In the United States, although Congress passed environmental legislation at a slower pace in the 1980s and '90s, some of the new laws were highly significant. The Superfund program began to clean up hazardous-waste sites in the '80s, for example, and the attack on acid rain began in the following decade.

Global warming has been the world's top environmental issue since the 1990s. Most — though not all — scientists believe that fossil-fuel emissions are causing the planet to heat up. Scientists can't make specific predictions about how much or how fast. Worst-case scenarios are truly catastrophic, forecasting drought, famine, floods, animal and plant extinctions, destruction of island and coastal communities — even massive human death.

The 1992 U.N. Framework Convention on Climate Change called on industrialized nations to reduce their emissions of "greenhouse gases," which are released when coal, oil and other fossil fuels are burned. The reduction was voluntary, however, and countries soon realized that the convention's goal — to stabilize emissions at 1990 levels by 2000 — would not be met.

The Kyoto Protocol, negotiated in 1997, set mandatory emissions reductions. But the United States — the world's largest greenhouse-gas emitter — has refused to ratify it, arguing that compliance would damage the economy. Critics warn that countries that have ratified may not meet the cuts because they aren't making sufficient changes in their consumption of fossil fuels. And rapidly industrializing countries — notably China and India — are expected to make major increases in their emissions.

CURRENT SITUATION

Democrats Take Over

Environmentalists celebrated the Democratic takeover of Congress on Nov. 7, 2006, and can point to growing signs of public support for environmental protection. But many environmental leaders remain focused on businesses for solutions to environmental problems, especially global warming.

Meanwhile, environmental groups are reporting recent increases in membership and financial contributions. The Sierra Club now has 800,000 members, a one-third rise in the last four years. [48] Between 2003 and 2006, membership jumped from 400,000 to 550,000 in the Natural Resources Defense Council and from 300,000 to 400,000 at Environmental Defense. Both reported substantial budget hikes as well. [49]

Overall, giving to environmental organizations increased by 7 percent from 2003 to 2004 and by 16.4 percent the next year — greater growth in both years than any other category of nonprofit organization tracked by the Giving USA Foundation. [50]

The Gallup Organization reports that the percentage of Americans who worry about the environment "a great deal" or "a fair amount" increased from 62 to 77 percent between 2004 and 2006. Since 1984, Gallup has asked Americans to choose between two sides in a mock debate: whether "protection of the environment should be given priority, even at the risk of curbing economic growth," or "economic growth should be given priority, even if the environment suffers to some extent." (*See graph, p. 160.*)

The pro-environment side has always prevailed, usually by a large margin. After falling precipitously during the early years of the Bush administration — from a 43-percentage-point pro-environment margin in 2000 to 5 percentage points in 2003 and 2004 — the pro-

Public Strongly Favors Action on Environment

Americans strongly favor environmental initiatives by both industry and government to cut pollution and increase energy efficiency.

Do you generally favor or oppose:

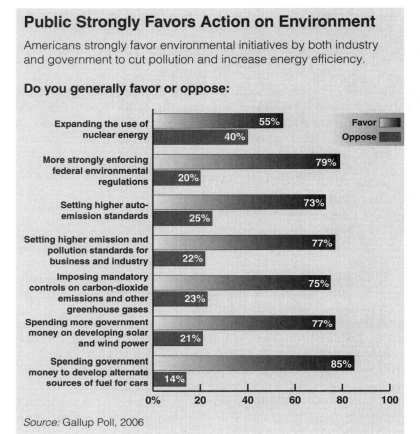

Expanding the use of nuclear energy — Favor 55%, Oppose 40%

More strongly enforcing federal environmental regulations — Favor 79%, Oppose 20%

Setting higher auto-emission standards — Favor 73%, Oppose 25%

Setting higher emission and pollution standards for business and industry — Favor 77%, Oppose 22%

Imposing mandatory controls on carbon-dioxide emissions and other greenhouse gases — Favor 75%, Oppose 23%

Spending more government money on developing solar and wind power — Favor 77%, Oppose 21%

Spending government money to develop alternate sources of fuel for cars — Favor 85%, Oppose 14%

Source: Gallup Poll, 2006

environment gap began widening again. Pro-environment respondents outnumbered pro-economy respondents by 17 percent in 2005 and 15 percent this year. [51]

Despite such positive signs, environmental activists don't expect major legislation to work its way through the House and Senate and survive presidential vetoes during the next two years. They also believe businesses are essential to the solutions, with or without government action.

Democratic congressional leaders tend to be more supportive of environmentalists' positions than Republicans. But Democrats didn't win large enough majorities to override vetoes or break GOP filibusters in the Senate. Indeed, the agenda Democratic leaders announced for the opening days of the next Congress, in 2007, does not include environmental legislation.

The loss of Republican power means environmentalists won't have to battle attempts to roll back environ-

mental protections, such as California Rep. Richard Pombo's efforts to weaken the Endangered Species Act, sell national park land in Alaska, open the Arctic National Wildlife Refuge to oil drilling and increase drilling off the nation's coasts. Pombo, who chaired the House Resources Committee, was defeated.

Individual representatives and senators will introduce environmental bills, including some to address global warming. But, said Sierra Club Executive Director Carl Pope, "I don't think we're going to see, at a national level, major progress, because Bush is still going to be there." [52]

Environmentalists "can't wait for the federal government, which is why you're seeing all these other players take the first steps," Sierra Club spokesman Antebi says.

Focus on Business

Environmentalists are drawing more sympathy from corporate executives, Public Affairs Council President Pinkham says, because "we've reached a tipping point where most business people agree that global warming is an issue that can't be ignored. Even companies with doubts are coming to realize you can't sit on the sidelines."

Environmental organizations are working with companies on a wide range of environmental challenges. Some relationships are cooperative, others confrontational. Environmentalists seek to apply pressure by winning support from companies' customers, employees and investors. They also appeal to executives' sense of social responsibility.

"We attempt to appeal to the most core, basic values that remind us that we're all human, that we all need to live on a healthy Earth together, and that some of us have far more decision-making power than others," says the Rainforest Action Network's Hogue. "If you're the CEO of a major bank or a government official or a logging

Are businesses better equipped than governments to address 21st-century environmental challenges?

YES
Margery Kraus
President and CEO, APCO Worldwide*

Written for *CQ Researcher*, November 2006

There is no doubt the environment is on people's minds: Used hybrid cars can fetch more than the original sticker price at resale; the *Oxford American Dictionary*'s word of the year for 2006 is "carbon neutral." However hip it may be, environmental responsibility is more than just the "flavor of the month," it is our future. And businesses not only can be the most efficient catalyst for creating a more sustainable planet but they also are increasingly expected to play that role.

A recent study conducted by APCO Worldwide reveals that the American public holds businesses to a higher standard on environmental issues than it does the U.S. government. There is a belief that business is less encumbered by politics and bureaucracy and has more resources to act and influence others to do so.

Today's progressive companies already know they have this responsibility and embrace it. Big corporations are larger than many nations. Major companies' global reach and standards allow them to directly impact environments beyond the boundaries of any one country. As they expand globally, businesses are able to build factories with proven technologies that often exceed the requirements of local governments.

Corporations have a tremendous opportunity to influence individual behavior. Employees can be offered incentives to use public transportation, recycle and contribute time to community environmental efforts. More broadly, businesses can sway consumer bases to adopt environmentally responsible behavior.

Finally, an increased number of businesses see sustainable products as a new part of their business. They are engineering or re-engineering those products to be recyclable and to incorporate recycled materials; they are employing clean production processes to create less waste and pollution.

Down the road, these forward-looking businesses will have a healthy, sustainable work force, clean water and quality of life that will enable them to have good employees and more consumers. Their ultimate incentive: You can't run a successful business in a failed world.

Obviously, safeguarding our environment is best accomplished by governments, businesses and individuals working together. However, businesses, especially multinational corporations, are well-positioned to take decisive leadership and have the infrastructure and resources to achieve measurable results — and consumers are expecting nothing less.

* The public-relations and strategic-communications firm represents many of the world's largest corporations.

NO
Michael Brune
Executive Director, Rainforest Action Network

Written for *CQ Researcher*, November 2006

Businesses and governments both have a vital role to play in addressing environmental challenges. We are beginning to see strong policies from a select number of high-profile businesses on issues such as forest protection and climate change. Meanwhile, state and local governments are responding to widespread public support for environmental protection, compensating for a disturbing lack of leadership in the White House and Congress.

One test for either businesses or governments is to determine to which constituency they are the most loyal. Most companies are guided by the old business axiom, "The customer is always right." These businesses realize that not only do consumers want to do business with companies that exhibit strong environmental values but also their own employees want to feel good about their employer's environmental record. Indeed, it is this view that has helped Home Depot, Lowe's, FedEx Kinko's and others to work with Rainforest Action Network to help protect endangered forests, and for Citigroup, Bank of America, JP Morgan Chase and Goldman Sachs to take principled stands on climate change and forest protection.

Conversely, many officials in Washington are stuck in the past, guarding the status quo. Within the last few years, the federal government has failed to enact, protect or enforce strong environmental policies, as evidenced by the attempted rollback of the Forest Service's "Roadless Rule" and the gutting of the Clean Water Act. Our politicians have fallen into the trap of believing they must choose between prosperity and the environment. Consequently, neither political party has stood up to the corporations whose policies are destabilizing and devastating our environment.

By leveraging public opinion and consumer choice to publicly stigmatize companies that refuse to adopt responsible environmental policies, environmental organizations are able to positively influence corporations' policies. This tactic strengthens marketplace democracy and empowers the consumer. It also has created significant progress and dramatic successes for environmental preservation. It gives consumers the ability to influence companies, stepping in where government has failed.

The reality is there is a new voice of business that shows how it is possible to do well by doing good, earning profits while upholding environmental principles. These businesses have shown a strong interest in working with government to meet the pressing environmental challenges of the 21st century. It's time for officials in Congress and the White House to listen and get to work.

Gov. Arnold Schwarzenegger, R-Calif., discusses his environmental initiatives as New York City Mayor Michael Bloomberg looks on at fuel-cell maker Bloom Energy in Sunnyvale, Calif., on Sept. 21, 2006. The mayor announced he is launching a citywide greenhouse-gas inventory and appointing an environmental advisory board. California just mandated cuts in motor vehicles' carbon-dioxide emissions.

executive, you are a human being first, and you don't want to do anything that you can't explain in good faith to your children and grandchildren."

In addition to its partnerships with FedEx, UPS and DuPont, Environmental Defense has struck agreements with numerous firms, including Wegmans Food Markets and Bon Appétit Management Company on implementing health and environmental standards for farmed salmon, McDonald's on reducing antibiotics in chicken, Compass Group food services on limiting antibiotics in pork and chicken, Bristol-Myers Squibb on incorporating environmental considerations into pharmaceutical development and packaging, and with other companies on other topics.

Having negotiated accords on environmentally friendly lending policies with Citigroup, JPMorganChase and Goldman Sachs, the Rainforest Action Network (RAN) now is running campaigns against Wells Fargo's investments in oil, coal, logging and mining operations. Among RAN's other campaigns to change corporate policies, it's pressing for revisions in Weyerhaeuser's logging practices and for increases in the fuel-efficiency of Ford vehicles.

"You're seeing tremendous leadership from the private sector right now," Environmental Defense's Yarnold says. But environmentalists continue to press for govern-

ment action because "businesses alone can't solve the global-warming problem."

Environmental groups want the federal government to require companies to meet environmental standards and to help them do so. New regulations are needed, environmentalists argue, not only to force recalcitrant companies to act but also to encourage corporations that want to act but can't afford to do more than their competitors.

"Many corporations, especially those active in international areas, are realizing they need to be more environmental and more progressive to stay competitive in the international arena," Oklahoma State University's Dunlap says. "A lot of American firms are caught in a bit of a dilemma. In some ways, they like having an administration that seems friendly to the market and keeping regulations minimal. On the other hand, they're not getting the incentives and the regulatory push to stay on the cutting edge."

Brune, of the Rainforest Action Network, describes companies that are "trying to lead by example and trying to pressure the government to wake up and step up to the plate."

The Sierra Club's Hamilton says he knows corporate executives "who have almost begged Congress to tell them what to do to reduce emissions, so they know how to plan for it. But companies are reluctant to take action on their own for fear of losing competitive advantage, because they don't know what is going to be required of them" when Congress finally does act.

"Businesses crave certainty," Yarnold explains. "Global businesses in particular crave certainty. To be operating in one regulatory environment in Europe and another in the United States is crazy. It's not good for business." Conflicts in state laws also will increase pressure for federal legislation, says Robert Brulle, an associate professor of sociology and environmental science at Drexel University, who is researching the 21st-century history of the environmental movement.

Environmentalists' top legislative goals are the cap-and-trading scheme for greenhouse gases and significant increases in vehicle fuel-economy standards. California Democrat Barbara Boxer, in line to chair the Senate Environment and Public Works Committee, said she plans "to roll out a pretty in-depth set of hearings on global warming. It isn't going to help any business, it isn't going to help anybody, if we do nothing" about the issue, she insisted.

Sen. McCain said he and Sen. Lieberman will re-introduce their global-warming bill and "absolutely" will push for a floor vote. McCain, a potential 2008 presidential candidate, also expressed optimism that President Bush would sign the legislation before he leaves the White House in January 2009.

"I think the president is coming around," McCain said. "He made a statement recently where he said that climate change is a significant issue. To tell you the truth, I'm worried more about [other] people in the administration than the president himself." [53]

In the past, Bush has said he agrees that human activity has contributed to climate change, but he has consistently rejected the idea of imposing mandatory curbs on carbon-dioxide emissions. Bush also has resisted calls to impose tougher standards on vehicle fuel economy, household appliances and building insulation — measures that could sharply reduce America's oil consumption.

Those Bush positions — plus opposition from other GOP lawmakers — lead other legislators to suggest that action is less likely than McCain predicts.

California Democrat Henry A. Waxman, incoming chair of the House Government Reform Committee, said environmentalists need to understand that "President Bush would veto any bill that ever got to him." [54] Oklahoma Republican James M. Inhofe, outgoing chair of the Senate Environment and Public Works Committee, expressed confidence that he can round up the 41 votes needed to sustain a filibuster against global-warming legislation.

Inhofe said he is seeing "an awakening" to his argument that harmful global warming is a myth. "People are realizing that [environmentalists] are saying things that are just flat not true," Inhofe said. [55]

Boxer, Inhofe's successor, acknowledged that passing legislation will be difficult. "Maybe I want to take the ball 50 yards," she said, "but I can take it only 30." [56]

OUTLOOK

Entrepreneurs in Spotlight

Environmentalists are counting on entrepreneurs to produce a future green world. Once governments impose restrictions on greenhouse-gas emissions, leaders of environmental organizations say, entrepreneurs will supply the technology that makes the restrictions work.

"It's going to look much the way it did during the information-technology gold rush at the advent of the Internet Age," Greenpeace Executive Director Passacantando says. "A whole new generation of entrepreneurs is going to lead us into the new era, and eventually we will have an economy that's built on low carbon-dioxide emissions or no carbon-dioxide emissions."

Environmental Defense's Yarnold sees hope in different pro-environment precedents — such as the restrictions on emissions that cause acid rain and deplete the ozone layer.

"Things were invented," he says. "Processes were created. People rise to the challenge. Investments get made. It creates economic activity. It creates jobs.

"Will there be solar panels made with nanotechnology? Are there chemical compounds that are better at conducting electricity than the materials we now have? I don't know. But I do know the circumstances under which those will be carried out. Efficient markets find low-cost, highly efficient solutions, and that's what will happen if the government puts a hard cap on carbon dioxide."

As Passacantando puts it, the choice of technologies "is not going to be Greenpeace's pick. It's going to be the entrepreneurs.' "

Environmentalists are most optimistic about conservation and renewable energies such as solar and wind.

"We have enough sunlight hitting the state of California every day to fulfill the country's energy needs," Oklahoma State's Brune says. "Enough wind flows through the Midwest to fulfill the country's energy needs. Both forms of energy are clean, create more jobs and have no greenhouse-gas emissions. Neither creates the environmental legacy of nuclear waste or the national-security problems associated with nuclear plants."

Some environmentalists acknowledge the possibility that new technology could make coal, oil and nuclear energy acceptable as well.

"There's great hope in low-carbon coal," Yarnold says, "and nuclear has to be on the table." Before new nuclear plants can be built, he adds, the industry must prove it can dispose of waste safely and prevent nuclear materials from being turned into weapons — obstacles that many environmentalists believe are insurmountable. Others caution that the transition away from fossil fuels won't be so simple. Envisioned solutions can be double-edged swords: windmill farms that deface the landscape and injure birds that fly too close; hydropower projects that dam waterways and injure fish; agriculture-based fuels that levy their own environmental costs and drive up the cost of food.

Critics from the left and the right warn against succumbing to pressure to take actions that don't really provide long-term solutions.

"You'll probably find that promises to do something about global warming will become more popular over time," the Cato Institute's Taylor says. "Politicians will make those promises, and voters will embrace politicians who make those promises. But the public doesn't seem to be willing to pay anything to reduce greenhouse gases. So politicians are going to find it's popular to propose programs but not popular to impose programs with costs, and I don't think greenhouse gases will be reduced much at all."

While Europe appears to be ahead of the United States in protecting the environment, Drexel University's Brulle says, Europe really is practicing "simulation of environmentalism. We have symbolic responses. But, when you look at carbon-dioxide emissions in Europe, they have not significantly gone down."

Brulle fears the United States will follow the same path. "We're not going to just stop using coal any more than we're going to destroy the economy of West Virginia," he says. Neither are Americans about to abandon a consumer culture that requires ever-higher energy consumption, he says.

"The way to reduce greenhouse-gas emissions now is to conserve big time, but I don't see any political will to do that," Brulle says. That leaves increased use of nuclear power as the only alternative for the foreseeable future, he argues.

"The question," he says, "is which is the worst poison. One will be absolutely fatal — climate change. One might be fatal, but is not always fatal — nuclear power.

"I'm not a fan of nuclear power, by any means. But, given the alternative of destroying the global eco-system for thousands of years, we have to seriously consider putting nuclear power into the mix."

NOTES

1. "Corporate Innovation: Changing the Way Business Thinks About the Environment," Environmental Defense; environmentaldefense.org/corporate_innovation.cfm. See also Jia Lynn Yang, "It's Not Easy Being Green — But Big Business Is Trying," *Fortune*, Aug. 7, 2006.

2. "For the Health of the Nation: An Evangelical Call to Civic Responsibility," National Association of Evangelicals, Oct. 7, 2004; www.nae.net/images/civic_responsibility2.pdf.

3. Elizabeth Keenan, "Plugging Into Nuclear," *Time*, June 19, 2006, p. 46; Andrew C. Revkin, "Updating Prescriptions for Avoiding Worldwide Catastrophe," *The New York Times*, Sept. 12, 2006, p. F2. For background, see Marcia Clemmitt, "Climate Change," *CQ Researcher*, Jan. 27, 2006, pp. 73-96.

4. Accessed at people-press.org/reports/display.php3? ReportID=280.

5. Accessed at www.pewtrusts.com/pdf/pew_research_economy_012506.pdf.

6. Accessed at www.harrisinteractive.com/harris_poll/index.asp?PID=607.

7. Accessed at www.foe.org/camps/intl/corpacct/wall-street/handbook/index.html and rockpa.org/wp-content/uploads/2006/06/Power%20of%20Proxy.pdf.

8. The Carbon Disclosure Project, "The $31.5 Trillion Question: Is Your Company Prepared for Climate Change?" www.cdproject.net/viewrelease.asp?id=8/.

9. Juliet Eilperin, "Cities, States Aren't Waiting For U.S. Action on Climate," *The Washington Post*, Aug. 11, 2006, p. A1.

10. *Ibid.* See also Karen Matthews, "States To Lower Greenhouse Gas Emissions," The Associated Press, Oct. 16, 2006.

11. Accessed at www.apolloalliance.org.

12. Accessed at www.apolloalliance.org/strategy_center/a_bold_energy_and_jobs_policy/ten_point_plan.cfm. For background on hydrogen, see Mary H. Cooper, "Alternative Fuels," *CQ Researcher*, Feb. 25, 2005, pp. 173-196.

13. Michael Schneider, "Leo's Green Builds Skein," *Daily Variety*, Oct. 17, 2006, p. 1.

14. Karen Krebsbach, "The Green Revolution: Are Banks Sacrificing Profits for Activists' Principles?" *US Banker*, Feb. 6, 2005.

15. Marc Gunther, "The Green Machine," *Fortune*, Aug. 7, 2006, p. 42.

16. *Ibid.*

17. Yang, *op. cit.*

18. Accessed at fedex.com/us/about/responsibility/environment/hybridelectricvehicle.html?link=4.

19. Steven Mufson, "As Power Bills Soar, Companies Embrace 'Green' Buildings," *The Washington Post*, Aug. 5, 2006, p. A1.

20. General Electric, press release, "GE Launches Ecomagination to Develop Environmental Technologies"; http://home.businesswire.com/portal/site/ge/index.jsp?ndmViewId=news_view&ndmConfigId=1002373&newsId=20050509005663&newsLang=en&ndmConfigId=1002373&vnsId=681.

21. "2005 Report on Socially Responsible Investing Trends in the United States," Social Investment Forum, Jan. 24, 2006; www.socialinvest.org/areas/research/trends/sri_trends_report_2005.pdf.

22. "Proxy Season Preview — Spring 2006," As You Sow Foundation and Rockefeller Philanthropy Advisors; www.asyousow.org/publications/2006_proxy_preview.pdf.

23. Carol Hymowitz, moderator, "Corporate Social Concerns: Are They Good Citizenship, Or a Rip-Off for Investors?" *The Wall Street Journal Online*, Dec. 6, 2005; http://online.wsj.com/public/article/SB113355105439712626.html?mod=todays_free_feature.

24. Testimony before U.S. House Energy and Commerce Committee, May 2, 2006.

25. Barbara Mantel, "Energy Efficiency," *CQ Researcher*, May 19, 2006, pp. 433-456.

26. *Ibid.*

27. The Coal Based Generation Stakeholders Group, "A Vision for Achieving Ultra-Low Emissions from Coal-Fueled Electric Generation," January 2005; www.nma.org/pdf/coal_vision.pdf.

28. Mantel, *op. cit.*

29. *Ibid.*

30. Daniel Gross, "Raise the Gasoline Tax? Funny, It Doesn't Sound Republican," *The New York Times*, Oct. 8, 2006.

31. Worldwatch Institute, *Vital Signs 2006-2007* (2006), p. 32.

32. U.S. Energy Department, "Annual Energy Review 2005," Energy Information Administration, July 27, 2006, Table 1.3; www.eia.doe.gov/emeu/aer/pdf/pages/sec1_9.pdf.

33. *Ibid.*, Table 8.4a; www.eia.doe.gov/emeu/aer/pdf/pages/sec8_17.pdf.

34. *Ibid.*, Table 2.1e; www.eia.doe.gov/emeu/aer/pdf/pages/sec2_8.pdf.

35. The Coal Based Generation Stakeholders Group, *op. cit.*

36. "Annual Energy Review 2005," *op. cit.*, Table 1.3.

37. Peter Schwartz and Spencer Reiss, "Nuclear Now! How Clean, Green Atomic Energy Can Stop Global Warming," *Wired*, February 2005.

38. U.S. Energy Department, op. cit., Table 10.1; www.eia.doe.gov/emeu/aer/pdf/pages/sec10_3.pdf.

39. Adriel Bettelheim, "Biofuels Boom," *CQ Researcher*, Sept. 29, 2006, pp. 793-816.

40. Revkin, *op. cit.*, p. 2.

41. Frank Clifford, "Alarmed by 'Cycle of Anti-Environmentalism,' " *Los Angeles Times*, Nov. 15, 2005, p. B2.

42. Unless otherwise noted, this "Background" section is based on "The Evolution of the Conservation Movement," Library of Congress; lcweb2.loc.gov/ammem/amrvhtml/conshome.html; Lorraine Elliott, "Environmentalism," *Encyclopaedia Britannica*, 2006; www.britannica.com/eb/article-224631; *History of the Environmental Movement*, Glen Canyon Institute; www.glencanyon.org/library/ movement-history.php; "History," U.S. Environmental Protection Agency; epa.gov/history/index.htm; Tom Arrandale, "National Parks Under Pressure," *CQ Researcher*, Oct. 6, 2006, pp. 917-840; Mary H. Cooper, "Environmental Movement at 25," *CQ Researcher*, March 31, 1995, pp. 273-296, and William Kovarik, "Environmental History Timeline," www.radford.edu/~wkovarik/envhist.

43. The Associated Press, "3 Plead Guilty to Ecoterror Charges," *Los Angeles Times*, July 21, 2006, p. A19.

44. "History of Earth Day," Earth Day Network; www.earthday.org/resources/history.aspx.

45. Beverly Beyette, "Earth Observance: The Day Politics Stood Still," *Los Angeles Times*, May 23, 1985, p. 5-1. Joanne Omang, " 'Sun Day,' Slated in May," *The Washington Post*, Sept. 19, 1977, p. A20.

46. Beyette, *op. cit.*

47. The Associated Press, April 23, 1970 (Lenin's birthday); Dan Eggen, "Earth Day: From Radical to Mainstream," *The Washington Post*, April 22, 2000, p. B1 (Daughters of the American Revolution).

48. Jerry Adler, "Going Green," *Newsweek*, July 17, 2006, p. 42.

49. *Encyclopedia of Associations*, 2003 and 2006.

50. *Giving USA 2006: The Annual Report on Philanthropy for the Year 2005*, published by the Giving USA Foundation.

51. The Gallup Organization, 2006.

52. Bettina Boxall, "Conservationist Clout," *Los Angeles Times*, Nov. 9, 2006. p. 27.

53. Darren Samuelsohn, "Sen. McCain Pledges Push for 'Long-Overdue' Emissions Bill," *Environment and Energy Daily*, Nov. 17, 2006.

54. *Ibid.*

55. *Ibid.*

56. Charles Babington, "Party Shift May Make Warming a Hill Priority," *The Washington Post*, Nov. 18, 2006, p. A6.

BIBLIOGRAPHY

Books

Bailey, Ronald, ed., *Global Warming and Other Eco Myths: How the Environmental Movement Uses False Science to Scare Us to Death*, Prima Publishing, 2002.
In this collection of essays the writers argue that many warnings about threats to the environment are way overblown.

Gore, Al, *An Inconvenient Truth: The Planetary Emergency of Global Warming and What We Can Do About It*, Rodale Books, 2006.
Former Vice President Al Gore urges action on global warming in this book written to accompany his surprisingly popular movie of the same name.

Savitz, Andrew W., and Karl Weber, *The Triple Bottom Line: How Today's Best-Run Companies Are Achieving Economic, Social and Environmental Success — and How You Can Too*, Jossey-Bass, 2006.
A business consultant and a freelance writer offer practical advice on how companies can profit from responding to environmental and other public needs.

Articles

Adler, Jerry, "Going Green," *Newsweek*, July 17, 2006, p. 42.
Adler looks at how individual Americans are taking action to protect the environment.

Gunther, Marc, "The Green Machine," *Fortune*, Aug. 7, 2006, p. 42.
Gunther reports on Wal-Mart's ambitious plans to become the world's greenest retailer and increase profits at the same time.

Holstein, William J., "Saving the Earth, And Saving Money," *The New York Times*, Aug. 13, 2006, p. 9.
Gwen Ruta, director of corporate partnerships for Environmental Defense, explains how her organization works with businesses.

Hymowitz, Carol, moderator, "Corporate Social Concerns: Are They Good Citizenship, Or a Rip-Off for Investors?" *The Wall Street Journal Online*, Dec. 6, 2005. Available online at http://online.wsj.com/public/article/SB113355105439712626.html?mod=todays_free_feature.
Debaters about corporations' environmental responsibility included Benjamin Heineman Jr., then senior vice president of GE; Ilyse Hogue, director of the Rainforest Action Network's Global Finance Campaign; and Fred Smith Jr., president and founder of the Competitive Enterprise Institute.

Pollan, Michael, "Mass Natural," *The New York Times*, June 4, 2006, p. 15.
Pollan fears Wal-Mart's plan to become an organic grocer and its massive purchasing power and lust for low prices will hurt organic farmers and consumers.

Schwartz, Peter, and Spencer Reiss, "Nuclear Now! How Clean, Green Atomic Energy Can Stop Global Warming," *Wired*, February 2005.
The authors argue that nuclear power can end global warming and the other environmental degradations associated with extracting and burning coal and oil.

Reports and Studies

Coal Based Generation Stakeholders Group, "A Vision for Achieving Ultra-Low Emissions from Coal-Fueled Electric Generation," January 2005; www.nma.org/pdf/coal_vision.pdf.
The coal industry and its customers tell how they plan to meet America's energy and environmental needs by cleaning up their acts.

Friends of the Earth, "Confronting Companies Using Shareholder Power: A Handbook on Socially-Oriented Shareholder Activism;" www.foe.org/camps/intl/corpacct/wallstreet/handbook/index.html.
The environmental organization urges corporate shareholders to press their companies to adopt environmentally friendly practices.

Hayward, Steven F., "Index of Leading Environmental Indicators 2006," American Enterprise Institute, 2006; www.aei.org/books/bookID.854/book_detail.asp.
The think tank's annual analysis of environmental statistics contends Earth is in much better shape than leading environmental organizations say.

National Association of Evangelicals, "For the Health of the Nation: An Evangelical Call to Civic Responsibility," Oct. 7, 2004; www.nae.net/images/civic_responsibility2.pdf.
Conservative religious leaders admonish believers that faith requires acting to relieve social ills and to protect the environment.

Price, Tom, "Activists in the Boardroom: How Advocacy Groups Seek to Shape Corporate Behavior," Foundation for Public Affairs, 2006.
The author examines how advocacy organizations influence companies' policies through both confrontation and cooperation.

Worldwatch Institute, *State of the World 2006: A Worldwatch Institute Report on Progress Toward a Sustainable Society*, W. W. Norton, 2006.
The environmental group reports on developments important to environmental protection and sustainability, including renewable alternatives to oil and the special challenges posed by rapid economic development in China and India.

For More Information

American Enterprise Institute, 1150 17th St., N.W., Washington, DC 20036; (202) 862-5800; www.aei.org. Conservative think tank that studies environmental and other issues.

Bullitt Foundation, 1212 Minor Ave., Seattle, WA 98101-2825; (206) 343-0807; www.bullitt.org. Philanthropic organization working to protect, restore and maintain the natural environment of the Pacific Northwest.

Cato Institute, 1000 Massachusetts Ave., N.W., Washington, DC 20001-5403; (202) 842-0200; www.cato.org. Libertarian think tank that questions environmental-protection measures that interfere with free markets.

Ecomagination, www.ge.ecomagination.com. Web site where General Electric explains its plans to profit from making environmentally friendly products.

Environmental Defense, 257 Park Ave. South, New York, NY 10010; (212) 505-2100; www.environmentaldefense.org. The advocacy group forms partnerships with corporations to promote environmentally friendly business practices.

League of Conservation Voters, 1920 L St., N.W., Suite 800, Washington, DC 20036; (202) 785-8683; www.lcv.org. Advocacy group that reports on government officials' actions on environmental issues.

Natural Resources Defense Council, 40 West 20th St., New York, NY 10011; (212) 727-2700; www.nrdc.org. Advocacy group that studies and acts on a wide range of environmental issues, with special focus on wildlife and wilderness areas.

Pew Center on Global Climate Change, 2101 Wilson Blvd., Suite 550, Arlington, VA 22201; (703) 516-4146; www.pewclimate.org. Funded by Pew Charitable Trusts.

Rainforest Action Network, 221 Pine St., 5th Floor, San Francisco, CA 94104; (415) 398-4404; www.ran.org. The activist group protests corporate practices that harm the environment and helps design pro-environment business practices.

Resources for the Future, 1616 P St., N.W., Washington, DC 20036; (202) 328-5000; www.rff.org. Independent scholarly organization that analyzes energy, environment and natural-resources issues.

Rockefeller Philanthropy Advisors, 437 Madison Ave., 37th Floor, New York, NY 10022; (212) 812-4330; www.rockpa.org. Studies and offers advice about shareholder activism by nonprofit organizations.

Sierra Club, 85 Second St., 2nd Floor, San Francisco, CA 94105; (415) 977-5500; www.sierraclub.org. Founded in 1892 to protect wilderness but now active on many environmental issues.

Social Investment Forum, 1612 K St., N.W., Suite 650, Washington, DC 20006; (202) 872-5319; www.socialinvest.org. The socially responsible investing industry's trade association.

Wal-Mart Sustainability, www.walmartfacts.com/featuredtopics/?id=1. Web site where Wal-Mart showcases its efforts to become environmentally friendly.

Worldwatch Institute, 1776 Massachusetts Ave., N.W., Washington, DC 20036-1904; (202) 452-1999; www.worldwatch.org. Studies environmental and economic trends.

8

Energy Efficiency

Barbara Mantel

Gas sells for over $3 a gallon in San Francisco in early May. Faced with unhappy motorists, lawmakers have proposed solutions ranging from investigating possible price-gouging to drilling for oil in the Arctic National Wildlife Refuge. But some experts say the best way to reduce prices is by reducing demand through improved energy efficiency.

From *CQ Researcher*,
May 19, 2006.

When members of Congress went home for spring break, angry constituents gave them an earful about gas prices that had risen to near or more than $3 per gallon. So when lawmakers returned to Washington in late April, they were determined to show voters their concern.

Republicans and Democrats alike threw out a flurry of energy proposals, including investigating possible price-gouging, opening the Arctic National Wildlife Refuge to oil drilling, easing environmental regulations on refineries and reforming fuel-economy standards.

But in a polarized Congress in an election year, getting agreement on any of these will be difficult, to say the least. And besides, some analysts say there's not enough emphasis on reducing demand. "With energy-supply markets tied in a straitjacket, moderating demand is our only real choice for the near term," said Steven Nadel, executive director of the American Council for an Energy-Efficient Economy, an independent policy group. The way to reduce demand, said Nadel, is to improve energy efficiency.

Increasing energy efficiency involves building buildings and developing appliances, industrial processes and vehicles that use less energy but deliver the same or better service. It doesn't mean turning down the thermostat and shivering; it means installing an energy-efficient furnace and keeping the thermostat setting the same.

Since government efficiency programs were created soon after the 1973 Arab oil embargo, America's "energy intensity" — the amount of energy the economy uses to produce a dollar of gross domestic product — has been reduced by more than 40 percent. [1]

Oil Is Largest U.S. Energy Source

More than 90 percent of the energy used in the United States in 2004 came from non-renewable sources, including 40 percent from oil. Renewable sources, such as wind and water power, produced 6 percent (left graph). Of the four main users of energy, industry accounted for one-third of total energy use (right graph).

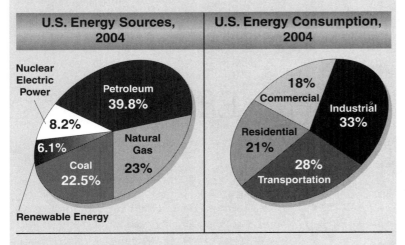

U.S. Energy Sources, 2004

- Petroleum **39.8%**
- Natural Gas **23%**
- Coal **22.5%**
- Nuclear Electric Power **8.2%**
- Renewable Energy **6.1%**

U.S. Energy Consumption, 2004

- Industrial **33%**
- Transportation **28%**
- Residential **21%**
- Commercial **18%**

Note: Percentages may not add to 100 due to rounding

Source: U.S. Energy Information Administration

- The average electricity used by new refrigerators has been cut by more than half since 1972.
- The energy used to produce a ton of paper has fallen 27 percent over 20 years. [2]

Despite the improved efficiency of appliances, vehicles and manufacturing, overall U.S. energy consumption has continued to increase — though at a slower rate — primarily because of population growth and economic expansion. American energy consumption has risen from about 75 quadrillion Btus in 1973 to about 100 quadrillion Btus in 2004, according to the Department of Energy, and will jump another 30 percent by 2025. [3]

But it doesn't have to be that way, some experts say. "Americans can still cost-effectively save half the electricity they use . . . and at least that much of the oil and gas," estimates the Rocky Mountain Institute, a research and consulting nonprofit. "Achieving these technical potentials . . . would take several decades, but pursuing them is clearly worthwhile." [4]

Meanwhile, energy costs have been climbing. The inflation-adjusted price of residential natural gas rose 29 percent this winter compared to last winter, and residential heating oil jumped 22 percent. [5] The inflation-adjusted price of gasoline in late April increased 27 percent over last year. [6]

But it's not just rising costs that are lending urgency to the call for reduced energy consumption. "The past decade was the hottest of the past 150 years and perhaps the past millennium," according to the nonpartisan Pew Center on Global Climate Change. [7] The Earth is warming, and a growing scientific consensus says it is partly due to the release of carbon dioxide and other greenhouse gases that result from burning fossil fuels. Rising sea levels and changes in precipitation are likely and, coupled with warming, could threaten ecosystems, biological diversity and even human health, according to the center.

In fact, a growing number of scientists believe the Earth may be approaching a "tipping point" — beyond

"If the U.S. were operating today at the same energy intensity as in 1973, we'd be consuming about 186 quadrillion Btus* each year, instead of the 100 quadrillion that we actually do," says Joe Loper, vice president of research and analysis at the Alliance to Save Energy, a coalition of business, government, environmental and consumer groups.

The nation's improved energy intensity is not due entirely to better energy efficiency. An estimated 25 to 50 percent of the reduction is due to structural changes in the economy, such as the shift away from manufacturing. Still, energy efficiency has played a significant role, and examples abound in all sectors of the economy:

- The average fuel economy of new cars and light trucks increased from 15 miles per gallon (mpg) in 1975 to 26 mpg by 1987, although that has dropped recently to 24 mpg.

---

* A Btu, or British thermal unit, is a measure of energy equal to the amount of heat required to raise the temperature of one pound of water by 1 degree Fahrenheit.

Energy-Saving Tips for Homeowners

Heating and Cooling: These use the most household energy. Clean filters, radiators, warm-air registers and baseboard heaters. Select ENERGY STAR furnaces when replacing equipment.

Insulation: Inspect insulation and then visit the Department of Energy's ZIP Code Insulation Program (www.ornl.gov/~roofs/Zip/ZipHome.html) to determine the recommended level for a locality. Add more if needed.

Ducts: Many duct systems are poorly insulated. Ducts that leak heated air into unheated spaces can add hundreds of dollars a year to bills. Seal leaky ducts with heat-approved tape and then insulate them. For new construction, run ducts through conditioned spaces rather than a crawl space or attic.

Appliances and Lighting: These account for the second-largest energy consumption. Compact fluorescent bulbs can reduce lighting energy use by as much as 75 percent and bulbs last 4-10 times longer than incandescent bulbs. Consider purchasing ENERGY STAR appliances when replacing equipment.

Laundry: Ninety percent of the energy used for laundry is for heating the water. Wash clothes in cold water, and only wash full loads. ENERGY STAR washing machines use 50 percent less energy than standard washers.

Water Heating: This is the third-largest home energy expense. Turn down the thermostat on the water heater. Install low-flow faucets. Insulate the water heater, being careful not to cover thermostat or the top, bottom and burner compartment of a gas heater. Insulate the first six feet of water pipes connected to heater. Drain a quart of water from tank every three months to remove sediment that impedes heat transfer. Consider buying an energy-efficient water heater.

Windows: Windows can account for 10-25 percent of the heating bill, and during the summer, sunny windows make the air conditioner work two-to-three times harder. Install storm windows to reduce heat loss in winter, and weatherize current ones. Keep South windows clean in winter and South-facing curtains closed in summer. Consider installing high-performance windows if renovating, although it will take many years to recoup the investment.

Home Office and Electronics: In general, ENERGY STAR office equipment — personal computers, monitors, printers, copiers and fax machines — use half the electricity of standard equipment. Laptops use much less energy than desktop computers. Three-quarters of the electricity used to power home electronics like televisions, stereos and computers is consumed while the products are turned off. Unplug equipment when not in use or switch off power strips.

which corrective action to reduce greenhouse gas emissions will be useless to prevent catastrophic disruptions. These concerns were heightened after release of a British report in January warning that a rise of 3 degrees C from current temperatures could lead to the irreversible destabilization of Arctic ice sheets or reversal of the Earth's ability to absorb carbon dioxide. This temperature level is well within most climate-change projections. [8]

Concern about air pollution, overloading the electrical grid and disruptions in oil supplies and subsequent price shocks are also cited as reasons to shrink energy demand.

Price shocks are a real threat, says Ann Korin, co-director of the Institute for the Analysis of Global Security. "Our most critical supply chain, our energy lifeline, is open to terrorism," she says. For instance, a quarter of the world's oil reserves is controlled by Saudi Arabia, whose reserves are concentrated in just eight oil fields. Most of its processing is concentrated in a single enormous facility.

While the utility, residential and commercial sectors of the U.S. economy have reduced their oil use dramatically since the 1970s, the transportation sector burns up 40 percent more than it did then and now accounts for more than two-thirds of total U.S. oil consumption. [9] Oil use "has become even more concentrated in the sector that . . . has historically demonstrated the least ability to respond to price shocks by switching to alternative fuels," noted a report by the Department of Energy's Oak Ridge National Laboratory. [10] "America is addicted to oil," said President Bush in his State of the Union address in February.

The United States must do a better job of developing alternative fuels and increase car and truck efficiency, the Oak Ridge report concluded.

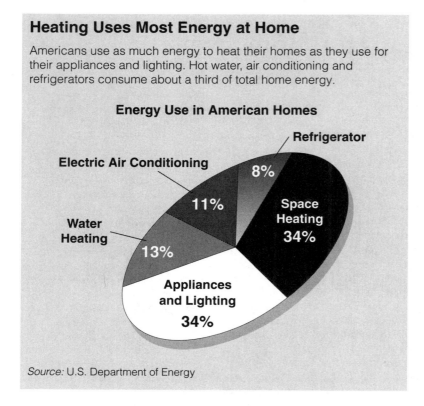

Heating Uses Most Energy at Home

Americans use as much energy to heat their homes as they use for their appliances and lighting. Hot water, air conditioning and refrigerators consume about a third of total home energy.

Energy Use in American Homes

Refrigerator 8%

Electric Air Conditioning 11%

Space Heating 34%

Water Heating 13%

Appliances and Lighting 34%

Source: U.S. Department of Energy

retary of Energy for energy efficiency and renewable energy under President Bill Clinton, calls the administration's decision to close all six regional energy-efficiency offices "one of the saddest examples of the administration's indifference to energy efficiency." The Energy Department contends the closings will reduce administrative overhead. But Reicher says the staff in those offices needs to be in the field to properly help homeowners, businesses and industry adapt energy-efficiency measures to local conditions.

While the federal government is cutting back its funding for efficiency programs, some states, like California, New York and Texas, are aggressively expanding their energy-efficiency requirements for appliances and equipment and are setting energy-saving targets for utilities. While some of these programs depend on state funding, others depend on federal money.

But federal funding for energy-efficiency research, development and demonstration projects has dropped 12 percent since 2002, and President Bush's proposed fiscal 2007 budget would slash such programs even more. [11] Facing a growing federal deficit, the president has proposed cutting funding by 9 percent for the voluntary ENERGY STAR program, which identifies and promotes energy-efficient products. He also would reduce by 30 percent funding for programs that help energy-intensive industries improve efficiency and that help local groups weatherize low-income homes. [12]

The proposal quickly came under attack from a coalition of companies, trade associations, environmental and energy-efficiency organizations, state and local government agencies and consumer advocates. "Now is the time to invest more, not less, in technologies and practices that promise the quickest, cleanest and cheapest means of addressing tight energy supplies and extraordinarily high prices," the group said in a statement to Congress. [13]

Critics are also concerned about staffing changes at the Department of Energy. Dan Reicher, former assistant sec-

As the nation grapples with budget cuts, rising energy prices and national security and climate concerns, here are some of the questions being asked:

Are homeowners and businesses doing enough to improve energy efficiency using existing technology?

Melanie and Mike Jones just couldn't get their house in Swansea, Ill., warm last winter. Despite a thermostat set at 74 degrees, she slept in socks, long pants and a sweatshirt. But when her toddler asked to sleep in a sweater too, Jones and her husband decided to take action, putting plastic on windows, caulking outside faucets, insulating light switches and having the furnace checked.

When the 1,940-square-foot ranch house did not get warmer, the Joneses called in a professional energy auditor. Not only did the heating ducts leak, but one section was split open. "Hot air was going into the crawl space," says Melanie Jones. "That's not where you want it to go!"

The Department of Energy recommends a host of ways to make residential and commercial buildings —

which account for 39 percent of U.S. energy consumption — more energy efficient. [14] They range from quick fixes like cleaning furnace filters and switching to compact fluorescent bulbs to long-term investments like sealing leaky ducts and adding insulation. (*See box, p. 172.*)

Despite major improvements in the energy efficiency of buildings since the 1970s, experts say much more can be done. The Alliance to Save Energy estimates buildings could be up to 30 percent more efficient within the next decade relying only on technologies "already in the market and known to be feasible and cost-effective." [15]

"There's tremendous potential," says Marilyn Brown, interim director of the engineering, science and technology division at the Oak Ridge laboratory. For example, commercial buildings could install reflective roofs to block heat in summer, she says. Although reflective roofs provide a quick return on investment, they are being installed on only "a small fraction" of commercial roofs today, according to Brown. Moreover, only 40 percent of residences and less than 30 percent of commercial buildings are well insulated, and less than a third of new windows purchased today are highly efficient, she says.

Obstacles — mainly upfront costs — must be overcome if energy-efficient products and construction techniques are to further penetrate the building sector, experts say. While options like switching to fluorescent light bulbs are relatively cheap, others are expensive. The Joneses spent $2,000 to repair their ductwork, and — depending on natural gas prices — won't recoup the costs for three years. They also spent considerable time on government Web sites learning about home energy use and energy audits. Many consumers and small-business owners don't have that kind of time or find the process daunting.

There is also the "split-incentive" problem: When a builder spends the extra money to make homes more energy efficient, it is the buyer who reaps the energy savings.

Many government programs are designed specifically to overcome these kinds of market barriers. They include the ENERGY STAR program, minimum energy-efficiency standards for appliances and programs to help industry improve efficiency. A National Academy of Sciences review of such programs concluded their net economic benefits exceeded their costs by more than 300 percent. [16]

The story is much the same in the industrial sector, which accounts for 33 percent of U.S. energy consumption. [17] Great strides have been made, but much more

Insulating the attic, along with sealing leaks to the outside with caulking and weather stripping, can reduce home heating and cooling bills up to 20 percent, according to the Alliance to Save Energy.

can be done, say efficiency experts. A Department of Energy report estimates that energy use in the industrial sector could be cut by 6 percent using currently available technology and improved equipment maintenance. [18] Even more energy could be saved with products and processes that require more research and development.

The Oak Ridge laboratory conducts energy audits of industrial plants, sending experts to review energy use and recommend ways to improve efficiency. "We have identified hundreds of millions of dollars in potential energy savings in just a couple of dozen plants," says Brown, "and these investments would have less than a two-year payback period — and some would be almost immediate." The measures range from replacing old motors with variable-speed models to sealing leaks in compressed air and steam systems.

As in the building sector, however, there are barriers. Many companies are large and complex, with no one accountable for energy-efficiency improvements. Even when someone is designated for the job, says Christopher Russell, director of the industrial team at the Alliance to Save Energy, that person often lacks clout. "I know people who were given the position of energy manager but didn't have the authority," he says, "and they quit."

Manufacturers also are reluctant to interrupt production to fix something they may not consider broken, especially if their energy costs are less than 5 percent of expenses.

Energy Efficiency Reduces U.S. Consumption

Since 1973, the United States has saved more energy through efficiency and conservation efforts than the amount of energy it consumed from petroleum.

Energy Conservation and Consumption, 1973-2004
(in quadrillion BTUs, or British thermal units)

	No. of Quads*
Energy efficiency and conservation	43.5
Petroleum	40.6
Natural gas	23.1
Coal	22.5
Nuclear electric power	8.2
Wood, waste, alcohol	2.9
Conventional hydroelectric	2.7
Geothermal	0.349
Solar and wind	0.205

* 1 Quad = 1 quadrillion BTUs (British thermal units) or 10^{15} BTUs

Source: Alliance to Save Energy, January 2006

" 'I've got only so many hours in the day,' " Russell hears from plant managers, " 'and do I want to use those hours to make widgets or to tune up my machinery?' "

Industrial plants adopt only 30-40 percent of the recommendations made during an energy audit, Russell says. "If fuel prices go up high enough, maybe you'll hear a different song," he says.

They certainly have had an impact at Pinehall Brick in Winston-Salem, N.C. Earlier this year, the company slightly increased the size of the holes in its bricks to reduce their weight in the kiln. "If you fire the same number of bricks, but they weigh less, you'll use less energy," said company President Fletcher Steele. The change has cut his energy use by 2.5 percent, he estimates. [19]

Should the federal government raise CAFE standards for cars?

After the Arab oil embargo of 1973, Congress passed the Energy Policy Conservation Act, requiring automakers to meet corporate average fuel economy (CAFE) standards set by the National Highway Traffic Safety Administration (NHTSA) and Congress. The near-term goal was to double the fuel economy of new cars by 1985 to 27.5 miles per gallon.

But there hasn't been much movement since. The CAFE standard for passenger cars has remained at 27.5 mpg for the past 16 years, and environmental groups say that's long enough. "We cannot simply drill our way out of our current gasoline-supply woes," says the Union of Concerned Scientists. [20] The group wants fuel-economy standards raised to more than 40 mpg by 2015, and 55 mpg by 2025.

While the idea of raising standards has gained some traction in Congress recently, the auto industry remains extremely skeptical, and technology — its feasibility, its cost and its desirability to consumers — is at the center of the debate.

In 2001, the National Academy of Sciences studied the efficacy of the CAFE program for Congress. It concluded that as the standards rose between 1975 and 1984, automakers used advances in the efficiency of engines, drive trains and aerodynamics to improve fuel economy. Fuel economy gained "62 percent without any loss of performance." But after 1985, as the government held CAFE standards steady, the industry concentrated technological advances "principally on performance and other vehicle attributes." Fuel economy remained essentially unchanged, while vehicles became 20 percent heavier and acceleration 25 percent faster. [21]

It wouldn't take hydrogen fuel cells, plug-in hybrids or space-age materials to raise fuel economy again, experts say. It could be done with current technology, and power and performance would not have to suffer, they say.

"Honda, Toyota and BMW are leading the pack," using such innovations as multi-valve engines, variable valve timing and lift, six-speed transmissions and low-rolling-resistance tires, says Alan Crane, a researcher who worked on the National Academy of Sciences report. "You would see a lot more implementation of these new technologies if the CAFE standards were raised."

Energy Policy Act Gets Mixed Reviews

In August 2005, President Bush signed the Energy Policy Act into law — the first major piece of federal energy legislation in 13 years.

It took Congress five years to draft the law after considering and then dropping several controversial provisions, including allowing oil drilling in the Arctic National Wildlife Refuge and raising fuel-economy targets for cars.

The law has its share of critics, from conservatives who say the government should not meddle in energy markets to consumers who say it did nothing to lower energy prices. But those who advocate energy efficiency as one of the most effective ways to reduce the nation's dependence on oil and cut greenhouse gas emissions gave the bill a cautious thumbs up.

"It's a modest down payment," says Steven Nadel, executive director of the American Council for an Energy-Efficient Economy. "But it doesn't do nearly enough and much more is needed." Nadel's organization estimates that the energy-efficiency sections of the law will reduce U.S. energy use by about 2 percent in 2020.

While the bill gives $2.6 billion in tax incentives to the oil and gas industry to promote energy development and distribution, it also contains several provisions designed to promote energy efficiency. For instance, it adopts energy-efficiency standards on 16 products, many of which were already subject to standards in some states, including dehumidifiers and traffic signals. The energy council estimates the standards will account for 40 percent of the anticipated energy savings in 2020.

The law also authorizes a variety of tax incentives. Consumers who buy hybrid vehicles between 2006 and 2010, for example, can receive up to $3,400 in tax credits, depending on the vehicle's fuel economy and weight. But the credit will be phased out once a manufacturer has sold 60,000 eligible vehicles. While some manufacturers probably won't reach that sales threshold for years, Toyota estimates it will have sold 60,000 hybrids by the second quarter of this year.

Bradley Berman, editor of hybridcars.com, doubts the tax credits will increase hybrid sales much. "It creates a general climate of acceptance of hybrids," says Berman, "but I don't believe it is increasing the number of hybrids on the road." The biggest problem for hybrids is lack of availability, he says, because demand for many models exceeds supply.

Homeowners, too, can receive tax credits for adding insulation, metal roofs, energy-efficient windows, furnaces, hot-water heaters and central air conditioners. The total credit cannot exceed $500, and the improvements must be made by the end of 2007.

"We're already seeing the manufacturers of these products advertising to contractors and pushing these incentives," says Nadel.

The law also encourages efficient construction of new homes and buildings. Builders whose new homes use 50 percent less energy for space heating and cooling than is required by current energy codes can receive a $2,000 tax credit. But the homes must be built by the end of 2007. Unfortunately, says Nadel, builders need much more time to learn how to construct such energy-efficient homes because very few exist today.

"If the credit expires in 2007," says Nadel, "it will nip this project in the bud." The same problem exists for the tax deduction offered to commercial builders, most of whom won't be able to design and build a qualifying project in such a short period.

Several other programs depend on federal funding, but Bush's proposed fiscal 2007 budget often doesn't supply it. For instance, the Energy Policy Act authorized $90 million for a major public-awareness campaign on how to save energy. "But it was not funded — not one cent," says Kara Saul Rinaldi, policy director at the Alliance to Save Energy.

Efficiency experts say such a campaign would be more than just good public relations. A similar $30 million campaign in California during that state's 2001 energy crisis contributed significantly to a 7 percent drop in energy use, according to the American Council for an Energy-Efficient Economy.[1] The law also authorized increased funding to help states develop and enforce energy-efficient building codes, but the president's budget zeroes out the entire program.

"That's terrible," says Rinaldi, because "every building built today may last 100 years."

House Energy and Commerce Committee Chairman Joe Barton, R-Texas, also criticized the president's budget. The administration "dropped the ball on everything in the Energy Policy Act," said Barton. ""I don't think there's a member of the committee on either side of the aisle who is happy with the budget."[2]

Testifying before Barton's committee in March, Energy Secretary Samuel Bodman said that cuts needed to be made to accommodate the president's increases in science-program funding and the initiative to increase nuclear power.[3]

---

[1] National Public Radio, "Talk of the Nation/Science Friday," Sept. 30, 2005.

[2] Quoted in Mary O'Driscoll, "Energy Policy: DOE 'dropped the ball' on EP Act Funding, Barton says," *Environment and Energy Daily*, March 10, 2006.

[3] *Ibid.*

According to the Union of Concerned Scientists, integrating these technologies into an SUV the same size and acceleration as the Ford Explorer could raise its fuel economy from 21 mpg to 36 mpg. But the improvements would add more than $2,000 to the cost of the vehicle and take up to five years to recoup through gasoline savings. [22]

"The technology is available, but will consumers pay for it?" asks Eron Shosteck, a spokesperson for the Alliance of Automobile Manufacturers. "What we have found is that some will and some won't, and some get very resentful [about buying] technology that they don't want to spend the money on."

Since CAFE standards are weighted to sales, it's not enough for carmakers to produce more fuel-efficient vehicles, says Shosteck. Consumers must buy them if carmakers are to meet government targets.

Safety is another concern. "The down-weighting and downsizing that occurred in the late 1970s and early 1980s, some of which was due to CAFE standards, probably resulted in an additional 1,300 to 2,600 traffic fatalities in 1993," the National Academy of Sciences reported. [23] Critics of CAFE standards have seized on that conclusion to argue against raising them.

But two members of the panel that wrote the report sharply challenged that conclusion. David Greene, a corporate fellow at the Oak Ridge laboratory, called the evidence of a link between fuel economy, weight reduction and traffic fatalities or injuries "highly dubious." Moreover, he said, weight reduction is just one way automakers can respond to higher CAFE standards. They can also adopt innovations in engine technology, transmission design and aerodynamics. [24]

Some of the greatest potential to reduce fuel consumption is in light trucks, which include SUVs, minivans and pickup trucks. Their CAFE standard, 21.6 mpg for this model year, is lower than for cars. But that is going to change for some of the smaller models. On March 29, NHTSA strengthened the light truck CAFE standard and overhauled the way the standards are set.

"The new standards represent the most ambitious fuel-economy goals for light trucks ever developed in the program's 27-year history," said Secretary of Transportation Norman Y. Mineta. "And more importantly, they close loopholes that have long plagued the current system." [25]

Under the plan, the heaviest SUVs — those weighing between 8,500 and 10,000 pounds, such as Hummers — for the first time will be subject to fuel-economy regulation. However, the heaviest pickup trucks, which make up 80 percent of the 8,500-10,000 pound weight class, will still be exempt.

In addition, instead of applying an average standard for light trucks as it has done in the past, NHTSA assigned a standard to each vehicle based on its size, or "footprint." The smaller the footprint, the more stringent the fuel-economy standard a vehicle would have to meet. Thus, the CAFE standard for the large Hummer 2 model will increase to 22 mpg in model year 2011, while the fuel-economy standard for the smaller Jeep Wrangler will rise to 28.6 mpg. The goal is to discourage automakers from designing smaller vehicles as light trucks instead of passenger cars just to take advantage of the truck category's historically lower CAFE standard.

While many environmental groups have long sought to close the light-truck loophole, the new regulations create their own problem: They may encourage carmakers to produce more of the largest SUVS and pickups because they have the lowest CAFE standards.

Environmentalists also attacked the administration's proposal on other fronts. The continued exemption of heavier pickup trucks is shortsighted, they said, and the fuel-economy standards are too low and the fuel savings too small. "You're talking about saving 11 billion gallons of gasoline over about 20 years," says David Friedman, research director of the Clean Vehicles Program at the Union of Concerned Scientists. "That's less than a month's worth of gasoline."

On May 2, 2006, California, Massachusetts and eight other states sued to force the Bush administration to toughen the standards for light trucks, alleging that it had failed to consider the standards' impact on air quality and greenhouse gas emissions. "The Bush administration is pushing for fuel-economy standards that appear to be authored by the oil and auto industries," said Massachusetts Attorney General Thomas F. Reilly. [26]

But the Alliance of Automobile Manufacturers called the new fuel-economy standards "a challenge." [27] It pointed out they are expected to cost the industry $6.7 billion during model years 2008-2011. As for raising fuel-economy standards for passenger cars, Transportation Secretary Mineta said the administration would oppose any increase without reforms to the program, such as tailoring fuel-economy standards to car size as it did for light trucks.

As an alternative to raising fuel-economy standards, economists often propose raising the excise tax on gasoline. Making gasoline more expensive would cause consumers to demand more fuel-efficient cars, they argue. But in the current environment of $3 gas, politicians are calling for lowering gasoline taxes, not raising them. (*See "At Issue," p. 185.*)

Can states do more to encourage energy efficiency?

States have long been the laboratories for energy-efficiency policies, often serving as the inspiration for federal programs. For instance, when the federal government declined to set minimum efficiency standards for appliances like refrigerators and room air conditioners in the early 1980s, several states set their own. The federal government eventually followed suit, after manufacturers said national standards were better than a patchwork of state rules.

States use various tools to encourage energy efficiency, ranging from appliance standards and energy codes for buildings to tax incentives and public education. But experts say states could be doing much more. Only half of the states have energy-efficiency programs, and many of them need to be strengthened, according to experts.

"We clearly are finding much more efficiency potential out there than any state is realizing," says Neal Elliot, industrial program director at the American Council for an Energy-Efficient Economy.

In response to rising energy prices, strains on electricity grids, environmental concerns and advances in technology, several states have begun to do more. Many have turned once again to appliance standards. Since 2004, 10 states have established new energy-efficiency standards for products. [28] And Congress, again taking its cue from the states, incorporated 16 of the state standards into the Energy Policy Act of 2005.

California, for example, set new standards for external-power supplies, swimming-pool pumps, home electronics, commercial refrigerators and lighting, while Massachusetts set new standards for residential furnaces, lighting and electronic equipment. The Northeast Energy Efficiency Partnerships, which works with states to promote efficiency, estimates that if all states in its region adopted new or updated energy-efficiency standards, by 2020 they could reduce projected growth in annual electricity consumption by 24 percent, cut projected growth in peak demand by as much as 55 percent and reduce annual carbon emissions by more than 6 million metric tons. [29]

Building energy codes — like efficiency standards — have been around for decades. California created the first state energy code in 1978. Florida soon followed, as did New York, Minnesota, Oregon, Washington and others.

Energy codes, which are included in state residential and commercial building codes, typically set standards for the thermal properties of windows, doors and skylights, for the amount of insulation in ceilings, walls and basements, and for proper size of heating and cooling equipment. But only 20 states have adopted the most up-to-date version of the model energy code endorsed by the Department of Energy, and enforcement remains a big problem.

While the code is set by the state, local officials conduct the building inspections. "Our best-guess estimate for the Northeast is that we have maybe 50-percent compliance with the energy component of the building code," says Jim O'Reilly, policy director of the Northeast partnerships. "A local building inspector is typically more concerned with making sure fire-retardant materials are used and making sure smoke detectors meet code."

California is an exception. Its building energy code is considered the nation's most stringent and best enforced, and the state says it is responsible for 25 percent of its electricity savings over the past 30 years. [30]

To improve local enforcement of energy codes, regional organizations like the partnerships train local officials, architects and builders, using Energy Department funds. But this funding would be eliminated by President Bush's budget request for 2007.

"That's potentially a big problem," says O'Reilly.

While appliance standards and building codes are mandates, states also try to transform the marketplace in other ways. They offer rebates to consumers who buy ENERGY STAR products and to businesses that buy high-efficiency motors; they pay to weatherize low-income homes and they mount education campaigns to promote efficiency and conservation.

States often pay for these programs by having local utilities assess customers a small surcharge, usually a fraction of a cent per kilowatt-hour, and then pool the money into "a public benefit fund." Sometimes the state administers the efficiency programs, sometimes the utility does; sometimes it's a quasi-state agency or nonprofit.

Twenty-five states have such funds, but they're all "running out of money," says Elliot of the American Council for an Energy-Efficient Economy. Once consumers and businesses learn about the rebates or the

CHRONOLOGY

1970s *Energy crises spark interest in conservation.*

1970 Domestic oil production begins to decline.

Oct. 20, 1973 Arab members of the Organization of Petroleum Exporting Countries (OPEC) embargo oil exports to the U.S., triggering energy crisis.

1975 Congress adopts CAFE (corporate average fuel economy) standards.

1977 President Jimmy Carter creates Energy Department and boosts funds for energy efficiency and renewable-energy research.

1978 CAFE standards take effect. . . . Congress passes National Energy Act of 1978, a comprehensive energy measure that includes energy-efficiency tax credits.

1979 Iranian revolution triggers second oil crisis, doubling crude oil prices.

1980s *As oil prices fall, interest in energy efficiency cools.*

Jan. 1981 Crude peaks at $34 a barrel. . . . Inflation leads to global recession.

1986 Crude prices plummet to $12 a barrel. . . . National Highway Traffic Safety Administration (NHTSA) relaxes CAFE standard for model years 1986-1989 as demand for small cars falls.

1987 President Ronald Reagan vetoes, then signs, National Appliance Energy Conservation Act. . . . CAFE standards are raised to 27.5 mpg for cars and 20.7 mpg for light trucks, including SUVs.

1990s *Clinton administration strengthens efficiency programs while GOP-controlled Congress reduces funds for them. . . . Falling oil prices spur demand for SUVs.*

1991 Persian Gulf War refocuses national attention on energy issues. . . . Environmental Protection Agency (EPA) launches Green Lights, the nation's first voluntary energy-efficiency effort and the precursor to the current ENERGY STAR program.

1992 President George H. W. Bush signs comprehensive Energy Policy Act.

1994 U.S. oil imports exceed domestic production for the first time.

1996 National energy-efficiency standard requires manufacturers to increase the energy efficiency of new refrigerators by 30 percent.

Dec. 1998 Crude prices fall to $10 a barrel, boosting consumer demand for SUVs and other gas guzzlers.

1999 President Bill Clinton orders federal government to reduce its energy use 35 percent from 1985 levels by 2010. . . . Honda releases the Insight, first hybrid car in U.S.

2000s *A Republican White House and sympathetic Congress reduce spending on government energy-efficiency programs while pressing for increased domestic production of fossil fuels.*

2000 Toyota releases the Prius, the first hybrid, four-door sedan in the U.S.

May 2001 President George W. Bush directs Vice President Dick Cheney to develop a national energy policy. Developed in secret, it calls for intensified domestic-energy production, including drilling in the Arctic National Wildlife Refuge. Courts later rule Cheney does not have to reveal the industry representatives he met with.

Aug. 2005 Bush signs Energy Policy Act, which includes incentives for improvements in energy efficiency and purchases of hybrid cars but does not increase vehicle fuel economy.

Feb. 2006 President Bush's fiscal 2007 budget proposes further reductions in funding for energy-efficiency programs.

March 2006 Federal government raises fuel-economy standards for light trucks.

April-May 2006 Gas prices climb above $3 a gallon. Bush temporarily halts purchases for the Strategic Petroleum Reserve, orders investigation into alleged price manipulation, asks Congress to repeal certain oil-industry tax incentives and suggests reforming CAFE standards for cars. Members of Congress introduce energy-conservation bills aimed at lowering energy prices.

weatherization programs, Elliot says, they rush to demand them and the programs "max out." In early 2005, heating and air-conditioning rebate programs in California ran short of cash, and later that year the state authorized utilities to increase the surcharge on customer bills.

In some states, legislatures have raided the funds. O'Reilly says the Connecticut legislature began to siphon off $1 million a month from its public benefit fund in 2003 to help pay the state's own energy bills. "Once they did that and there wasn't a great hue and cry, they went and grabbed the whole thing," he says. Some of the money was eventually returned, but the program was cut in half.

"Even if you had public programs that weren't threatened by funding diversion," says O'Reilly, "even if you had building energy codes that were more effectively enforced and even if you had a list of product and appliance standards being set in all states, we as a region are still capturing only a fraction of what is technically achievable in terms of energy efficiency."

Energy-efficiency advocates would like to see states follow the lead of Texas, California and Connecticut, which have adopted energy-efficiency "portfolio standards" that set firm targets for energy savings by electric utilities. Texas, for instance, requires utilities to use energy-efficiency measures to meet 10 percent of the growth in energy demand each year. The rule became effective in 2004. New Jersey is developing an efficiency portfolio standard, and Rhode Island and Maine are considering them as well. Energy-efficiency portfolio standards are similar to the renewable portfolio standards that already exist in 21 states and which require utilities to meet a certain percentage of energy demand through renewable sources.

BACKGROUND

Rapid Change

Wood fuel was America's primary source of energy for 200 years, but after a rapid period of industrialization in the late 1800s, coal came to dominate and by the end of World War I accounted for 75 percent of the nation's energy use. [31]

Petroleum and natural gas grew in importance after discovery of the vast Spindletop oil reserve in Texas in 1901 and the advent of mass-produced automobiles. Americans turned to automobiles as their chief form of

President Bush asked lawmakers in April to approve energy exploration in the Arctic National Wildlife Refuge as part of his plan to ease rising prices. He also asked Congress to repeal $2 billion in tax breaks for energy companies and expand tax breaks to buyers of hybrid cars.

U.S. Fish and Wildlife Service/Getty Images

transportation, spurring suburban development and the construction of a vast network of roads and highways. [32] Trucks took business away from railroads, and railroads themselves began switching from coal to diesel. Homeowners began to use cleaner-burning natural gas in their furnaces and ranges. By 1947, annual consumption of petroleum and natural gas exceeded that of coal and then quadrupled in a single generation.

"Neither before nor since has any source of energy become so dominant so quickly," according to the Department of Energy. [33]

For much of this time, the country produced almost all the energy it consumed. But by the late 1950s, it began to rely more heavily on imported oil. Economic growth, rising personal income and a growing number of automobiles on the road stimulated the demand for oil, just as domestic production began to decline. Between 1970 and 1973, imports of crude oil and petroleum products doubled.

That rising dependence on imports proved critical when on Oct. 20, 1973, the Arab members of the Organization of Petroleum Exporting Countries (OPEC) cut off all shipments to the United States for five months in retaliation for its support of Israel in the Yom Kippur War. [34] By November, oil supplies were critically low, prompting panic buying and long lines at the pump. Energy shortages threatened almost every sector of the economy.

More Builders Going "Green"

When the Alta Ski Resort in Utah's Wasatch Mountains was planning a new mid-mountain ski shelter, it decided to "go green."

"We're on public land," says Tom Whipple, Alta's facilities supervisor. "So I think we've always been good stewards, and this is the next step."

The three-level Watson Shelter opened this season. To reduce the impact on the environment, the deck is made of recycled materials, and water is sterilized with ultraviolet light instead of chemicals. The restrooms use waterless urinals, automatic faucets and low-flow toilets. To save on energy, the building makes maximum use of daylight, uses fluorescent bulbs with occupancy sensors and contains energy-efficient windows, high-efficiency boilers and a computer-controlled heating and ventilation system.

Building "green" is catching on, but for a while no one knew exactly what the term meant. Then in 1993, a group of architects and building professionals founded the U.S. Green Building Council to define and standardize the process. Seven years later, the organization, now a coalition of architects, building professionals, environmentalists, utilities and government officials, introduced a rating system for sustainable building that has quickly become a sought-after imprimatur.

The system is called LEED — Leadership in Energy and Environmental Design — and buildings are rated in five categories:

- site sustainability
- water efficiency
- materials and resources
- indoor environmental quality, and
- energy efficiency.

A commercial building receives points in each category, and the total determines its rating, ranging from certified, silver and gold to platinum — the highest.

"Energy efficiency plays the largest role in terms of points," says Tom Hicks, the council's LEED vice president. "This reflects not only the impact to the bottom line but also the broader impacts to the environment."

To receive a LEED rating, the owners of a planned building must first register it. The number of registrations has climbed dramatically since LEED was introduced — from 400 in 2003 to 1,000 last year, bringing the total number of registered buildings to more than 4,000. Once a building is complete, it can be rated. About 400 buildings currently have LEED ratings.

Several are in New York City. In March, 7 World Trade Center — the last building to fall in the 2001 terrorist

---

The public looked to government for solutions, and two years later Congress passed the Energy Policy Conservation Act of 1975, which created the Strategic Petroleum Reserve to soften the economic impact of future disruptions in oil supplies. To encourage domestic production, the law began a phased deregulation of U.S. oil prices, which had risen much less than world prices during the embargo, largely due to price controls imposed by President Richard M. Nixon.

The law also promoted energy efficiency, and automobiles were a natural target. The oil embargo and the resulting energy shortages had brought into sharp focus the fuel inefficiency of U.S. cars. The average fuel economy of new cars had fallen from 14.8 mpg in model year 1967 to 12.8 mpg in 1974. [35] The law established corporate average fuel economy (CAFE) standards for new cars.

In early 1977, newly elected Democratic President Jimmy Carter devised a National Energy Plan and called the challenge of reducing America's dependence on foreign oil the "moral equivalent of war." At the president's request, Congress created the Department of Energy to coordinate energy policy and, after much negotiation, passed the National Energy Act of 1978, which significantly increased funding for energy efficiency and renewable-energy research and development.

Carter could have used a period of energy stability to organize his new department and implement its programs, but in January 1979 the Iranian revolution triggered a second oil crisis, greatly disrupting the flow of oil to world markets and sending world oil prices soaring. In response, Carter called for increased production, conservation and development of alternative fuels as well as the continued decontrol of U.S. oil prices.

attacks and the first to be rebuilt — received a gold LEED certification. Its developer, Larry A. Silverstein, said certification won't stop there.

"Everything we do at 7 World Trade Center we will do at the Freedom Tower . . . and at all subsequent World Trade Center buildings," said Silverstein. [1] The 7 World Trade building has a public park, state-of-the-art clear glass, a high-efficiency air-filtration system, high-efficiency steam-to-electricity turbine generators and a system to harvest rainwater for cooling the building and irrigating the park.

Just a few blocks away, a 292-unit luxury apartment building that opened in 2003, the Solaire, is also certified gold, and the neighborhood expects seven other LEED-certified apartment buildings to be completed in the next few years. Solaire leasing manager Lydia Haran said green features were the primary selling point. "We learned from the leasing process that . . . other factors were secondary; that there was a pent-up demand for green luxury high rises." [2]

It's not just private developers who are registering for LEED certification. More than two-dozen U.S. cities now require municipal buildings to meet LEED standards, and nearly a dozen states have done the same for state-owned buildings. [3]

Still, LEED-registered buildings represent just 5 percent of the commercial building market, and most of those buildings are large, averaging 100,000 square feet. The average commercial building in the United States is 15,000 square feet.

"Smaller builders may not have the same financial abilities as the larger builders," says Hicks. But he adds, the costs are surprisingly low. "People think that these buildings must cost 20 percent more to build, but it's actually less than 2 percent more." The time it takes to recoup these added costs depends on several factors, including the amount of water and energy saved and their costs.

Currently, LEED ratings are available only for commercial and institutional buildings, but the U.S. Green Building Council is developing LEED ratings for homes as well.

Meanwhile, the National Association of Home Builders has issued a set of guidelines for builders interested in constructing green homes. According to an association survey, interest is climbing: In 2005, green building represented $7.4 billion worth of the residential market, or 2 percent of housing starts. In 2010, green building will represent $19-$38 billion worth of the residential market, or 5-10 percent of housing starts. [4]

[1] U.S. Green Building Council, 7 World Trade Center Earns LEED Certification, March 27, 2006. www.usgbc.org/News/USGBCNews Details.aspx?ID=2225.

[2] Gracella Hapgood, "Green Gets Green," *Continental.com/magazine*, December 2005, p. 72.

[3] U.S. Green Building Council, "LEED Initiatives in Governments and Schools," March 21, 2006.

[4] National Association of Home Builders, "Key Points from the Green Building Survey," www.nahb.org/fileUpload_details.aspx?content ID=56262.

This second energy crisis combined with Carter's inability to free American hostages from the U.S. Embassy in Tehran contributed to Carter's loss to Republican Ronald Reagan in the 1980 presidential election. [36]

Falling Prices

Reagan reversed Carter's emphasis on energy efficiency and alternative fuels and even advocated abolishing the Department of Energy, which he said had not "produced a quart of oil or a lump of coal or anything else in the line of energy." [37]

Funds for efficiency and conservation programs at the Department of Energy were slashed by more than 50 percent — from $730 million in 1981 to $333 million in 1989 — and funding for alternative-energy research plummeted from $1 billion to $116 million. [38] Reflecting his GOP administration's free-market philos-

ophy, Reagan accelerated the schedule for energy price decontrol.

The public's interest in energy efficiency flagged along with the president's. After OPEC increased production in 1986, oil prices plunged from $30 a barrel to $12. Consumers began to turn away from smaller, more fuel-efficient cars and began their love affair with mini-vans and SUVs.

Paradoxically, just as energy prices were falling President Reagan did support one of the country's most far-reaching energy-efficiency programs. In 1987, he signed the National Appliance Energy Conservation Act, which set federal energy-efficiency standards for commonly used appliances.

Reagan's successor, Republican George H. W. Bush, continued the emphasis on deregulating oil and gas, but he also renewed funding for research and development of

Installing a high-efficiency natural gas furnace can help lower home heating bills. Heating accounts for the biggest chunk of the energy used in a typical home.

When Democrat Bill Clinton took over the White House in 1993, his energy policy reflected the growing concern about the dangers of global warming and the part played by the burning of fossil fuels in creating greenhouse gas emissions. In his first Earth Day address on April 21, Clinton announced that the United States would stabilize greenhouse gas emissions at 1990 levels by the year 2000. In October, the administration unveiled its Climate Change Action Plan. Energy efficiency and conservation measures counted for about 70 percent of the plan's anticipated emissions reductions. [39]

Sustained Price Rise

In the late 1990s, energy prices began to rise again. In March 1999, OPEC production cuts sent the price of world crude oil from less than $11 a barrel to $24.50 a barrel by December. [40] Disruptions in the flow of oil from Venezuela and Nigeria further restricted production. Meanwhile, world demand for oil increased, propelled in part by rapid economic growth in China and India, which were becoming major energy consumers.

Natural gas prices in the United States also were rising. The bitterly cold winter of 2000-2001 caused a surge in demand for gas for home heating and electrical generation, and by the beginning of the decade, demand exceeded domestic supplies.

In May 2001, against this backdrop of shortage and rising prices, newly elected President George W. Bush presented his national energy policy emphasizing increasing domestic production of oil, gas, coal and nuclear power. The president called for opening the Arctic National Wildlife Refuge to oil and gas exploration, reducing barriers to drilling on other public lands and easing regulations for the licensing of power plants and gas refineries. Bush's plan also called for an expansion of the ENERGY STAR program and efficiency standards for appliances. [41]

"Energy production and environmental protection are not competing priorities," said the president. [42]

Environmental groups and congressional Democrats immediately attacked the plan. "Who would benefit?" asked David Hawkins, director of the Climate Center at the Natural Resources Defense Council, an environmental group. "The oil, coal and auto industries, which shoveled millions of dollars into Bush campaign coffers. Who loses? Anyone who likes to breathe." [43]

Not until the summer of 2005, with oil reaching almost $60 a barrel and gasoline just under $2.50 a gallon, did

energy efficiency and alternative fuels. The Bush administration also ushered in a non-regulatory approach. In 1992, the Environmental Protection Agency (EPA) launched ENERGY STAR, a voluntary labeling program designed to identify and promote energy-efficient products to reduce greenhouse gas emissions. Computers and monitors were labeled first, eventually followed by office equipment, major appliances, lighting and home electronics.

That same year, Bush signed the Energy Policy Act. It encouraged oil and gas exploration in coastal U.S. waters while improving building energy codes, equipment standards and the management of energy use by the federal government — the nation's biggest energy consumer.

Congress approve the Energy Policy Act of 2005. "After years of debate and division, Congress passed a good bill," President Bush said as he signed it on Aug. 8. "I'm confident that one day Americans will look back on this bill as a vital step toward a more secure and more prosperous nation that is less dependent on foreign sources of energy."

The law provides $2.6 billion in tax credits for oil and gas production and refining, streamlines approval procedures for drilling on public lands, expedites federal judicial review for permitting natural gas pipelines and liquefied natural gas terminals and promotes the development of clean coal. Consumer advocates and environmental groups promptly attacked the plan as doing little to lower gasoline prices, while conservatives attacked it for doing too much. "With oil flirting with $60 a barrel, you don't need to provide new incentives for development, new incentives for production and exploration," said Jerry Taylor, a senior fellow at the libertarian Cato Institute. [44]

With regard to energy efficiency, the law gives manufacturers and consumers tax incentives to speed the adoption of energy-efficient technologies and sets minimum energy-efficiency standards for 16 products.

By the spring of 2006, energy prices had reached new historic highs. Crude oil breached the $70 per barrel mark, and gasoline climbed above $3 a gallon in some regions. In April, Bush announced a plan that he said would ease rising prices. He directed the Justice Department to investigate possible price gouging and temporarily halted government purchases of oil to fill the Strategic Petroleum Reserve. He also asked Congress to repeal $2 billion in tax breaks for energy companies, expand tax breaks to buyers of hybrid cars and approve energy exploration in the Arctic National Wildlife Refuge.

CURRENT SITUATION

Efficiency Lawsuit

Environmentalists, 15 states and two consumer groups are suing the Energy Department for failing to toughen minimum energy-efficiency standards for 22 household and commercial products. The department is between six and 13 years behind schedule updating federally mandated standards for products like dishwashers, central air conditioners and furnaces. For instance, a new, stronger energy-efficiency standard for home furnaces is 12 years overdue.

The department blames its own internal rulemaking process for the delays. Congressional Democrats blame the delays on mismanagement, and efficiency advocates cite budget cuts. Almost everyone agrees the delays will cost consumers money.

According to the American Council for an Energy-Efficient Economy, existing standards will save nearly 400 billion kilowatt-hours per year by 2020 or about $34 billion at current electricity and natural gas prices. "Updating all the standards now pending at the Department of Energy could save another 180 billion kilowatt-hours per year by 2030 . . . worth about $15 billion per year at current prices." [45]

While the delays straddle three different administrations, past administrations at least caught up on some. The Clinton administration issued 10 efficiency standards, says Katherine Kennedy, a senior attorney at the Natural Resources Defense Council, one of the parties in the lawsuit. "Bush senior's administration issued five standards," she continued. "But the current administration has not issued any strengthened energy standards at all."

On Jan. 31, 2006, the Energy Department released a schedule for bringing the standards up to date. "This aggressive schedule shows our commitment to greater efficiency by issuing new standards for all products in the backlog by June of 2011, just five years from now," said Acting Assistant Secretary for Energy Efficiency and Renewable Energy Douglas L. Faulkner. [46]

But the groups suing the department were far from mollified. "It leaves aside until after 2011 any action on two of the standards that have the potential for the biggest energy savings — residential refrigerators and residential furnace fans," says Andrew deLaski, executive director of the nonprofit Appliance Standards Awareness Project.

In addition, the schedule is voluntary. "There is no reason to believe that [the Department of Energy] will meet the deadlines in this plan," says Kennedy, "when they have missed so many deadlines in past plans."

The plaintiffs in the lawsuit have proposed their own schedule with earlier deadlines and are asking the court to make those deadlines binding.

Automakers Sue California

While California is one of the states suing the federal government over appliance standards, automakers are suing California over its anti-climate-change law.

Gas Tax Hasn't Changed in a Decade

The federal excise tax on gasoline has remained virtually unchanged — at about 18 cents per gallon — since 1994. Today, many economists want Congress to raise the tax in hopes it will force consumers to demand more fuel-efficient cars. But with gas currently selling for more than $3 a gallon, politicians want the tax lowered, not raised.

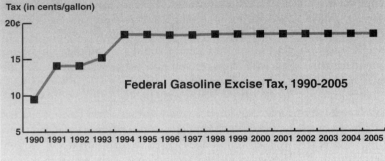

Tax (in cents/gallon)

Federal Gasoline Excise Tax, 1990-2005

Source: Congressional Research Service, Tax Foundation

In July 2002, former Democratic California Gov. Gray Davis signed the nation's first law to control the amount of greenhouse gases emitted in auto exhaust. Two years later, the California Air Resources Board issued regulations to implement the law, which gives automakers until 2009 to develop an auto fleet emitting 22 percent fewer greenhouse gases by 2012 and 30 percent fewer by 20016.

Automakers immediately protested, and in December 2004 the Alliance of Automobile Manufacturers, the Association of International Automobile Manufacturers and California auto dealers challenged the law in federal court. "This regulation is inconsistent with federal law, as well as fundamental principles for sound regulation of motor vehicles," said Fred Webber, president and CEO of the manufacturers' alliance. [47]

California and the automakers disagree on almost every point: the legality of the law, its cost to consumers and its impact on vehicle choice.

Virtually all vehicle greenhouse gas emissions are carbon dioxide, and the only way to reduce those is to improve fuel economy, say automakers. But only the federal government can set fuel-economy standards, the manufacturers' alliance says and calls the California law a backdoor attempt by a state to set fuel-economy standards. [48]

California lawmakers counter that the state is setting emissions, not fuel-economy standards, and that it has authority to do so under the federal Clean Air Act. California regulators say the technology to reduce vehicles' greenhouse emissions is readily available and would add less than $400 to the cost of a car or small SUV in 2012 and just over a $1,000 in 2016. Moreover, they estimate that car buyers would more than recoup these costs over the lifetime of the vehicle with savings at the gas pump.

The Alliance of Automobile Manufacturers, however, puts the cost at triple those amounts and says drivers would never completely recoup them. It also says Californians would see fewer models on sales lots and full-size pickup trucks might disappear altogether.

Nine states, including New York, have pledged to adopt the California standards. And after Canada threatened to copy the California law, automakers and the Canadian government reached a voluntary agreement in March 2005 to reduce greenhouse gas emissions from cars sold there. Automakers already have a voluntary agreement with the European Union.

Environmental groups say the Canadian pact weakens the carmakers' lawsuit. "When they go into court and say, 'Your honor, we can't do this,' we can point out that they have agreed to do this just north of us in Canada," said Daniel Becker, director of the Sierra Club's global warming program. [49]

But automakers say the Canadian pact has no bearing on the U.S. lawsuit. Canada has the authority to reach a voluntary agreement with carmakers, but states, automakers argue, don't have the authority to set fuel-economy standards. "So it is apples and oranges," said Gloria Bergquist, a spokeswoman for the Alliance of Automobile Manufactures. [50]

Hybrid Potential

The California law comes at a particularly difficult time for U.S. automakers. General Motors and Ford plan to cut 60,000 jobs and close or idle more than two-dozen facilities in the next several years. These restructuring plans are designed to reverse billions of dollars of losses

Should gas taxes be raised to encourage energy conservation?

YES

Robert H. Frank
Professor of Economics, Johnson Graduate School of Management, Cornell University

Written for *CQ Researcher*, May 2006.

Suppose a politician proposed a policy that would, if adopted, produce hundreds of billions of dollars in savings for American consumers, significant reductions in traffic congestion, major improvements in air quality, large reductions in greenhouse gases and substantially reduced dependence on Middle East oil. This policy would also require no net cash outlays from American families, no additional regulations and no expansion of the bureaucracy.

Although it sounds too good to be true, such a policy could be enacted by Congress tomorrow — namely, a $2-a-gallon tax on gasoline whose proceeds were refunded to American families in reduced payroll taxes.

On average, a family of four currently consumes almost 2,000 gallons of gasoline annually. If all families continued to consume gasoline at the same rate after the imposition of a $2-a-gallon tax, the average family would pay $4,000 in additional gasoline taxes annually. A family with two earners would then receive an annual payroll tax refund of $4,000.

But that is not how things would play out. Suppose, for example, that the family was about to replace its aging Ford Explorer, which gets 15 mpg. It would have a strong incentive to consider Ford's new Focus wagon, which can haul almost as much cargo and gets more than 30 miles per gallon.

Experience from the 1970s confirms that consumers respond to higher gasoline prices not just by buying more efficient cars but also by taking fewer trips, forming carpools and moving closer to work. If families overall bought half as much gasoline as before, the rebate would be only $2,000 for the representative two-earner family. In that case, this family could not buy just as much gasoline as before unless it spent $2,000 less on everything else.

One barrier to the adoption of higher gasoline taxes has been the endless insistence by proponents of smaller government that all taxes are bad. But as even the most enthusiastic free-market economists concede, current gasoline prices are far too low, because they fail to reflect the environmental and foreign policy costs associated with gasoline consumption. Government would actually be smaller, and we would all be more prosperous, if not for the problems caused by what President Bush has called our addiction to oil.

In the warmer weather they will have inherited from us a century from now, perspiring historians will struggle to explain why this proposal was once considered politically unthinkable.

NO

Ben Lieberman
Senior policy analyst, Heritage Foundation

Written for *CQ Researcher*, May 2006.

Raising the excise tax on gasoline is clearly not the solution to the energy challenges Americans face. The last thing drivers struggling with $2.90-a-gallon gas need is the government deliberately raising the price even higher.

There is no doubt that a large enough tax increase on motor fuels would reduce consumption by forcing the public — low-income persons disproportionately — to drive less, and pricing some at the margins off the roads entirely. Indeed, the gas tax may well be the most regressive tax in existence, especially for those who drive to low-wage jobs. But the goal of our nation's energy policy should not be reductions in use per se, especially if achieved by punishing the American consumer. The aim should be to help people, not hurt them, and for that we want energy that is more affordable, not less.

Some argue that a higher gasoline tax would encourage people to drive more fuel-efficient cars. It would, but those cars are already available for those who want them. Coercing people through economic necessity to choose smaller and less safe vehicles can hardly be considered a favor to them.

Others believe that a heftier gas tax is needed to encourage alternative fuels and vehicles. But are we better off with alternatives that are so expensive that they can't compete with oil even at today's high prices? Granted, petroleum use has its costs — geopolitical as well as economic — but that does not mean that alternatives are necessarily better.

An economically viable alternative would be a very good thing, but there is no reason to believe that high gasoline taxes will spur any rapid technological advances toward that end. Consider the fact that Europe has for years accepted the "wisdom" of higher fuel taxes — in many nations there the taxes alone exceed $3 per gallon. Yet despite years of such high prices, European automotive engineers — including the vaunted Germans — have failed to come up with a gasoline or diesel alternative that can grab significant market share. Similarly, high taxes on gasoline here are unlikely to lead to miracle breakthroughs, just a bigger cost burden for motorists.

Rather than raising taxes, Congress should be taking steps to ensure that energy is as affordable as market forces will allow. These steps include removing the stiff restrictions on new, domestic oil production in the Arctic National Wildlife Refuge and offshore, and streamlining regulations that hamper needed refinery expansions and make gasoline more expensive to produce. Affordable energy should be seen as the solution, not the problem.

Department of Energy Efficiency Programs

Building Technologies Program: Conducts research and development of emerging building technologies and promotes integration of new technologies. Helps states to implement and enforce building energy codes and sets energy-efficiency standards for appliances and equipment.

ENERGY STAR: Identifies and promotes energy-efficient products, buildings and practices through a voluntary labeling program. ENERGY STAR labels exist for more than 35 products, including office equipment, residential heating and cooling equipment, lighting, home electronics and major appliances.

Industrial Technologies Program: Partners with energy-intensive industries to reduce energy consumption. Conducts research and development of technologies common to many industries, like sensors and combustion, to increase efficiency. Works with industry to implement energy-management practices in plants.

Distributed Energy and Electric Reliability Program: Develops advanced technologies to strengthen the nation's electric-energy infrastructure. Conducts research, development, demonstration, technology transfer and educational activities in partnership with utilities, state agencies, universities and national laboratories.

Weatherization Assistance Program: Enables low-income families to permanently reduce their energy bills by making their homes more energy efficient.

State Energy Program: Provides funding to states to design and carry out their own energy-efficiency and renewable-energy programs.

FreedomCAR and Fuel Partnership: Focuses on the research needed to develop technologies, such as fuel cells and advanced hybrid propulsion systems, needed to produce vehicles using little or no gasoline and producing few emissions.

---

suffered as health-care costs have climbed and sales of SUVs and pickups have slumped in the face of rising gasoline prices.

Analysts say rising gasoline prices pose a serious threat to domestic automakers. "If the automakers do not change the fuel economy from where it is today, they will lose a lot of money," says Walter S. McManus, director of the Automotive Analysis Division at the University of Michigan Transportation Research Institute. McManus expects high or rising oil prices to be the norm for the next two decades.

The institute modeled the potential effects of average gasoline prices at $3.37 a gallon compared to a baseline of $1.96 a gallon. The report predicted that sales of cars and light trucks in North America would decline 14 percent in model year 2009 and profits would shrink by $17.6 billion, with U.S. automakers absorbing the brunt of the reductions "because of their dependence on SUV and pickup sales." [51]

McManus and other auto analysts say the technology is there to improve fuel economy, although retooling plants could cost billions of dollars. Among the available technologies are things like six-speed automatic transmissions, automated manual transmissions,

variable valve lift, dual cam phasers, turbocharging and hybrids. Of them all, hybrids may offer the most fuel savings.

Hybrid vehicles run off a rechargeable battery and gasoline. Their engines are smaller, and when the vehicle is stopped, the gasoline motor shuts off and the electric motor and battery take over. Hybrids often recover braking energy and use it to charge the battery.

But hybrid vehicles are currently less than 1.5 percent of the U.S. market, and Toyota dominates. The sales of its Prius alone are more than all other hybrids combined. Next is Honda and then Ford. Trailing far behind are General Motors and DaimlerChrysler. "What I'm afraid of is that some of these companies are setting themselves up for a repeat of the 1970s," says Friedman, of the Clean Vehicles Program at the Union of Concerned Scientists, "when there was an oil embargo, gas lines and gas-price spikes and the Big Three automakers didn't have the products that consumers needed."

All the automakers plan to introduce more hybrids. "We expect roughly half of our lineup to be available as a hybrid option," says Mike Moore, a Ford spokesman. General Motors is adding three hybrid models in model year 2007, and DaimlerChrysler plans to unveil a hybrid Dodge Durango. The forecasting firm J.D. Powers expects hybrids to account for 3.5 percent of U.S. sales by 2012. [52]

Bradley Berman, the editor of hybridcars.com, an informational Web site, calls that estimate conservative. "It's not based on market potential," says Berman.

But predicting market potential is difficult. Hybrid technology can add several thousands of dollars to the price of a vehicle, and the length of time needed to recoup that cost depends on how much one drives, the price of gasoline and the vehicle's fuel economy. *Consumer Reports*, a product-rating publication, tested hybrids in city and highway driving and found that most fell far short of the estimates published on their fuel-economy labels. [53]

If hybrids are to go mainstream, automakers say they must get the price of the vehicles down. "We've said we want to sell 1 million hybrids a year by about 2012," explained Dave Hermance, executive engineer for advanced-technology vehicles at Toyota. "To do that, we need to reduce costs and thus reduce the manufacturer's suggested retail price premium by about $1,000." [54]

But many environmental groups are concerned that some automakers are reducing that price premium by weakening the hybrid technology and barely improving gas mileage. "There are good hybrids and bad hybrids in the marketplace," says Friedman of the Union of Concerned Scientists.

For instance, says Friedman, the hybrid Chevrolet Silverado pickup truck doesn't deserve the name hybrid. The engine does idle-off at stops, but it doesn't accelerate from stops using the electric motor, it doesn't have regenerative braking and it can't run on just the electric motor and the battery, as the most advanced hybrids do. "And the Silverado only gets a 10 percent increase in fuel economy over the conventional version, whereas the Honda Civic and the Toyota Prius do much better than that," says Friedman.

"This is the part where the market hasn't quite adjusted. They think hybrids should get 50 miles per gallon," said Steve Poulos, a General Motors hybrid engineer. "The reality is you have to look by class of vehicle." The Silverado is a full-size pickup, and owners tend to drive a lot of miles, said Poulos. [55] Thus, even a 10 percent improvement in fuel economy would save them a lot of money.

Toyota Motor Co.

The Toyota Prius outsells all other hybrids combined. Hybrid vehicles now account for less than 1.5 percent of the U.S. market, but that's expected to rise to 3.5 percent by 2012.

OUTLOOK

Will Congress Act?

Since late April, lawmakers in Congress have been responding to voters' complaints about rising gasoline prices by scrambling to put together an energy bill. Fearing how gasoline prices will play in the November elections, Republicans and Democrats have been floating a variety of ideas and sharp words.

In early May, House Republicans called a Senate Republican proposal to mail American households a $100 rebate "silly" and "insulting." The Senate leadership promptly shelved it.

The remaining proposals being seriously debated would not have an immediate impact on gasoline prices. In fact, their impact could take years to be felt. They include giving the Federal Trade Commission greater authority to crack down on price gouging, withdrawing $2 billion in oil-industry tax breaks, streamlining refining regulations, drilling in the Arctic National Wildlife Refuge (ANWR), expanding tax credits for hybrid vehicles and raising the fuel-economy standards for passenger cars.

However, it is uncertain which proposals will make it out of Congress. "The House has the capacity to pass bills that very strongly favor the producer-based solutions, but you can't get enough votes in the Senate to pass those," says Bruce Oppenheimer, a professor of political science at Vanderbilt University. "And the House is unwilling to adopt solutions that the Senate would tolerate that are more heavily weighted toward conservation and alternative-fuels-based solutions."

"It's really a question of whether the frustration of the public with energy prices will be enough to bring forth a bipartisan legislative initiative," says Kara Saul Rinaldi, director of policy at the Alliance to Save Energy. "And something that would pass this Congress could not have a lot of the most contentious issues in there."

Those contentious issues include drilling for oil in ANWR and raising the fuel-economy standards for passenger cars. Although several Republicans who formerly opposed raising standards have now said they would consider it, past proposals have failed by wide margins.

Moreover, Transportation Secretary Mineta said the administration opposes any hikes in fuel-economy standards until Congress gives the department the authority to reform the program. Mineta would like to replace the average fleetwide standard of the current system with different standards for each size car, as it did for light trucks in March. But several prominent Democrats, including Rep. John Dingell, D-Mich., have expressed reluctance to give Congress such authority, and the Alliance of Automobile Manufacturers said it may be premature to adopt a new system for cars with "the ink barely dry on the recent light-truck rule." [56]

This is not the first time the current Congress has responded to rising energy prices with a flurry of proposals. After Hurricane Katrina interrupted the flow of energy supplies last September, more than 40 energy bills were introduced. Several were aimed at increasing efficiency.

The Health Care for Hybrids Act, introduced by Sen. Barack Obama, D-Ill., would help automakers meet rising health-care costs if at least half of the savings were reinvested in hybrids and alternative-fuel vehicles or in retooling manufacturing plants. Two broader bills would set specific oil-saving targets and would increase incentives for the purchase of efficient vehicles, provide incentives for fuel stations to install alternative-fuel pumps and provide incentives to speed the commercialization of technologies that could reduce gasoline use.

Congress will continue to hold hearings on energy policy, and the fate of any of these proposals depends, partly, on the course of energy prices this summer.

"The rug gets pulled back out of everything if energy prices go down again," says Oppenheimer.

NOTES

1. Energy Information Administration, "Monthly Energy Review March 2006." Gross domestic product is the annual output of goods and services in the United States.

2. American Council for an Energy-Efficient Economy, "Energy Efficiency Progress and Potential;" www.aceee.org/energy/effact.htm.

3. Energy Information Administration, "Annual Energy Outlook 2006."

4. Rocky Mountain Institute, "Meeting Our Needs With Efficiency," www.rmi.org/site-pages/pid318.php.

5. Energy Information Administration, March 2006, *op. cit.*

6. American Petroleum Institute, "U.S. Pump Price Update — April 26, 2006," http://api-ec.api.org/filelibrary/PumpPriceUpdate.pdf.

7. Pew Center on Global Climate Change, "Basic Science;" www.pewclimate.org/global-warming-basics/basic_science/.

8. Department for Environment, Food and Rural Affairs, United Kingdom, "Avoiding Dangerous Climate Change," *Executive Summary*, Jan. 30, 2006, pp. 2-3. See also Juliet Eilperin, "Debate on Climate Shifts to Issue of Irreparable Change; Some Experts on Global Warming Foresee 'Tipping Point' When It Is Too Late to Act," *The Washington Post*, Jan. 29, 2006, p. A1.

9. Energy Information Administration, "Annual Energy Review 2004."

10. David L. Greene and Nataliya I. Tishchishyna, "Costs of Oil Dependence: A 2000 Update," Oak Ridge National Laboratory, p. 3.

11. "Federal Energy-Efficiency Programs Deserve Significant Increases in FY 2007 Funding," Alliance to Save Energy; www.ase.org/files/2903_file_Budget_Statement.pdf.

12. Alliance to Save Energy, Legislative Alert, "President's FY2007 Budget Would Cut Energy-Efficiency Funding," pp. 2-3.

13. *Ibid.*

14. Alliance to Save Energy, "Building on Success: Policies to Reduce Energy Waste in Buildings," July 2005, p. 6.

15. *Ibid.*, p. 8.

16. National Academy of Sciences, "Energy Research at DOE: Was it Worth It?" 2001, p. 6.

17. National Association of Manufacturers, "Efficiency and Innovation in U.S. Manufacturing Energy Use," 2005, p. 3.

18. Department of Energy, "Energy Use, Loss and Opportunities Analysis: U.S. Manufacturing & Mining," 2004, pp. 1, 72.

19. Timothy Aeppel and Melanie Trottman, "As Energy Costs Soar, Companies Retool Operations," *The Wall Street Journal*, April 22, 2006, p. A1.

20. Union of Concerned Scientists, "Clean Vehicles," www.ucsusa.org/clean_vehicles/fuel_economy/.

21. National Academy of Sciences, "Effectiveness and Impact of Corporate Average Fuel Economy (CAFE) Standards," 2002, p. 3.

22. Union of Concerned Scientists, "Building a Better SUV," September 2003, p. 3.

23. National Academy of Sciences, 2002, *op. cit.*

24. David L. Greene, "Improving the Nation's Energy Security: Can Cars and Trucks Be Made More Fuel Efficient?" testimony before House Science Committee, Feb. 9, 2005, p. 7.

25. U.S. Department of Transportation, www.dot.gov/affairs/cafe032906.htm.

26. Danny Hakim, "10 States, in Challenge to U.S., Plan Suit to Force Better Mileage Rules for S.U.V.'s," *The New York Times*, May 2, 2006. The article came out the day before the formal filing of the suit.

27. "Statement of the Alliance of Automobile Manufacturers before House Committee on Energy and Commerce," May 3, 2006, p. 7.

28. Appliance Standards Awareness Project, press release, March 15, 2006; www.standardsasap.org/press21.htm.

29. Northeast Energy Efficiency Partnerships, "Energy Efficiency Standards: A Low-Cost, High Leverage Policy for Northeast States," pp. i-ii.

30. American Council for an Energy-Efficient Economy, "Energy Efficiency's Next Generation: Innovation at the State Level," November 2003, p. 9.

31. Energy Information Administration, "History of Energy Use in the United States," www.eia.doe.gov/emeu/aer/eh/frame.html.

32. For background, see Mary H. Cooper, "Alternative Energy," *CQ Researcher*, Feb. 25, 2005, p. 182. For background, see "Ten Years of Federal Aid in Road Building," *Editorial Research Reports 1927* (Vol. III), available in *CQ Researcher Plus Archive*, http://library.cqpress.com.

33. Energy Information Administration, "History of Energy Use in the United States;" www.eia.doe.gov/emeu/aer/eh/frame.html.

34. Daniel Yergin, *The Prize* (1991), p. 608. For background, see Sandra Stencel, "Middle East Reappraisal," *Editorial Research Reports*, Dec. 12, 1973, available in *CQ Researcher Plus Archive*, http://library.cqpress.com.

35. Congressional Research Service, *CRS Issue Brief*, "Automobile and Light Truck Fuel Economy: The CAFE Standards," June 19, 2003, p. 2.

36. Yergin, *op. cit.*, pp 699-702.

37. Department of Energy, Energy History Series, "Department of Energy 1977-1994," November 1994, p. 31.

38. White House, "Budget of the United States Government, Fiscal Year 2007."

39. Department of Energy, November 1994, *op. cit.*, p. 85.

40. Congressional Research Service, "Energy Policy: Conceptual Framework and Continuing Issues," Jan. 18, 2006, p. 1.

41. For background, see Mary H. Cooper, "Energy Policy," *CQ Researcher*, May 25, 2001, pp. 441-464; and Cooper, "Alternative Energy," *op. cit.*

42. The White House, "Remarks by the President to Capital City Partnership," May 17, 2001; www.whitehouse.gov/news/releases/2001/05/20010517-2.html.

43. Natural Resources Defense Council, press release, "NRDC Offers Responsible Alternative to Bush Energy Plan," May 17, 2001.

44. CNBC, "Morning Call," Aug. 1, 2005.

45. American Council for an Energy-Efficient Economy, press release, "Coalition Praises DOE for First Step Toward Setting New Energy-Saving Appliance Standards," Feb. 1, 2006.

46. Department of Energy, press release, "Department Sets Aggressive Schedule for New Appliance Standards," Feb. 1, 2006.

47. Alliance of Automobile Manufactures, "Automakers and Dealers Cite Federal Law, Marketplace Principles in Challenging Carbon Dioxide Law," Dec. 7, 2004.

48. *Ibid.*

49. Miguel Bustillo, "Canada OKs Auto Emissions Pact," *Los Angeles Times*, March 24, 2005.

50. *Ibid.*

51. University of Michigan Transportation Research Institute, "How Oil Prices Threaten Automakers' Profits and Jobs," July 2005, p. iv.

52. J. D. Power and Associates, "44 Hybrid and 26 Diesel Models Anticipated in U.S. Market by 2012," June 28, 2005.

53. ConsumerReports.org, "High Cost of Hybrid Vehicles, Sizing Up the Savings & Costs," April 2006.

54. *Ibid.*

55. hybridCARS.com; www.hybridcars.com/silverado-sierra.html.

56. "White House Plan On CAFE Reform Legislation Faces Stiff Opposition," *Energy Washington Week*, May 10, 2006.

BIBLIOGRAPHY

Books

Kemp, William H., *Smart Power: An Urban Guide to Renewable Energy and Efficiency*, New Society, 2006.
Kemp, a developer of control systems for low-environmental-impact hydroelectric utilities worldwide, has written an accessible guide for homeowners interested in using less energy or adopting renewable-energy technologies.

Wulfinghoff, Donald R., *Energy Efficiency Manual*, Energy Institute Press, 2000.
Wulfinghoff, an engineer and publisher of Energy Institute Press, has written a technical how-to guide for anyone interested in improving energy efficiency in a home, commercial building or industrial plant.

Yergin, Daniel, *The Prize: The Epic Quest for Oil, Money & Power*, Free Press, 1991.
Yergin, the co-founder and chairman of Cambridge Energy Research Associates, won a Pulitzer Prize for his account of the struggle for wealth and power that surrounds the quest for oil in the 20th century.

Articles

Aeppel, Timothy, and Melanie Trottman, "As Energy Costs Soar, Companies Retool Operations," *The Wall Street Journal*, April 22, 2006, p. A1.
Industrial companies are examining energy use and finding ways to improve energy efficiency in order to cut costs as energy prices continue to rise.

Freeman, Sholnn, "Light Trucks' Mileage Rules Toughen," *The Washington Post*, March 30, 2006, p. D1.
The federal government raised the fuel-economy standards for light trucks and reformed the process for setting those standards, but environmentalists say the rules are too lax and the fuel savings too low.

"Gentlemen, Start Your Engines," *The Economist*, Jan 21, 2006, p. 77.
Hybrid vehicles may not be all they are cracked up to be, but U.S. drivers are interested in more fuel-efficient cars.

Hulse, Carl, "Plan for $100 Gas Rebate Appears to Be All but Dead," *The New York Times*, May 3, 2006, p. A16.
To deal with rising gas prices, congressional Republicans proposed giving taxpayers a $100 rebate, but the plan met with scorn.

Simon, Richard, "Congress Ready to Approve Energy, Highway Measurers," *Los Angeles Times*, July 29, 2005, p. A18.
After years of negotiations and many compromises, Congress approves the Energy Policy Act of 2005.

Reports and Studies

Alliance to Save Energy, *Building on Success: Policies to Reduce Energy Waste in Buildings*, July 2005.
The alliance discusses and recommends more than 40 government policies that it says would help cut energy use in buildings.

American Council for an Energy-Efficient Economy, *Energy Efficiency's Next Generation: Innovation at the State Level*, November 2003.

The council presents innovative policies and programs at the state level that it says can make a substantial difference in improving energy efficiency.

Congressional Research Service, *Energy Policy: Conceptual Framework and Continuing Issues,* **Jan. 18, 2006.**
This report examines the many issues that shaped U.S. energy policy from the 1973 Arab oil embargo to the present, and includes a discussion of unresolved energy issues such as drilling in the Arctic National Wildlife Refuge.

National Academy of Sciences, *Effectiveness and Impact of the Corporate Average Fuel Economy (CAFE) Standards,* **2001.**
Researchers determined that CAFE standards helped to raise fuel economy while also contributing to an increase in fatalities in the late 1970s and 1980s as carmakers reduced the size and weight of cars.

National Association of Manufacturers, *Efficiency and Innovation in U.S. Manufacturing Energy Use,* **2005.**

The association describes opportunities for manufacturers to become more energy efficient and presents case studies of best practices.

Northeast Energy Efficiency Partnerships, *Energy Efficiency Standards: A Low-Cost, High-Leverage Policy for Northeast States.*
The authors say that energy-efficiency standards for appliances and equipment are among the lowest-cost, highest-benefit energy policies that states have ever adopted and recommend that states adopt standards for 10 additional products.

University of Michigan Transportation Research Institute, *In the Tank: How Oil Prices Threaten Automakers' Profits and Jobs,* **July 2005.**
The authors discuss how high gasoline prices and the resulting slump in SUV sales are cutting into profits and jobs at domestic automakers, who need to make fuel efficiency their top priority.

For More Information

Alliance to Save Energy, 1850 M St., N.W., Suite 600, Washington, DC 20036; (202) 857-0666; www.ase.org. A nonprofit organization that promotes energy efficiency worldwide to achieve a healthier economy, a cleaner environment and greater energy security.

Alliance of Automobile Manufacturers, 1401 I St., N.W., Suite 900, Washington, DC 20005; (202) 326-5500; www.autoalliance.org. A trade association of nine car and light truck manufacturers including BMW group, DaimlerChrysler, Ford, General Motors, Mazda, Mitsubishi Motors, Porsche, Toyota and Volkswagen.

American Council for an Energy-Efficient Economy, 1001 Connecticut Ave., N.W., Suite 801, Washington, DC 20036; (202) 429-8873; www.aceee.org. A nonprofit organization dedicated to advancing energy efficiency.

American Petroleum Institute, 1220 L St., N.W., Washington, DC 20005; (202) 682-8000; www.api.org. The primary trade association of the oil and natural gas industry.

Environmental Protection Agency, ENERGY STAR Web site, www.energystar.gov. Provides information about the government's voluntary labeling program that promotes energy-efficient products and buildings.

Edison Electric Institute, 701 Pennsylvania Ave., N.W., Washington, DC 20004; (202) 508-5000; www.eei.org. An association of U.S. shareholder-owned electric companies, international affiliates and industry associates worldwide.

Hybridcars.com, www.hybridcars.com. A Web site providing information about hybrid vehicles and the hybrid-vehicle marketplace.

Rocky Mountain Institute, 1739 Snowmass Creek Road, Snowmass, CO 81654-9199; (970) 927-3851; www.rmi.org. A nonprofit that works with businesses, individuals, governments and communities to promote the efficient use of resources.

The Tax Incentive Assistance Project, www.energytaxincentives.org. A Web site that provides information to consumers and businesses about federal income-tax incentives for energy-efficient products and technologies.

Union of Concerned Scientists, 2 Brattle Square, Cambridge, MA 02238; (617) 547-5552; www.ucsusa.org. A nonprofit partnership of scientists and citizens combining scientific analysis, policy development and citizen advocacy to achieve practical environmental solutions.

U.S. Department of Energy, Energy Efficiency Web site, www.energy.gov/energyefficiency/index.htm. Describes energy-efficiency programs and provides an extensive list of homeowner tips for saving energy.

U.S. Green Building Council, 1800 Massachussetts Ave., N.W., Suite 300, Washington, DC 20036; (202) 828-7422; www.usgbc.org. A coalition of building-industry leaders working to promote buildings that are environmentally responsible, profitable and healthy.

9

National Parks Under Pressure

Tom Arrandale

O n a steep mountain road in Wyoming's Yellowstone National Park, biologist Emily Almberg is telling a group of tourists how wolves have returned to the huge park. Suddenly, in the grassy meadow along Antelope Creek, two wolf pups pop up, stretch and yawn and begin chasing one another.

Almberg cranks her tripod-mounted Nikon telescope down to eye level for a 4-year-old boy from Libertyville, Ill. "Do you have a dog at home?" she asks. "When you come home, does it ever lick you in the face?"

Face licking is a greeting and a way of asking for food, Almberg explains. "That's what wolf pups do when the adults arrive," she says. "They lick the adults to get them to spit out the meat they've carried back from a carcass to feed their pups."

To many Americans, the chance to glimpse and learn about wolves, grizzly bears, moose, elk and other wildlife defines why protecting U.S. national parks is so important. Yellowstone's estimated 150 wolves draw visitors from around the world and often star in TV nature documentaries. For biologists like Almberg, the Yellowstone Wolf Project has been an unprecedented opportunity to study wolves in the wild.

But Yellowstone no longer can afford to pick up the tab for one of the world's most celebrated biological experiments. The federal government pays three staff biologists, but wolf-project managers must raise $250,000 a year from private foundations and businesses to place radio collars on the wolves, monitor pack movements and station biologists along park roads where visitors gather to watch the wolves.

"It's tragic that the premier endangered-species effort in the United States right now has to go to private donors, hat in hand,"

Private donations help biologists place radio collars on the wolves at Wyoming's Yellowstone National Park and monitor wolf-pack movements. Budget shortages are forcing national parks around the country to seek private and corporate funding not only to continue scientific research but also to accommodate the parks' 274 million annual visitors, while at the same time preserving treasured lands for future generations.

From *CQ Researcher*,
October 6, 2006.

193

Most-Popular Attractions Are in the East

Seven of the 10 most-popular National Park Service units are in the Eastern United States (top). Four times more people visit the Blue Ridge Parkway than the Grand Canyon, for example. But most of the most popular national parks are in the West (bottom).

Park Unit	Location	Visits in 2005
The 10 Most-Visited Units in the National Park System		
Blue Ridge Parkway	N.C., Va.	17,882,567
Golden Gate National Recreation Area	San Francisco	13,602,629
Great Smoky Mountains National Park	N.C., Tenn.	9,192,477
Gateway National Recreation Area	New York City	8,294,353
Lake Mead Nat. Recreation Area	Nev., Ariz.	7,692,438
George Washington Memorial Parkway	Washington, D.C., Va.	7,284,165
Natchez Trace Parkway	Miss., Ala., Tenn.	5,482,282
Delaware Water Gap National Recreation Area	N.J., Pa.	5,052,264
National World War II Memorial	Washington, D.C.	4,410,379
Grand Canyon National Park	Ariz.	4,401,522
The 10 Most-Visited National Parks		
Great Smoky Mountains	N.C., Tenn.	9,192,477
Grand Canyon	Ariz.	4,401,522
Yosemite	Calif.	3,304,144
Olympic	Near Seattle	3,142,774
Yellowstone	Wyo., Mont., Idaho	2,835,651
Rocky Mountain	Colo.	2,798,368
Zion	Utah	2,586,665
Cuyahoga Valley	Ohio	2,533,827
Grand Teton	Wyo.	2,463,442
Acadia	Maine	2,051,484

Source: National Park Service

274 million visitors a year — two-thirds more than in 1970 — and at the same time fulfill the historic mandate to keep the nation's most treasured lands "unimpaired for the enjoyment of future generations."

Now environmental organizations, retired park superintendents and rangers have begun speaking out against budget restrictions and subtle management pressures they contend undercut that mission.

"For the last [several] presidential administrations, the Park Service hasn't received the funding that would be needed to do the three things national parks were created to do — provide a quality visitor experience, protect resources for the future and have a productive relationship with park interest groups," says Rick Smith, a former superintendent at Carlsbad Caverns-Guadalupe Mountains National Park.

The Park Service receives about $2.5 billion a year — up from $1.7 billion in 1997 — to manage 84 million acres in 390 park units, which include 58 national parks and a growing number of historic sites, battlefields and public recreation areas. It employs 20,000 rangers, interpreters, biologists, historians, archeologists, clerks, maintenance workers and other staff.

But funding hasn't kept up with the Park Service's expanding responsibilities, say service supporters, including a $5 billion maintenance backlog and implementation of anti-terrorism plans — despite a 35 percent increase in anti-terrorism funds since 2000. And because Congress added new units to the system without providing additional maintenance funds, campgrounds, toilets, trails, visitor centers, historic lodges and headquarters buildings have fallen into disrepair, according to Park Service advocates. They point to such

says Tim Stevens, Yellowstone program manager for the National Parks Conservation Association (NPCA).

All around the country, America's beloved national parks are falling on hard times. The Park Service is still among the most widely respected government agencies, but the NPCA says federal funding now falls $800 million a year short of what the parks need to accommodate

problems as washed out trails at Mount Rainier National Park in Washington, decaying fortifications at Florida's Dry Tortugas National Park and collapsing ancient structures at New Mexico's Chaco Culture National Historical Park. [1]

What's more, a recent Government Accountability Office (GAO) report said funding for daily park operations comes nowhere near the amount needed to keep pace with fixed costs. [2] "Looking at federal dollars, they're not going up," Yellowstone Superintendent Suzanne Lewis told the Cody, Wyo., Chamber of Commerce in September. "In the National Park Service, we've been fortunate; our budget hasn't nose-dived. But every year we tend to get a little bit of money that will not quite cover the fixed costs for another year."

Faced with skyrocketing fuel and utility costs and a new, more generous retirement system for younger employees, superintendents at national parks around the country have had to cut education, maintenance activities and visitor and resource protection, the GAO report said. For example, Maine's Acadia closed seven restrooms during the popular winter season, Shenandoah in Virginia shut down a visitor center and Grand Canyon canceled 12 daily interpretative programs.

Moreover, Bryce Canyon National Park in Utah curtailed backcountry patrols, despite suspicions of wildlife poaching, and Yellowstone eliminated six law-enforcement rangers. "Visitors and resources at national parks will be put at greater risk this summer than in the past," said a Coalition of National Park Service Retirees report. [3]

Faced with such fiscal challenges, the Park Service is developing a systemwide scorecard for measuring how parks are performing, and some parks are devising business plans and setting priorities for the next five years at current budget levels. But, worries Blake Selzer, chief budget analyst for the NPCA, "are they only just looking at ways to operate parks at a bare-bones minimum?"

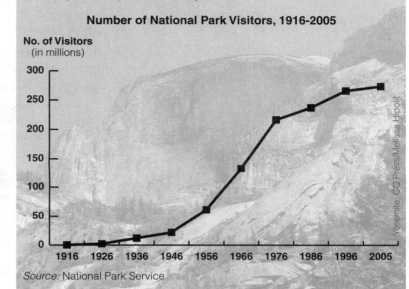

Number of Park Visitors Levels Off

The number of people visiting national parks grew steadily after World War II but leveled off in the last 10 years, despite population growth and the addition of new park units. Higher gas prices and entrance fees may have kept visitors away.

Number of National Park Visitors, 1916-2005

Source: National Park Service

In addition to the budget cutbacks, environmental threats — including climate change, air and water pollution, invasive species and encroaching development — are taking a toll on the parks. By 2030, scientists warn, global warming could melt the remaining glaciers in Montana's Glacier National Park and the snow-capped peaks at Washington state's Mt. Rainier National Park and others; dry up lakes and flood shorelines at popular national recreation areas; and kill the ancient trees at California's Joshua Tree National Park. [4]

"A disrupted climate is the single greatest threat" to ever face national parks in the Rocky Mountains, along the Pacific Coast and in Southwestern deserts, said a report by the Natural Resources Defense Council and the Rocky Mountain Climate Organization. [5]

More immediately, cars, trucks and industrial smokestacks are throwing vast pollution clouds over the Grand Canyon and Great Smoky Mountains, while pollution surpasses federal air-quality standards in 150 of the park system's 390 units, according to the NPCA. [6] "Air pollution threatens the very essence of what Americans value

Several golf courses, 20,000 homes and a giant landfill for trash from Los Angeles are planned near California's Joshua Tree National Park. In the next three decades, the park's ancient trees could be killed by global warming, scientists warn.

most about our national parks," said Mark Wenzler, NPCA's clean-air director.

Water pollution also threatens the system's rivers, wetlands, beaches and marine sanctuaries, while non-native species endanger the system's 398 threatened or endangered plants and animals. For example, South American boa constrictors and Burmese pythons — apparently released by pet owners — now thrive in the Everglades, and lake trout illegally released in Yellowstone Lake are preying on native cutthroat trout.

Meanwhile, new homes, roads and businesses around Yellowstone and Glacier parks are cutting wildlife off from traditional migration routes; subdivisions are going up right on the edge of West Virginia's New River Gorge

National River; 6,000 new homes may be permitted near Everglades National Park, and 20,000 homes, several golf courses and a giant landfill for Los Angeles' trash are planned near Joshua Tree National Park, northeast of Palm Springs. [7]

As park officials try to cope with the multitude of pressures, government officials and advocates for the national parks are asking:

Should visitors and donors bear more of the costs of running the parks?

With federal budgets expected to remain tight, the Park Service is seeking other resources to cover costs — raising serious questions about whether it's appropriate for the service to cash in on the national parks' popularity by charging higher fees and courting corporate and charitable sponsors.

Although entrance to many historic sites and small park units is still free, other less popular sites now charge $5-$10, and most large parks charge $20 per car for a one-week pass. Last year, however, Yellowstone, Glacier, Grand Teton and Grand Canyon national parks raised their weekly fees to $25. That's still a bargain compared to what vacationers pay for a day at Disneyland or other major leisure destinations, but the Park Service's growing reliance on fees could eventually price some Americans out of their national parks, say critics. And, since individual parks now can keep most of their receipts to build and maintain their own facilities, critics worry that managers will feel compelled to court increasing numbers of visitors by investing in facilities at the expense of protecting natural and cultural resources.

In fiscal 2005, the agency collected $160 million in entrance fees at 151 park units, plus additional charges for campgrounds and other facilities. Hospitality companies paid another $47 million in franchise fees to operate more than 600 lodges, restaurants, souvenir shops, gasoline stations, campgrounds, river rafting trips, horseback rides and other services. Parks require those businesses to plow the bulk of those concession revenues back into improving the park-owned facilities they operate.

In fact, the Interior Department's initiatives to collect visitors' fees to supplement park budgets have been stirring controversy since they were initiated a decade ago. Three years ago, for instance, Yellowstone began charging adults $15 for popular day hikes led by park rangers through some geyser basins, lakes and backcountry valleys.

Tourism and recreation-industry groups support visitors' fees, pointing out that those who drive recreation vehicles and other outdoor equipment welcome the chance to help pay for the facilities they're using. "The cost of many things should be borne by the people who are the direct beneficiaries," says Derrick A. Crandall, president of the American Recreation Coalition, which represents travel businesses, recreation organizations, campgrounds, marinas, hotels and manufacturers of snowmobiles, off-road and recreational vehicles and small watercraft.

In 1996, Congress approved a "fee demo" program, which allowed national parks and other public lands to keep 80 percent of their fee receipts and plow them back into infrastructure improvements. Most participating parks doubled their entrance fees, and in fiscal 2006 the Park Service is expected to generate more than $137 million in fees that park managers can use for maintenance and construction. During the last decade, more than $1 billion, mostly from entrance fees, has been poured back into the parks to upgrade and replace aging facilities, of which $473 million went towards maintenance, $228 million to rehabilitate historic structures, maintain cultural landscapes and protect museum collections, $103 million to improve visitor centers and exhibits and $123 million to upgrade campgrounds, trails and backcountry facilities.

For instance, Yosemite National Park used fee receipts to build a visitor-center theater, replace leaky sewer lines, install new campground picnic tables and fire rings and expand its shuttle-bus fleet. Yellowstone spent $8.6 million to expand and refurbish a 1958 visitor-education center with state-of-the-art models and computer-generated exhibits on volcanic geology, which forms the park's unique geysers.

Dedicating the center on Aug. 25, 2006, Secretary of the Interior Dirk Kempthorne noted that it was built with funds contributed by 20 million Yellowstone visitors between 1997 and 2005. "To put it a different way, each visitor contributed 43 cents," Kempthorne said. "It's amazing what pocket change will do."

In some Western states, local hunters, fishermen and other groups have protested when the U.S. Forest Service began raising fees and imposing new charges at national forest facilities. But a 2003 Park Service survey found that 80 percent of park visitors thought entrance fees were "just about right" and that 92 percent preferred that their money stay in the parks they had visited. Economists contend that keeping a share of fees gives managers a direct incentive to keep facilities repaired and attractive. "They're getting into it, because they know they get to spend the money themselves instead of just sending it back to Congress," says Holly Fretwell, a Montana State University economist.

In 2004 Congress extended the fee demo program another 10 years, and revenues are climbing. In its fiscal 2007 budget, the Park Service predicts that visitor fees will generate almost $165 million a year — 29 percent more than two years ago.

For some parks, however, the fees have not produced much income. For instance, when the federal government created Great Smoky Mountains National Park by buying privately owned forests, Tennessee prohibited entrance fees so motorists could drive on park highways for free. And small units with relatively few visitors do not collect much.

The NPCA backs the fee demo concept. But some environmentalists worry that the program creates incentives for empire-building park managers to invest in infrastructure to attract more fee-paying visitors, damaging natural and cultural resources in the process. Park Service policy also prohibits using fee demo revenues to cover operating costs. As a result, notes NPCA budget expert Selzer, some heavily traveled parks have applied fee demo receipts to building new facilities, but Congress hasn't provided sufficient funds for the salaried staffs needed to run them.

"They're taking in a lot of money," says Smith, the retired superintendent, but "by and large it ends up being put into bricks and mortar, and in many parks, infrastructure is not the problem."

Another concern about entrance fees, says former Shenandoah National Park Superintendent Bill Wade, who chairs the retirees' group, is that "The more you rely on recreation fees, the more you're pricing some people out of the market. I think entrance fees ought to be ended altogether."

Yellowstone Superintendent Lewis notes that park attendance declined barely 1 percent after the $5-per-car fee increase was imposed last year. "We're really still getting a bargain," Stevens, the NPCA's Yellowstone representative, concurs. "But there may be a tipping point, and we don't want to make parks inaccessible to any Americans."

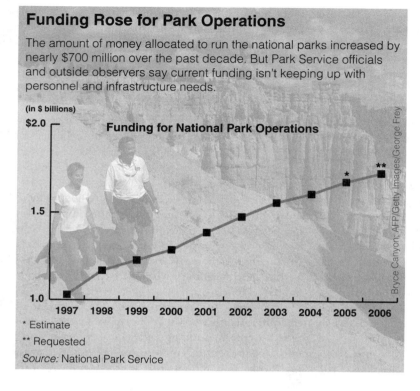

Funding Rose for Park Operations

The amount of money allocated to run the national parks increased by nearly $700 million over the past decade. But Park Service officials and outside observers say current funding isn't keeping up with personnel and infrastructure needs.

Funding for National Park Operations

(in $ billions)

$2.0

1.5

1.0

1997 1998 1999 2000 2001 2002 2003 2004 2005 2006

* Estimate

** Requested

Source: National Park Service

Bryce Canyon, AFP/Getty Images/George Frey

Then-Yellowstone Superintendent Michael Finley helped set up the Yellowstone foundation in 1995, making it the first organization created to raise funds for a specific national park. Now, similar partner organizations are helping to upgrade facilities and keep some of the country's most popular parks running. For instance, the Friends of Acadia raised $9 million to restore 130 miles of trails inside Acadia National Park, and private education groups created an environmental learning center at Indiana Dunes National Lakeshore.

The Yellowstone foundation contributed $1 million for the park's recently reconstructed Canyon Visitor Center and just finished raising $15 million to supplement $11 million in federal funding for the new visitor center at Old Faithful Geyser. In all, the foundation has raised more than $36 million for programs "that would not be likely to get congressional allocations," says Michael Cary, the organization's president.

For the wolf project, the foundation pays for collaring devices, staff members to track wolves' movements from helicopters and graduate students to study how predators affect elk and bison populations. Primarily, "we fund the science," Cary says, "and there's a lot of good scientific information being generated."

In May, the Park Service backed off from a proposal allowing employees to actively solicit donations from visitors and the private sector, including from park concessions. Critics had argued the policy might pave the way for corporate donors to display commercial logos on kiosks and other park structures. "There will be few places in the common areas of national parks . . . off-limits to the Nike swoosh or the McDonald's arches," contended Public Employees for Environmental Responsibility, a whistleblowers' organization representing government workers. [9]

The Park Service retirees' group shares concern about parks getting too close to private benefactors. "The less the national parks rely on public funds, the greater the

In Yellowstone, Stevens adds, the park has crossed that line by charging adults $15 for the popular day hikes that rangers lead to backcountry lakes, and across wild valleys on trails that lead away from crowded roads and visitor facilities. "That's part of the whole national park experience," but even with discounts for children, "for my family that would be $50, and we probably couldn't afford that," Stevens says.

Parks also depend increasingly on donations from foundations and wealthy citizens. The National Park Foundation, chartered by Congress in 1967, collects $30 million a year from foundations and large corporations such as Unilever, American Airlines, Ford Motor Co., and the Discovery Channel. In addition, 150 "friends" groups affiliated with individual parks raise another $17 million a year, and 65 nonprofit associations pass along another $26 million in receipts from book stores they run in the parks. And through the service's Volunteers in the Parks program, 122,000 citizens work 4.5 million hours a year helping rangers greet visitors and distribute maps and information. [8]

risk that they'll be less national and less public," Wade says. Adds former Carlsbad Superintendent Smith: "We shouldn't turn parks and park superintendents into beggars and panhandlers. The parks are for the American people, and they deserve public funding."

Is recreation compatible with keeping parks "unimpaired"?

The 1916 National Park Service Organic Act directed the agency to keep parks "unimpaired" while still accommodating human visitors. But the continuing funding shortages are intensifying the debate over whether the Park Service's concern about conserving natural resources has pushed aside its obligation to give ordinary Americans opportunities to enjoy the parks.

That debate has come into clear — and noisy — focus as the service considers allowing snowmobiles, off-road vehicles and small personal watercraft to explore areas previously unreachable except by foot or horseback. As motorized vehicles have become more popular, the Park Service has encouraged snowmobiles on Yellowstone's unplowed roads during winter months and has tolerated jet skis on heavily used recreation-area waters.

But the noisy vehicles spew exhaust fumes and can erode trails, tear up beaches and other wild areas. The federal Wilderness Act of 1964 bars motor-driven vehicles from the nation's protected wilderness, including the backcountry in national parks. But even in developed park areas, rangers and conservationists contend the machines have begun disrupting the silence and natural conditions of the parks. In 2000, as the Clinton administration moved to strengthen the Park Service's focus on conservation, the agency proposed phasing snowmobiles out of Yellowstone and barring jet skis from national park waters.

Most of Yellowstone remains impassable to automobiles in winter, except for a single road the Park Service keeps open to two isolated Montana communities. Starting in the 1950s, tourists began riding multi-passenger over-snow coaches over unplowed park roads; and snowmobiles began roaring into the park in 1963. Businesses in gateway communities promoted the sport to generate winter customers, and by the 1990s some 1,400 motorized sleds were entering the park on peak winter days. Winter visitors were spending $30 million a year in West Yellowstone, Mont., the most popular park entrance for snowmobilers. [10]

By the mid-1990s, the Park Service had become concerned that growing snowmobile traffic was causing air pollution and road overcrowding while disturbing the park's elk and bison. Prodded by a lawsuit by the Fund for Animals, Yellowstone Superintendent Finley proposed in November 2000 to exclude snowmobiles from the park after three more winters. Snowmobile manufacturers promptly challenged the decision in court, and several contending lawsuits were filed over the following years.

Eventually, the park set a limit of 720 snowmobiles a day through the upcoming 2006-2007 winter and required snowmobilers to hire trained guides and use clean-burning, four-stroke engines. The plan bars snowmobiles from park roads at night and sets 14 miles of side roads aside for the big snow coaches. Legal disputes remain on hold, and Yellowstone planners are now working on a permanent snowmobile policy that's likely to face additional court challenges.

Meanwhile, other park-system units are struggling through similar controversies. After settling an environmental group's lawsuit in 2002, the service permanently closed five seashore and recreation areas to personal watercraft and moved to keep them out of 16 other units while park managers assessed their impact. Ten units were reopened in 2005, and in May the craft were permitted again at Gulf Islands National Seashore off the Florida and Mississippi coasts and in September at Cape Lookout National Seashore in North Carolina.

Park managers in both units wanted to continue banning jet skis but were overruled by President George W. Bush's first secretary of the Interior, Gale Norton, according to *National Parks Traveler* magazine. [11] Recreation interests contended the Clinton-administration rule had needlessly harmed gateway towns and motorized-equipments sales without proving the parks were being damaged.

The jet ski deliberation process "has been delayed too long, and in the meantime millions of Americans have been denied access to their national parks, thousands of small businesses have suffered and thousands of jobs have been lost," Maureen Healey, director of the Personal Watercraft Industry Association, said recently. [12]

Just before Bill Clinton left office in 2001, the Park Service rewrote its official 280-page operations manual, reaffirming that conservation is the service's top priority, even if it requires limiting access. Recreation users have challenged that focus, arguing that Clinton-era policies excluded millions of Americans from enjoying their national parks with motorized vehicles.

"The 2001 policies were driven by a belief that the American public is loving the parks to death, and we do not share that belief," says Crandall, of the American Recreation Coalition. As Crandall told Park Service Director Fran Mainella in February, the group is concerned that the revised operations manual sets out a "simplistic, single-focused mission" that ignores the agency's long history of building roads, visitor centers, lodging and other infrastructure "that has long enhanced visitation to the parks while providing protection for park features and qualities." [13]

William P. Horn, an assistant Interior secretary during the Reagan administration, contends the revisions misinterpret the 1916 Organic Act. "Congress has never intended that parks be managed as biospheres under glass or managed in an exclusionary manner," Horn told the Senate National Parks Subcommittee in 2005. "In contrast, imagine today trying to build a fraction of Yellowstone's road system or even one of its historic hotels or lodges. It is an absolute certainty that impairment, especially the very-low-impact threshold [allowed] in the Clinton-era policies, would be the basis for objections."

In Crandall's view, current management policies overlook the different purposes of the various parks, historic sites and recreation areas. In 2005, the nation's 58 national parks drew 63 million visitors — less than a quarter of the total that year for all Park Service units. Seventeen national recreation areas and 10 national seashores attracted roughly as many, mostly from nearby metropolitan areas. Virginia's Blue Ridge Parkway and San Francisco's Golden Gate National Recreation Area are by far the most heavily visited units; only two national parks, Grand Canyon and Great Smoky Mountains, ranked in the top 10 most-visited units in 2005. (*See chart, p. 194.*)

"Not every unit is a Grand Canyon, a Yellowstone or a Grand Teton," Crandall says. Even in such natural parks, he adds, "90-plus percent of visitors never get beyond an eighth of a mile from the paved surface of the road system." By giving conservation priority over recreation opportunities throughout all 390 units, the Clinton policies "reduce the value of the system to the American public by providing fewer opportunities for physical, mental and spiritual fulfillment."

In 2005, Paul Hoffman, then the Interior Department's deputy assistant secretary for fish, wildlife and parks, drafted a new version of the management manual giving recreation equal standing with conservation. A former aide to Vice President Dick Cheney, Hoffman had also been director of the Chamber of Commerce in Cody, a gateway community leading to Yellowstone.

The park retirees' group leaked Hoffman's draft to the press and claimed it would open the parks to inappropriate commercial uses. Jon Catton — a leading critic of snowmobiles in Yellowstone — says Hoffman apparently went through the manual line-by-line and removed key phrases giving park officials authority to find that noise, air pollution and wildlife impacts from motorized recreation unacceptably impair the parks.

Park Service officials quickly disowned Hoffman's proposals and issued yet another revised manual, allowing recreation only at levels that never imperil natural or cultural values.

Should "gateway communities" help decide how national parks are managed?

While all Americans have a stake in park-management decisions, nearby communities feel the consequences most acutely. "We're a big player in any community," says Yellowstone Superintendent Lewis, who previously ran Glacier National Park and Chattahoochee National Recreation Area, near Atlanta. "The wildlife doesn't stop at the park boundary. The visitors don't stop at the park boundary. Nothing stops at the park boundary."

Superintendents often come under pressure to take local interests into account when they decide whether recreation activities will impair natural or cultural resources.

Since Yellowstone became the first national park in 1872, towns near national parks have catered to tourists arriving first by railroad and then automobile. In addition to providing motels, restaurants and gas stations for tourists, neighboring communities share the costs of police and fire protection and medical care with the parks. In turn, some parks help maintain and plow nearby scenic highways.

Visitors spent $10.3 billion in gateway communities in 2005, supporting 211,000 jobs paying $3.9 billion in wages and salaries, according to a 2006 Park Service study. [14] Park visitors have long been crucial economic mainstays for gateway communities like Gatlinburg,

Tenn. (Great Smoky Mountains National Park); Bar Harbor, Maine (Acadia); Estes Park, Colo. (Rocky Mountain) and Springdale, Utah (Zion). And many communities have grown even more reliant on park tourism in recent decades as mining, logging and ranching opportunities have declined.

What's more, Lewis told the Cody chamber, Yellowstone's own 400-person payroll "runs upwards of $20 million a year, and all of these people live and shop and interact in these local communities" at park entrances.

"There is a very significant, tight, symbiotic relationship" between the Park Service and adjacent towns and counties, says Bill Murdock, a county commissioner in Gallatin County, Mont., on Yellowstone's northwest border. But too often the parks have "taken those communities for granted."

Park Service officials agree that some superintendents haven't spent enough time talking with surrounding communities. "In the past we had an attitude that we just want to run the parks," says Stephen P. Martin, deputy director for operations.

Conflicts have escalated — particularly around big parks — since the Park Service began giving higher priority to protecting natural resources in the 1960s. Nearby communities sometimes feel they're losing out, for instance when park decisions ban or limit motorized snowmobiles and jet skis that gateway businesses sell, maintain and rent to vacationers. And 10 years after federal biologists brought wolves back into Yellowstone, ranchers, big-game outfitters and county commissioners complain the predators kill livestock and reduce elk herds as they move outside the park.

The Park Service has also worked with federal and state livestock agencies to cull 1,000 bison from Yellowstone's expanding herds because ranchers' fear they carry the livestock disease brucellosis. And businesses in California gateway communities complain that Yosemite's long-debated plans to limit traffic and possibly visitor numbers in the Yosemite Valley "have left a significant portion of the public searching for a more convenient alternative for vacations and getaways," Bob Warren, chairman of the National Alliance of Gateway Communities, told Congress in May. [15]

Legislation proposed by Rep. George Radanovich, a California Republican whose district lies near Yosemite, would require the Park Service to give gateway communities formal roles in park-management decisions. The measure has gone nowhere, but in revising its systemwide management policies in August, the service instructed park superintendents to engage more regularly with gateway communities as well as other groups with interest in park operations.

"Some superintendents are better at that than others," points out Martin. Yellowstone's Lewis, for instance, "has been very accessible to gateway communities," says Gene Bryan, director of the Cody Chamber of Commerce. "We don't always agree, but we can sit and talk and not be disagreeable."

In Cody, West Yellowstone and other gateway towns, business leaders are counting on continued snowmobile access to Yellowstone to keep winter visitors coming. Murdock and Bryan agree that tighter regulation is required, including clean-running sleds and limits on the number of visitors. Some established West Yellowstone operations already have begun upgrading rental fleets and offering snowcoach tours as alternatives to snowmobiles. "We're not asking for throwing the park wide open," Bryan says. "None of us who have been in this business very long wants to do anything to harm the very reason we live here."

At some other national parks, local governments have worked closely with park administrators on mutually beneficial projects, such as traffic management. Environmental groups realize that over the long term, wild and natural landscapes are gateway regions' economic salvation. People increasingly are moving into communities near national parks and other natural lands — precisely because the parks offer compelling scenery, fascinating wildlife and undeveloped lands where they can hunt, fish, hike or ride horses or motorized off-road vehicles.

"More and more gateway communities are finding that adjoining parks, wildlife refuges or wilderness areas can be powerful economic assets," wrote three land-conservation advocates in a 1997 book on gateway towns. [16]

Between 1970 and 2000, the population in 20 counties surrounding Yellowstone National Park grew 62 percent, and "demographers believe that this rapid migration will continue in areas . . . rich in natural amenities," noted a 2005 study by the Sonoran Institute and Montana State University. [17] A separate National Parks Conservation Association report on six Yellowstone gateway counties found that the region's wild landscapes "do far more than simply draw tourists in large numbers. Much of the area's success is driven by the region's spectacular setting, abun-

C H R O N O L O G Y

1860s-1890s *Federal government begins setting aside scenic public lands.*

1864 President Abraham Lincoln gives Yosemite Valley to California "for public use, resort and recreation."

1872 President Ulysses S. Grant establishes world's first national park at Yellowstone.

1886 U.S. Army assigned to Yellowstone to protect natural features and arrest poachers. Congress passes the Lacy Act, strengthening federal control of national park resources.

1890 Congress sets aside Yosemite National Park.

1900s-1950s *Federal government creates National Park Service and dramatically increases national park acreage.*

1906 President Theodore Roosevelt signs the Antiquities Act, authorizing presidents to proclaim federal lands as natural and historic monuments. The size of the national parks doubles during his tenure.

1913 Over conservationist John Muir's objections, Congress approves damming Yosemite's Hetch Hetchy Valley to supply water to San Francisco.

1916 President Woodrow Wilson signs Organic Act, creating National Park Service.

1919 The East's first national park — Lafayette, later renamed Acadia — is created in Maine.

1926 Congress authorizes Great Smoky Mountains National Park.

1933 Park Service is given responsibility for national battlefields and historic sites.

1956 Park Service launches Mission 66, a 10-year, $1 billion project to upgrade park facilities for Park Service's 50th anniversary in 1966.

1960s-1990s *Park Service expands, switches from managing wildlife to "natural regulation" of ecosystems.*

1963 Park Service stops controlling elk and bison herds in Yellowstone, allows natural regulation instead; policy eventually expands to other park ecosystems.

1964 Wilderness Act protects wild landscapes in national forests and on public lands around national parks.

1980 President Jimmy Carter signs landmark Alaska Lands law, increasing Alaska's national park acreage six-fold.

1988 Wildfires burn nearly a third of Yellowstone, testing the service's resolve to let natural forces regulate park ecosystems.

1995 Wolves are returned to Yellowstone National Park.

2000s *Conflicts continue between conservation and recreation.*

2000 Yellowstone National Park proposes banning snowmobiles.

2001 President Bill Clinton uses Antiquities Act to create new monuments. . . . Park Service strengthens policy of giving conservation priority over recreation. . . . President George W. Bush names Gale Norton as Interior secretary and Fran Mainella as Park Service director.

2004 After court battles, Yellowstone allows snowmobiles temporarily, through winter 2006-2007; rule limits numbers, requires guided tours and cleaner engines.

2005 Critics claim proposed Interior policy could allow commercial development and motorized recreation to ruin the parks' resources.

2006 Norton and Mainella resign. Former Idaho Gov. Dirk Kempthorne becomes Interior secretary; Mary Bomar becomes Park Service director. . . . Park Service maintains 2001 focus on conservation. Kempthorne promises to develop 10-year Centennial Challenge program to improve the system by the agency's 100th anniversary in 2016.

dant wildlife, easy access to outdoor recreation and small, friendly towns." [18]

That success, however, threatens to encircle parks with resorts and subdivisions that cut off wildlife-migration corridors along park boundaries. Long-term land-use decisions by local governments could be critical to preserving Yellowstone's ecosystem, says Murdock, the Montana county commissioner. "The elk don't stop at the park boundary when they migrate, nor do the grizzlies or the wolves," he says.

Because of that interdependence, "it's very, very important that the communities understand what the park can and cannot do with its resources — and [understand] what the connection is between the community and the value of living in the community relative to keeping those resources healthy," Lewis told Cody business leaders."

The NPCA has proposed that the Park Service participate in land-use planning around gateway communities. Meanwhile, as they implement the revised management policies, park superintendents will try to step up their outreach to adjacent communities while maintaining their "fundamental mission of long-term conservation of resources," says NPCA President Kiernan. "You can do both."

BACKGROUND

Promoting the Parks

Protecting a national park against development was a new idea in 1872 when Congress set Yellowstone National Park aside at the headwaters of the Yellowstone River "as a public park or pleasuring ground for the benefit and enjoyment of the people." Ever since, the government has been trying to balance promoting recreation with preserving the parks' natural resources. [19]

The federal government assigned the U.S. Army to manage the park in 1886 to bring rampant wildlife poaching under control and protect natural features. To attract vacationing passengers, Western railroads began advertising the scenic wonders of Yellowstone and helped convince Congress to protect other natural areas as national parks, including the Yosemite, Sequoia and General Grant parks in California. President Theodore Roosevelt, an ardent outdoorsman who frequently visited the parks, doubled the nation's park acreage during his administration, and Congress in the 1906 Antiquities

Act authorized presidents to protect threatened lands by declaring them national monuments.

In 1913, however, in a portent of future conflicts between using park resources and preserving them, Congress approved damming the Hetch Hetchy Valley inside Yosemite to supply water to San Francisco, despite the objections of Sierra Club founder John Muir.

The tension between preservation and development continued after Congress established the National Park Service in 1916. The Organic Act declared that the fundamental purpose of the parks was "to conserve the scenery and the natural and historic objects and the wildlife therein and to provide for the enjoyment of the same in such manner and by such means as will leave them unimpaired for the enjoyment of future generations." Although that mission remains on the books, how the Park Service applies it has evolved over the last nine decades.

President Woodrow Wilson appointed Stephen T. Mather, a Chicago borax manufacturer who had campaigned for the Organic Act, as the first Park Service director. He served until 1929, when his longtime aide Horace Albright took over. Both worked to solidify public support for the parks by encouraging tourists to visit and by courting influential businessmen and conservation leaders.

While Mather rejected a plan to string a cable car across the Grand Canyon, he and Albright encouraged more park visitors by building roads, campgrounds and large, rustic lodges and restaurants. The service granted concessions to private businesses to run lodges, cabins, stores, restaurants and gasoline stations inside the parks.

Visitors have paid fees to enter national parks since Mount Rainier National Park began charging an entrance fee in 1908. When the Park Service was created in 1916, seven of the system's 14 units already charged entrance fees to drive an automobile into the park, including $10 a year at Yellowstone and $2 a year at Glacier and Mesa Verde national parks. Mather thought the agency could finance all park operations and improvements from concession revenues and entrance fees.

But in 1918 Congress directed the Park Service to deposit revenues directly into the federal Treasury. "This broke the link between park revenues and park spending, and expenditures have become political footballs ever since," conservative economists Donald R. Leal and Montana State University's Fretwell argued in a 1997 study for the Property and Environment Research

"We Have to Be Relevant to the Kids"

When she was a child in suburban Ohio, Suzanne Lewis remembers playing in the nearby woods all the time.

"But we don't tell our kids to go play in the woods after school anymore," says Lewis, who grew up to become superintendent of the National Park System's crown jewel, Yellowstone National Park.

As a result, "We've got a lot of kids today who aren't comfortable in the outdoors," she continues, a condition some researchers have dubbed "nature-deficit syndrome." Researchers recently have found that the symptoms of attention deficit hyperactivity disorder in children can be alleviated if they spend less time watching television or playing video games and more time outdoors. [1]

The trend away from outdoor activities for children worries Lewis and other Park Service officials. "Who is going to come to the national parks?" Lewis asked in a recent speech to the Cody, Wyo., Chamber of Commerce. "And when they do come, what will be their comfort level in these parks and what will they want from these wild places?" For the future of the National Park System "that's a very, very significant question."

Indeed, the total number of park visitors has leveled off in the last decade — even at Yellowstone — even though more park units have been added and the U.S. population has grown.

While Lewis attributes this year's decline to summer gasoline prices that topped $3 a gallon, some Park Service officials are beginning to worry that the national treasures they manage are losing their allure to new generations of Americans.

"The thing I am most concerned about is the demographics of who's coming to the parks — and who's going to come in the future," she told the Cody chamber.

Visits to the national park system grew steadily after World War II, peaking at 287 million in 1987. In the last 20 years, however, despite the addition of 80 new units to the system and a 23 percent increase in the nation's population to nearly 300 million people, park visitation had fallen to 274 million in 2005.

New Mexico Tourism Secretary Michael Cerletti blamed the falloff on fee increases and overcrowding. Plus, he said in April testimony to Congress, people aren't visiting the parks because they find them overcrowded, the facilities degraded and the interpretive programs boring.

But recreation-industry officials argue that policies designed to protect the parks from crowds and noise — such as higher entrance fees and restricting snowmobiles, jet skis and off-road vehicles — have discouraged visitors.

"Fewer Americans are visiting and benefiting from our parks, and the failure to deliver these benefits to urban Americans, youth, senior citizens, the disabled and Americans of diverse ethnicity should be of particular concern," the American Recreation Coalition told Secretary of the Interior Dirk Kempthorne in a letter in August.

The Park Service has focused too much on preserving natural conditions and lost touch with modern-day Americans who have grown up watching television, using computers and cell phones and enjoy riding motorized equipment and camping out in trailers and recreation vehicles, say tourism- and recreation-equipment manufacturers.

"Gone are the days of taking the station wagon for a two-week camping trip to a national park," Bob Warren, a Northern California tourism official, told an April congressional hearing on park-visitation trends. "Hiking, cookouts, sleeping in tents and watching deer is just not stimulating enough for those who have grown up with constant and

Center, which contends that private interests provide the most effective incentives for environmental protection. [20]

The Park Service expanded its political base when Congress created Acadia National Park in Maine and Great Smoky Mountains National Park in the Southeast. In the 1930s, President Franklin D. Roosevelt doubled the system by giving the Park Service control over national monuments, battlefields, historic sites and national shrines and parks in Washington, D.C.

During World War II, park funding was constricted, leaving the service with a backlog of facilities in disrepair just as tourism boomed with the nation's postwar prosperity. In the 1950s, Director Conrad Wirth responded with his crash "Mission 66" initiative to make the parks more accessible by 1966, the 50th anniversary of the Organic Act. The project built or improved 2,000 miles of roads and constructed 114 visitor centers, many with cafeterias, souvenir shops and auditoriums.

instant multimedia stimulation. Their definition of an outdoor experience includes jet skis, ATVs [all-terrain vehicles], motorcycles and jet boats — all part of activities that are largely prohibited in national parks."

Currently, the nation's 58 national parks draw 23 percent of the system's visitors, while units near major metropolitan areas — created primarily for recreation — now attract just as many.

Some critics say the tradition-bound Park Service has been slow to adapt to social and economic changes. "There is a tremendous value in the legacy and esprit de corps in the service," says recreation coalition Director Derrick A. Crandall. But "many recent superintendents have been too much focused backward and not enough on changes" in the public who visits parks. Crandall admires some business-minded managers of popular parks who "are not quite as wedded to the past."

Advocates of the Park Service, on the other hand, attribute dropping attendance to high gasoline prices, fears of terrorism and economic changes that leave families with less time for extended vacations in the parks.

However, Laura Loomis, director of visitor experience at the National Parks Conservation Association, notes that

Yosemite Ranger Adrienne Freeman shows off an animal skull during National Parks Family Day. Budget cutbacks have forced many parks to reduce ranger staffs and programs.

surveys show that 95 percent of visitors say they've enjoyed the time they spent in the parks. "Overall, they're in support of staying the course and keeping the parks the same," she says.

Others question the claim that visitation is off, pointing out that visitors to the Gulf Islands National Seashore dropped 2.5 million during the extraordinary 2005 hurricane season — accounting for three-quarters of that year's nationwide decline. [2]

In any case, says Lewis, parks must adapt to the changing interests and expectations of modern park visitors in addition to preserving natural experiences. Yellowstone's recently redesigned Canyon visitor center, for example, features state-of-the-art educational displays depicting the volcanic geology beneath that park. "We have to be relevant to the kids," Lewis says. "We can't tell them not to bring their Ipods."

---

[1] Frances E. Kuo and Andrea Faber Taylor, "A Potential Natural Treatment for Attention-Deficit/Hyperactivity Disorder: Evidence From a National Study," *American Journal of Public Health*, www.ajph.org/cgi/content/abstract/94/9/1580. For background on attention deficit disorder, see Kathy Koch, "Rethinking Ritalin," *CQ Researcher*, Oct. 22, 1999, pp. 905-928.

[2] Kurt Repanshek, "Keeping Track of Visitors No Easy Task," *National Parks Traveler*, Oct. 2, 2006, www.nationalparkstraveler.com.

The tourism industry and philanthropists continued playing important roles in expanding and popularizing the park system. John D. Rockefeller Jr. contributed $25 million of his own fortune, providing land for Grand Teton, Great Smoky Mountains, Shenandoah and Yosemite.

In keeping with prevailing feelings about wildlife, the Park Service promoted picturesque wildlife — like elk and deer — but eliminated predatory wolves and moun-

tain lions from Yellowstone. Rangers there also allowed tourists to feed black bears begging for handouts along roadsides and erected bleachers where visitors gathered to watch grizzlies feed at open garbage dumps.

Conserving the Parks

Public attitudes about wilderness began shifting in the 1950s and early '60s. The Sierra Club and other environmental groups rallied to the park system's defense to

Snowmobiles await riders in Yellowstone National Park. Concern that growing snowmobile traffic was causing air pollution and disturbing wildlife prompted the Park Service to set a limit this year of 720 snowmobiles per day and require snowmobilers to hire trained guides and use clean-burning, four-stroke engines.

block construction of a dam in Dinosaur National Monument and others on the Colorado River inside the Grand Canyon. The Park Service continued to struggle with the growing tension between recreation and preservation.

With natural predators eliminated, Yellowstone's plentiful elk population threatened to denude the park's northern range. But public outcry forced rangers to stop shooting the elk to cull the herd to sustainable levels. Zoologist A. Starker Leopold, son of legendary wilderness advocate Aldo Leopold, recommended that the Park Service shift away from artificially manipulating wildlife and natural conditions. The 1963 Leopold report proposed letting natural forces run their course as much as possible inside park boundaries in order to "maintain a vignette of primitive America."

Stewart L. Udall, the conservation-minded Interior secretary during the Kennedy and Johnson administrations, embraced the report and pushed the Park Service to stress conservation. Congress reinforced the effort over the following decade by enacting laws setting out national goals for cleaning up air and water pollution and saving endangered species. Since then, superintendents, biologists and rangers have embraced a preservationist view of their work. Following the new philosophy, Yellowstone closed its dumps in the 1960s, fined tourists for feeding bears and let elk and bison herds expand and migrate outside the park in winter.

On Dec. 2, 1980, during his lame-duck tenure, President Jimmy Carter signed the landmark Alaska Lands legislation into law, culminating an intense, nine-year congressional battle. While restricting development on more than 100 million acres of land in Alaska, the massive bill also expanded three existing Alaskan national parks and created 10 new parks — increasing the state's national park acreage sixfold, from 7.5 million acres to 43.6 million acres.

Dubbed the "conservation vote of the century" by environmentalists, the bill more than doubled the size of the country's national park and wildlife refuge systems and nearly tripled the amount of U.S. territory designated as wilderness. [21]

Six weeks later, Ronald Reagan was inaugurated, and his administration took a decidedly different tack on park conservation. His Interior secretary, James Watt, disdained the preservation trend. Watt snowmobiled through Yellowstone, proclaimed himself bored while rafting through the Grand Canyon and scoffed at hikers and other environmentalists. Watt forced the Park Service to transfer managers after they resisted hunting in some of the new Alaskan national parks and others who tried to restrict Glacier Bay boat tours that disturbed endangered humpback whales. [22]

But while Watt pushed other Interior agencies to accelerate logging and oil and gas drilling, the Park Service continued its shift toward standing aside while natural forces took their course, for instance by maintaining a policy of allowing many lightning-sparked wildfires to burn themselves out. In 1988, however, Yellowstone Superintendent Bob Barbee came under intense criticism when fires burned across more than a third of the park's 2.2 million acres, threatening the historic Old Faithful Inn, coming close to gateway towns and forcing visitors to evacuate.

Can Cell Phones and Wilderness Coexist?

For generations, Americans visited their national parks to get away from it all. That experience didn't include receiving instant BlackBerry messages from the office, nor could visitors overhear others ordering pizza by cell phone while watching — and trying to hear — geysers erupt in Yellowstone National Park's remote thermal basins.

Today, however, as wireless technologies have changed how millions of Americans live, the National Park Service is deciding whether visitors should be able to stay in touch with the outside world — and possibly ruin the solitude and scenic vistas that others hope to find when they cross national park boundaries.

Two years ago, environmental groups and Wyoming historic preservation officials complained that a 100-foot-tall tower was marring the landscape within sight of Yellowstone's Old Faithful geyser. Park officials lopped 20 feet off the structure last year — and coated the steel with vinegar and water to dull its shine. They also began studying whether blanketing Yellowstone with wireless service is compatible with keeping the national parks unimpaired.

Yellowstone Superintendent Suzanne Lewis said the park's challenge "is how to respond appropriately to visitor expectations" for convenient wireless service while still "protecting the historic, rustic, outdoor experience of a visit to the world's first national park."

Park officials lopped 20 feet off a cell phone tower in Yellowstone park last year after preservationists complained it was marring the view of Old Faithful geyser.

Cell towers have been installed in the Grand Canyon, Everglades and Yosemite national parks and other units, pursuant to the Telecommunications Act of 1996, which ordered government agencies to allow cell companies to build towers on federally owned lands. But Sen. Lamar Alexander, R-Tenn., has blocked a proposal to build three 120-foot towers inside Great Smoky Mountains National Park, and cell projects in other parks have begun encountering similar opposition.

Yellowstone imposed a moratorium on new towers in 2004 and is reviewing wireless technologies used inside the park — including two-way radios, Web cams, seismic monitors and radio collars on wolves and grizzly bears. The assessment likely will set a precedent for how other parks respond when cell-phone companies propose building new towers to expand service coverage.

Yellowstone rangers still communicate with handheld radios, a 1930s-era technology that involves "many dead zones where they can't receive communications," says Eleanor Clark, Yellowstone's chief of planning. After the first cell towers were installed in the mid-1990s, some park rangers began carrying cell phones, but they only work in 5 percent of Yellowstone's 2.2 million acres. "We know where to stop to get reception," says Stephen Swanke, Yellowstone's assistant chief ranger.

With better cell coverage, Yellowstone visitors could summon help by dialing 911, and park staff could stay in closer touch while on backcountry patrols. But environmentalists are urging the park to consider giving rangers satellite phones instead or perhaps limiting public cell access to 911 emergency calls. Cell phones may make visitors feel safer, but they could also encourage "reckless behavior based on a false sense of security" if visitors grow overconfident when they wander through active thermal areas or hike into backcountry grizzly-bear habitat, says Amy E. McNamara, the national parks director for the Greater Yellowstone Coalition.

Tim Stevens, the National Parks Conservation Association's Yellowstone program director, says the park should consider tearing down the Old Faithful cell tower and remind visitors they shouldn't enter a wild and natural park expecting all the modern-day conveniences.

"It's not like spending a day in the city," Stevens says. "There are plenty of people who would rather protect the silence and solitude of Yellowstone Park."

National Park Service (all)

The Great Outdoors, from East to West

The National Park Service manages 84 million acres in 390 park units, including 58 national parks ranging from Dry Tortugas in Florida (top) to Acadia in Maine (middle) to Mesa Verde in Colorado (bottom). The park system also includes a growing number of historic sites, battlefields and public recreation areas and employs 20,000 rangers, interpreters, biologists, historians, archeologists, clerks, maintenance workers and other staff.

In the 1990s, funding problems continued to plague the parks, and a $34 million shortfall in 1993 led the service to close campgrounds and eliminate other services. Congress created the fee demo program in 1996, and in 2000 the Park Service began selling $50-a-year National Parks Passes that allow access to all units. But President Clinton's Interior secretary, Bruce Babbitt, a former Arizona governor who later led the League of Conservation Voters, reaffirmed the federal commitment to keeping park lands wild and pristine, protecting and, if possible, restoring ecosystems.

Over the objections of neighboring states, Babbitt in 1995 approved transplanting Canadian wolves into Yellowstone to help keep elk and bison in check. After 1997 floods washed away two popular Yosemite campgrounds, Babbitt approved a long-term plan to restore natural woodland habitat and native aquatic species along the Merced River.

Before Babbitt left office, he and Park Service scientists helped negotiate a comprehensive federal-state plan that attempts to rescue Everglades National Park and three nearby parks by partially restoring natural water flows that federal flood-control projects had diverted from the Everglades. [23] During the Clinton administration's final year, the Park Service set the stage for recent controversies when it barred snowmobiles and jet skis from certain parks and redrafted its management manual to give park superintendents a strengthened hand to restrict recreation in order to protect natural and cultural resources.

Many of Babbitt's decisions were controversial, particularly in the recreation industry and gateway communities. But in those years, the agency had shifted its goal to embrace more actively protecting park resources. In 1999, the Park Service launched a five-year "Natural Resources Challenge" to strengthen scientific research, inventory native ecosystems, monitor natural conditions and control invasive species.

"For most of the 20th century, we have practiced a curious combination of active management and passive acceptance of natural systems and processes, while becoming a superb visitor-services agency," the Park Service declared in a plan signed by Robert Stanton, Clinton's Park Service director, authorizing the challenge effort. "In the 21st century, that management style clearly will be insufficient to save our natural resources." [24]

Are Park Service policies keeping people out of the parks?

YES
Derrick A. Crandall
President, American Recreation Coalition

From letter to National Park Service Director Fran Mainella, Feb. 17, 2006

The 2001 version of NPS [National Park Service] management policies was developed under Interior [Department] leadership that repeatedly expressed concerns about visitors "loving the parks to death" and suggested the likelihood of continuing large increases in park visitation.

We believe that philosophy was based on a false premise. In fact, recent data suggest that visitation to the National Park System is not increasing. Visitation in 2005 was down 2.1 percent for the year, and visitation to the small portion of the 388-unit system comprised of national parks has been stable or trending downward for several years. We have real fear that the mental, physical and spiritual benefits of visits to our National Park System will be realized by a declining portion of the public — and that the system will have little meaning for some of the U.S. population cohorts experiencing the fastest growth — ethnic minorities, urban residents and young people.

We believe that the 2001 policies erred in responding favorably to an understandable desire among some park managers and park advocates for a simplistic, single-focused mission. [The manual] does not reflect the direction of the Organic Act and ignores the management precedents of the agency's most respected early leaders. The vision of those leaders resulted in design and construction of infrastructure that has long enhanced visitation to the parks while providing protection for park features and qualities.

The mission of the agency cannot be effectively implemented through appropriations alone. We feel increased attention can and should be placed upon using fees to increase agency resources. We firmly believe that increased use of technology to educate, interpret for and manage visitors — often through partnerships — is a preferred course for the National Park Service.

The extraordinary diversity of the National Park System must be reflected in the operations of these units. Man-altered environments like Lake Mead, much of Golden Gate National Recreation Area and the National Mall, for example, must be managed much differently than park units with extensive wilderness and backcountry zones. These are the units that many Americans will first encounter when they visit the National Park System and play a special role in creating an understanding of the value of the priceless outdoor legacy we enjoy today.

NO
Denis Galvin
Retired Deputy Director, National Park Service

On behalf of the National Park Conservation Association, from testimony before the House Subcommittee on National Parks, Feb. 15, 2006

What is needed is for a broad constituency of interests that are engaged with the National Park Service — recreation, tourism, gateway communities, conservation, preservation and regular "good citizens" — to step up their support for their national parks as they are, and as they are intended to be: preserved unimpaired for future generations to enjoy.

Nearly 300 million people visited the parks last year, and we know from surveys that they "enjoyed" them. NPS concessionaires grossed over $1 billion in 2004; surrounding gateway communities and businesses grossed over another $11 billion attributable to national park visitors.

Despite this, there are those who suggest that NPS management of the parks is too restrictive, or that the parks are locked up, or lack access. Nothing could be further from the truth.

The national parks do not have to sustain all recreation; that is why we have various other federal, state, local and private recreation providers. The NPS mission is different from that of state park agencies, or of county or city park agencies. Together, these agencies provide for many forms of public recreation — but not all forms of recreation are appropriate in national parks.

There is no credible debate over whether parks should be used by the American people; the debate centers on how the use occurs, or sometimes when or where.

For the NPS professionals, conserving the parks unimpaired for future generations is synonymous with offering park visitors a high-quality experience. Scenic vistas should be clear, natural sounds should dominate over man-made noises, native wildlife should be abundant and visible for visitors, historic sites such as battlefields should look like they did when the historic events occurred, park visitor facilities should not be so located as to disturb the natural scene or the cultural landscape.

Preservation is the key to continued success of the NPS in fulfilling its statutory mandate, and also to sustaining the core destinations that fuel the tourism industry.

CURRENT SITUATION

Budget Woes

Six years into the Bush administration, debate continues over whether the National Park Service has been able to give the national parks the protection they require. [25]

In tough fiscal times during the Reagan administration, the service's sterling reputation with the American public helped fend off debilitating funding cuts. But since 2001, managers have been handling ever more difficult responsibilities with shrinking budgets, sometimes under what Park Service veterans say has been unprecedented political duress.

"We certainly did better during the Reagan administration than anybody else in Interior, but that's not the case now," says former Superintendent Smith. Former Secretary Norton, her deputy Steven Griles and NPS Director Mainella were regarded within the service as sympathetic to recreation interests and distrustful of longtime agency employees. Like Watt, a former mentor, Norton took a snowmobiling trip through Yellowstone. The administration also declared that the Park Service would focus on catching up with a much-discussed backlog in repairing lodges, campgrounds, restrooms and other visitor facilities.

Since fiscal 2002, the Park Service has poured $4.9 billion into deferred maintenance work on nearly 6,000 facilities, according to the agency's fiscal 2007 budget proposal. For fiscal 2007, the Park Service has asked Congress for $393.5 million for maintenance, $229.3 million for new facilities and $210 million in highway funds to upgrade park roads. The budget request included $10 million a year for routine repairs to keep facilities from deteriorating. Overall, with funds expected through 2009, park assets "will be brought into acceptable condition," according to the agency's fiscal 2007 Park Service budget, nicknamed the Green Book. [26] But in 2005, the Congressional Research Service (CRS) said there was still a $7.1 billion backlog of repairs through 2004. [27]

At the same time, the White House and Congress have slashed federal funding for daily park operations well below what superintendents say they need. Between fiscal 2001 and 2005, the amounts allocated for daily operations rose by $100 million — to more than $1 billion a year, but that doesn't keep up with inflation, according to the CRS.

"The Park Service has been something of a thorn in the side of this administration," says Smith. And although current officials talk guardedly about funding cuts, in the past year retired park managers have gone public with complaints that Congress and Interior Department superiors are meddling in Park Service efforts to preserve threatened national parks. In 2003, more than 500 retired park officials formed the Coalition of National Park Service Retirees, which has harshly criticized the way the administration is trying to change how the parks are managed.

By speaking out, says John Varley, a former Yellowstone Resources Center director who retired in 2005, the retirees demonstrate the dismay within current Park Service ranks about budget cuts and political interference they contend have kept the agency from protecting the parks against serious threats.

Ecological Integrity

In recent decades, it has become clear that even the largest parks are not big or isolated enough to be immune from environmental damage, particularly from air and water pollution, invasive species and human development.

Serious ecological problems are threatening the park system's biodiversity, particularly the 398 threatened or endangered species of plants and animals. "The mission to preserve parks unimpaired includes the ecological integrity of park resources," the NPS' Science Advisory Committee declared in a 2004 study. "National parks with decreased biological diversity and diminished natural systems can in no way be considered unimpaired." [28]

A recent NPCA study also found that the air in California's Sequoia and Kings Canyon national parks violated federal ozone standards for an average of 61 days a year, making hiking, biking and rock climbing potentially hazardous. Yellowstone and Grand Teton national parks are threatened by emissions from new coal-fired power plants and 8,700 oil and gas wells being drilled in surrounding regions, while a new power plant 50 miles west of Kentucky's Mammoth Cave National Park will increase mercury concentrations already found in the park's endangered Indiana bats. [29]

Preserving ecosystems inside parks is also complicated by exotic plants and animals. Feral pigs run through the Great Smoky Mountains National Park and park units in Hawaii. The service now deploys 16 mobile exotic-plant management teams, including experts trained to tackle tamarisk in the Rio Grande Valley, leafy spurge in Great Plains parks and lygodium, an Old World climbing fern that's killing native trees in the Everglades.

Michael Soukup, the service's long-time associate director for natural stewardship and research, sees invasive species and housing developments surrounding park boundaries as the most severe threats. Moreover, he adds, global climate change and loss of habitat overseas may be changing park ecosystems. Migratory birds are losing South American wintering grounds, he says, and "it will be sad if our parks don't have some of their songbirds in the future." If concerns about global warming are realized, Soukup adds, "there will be some big changes afoot that will affect the distribution of wildlife."

The Clinton administration's Natural Resource Challenge called for funding to be channeled into improving scientific research in the system's natural parks. The challenge is conducting inventories of ecological resources, monitoring for changes and improving environmental conditions. The service now is working with biologists from universities and other government agencies to study all the birds, mammals, reptiles, amphibians, fish and plants in the parks.

The initiative expanded efforts to remove invasive species that threaten native wildlife and created 13 research learning centers for scientists conducting studies in parks around the country. The Bush administration has continued funding the Natural Resource Challenge and has proposed spending an additional $1 million for fiscal 2007 to establish the last two of 32 networks for monitoring the vital signs of park ecosystems.

Fear and Whistleblowers

The Natural Resource Challenge "is having an enormous impact," says Soukup, but "it's going to take a long time to realize the full importance of what it accomplishes."

But while the 1999 initiative proposed doubling natural-resource spending from $85 million to $170 million a year, Varley says funding has begun drying up. Inside the parks, experts say budget cuts are taking a toll on biological research and resource-management programs. [30]

For instance, Yellowstone has kept its wolf program funded through private support, "but most projects don't have that charisma," says Varley. While the agency focuses on protecting endangered species and controlling invasive pests, "You have smaller programs that just vanish — any programs on bats, for example. They're not

on anybody's radar screen, but they're a good indicator species for environmental quality."

In the short term, most wildlife "is resilient enough that it's not going to hell in a handbasket tomorrow," Varley says. For the long term, however, he fears funding cutbacks will prevent park scientists from spotting ecological trends before they become dire threats. "You can't measure that from one year to the next," he says. Consistent monitoring year after year "is the only way you can figure out there's a problem for grizzlies, wolves and elk — and for bats and songbirds. You can't go back in time and get the numbers, so you don't know what's increasing or decreasing."

In some cases, park managers have felt subtle pressure not to speak publicly about resource threats for fear of retribution. For example, the White House does not accept that global warming is a major threat, Varley says, "but anybody who's been in the park and worked in the field believes it's real. I was never asked not to say anything, but I never tested it. If I couldn't tell the truth, I didn't speak. I was too close to retirement."

Meanwhile, Varley adds, "I don't know anybody [inside the Park Service] who's talking. This cast of [Bush administration] characters knows Old Testament vengeance."

In one incident, Hoffman, author of the controversial manual revision, reportedly challenged Death Valley National Park Superintendent J. T. Reynolds' policy of keeping off-road enthusiasts from driving jeeps up steep canyons. Then in 2005, after Reynolds criticized Hoffman's proposed manual revisions, the service conducted three investigative reviews of how Death Valley is managed but found no significant problems. At the Mojave National Reserve, a new California unit that allows hunting, Hoffman questioned Superintendent Mary Martin, who resisted pressure from Hoffman and congressional staffers to reopen artificial water "guzzlers' to attract game animals for hunters. Martin eventually transferred to become superintendent of Lassen Volcano National Park and the guzzler decision is still disputed. [31]

The National Parks Conservation Association came to Reynolds' defense by giving him its 2005 Stephen T. Mather Award for protecting national parks. Most current employees feel compelled to keep silent to protect their jobs, but Smith says some high-ranking officials, including park superintendents, have been quietly passing tips along to the retiree group's whistleblowers. [32]

Over time, Park Service veterans are beginning to worry that tight budgets and political pressures are producing a "not very attractive" evolutionary change in park managers, Smith says. Now an official can rise through the Park Service ranks "if your park makes money because you're able to collect fees or you're a great fund-raiser, or if your park has a congressman or congresswoman on an appropriations committee you get palsy-walsy with," he says. "I would prefer a park manager who has real dedication to preserving and protecting the resource."

OUTLOOK

Back to Basics?

On Aug. 25, as the Park Service celebrated the 90th anniversary of the Organic Act, new possibilities seemed to be in the crisp Yellowstone air as Kempthorne traveled to the park to dedicate its new Canyon Visitor and Education Center. He announced a new 10-year Centennial Challenge initiative "to prepare national parks for another century of conservation, preservation and enjoyment" before the 100th anniversary in 2016.

"The challenge facing the National Park Service — at Yellowstone and all our parks — is to conserve what is timeless while keeping pace with the modern needs and expectations of the American people," Kempthorne said, citing the Mission 66 project as a precedent. In an accompanying message, the president directed the service to set performance goals and signature projects for improving the parks "that continue the . . . legacy of leveraging philanthropic partnerships and government investments for the benefit of national parks and their visitors." [33]

The administration has given the Park Service until May 31, 2007, to figure out how that will be accomplished. Deputy Director Martin says the agency will need additional appropriations and revenues from fees and private contributions. "Fee demo will be part of it, but it can't be all of it," Martin says. "It's not enough to meet the fundamental missions of the parks."

In September, Sen. Craig Thomas, R-Wyo., chairman of the Senate Subcommittee on National Parks, joined with Hawaii's Sen. Daniel Akaka, the committee's ranking Democrat, to circulate a draft letter to Bush among Senate colleagues calling for increases in park operating budgets. Taking note of President Dwight D. Eisenhower's $1 billion

Mission 66 program, the draft letter called for "a proportional investment in our national parks as we embark on their 100th anniversary." [34]

In the House, Rep. Mark Souder, an Indiana Republican, has been pushing a proposed National Park Centennial Act to create a federal income tax check-off allowing Americans to donate tax refunds to park system funding. NPCA President Kiernan welcomed the administration's plan but cautioned that it won't be enough to repair and build facilities, nor will it cover operating funds. In the four decades since Mission 66 was completed, "we've learned a lot about what it means to protect the natural and cultural resources in the parks," Kiernan says. "We need to do this in a very sensitive way."

Meanwhile, the parks still struggle to balance conflicting missions. On Aug. 31, NPS Director Mainella signed updated management policies that she says "make clear the National Park Service's desire for people to visit and enjoy their national parks" while steering the agency toward "cooperative conservation and civic engagement in our decision-making." The revisions encourage park superintendents to reach out to gateway communities and other interested groups "trying to move to the center so we can make long-term sustainable decisions," says NPS Deputy Director Martin, a former Grand Teton superintendent.

"But it's a two-way street," Mainella continues. "The outside groups need to understand what our fundamental mission is and come up with solutions that work for the mutual benefit of everybody."

The new version of the management manual maintains the 2001 directive giving conservation top priority, leaving it up to park managers to make tough calls balancing recreation with preservation. Catton, the Montana snowmobile critic, expects park managers will still come under pressure to define potential impacts in ways that subtly bypass the 1916 Organic Act's ban on impairing park resources.

Recreation interests and some gateway communities "will continue the pressure on the Park Service and in some cases on individual park superintendents," says retired Shenandoah Superintendent Wade. "It's going to come down to how the management policies are implemented."

Meanwhile, environmentalists keep pushing the parks for more stringent preservation. California advocates are in court demanding that Yosemite limit visitor numbers as it redesigns roads and facilities damaged by Merced River floods nine years ago. In 2007, more legal challenges will be likely as Yellowstone planners try to settle on a permanent snowmobile policy.

"We need to be brave enough to recognize that park resources have limits," says Yellowstone's Lewis. "Those limits aren't intended to have negative impacts on the economies of these local communities," but accepting them will be essential for "making those resources last for a long, long time."

NOTES

1. "The Burgeoning Backlog," National Parks Conservation Association, May 2004.

2. Government Accountability Office, "National Park Service, Major Operations Funding Trends and How Selected Park Units Responded to Those Trends for Fiscal Years 2001 through 2005," March 2006.

3. Coalition of National Park Service Retirees, "Reality Check: What Visitors to America's National Parks Will Experience During Summer 2006," June 15, 2006.

4. For background see Marcia Clemmitt, "Climate Change," *CQ Researcher*, Jan. 27, 2006, pp. 73-96; Stephen Saunders and Tom Easely, "Losing Ground, Western National Parks Endangered by Climate Disruption," Natural Resources Defense Council (NRDC) and the Rocky Mountain Climate Organization, July 2006, p. v.

5. *Ibid.*, NRDC.

6. "Turning Point," National Parks Conservation Association, August 2006.

7. See Benjamin Spillman, "Developers Covet Areas Surrounding National Parks," *USA Today*, March 21, 2006.

8. Kurt Repanshek, "Life in America's National Parks," *National Parks Traveler*, www.nationalparkstraveler.com, Nov. 15, 2005.

9. Public Employees for Environmental Responsibility, "Comments on Proposed Rewrite Director's Order #21 Donations and Fundraising," Nov. 30, 2005.

10. Michael Lanza, "Still Buzzing," *Backpacker*, February 2006, p. 71.

11. Kurt Repanshek, "Jet Skis in the Parks: Congresswoman Miller Wants Them," *National Parks Traveler*, www.nationalparkstraveler.com, Feb. 4, 2006.

12. Press release, May 4, 2006.

13. Derrick A. Crandall, letter to National Park Service Director Fran Mainella. Feb. 17, 2006.

14. "National Park Service Social Science Program, FY 2005 Money Generation Model Briefing Statement," March 2006.

15. Prepared testimony, Senate Subcommittee on Public Lands and Forests, May 10, 2006.

16. Jim Howe, Ed McMahon and Luther Probst, *Balancing Nature and Commerce in Gateway Communities* (1997), p. 6.

17. Patricia Gude, "Yellowstone 2020, Creating our Legacy," Sonoran Institute, 2005.

18. "Gateways to Yellowstone, Protecting the Heart of Our Region's Thriving Economy," National Parks Conservation Association, May 2006.

19. For background, see Rachel S. Cox, "Protecting the National Parks," *CQ Researcher*, June 16, 2000, pp. 521-544, and Richard L. Worsnop, "National Parks," *CQ Researcher*, May 28, 1993, pp. 457-480.

20. Donald R. Leal and Holly L. Fretwell, "Back to the Future to Save Our Parks," *PERC Policy Series Issue No. PS-10*, Property and Environment Research Center, June 1997.

21. For background see "Alaska Lands," *1980 Congress and the Nation, Vol. V*, pp. 577-583, or online at http://library.cqpress.com/catn/.

22. For background see Tom Arrandale, "Access to Federal Lands," in *Editorial Research Reports 1981* (Vol. II), available at *CQ Researcher Plus Archive*, CQ Electronic Library, http://library.cqpress.com.

23. See Michael Grunwald, *The Swamp, The Everglades, Florida, and the Politics of Paradise* (2006). See also David Hosansky, "Reforming the Corps," *CQ Researcher*, May 30, 2003, pp. 497-520, and Mary H. Cooper, "Water Quality," *CQ Researcher*, Nov. 24, 2000, pp. 953-976.

24. "The Natural Resources Challenge, The National Park Service's Action Plan for Preserving Natural Resources," National Park Service, August 1999, p. 2.

25. For background, see Mary H. Cooper, "Bush and the Environment," *CQ Researcher*, Oct. 25, 2003, pp. 865-896.

26. "Budget Justifications and Performance Information, Fiscal Year 2007, Overview," National Park Service.

27. Carol Hardy Vincent, "National Park Management," Congressional Research Service, March 11, 2005.

28. "National Park Service Science in the 21st Century," National Parks Science Committee, March 2004, p. 3.

29. "Turning Point," *op. cit.*

30. For background, see Marcia Clemmitt, "Budget Deficit," *CQ Researcher*, Dec. 9, 2005, pp. 1029-1052.

31. See Michael Shnayerson, "Who's Ruining Our National Parks," *Vanity Fair*, June 2006.

32. For background, see "Peter Katel, "Protecting Whistleblowers," *CQ Researcher*, March 31, 2006, pp. 265-288.

33. "Memorandum for the Secretary of the Interior," President George W. Bush, Aug. 24, 2006.

34. Quoted in Noelle Straub, "Thomas urges Bush's help on national parks," *Billings Gazette*, Sept. 9, 2006, p. 7B.

BIBLIOGRAPHY

Books

Chase, Alston, *Playing God in Yellowstone, The Destruction of America's First National Park*, Atlantic Monthly Press, 1986.
A Montana-based writer with a long association with Yellowstone National Park takes a critical look at how park officials shifted away from actively managing park wildlife to adopt "natural regulation" policies.

Grunwald, Michael, *The Swamp: The Everglades, Florida, and the Politics of Paradise*, Simon & Schuster, 2006.
Washington Post reporter Grunwald traces the history of development in South Florida's unique Everglades system, including how preserving Everglades National Park spurred comprehensive change in government water policy.

Howe, Jim, Ed McMahon and Luther Probst, *Balancing Nature and Commerce in Gateway Communities*, Island Press, 1997.
Conservation experts from the Conservation Fund and the Sonoran Institute summarize case studies of how gateway communities prosper because of proximity to wild landscapes in national parks.

Rettie, Dwight F., *Our National Park System*, University of Illinois Press, 1995.
A former chief of the National Park Service's Policy Development Office provides an insider's look at the agency's organization and argues for a more coherent vision for managing the national parks.

Sellers, Richard West, *Preserving Nature in the National Parks, A History*, Yale University Press, 1997.
A historian with the National Park Service discusses the history of the service and traces the continuing conflict between encouraging tourism and managing resources scientifically.

Articles

Lanza, Michael, "Still Buzzing," Backpacker, February 2006.
The magazine's Northwest editor looks at the continuing fight over snowmobiles in Yellowstone National Park and sees room for both the machines and quieter, non-motorized recreation.

Mitchell, John G., "Our National Parks in Peril," *National Geographic*, October 2006, p. 68.
The author says "veiled hostility" directed at national parks by high-level political appointees has not only rattled the morale of many career professionals but also assaulted the legal and regulatory fabric that has held the National Park System together for 90 years.

Schnayerson, Michael, "Who's Ruining Our National Parks?" *Vanity Fair*, June 2006.
Contributing Editor Schnayerson provides a critical report on the role of Paul Hoffman, an Interior Department political appointee, in a controversial effort to rewrite national park policies to favor recreation over conservation.

Reports and Studies

National Park Service, U.S. Department of the Interior, *Budget Justifications and Performance Information*, Fiscal Year 2007.
The Park Service's "Green Book" outlines funding trends and goals for the agency's annual operations.

National Park Service, U.S. Department of the Interior, *Management Policies, the Guide to Managing the National Park System,* **Aug. 31, 2006.**
The final 2006 revision of the service's manual maintains most of the Clinton administration's 2001 changes affirming that keeping parks unimpaired remains the overriding objective in managing national parks.

National Parks Conservation Association, *Endangered Rangers,* **March 2004.**
The advocacy group traditionally closely aligned with the National Park Service outlines how it believes federal budget cuts are damaging the national parks.

National Parks Conservation Association, *Gateway to Glacier,* **2003;** *Gateways to Yellowstone,* **May 2006;** *National Treasures and Economic Engines, The Economic Impact of Visitor Spending in California's National Parks,* **undated.**

The park advocacy group's regional offices contend that the ecological attractions of Western national parks serve as the chief economic assets for gateway communities and counties.

The Trade Partnership, *Analysis of the Economic Impact of the Ban on Use of Personal Watercraft by the National Park Service,* **February 2006.**
Commissioned by personal-watercraft manufacturers, the study says restrictions on using jet skis in national parks cost the country $567 million and 3,300 jobs a year but offer few environmental benefits.

U.S. Government Accountability Office, *National Park Service, Major Operations Funding Trends and How Selected Park Units Responded to Those Trends for Fiscal Years 2001 through 2005,* **March 2006.**
The report to Congress lays out trends in overall Park Service operating funds and outlines how 12 park units cut operations or shifted priorities because of fiscal cutbacks.

For More Information

American Recreation Coalition, 1225 New York Ave., N.W., Suite 450, Washington, DC 20005-6405; (202) 682-9530; www.funoutdoors.com. Fosters public/private partnerships to enhance and protect outdoor recreational opportunities.

Coalition of National Park Service Retirees, 5625 North Wilmot, Tucson, AZ 85750; (520) 615-9417; www.npsretirees.org. Former National Park Service employees work to improve parks funding and other aspects of parks management.

National Parks Conservation Association, 1300 19th St., N.W., Suite 300, Washington, DC 20036; (800) 628-7275; www.npca.org. A citizens' interest group that seeks to protect national parks.

National Park Foundation, 1201 Eye St., N.W., Suite 550B, Washington, DC 20005; (202) 354-6460; www.nationalparks.org. Chartered by Congress and chaired by the Interior secretary; encourages private-sector support of the National Park System.

National Park Service, U.S. Department of the Interior, 1849 C St., N.W., Washington DC 20240; (202) 208-3100; www.doi.gov. Cares for the nation's nearly 400 national parks, historic monuments and recreation sites.

Public Employees for Environmental Responsibility, 2000 P St., N.W., Suite 240, Washington, DC 20036; (202) 265-7337; www.peer.org. An alliance of local, state and federal scientists, law-enforcement officers, land managers and other professionals dedicated to upholding environmental laws and values.

Sonoran Institute, 7650 E. Broadway, Suite 203, Tucson, AZ 85710; (520) 290-0828; www.sonoran.org. Works with communities to conserve and restore important natural landscapes in Western North America.

Yellowstone Park Foundation, 222 East Main St., Suite 301, Bozeman, MT 59715; (406) 586-6303; www.ypf.org. Works with the National Park Service to protect, preserve and enhance the natural and cultural resources and the visitor experience at Yellowstone National Park.

10

Privacy in Peril

Marcia Clemmitt

Police inversigators discovered that before killing his wife, business consultant Justin Barber of Jacksonville, Fla., at left, searched the Internet for famous murder cases and ways to avoid extradition. He was convicted in June 2006 and sentenced to life in prison. Privacy advocates warn that while personal information can help solve crimes, its misuse by criminals and corporations violates citizens' privacy on a vast scale.

AP Photo/The Record, Peter Willott

W hen Thelma Arnold of Lilburn, Ga., used AOL's search engine last year, she certainly hoped the information she was looking for would stay private. After all, in addition to seeking help in buying school supplies for Iraqi children, she wanted to know what to do about a "dog that urinates on everything" and where to find single men over 60.

Unfortunately for Arnold, AOL had posted details of her searches on the Internet last summer, along with 20 million other queries submitted to AOL by some 657,000 customers. * Although AOL had replaced the searchers' names with numbers to protect their identities, many of the queries included personal information, such as Social Security numbers and date of birth.

Within days, Arnold got a phone call from a *New York Times* reporter, who read her a list of search terms and asked if she was customer number 4417749. Arnold confirmed that she was. Her searches for "landscapers in Lilburn, Ga.," as well as for several people with her last name, helped the reporter figure out her identity.

"My goodness, it's my whole personal life," she said. "I had no idea someone was looking over my shoulder." [1]

As computer databases and electronic-surveillance technologies continue to proliferate, governments and businesses are finding more and more opportunities to develop detailed dossiers on anyone who buys a product, signs up for a government program or logs

From *CQ Researcher,*
November 17, 2006.

---

* AOL said it posted the information to help researchers studying consumers. Cynics speculated that AOL wanted to show that it was competing with Google and other popular search engines.

217

Most States Require Notification After ID Theft

More than 200 major cases of identity theft have been reported in the United States since 2005. Since California passed the first breach-notification law in 2003, 31 states have adopted breach laws.

States with no breach-notification laws (18)

States with breach-notification laws applying to any agency or company (21)

States with breach-notification laws that do not apply to public agencies (11)

Major security breaches since 2005:

Between 500,000 and 2 million people affected

More than 2 million people affected

Source: Stateline.org, "States Failing to Secure Personal Data," July 12, 2006

theft easy and devastating and threaten the speedy approach "of a Big Brother society."

Today, data-gathering is ubiquitous. The Electronic Privacy Information Center estimates that Londoners are photographed more than 300 times a day by more than 1.5 million surveillance cameras throughout the city. [2] Within a few years, all new cars will be equipped with "black boxes" that record data like speed, steering-wheel movement and how hard brakes are pressed; 64 percent of 2005 cars had them. [3]

In September the social-networking Web site Facebook faced a user revolt after it began instantly reporting any changes in members' pages to all their Facebook "friends." [4] In 2005, Walt Disney World's Florida theme parks began fingerprint scans for all visitors to prevent ticket sharing. [5]

Beginning in 2008, the Real ID Act enacted by Congress last year will require states to electronically link all driver's licenses to personal information in a database accessible to all other states. The new database will make all other existing databases "look minuscule by comparison," says Nehf.

onto a computer. National-security and law-enforcement agencies say they need the information to head off terrorism and fight crime, while businesses seek purchasing data in order to better target their marketing efforts. The growing demand for and increasing supply of personal information available today make for what privacy advocates call a "perfect storm" of privacy breaches.

Eventually, says James P. Nehf, a professor at the Indiana University School of Law, "Our movements will be tracked so that people will know where you've been and what time of day you were there" through machine-readable chips in driver's licenses and passports and even implanted in our bodies.

If, as is likely, "all this information that's picked up goes into a database" where it's linked with other personal information on file, "the potential for abuse is enormous," he says. Such databases will make identity

With so many public and private databases cropping up, privacy advocates say opportunities are rife for government to buy or subpoena unprecedented amounts of personal information and for private companies and individuals to buy or steal it.

The potential for abuse is significant, explains Illinois Attorney General Lisa Madigan. Earlier this year she sued several so-called data brokers, or aggregators, for allegedly selling fraudulently obtained cellular-phone records that reveal not only whom phone owners spoke with but also their location. (*See sidebar, p. 228.*)

"Imagine that you are a victim of domestic violence" who has "found the courage and the means to flee" an abusive spouse, said Madigan. With cell-phone records available for sale by shady data brokers, "your abuser . . . will know when you pick the kids up at school and when you get home. Now he can find you." [6]

At the same time, other experts say the vast, new databases also help solve crimes and streamline business transactions. In fact, the same kind of cell-phone records that can enable a stalker to track a victim have also helped to catch wanted criminals, including kidnapping suspects. [7]

Cell-phone records, for instance, quickly helped North Dakota police focus on Alfonso Rodriguez as a suspect in the 2003 kidnapping and murder of University of North Dakota student Dru Sjodin. Rodriguez was sentenced to death in September. And in Maryland, investigators are narrowing down leads in the mysterious 2003 death of Maryland Assistant U.S. Attorney Jonathan Luna, using cell-phone records and data from his EZ-Pass toll card.

Internet searches for terms like murder, missing corpse and presumed dead led Florida police to business consultant Justin Barber, convicted in June for the 2002 murder of his wife, April. [8] Google searches for words like neck and snap also led North Carolina investigators to computer consultant Robert Petrick, who was convicted in November 2005 for the 2003 murder of his wife, Janine. [9]

Hackers Have Easy Access to Personal Data

More than 97 million records containing Americans' personal information have been involved in security breaches at universities, corporations and government agencies since 2005.

Selected Recent Data Breaches in the United States

Name	Date Made Public	Nature of Breach	No. of Records Involved
Starbucks Corp.	Nov. 3, 2006	Two laptops with employees' addresses and Social Security numbers were lost.	60,000
University of Minnesota	Sept. 8, 2006	Two computers stolen containing information on students from 1992-2006.	13,084
Circuit City, Chase Card Services	Sept. 7, 2006	Five computer data tapes were lost containing cardholders' personal information.	2.6 million
University of Tennessee	July 7, 2006	Hacker accessed computer data on past and current employees.	36,000
Texas Guaranteed Student Loan Corp.	May 30, 2006	A subcontractor's worker lost a computer with borrowers' data.	1.7 million
Dept. of Veterans Affairs	May 22, 2006	A laptop containing data on all U.S. veterans was stolen.	28.6 million
Vermont State Colleges	March 24, 2006	Laptop stolen containing data of students, faculty and staff.	14,000
General Electric	Sept. 25, 2005	Laptop containing Social Security numbers of GE employees stolen.	50,000
CardSystems	June 16, 2005	Hacking	40 million

Source: Privacy Rights Clearinghouse, "A Chronology of Data Breaches"

Last spring, Congress began investigating companies and individuals who obtain personal information by "pretexting" — or claiming to be someone they're not. The practice came under scrutiny last summer, when a scandal erupted at Hewlett Packard (HP). Private investigators hired by the computer giant to determine who leaked secret information apparently used pretexting to obtain journalists' and board members' phone records.

Although the House Energy and Commerce panel held hearings about the HP scandal in September, it had already, in fact, overwhelmingly approved a bill to outlaw pretexting last spring. But the measure has stalled, despite the new media attention from the HP affair.

Also stalled are Bush administration efforts to get Internet companies, phone companies and Web sites to retain consumer information — including lists of Web sites visited — that might help fight child pornography and other crimes. While some lawmakers introduced measures to mandate such data retention, others proposed banning it. Meanwhile, the European Union in

Smile, Your Employer May Be Watching

After 14 years at Weyco, an insurance consulting firm near Lansing, Mich., Anita Epolito was summarily fired last year for a reason she never expected — smoking cigarettes. Her boss had given employees 15 months to quit smoking and then in January 2005 began firing workers if random screenings showed they still used nicotine.

But Epolito says the smoking was just a "smoke screen" obscuring the true issue. "This is about privacy," said Epolito. "This is about what you do on your own time that is legal, that does not conflict with your job performance."

But her boss, Howard Weyers, said the policy was about smokers who develop illnesses that drive up the cost of health insurance. The random nicotine tests are perfectly legal and in the best interests of his business, Weyers said, adding, "I'm not going to bend from the policy." [1]

Many other kinds of worker-surveillance methods — both electronic and more low-tech — are available to employers today. Software can monitor anything sent from workplace computers, including Internet browsing, chat room comments and even e-mails sent from workers' private e-mail accounts accessed on office computers. Keystroke loggers can record everything typed on a workers' computer, including deleted material. In some companies, so-called smart ID cards track employees' location throughout the workplace, including how long they spend in the bathroom. And while lie-detector tests are banned in hiring, lengthy psychological tests are permitted and frequently used.

The number of employers who snoop on workers is increasing, according to periodic surveys by the American Management Association (AMA). In 2005, 76 percent of employers told the AMA they monitored workers' Web connections. (*See graph, p. 221.*) [2]

While older workers often bristle at surveillance, those in their teens and 20s take it in stride, says Camille Hebert, a professor at Ohio State University's Moritz College of Law. "I'm 47 and have never taken a drug test," she says. "My 21-year-old has taken a test several times. After a while, it seems normal."

Some scholars of workplace behavior say excessive snooping could backfire on employers. Workers who feel their privacy is being invaded are more likely to withhold information from employers and, generally, lose their commitment to the organization, argue Bradley J. Alge, an associate professor of management at Purdue University, and Jerald Greenberg, a professor of management at Ohio State University. Loss of commitment leads to behaviors like increased absenteeism, "checking out" during meetings and being less willing to exercise creativity on the job, Alge and Greenberg write. Monitoring perceived as unjust by workers "can have particularly dire consequences . . . potentially undermining the very safety and security the monitoring system is designed to ensure in the first place." [3]

As surveillance technologies like video cameras and computer-keystroke monitors become cheaper and more effective, employers are increasingly viewing worker surveillance as a key cost-containment strategy. [4]

Although the Constitution prohibits government agents from searching citizens' homes without a warrant showing "cause," no such protection exists for employees. Courts generally give employers broad latitude to monitor workers, arguing that they have the right to ensure that people they hire perform their jobs as well as possible, says Hebert. In essence, "employers can do whatever they want," she says.

Worker privacy is "not a very coherent area of the law," she adds. "There is no federal statute that provides for pri-

December 2005 required companies operating in Europe to retain such information.

In perhaps the year's highest-profile privacy-related controversy, the Bush administration asked for expanded anti-terrorism powers to wiretap Americans' overseas phone calls and e-mails without seeking warrants. Despite vocal opposition from privacy advocates and congressional Democrats, both the House and Senate considered legislation expanding the president's wiretapping powers, and the full Senate approved a bill in September.

As the means and motives for collecting personal data proliferate, some privacy advocates and even some businesses — including computer companies such as Microsoft, Intel and eBay — have called for federal privacy-protection legislation. The United States needs "a national data-protection office, like every other country in the industrialized world," said Simson L. Garfinkel, a postdoctoral fellow at Harvard's Center for Research on Computation and Society. [10]

Regardless of whether Congress acts to curb information gathering and sharing, technology eventually will

vacy protection." Instead, some protection is offered by a variety of more general federal laws, such as those covering wiretapping, and state laws that govern the way drug tests are given, for example. However, courts do uphold a few strong privacy standards, such as banning cameras in places where workers may disrobe. A federal law bans the use

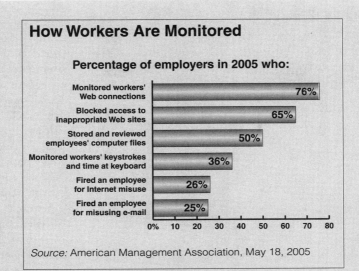

How Workers Are Monitored

Percentage of employers in 2005 who:

Monitored workers' Web connections	76%
Blocked access to inappropriate Web sites	65%
Stored and reviewed employees' computer files	50%
Monitored workers' keystrokes and time at keyboard	36%
Fired an employee for Internet misuse	26%
Fired an employee for misusing e-mail	25%

0% 10 20 30 40 50 60 70 80

Source: American Management Association, May 18, 2005

tions. Setting the tone for today's hands-off approach on workplace privacy, the Privacy Protection Study Commission concluded that employers set workplace policies — including privacy standards. And, because workers are free to work for an employer or not, they are generally obligated to abide by the boss' rules.

of lie-detector tests for general screening, allowing polygraphs only when some specific wrongdoing is suspected.

Otherwise, courts and legislators generally maintain that "if an employer hires you, they have a right to have you be on time and be efficient," which a business may conclude requires monitoring, says Hebert.

From time to time Congress considers strengthening safeguards on worker privacy. In 2000, for example, Rep. Charles Canady, R-Fla., and Sen. Charles Schumer, D-N.Y., introduced a measure that would have allowed workers to sue employers who didn't notify them that their electronic communications were being monitored. "Everybody has the right to know when they're being watched," said Schumer. [5] However, although House and Senate panels debated the bills, they never made it to the floor. [6]

In the 1970s, Congress created a panel to examine whether consumers and workers needed privacy protec-

[1] "Whose Life Is It Anyway?" CBS News, Oct. 30, 2005, www.workrights.org/in_the_news?in_the_news_cbs60minutes.html.

[2] "2005 Electronic Monitoring and Surveillance Survey: Many Companies Monitoring, Recording, Videotaping — and Firing — Employees," American Management Association, May 18, 2005, www.amanet.org.

[3] Bradley J. Alge, Jerald Greenberg and Chad T. Brinsfeld, "An Identity-Based Model of Organizational Monitoring: Integrating Information Privacy and Organizational Justice," *Research in Personnel and Human Resources Management, 2006,* pp. 71, 120.

[4] For background see "Privacy in the Workplace," *Editorial Research Reports,* 1986, and Patrick G. Marshall, "Your Right to Privacy," *CQ Researcher,* Jan. 20, 1989, both available at *CQ Researcher Plus Archive,* www.cqpress.com; and Richard L. Worsnop, "Privacy in the Workplace," *CQ Researcher,* Nov. 19, 1993, pp. 1009-1032.

[5] Quoted in "Congressional Alert: Bill S. 2898, HR 4908," *The Internet Party* blog; www.theinternetparty.org/congress/index.php?section_type=con&cat_name=Privacy&td=20011015162238&page_sort=3.

[6] "Workplace Privacy," Electronic Privacy Information Center, www.epic.org/privacy/workplace.

allow agencies and corporations to track individuals' activities by linking data such as cell-phone records and surveillance videos to credit-card numbers, voting records and Internet search queries. Once those databases are integrated — as they will be — "your life will be pretty much an open book," says Nehf.

With computer databases swelling and electronic-surveillance technology evolving rapidly, here are some of the questions lawmakers and privacy advocates are asking:

Should Congress make warrantless wiretapping easier?

Late last year, reporters discovered that President George W. Bush had authorized government agencies to wiretap Americans without first obtaining warrants, arguing the power to quickly authorize such surveillance was vital to fighting terrorism. Despite an outcry by civil-liberties advocates who said the wiretaps were illegal, Congress this year has considered giving the president expanded wiretapping powers.

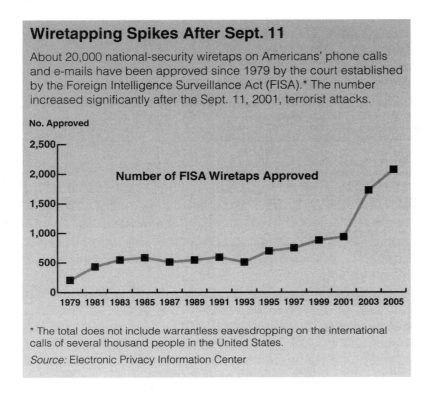

Wiretapping Spikes After Sept. 11

About 20,000 national-security wiretaps on Americans' phone calls and e-mails have been approved since 1979 by the court established by the Foreign Intelligence Surveillance Act (FISA).* The number increased significantly after the Sept. 11, 2001, terrorist attacks.

No. Approved

Number of FISA Wiretaps Approved

1979 1981 1983 1985 1987 1989 1991 1993 1995 1997 1999 2001 2003 2005

* The total does not include warrantless eavesdropping on the international calls of several thousand people in the United States.

Source: Electronic Privacy Information Center

secret panel of judges empowered to review government requests for security-related domestic surveillance. The FISA court fast-tracks government requests for surveillance warrants in national-security cases, although information gleaned from such surveillance can not be shared with agents working on criminal cases. The law also allows the government to wiretap citizens without a warrant for a limited number of days in certain circumstances.

Attorney General Alberto R. Gonzales contends that expanded power to wiretap Americans making overseas phone calls is crucial because the nation is at war against terrorists. "The terrorist-surveillance program is an essential element of our military campaign against al Qaeda," he told the Senate Judiciary Committee. [12] Obtaining FISA warrants currently takes too long and requires the government to submit too much information, and the warrantless wiretaps allowed are too restrictive, he contends.

Enabling the president to authorize speedy and long-term wiretapping on American soil "allows us to collect more information regarding al Qaeda's plans, and, critically, it allows us to locate al Qaeda operatives, especially those already in the United States and poised to attack," said Gonzales. "We cannot defend the nation without such information, as we painfully learned on Sept. 11."

Intelligence and military professionals, not courts, are best suited to decide who should be wiretapped, he said. "The optimal way to achieve the speed and agility necessary to this military-intelligence program . . . is to leave the decisions about particular intercepts to the judgment of a professional intelligence officer," said Gonzales. If an intelligence officer is required to navigate through the FISA procedures, "there would be critical holes in our early-warning system."

Following the Democrats' Nov. 7 electoral takeover of both houses of Congress, Bush said he still hopes to sign a bill giving him broader discretion to wiretap U.S. residents suspected of terrorist ties. Presumptive House Speaker Rep. Nancy Pelosi, D-Calif., however, said it's possible the White House and congressional Democrats will reach common ground on wiretapping but that Democrats will insist on some kind of judicial oversight of each individual case rather than the blanket approval the White House seeks. [11]

Wiretap opponents say snooping on Americans without adequate judicial oversight compromises their privacy and violates their Fourth Amendment constitutional protections against government searches without reasonable "cause" for such a search being shown first. About 30 lawsuits have been filed around the country challenging the searches "on constitutional grounds," says Nancy Libin, staff counsel at the Center for Democracy and Technology (CDT).

Revelations that the government had wiretapped dissidents' conversations during the turbulent 1960s and '70s led Congress in 1978 to pass the Foreign Intelligence Surveillance Act (FISA), which set up a

Historically, presidents have been allowed to conduct warrantless surveillance against wartime enemies on home soil, said Douglas W. Kmiec, a professor of constitutional law at Pepperdine University. "Neither Congress nor the president has required the armed forces to seek a battlefield warrant to conduct visual electronic surveillance," said Kmiec. "The Civil War is . . . the main historical battle fought on our soil, and there is no history suggesting that any search or observation of Confederate forces . . . was subject to a warrant requirement." [13]

There's no reason to imagine that the power to wiretap without a warrant would be misused for political purposes, said Robert F. Turner, associate director of the University of Virginia School of Law's Center for National Security Law. President Bush's critics "have done a grave disservice to our nation in drawing comparisons with President [Richard M.] Nixon's 'enemies list' and suggesting there is something evil about the program," he said, referring to a "watch list" of political opponents maintained by Nixon. [14]

Most Americans would gladly trade some privacy to help defeat terrorists, Turner continued. "I find it unimaginable that many rational Americans who are not intentionally assisting foreign terrorists would favor a policy by which the [National Security Agency] would ignore communications between known or suspected al Qaeda operatives abroad and . . . people within this country," he said. "They would be asserting that their privacy interests are of greater importance than the right to exist of perhaps tens- or hundreds-of-thousands of their fellow citizens."

But opponents of expanded wiretapping power say allowing a single government branch to breach Americans' privacy without sufficient oversight is a recipe for abuse. "This is not a debate about whether we ought to be wiretapping terrorists. The government had better be," says the Center for Democracy and Technology's Libin. "It's a debate over whether there should be checks" on the wiretapping power.

It's even more important to retain such checks in national-security cases than in criminal cases, where "you have a trial at the end that acts as a check" with public exposure of evidence, she says, whereas terrorism cases often are handled in secret military tribunals. " 'Trust us' is not the principle on which our country was founded."

She notes that since the FISA court was established, it has reviewed about 20,000 requests for FISA warrants and rejected only four — all in 2002. In that year, the Bush administration began bypassing the court and using warrantless wiretapping of U.S. residents.

Harold Hongju Koh, dean of Yale Law School, argues that proposed legislation to expand presidential wiretap-

ping power "would make matters far worse by giving Congress' blanket pre-authorization to a large number of unreasonable searches and seizures." (*See "At Issue," p. 233*.) Further, he added, the wiretapping bill approved by the Senate this fall "ratifies an illegal ongoing program without demanding first a full congressional review of what is now being done and more executive accountability going forward." It also would provide "neither the congressional oversight nor the judicial review that this program needs to restore . . . confidence in our constitutional checks and balances." [15]

Kenneth Gormley, professor of constitutional law at Pittsburgh's Duquesne University, said unless the government adheres to the Bill of Rights' ban on unreasonable government searches, officials would be destroying the very democracy they claim to be protecting from terrorists. [16]

The president's wiretapping program and congressional proposals to authorize it are vague enough to allow many abuses, say critics. "If, as they claim, the Bush administration can ignore FISA's express prohibition of warrantless wiretapping, can the government also eavesdrop on purely domestic phone calls?" asked Vermont Sen. Patrick J. Leahy, the top-ranking Democrat on the Senate Judiciary Committee and its incoming chairman. "Can it search or electronically bug an American's home or office?" [17]

Since combating terrorism is neither a declared war nor a time-limited activity, extra presidential powers granted in that context would essentially be eternal, Gormley pointed out. "When does this emergency cease?" he asked. Are "we prepared to say that the president may unilaterally suspend the Constitution for an indefinite period of time in order to deal with emergencies that have no ending point?"

Wiretapping under a FISA warrant is as effective as warrantless wiretapping, *The New York Times* editorialized last January. "The nation's guardians did not miss the 9/11 plot because it takes a few hours to get a warrant to eavesdrop on phone calls and e-mail messages," the paper said. "They missed the plot because they were not looking. Nothing prevented American intelligence from listening to a call from al Qaeda to the United States, or a call from the United States to al Qaeda, before Sept. 11, 2001, or since."

FISA "simply required the government to obey the Constitution in doing so," the editorial continued. "And FISA was amended after 9/11 to make the job much easier." [18]

Should companies be required to save data on customers' phone calls and Web searches?

To aid law enforcement, especially in child-pornography cases, President Bush has asked Internet and phone companies to save information on customers' Internet searches and phone calls. Attorney General Gonzales told the Senate Banking Committee that data retention "helps us make cases" against child pornographers and sex predators. "We have to find a way for Internet service providers (ISPs) to retain information for a period of time so we can go back with a legal process to get them." [19]

Although the Bush administration hasn't specifically mentioned the war on terrorism as a rationale for asking companies to retain Web-search data, the European Union (EU) directed telecommunications companies and ISPs in Europe to retain such data in order to put "a vital tool against terrorism and serious crime" in the hand of law-enforcement agencies," said British Home Secretary Charles Clarke. "Modern criminality crosses borders and seeks to exploit digital technology." [20]

Privacy advocates, however, argue that while such databases might help police they also could endanger privacy by allowing others, such as divorce lawyers, to conduct "fishing" expeditions into personal information. "If you have a huge database, then it becomes a huge target," says Indiana University's Nehf. "Unauthorized access by computer hacking," for example, is a huge problem now, but once the information is available, businesses, law-enforcement agencies, attorneys in civil cases and others "will start wanting to use it for 85 different purposes," he says.

However, state attorneys general agree with Gonzales that access to computer searches is critical for law enforcement. Last June, 49 attorneys general asked Congress to require ISPs to retain more data, citing the "growing crisis of Internet-based sex crimes against children and, in particular, the problem of insufficient data-retention policies" by ISPs.

"While law enforcement is doing more to catch online predators, their investigations often tragically dead-end at the door of [ISPs] that have deleted information critical to determining a suspect's name and physical location," the National Association of Attorneys General wrote in a letter to Congress. Although the group declined to specify how long subscriber information and content should be retained, "it is clear that something must be done," it said. [21]

Retaining phone records is especially important now that many phone companies are adopting flat-rate billing rather than charging by the call, according to the International Association of Chiefs of Police. Migration to flat-rate billing "has substantially eroded" law enforcement's ability to lawfully obtain telephone records "critical to the identification, detection and prevention" of terrorist and criminal conspiracies, the group said in a resolution endorsed in October. [22]

The EU's data-retention directive would also help music and media companies fight music and video theft. "We would appreciate your support in ensuring that this becomes an effective instrument in the fight against piracy," said the Creative and Media Business Alliance, whose members include such companies as EMI, SonyBMG and TimeWarner. [23]

But opponents argue that additional data retention threatens consumers' privacy and would turn phone and Internet companies into unofficial government agents. The government has asked ISPs to retain all of their records "just in case, someday, somehow, for some reason, the government may want them in some future case," said Mark Rasch, chief security counsel of the Omaha-based computer firm Solutionary. The proposal "represents a dangerous trend of turning private companies into proxies for law enforcement or intelligence agencies against the interest of their clients or customers." [24]

ISPs create short-term records of "virtually everything that virtually everyone does virtually," said Rasch, from blog posting and shopping online to editing a MySpace account or downloading music. But those records are frequently purged because they serve no real function for the ISP, he said.

Moreover, law-enforcement agencies already have the right to demand that ISPs retain specific records for between three and six months, he pointed out.

If such records are retained indefinitely, all Internet travels will become fair game for "criminal or civil subpoena, investigative demand, national security letter, grand jury subpoena, search warrant [and] administrative demand" in matters ranging from criminal investigations to divorce, according to Rasch. "If records exist, they will be subpoenaed, stolen, lost or hacked."

Furthermore, the Center for Democracy and Technology worries that ISPs, to recoup some of the expense of storing all that new data, "might be tempted to use the stored information for a range of currently unanticipated purposes," exposing customers to additional privacy threats. [25]

A list of an individual's Internet browsing — called a clicktrail — is "the equivalent of being tailed everywhere you go," undermining one's ability to remain anonymous, because analysts of that data "are likely to identify you," according to William McGeveran a fellow at Harvard Law School's Berkman Center for Internet and Society. [26]

Data retention could also breach the privacy of police work, according to Peter P. Swire, a law professor at Ohio State University. "Commercial ISPs would retain detailed records of communications to and from the FBI or the local police department," becoming "a honey pot for attacks" from ISP employees working for or bribed by criminals or from outside hackers, Swire said. "Organized-crime groups . . . might find it irresistible to place a spy in ISPs in cities where they operate." [27]

Other critics argue that businesses already save too much information. For example, companies like Google and MSN archive search-engine queries, as Thelma Arnold discovered when a reporter tracked her down in Lilburn, Ga.

"Search engines can only regain the trust of the public if they delete the search queries as soon as they get them," said British technology reporter Andrew Orlowski. In many cases, "these questions . . . would only have been made with the assumption that no one would ever see them. So what business do . . . organizations have hoarding this information?" [28]

Should Congress criminalize pretexting?

Obtaining access to confidential information by pretending to be another person — or pretexting — became news this year when investigators for HP used the tactic to obtain phone records of board members and journalists.

A pending House bill would ban pretexting to obtain phone records and require phone companies to do more to prevent the practice. Supporters of the measure say it's needed because some lawyers believe pretexting is legal. But opponents say it would unfairly increase phone companies' privacy-protection responsibilities. Others say lawmakers should spend their energy developing a broader consumer-privacy law.

"Even though most experts agree" that pretexting is already illegal under state and federal laws, the HP case indicates that there is "confusion in the highest echelons of corporate America and among their legal counsel" about that fact, said Rep. Dianne DeGette, D-Colo. [29]

The legislation also pressures phone companies to do more to safeguard customers' data, supporters say. Without the bill, it's too easy for scam artists to get the personal phone logs of others, said Rep. Jan Schakowsky, D-Ill. [30]

"We are putting obligations on you to protect our constituents' privacy," Rep. Jay Inslee, D-Wash., told telephone executives at a Sept. 29 House Commerce Subcommittee on Oversight and Investigations hearing. "It's entirely appropriate . . . to have a more uniform system so that we can have the highest level of anti-pretexting technologies in use. That is a fair obligation on the industry." [31]

A new law would help clarify "the illegality of this practice," Joel Winston, the Federal Trade Commission's associate director for privacy protection, told the subcommittee. Moreover, he added, the law should apply not only to the pretexters but also to anyone who solicits their services "when they know or should know that fraudulent means are being deployed." [32]

However, private investigators, corporate boards and others who want to access phone records now legally accessible only to law-enforcement agencies armed with a judicial warrant, argue that sometimes their need for information trumps privacy worries.

Rep. Ed Whitfield, R-Ky., told fellow subcommittee members that after one of the panel's hearings on the HP pretexting scandal, two legislators warned him that corporate boards "should have the right to determine who's leaking information." [33]

Jimmie Mesis, editor in chief of *PI Magazine*, said banning pretexting would cripple the ability of private investigators to solve important cases. He said he had warned private detectives to stop "blatantly" advertising that they can obtain unpublished numbers or phone records or risk a new law that "will eventually prevent us from using an amazing investigative resource." [34]

Although phone companies oppose pretexting and have sued pretexters, they are reluctant to endorse a new law because they think consumers would find tougher security measures inconvenient. Customers "don't want another password," said Tom Meiss, associate general counsel of Cingular Wireless. "Ironically, the stronger you make the security, the more likely it is that people are going to get locked out" of their own accounts. That would just play into pretexters' plans, he said, because many pretexters get the records by telling customer-service representatives they are customers who have forgotten their passwords. [35]

C H R O N O L O G Y

1890s-1960s *Law-enforcement agencies raise privacy concerns when they wiretap phones.*

1895 New York City police looking for criminal evidence figure out how to wiretap telephones.

1928 Supreme Court declares in *Olmstead v. United States* that warrantless police wiretaps don't violate the Constitution's ban on "unreasonable searches and seizures."

1956 FBI launches COINTELPRO counterintelligence program to keep tabs on the Communist Party and other dissident groups.

1967 Supreme Court in *Katz v. United States* overturns *Olmstead*, requiring warrants before police can wiretap.

1970s-1980s *Government surveillance in national-security matters draws scrutiny, and personal information begins to migrate into computer databases.*

1972 Supreme Court in *United States v. United States District Court* requires warrants for wiretapping in national-security cases.

1974 Privacy Act requires federal agencies to safeguard privacy when they collect personal information; attempts to extend privacy requirements to commercial businesses fail.

1976 The so-called Church committee concludes that from World War I through the 1970s U.S. presidents have claimed national-security reasons for spying on political enemies.

1978 Foreign Intelligence Surveillance Act creates a special court to secretly assess government requests for national-security wiretaps.

1986 Electronic Communications Privacy Act prohibits warrantless government wiretaps of electronic communications.

1990s *The booming Internet and cell-phone industries make more private data vulnerable to computer hacking and*

other misuse. Australia, Canada, New Zealand and most European countries enact wide-ranging consumer-privacy laws.

1995 European Union adopts a privacy directive establishing a minimum standard of data-privacy protection across Europe.

1999 A woman is shot to death in New Hampshire after a business obtains her personal data by trickery and sells it to a stalker. . . . The Gramm-Leach-Bliley law makes it a federal crime to obtain financial records by pretexting — claiming a false identity.

2000s *Terrorism fears and burgeoning electronic technology increase government-surveillance initiatives. Data aggregators sell personal information gained from multiple public and private sources.*

2001 Terrorist attacks on Sept. 11 shift attention from privacy protection to national security. . . . USA Patriot Act passed on Oct. 25, giving government sweeping surveillance powers.

2005 Atlanta-based data aggregator Choice-Point sells data on 163,000 people to a crime ring and later faces a $15 million fine. . . . Computers are hacked at CardSystems Solutions, which manages credit-card money transfers, potentially exposing financial data on 40 million people. . . . AT&T is accused of helping the Bush administration wiretap Americans' phone calls without warrants. . . . Real ID Act requires nationally standardized driver's licenses to be electronically linked to personal data and available to all states. . . . Congress reauthorizes Patriot Act but with new surveillance limits.

2006 Federal judge strikes down National Security Agency domestic-surveillance program, but its wiretaps continue under appeal. . . . Congress considers increasing the president's power to order wiretaps. . . . AOL posts 650,000 supposedly anonymous search-engine queries online, but researchers identify customers using Social Security and credit-card numbers in the data. . . . A Department of Veterans Affairs laptop computer with veterans' personal data is stolen. . . . Investigators working for computer giant HP in a leak investigation use pretexting to get journalists' and board members' phone records.

Many legal scholars and privacy advocates point out that pretexting is already clearly illegal and that many other privacy issues deserve lawmakers' attention but are not being addressed by current laws or regulations.

"Congress might pass a law making [pretexting for phone records] illegal, but it's already illegal, so I don't think that gets you very far," says Nehf.

BACKGROUND

Behind Closed Doors

In the days before the telegraph and telephone, privacy was defined as the right to be free from unreasonable intrusions into one's own home. But with people's lives increasingly dominated by electronics, the question of what is private has become harder to answer. For example, once a customer enters a credit-card number into a database that belongs to a commercial business, who owns that information — the customer or the business owner? Or has the customer made it public record by giving it away? [36]

Starting in the 15th century, the British government began challenging citizens' views that their homes were effectively their castles — where privacy was sacrosanct — by authorizing government agents to search homes and businesses if they suspected the owners of criminal activity, heresy or political dissent.

Eventually, England began regularly issuing "general warrants" authorizing searches of houses and businesses without any proof that owners had done anything wrong and without even naming the object of the search.

By the mid-18th century, however, English citizens fed up with general warrants successfully sued government agents for trespassing. In one case, England's Court of Common Pleas found that the defendants had no right to use the warrants, asserting "there is no law in this country to justify the defendants in what they have done. If there was, it would destroy all the comforts of society." [37]

At about the same time, the American colonists were outraged by similar general warrants — so-called writs of assistance — issued to British customs officers searching for smuggled goods. The writs had no time limit, allowed officers to search anyplace they wanted without responsibility for damages and could be transferred from officer to officer.

The writs were among the grievances the colonists listed when they declared their independence from England in 1776. The Constitution's Fourth Amendment — citizens' primary protection against unreasonable government searches — banned general search warrants.

Electronic Intrusion

As technologies advanced, however, the meaning of a guarantee against "unreasonable searches" became murkier. When private information is transmitted long distances over a wire, for instance, it is unclear whether it remains protected private information. [38]

In the second half of the 19th century, some states made it a crime for a telegraph company to disclose a telegram's contents to anyone but its authorized recipient. And in 1877, Western Union President William Orton resisted a congressional subpoena seeking telegrams for evidence in an investigation of voting irregularities.

The subpoena asked his company "to become spies and . . . informers against the customers who have reposed in us the gravest confidence concerning both their official and their private affairs," Orton said. [39] After being declared in contempt of Congress and arrested, however, he gave in and handed over 30,000 telegrams. To avoid similar future troubles, Western Union reduced the amount of time it kept copies of messages.

By the late 1880s, a new technology — the telephone — was transmitting a million messages a day in the United States. Original users of the telephone had little expectation of confidentiality, though, because initially four or more neighbors shared the same "party line," and operators knew exactly who was talking to whom, since the operators placed most calls manually.

Meanwhile, police agencies were quick to see the telephone's potential for evidence gathering, and by the 1890s police had figured out how to "tap" phones. The public remained largely unaware of this development until a 1916 investigation into New York public utilities turned up evidence of the taps, which were being used to keep tabs on resident aliens who might be spying for enemy governments during World War I.

The government had set up "a complete central-office switchboard . . . in the New York Custom House, with taps running into it from all parts of the city. Every time a suspected alien lifted his receiver a light showed . . . and a stenographer . . . took a record of the conversation." [40]

Attacks on Privacy Getting More Ingenious

Companies are creating increasingly ingenious ways to monitor consumers' buying habits. Many supermarkets and drug stores, for instance, now offer discounts on certain products to those who sign up for the stores' frequent-buyer cards. But to get that card — and a few bucks off on their purchases — customers must give the store their names, addresses and phone numbers. The store's computers then track the buyers' purchasing preferences and sell the information to other marketers.

But besides collecting data for commercial purposes, a growing number of companies — legitimate and illegitimate — are in the business of selling personal information. These data aggregators (also called data brokers or information resellers) sometimes collect information under false pretenses — known as pretexting — and sell it to all comers. Law-enforcement agencies around the country have recently tried to shut down such companies.

In March, for example, Florida Attorney General — now governor-elect — Charlie Crist charged the Global Information Group with pretexting to obtain customer phone records. [1] Between Sept. 14 and Oct. 19, 2005, the company allegedly made more than 5,100 calls to Florida Verizon Wireless customers, attempting to obtain confidential information "through deceit, either by impersonating a customer or employee, or otherwise convincing the customer-service representative to provide private information . . . without the customer's consent or knowledge," the lawsuit claims. [2]

"Why do these people sell this data — and, apparently, sell it to anyone? Frankly, greed is the name of the game," said information-security consultant Robert Douglas, CEO of PrivacyToday.com. Individuals ranging from lawyers and private investigators to vengeful ex-spouses, obsessed stalkers or identity thieves will pay top dollar for personal data, he said. [3]

Beyond the underworld of information thieves there is the fast-growing world of large, legitimate data aggregators. Companies such as ChoicePoint, Acxiom and InfoUSA assemble for resale detailed personal profiles from government sources including birth and death records, property records, voter registrations and court files, publicly available information like telephone and business directories and proprietary sources such as credit files and product-warranty questionnaires.

Law-enforcement agencies and government offices buy information from data aggregators, according to the Government Accountability Office (GAO). In fiscal 2005, for example, the Justice, Homeland Security and State departments, as well as the Social Security Administration,

---

Discovery of the taps triggered public outrage, and the telephone company ended its cooperation with the government. But police wiretapping continued unchecked.

By the 1920s, most U.S. phone calls were placed by automatic switchboards, not live operators, and the public began to expect that telephone conversations were confidential. But as more and more conversations about activities — legal and illegal — began traveling over telephone lines, police saw more reason to wiretap. Eventually, the Supreme Court was asked to consider whether the Fourth Amendment restricted wiretapping.

During Prohibition, Seattle police Lt. Roy Olmstead was arrested for bootlegging. But because federal agents had not sought a warrant before tapping phones at his home and the homes of three associates, he claimed the taps violated his constitutional protection against war-

rantless searches. But a 5-4 Supreme Court decision in 1928 held that the taps were not an "unreasonable search" under the Constitution. [41]

"There was no searching. There was no seizure," wrote Chief Justice William Howard Taft for the majority. "The evidence was secured by the sense of hearing and that only."

In a strong and seemingly prescient dissent, Justice Louis D. Brandeis protested that "subtler and more far-reaching means of invading privacy have become available to the government. . . . The progress of science . . . is not likely to stop with wiretapping. Can it be that the Constitution affords no protection against such invasions of individual security?" Surely, Brandeis continued, the Constitution protects against "every unjustifiable intrusion by the Government upon the privacy of the individual, whatever the means employed." [42]

spent $30 million buying personal information from resellers, according to GAO. The agencies used the information for purposes like tracking down potential witnesses and making sure that people are entitled to the government benefits they receive. [4]

It's far cheaper for government to use commercially aggregated data, Consumer Data Industry Association President Stuart Pratt told the House Judiciary Committee in April. "One commercial database provider charges just $25 for an instant comprehensive search of . . . more than 100 million criminal records across the United States," said Pratt. "An in-person, local search of one local courthouse for felony and misdemeanor records takes three . . . days and costs $16 [in] courthouse fees," adding up to a $48,544 tab for an in-person search of every county courthouse nationwide. [5]

But critics say that as commercial — but largely unregulated — data aggregators replace public records as the preferred information source for business and government, oversight is needed to protect individuals' privacy.

For example, 41 states allow some people accused or convicted of crimes to expunge their criminal records under certain circumstances. But removing a crime from one's record is much more difficult now that private companies serve as key providers of public data. Unlike government offices, private companies are not legally required to ensure the accuracy of their data. Consequently, many databases "are updated only fitfully, and expunged records now often turn up in criminal background checks ordered by employers and landlords." [6]

For the interconnected world of government and commercial data keeping, a new legal framework to protect personal information is needed, say some analysts.

In the case of criminal-record expungement, for example, "the solution . . . is for states . . . to require" commercial data brokers "to promise that they will delete records when they are expunged" from the public records, according to Daniel J. Solove, an associate professor of law at The George Washington University." [7]

---

[1] "Crist Charges Second Data Broker Over Sale of Phone Records," press release, Office of the Attorney General of Florida, Feb. 24, 2006, http://myfloridalegal.com.

[2] *Florida v. Global Information Group, Inc.,* http://myfloridalegal.com/webfiles.nsf/WF/MRAY-6M9RY3/$file/Global_Complaint.pdf.

[3] Testimony before House Committee on Energy and Commerce, Feb. 1, 2006.

[4] Linda D. Koontz, "Personal Information: Agencies and Resellers Vary in Providing Privacy Protections," Government Accountability Office, April 4, 2006.

[5] Testimony before House Judiciary Subcommittees on Commercial and Administrative Law and on the Constitution, April 4, 2006.

[6] Adam Litpak, "Expunged Criminal Records Live to Tell Tales," *The New York Times*, Oct. 17, 2006.

[7] Daniel J. Solove, "The Reincarnation of Expunged Criminal Records," *Concurring Opinions* blog, Oct. 17, 2006; www.concurringopinions.com.

For nearly four decades, the court's declaration that warrantless wiretaps were constitutional held sway. By 1967, however, with the world firmly entrenched in the electronic era, the court came around to Brandeis' view. In *Katz v. United States* the court ruled that FBI agents had violated the Fourth Amendment by not requesting a judicial warrant before installing a listening device on a phone booth to record calls made by Charles Katz, a small-time Los Angeles gambler.

The *Katz* decision reflected how advancing technology had changed the concept of privacy. No longer did invasion of privacy require intrusion into one's home or a sealed letter. "Once it is recognized that the Fourth Amendment protects people — and not simply 'areas' — against unreasonable searches and seizures, it becomes clear that the reach of that Amendment cannot turn upon the presence or absence of a physical intrusion into any given enclosure," said the court majority in *Katz*. [43]

National Security

For nearly as long as there have been telephones, government agencies have argued that national security requires eavesdropping on electronic communications. The FBI, NSA and other executive-branch agencies say they need secrecy and know more than the courts about security threats so they should be free to conduct surveillance — including of American citizens — without seeking warrants.

In the 1950s and '60s, the FBI, under orders from Director J. Edgar Hoover, set up a nationwide counterintelligence program — COINTELPRO — to investigate dissident political organizations ranging from the Communist Party to the Black Panthers. Eventually, COINTELPRO expanded to spy on the Ku Klux Klan and anti-war groups such as Students for a Democratic Society.

Meanwhile, NSA's "Project Shamrock" searched for key words in every telegram sent into or out of the

Shhhhh!

Keep silent while we rifle through your personal records.

The Patriot Act

Here to protect YOU from your freedoms.

ACLU www.aclu.org   ALA American Library Association   www.alawash.org

ACLU/ALA

A poster sponsored by the American Civil Liberties Union and the American Library Association condemns so-called third-party searches permitted by the 2001 USA Patriot Act. The controversial law allowed the government to obtain data on which books patrons checked out and prohibited librarians from revealing that a search had occurred. Protests by privacy activists led Congress in 2005 to tighten the requirements for such searches.

United States in search of communist sympathizers — another example of massive domestic surveillance conducted without a judicial warrant.

By the early 1970s, worries were growing about how such programs compromised Americans' privacy. And in 1971, U.S. Court of Appeals Judge Damon J. Keith ruled in the Michigan criminal trial of the White Panther Party that national-security concerns were not an adequate justification for warrantless wiretapping of Americans. [44]

In the case, which involved the bombing of CIA offices in Ann Arbor, the government claimed that the president and attorney general had the power "to authorize without judicial warrant electronic surveillance in 'national security' cases and to determine unilaterally whether a given situation is a matter . . . of national security," wrote Keith. [45]

But "we are a country of laws and not of men," Keith said. "If the president is given power to delegate who shall conduct wiretaps, the question arises whether there is any limit on this power."

In 1972, the Supreme Court unanimously upheld Keith's ruling. "We cannot accept the government's argument that internal security matters are too subtle and complex for judicial evaluation," wrote Justice Lewis F. Powell. [46]

In 1976, the Senate launched an investigation of national-security surveillance. The Select Committee to Study Governmental Operations with Respect to Intelligence Activities — known as the Church committee after its chairman, Sen. Frank Church, D-Idaho — examined millions of pages of documents and concluded that abusive domestic spying by federal agencies went as far back as World War I.

"The constitutional system of checks and balances has not adequately controlled intelligence activities," the committee's report said. "Too many people have been spied upon by too many government agencies, and too much information has been collected. . . . The government has often undertaken the secret surveillance of citizens on the basis of their political beliefs, even when those beliefs posed no threat of violence or illegal acts on behalf of a foreign power." [47]

To prevent such abuses in the future, the Supreme Court and members of Congress declared that lawmakers should set up a system for issuing national-security warrants. The 1978 Foreign Surveillance Intelligence Act (FISA) established the Foreign Surveillance Intelligence Court (FISC) — a secret panel of judges empowered to review government requests for security-related domestic surveillance.

FISA fast-tracks government requests for warrants for national-security surveillance on the condition that information gained through FISA warrants not be shared with agents working on criminal cases. Since the Sept. 11, 2001, terrorist attacks, Congress has amended the law five times at the request of both Congress and the administration. Among other things, the changes:

Tips on Protecting Your Privacy

Many experts argue that surveillance and database technologies have proliferated to such an extent that Americans have little privacy left to protect. Nevertheless, here are some ways consumer and advocacy groups say citizens can protect their personal information:

Be on the lookout for pretexting. Many unscrupulous individuals and businesses try to get private information under false pretenses, says the Federal Trade Commission (FTC). To avoid being victimized, never give out your Social Security number, mother's maiden name, bank account numbers or other personal information to a telephone caller or e-mailer, no matter who they claim to be, says the FTC.

"Pretexters may pose as representatives of survey firms, banks, Internet service providers and government agencies" to get you to reveal your data. But "legitimate organizations with which you do business have the information they need and will not ask you for it." [1]

The FTC also advises consumers to ask banks and other companies that gather personal information what measures they take to prevent pretexting.

Don't use your Social Security number (SSN) or birth date as a password. The technology magazine *Wired* says both are too easily discovered to make for good security, and using them as passwords only makes it easier for someone to steal them. Insist that your health-insurance provider and phone companies allow you to use a customer-designated password, and use different passwords for different accounts, the magazine advises. [2]

Use unique passwords. Thieves can easily discover passwords like a pet's name or consecutive numbers, says the Privacy Rights Clearinghouse, "Think of a favorite line of poetry, like 'Mary had a little lamb.' Use the first or last letters to create a password. Use numbers to make it stronger. For example, MHALL, or better yet, MHA2L." [3]

Use a prepaid disposable cell phone. If you're worried about your phone records becoming available to third parties, such as stalkers, buy a disposable phone and add calling minutes through the phone company rather than through a Web site, which might track your computer's address. [4]

Use a Web-accessible e-mail account for personal e-mails. While employers may still be able to read your e-mails if you access the account from a workplace computer, they won't be automatically stored in the company's main computer server, says the Center for Democracy and Technology (CDT). All mail sent through your workplace e-mail is stored there, even if you access your work e-mail from a home computer. [5]

Clear your computer's memory cache frequently. While keeping a cache of recently visited Web pages makes it easier to call the pages up again, failing to periodically erase it can have "grave implications for personal privacy," especially if you share a computer, says CDT. Go to the "preferences" folder in your Internet browser and click "empty cache" to delete your browsing list. In Internet Explorer, call up "Internet options" from the "tools" menu, and then click "clear history." [6]

Ask your bank how much personal data it shares about you. The Federal Reserve Board (FRB) points out that banks, insurance companies and other financial-services companies can share customer information with other businesses, but they must first send privacy notices to customers offering them a chance to opt out. If you didn't opt out when you received your privacy notification, "it's not too late," says the FRB. "You can always change your mind." Just call the company for instructions on opting out of future data-sharing. [7]

Use other "opt-out" tools to protect your information. To limit the number of preapproved credit-card offers you receive, opt out of credit-reporting bureaus' marketing lists at www.optoutprescreen.com or call 888-5OPTOUT. To opt out of calls from nationwide marketers, contact the FTC's National Do Not Call Registry at www.donotcall.gov or call (888) 382-1222. [8]

---

[1] "Pretexting: Your Personal Information Revealed," *Facts for Consumers*, Federal Trade Commission, www.ftc.gov.

[2] Kim Zetter, "Protect Yourself From Pretexting," *Wired News*, Sept. 14, 2006; www.wired.com.

[3] "Coping With Identity Theft: Reducing the Risk of Fraud," *Fact Sheet 17*, Privacy Rights Clearinghouse, September 2006, www.privacyrights.org.

[4] *Ibid.*

[5] "Getting Started: Top Ten Ways to Protect Privacy Online," Center for Democracy and Technology, www.cdt.org.

[6] *Ibid.*

[7] "Privacy Choices for Your Personal Financial Information," Federal Reserve Board, www.federalreserve.gov/pubs/privacy/.

[8] Privacy Rights Clearinghouse, *op. cit.*

- Permit extending wiretaps to other phones a suspect may be using, even if the phone owners are not under investigation;
- Lengthen the time warrants are valid for both wiretaps and physical searches;
- Allow surveillance of e-mails under the same wiretapping warrant;
- Allow FISA wiretapping for a broader range of investigations by allowing foreign-intelligence gathering to be only "a significant purpose" rather than "the purpose" of the investigation;
- Protect from legal liability anybody who helps with FISA wiretapping. [48]

By 2005 the FISA court had granted some 20,000 warrants during its 27-year existence. It had turned down government requests for warrants only four times — in 2002. Last year the court approved 2,072 warrant requests — the highest annual total ever and 18 percent more than in 2004. [49]

Yet in December 2005 *The New York Times* reported that since early 2002 President George W. Bush had secretly authorized the NSA to bypass the FISA court and conduct warrantless eavesdropping on U.S. citizens' international telephone calls and e-mails. Through the end of 2005, several thousand people in the United States had had their international communications monitored, with about 500 Americans under surveillance at any given time, government officials told the paper. [50]

The administration says the program has been successful in slowing terrorists. For example, officials said, it helped uncover a plot by a naturalized citizen in Ohio, Iyman Faris, who pled guilty in 2003 to plotting to destroy the Brooklyn Bridge. [51]

In August 2006, however, a U.S. district judge ruled that the NSA eavesdropping program was unconstitutional. The government has appealed the decision, and a court has said the eavesdropping may continue while the appeal proceeds. [52]

Another post-9/11 security measure — the USA Patriot Act — allowed government agents to obtain personal records held by "third parties," such as library records of what books an individual has borrowed, and prohibited anyone — librarians, for instance — from revealing that such a search had occurred. [53]

When Congress reauthorized the measure in 2005, it barred third-party searches without the approval of top FBI officials and required the Justice Department's

inspector general to audit each search request. Congress also recommended that citizens be able to challenge the search orders in court. [54]

Database Era

Before the computer age, privacy advocates worried most about concentrations of personal information at government agencies. But with computers came a new age of information gathering, with government agencies and private businesses accumulating, analyzing, sharing and selling personal information of all kinds.

We are in a period of "surveillance creep" — where personal information is demanded not by a policeman's knock on the door but through various kinds of "soft surveillance," in which people are persuaded to give up their privacy on the grounds that it's in the best interests of themselves and society, according to Gary T. Marx, a professor emeritus of sociology at the Massachusetts Institute of Technology.

For example, more buildings now post signs stating that "in entering here you have agreed to be searched," says Marx. In the Justice Department's "Watch Your Car" auto-theft-prevention program, owners place decals on their cars inviting police anywhere to stop the car if it is driven late at night.

"There is a chilling and endless-regress quality in our drift into a society where you have to provide ever-more-personal information in order to prove that you are the kind of person who does not merit even more intensive scrutiny," he contends. [55]

Private information that allows government and business to profile and track individuals is being collected in a variety of new ways and used for many purposes. For example, Illinois' E-Z Pass — an electronic card that allows drivers to pass quickly through highway toll booths — has taken center stage in some family-court cases. Divorce attorneys subpoena E-Z Pass records to see if travel patterns demonstrate that a spouse had an extramarital affair or spends too much time on the road to be awarded child custody. [56]

"When a guy says, 'Oh, I'm home every day at 5, and I have dinner with my kids every single night,' you subpoena his E-Z Pass, and you find out he's crossing that bridge every night at 8:30. Oops!" said Philadelphia lawyer Lynn Gold-Bikin. [57]

Now even more extensive databases are coming. Under the 2005 Real ID Act, states must issue standard-

Should Congress expand the president's authority to wiretap Americans to combat terrorism?

YES
Steven G. Bradbury
Acting Assistant Attorney General

Testimony before the Senate Committee on the Judiciary, July 26, 2006

Foreign-intelligence surveillance is a critical tool in our common effort to prevent another catastrophic terrorist attack on the United States. The enemies we face operate in obscurity, through secret cells that communicate globally while plotting to carry out surprise attacks from within our own communities.

The past 28 years since the enactment of the Federal Intelligence Surveillance Act (FISA) have seen perhaps the greatest transformation of modes of communication of any period in history. At that time, Congress did not anticipate the technological revolution that would bring us global high-speed fiber-optic networks, the Internet, e-mail and disposable cell phones.

Innovations in communications technology have fundamentally transformed how our enemies communicate, and therefore how they plot and plan their attacks. Meanwhile, the United States confronts the threat of al Qaeda with a legal regime designed for the last century and geared more toward traditional case-by-case investigations.

In times of national emergency and armed conflict involving an exigent terrorist threat, the president may need to act with agility and dispatch to protect the country by putting in place a program of surveillance targeted at the terrorists and designed to detect and prevent the next attack. Article II of the Constitution gives the president authority to act in this way to defend the nation.

[Legislation] sponsored by Judiciary Committee Chairman Arlen Specter, R-Pa., would create for the first time an innovative procedure whereby the president will be able to bring such a surveillance program promptly to the FISA court for a judicial determination that it is constitutional and reasonable. *

Chairman Specter's bill includes several important reforms to update FISA for the 21st century. The bill would change the definition of "agent of a foreign power." Occasionally, a foreign person who is not an agent of a foreign government or a suspected terrorist will enter the United States in circumstances where the government knows that he possesses potentially valuable foreign-intelligence information, and the government currently has no means to conduct surveillance of that person under FISA.

The chairman's legislation would limit the amount of detail required for applications for FISA warrants. And, very importantly, the "emergency authorization" provisions would be amended to permit emergency surveillance for up to seven days, as opposed to the current three days.

NO
Harold Hongju Koh
Dean, Yale Law School

Testimony before the Senate Committee on the Judiciary, Feb. 28, 2006

For nearly 30 years, the Foreign Intelligence Surveillance Act of 1978 (FISA) has guaranteed compliance with constitutional requirements by providing a comprehensive, exclusive statutory framework for electronic surveillance. Yet apparently, the National Security Agency (NSA) has violated these requirements repeatedly by carrying on a sustained program of secret, unreviewed, warrantless electronic surveillance of American citizens and residents.

Unfortunately, [legislation] sponsored by Judiciary Committee Chairman Arlen Specter, R-Pa., would not improve the situation. *

The proposed law would simply amend FISA to increase the authority of the president to conduct surveillance, based on a showing of "probable cause" that the entire surveillance program — not any particular act of surveillance — will intercept communications of a foreign power or agent, or anyone who has ever communicated with a foreign agent.

While perhaps legalizing a small number of reasonable searches and seizures, the statute would make matters far worse, giving Congress' blanket pre-authorization to a large number of unreasonable searches and seizures, and providing neither the congressional oversight nor the judicial review that this program needs.

We must not forget the historical events that led to enactment of the 1978 FISA statute. When American ships were attacked in the Gulf of Tonkin in 1964, President [Lyndon B.] Johnson asked Congress for a resolution that gave him broad freedom to conduct a controversial, undeclared war in Indochina. That war traumatized our country and triggered a powerful antiwar movement. It soon came to light that to support the war effort, three government agencies — the FBI, the CIA and the NSA — had wiretapped thousands of innocent Americans suspected of committing subversive activities against the U.S. government.

To end these abuses, Congress passed FISA, which makes it a crime for anyone to wiretap Americans in the United States without a warrant or a court order.

Drafted with wartime in mind, FISA permits the attorney general to authorize warrantless electronic surveillance in the United States for only 15 days after a declaration of war, to give Congress time to pass new laws to give the president any new wiretap authority he may need to deal with the wartime emergency.

In short, FISA was based on simple, sensible reasoning: Before the president invades our privacy, his lawyers must get approval from someone who does not work for him.

* The proposed legislation is S2453.

ized driver's licenses with digital photographs and machine-readable chips beginning in 2008. States must verify that all license holders are in the country legally, retain the proofs of identity on file for up to a decade and maintain all license information in a database accessible to all other states.

"The average person does not see the privacy consequences" of the massive, interconnected databases that will result, said James W. Harper, director of information studies at the libertarian Cato Institute. "The one that I prioritize most is the likelihood that Real ID will be used for tracking and surveillance. That's not an immediate concern, but down the line you can be sure it will be used that way." [58]

In the early 1970s, when the era of databases was just beginning, Sen. Samuel J. Ervin, D-N.C., proposed enacting a comprehensive privacy bill that would apply to both the government and the private sector. Businesses objected, however, claiming it would be expensive and was unnecessary.

In the end, the Privacy Act of 1974 applied only to federal agencies. Companies were allowed to self-regulate based on a consensus list of Fair Information Practice Principles (FIPP) that business, government and privacy advocates developed. The principles are designed to make sure agencies collect only the information needed for a specific purpose and to ensure citizens' access to the data collected about them so they can check it periodically for accuracy. [59]

As a result of the Privacy Act's limitations — and unlike most industrial nations — the United States has no comprehensive privacy law today. A piecemeal collection of state and federal laws does set data-handling standards for certain industries, however.

For instance, the Health Insurance Portability and Accountability Act of 1996 (HIPAA) established some privacy safeguards for medical records. The Gramm-Leach-Bliley Act of 1999 sets customer-notification standards and outlaws pretexting for financial records.

Meanwhile, private databases continue to grow, filled with information used by both businesses and government.

Such large databases of personal information speed up business, to everyone's benefit, according to technology writer Declan McCullagh, chief political correspondent for the tech-news Web site News.com. [60] "A few decades ago, applying for credit meant an in-person visit. . . . If the loan officer didn't know you personally, he or she would contact your references and . . . eventually make a decision a few weeks later. . . . It was a slow, painful process that was hardly consumer-friendly.

"Today, not only can you get a loan nearly instantly, you'll pay less for it than in countries that prevent the free flow of information," McCullagh continues. Economist Walter Kitchenman, of Purchase Street Research in New York, estimates that U.S. mortgage rates are up to two full percentage points lower than they would be otherwise, thanks to information sharing among financial firms.

CURRENT SITUATION

Spying Bills Stall

Congress has been considering bills this year that would give the president more leeway to wiretap Americans without a warrant and outlaw the use of a false identity to obtain phone records. A group of high-tech companies has also been pushing for a wide-reaching consumer-privacy law.

Both the Senate and the House considered — but did not pass — bills to make it easier for the president to eavesdrop on international phone calls and Internet messages in order to combat terrorism. Despite repeated amendments to FISA procedures since September 2001, administration officials say the federal framework of issuing national-security warrants still doesn't work for anti-terror efforts.

"Frankly, I don't think anyone can make the claim that the FISA statute was designed to deal with 9/11 or to deal with a lethal enemy who likely already had armed combatants inside the United States," CIA Director Gen. Michael V. Hayden told the Senate Judiciary Committee in July. [61]

Several lawmakers agreed, proposing bills that would give the president wider eavesdropping latitude. For example, a bill introduced in the House by Rep. Heather Wilson, R-N.M., would reduce the amount of information federal agents must give to the FISC before the court issues a warrant. The measure also would expand the amount of time the president may conduct surveillance before obtaining a warrant and would allow warrantless surveillance after any "armed attack" on the United States.

"You can't get the information for probable cause . . . fast enough" to meet current FISC requirements, Wilson said at a House Intelligence Committee hearing in July. [62]

Privacy advocates say the FISA system does not need such a broad overhaul and argue that many proposed changes leave too much room for interpretation and unchecked action by the president. For example, allowing warrantless surveillance in cases of "armed attack" against the United States rather than only during wartime opens the possibility that a president could snoop on U.S. citizens for months if a U.S. embassy abroad were attacked, says the Center for Democracy and Technology's Libin.

This is not to say that FISA shouldn't be "streamlined" to keep up with current developments, she says. For example, a bipartisan bill sponsored by Sens. Dianne Feinstein, D-Calif., and Arlen Specter, R-Pa., would allow wiretapping without a warrant in some emergency cases for seven days rather than 72 hours as is currently allowed. The extension would give the government more time to demonstrate that it needs a warrant in complex terrorism investigations. "By all means, let's have a discussion about whether changes like that are needed," Libin says.

This year, Congress also failed to pass several consumer-privacy proposals. The full House failed to consider the House Energy and Commerce Committee's bipartisan bill to outlaw pretexting to obtain phone records. "There are people who think the phone record is not your personal property, it is the company's property," said Commerce Committee Chairman Rep. Joe L. Barton, R-Texas, in explaining why the measure did not progress. [63] If the records belong to the company, companies do not want responsibility for protecting their confidentiality, as the Commerce-passed bill would do, he said.

Congress also failed to pass data-retention requirements for Internet service providers. Colorado Rep. DeGette sponsored legislation similar to the administration's request: It required Internet companies to retain records of customer Web searches for at least a year in order to help solve child-pornography cases.

Neither did Congress pass legislation on the "other side" of the privacy question proposed by Rep. Edward J. Markey, D-Mass., the top-ranking Democrat on the House Telecommunications and Internet Subcommittee. In the wake of numerous incidents in which data thieves stole personal information from companies, Markey's bill would "prevent the stockpiling of private citizens' personal data" by requiring Web-site owners to quickly destroy any identifiable personal information such as credit-card numbers. [64]

Most observers expect the new Democrat-led Congress next year to push harder for consumer-privacy measures, but with a crowded agenda and different White House priorities it is unclear how much the 110th Congress will be able to accomplish.

States Act

Legal analysts say a comprehensive privacy law is needed, rather than today's piecemeal approach.

Lawmakers must examine the many types of electronic data-sharing — from business transactions to personal shopping to instant messaging and chat-room conversations — and decide what level of privacy protections are required for the various modes, says Ric Simmons, an assistant professor at Ohio State University's Moritz College of Law. "Not everything deserves the same level of protection," he adds, but with sound technical advice lawmakers should be able to create a comprehensive outline of what needs to be protected at what level and why.

Such comprehensive privacy-protection standards should cover all business sectors, says Center for Democracy and Technology Deputy Director Ari Schwartz. "The current model — that every sector's data has to have its own standard — doesn't work," he says. Businesses aren't yet talking about it publicly, Schwartz says, but in private some companies now favor standards, and leading lawmakers on key committees are interested in broad consumer-privacy protections. "We're going to have much more serious debate of a consumer-privacy law" in the near future.

States and businesses are helping create momentum for consumer-privacy regulation, especially after a series of highly publicized data breaches in the past few years raised fears among lawmakers and advocacy groups that the immense personal databases companies are amassing are not being adequately protected from hackers and data and identity thieves.

As a result, companies now face lawsuits and a patchwork of state laws. Beginning with California, 32 states have enacted laws requiring companies to notify consumers when their information is compromised; 22 of the laws apply to government agencies as well as to private companies. Lawmakers in California, Illinois, Florida and Washington also have introduced bills banning the sale and acquisition of cell-phone records. [65]

Other states are suing to block Web sites from selling records and are prosecuting companies that gain records on false pretenses. In January, Illinois became the first state to sue a rogue data-collection company when Attorney General Madigan sued Florida-based 1st Source Information Specialists. [66]

Perhaps because of the widely divergent maze of state laws that has emerged, a group of high-tech companies — including eBay, Google, HP, Intel, Microsoft, Oracle, Sun Microsystems and Symantec — recently reversed their long-held opposition to federal consumer-privacy laws and formed the Consumer Privacy Legislative Forum to help enact a multisector nationwide privacy law.

A May 2006 survey revealed that 94 percent of Americans view identity theft as a serious problem, and only 24 percent think businesses are doing enough to protect their information. [67] "The time has come . . . to consider comprehensive harmonized federal privacy legislation to create a simplified, uniform but flexible legal framework," said the forum. [68]

In the meantime, insurance companies, state agencies and universities — largely at the behest of state legislatures — already are tightening controls on personal data, mainly by ending the use of Social Security numbers as all-purpose passwords, says Indiana University's Nehf. "The easy days of having one number" to access multiple databases "are going away," he says.

Several Democrat-sponsored privacy bills are waiting in the wings and are likely to be considered by the new Democratic Congress, according to Libin. For example, a bill cosponsored by Vermont's Sen. Leahy, incoming chairman of the Senate Judiciary Committee, and current Chairman Specter would allow individuals to access and correct personal information held by commercial data brokers and require private and public organizations holding personal data to establish privacy-protection policies.

A bill introduced by Specter and Sen. Feinstein would "streamline the FISA apparatus" without giving the president expansive new wiretapping powers, as Republican-sponsored legislation would do, Libin says. Specter "hasn't been touting that bill" in this Congress, but its chances would greatly improve in a Democrat-led Senate, she says. In addition, some Democratic leaders

have already vowed to hold oversight hearings on the NSA's surveillance of U.S. citizens.

OUTLOOK

Good-bye Privacy?

Some scholars predict that as new means of electronic data-gathering continue to proliferate, the concept of "private" data will disappear. Computer databases and electronic-surveillance devices such as radio-frequency identification devices (RFIDs) — machine-readable chips already being implanted in everything from supermarket products to pets and people — are spreading so rapidly that privacy will soon be an alien concept, say some scholars.

Surveillance technologies are already so ubiquitous, said Hal Varian, professor of information at the University of California, Berkeley, that privacy "is a thing of the past. Technologically, it is obsolete." As humanity adjusts, however, "social norms and legal barriers will dampen out the worst excesses." [69]

Michael Dahan, a professor at Israel's Sapir Academic College, predicts that by 2020 — just 14 years from now — every newborn child in industrialized countries will be implanted with a machine-readable chip that can track that person from a distance. "Ostensibly, providing important personal and medical data may also be used for tracking and surveillance."

Others argue that as privacy vanishes in a world with vast databases containing everything known about each individual, people will come to value privacy more. "Privacy will be seen more and more as a basic human right, and there will be growing pressure to define this in an international . . . convention and to have states enforce it," said Robert Shaw, policy adviser for the International Telecommunication Union. [70]

Still others are skeptical. Young people currently seem to have less interest in privacy than older generations, as they post personal revelations on Web sites like MySpace, some scholars point out.

"Historians have said that 300 and 400 years ago, nobody had any privacy," says Indiana University's Nehf. "Today we value it. But it might be that in another 100 years we will have lost it again as a value."

NOTES

1. For background, see Michael Barbaro and Tom Zeller, Jr., "A Face Is Exposed for AOL Searcher No. 4417749," *The New York Times*, Aug. 9, 2006.

2. Peter Monaghan, "Watching the Watchers," *Chronicle of Higher Education*, March 17, 2006; http://chronicle.com.

3. "New Rule: Car Buyers Must Be Told About 'Black Boxes,'" CNN Money, Aug. 22, 2006; www.cnn.com/2006/AUTOS/08/21/event_data_recorder_rule/index.html.

4. For background, see Danah Boyd, "Facebooks' 'Privacy Trainwreck': Exposure, Invasion, and Drama," *Apophenia Blog*, Sept. 8, 2006; www.danah.org/papers/FacebookAndPrivacy.html.

5. "Disney World Mandates Fingerprint Scans," *NetWorkWorld Weblogs*, July 18, 2005; www.networkworld.com/weblogs/layer8/009514.html.

6. Testimony before House Committee on Energy and Commerce, Feb. 1, 2006.

7. Tresa Baldas, "High-Tech Evidence: A Lawyer's Friend or Foe?" *The National Law Journal*, Aug. 24, 2004; www.law.com.

8. "Against Jury's Recommendation, Judge Spares Justin Barber Death Penalty for Wife's Murder," "Court TV News," Sept. 15, 2006; www.courttv.com.

9. "Patrick Googled 'Neck,' 'Snap,' Among other Words, Prosecutor Says," *WRAL.com*, Nov. 9, 2005; www.wral.com.

10. Quoted in Monaghan, *op. cit.*

11. Michael Abramowitz and Jonathan Weisman, "Bush Meets With Pelosi; Both Pledge Cooperation," *The Washington Post*, Nov. 10, 2006, p. A1.

12. Testimony before Senate Committee on the Judiciary, Feb. 6, 2006; http://judiciary.senate.gov.

13. *Ibid.*

14. *Ibid.*; for background on Nixon's enemies list, see "List of White House 'Enemies' and Memo Submitted by Dean to the Ervin Committee," *Watergate and the White House, Vol. 1, Facts on File*, pp. 96-97; http://web.archive.org/web/20030621235432/www.artsci.wustl.edu/~polisci/calvert/PolSci3103/watergate/enemy.htm.

15. *Ibid.*

16. *Ibid.*

17. Remarks to 16th Annual Conference on Computers, Freedom & Privacy, May 3, 2006; http://leahy.senate.gov.

18. "Spies, Lies and Wiretaps," *The New York Times*, Jan. 29, 2006.

19. Quoted in "Gonzales Calls for ISP Data Retention Laws," *The Register*, Sept. 20, 2006; www.theregister.co.uk.

20. Quoted in Jo Best, "Europe Passes Tough New Data Retention Laws," *C/Net News.com*, Dec. 14, 2005; http://news.com.com.

21. Letter to congressional leaders, National Association of Attorneys General, June 21, 2006; www.naag.org.

22. International Association of Chiefs of Police, resolution adopted at 113th annual conference, Oct. 17, 2006; www.politechbot.com.

23. Quoted in Graeme Wearden and Karen Gomm, "Entertainment Industry 'Trying to Hijack Data Retention Directive,'" *ZDNet.UK*, Nov. 24, 2005; www.zdnet.co.uk.

24. Mark Rasch, "Retain or Restrain Access Logs?" *Security Focus* blog, www.securityfocus.com/print/columnists/406.

25. Nancy Libin and Jim Dempsey, "Mandatory Data Retention — Invasive, Risky, Unnecessary, Ineffective," Center for Democracy and Technology, June 2, 2006; www.cdt.org.

26. William McGeveran, "Some Objections to DOJ's Data Retention Proposal," *Harvard Law School Info/Law* blog, June 5, 2006; http://blogs.law.harvard.edu.

27. Peter P. Swire, "Is Data Retention Secure?" *Federal Computer Week*, June 12, 2006; www.fcw.com.

28. Andrew Orlowski, "Google Vows: We'll Keep Hoarding Your Porn Queries," *The Register*, Aug. 12, 2006; www.theregister.co.uk.

29. Quoted in "House Energy and Commerce Subcommittee on Oversight and Investigations Holds Hearings on Hewlett-Packard Pretexting Scandal," *Congressional Quarterly Congressional Transcripts*, Sept. 29, 2006.

30. Quoted in Roy Mark, "Telecoms Refuse to Endorse Pretexting Bill," internetnews.com, Sept. 29, 2006; www.internetnews.com/bus-news/article.php/3635241.

31. Quoted in *ibid*.

32. Testimony before House Energy and Commerce Subcommittee on Oversight and Investigations, Sept. 29, 2006.

33. Quoted in "House Energy and Commerce Subcommittee on Oversight and Investigations Holds Hearings on Hewlett-Packard Pretexting Scandal," *op. cit.*

34. Quoted in Chris Jay Hoofnagle, testimony before California State Assembly Committee on Public Safety, March 7, 2006; www.epic.org.

35. Quoted in "House Energy and Commerce Subcommittee on Oversight and Investigations Holds Hearing on Hewlett-Packard Pretexting Scandal," *op. cit.*

36. For background, see Susan W. Brenner, "The Fourth Amendment in an Era of Ubiquitous Technology," Dec. 13, 2005; www.olemiss.edu/depts/law_school/ruleoflaw/pdf/01-BRENN.pdf; Robert Ellis Smith, "Ben Franklin's Web Site; Privacy and Curiosity from Plymouth Rock to the Internet," *Privacy Journal* (2004); J. Hamer, "Rights to Privacy," *Editorial Research Reports*, 1974, in *CQ Researcher Plus Archive*; www.cqpress.com.

37. Chief Justice of the Common Pleas, Charles Pratt, First Earl Camden, *Entick v. Carrington*, 2 Wils. K. B. 275,291. Quoted in *ibid*. For background, see www.constitution.org/trials/entick/entick_v_carrington.htm.

38. For background, see H. B. Shaffer, "Eavesdropping Controls," *Editorial Research Reports*, 1956; H. B. Shaffer, "Wiretapping in Law Enforcement," *Editorial Research Reports*, 1961, and J. Kuebler, "Wiretapping and Bugging," *Editorial Research Reports*, 1967, all in *CQ Researcher Plus Archive*; www.cqpress.com.

39. Quoted in Brenner, *op. cit.*

40. "Tapping the Wires," *The New Yorker*, June 18, 1938; www.spybusters.com/History_1938_Tapping_Wires.html.

41. *Olmstead v. United States*, 277 U.S. 438 (1928).

42. Louis D. Brandeis, Dissenting Opinion, *Olmstead v. United States*, 277 U.S. 438 (1928); www.law.cornell.edu/supct/html/historics/USSC_CR_0277_0438_ZD.html.

43. *Katz v. United States*, 389 U.S. 347, 348 (1967).

44. The case was *U.S. v. Sinclair*.

45. Quoted in Spencer Overton, "No Warrantless Wiretaps of Citizens," *blackprof.com blog*, Dec. 18, 2005; www.blackprof.com.

46. *United States v. United States District Court* 407 U.S. 297 (1972).

47. "Final Report of the Select Committee to Study Governmental Operations With Respect to Intelligence Activities," April 26, 1976; www.icdc.com/~paulwolf/cointelpro/churchfinalreportIIa.htm.

48. "Amendments to the Foreign Intelligence Surveillance Act," Congressional Research Service, July 2006; www.fas.org/sgp/crs/intel/m071906.pdf. The FISA amendments were included in the Patriot Act of 2001, the Fiscal Year 2002 Intelligence Authorization Act, the Homeland Security Act of 2002, the Intelligence Reform and Terrorism Prevention Act of 2004, and the USA Patriot Improvement and Reauthorization Act of 2005.

49. Foreign Intelligence Surveillance Act Orders, 1979-2005; Electronic Privacy Information Center; www.epic.org/privacy/wiretap/stats/fisa_stats.html.

50. James Risen and Eric Lichtblau, "Bush Lets U.S. Spy on Callers Without Courts," *The New York Times*, Dec. 16, 2005, p. A1.

51. *Ibid.*

52. Grant Gross, "NSA Wiretapping Program Can Continue," *InfoWorld*, Oct. 4, 2006; www.infoworld.com/article/06/10/04/HNnsasurveillance_1.html.

53. For background, see Kenneth Jost, "Civil Liberties Debates," *CQ Researcher*, Oct. 24, 2003, pp. 893-916.

54. "Print Shop," House Committee on the Judiciary; http://judiciary.house.gov/Printshop.aspx?Section=232.

55. Quoted in Monaghan, *op. cit.*

56. Tresa Baldas, "High-Tech Evidence: A Lawyer's Friend or Foe?" *The National Law Journal*, Aug. 24, 2004; www.law.com.

57. Quoted in *ibid*.

58. Quoted in Mike Stuckey, "Where Rubber Meets the Road in the Privacy Debate," MSNBC.com, Oct. 20, 2006; www.msnbc.com.

59. "Fair Information Practice Principles," Federal Trade Commission; www.ftc.gov/reports/privacy3/fairinfo.htm.

60. Declan McCullagh, "Database Nation: The Upside of 'Zero Privacy,'" *Reason*, June 2004.

61. Quoted in "Senate Judiciary Committee Holds Hearing on Foreign Intelligence Surveillance," *Congressional Quarterly Congressional Transcripts*, July 26, 2006; www.cq.com.

62. Quoted in "House Intelligence Committee Holds Hearing on Foreign Intelligence Surveillance Act," *Congressional Quarterly Congressional Transcripts*, July 27, 2006; www.cq.com.

63. Quoted in "House Energy and Commerce Subcommittee on Oversight and Investigations Holds Hearing on Hewlett-Packard Pretexting Scandal," *op. cit.*

64. Quoted in Bill Brenner, "Security Blog Log: Data Storage Bills Go To Extremes," *Search Security.com*, May 21, 2006; http://searchsecurity.techtarget.com.

65. *Stateline.org*; www.stateline.org/live/ViewPage.action?siteNodeId=137&languageId=1&contentId=126215#map.

66. John Gramlich, "States, Feds, Go After Online Records Brokers," *Stateline.org*, Feb. 4, 2006; www.stateline.org.

67. For background, see Peter Katel, "Identity Theft," *CQ Researcher*, June 10, 2005, pp. 517-540.

68. Peter P. Swire, testimony before House Energy and Commerce Subcommittee on Commerce, Trade and Consumer Protection, June 20, 2006.

69. Quoted in *Future of the Internet II*, Pew Internet & American Life Project, 2006.

70. Quoted in *ibid.*

BIBLIOGRAPHY

Books

Lane, Frederick, *The Naked Employee: How Technology Is Compromising Workplace Privacy*, American Management Association, 2003.
A technology writer describes the growth of employer surveillance of workers, a trend he says federal law allows to proceed unchecked.

O'Harrow, Robert, *No Place To Hide: Behind the Scenes of Our Emerging Surveillance Society*, Free Press, 2005.
A *Washington Post* technology reporter describes the burgeoning public and private use of surveillance and data-storage technologies.

Rosen, Jeffrey, *The Naked Crowd: Reclaiming Security and Freedom in an Anxious Age*, Random House, 2005.
A George Washington University law professor uses sociological and psychological descriptions of how people respond to unsettling events to explore how the terrorist attacks of 2001 changed Americans' attitudes toward privacy and security.

Smith, Robert Ellis, *Ben Franklin's Web Site: Privacy and Curiosity from Plymouth Rock to the Internet*, Privacy Journal, 2004.
The editor of the *Privacy Journal* newsletter recounts the social history of privacy in America, including chapters on how Americans have viewed privacy in relation to sex, government snooping and tabloid-press invasions of celebrities' privacy.

Solove, Daniel J., *The Digital Person: Technology and Privacy in the Information Age*, New York University Press, 2004.
An associate professor of law at The George Washington University argues that ignorance of and indifference to the collection of personal data by businesses and public agencies are the main barriers to creating a legal framework to protect privacy.

Articles

"AT&T Whistle-Blower's Evidence," *Wired News* online, May 17, 2006; www.wired.com/news/technology/1,70908-0.html.
An AT&T technician explains what he observed in the company's San Francisco offices to convince him that the phone company was illegally cooperating with the National Security Agency's warrantless surveillance program.

Meredith, Peter, "Facebook and the Politics of Privacy," *Mother Jones*, **Sept. 14, 2006; www.motherjones.com.**
In an interview, a University of California student explains his privacy concerns about Facebook's new "news feed" feature.

Richtel, Matt, and Miguel Helft, "An Industry Is Based on a Simple Masquerade," *The New York Times*, **Sept. 11, 2006, p. C1.**
Some small companies gather personal data by tricking telephone companies and other holders of consumer records, but awareness of these fraudulent businesses is growing.

Risen, James, and Eric Lichtblau, "Bush Lets U.S. Spy on Callers Without Courts," *The New York Times*, **Dec. 16, 2005, p. A1.**
Federal officials reveal that President Bush authorized warrantless wiretaps of some Americans' international phone calls and e-mails, beginning in 2002.

Sullivan, Bob, "Who's Buying Cell Phone Records Online? Cops," MSNBC.com, June 20, 2006, www. msnbc.msn.com.
Shady data brokers claim that police agencies, including the FBI, are among their customers.

Reports and Studies

Anderson, Janna Quitney, and Lee Rainie, *The Future of the Internet, II*, **Pew Internet & American Life Project, September 2006; www.pewinternet.org/ pdfs/PIP_Future_of_Internet_2006.pdf.**
Internet analysts and Internet-business leaders predict that by 2020 Internet information gathering and electronic surveillance will facilitate many government and business functions but will also threaten personal privacy.

Brenner, Susan W., "The Fourth Amendment in an Era of Ubiquitous Technology," December 2005; www.olemiss.edu/depts/law_school/ruleoflaw/pdf/01 -BRENN.pdf.
A professor of law and technology at Ohio's University Dayton School of Law explains how then-current technologies helped shape legal interpretations of privacy from the 12th century to the present.

"Digital Search and Seizure: Updating Privacy Protections to Keep Pace with Technology," Center for Democracy & Technology, February 2006.
A privacy-advocacy organization argues that due to new developments in information storage and surveillance technology, new regulations are needed to allow government surveillance without swamping civil rights.

"Privacy and Human Rights 2005," Electronic Privacy Information Center and Privacy International, 2006.
In the current edition of this annual report, two privacy-advocacy groups describe the privacy landscape in more than 60 countries, including new legislation, emerging technology issues and post-9/11 security concerns that are leading some governments to forgo privacy protections.

For More Information

American Civil Liberties Union, 125 Broad St., 18th Floor, New York, NY 10004; (212) 549-2500; www.aclu.org/. Advocates for protection of individuals' privacy and other rights.

ARMA International, 13725 W. 109th St., Suite 101, Lenexa, KS 66215; (913) 341-3808; www.arma.org. An organization for information-management professionals that develops standards for privacy protection.

Berkman Center for Internet and Society at Harvard Law School, 23 Everett St., 2nd Floor, Cambridge, MA 02138; (617) 495-7547; http://cyber.law.harvard.edu. Investigates legal, technical and social issues surrounding the Internet, including privacy.

Center for Democracy and Technology, 1634 I St., N.W., #1100, Washington, DC 20006; (202) 637-9800; www.cdt.org. Advocates preservation of privacy and other constitutional freedoms in the developing digital world.

Consumer Data Industry Association, 1090 Vermont Ave., N.W., Suite 200, Washington, DC 20005-4905; (202) 371-0910; www.cdiaonline.org. Represents businesses involved in database aggregation, such as credit agencies and security firms.

Electronic Frontier Foundation, 454 Shotwell St., San Francisco, CA 94110; (415) 436-9333; www.eff.org. Advocates for and litigates on technological issues involving privacy, free speech, freedom to innovate and consumer rights.

Electronic Privacy Information Center, 1718 Connecticut Ave., N.W., Suite 200, Washington, DC 20009; (202) 483-1140; www.epic.org. Provides information and advocacy on privacy as a civil right.

Pew Internet & American Life Project, 1615 L St., N.W., Suite 700, Washington, DC 20036; (202) 419-4500; www.pewinternet.org. Provides data and analysis on social issues surrounding Internet usage, such as threats to privacy.

Privacy International, 6-8 Amwell St., Clerkenwell, London EC1R 1UQ UK; 44 208 123 7933; www.privacy-international.org. Advocates for privacy rights and tracks privacy issues worldwide.

11

Death Penalty Controversies

Kenneth Jost

Former death row inmate Aaron Patterson is one of 17 wrongfully convicted men freed in Illinois, the only state with a death penalty moratorium. The American Bar Association has called for a nationwide moratorium on executions, citing documented problems in capital trials and sentencing such as racial discrimination, inadequate legal representation and other constitutional violations.

From *CQ Researcher,*
September 23, 2005. (Updated May 21, 2007)

Robin Lovitt says he didn't do it. He says Clayton Dicks was already lying mortally wounded on the floor of the Arlington, Va., pool hall when he came out of the restroom in the early morning hours of Nov. 18, 1998.

The jury in Lovitt's capital murder trial in September 1999 decided instead to believe a witness who testified he was "80 percent" certain he saw Lovitt stab Dicks and a jailhouse informant who said Lovitt later confessed to the crime while in custody.

Lovitt was sentenced to death, and his conviction and sentence upheld on appeal in the state courts. But court-appointed lawyers handling his federal habeas corpus case now say the state has made it impossible for Lovitt to prove his innocence by throwing away the physical evidence introduced at trial.

The evidence that a deputy court clerk discarded — ostensibly to save space in a crowded storage room — included a bloody pair of scissors that prosecutors depicted as the murder weapon. Lovitt's legal team, headed on a pro bono basis by former Whitewater special prosecutor Kenneth Starr, says the clerk's action prevents them from arranging for sophisticated DNA testing that could refute the prosecution's effort to link the scissors to Lovitt.

"The DNA along with the other evidence has been destroyed and destroyed in a very intentional way," says Starr, now dean at Pepperdine University School of Law in Malibu, Calif. Starr remains affiliated with the Washington office of Kirkland & Ellis, which is representing Lovitt, along with Rob Lee of the Virginia Capital Representation Resource Center in Charlottesville.

Lawyers for the state say discarding the evidence was an honest mistake that doesn't matter because the other evidence against

U.S. Executions Declined in Recent Years

The number of executions in the United States in the past three decades peaked at 98 in 1999 and then fell to 53 in 2006. Capital punishment opponents say the innocence issue contributed to the decline.

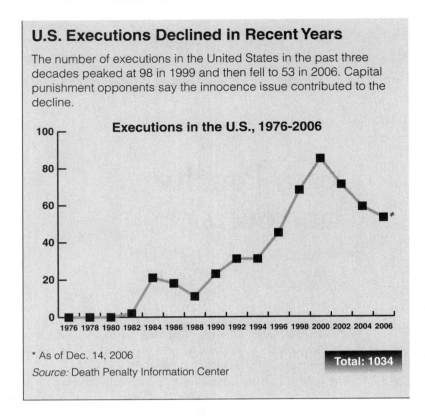

Executions in the U.S., 1976-2006

* As of Dec. 14, 2006

Total: 1034

Source: Death Penalty Information Center

Lovitt was so strong. "This case is not a DNA case," says Emily Lucier, a spokeswoman for the Virginia attorney general's office. [1] But the U.S. Supreme Court saw Lovitt's plea as strong enough to order a stay of execution on the evening of July 11, only four-and-a-half hours before Lovitt was scheduled to die by lethal injection. Four months later, Virginia Gov. Mark Warner commuted Lovitt's sentence to life in prison. [2]

The advent of DNA testing — which has been credited with "exonerating" more than 160 prison inmates over the last 15 years, including 14 men on various states' death rows — has focused attention on using new technology to prevent executions of innocent defendants. [3]

"These DNA exonerations have proven to everybody that there are far more innocent persons in our criminal justice system than anyone had imagined," says Barry Scheck, the New York defense lawyer who pioneered the use of DNA evidence to support innocence claims. He helped found the Innocence Project at Yeshiva University's Cardozo School of Law to investi-

gate such cases on an ongoing basis and is also president of the National Association of Criminal Defense Lawyers.

More broadly, the Death Penalty Information Center, which opposes capital punishment, claims that 123 people have been "released from death rows with evidence of their innocence" since 1973. The center calls these releases "exonerations" and counts 38 such cases just since 2000.

Death penalty supporters acknowledge the importance of DNA testing as a forensic technique for both the prosecution and the defense. But they dispute the broad characterization of the death row releases as exonerations and depict "actual innocence" — as opposed to exoneration through a technicality issue — as only a minor aspect of the protracted death penalty litigation in state and federal courts.

"The intense scrutiny that capital cases receive in the present system is finding and correcting the few cases of wrongful convictions," says Kent Scheidegger, legal director for the pro-death penalty Criminal Justice Legal Foundation in Sacramento. "Our criminal justice system should be paying more attention to actual guilt and innocence and spending less resources litigating issues that have nothing to do with guilt."

Law enforcement groups emphasize in particular that anti-death penalty groups have yet to document a case in the modern era of someone who was executed and later proven conclusively to have been innocent of the crime.

"They're looking for the innocent defendant who was executed," says Joshua Marquis, district attorney in Clatsop County (Astoria), Ore., and chairman of the National District Attorneys Association's capital litigation committee. "They haven't found one yet. I don't think they're going to find one."

Nevertheless, death penalty opponents credit the innocence issue with contributing to a decline in the number of death sentences and the number of executions

Texas Leads States in Executions

Prisons in California, Texas and Florida alone hold 42 percent of the nation's 3,415 death row inmates. Since 1976 there have been 981 executions in the United States, including 37 so far this year. Texas has executed 348 people since 1976, far more than any other state.

Current Death Row Population and Executions Since 1976
(No. of inmates/no. of executions)

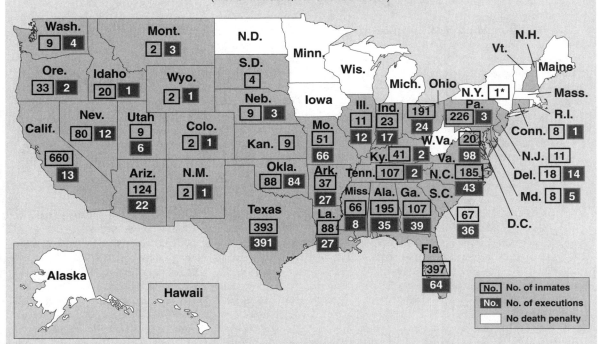

Legend	
No.	No. of inmates
No.	No. of executions
	No death penalty

State data (No. of inmates / No. of executions):
- Wash.: 9 / 4
- Ore.: 33 / 2
- Calif.: 660 / 13
- Nev.: 80 / 12
- Idaho: 20 / 1
- Mont.: 2 / 3
- Wyo.: 2 / 1
- Utah: 9 / 6
- Ariz.: 124 / 22
- Colo.: 2 / 1
- N.M.: 2 / 1
- N.D.: —
- S.D.: 4
- Neb.: 9 / 3
- Kan.: 9
- Okla.: 88 / 84
- Texas: 393 / 391
- Minn.: —
- Iowa: —
- Mo.: 51 / 66
- Ark.: 37 / 27
- La.: 88 / 27
- Wis.: —
- Ill.: 11 / 12
- Ind.: 23 / 17
- Miss.: 66 / 8
- Ala.: 195 / 35
- Ga.: 107 / 39
- Mich.: —
- Ohio: 191 / 24
- Ky.: 41 / 2
- Tenn.: 107 / 2
- S.C.: 67 / 36
- N.C.: 185 / 43
- W.Va.: 20
- Va.: 98
- Pa.: 226 / 3
- N.Y.: 1*
- N.H.: —
- Vt.: —
- Maine: —
- Mass.: —
- R.I.: —
- Conn.: 8 / 1
- N.J.: 11
- Del.: 18 / 14
- Md.: 8 / 5
- D.C.: —
- Fla.: 397 / 64
- Alaska: —
- Hawaii: —

* One inmate remain on death row in New York even though the state legislature failed to enact a new death penalty statute after the state's law was invalidated in June 2004.

Source: Death Penalty Information Center

in the United States in the past few years. After peaking at 98 in 1999, the number of executions fell steadily to 53 in 2006, according to the death penalty center, representing a 47 percent drop over seven years.

"A large part of that is due to revelations about problems with the death penalty — in particular because innocent people were convicted and sentenced to death and in some cases came close to being executed," says Richard Dieter, the center's executive director. "That kept pushing the problem of the death penalty into the public eye."

Prosecutor Marquis acknowledges that the innocence issue has been useful for death penalty opponents. "They succeeded in driving the debate away from the legal or moral issue, which they were losing," he says. But, he notes, polls show a substantial majority of Americans still support capital punishment.

Public ambivalence about the death penalty is reflected in the seemingly conflicting mix of pending federal and state cases and proposals in Congress and state legislatures. The federal Justice Department has become more aggressive about pursuing capital cases, including

Is the Defendant Mentally Retarded?

Daryl Atkins won a landmark ruling from the U.S. Supreme Court in 2002 barring the execution of mentally retarded offenders. When Atkins' case returned to Virginia courts, however, a jury found that he is not mentally retarded and left him on death row for a 1996 robbery-murder.

The jury in Yorktown, Va., heard seven days of testimony and deliberated for 13 hours before deciding on Aug. 5 that Atkins is not mentally retarded under Virginia law. Jurors apparently credited testimony offered by prosecution witnesses that the 27-year-old Atkins manages to perform daily life functions over evidence introduced by the defense, including IQ scores below the threshold of 70 set by Virginia law to define mental retardation. [1]

Atkins' lawyers say they will appeal the panel's decision. For now, however, the result is one sign that the Supreme Court's decision in the case that bears his name will not produce the benefits that advocates for the mentally retarded had hoped or expected.

"The promise of Atkins has not been realized," says Robin Maher, director of the American Bar Association's death penalty representation project.

States faced no such difficult implementation decisions in applying the Supreme Court's March 2005 decision barring execution of juvenile offenders. The ruling in Roper v. Simmons means that anyone convicted of an offense committed under the age of 18 is ineligible for the death penalty. But in banning the death penalty for mentally retarded defendants in Atkins v. Virginia, the high court left it to the states to establish their own definitions of retardation.

Since the Atkins case, Virginia and seven other states — California, Delaware, Idaho, Illinois, Louisiana, Nevada and Utah — have changed their statutes to comply with the ruling, according to a compilation by the Death Penalty Information Center. In seven of the states, the judge determines if the defendant is mentally retarded; only in Virginia does the jury decide. [2]

The eight states consider offenders as mentally retarded if their IQ falls below a certain level, generally between 70 and 75, and if they demonstrate deficits in adaptive behavior before the age of 18.

Richard Dieter, executive director of the anti-death penalty group, calls the Virginia procedure "unusual" because mental retardation is determined in other states before the trial begins. Virginia's procedure calls for a trial on guilt or innocence with a hearing on mental retardation afterward before the same jury.

The procedure "colors the decision-making process," Dieter says, because it is hard for jurors to make an objective decision "once you tell the jury they're letting somebody off for the worst punishment."

Atkins was convicted of capital murder for abducting a U.S. airman outside a store, forcing him to withdraw $200 from an automated teller machine, and then shooting him eight times. A co-defendant who pleaded guilty in exchange for reduced charges claimed — but Atkins denied — that it was Atkins who did the shooting.

cases in states that have no death penalty law themselves. By mid-2007, there were 50 inmates sentenced to death under federal law, up from 18 when the decade began.

Courts and governors shut down the death penalty in 11 states in 2006 and 2007, imposing moratoriums because of concerns that sometimes-botched lethal injections violated constitutional protections against cruel and unusual punishment. Some of those states scrambled to find more acceptable methods.

But a number of states, including Maryland, Montana and New Jersey, considered outright abolition of the death penalty. In Maryland, Gov. Martin O'Malley made elimination of the death penalty a key priority upon taking office in 2007. O'Malley testified before separate state House and Senate committees on the same day, calling capital punishment "inherently unjust." The abolition bill died in a tied vote in the Senate committee, but supporters predict an abolition bill will pass in that state, and perhaps a few others, sometime over the next several years. [4]

In states that have used the death penalty with greater regularity, however, there has been a bit of a backlash against the abolitionist movement. Several have expanded the categories of crimes punishable by death. Oklahoma and South Carolina in 2006 each passed death penalty laws to cover those who rape children,

The ABA's Maher says procedures in other states are also unfair to mentally retarded offenders. "Almost all the statutes inappropriately place the burden of persuasion on the mentally retarded prisoner or require proof that does not comport with professional standards," Maher says. In addition, Maher says that several states with relatively large numbers of death penalty cases — including Texas, Alabama, Mississippi and Oklahoma — have refused to enact laws to protect the mentally retarded from executions.

A leading prosecutor, however, blames the Supreme Court for problems in implementing the decision. "States are lurching along trying to come up with statutes that comply with *Atkins*, but they're having problems because the court didn't really say what they needed to do," says Joshua Marquis, district attorney in Clatsop County, Ore., and chair of the National District Attorneys Association's capital litigation committee.

Courts in Texas, the state with the highest number of executions, have upheld death sentences in several cases involving mental retardation issues following guidelines set by the Texas Court of Criminal Appeals. In a ruling in February 2004, the

Darryl R. Atkins

Virginia Dept. of Corrections

Texas court rejected a mental retardation plea in upholding the death sentence imposed on Jose Briseno for the 1991 slaying of a local sheriff. The court reasoned that Briseno was not mentally retarded because he was able to devise plans and adjust to his surroundings. [3]

Prosecutors in Atkins' case made a similar argument about his problem-solving ability by offering testimony that while in prison, Atkins had been observed placing his soup bowl in a sink containing hot water to keep it warm. A defense expert, however, reached a different conclusion from the incident, saying that Atkins apparently failed to appreciate that the water would soon cool.

— *Melissa J. Hipolit*

[1] See Maria Glod, "Virginia Killer Isn't Retarded, Jury Says," *The Washington Post*, Aug. 6, 2005, p. A1; Donna St. George, "A Question of Culpability: Mental Capacity of Convicted Virginia Man Is a Murky Legal Issue," *The Washington Post*, July 23, 2005, p. A1.

[2] Death Penalty Information Center, www.deathpenaltyinfo.org/article.php? scid=28&did=668.

[3] Martha Deller and Max B. Baker, "Texas Courts Try to Set Rules for Executing Mentally Retarded Inmates," *Fort Worth Star-Telegram*, July 13, 2005.

even when murder is not involved. In 2007, Utah enacted two new laws to expand the death penalty in cases involving children. The Virginia legislature passed five death-penalty expansion bills that year, overriding Gov. Tim Kaine's vetoes of three of the bills.

Meanwhile, the perennial issue of deterrence is drawing renewed attention with efforts by some researchers to show that abolishing or suspending the death penalty leads to an increase in murders. Other academics sharply dispute the studies.

As the various death penalty debates continue in Washington and around the country, here are some of the other specific questions at issue:

Should the Supreme Court ease the rules for death row inmates to raise innocence claims?

A jury in rural East Tennessee convicted Paul House of murder in 1986 in the beating death of a neighbor, Carolyn Muncey. Prosecutors argued that House, a paroled sex offender from Utah, killed Muncey after an attempted rape. As evidence, the prosecutors showed that semen found on Muncey's body matched House's blood type.

More than a decade later, however, DNA testing — unavailable at the time of trial — conclusively established that the semen came not from House, but from Muncey's husband, Herbert. Lawyers working on House's federal habeas corpus petition also uncovered

Most Americans Support the Death Penalty

Nearly two-thirds of Americans support the death penalty, but about as many believe that innocent people have been executed within the past five years.

Are you in favor of the death penalty for a person convicted of murder?

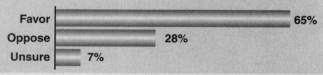

Favor — 65%
Oppose — 28%
Unsure — 7%

If you could choose between the following two approaches, which do you think is the better penalty for murder: The death penalty or life imprisonment with absolutely no possibility of parole?

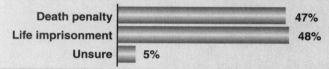

Death penalty — 47%
Life imprisonment — 48%
Unsure — 5%

Generally speaking, do you believe the death penalty is applied fairly or unfairly in this country today?

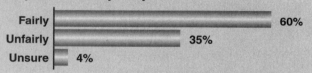

Fairly — 60%
Unfairly — 35%
Unsure — 4%

How often do you think that a person has been executed under the death penalty who was, in fact, innocent of the crime he or she was charged with? Do you think this has happened in the past five years, or not?

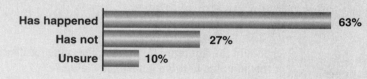

Has happened — 63%
Has not — 27%
Unsure — 10%

Source: USA Today/Gallup Poll, May 5-11, 2006, based on telephone interviews with 1,523 randomly selected adults ages 18 and over

other evidence casting doubt on the verdict, including testimony by two neighbors that Herbert Muncey had confessed to killing his wife long after the event.

Despite the evidence, the federal appeals court for Tennessee refused, by an 8-7 vote, to give House a chance to have his newly substantiated claim of innocence heard in federal court. Now, the U.S. Supreme Court is poised to consider House's case in order to decide how to balance the states' interest in maintaining the finality of criminal convictions against what death penalty critics contend is the real possibility of executing an innocent person.

The high court dealt with the issue in two decisions in the 1990s: *Herrera v. Collins* (1993) and *Schlup v. Delo* (1995). [5] In the first case, the court rejected a Texas death row inmate's effort to reopen his murder case based on late evidence blaming the offense on his brother, who had since died. In the second ruling, however, the court allowed a Missouri death row inmate a hearing to determine whether his innocence claim was strong enough to justify a second chance to challenge his conviction on constitutional grounds.

Together, the two cases created a narrow window for lower federal courts to use an inmate's actual innocence claim — if sufficiently strong — as a "gateway" to belatedly raising a federal constitutional issue. They left open the question whether a freestanding innocence claim — apart from any constitutional violation — could be the basis for a successful request for federal habeas corpus relief.

Death penalty critics emphasize that the first of the decisions was handed down the same year the first death row inmate was released for DNA-related reasons. The number of DNA exonerations since then demonstrates the need for the court to re-examine the decisions, they say.

"They set some very strict standards for actual innocence claims independent of any other constitutional claim," says Dieter of the Death Penalty Information Center. "In light of what we now know, it is time for the court to reflect on the revelations of science and what's happened in the death penalty world and give the lower courts some guidelines."

Prosecutors and law enforcement supporters, however, say the high court should maintain strict standards for state prisoners to meet before asking federal judges in effect to give them a second trial. "If you're going to retry every capital case, you're going to have an even more inefficient system than you have now," says Barry Latzer, a professor at City University of New York's John Jay College of Criminal Justice.

"It's natural for the system to have a very high hurdle for retrial of innocence claims," Latzer says. "The place for that is in the original trial, not on appeal."

But Scheck says there is "no evidence" that states with liberal rules on the use of newly discovered evidence are having significant problems.

In House's case, lawyers with the Federal Defenders Service in Knoxville contend that the Sixth U.S. Circuit Court of Appeals rejected his petition based on a stricter rule than required by the Supreme Court. "The *Schlup* case does not require the elimination of all evidence of guilt," says attorney Stephen Kissinger. "The real test is what [the jury] would have done given all this evidence. The truth of the matter is that no jury has passed on the vast majority of the new evidence in this case."

Lawyers for the state, however, say the appeals court majority correctly followed the rule established in *Schlup*. Under that decision, they argue, House had to show that "in light of the new evidence, no juror, acting reasonably, would have voted to find him guilty beyond a reasonable doubt." They contend that the new DNA evidence does not contradict the prosecution's case against House and that the appeals court properly discounted other evidence, including Muncey's purported confession.

For his part, Scheidegger says new claims of actual innocence should normally be considered in executive clemency proceedings with federal court review available only as "a last-ditch backup."

"Any time a new avenue for review of capital cases is opened up, the possibility of abuse exists," he says.

But Dieter says governors rarely grant clemency, deferring instead to the courts. "It seems to be a passing of the buck on this issue," he says. In any event, he adds, "Clemency is for the extraordinary case where mercy or reduction of sentence is appropriate. Guilt or innocence is for the courts."

Illinois Gov. Rod R. Blagojevich signs the final piece of the state's death penalty reform package on Jan. 20, 2004, as state legislators observe. The most comprehensive death penalty reform package in that state's history was prompted by newspaper investigations showing that at least 13 innocent people had been convicted and sentenced to death in Illinois due to bias, errors and incompetence.

Should Congress pass legislation to limit federal habeas corpus claims?

In an attempt to deal with a growing flood of death row appeals, Congress passed a major overhaul of federal habeas corpus law in 1996 aimed at cutting back death row inmates' use of the procedure to challenge their convictions or sentences. The Antiterrorism and Effective Death Penalty Act — known as AEDPA — gives state inmates a one-year deadline to file a federal habeas corpus petition after all state proceedings are finished. It also generally bars the filing of a second federal petition and requires federal judges to defer to state rulings unless clearly mistaken or unreasonable.

In a steady stream of densely technical cases over the past nine years, the U.S. Supreme Court has been relatively strict in interpreting the act's major provisions. But supporters of the law say some federal appeals courts — especially the Ninth Circuit, which covers California and eight other Western states — have liberally interpreted the act to allow inmates opportunities for hearings that it was intended to preclude.

To fix the supposed problem, two Republican lawmakers — Sen. Jon Kyl of Arizona and Rep. Dan Lungren of California — introduced a bill, the Streamlined Procedures Act, aimed at tightening the deadlines and standards for obtaining federal habeas relief. But an array of opponents — including death penalty critics, the American Bar Association and state and federal judicial bodies — say the bill would do little to speed death penalty challenges while cutting off access to federal courts for legitimate legal challenges and risking execution of innocent persons. [6]

Some supporters of the bill question the need for federal habeas review at all. "It's by and large unnecessary because the cases have already been thoroughly reviewed at the state level," says Latzer. "But if you must have it, it should be more efficient." Others do not go quite that far, but say the bill is needed because of what Scheidegger calls "the evasions" of AEDPA's restrictive provisions by some federal courts.

In introducing the bill, Kyl cited statistics showing that the number of habeas cases pending in federal courts increased from 13,359 in fiscal year 1994 to 23,218 in fiscal year 2003. But opponents of the measure say the figures do not show that AEDPA has failed to make it harder for inmates to actually get hearings in federal court or to win their cases. "You're never going to stop prisoners from filing petitions," says Virginia Sloan, president of the bipartisan Constitution Project, who is coordinating a campaign against the bill.

Among its many provisions, the bill would narrow grounds for habeas petitions and limit inmates' ability to amend claims. It would bar federal courts from considering any claim not properly raised in state courts unless an inmate had a "clear and convincing" claim of actual innocence. And it would require federal appeal courts to rule on habeas claims within 300 days of the filing of the inmate's legal brief.

The bill's provisions are "carefully crafted, common sense responses to some of the worst abuses we face," Tom Dologenes, head of the habeas corpus unit in the Philadelphia district attorney's office, told the Senate Judiciary Committee in July.

But opponents argue the bill goes in the wrong direction. "With all the exonerations we've seen in recent years, we should be expanding instead of cutting back on review," says Sloan.

Scheck particularly criticizes the provision that raises the standards for actual innocence claims. "This bill makes everything worse in terms of innocence litigation," he says.

Both the U.S. Judicial Conference and the National Conference of State Chief Justices and Court Administrators opposed the bill. In a letter to Senate Judiciary Committee Chairman Arlen Specter, R-Pa., the federal judges said the bill could "complicate" habeas cases and "lead to more, rather than less, litigation." For their part, the state judges adopted a resolution in August warning that the provisions restricting federal habeas relief would have "unknown consequences for the state courts and the administration of justice."

Supporters of the bill, however, argued that state courts do not need the additional oversight entailed in federal habeas cases. "The issue is whether there is confidence in the state courts, whether they can protect the rights of criminal defendants and death penalty defendants in particular," says Latzer. "I have confidence in them, and that diminishes the need for federal review in my mind."

Should states impose moratoriums on executions?

Illinois Gov. George Ryan, a conservative Republican, had supported the death penalty throughout his 20-plus years in politics. But investigations by Northwestern University journalism students and *Chicago Tribune* reporters during Ryan's first year as governor in 1999 convinced him that the state's system for sending people to death row was "fraught with error."

So in January 2000 Ryan took the then-unprecedented step of imposing an official moratorium on executions in the state. "Until I can be sure that everyone sentenced to death in Illinois is truly guilty, until I can be sure with moral certainty that no innocent man or woman is facing a lethal injection, no one will meet that fate," Ryan said. Three years later, just as he was about to leave office, Ryan went further: He pardoned four death row inmates and commuted the death sentences of 164 others to life imprisonment. [7]

Ryan's initial step drew wide praise, even from State's Attorney Dick Devine, the chief prosecutor in Cook County (Chicago). But Devine sharply criticized Ryan's later clemency action as "outrageous and unconscionable." [8]

Ryan followed up the moratorium by appointing a commission to make recommendations for improving the handling of death penalty cases, including providing better legal representation for defendants. Ryan's successor as governor, Democrat Rod R. Blagojevich, has kept the moratorium in effect pending an evaluation of some of the reforms adopted in November 2003. As of September 2005, however, only one other governor — Maryland's Parris Glendening — had followed Ryan's lead; and the move by Democrat Glendening was revoked in 2003 by his Republican successor, Robert Ehrlich.

As noted earlier, 11 states imposed moratoriums in 2006 and 2007 — or had moratoriums imposed on them by federal courts — due to concerns about lethal injection, the primary means of execution in nearly every death penalty state. Many of those moratoriums, however, were temporary and did not represent a change in policy. Several states have considered outright bans on executions, but only New Jersey has joined Illinois in creating an open-ended moratorium.

Moratorium supporters include the American Bar Association, which called for the step in February 1997. Ron Tabak, a lawyer with a prestigious New York firm who works with the ABA committee created to push the proposal, says moratoriums are needed because of the variety of documented problems in capital trials and sentencing, including racial discrimination, inadequate legal representation and other constitutional violations.

"Every jurisdiction should have a moratorium, study the issues carefully, and try to see if they can fix the problems or decide on some other course of action," Tabak says.

Death penalty supporters, however, question the need for further studies and sharply criticize Ryan's actions in Illinois or other proposals for suspending capital punishment. "I don't see any new problems that would call for studies," says Latzer. "This has been studied to death. I don't see any new problem except the problem of delays in carrying out executions."

"That's an abuse of the clemency power," says Scheidegger. "That's not why the governor has a clemency power: to issue a de facto repeal of the capital punishment statute."

"A moratorium is a moral dodge," says prosecutor Marquis. "We [already] have one in this country," he adds. "It's the 12 to 15 to 20 years it takes to get these cases through the courts."

Death penalty critics and opponents, however, echo the ABA's position that flaws in the system — and specifically the risk of executing an innocent person — demand careful study and a suspension of executions in the meantime.

"State moratoriums are an excellent idea," says Stephen Saloom, policy director of the Innocence Project. "They will allow states to stop and take a look at all the factors to be considered in assessing the accuracy of those death verdicts that have been handed down and even more so the potential for error in various parts of their system."

"We don't yet have a system that's totally reliable," says Dieter. "It would be a healthy process for the country to decide how much error we're going to allow, how to get that error down to an absolute minimum, and — knowing these changes are going to cost something — to decide whether it's worth it."

Scheidegger counters by citing a study by University of Houston economist Dale Cloninger that purportedly shows the Illinois moratorium resulted in an increase in murders as a result of reduced deterrence. Instead of adopting a moratorium to guard against a wrongful execution, Scheidegger says, the better step is "a more careful review of the cases to make sure they have the right guy."

For his part, Latzer warns that officials who favor moratoriums risk political retaliation. "If people in the state support the death penalty and the governor circumvents it, he has to face the consequences in the next election," Latzer says. *

In Illinois, however, initial polls indicated public approval of Ryan's moratorium. Public support for the death penalty remains strong nationwide, but has slipped from its mid-1990s peaks. Several openly anti-death penalty governors have been elected in recent years, including Kaine in Virginia and Deval Patrick in Massachusetts.

Tabak says public support for the idea of a moratorium has increased over time. "There's been a lot more public education and public understanding since then," he says. "As these efforts get more pronounced, there will be further results along these lines."

---

* *Habeas corpus* — Latin for "you have the body" — is a procedure dating from England's *Magna Carta* (1215) that ensures the right of a defendant to petition a judge to determine the legality of his or her incarceration or detention by the government.

* Ryan decided not to seek re-election in 2002 in the midst of a federal investigation of corruption in his administration. He was later indicted on 22 counts of racketeering, mail and tax fraud and other charges; he pleaded not guilty, and jury selection began on Sept. 19, 2005.

C H R O N O L O G Y

1950s-1960s *Support for death penalty falls, along with number of executions.*

1953 Gallup Poll finds 68 percent support for capital punishment; executions average around 100 per year in early 1950s.

1966 Support for death penalty falls to 42 percent; two executions in a year are the last for more than a decade.

1970s-1980s *Supreme Court first abolishes, then reinstates capital punishment; begins to cut back on use of federal habeas corpus to challenge death sentences.*

1972 Supreme Court, in 5-4 ruling, invalidates all existing death sentences; public backlash boosts support for death penalty, while states move to revise capital punishment statutes.

1976 Supreme Court upholds capital punishment under "guided discretion" statutes, but bars mandatory death sentences.

1987 Supreme Court rejects effort to invalidate death penalty because it is most often imposed in murder cases where victim is white.

1989 Supreme Court limits use of new constitutional rulings in federal habeas corpus cases; upholds execution of mentally retarded offenders, older teens (16- or 17-year-olds).

1990s *Supreme Court, Congress tighten rules on habeas corpus; death penalty critics warn against risk of executing innocent persons.*

1991 Supreme Court says state inmates cannot raise constitutional claims in federal habeas corpus action if they miss deadlines for raising issue in state courts.

1992 Innocence Project founded to use DNA testing of post-conviction claims. . . . Supreme Court limits federal courts' duty to hold hearing in habeas corpus cases unless inmate raises factual innocence claim.

1993 Supreme Court sidesteps question whether stand-alone "actual innocence" claim can be grounds for habeas corpus review in federal court. . . . First wrongly convicted defendant is released based on DNA test results.

1994 Support for death penalty peaks at 80 percent.

1995 Supreme Court slightly eases test for death row inmate to use "actual innocence" claim to revive constitutional challenge to conviction or sentence.

1996 Congress passes Anti-terrorism and Effective Death Penalty Act (AEDPA) limiting and setting one-year deadline for federal habeas corpus petitions.

1997 American Bar Association calls for national moratorium on executions.

1998 Number of executions peaks at 98.

2000-Present *Death penalty critics use "innocence" cases to attack flaws in system; supporters say court reviews catch most errors.*

2000 Illinois Gov. George Ryan imposes moratorium on executions in state, citing risk of executing innocent person; as he leaves office three years later, commutes 164 death sentences to life imprisonment.

2002 Supreme Court bars death penalty for mentally retarded offenders; three years later, the defendant in the case, Daryl Atkins, is kept on death row after a Virginia jury rules he is not mentally retarded.

2004 New York court rules state death penalty law unconstitutional in June; nine months later, state legislative committee rejects bill to reinstate capital punishment, reducing number of death penalty states to 37. . . . Congress passes law to guarantee inmates right to post-conviction DNA testing.

2005 Supreme Court bars death penalty for juvenile offenders, throws out death sentences in four individual cases. . . . Justice John Paul Stevens says death penalty procedures entail "risks of unfairness." . . . High court due to open term on Oct. 3 with new chief justice, "actual innocence" cases on docket.

BACKGROUND

Running Debates

The death penalty has enjoyed popular approval and acceptance throughout U.S. history, but opposition on various moral and practical grounds dates from the nation's founding. Anti-death penalty sentiment rose to a near majority during the 1950s and '60s, and the number of executions declined. But support increased after the controversial 1972 Supreme Court decision to outlaw capital punishment as then administered and has remained generally strong since the court four years later upheld re-enacted death penalty laws. [9]

Capital punishment procedures were significantly changed during the 19th and 20th centuries, sometimes in evident response to public opinion. Abolitionist opponents helped bring about the division of murder into two degrees with the death penalty reserved only for the more serious, first-degree offense. The power to sentence defendants to death was also transferred from judges to juries in the 19th century. Death penalty opponents successfully campaigned against public executions and in favor of replacing the gallows with the supposedly more humane electric chair.

The first scientific poll on the subject, conducted in the mid-1930s, found that Americans supported the death penalty for murder by a substantial margin: 61 percent to 39 percent. [10] Subsequent annual Gallup Polls showed that support peaked at 68 percent in 1953, but fell over the next decade to a low of 42 percent in 1966. A Harris survey that year found near-majority disapproval: 47 percent. The decline coincided with civil rights and criminal-justice reform movements that focused public attention on racial discrimination and procedural injustices in capital trials and sentencing.

Increasing public disquiet about the death penalty also can be inferred from the decline in the number of executions during the same period. From a peak of around 190 a year in the late 1930s, the number of executions dropped to slightly more than 100 per year in the early 1950s and then fell by the mid-1960s to only one in 1965, two in 1966, and none during the decade starting in 1967.

As early as the 1930s some notorious death penalty cases had drawn the Supreme Court into overseeing state criminal justice systems. Most notably, the court in the so-called Scottsboro cases twice intervened to overturn the convictions and death sentences of nine young black men tried in a racially charged atmosphere in Alabama for allegedly raping two white women. By the 1960s, death penalty opponents — including the NAACP Legal Defense Fund — were mounting broader attacks that claimed the death penalty was unconstitutional under either the 14th Amendment's Equal Protection Clause or the Eighth Amendment's prohibition against cruel and unusual punishment.

The campaign climaxed on June 29, 1972, with the Supreme Court's decision in *Furman v. Georgia*, which invalidated all existing death sentences and death penalty statutes. The five justices in the majority each wrote separately: Two found the death penalty unconstitutional as "cruel and unusual punishment" under all circumstances, while three others objected to its arbitrary use. The four dissenters argued that the issue was for state legislatures, not the courts. [11]

However, public support for the death penalty was already growing by the late 1960s, and the Supreme Court's decision created a backlash that accelerated the shift. Gallup Polls conducted in 1972 before and after the *Furman* decision recorded an increase in pro-death penalty responses from 50 percent in March to 57 percent in November. For their part, state legislatures responded to the decision by adopting new laws aimed at curing the defects identified by the high court. Some states passed mandatory death penalty statutes, while others adopted so-called guided-discretion laws that gave juries aggravating and mitigating factors to consider in capital sentencing hearings. In 1976 the Supreme Court ruled the mandatory death penalty laws unconstitutional, but the justices upheld the guided-discretion statutes by a 7-2 vote. [12]

The ruling allowed the resumption of executions, which came slowly at first but gradually reached a peak of 98 in 1999. Public support for the death penalty also continued to rise, peaking at 80 percent in 1994. For its part, the Supreme Court rejected broad challenges to the death penalty, though it somewhat narrowed application of capital punishment and also established complex procedural rules for capital sentencing hearings. In one significant line of decisions, the court generally held that juries must be given broad discretion to consider any mitigating factors put forward by the defendant in an effort to avoid a death sentence, such as personal character, social background or minimal responsibility for the offense. [13]

Do Executions Deter Killings?

A dozen statistical studies have been published over the past decade claiming to show that capital punishment deters capital crimes. But some researchers say the studies are conceptually and technically flawed. In any case, say death penalty opponents, the question of deterrence has little influence today on public attitudes toward capital punishment. [1]

The effectiveness of executions as a deterrent has been argued at least since 18th-century England when, reportedly, pickpocketing — itself a capital crime — spiked at public hangings. More recently, *The New York Times* published a much-noticed report in 2000 showing that states with the death penalty had higher murder rates than states without capital punishment. [2]

Statistical work on the issue by U.S. economists dates back to the 1970s. Dale Cloninger, one of the earlier researchers in the field and now a professor at the University of Houston's School of Business in Clear Lake, says those early studies showed a deterrent effect. But Joanna Shepherd, an assistant professor at Emory University School of Law in Atlanta and a recent entrant in the field, describes the early studies as inconclusive and unsophisticated by present-day standards.

With more advanced techniques, however, Shepherd says new statistical studies — published in peer-reviewed economics journals — show a deterrent effect from executions. "We controlled for every conceivable factor that we thought might influence murder rates," Shepherd says of the work, including her studies.

Cloninger continues to write on the issue, including two studies linked to death penalty moratoriums: an unofficial, court-imposed lull in executions in Texas in the mid-1990s and Illinois' more recent official moratorium. In each instance, Cloninger says, the state's homicide rate increased during the moratorium; and killings in Texas fell after executions resumed. [3]

In her newest study, however, Shepherd says the effect of executions appears to vary from state to state. She finds a deterrent effect in only six states with comparatively more executions, no effect in others and a so-called "brutalization effect" in some other states — where executions appear to be associated with higher homicide rates. [4] While calling for additional studies, Shepherd suggests that the data show that a state needs to reach a certain threshold number of executions for the "deterrence effect" to outweigh the "brutalization effect."

Conflicting Goals?

With the constitutionality of capital punishment settled, supporters and critics of the death penalty pursued seemingly conflicting goals during the 1990s. Supporters, frustrated by the growing number of death row inmates awaiting execution, lobbied Congress successfully for restrictive procedural requirements on the use of federal habeas corpus to challenge state convictions or sentences. Meanwhile, critics and opponents of the death penalty called for more rigorous review of capital cases because of what they depicted as a large number of death row "exonerations" — cases in which condemned inmates had won reversals of their convictions or sentences. [14]

In the 1960s the Supreme Court had opened the door for state inmates to make greater use of federal habeas corpus petitions to try to overturn their convictions or sentences on federal constitutional grounds. By the 1980s, however, a more conservative high court under

Chief Justice William H. Rehnquist was moving to limit habeas corpus. In one significant decision, the Rehnquist Court in 1989 generally blocked the use of new constitutional rulings as a basis for overturning convictions or sentences in habeas corpus proceedings. In two others, the court in the early 1990s barred inmates from filing federal habeas corpus petitions if they failed to abide by state procedural rules and made it harder for inmates to have federal courts rule on factual issues unless they raised a claim of actual innocence. [15]

Congress imposed further restrictions in the major overhaul of federal habeas corpus passed in 1996 as part of an anti-terrorism bill. The Antiterrorism and Effective Death Penalty Act generally required state inmates to file federal habeas corpus petitions within a year of exhausting state appeals and post-conviction proceedings. The law also barred a second or successive petition except in narrow circumstances as determined by a federal appeals

Richard Berk, a professor of statistics and sociology at the University of California, Los Angeles, and Jeffrey Fagan, a professor of law and public health at Columbia University in New York City, are two veteran academics who sharply dispute the claims of deterrence. In a new analysis of the data, Berk says the claimed deterrent effect exists in only one state — Texas — and is not large there. "If you throw Texas out of the mix," he says, "there's nothing going on."[5]

Fagan, who is studying the issue under a grant from the Soros Foundation-funded U.S. Justice Fund told a legislative committee in Massachusetts in July that the deterrence studies are "fraught with technical and conceptual errors." He says other research also shows that better detection and apprehension would be more effective deterrents.

Cloninger says the deterrence studies show what most economists would expect: that the risk of punishment affects criminal behavior. "To an economist, it's sensible that murderers are sensitive to risk," he says. "Other people are." But Berk and Fagan both say would-be killers are unlikely to know the execution rate in a specific state or, in any event, to think about it before a crime. "This information is not available even if your criminal is a calculating machine," Berk says.

Death penalty supporters say the evidence of deterrence strengthens their position in countering fears of executing an innocent person. "If that were the only consideration as far as tradeoffs are concerned, it would be a very weighty one," says Kent Scheidegger, legal director of the pro-law enforcement Criminal Justice Legal Foundation in Sacramento, Calif. "But you have on the opposite side the very weighty consideration that you might be costing innocent lives" by not enforcing the death penalty.

Death penalty opponents, however, call the academic argument a standoff that does not matter to the overall public debate. "The death penalty is more about punishment and retribution and just deserts," says Richard Dieter, executive director of the Death Penalty Information Center. "Deterrence is not going to be the decisive factor as to whether we keep the death penalty or get rid of it."

---

[1] The pro-death penalty Criminal Justice Legal Foundation has listed the studies on its Web site: www.cjlf.org.

[2] Raymond Bonner and Ford Fessenden, "Absence of Executions: States With No Death Penalty Share Lower Homicide Rates," *The New York Times*, Sept. 22, 2000, p. A1.

[3] See Dale O. Cloninger and Roberto Marchesini, "Execution Moratoriums, Commutations, and Deterrence: The Case of Illinois," working paper, August 2005 (http://econwpa.wustl.edu/eprints/le/papers/0507/0507002.abs); "Execution and Deterrence: A Quasi-Controlled Group Experiment," *Applied Economics*, Vol. 33 (2001), pp. 569-576.

[4] Joanna M. Shepherd, "Deterrence versus Brutalization: Capital Punishment's Differing Impacts Among States," *Michigan Law Review*, Vol. 4, Issue 2 (November 2005).

[5] Richard A. Berk, "New Claims about Executions and General Deterrence: Déjà Vu All Over Again?" *Journal of Empirical Legal Studies*, Vol. 2, No. 2 (July 2005), pp. 303-330.

---

court. And — in a major jurisdictional change — the act required federal courts to defer to state court rulings unless the decision was "contrary to, or involved an unreasonable application of, clearly established Federal law, as determined by the Supreme Court of the United States."[16]

Meanwhile, critics and opponents of capital punishment were mounting a documented attack on the reliability of judicial proceedings that led to the growing number of death sentences. A combination of events brought the innocence issue to the forefront of public debate.[17] Most important was the new technology of DNA testing, which defense lawyers initially resisted but eventually recognized as potentially valuable to support claims of innocence by convicted defendants, including some on death row.

Two of the defense lawyers who pioneered the use of DNA testing — Scheck and Peter Neufeld — founded the Innocence Project as a nonprofit legal clinic to use post-conviction DNA testing to support innocence claims. By 1999, they claimed in a book that the project had provided "stone-cold proof" that 67 people had been sent to prison for crimes they did not commit, including 11 sentenced to death.[18] In April 2007, the project claimed its 200th "exoneration," including 14 in death penalty cases.

In addition, in-depth investigations have uncovered evidence of seriously flawed capital cases in Illinois and Oklahoma. In Illinois, students in a journalism course at Northwestern University helped uncover 13 cases of innocent defendants on death row, who were later exonerated. *The Chicago Tribune* put a dramatic headline on its own later, staff-written story: "Death Row Justice Denied: Bias, Errors and Incompetence Have Turned Illinois' Harshest Punishment Into Its Least Credible."[19]

Two years later, a March 2001 FBI report questioned testimony in eight cases by an Oklahoma City police laboratory scientist, Joyce Gilchrist, leading to an extensive

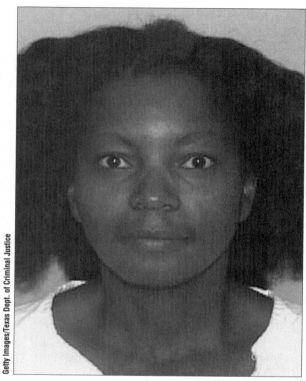

Texas executed Frances Newton on Sept. 14, 2005, for the 1987 murder of her husband and two children, becoming the third woman — and the first black woman — executed in Texas since 1982.

re-examination of her role in some 23 capital cases, including 12 in which defendants had actually been executed. But state authorities who reviewed the capital cases expressed confidence that all of the defendants had been properly convicted without regard to Gilchrist's evidence in the cases. The investigation also resulted in May in the release of a defendant serving a sentence for rape. Gilchrist was fired in September because of "flawed casework testimony." [20]

The Supreme Court's two mid-decade rulings in "actual innocence" cases reflected a tentative approach. In the first — *Herrera v. Collins* — Chief Justice Rehnquist's opinion for the 6-3 majority in 1993 held that federal courts had no authority in habeas corpus cases to consider actual innocence claims apart from some independent constitutional violation. But he qual-

ified the holding by saying that even if a "truly persuasive demonstration of 'actual innocence' after trial would render an execution unconstitutional," the inmate's evidence in the case fell "far short of any such threshold."

Two years later, though, a liberal majority held in *Schlup v. Delo* that a death row inmate was entitled to a hearing on a second federal habeas petition if he or she could show that a constitutional violation "probably resulted" in the conviction of an innocent person. Rehnquist led the dissenters in the 5-4 ruling.

After the decade's end, the pivotal justice in the two cases — Sandra Day O'Connor — acknowledged her own concerns about the issue. Speaking to a meeting of women lawyers in Minneapolis in July 2001, O'Connor said, "If statistics are any indication, the system may well be allowing some innocent defendants to be executed." After noting that Minnesota had no death penalty, O'Connor added, "You must breathe a sigh of relief every day." [21]

Changing Views?

Support for capital punishment sagged somewhat in the early years of the 21st century, seemingly in response to the work of death penalty critics and opponents. In the most dramatic event, Illinois Gov. Ryan specifically cited the risk of executing innocent persons in declaring his death penalty moratorium in January 2000 and then, as he left office in January 2003, commuting death sentences for the state's 164 condemned inmates. Meanwhile, the Supreme Court became somewhat more receptive to death row inmates' pleas by barring capital punishment for mentally retarded and juvenile offenders and setting aside death sentences in some individual cases because of racial discrimination, trial errors or inadequate legal representation.

During the Illinois moratorium, the commission Ryan created to study the state's flawed capital trials and sentencing procedures recommended a broad reform package, adopted in November 2003 after Ryan had left office. [22] The law gave defense lawyers access to all police notes, tightened police lineup procedures and mandated pretrial hearings on reliability of testimony from jailhouse informants. It also provided funding for pretrial or post-conviction DNA testing and removed the time limit on actual innocence claims in state courts.

Death penalty critics described the package as "historic," though it fell short of some recommended

Group Says Innocent Man Was Executed

L arry Griffin maintained his innocence until the day he was executed in 1995 for a drug-related, drive-by shooting 15 years earlier. Now the St. Louis prosecutor's office is re-examining the case after a year-long investigation by a civil rights advocacy group concluded Griffin was innocent. [1]

The law professor who supervised the NAACP Legal Defense Fund (LDF) investigation says Griffin's case is an actual instance of a wrongful execution. If true, Griffin would be the first man in modern times proven to have been executed for a crime he did not commit. But the original prosecutor defends Griffin's 1981 verdict, and says the LDF just wants to use Griffin as "the poster child for the proposition that an innocent man was executed." [2]

Griffin was convicted of the June 26, 1980, shooting death of Quintin Moss, shot 13 times by men firing from a slow-moving car as Moss was selling drugs to another man, Wallace Conners, in a neighborhood used as an open-air drug market.

The case against Griffin consisted chiefly of identification by an eyewitness, Robert Fitzgerald, and evidence of motive: Moss was suspected of having murdered Griffin's older brother. Conners never identified Griffin, however, and moved away.

Moss' family, which had always doubted the case against Griffin, sought the LDF's help. Fund investigators found Conners in Los Angeles, where he told them Griffin was not among the shooters and that eyewitness Fitzgerald was not at the scene.

"He's innocent, and we've got very strong proof of it," says University of Michigan law professor Samuel Gross. If the case were brought to trial now, he added, "We'd win hands down."

But Gordon Ankney, the prosecutor in the case and now a private attorney in St. Louis, still believes in the verdict. "The truth . . . was presented in the courtroom under oath," he said recently.

After the LDF's report was released in June, St. Louis Circuit Attorney Jennifer Joyce assigned two lawyers to re-investigate the case. The investigation is expected to take several months.

---

[1] The 11-page report — a June 10, 2005, memorandum to attorneys representing the family of the homicide victim — can be found on the Web site of the *St. Louis Post-Dispatch* (www.stltoday.com) or on sites maintained by anti-death penalty groups, including Truth in Justice (www.truthinjustice.org). Account drawn from Terry Ganey, "Case Is Reopened 10 Years After Execution," *St. Louis Post-Dispatch*, July 12, 2005, p. A1.

[2] See Ganey, *op. cit.*; Gordon Ankney, "Judge Him on Evidence, Not on Opinion," *St. Louis Post-Dispatch*, July 25, 2005, p. B7.

---

changes — including statewide oversight of death penalty cases. For his part, Gov. Blagojevich said he would keep the death penalty moratorium in place while the changes were put into effect.

In Maryland, Democrat Parris Glendening followed a different sequence from Ryan's in first commissioning a study of racial bias in capital sentencing in 2001 and then imposing a death penalty moratorium in May 2002 while awaiting the results. The study found evidence that the death penalty was more likely to be sought in cases with white victims than in cases with black victims. But it was released in January 2003 — after Glendening had been defeated for re-election by the conservative Republican Ehrlich, who had vowed during his campaign to lift the moratorium. [23] The state carried out one execution during Ehrlich's tenure: the lethal injection of convicted triple murderer Steven Oken on June 17, 2004. [24] At the end of 2006, Maryland became one of the states where executions have been put on hold due to judicial concerns about lethal injections. Gov. Martin O'Malley, who unseated Ehrlich in 2006, is a death penalty critic but failed in 2007 to convince the legislature to abolish the punishment.

In Washington, death penalty critics were using the innocence issue to lobby for legislation to help inmates have access to post-conviction DNA testing. The five-year legislative fight culminated in October 2004 with passage of the Innocence Protection Act, which guarantees federal inmates the right to DNA testing within specified time limits or with court approval. The act also uses federal grants to encourage states to make DNA testing available to state inmates as well. [25]

Meanwhile, the Supreme Court was moving to narrow application of the death penalty and to exercise more critical oversight of state courts' handling of capital cases. In two landmark decisions, the court in 2002 and 2005 ruled that the Eighth Amendment's prohibition on cruel and unusual punishment barred the death penalty for mentally retarded or juvenile offenders. [26] In another case with broad application, the court in 2002 ruled that only juries, not judges, could make factual determinations needed to make defendants eligible for the death penalty. [27]

Equally significant, the court set aside death sentences in several individual cases. Many of the reversals appeared to rebuke two of the most conservative federal appeals courts that handled cases from states with large numbers of executions: the New Orleans-based Fifth Circuit with jurisdiction over Texas and the Richmond-based Fourth Circuit with jurisdiction over Virginia. In two Virginia cases, for example, the court upheld death row inmates' pleas — rejected by the Fourth Circuit — that their lawyers had provided constitutionally inadequate representation by failing to investigate social histories potentially useful as mitigating evidence to avoid the death penalty. In two Texas cases, the court ordered new hearings — refused by the Fifth Circuit — for condemned inmates' claims of racial discrimination in jury selection and improper withholding of damaging information about a key prosecution witness. [28]

The high court's critical scrutiny of capital cases peaked during the 2004-05 term. In addition to the ruling on juvenile offenders, the justices in four other cases set aside death sentences that had been upheld through appeals or post-conviction proceedings in federal and state courts:

- In a Pennsylvania case, the court somewhat strengthened the requirement that defense lawyers investigate defendants' background for potential mitigating evidence.
- In a Missouri case, the court ruled that the defendant was improperly shackled during the sentencing hearing.
- In a Texas case, the court summarily threw out a death sentence because the trial judge's instructions did not allow jurors to consider the defendant's mental retardation as a mitigating factor.
- And in a follow-up to the earlier Texas racial discrimination case, the court sharply set aside the Fifth Circuit's decision to uphold the death sentence in the face of the high court's earlier ruling. [29]

Death penalty critics took heart from the high court's rulings as well as a decline in the number of executions and a dip in approval of the death penalty. Executions fell from a high of 98 in 1999 to 53 in 2006, according to the Death Penalty Information Center. Meanwhile, support for the death penalty in Gallup Polls fell to 66 percent in 2002. Two-thirds of respondents still support the death penalty, but for the first time a 2006 poll showed that more people favored life sentences, as opposed to executions, as a primary means of punishment. And a majority of respondents — 73 percent in 2003, 59 percent in 2004 — said they believed an innocent person had been executed in recent years.

Supporters of capital punishment, however, emphasized the poll results showing that most Americans continue to support the death penalty. "They are concerned about executing an innocent person," says Latzer of the John Jay College of Criminal Justice. "But notwithstanding their concerns, they still overwhelmingly favor the death penalty."

CURRENT SITUATION

A Drop in Support

The tide has been running primarily against the death penalty in states in recent years. As mentioned earlier, states such as Maryland, Montana and Nebraska have given serious consideration to abolishing the death penalty, while New Jersey's legislature became the first to impose a moratorium on the practice. A commission created by that legislature recommended in January 2007 that the state's little-used death penalty system be abolished altogether. "As a practical matter, we are already operating under the system that the commission has proposed, namely a system in which we have life sentences without parole," said Peter G. Verniero, a former state Supreme Court justice and Republican attorney general. "Capital punishment is not something that you should have on the books unless there is a very clear consensus that it is the correct policy." [30]

All but a dozen states have death penalty statutes in place, but these laws are moribund in many places. The death penalty became a hot political issue in New York after two consecutive governors vetoed capital punishment legislation every year between 1978 and 1994. Republican George E. Pataki's successful 1994 gubernatorial campaign was built largely on the issue and he was proud to sign a death penalty bill into law during his first year in office. It was seldom used, however. No one

Should states adopt moratoriums on executions?

YES

Barry Scheck
Co-founder/Co-director, The Innocence Project, www.innocenceproject.org

Written for *CQ Researcher*, September 2005

Post-conviction DNA testing has exonerated 162 inmates (and counting), identified numerous real assailants and proved the innocence of 14 men sentenced to death. These exonerations have not just demonstrated the real risk of executing an innocent person but also exposed serious weaknesses in the state criminal-justice systems, indicating that moratoria are needed on executions.

DNA testing is not a panacea; it will not make any state's death penalty fair, accurate or just. It does not offer probative evidence in the vast majority of criminal cases.

Indeed, DNA exonerations have created a learning moment, an opportunity to deal with the causes of wrongful conviction that victimize the innocent and allow the real criminals to go free: Mistaken eyewitness identification, false confessions, incompetent defense lawyers, poor forensic science and law enforcement misconduct. These issues can and must be addressed to prevent execution of the innocent.

This is the heart of the death penalty moratorium debate. Reasonable people can differ about the morality of capital punishment. But it is not reasonable to excuse inequities in the administration of capital punishment. As the president has acknowledged, capital lawyers are not adequately trained or properly funded. Until the American Bar Association's Guidelines for the Administration of Capital Punishment are implemented, no citizen can be confident about the guilt of all death row inmates.

Consider as well scientific advances that come too late. Texas executed Cameron Willingham in 2004 despite exhortations from a leading expert that the arson evidence underlying Willingham's murder conviction was proven false by new scientific data. Soon afterward, Texas exonerated Ernest Willis from his arson murder death sentence when prosecutors agreed with the same expert and science offered in Willingham's case. Nothing could be done for Willingham — likely an innocent man — because the state had already killed him.

Are fair-minded supporters of capital punishment willing to make the system fair and accurate? Should Louisiana, whose indigent-defense system was already in fiscal crisis, spend millions now to pursue executions? Why not invest in better crime labs, decent defense counsel and eyewitness and police reforms? How can states fail to enact these good law enforcement measures that protect against wrongful executions and help apprehend real murderers?

Until states address these known systemic failures, they must impose moratoria on executions.

NO

Kent Scheidegger
Legal Director, Criminal Justice Legal Foundation, www.cjlf.org

Written for *CQ Researcher*, September 2005

Should the execution of Danny Rolling stay on hold when his current, and hopefully last, appeal is decided? That is what the moratorium backers propose. They want to hold every execution in America, regardless of how clear the murderer's guilt or how clearly deserved his sentence. They have yet to come up with a single convincing reason for such a drastic step.

There is no doubt whatever of Rolling's guilt. It was proven by both DNA and his confession. In a spree of rape, mutilation and murder he killed five college students in Gainesville, Fla., in 1990. Eleven years have passed since his sentence, while multiple courts have repeatedly considered and rejected arguments that have nothing to do with guilt or innocence.

This is not unusual. Only a handful of capital cases involve genuine questions of innocence. By all means, we should put those few on hold as long as it takes to resolve the questions, and the governor should commute the sentence if a genuine doubt remains. At the same time, we should proceed with the justly deserved punishment in the many cases with no such questions, and considerably faster than we do now.

The other arguments against the death penalty have failed. The claim of discrimination against minority defendants is refuted by the opponents' own studies. So, too, is the claim of bias on the race of the victim, when the data are properly analyzed.

It has also been shown that lawyers appointed to represent the indigent get the same results on average as retained counsel. For example, Scott Peterson, with the lawyer to the stars, sits on death row, while the public defender got a life sentence for the penniless Unabomber. The mitigating circumstance of Theodore Kaczynski's mental illness made the difference, not the lawyers.

On the other hand, a powerful reason for the death penalty becomes clearer every year. Study after study confirms that the death penalty does deter murder and does save innocent lives when it is actually enforced.

Conversely, delay in execution and the needless overturning of valid sentences sap the deterrent effect and kill innocent people.

To minimize the loss of innocent life, the path is clear. Take as long as we need in the few cases where guilt is in genuine question and proceed to execution in a reasonable time in a great bulk of cases where it is not.

was ever executed by the state under the new law, and most of the few death sentences that were handed down were thrown out quickly on appeal. After the state's highest court struck down the statute in 2004, once-eager legislators showed little interest in reviving it. A legislative study found that the death penalty law had cost the state $170 million, although no executions had been carried out.

Capital cases are enormously expensive — and they are hard to win. The average case eats up more than a decade in appeals from the time of conviction to execution — and can take twice that long. These factors have made prosecutors less eager to pursue death sentences. In Indiana, for instance, prosecutors sought the death penalty in 17 cases in 1994. In recent years, however, they have sought it only two or three times a year.

With public opinion softening, prosecutors wary of the difficulty of cases and more politicians winning office despite their opposition to the death penalty (including 10 Democratic governors elected in 2005 and 2006), the death penalty appears in some places to be losing its political salience. DNA testing and other new techniques have led not only to overturned convictions, but a sense of doubt that society can be certain in every case that it is executing the right person. "We're in a period of national reconsideration of capital punishment," says Austin D. Sarat, an Amherst College political scientist who has written extensively about the subject. "It's become possible to say, 'I'm in favor of the death penalty in the abstract, but I'm against executing the innocent.'"

"The Hippocratic Paradox"

The most pressing concern about the death penalty centers on the actual means of execution. Some capital punishment advocates argue that murderers should not be treated any more humanely than they treated their victims, but the Eighth Amendment's ban on cruel and unusual punishment has meant that the hunt for a quick and possibly pain-free procedure has lasted for more than a century.

States hoped they had cracked the problem 30 years ago with the development in Oklahoma of a protocol for lethal injection that was soon widely adopted. Three drugs are injected intravenously: the first leads to unconsciousness, the second prevents movement (to avoid jerking motions that could upset witnesses) and the third stops the heart.

Lethal injection is now the preferred method of execution in every death penalty state except Nebraska, which uses electrocution. But because of rising complaints about botched injections, the death penalty has been put on hold in 11 states, either by courts or the governor, as lawmakers try to come up with a new, safer protocol.

Details about death penalty procedures are closely guarded secrets, so it has been difficult for outside experts to know whether correct doses have been given. (Veterinary euthanasia is more uniformly regulated.) Injections are typically administered by guards or other prison volunteers, not by doctors or nurses. And because of the high incidence of past drug use among death row felons, it is sometimes hard for the guards to find a usable vein. Needles stuck into tissue rather than veins have resulted in many instances of the condemned enduring gruesome and long-lasting pain before dying.

It was once difficult for attorneys for death row inmates to get any information about how lethal injections were used — the first evidentiary hearing about the method was not held until 15 years after states began to use it — but they have pieced together a considerable body of evidence that has recently led judges in several states to call the practice into question. Some states, such as South Dakota, are now working on legislation to clarify the rules surrounding the procedure. Lawmakers in other states, Missouri among them, are having to negotiate with judges to find altered methods that will pass muster. That task has been made more difficult by the unwillingness of the medical community to participate.

"We've called this the Hippocratic paradox," says Jonathan Groner, a physician at Ohio State University opposed to the death penalty. "It's immoral for health care professionals to participate because of their irreversible obligation only to use their skills for healing and not for killing." And, says Groner, it is just as immoral for prison guards without medical training to use the necessary equipment.

Others dispute that, but the resistance of the medical profession to capital punishment is having effects throughout the system. A 2005 article in the British medical journal *The Lancet* has also had a wide influence in the battle against "medical collusion."

A federal judge in California found the state's injection method unconstitutional, forcing it to call off the most recently scheduled execution at nearly the last minute in February 2006. The long-standing refusal of the California Medical Association to allow physicians to administer the death penalty — the group won statutory protection in 2001 to prevent physicians from being forced to participate directly in executions — has made the state's job of finding a workable compromise more difficult.

"That's absolutely going to slow us down, because the courts want to see the medical profession weigh in on how you make sure they're not feeling pain while you stop their heart," said Lance Corcoran, chief of governmental affairs for the California Correctional Peace Officers Association, a prison guard union.

Kent Scheidegger, legal director for the Criminal Justice Legal Foundation in Sacramento, which supports capital punishment, is confident the problems regarding methodology will be resolved. The complaints about lethal injection spread quickly, he said, "but once a state comes up with an acceptable method, that will be approved and copied by other states."

But Deborah W. Denno, a Fordham University law professor, says the concerns about lethal injections will not fade away. "No responsible death penalty attorney these days would not challenge it," she said. "Not every inmate is going to be innocent, and not all of them are affected by questions about racial disparities, but all of them are going to be able to make this appeal."

Death Penalty Supporters

The death penalty is clearly an issue that wins less than universal support — which it nearly enjoyed during the 1990s. For all the problems that have come to be associated with it, however, the death penalty still retains a strong majority of public support — including in those states where political opposition to the practice runs strongest. In states that have been most ardent in pursuing executions, political support for the death penalty runs as strong as ever, with legislators seeking to expand the law to allow for capital punishment in more cases.

As mentioned earlier, the death penalty has recently been expanded in several states, including South Carolina and Oklahoma, to cover sex crimes against children. Missouri Gov. Matt Blunt, a Republican, has called for the death penalty to be automatically invoked against cop killers, even though executions are on hold in his state due to problems with lethal injections.

In 2007 Utah enacted two new laws, including one that makes the murder of children younger than 14 a capital crime, while the other would impose the death penalty on those who killed children as a result of abuse, even if they did not intend to kill. The second measure was prompted by the death of a 10-year-old girl who had been abused over a two-week period and whose body was found covered with bites and bruises. "We couldn't get it declared a capital offense, even though this one absolutely deserved it," said state Rep. Paul Ray, the legislation's sponsor. "Both the father and mother were monsters."

The death penalty in recent decades has always involved questions of geography, with the practice much more prevalent in the South and West than elsewhere. Since the Supreme Court's 1976 decision allowing reinstatement of the death penalty, three out of every eight executions have occurred in Texas alone. In 2006, all but eight of the 53 executions took place in six states: Texas, Ohio, Virginia, Oklahoma, North Carolina and Florida.

"We found a tremendous difference between jurisdictions, even ones side by side," says former Maryland Gov. Parris Glendening. "It became clear to me that the death penalty had become almost a lottery of jurisdiction."

Federal Cases

If death penalty opponents like Glendening are disturbed by the variations among states and within states in application of the death penalty, they are none too pleased by the Bush administration's attempt to apply the death penalty more uniformly across the country. Federal prosecutors have stepped up their pursuit of capital cases, including in some states with no death penalty statutes of their own. "The willingness to pursue federal death cases reflects national public opinion," says John C. McAdams, a Marquette University political scientist who supports the death penalty.

In February 2007, a federal jury in Brooklyn sentenced Ronell Wilson to die for shooting two undercover detectives in the back of the head. Federal prosecutors had taken over the case after New York's death penalty law was invalidated. After consulting with families of the victims, Daniel Donovan, the district attorney on Staten Island in New York City, approached the U.S. attorney for the Eastern District of New York and asked her to take over the case, in hopes that a federal jury would return a sentence of death. "The district attorney made a conscious decision," said his spokesman, "to see whether the death penalty as part of the federal prosecution would be appropriate."

It was no sure thing. Wilson's case was the first time a federal grand jury in New York had handed down a death sentence since 1954. Federal prosecutors had failed in 14 previous attempts to win a capital conviction. But the sentence came down only a few days after an almost equally surprising death sentence in North Dakota. Alfonso Rodriguez Jr. was sentenced to die in a rape and murder case — becoming the first person sentenced to die in that state since 1915. Even his prosecutor sounded a little bit surprised. "It's just not part of the culture up here really at all," said U.S. Attorney Drew Wrigley.

OUTLOOK

George W. Bush had been a strong supporter of the death penalty while serving as Texas governor. As president, his attorneys general have also been rigorous in pursuing capital cases. Despite some local opposition, they have argued that the same federal laws apply in abolitionist states such as North Dakota, Michigan and Iowa as in pro-death penalty states such as Missouri and Oklahoma. "The decision to seek the death penalty is made based on the unique facts of each case," says Erik Ablin, a Justice Department spokesman. "We do have a review process in place to ensure that the death penalty is applied in a consistent and fair manner nationwide."

Seeking the death penalty, of course, is not the same thing as getting it. Notwithstanding the desire in Washington to seek uniformity in applying the law, most federal death sentences are still handed down in states where capital punishment is widely accepted. By far the largest share of federal death penalty crimes have occurred in Texas, which in turn is easily the leading death penalty state in the union. "The death penalty is a much harder sell in New York or Minneapolis or Boston than in Houston or Dallas or Montgomery, Alabama," says Franklin E. Zimring, a Berkeley law professor who has written about the topic.

It is clearly becoming harder to convince juries about the necessity for death sentences, which are in decline nationwide. Tangible problems have cut into support for capital punishment, including instances of DNA evidence revealing the innocence of some death row inmates, questions about racial and geographic disparities in the application of the death penalty, and complaints that many convicted killers have not received adequate legal representation.

Death penalty abolitionists feel they are making more headway with their arguments than they had for a generation. That has, in part, been the result of a fundamental change in their approach: from labeling immoral the idea of the state killing anyone to flagging problems in how the death penalty is administered. By pointing out practical concerns, they have managed to put death penalty supporters on the defensive.

But even as abolitionists have largely abandoned moral arguments in favor of drawing attention to legal and practical problems, death penalty supporters now often couch their arguments not in terms of deterrence but in terms of the moral necessity of executing killers whose crimes scour the heart.

Corcoran, the guard union official in California, cites the example of Richard Ramirez, known as the Night Stalker, who was convicted of 13 murders in 1989. "If we execute Richard Ramirez, we can debate all day whether it's going to have an impact on other psychopaths," he says. "But when we execute Richard Ramirez, he is specifically deterred from ever murdering anyone again."

It is the most brutal killers that most people think about when they think about preserving the death penalty. It is because of them — the Jeffrey Dahmers and the Osama bin Ladens — that the death penalty, for all its flaws and declining application, is unlikely to disappear entirely in this country.

A few states may in fact abolish it, determining that it is better to wipe it from the books after years of not using it. That is what happened in Europe, where after several years of moratoriums politicians decided they might as well abolish it.

But in most states, even the ones that impose capital punishment rarely or not at all, the death penalty serves a symbolic purpose, says Dieter of the Death Penalty Information Center. "I don't think all states are going to be falling like dominoes and eliminating the death penalty after a few states do," he says. "We need it for those worst offenses, to keep anarchy from slipping in the door."

NOTES

1. Quoted in Donna St. George, "Va. Man Nears Execution in Test of Destroyed DNA," *The Washington Post*, July 12, 2005, p. A1.

2. For previous coverage, see these *CQ Researcher* reports: Kenneth Jost, "Rethinking the Death Penalty," Nov. 16, 2001, pp. 945-968; Mary Cooper, "Death Penalty Update," Jan. 8, 1999, pp. 1-24.

3. For background, see Kenneth Jost, "DNA Databases," *CQ Researcher*, May 28, 1999, pp. 449-472.

4. Alan Greenblatt, "Death From Washington," *Governing*, May 2007, p. 36.

5. *Herrera v. Collins*, 506 U.S. 390 (1993), and *Schlup v. Delo*, 513 U.S. 298 (1995).

6. The bill numbers are S 1088 and HR 3035.

7. For coverage, see Ken Armstrong and Steve Mills, "Ryan: 'Until I Can Be Sure.' Illinois Is First State to Suspend Death Penalty," *The Chicago Tribune*, Feb. 1, 2000, p. 1; Maurice Possley and Steve Mills, "Clemency for All: Ryan Commutes 164 Death Sentences to Life in Prison Without Parole," *The Chicago Tribune*, Jan. 12, 2003, p. 1. *The Tribune's* five-part investigative series was published in November 1999 under the title "The Failure of the Death Penalty in Illinois."

8. Quoted in Bill Kurtis, *The Death Penalty on Trial: Crisis in American Justice* (2004), p. 9.

9. For a concise history by a confirmed opponent, see Hugo Adam Bedau, "An Abolitionist's Survey of the Death Penalty in America Today," in Hugo Adam Bedau and Paul G. Cassell, *Debating the Death Penalty: Should America Have Capital Punishment?* (2004), pp. 15-24.

10. Public opinion data taken from Robert M. Bohm, "American Death Penalty Opinion: Past, Present, and Future," in James R. Acker, Robert M. Bohm, and Charles S. Lanier (eds.), *America's Experiment with Capital Punishment* (2d ed.), 2003, pp. 27-54. For current polling data, see the Web site of the Death Penalty Information Center (www.death-penaltyinfo.org).

11. The citation is 408 U.S. 238 (1972). For background on this and subsequent Supreme Court deci-

sions, see David G. Savage, *Guide to the U.S. Supreme Court* (4th ed.), 2004, pp. 655-662.

12. The citation is 428 U.S. 153 (1976). The 5-4 ruling to bar mandatory death penalty laws is *Woodson v. North Carolina*, 428 U.S. 280 (1976).

13. See, e.g., *Lockett v. Ohio*, 438 U.S. 586 (1978).

14. Some background drawn from Franklin E. Zimring, *The Contradictions of American Capital Punishment* (2003). Zimring, a professor at the University of California's Boalt Hall School of Law in Berkeley, is a strong opponent of the death penalty.

15. The decisions are *Teague v. Lane*, 489 U.S. 288 (1989); *Coleman v. Thompson*, 501 U.S. 722 (1991); and *Keeney v. Tamayo-Reyes*, 504 U.S. 1 (1992). For more background, see Savage, *op. cit.*, pp. 295-300.

16. See *1996 CQ Almanac*, p. 5-18.

17. See Zimring, *op. cit.*, pp. 157-162.

18. Barry Scheck, Peter Neufeld and Jim Dwyer, *Actual Innocence: Five Days to Execution and Other Dispatches from the Wrongly Convicted* (1999).

19. Ken Armstrong and Steve Mills, "Death Row Justice Denied: Bias, Errors and Incompetence in Capital Cases Have Turned Illinois' Harshest Punishment into Its Least Credible," *The Chicago Tribune*, Nov. 14, 1999, p. 1.

20. See Jim Yardley, "Oklahoma Retraces Big Step in Capital Case," *The New York Times*, Sept. 2, 2001, p. 12.

21. "O'Connor Questions Death Penalty," The Associated Press, July 3, 2001.

22. For coverage, see John Chase and Ray Long, "Death Penalty Reform Passes," *The Chicago Tribune*, Nov. 20, 2003, p. 1. For more complete information, see the Center for Wrongful Convictions' Web site, www.law.northwestern.edu/wrongfulconvictions.

23. For coverage, see Lori Montgomery, "Maryland Suspends Death Penalty," *The Washington Post*, May 10, 2002, p. A1; Susan Levine and Lori Montgomery, "Large Racial Disparity Found by Study of Md. Death Penalty," *The Washington Post*, Jan. 8, 2003, p. A1.

24. See Susan Levine, "Maryland Executes Oken," *The Washington Post*, June 18, 2004, p. A1.

25. Jennifer A. Dlouhy, "Add-Ons End Years of Wrangling, Clear Path for DNA Testing Bill," *CQ Weekly*, Oct. 16, 2004, p. 2442.

26. The decisions are *Atkins v. Virginia*, 536 U.S. 304 (June 20, 2002); and *Roper v. Simmons*, — U.S. — (March 1, 2005).

27. The case is *Ring v. Arizona*, 536 U.S. 584 (June 24, 2002).

28. The cases are, respectively, *Terry Williams v. Taylor*, 529 U.S. 362 (April 18, 2000); *Wiggins v. Smith*, 539 U.S. 510 (June 26, 2003); *Miller-El v. Cockrell*, 537 U.S. 322 (Feb. 25, 2003); and *Banks v. Dretke*, 540 U.S. 668 (Feb. 24, 2004).

29. The cases are, respectively, *Rompilla v. Beard* (June 20, 2005); *Deck v. Missouri* (May 23, 2005); *Smith v. Texas* (Nov. 15, 2004); and *Miller-El v. Dretke* (June 13, 2005). Citations to U.S. Reports not yet available.

30. Alan Greenblatt, "The Capital Punishment Crossroads," *CQ Weekly*, Feb. 19, 2007, p. 538.

BIBLIOGRAPHY

Books

Acker, James R., Robert M. Bohm and Charles S. Lanier (eds.), *America's Experiment with Capital Punishment: Reflections on the Past, Present, and Future of the Ultimate Penal Sanction* (2d ed.), Carolina Academic Press, 2003.
More than 30 contributors provide comprehensive coverage of death penalty issues being debated in the United States. Includes notes and references for each chapter, tabular materials. Acker is a professor at the University of Albany, Bohm at the University of Central Florida; Lanier is co-director of the Capital Punishment Research Initiative at the University of Albany.

Bedau, Hugo Adam, and Paul G. Cassell (eds.), *Debating the Death Penalty: Should America Have Capital Punishment?* Oxford University Press, 2004.
Eight contributors, evenly split between supporters and critics of the death penalty, examine various aspects of the capital punishment debate. Bedau is professor emeritus of philosophy, Tufts University, and a confirmed opponent of the death penalty; Cassell, a former law professor at the University of Utah and now a federal district court judge, supports capital punishment.

Kurtis, Bill, *The Death Penalty on Trial: Crisis in American Justice*, Public Affairs, 2004.
The veteran television correspondent provides a journalistic account of two exoneration cases originally used in a program for A&E Television Network.

Scheck, Barry, Peter Neufeld and Jim Dwyer, *Actual Innocence: Five Days to Execution and Other Dispatches from the Wrongly Convicted*, Doubleday, 2000.
Defense lawyers Scheck and Neufeld — founders of the Innocence Project — and Pulitzer Prize-winning columnist Dwyer recount stories of helping 10 men, including some death row inmates, prove their innocence after wrongful convictions.

Zimring, Franklin E., *The Contradictions of American Capital Punishment*, Oxford University Press, 2003.
The longtime death penalty opponent and University of California at Berkeley law professor examines what he calls the contradictions of public support for speeding death penalty cases while trying to minimize the risk of wrongful executions.

Articles

Armstrong, Ken, and Steve Mills, "Death Row Justice Denied: Bias, Errors and Incompetence in Capital Cases Have Turned Illinois' Harshest Punishment into Its Least Credible," *The Chicago Tribune*, Nov. 14, 1999, p. 1.
This is the first of five articles describing the newspaper's investigation of all 285 Illinois death penalty cases since the state reinstated capital punishment 22 years ago; the paper found serious flaws in the state's criminal justice system.

Dlouhy, Jennifer A., "Add-Ons End Years of Wrangling, Clear Path for DNA Testing Bill," *CQ Weekly*, Oct. 16, 2004, p. 2442.
Congress completed work on a DNA testing bill, which would give federal inmates access to genetic testing and seek to ensure defendants in capital cases have sufficient legal representation.

Ganey, Terry, "Was the Wrong Man Executed?" *St. Louis Post-Dispatch*, **July 11, 2005.**
St. Louis Circuit Attorney Jennifer Joyce reopened an investigation into the case of Larry Griffin, who was sentenced to death for a drive-by murder 25 years ago.

Levine, Susan, and Lori Montgomery, "Large Racial Disparity Found by Study of Md. Death Penalty," *The Washington Post*, **Jan. 8, 2003, p. A1.**
Maryland Gov. Parris Glendening commissioned a study to investigate racial bias in the state's capital sentencing in 2001, which found the death penalty was more likely to be sought in cases involving white victims than in cases with black victims.

Reports & Studies

Berk, Richard A., "New Claims About Executions and General Deterrence: Déjà Vu All Over Again?" *Journal of Empirical Legal Studies*, **Vol. 2, No. 2 (July 2005), pp. 303-330.**

This analysis claims the deterrent effect exists in only one state — Texas — and is not particularly influential there.

Shepherd, Joanna, "Deterrence versus Brutalization: Capital Punishment's Differing Impacts Among States," *Michigan Law Review*, **Vol. 4, Issue 2 (November 2005).**
The effects of capital punishment vary from state to state, the researcher finds.

Zimerman, Paul R., "State Executions, Deterrence and the Incidence of Murder," *Journal of Applied Economics*, **Vol. 7, No. 1 (May 2004), pp. 163-193.**
This study by the Criminal Justice Legal Foundation finds that the announcement of capital punishment creates a deterrence rather than the death penalty itself. Other studies showing that executions deter capital crimes can be found on the group's Web site, www.cjlf.org.

For More Information

American Association on Intellectual and Developmental Disabilities, 444 N. Capitol St., N.W., Suite 846, Washington, DC 20001; (800) 424-3688; www.aamr.org. The largest and oldest organization devoted to mental retardation and related disabilities.

Criminal Justice Legal Foundation, P.O. Box 1199, Sacramento, CA 95812; (916) 446-0345; www.cjlf.org. A pro-death penalty public-interest law organization working to ensure that the courts respect the rights of crime victims and law-abiding society.

Death Penalty Information Center, 1101 Vermont Ave., N.W., Suite 701, Washington, DC 20005; (202) 289-2275; www.deathpenaltyinfo.org. An anti-death penalty organization furnishing analysis and information on issues concerning capital punishment.

Innocence Project, 100 5th Ave., 3d Floor, New York, NY 10011; (212) 364-5340; www.innocenceproject.org. Seeks to exonerate the wrongfully convicted through DNA testing and to effect reforms to prevent wrongful convictions.

National Association of Criminal Defense Lawyers, 1150 18th St., N.W., Suite 950; Washington, DC 20036; (202) 872-8600; www.criminaljustice.org. Works to ensure justice and due process to persons accused of crimes.

National Conference of State Legislatures, 7700 East 1st Pl., Suite 700, Denver, CO 80230; (303) 364-7700; www.ncsl.org. A bipartisan organization that provides a forum for state legislators and their staffs to discuss state issues.

National District Attorneys Association, 99 Canal Center Plaza, Suite 510, Alexandria, VA 22314; (703) 549-9222; www.ndaa.org. Helps prosecutors by providing training, research and legislative advocacy.

12

Consumer Debt

Barbara Mantel

Chicago bankruptcy attorney Melvin James Kaplan displays the hundreds of credit cards abandoned by his clients. Consumer debt has grown so fast that Americans now owe more money — $1.2 trillion — than they make. The new, Democrat-controlled Congress already has held several hearings on credit card debt and mortgage lending and plans to hold more, questioning whether lenders extended too much credit to people of limited means.

From *CQ Researcher*, March 2, 2007.

AP Photo/Charles Rex Arbogast

aul and Kristi Miller of Lancaster, Pa., have struggled with debt for most of the 11 years they have been married. After the birth of their twins just 13 months after the wedding, they started using credit cards, mostly for necessities like diapers, food and clothing for the children.

"The kids ate the food in five minutes," says Kristi, "but we would pay for that food for years and years."

More children followed, but with Paul earning less than $50,000 a year as a supervisor at a medical equipment supplier, the family's income often fell short. At one point, the Millers' credit card bills totaled $5,000, and they asked Kristi's parents for help. But it was a brief respite. "We turned to credit cards again, and we were very embarrassed about that," she says. When their credit card debt ballooned to $9,000, they took out a home equity loan to pay that off as well as their $8,000 car loan.

But the cycle continued, and about three-and-a-half years ago, with their four credit cards maxed out, the Millers sought credit counseling. They cut up their cards, sold their house to pay off the home equity loan and became renters. Recently, they used a tax refund to finally pay off the last of their debt.

"We're kind of back to square one," says Kristi. "We no longer have debt, but we don't have any savings or investments either."

A chorus of voices now warns that many American households, like the Millers, are dangerously overextended. Others disagree and say most people are managing their debt just fine. But everyone agrees that households have dramatically increased the amounts they borrow.

In 1990, American households borrowed $231 billion and increased their borrowing at a steady 6 or 7 percent a year during

Household Debt Gobbling Up Disposable Income

The percentage of disposable income used to make monthly debt payments rose from about 11 percent to more than 14 percent.

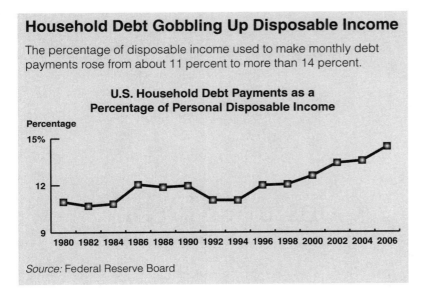

U.S. Household Debt Payments as a Percentage of Personal Disposable Income

Source: Federal Reserve Board

the 1990s. In 2000, however, households began adding to their debt at a much faster pace — first by 9, then 10 and recently by almost 12 percent a year. By 2005, Americans were $1.2 trillion in debt. [1] The Federal Reserve Board facilitated the increase in debt by dramatically lowering interest rates, and thus the cost of borrowing, to avoid a deep recession after the dot-com and stock market busts of early 2000.

Debt has grown so fast that — for the first time since the government began collecting data in the 1950s — Americans now owe more money than they make. The ratio of household debt to personal disposable income first breached 100 percent in 2001 and has since climbed to 131. [2] (*See graph, p. 272.*)

Americans are now drowning in debt, says Elizabeth Warren, a professor of bankruptcy law at Harvard University and author of *The Two-Income Trap.* "Debt is an insidious cancer that eats away at a family's independence," she says. It has grown so dramatically, she says, because families are being squeezed between stagnant real incomes and the growing costs of housing, health care, energy and food. So they borrow.

"If anything goes wrong, like illness, loss of a job or divorce, families can quickly find themselves in a position where they can't make their payments on their outstanding loans," Warren continues.

Home loans represent the largest and fastest growing slice of household debt, which is not surprising since home

prices have skyrocketed this decade. In 2004, the latest year for which data are available, the median home loan was $97,000, an increase of 26.5 percent over the 2001 amount. Student loans were a close second, increasing 26.3 percent. And credit card debt and car loans grew, respectively, by 20.9 percent and 11.1 percent. (*See graph, p. 270.*) [3]

But the level of debt by itself does not necessarily indicate that consumers are in trouble and about to default. To judge whether families can manage their debt, economists look to other kinds of statistics that better indicate financial stress. Based on those indicators, there may be cause for concern.

For instance, according to the Federal Reserve Board, as debt rose between 2001 and 2004, families devoted more of their incomes to servicing that debt, despite the general decline in interest rates. (*See graph, p. 269.*) In addition, the fraction of families with very large debt payments relative to their income increased and so did the percentage of families that were 60 days late or more in making payments. [4]

But analysts at Third Way, a progressive, nonpartisan think tank focusing on economic and national security issues, said in a recent report that none of this is alarming and called the increases in signs of financial stress small and "scant."

"Americans, contrary to myth, are not 'drowning in debt,' " the report said. While it's true that household debt, particularly mortgage debt, has risen significantly, "most families would consider buying a house an investment, not a negative event." [5]

In fact, the value of Americans' homes has increased significantly, pushing up the real net worth for Americans at every income level. The recent housing boom — although now stalled — played a large part. "The typical American household is in better financial shape than it was a decade ago," said James Sherk, a policy analyst at the Heritage Foundation, a conservative think tank. [6]

But Christian Weller, senior economist at the Center for American Progress, a liberal think tank, says the signs of financial stress are worrisome and that the concentration of family wealth in housing bodes ill.

"Families have so much money now tied up in their homes that they don't save money or save very little," he says. In fact, Americans overall spent more than they earned in 2005 for the first time since the Great Depression.

Weller says families have built up housing wealth at the expense of more liquid financial assets, leaving them little cushion if the economy sours. The share of families whose financial wealth equals three months' worth of income rose steadily during the 1990s, from 32.8 percent to 38.8 percent, but it dropped dramatically between 2001 and 2004. "In took just three years to erase all the gains of the previous 12," says Weller. Moreover, housing wealth created after 2000 could significantly shrink if the recent housing slump continues much longer.

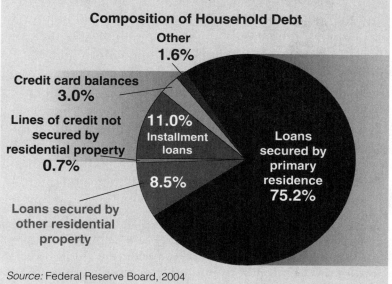

Home Loans Make Up Most Family Debt

Residential mortgages and home equity loans account for three-quarters of U.S. household debt, while installment loans and credit card balances make up another 14 percent, according to the most recent Federal Reserve Board "Survey of Consumer Finances."

Composition of Household Debt

Other **1.6%**

Credit card balances **3.0%**

Lines of credit not secured by residential property **0.7%**

11.0% Installment loans

Loans secured by other residential property **8.5%**

Loans secured by primary residence **75.2%**

Source: Federal Reserve Board, 2004

Already, more than 20 regional mortgage companies that specialize in the riskiest borrowers have filed for bankruptcy or closed. Larger lenders, like Britain-based HSBC, have announced losses as a result of a steady rise in default rates among high-risk borrowers, a group assiduously courted in the past several years.

The new, Democrat-controlled Congress already has held several hearings on credit card debt and mortgage lending in 2007 and plans to hold more, questioning whether lenders expanded credit too aggressively to people of limited means. That's quite a shift from two years ago, when the Republican-controlled Congress was more concerned about the impact of defaulting customers on lenders and passed legislation making it more difficult for borrowers to file for bankruptcy to discharge debts.

Banking regulators are also cracking down. Last fall, they issued guidelines requiring mortgage lenders to be more careful when making loans. Meanwhile, the House has voted to cut the interest rate on federally guaranteed student loans — a major source of debt for young people — and the Senate is considering similar action.

As consumer debt rises, these are some of the questions economists, consumer advocates, financial institutions and policymakers are debating:

Are lenders giving mortgages to people who can't afford them?

Each month seems to bring more bad news from mortgage lenders. Texas-based Sebring Capital ceased operations in early December. In California, Ownit Mortgage Solutions filed for bankruptcy just after Christmas, and ResMae Mortgage filed in January. In all there have been more than 20 recent casualties among "subprime" lenders, who cater to borrowers with blemished credit histories.

This segment of the market has been growing rapidly in the past three years, as lenders raced to find new borrowers to keep the housing boom on track. Starting as a niche market in the mid-1990s, subprime lending has grown into a major economic force, now representing about one-quarter of all home loans made in the United States.

It has turned many families with sketchy credit histories, including millions of minorities, into first-time

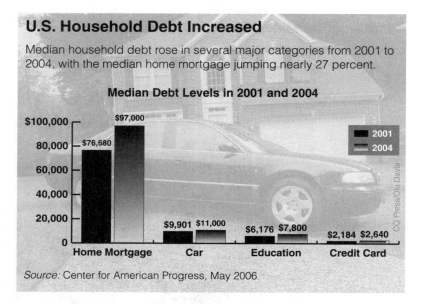

U.S. Household Debt Increased

Median household debt rose in several major categories from 2001 to 2004, with the median home mortgage jumping nearly 27 percent.

Median Debt Levels in 2001 and 2004

- 2001
- 2004

Home Mortgage: $76,680 / $97,000
Car: $9,901 / $11,000
Education: $6,176 / $7,800
Credit Card: $2,184 / $2,640

Source: Center for American Progress, May 2006

CQ Press/Olu Davis

economist at the Ford Foundation. It measures whether a mortgage will ever go into foreclosure over its lifetime. A study from the Center for Responsible Lending projects that nearly 20 percent of subprime loans originated in the past two years will end in foreclosure — up from 13 percent of loans originated in 2000. "That's astounding," says McCarthy.

But Fratantoni of the Mortgage Bankers Association calls the center's projection "unduly pessimistic." Delinquencies and foreclosures are increasing modestly and primarily in the Midwest, where the job market and the housing market are particularly weak, he says. But the Center for Responsible Lending predicts foreclosures will spread to other regions, and that the cause is not just regional job loss but the mortgage products themselves. "If these loans were really affordable, then even given a shock like job loss, people might still be able to make the payment," says Debbie Goldstein, the center's executive vice president.

homebuyers or allowed them to refinance their homes at initially lower interest rates. "A lot of people who would not have qualified for any credit at all are now able to get a mortgage and buy a home," says Michael Fratantoni, a senior economist at the Mortgage Bankers Association.

The expansion in the subprime market has been driven by several factors, notably computerization, automation and the sophisticated use of credit scores that rank a borrower's risk of default. (*See graph, p. 272.*) These developments have allowed lenders to create an array of non-traditional mortgages and tailor them to a homebuyer's credit profile. Professionals call it "risk-based pricing."

But what once was a boon to people with weak credit may turn out to be a bane. The bulk of loans in the subprime market are adjustable-rate mortgages (ARMs), and as interest rates have risen in the past year and the housing market has slowed, delinquencies and foreclosures have increased. According to the Mortgage Bankers Association, the delinquency rate for subprime loans in the third quarter of last year was 12.56 percent, nearly a percentage point higher than the previous quarter. The foreclosure rate was 3.86 percent, up about a third of a percentage point. [7]

But those figures give only a snapshot of how mortgages are doing at one point in time. "A more telling statistic, and one that is really troubling, is the 'ever-foreclosure rate,'" says George McCarthy, a housing

The most common loan made to homebuyers with checkered credit histories is a "2/28" adjustable-rate mortgage. These mortgages usually have a low, fixed "teaser" rate for the first two years, followed by rate adjustments every six months. When lenders qualify borrowers for such loans, they generally only look at "whether the borrower can make the payments in the initial two years," says Goldstein, "and not whether they can make the payment when the rate goes up — and it can go up by 30 or 50 percent." The loans are complicated and the disclosure forms confusing, she says, so home buyers often don't understand that they are in for future payment shock.

The structure of mortgage lending compounds the problem, say consumer advocates. Brokers, not bankers, now originate about 80 percent of mortgages. A broker screens prospective borrowers, recommends loan products, prepares and submits loan applications to lenders, who fund the loan if approved. When the loan closes, the broker collects a fee from the borrower and may also collect a cash bonus from the lender if he brings in a loan with a higher interest rate than the borrower's credit profile would indicate. Advocates say, as a result, brokers have incentive to close as many loans as possible at the highest interest rate possible.

"Risk-based pricing only happens if you have a broker who matches the borrower to the right product," says McCarthy. "But that's not what brokers do. They match borrowers to the product that benefits the broker most."

"To say that we are pushing higher-priced product so that we can earn more is an unfair statement," says Harry Dinham, president of the National Association of Mortgage Brokers. "It's a very competitive marketplace, and it's very hard to overcharge the customer."

Industry professionals also say the creation of mortgage-backed securities — known as securitization — discourages the practice of making unaffordable loans. A firm that originates mortgages doesn't necessarily keep those loans. It often sells its mortgages to financial institutions that then package them into mortgage-backed securities to sell to investors. "If you originate a loan that has a delinquency early in its life, most investors will make originators buy back the loan," says Fratantoni. "It's market discipline at work." In fact, it's exactly what put ResMae into bankruptcy in February, when it said buying back defaulted mortgages from Merrill Lynch would cripple it.

But consumer advocates say market discipline comes too late for borrowers who shouldn't have been placed in unaffordable loans in the first place. The advocates want greater regulation of such lending.

Last September, in response to the proliferation of two other kinds of risky mortgages, federal bank regulators issued guidelines to help protect homebuyers. Like 2/28 loans, interest-only loans (in which payment on the principal is deferred for the first three to five years) and payment-option ARMS (in which initial monthly payments can be very low) result in higher payments at the back end. Though they've been traditionally marketed to prime customers, interest-only loans are making inroads into the subprime market. The new guidelines require more stringent underwriting standards and better disclosure, and consumer advocates would like to see the new rules extended to 2/28 loans as well.

But lenders are even more worried about calls by some for Congress to establish suitability standards for the mortgage industry, which would make brokers and bankers legally culpable for placing someone in a mortgage that they couldn't afford to pay back.

Christmas shoppers wait in line with their purchases in Philadelphia. Some economists worry that Americans' credit card debt rose too fast from 2001 to 2004 — about 21 percent — and that they have so much money tied up in their homes they don't save, or save very little.

"Who's going to decide what's suitable?" asks Dinham. "It's going to end up in the courts. A borrower is perfectly happy with a loan, then loses his job and can't make payments and will try to blame the lender." A suitability standard could result in some lenders pulling out of the subprime market or substantially reducing the number of loans they make, Dinham says. That's already happening, even without additional regulation, as rising subprime defaults lead lenders to tighten the standards used to qualify risky borrowers for loans.

Are Americans piling up too much credit card debt?

After she divorced two years ago, 48-year-old Tracie Anderson of Beaverton, Mich., got her first credit card. And then her second. And then her third, fourth and fifth. "After the third one, I knew I shouldn't really have more," says Anderson. "But I figured they knew my credit score, and maybe they knew better than me; maybe I was looking at it all wrong."

Anderson faced a series of seasonal layoffs from her job on the assembly line of a small manufacturer and a growing list of hard-to-pay bills. "Rent, phone, Internet, car repairs, gasoline, food, clothes." she says. Her card debt eventually reached $20,000, and she moved in with a relative. After she got laid off again this past November,

Your FICO Score — and Why It Matters

Consumers' credit ratings are measured by their FICO scores, and most lenders base loan approvals on them. Scores range from 300-850, with higher numbers reflecting better credit. FICO scores are based on several categories but mainly the consumer's payment history and the amount of debt owed (graph). Consumers with better credit ratings (higher FICO scores) are able to get lower rates on mortgage and auto loans (table at bottom).

Factors Used in Calculating Ratings

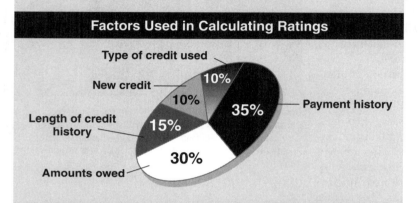

How FICO Scores Affect Loan Payments

30-year fixed $300,000 mortgage (as of Feb. 23, 2007)				Three-Year $25,000 Car Loan (as of Feb. 23, 2007)		
FICO Score	Interest Rate	Monthly Payment		FICO Score	Interest Rate	Monthly Payment
760-850	5.88%	$1,818		720-850	7.16%	$774
700-759	6.10	1,819		690-719	7.96	783
660-699	6.38	1,874		660-689	9.47	801
620-659	7.19	2,036		620-659	11.01	819
580-619	8.52	2,312		590-619	14.46	860
500-579	9.42	2,506		500-589	15.14	868

Source: MyFICO.com

Anderson finally arranged a payment plan and hopes she can be out of debt within two years. But it all depends on finding a job. "Michigan is really bad right now," she says. "There are not too many manufacturing jobs for people like me."

Demos, a public policy and advocacy organization, found that seven out of 10 low- and middle-income households it surveyed reported using their credit cards for basic living and medical expenses and for car and house repairs. [8]

"We have a negative savings rate in this country," says Tamara Draut, director of Demos' economic-opportunity program. "So when you don't have savings for a car repair, you turn to your Visa card."

Between 1980 and 2005, the amount that U.S. consumers charged to their credit cards grew from $69 billion a year to more than $1.8 trillion, and credit card debt more than tripled. That rate of growth has slowed in the past five years as homeowners took advantage of soaring property values to tap into equity and pay down their more expensive card debt. [9]

Not everyone with a card, however, racks up debt. Nearly half pay their balance in full each month. But for those who don't, credit card debt can sometimes be debilitating, even though on average, it accounts for less than 10 percent of household borrowing. "In the aggregate, I don't think credit card debt is a major threat to households," says Weller of the Center for American Progress. "But because its costs can quickly spiral out of control, it can pose a particular threat for some, like low-income families." According to Weller's calculations, low-income families have seen a disproportionate increase in credit card payments, heavy indebtedness and delinquency rates from 1989 to 2004. [10]

It used to be that only households with the highest credit ratings could get a credit card, and the terms were the same for everyone. But after 1990, the credit card industry began using sophisticated credit risk analysis to tailor products to an individual's risk, just as the mortgage industry has. "If you have a decent credit history, you can have access to a credit card," says James Chessen, chief economist at the American Bankers Association.

"That's a very good thing because it allows you to be like any other adult in our society."

With increased competition during the 1990s — there are now more than 6,000 companies issuing credit cards — companies lowered their interest rates and many eliminated annual fees. But credit cards became much more complex in the process: Now issuers offer cards with a variety of interest rates and fees, depending on a borrower's risk. For many cardholders, that has meant escalating costs.

For instance, an average penalty fee of $34 is often charged for late payments or for exceeding a credit limit. Late payment can also trigger a penalty interest rate, which can bring an interest rate from something like 8 percent to more than 30 percent. "Tripling and quadrupling the interest rate is capricious and doesn't reflect a real relation to risk," says Draut. "Being a day or two late doesn't mean you are that much riskier than you were before."

But the American Bankers Association defends those fees. "There is no question that the fees have gone up over time," says Chessen. "But they're called penalty fees because someone missed their obligation." Besides, he says, if a cardholder is unhappy with his credit card, he can shop for another one.

But comparison shopping is extremely difficult, concluded a recent Government Accountability Office report. Mandatory disclosure statements in credit card agreements have "likely reduced consumers' ability to understand the costs of using credit cards," the report said. The disclosures often bury important information in text; scatter information about a single topic in numerous places; use hard-to-read typefaces and are written at a 10th- or 12th-grade level even though nearly half of American adults read at an 8th-grade level.

In January several consumer advocacy groups asked the Senate Banking Committee to regulate industry practices more stringently by requiring, among other things:

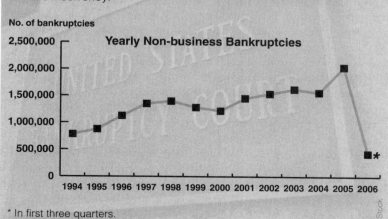

Bankruptcies Plummet After Steady Rise

The number of bankruptcies filed by individuals rose steadily over the past decade to a record high in 2005 before dropping precipitously in 2006. A federal law passed in 2005 made it harder for individuals to declare insolvency.

No. of bankruptcies

Yearly Non-business Bankruptcies

* In first three quarters.

Source: American Bankruptcy Institute

- Fees that closely match the true cost borne by the card issuer.
- A ban on retroactive rate increases: Currently, issuers often apply penalty interest rates to past balances as well as those going forward.
- A ban on universal default: Issuers sometimes apply a penalty interest rate to cardholders who are current on their payments with that issuer but who have made missteps with other lenders.
- A ban on late fees for payments mailed on time: Issuers currently do not accept the postmarked date as proof of on-time payment.
- Real warnings on minimum payments: Tell consumers exactly how much their total interest costs will be and how long it will take to pay back the debt if only the minimum payment is made. [11]

The Federal Reserve Board is reviewing disclosure requirements, and the American Bankers Association agrees disclosure needs to be improved. But it is opposed to the other changes proposed by consumer advocates. (*See "At Issue," p. 283.*)

With Democrats now in control of Congress, many observers expect more scrutiny of the credit card industry. While no legislation is guaranteed, the increased glare by itself could encourage some card issuers to change their practices.

Will the explosion in consumer debt deepen the next recession?

Consumer spending accounts for about 70 percent of economic activity in the United States, and it has been growing strongly each year since the mild recession of 2001. That strength has significantly contributed to the country's steady improvement in overall economic growth — from 1.6 percent in 2002 to 2.5 percent in 2003 and above 3 percent each year since then. [12]

But while American households have been spending more and more each year, they've been saving less and less; overall, household spending has not been keeping up with income, and U.S. consumers have turned to debt — specifically mortgage debt — to finance their purchases.

"The values of homes were going up, and people were using their homes as ATM machines," says Nouriel Roubini, a professor of economics at New York University and the head of Roubini Global Economics.

The Federal Reserve helped the process along. To soften the recession of 2001, the "Fed" aggressively eased credit, holding its key short-term interest rate below 2 percent from the end of 2001 through 2004. A real estate boom followed, fueled by mortgage lending at low interest rates. New home construction rose by a third, and sales increased by nearly 40 percent.

Not surprisingly, as the value of their homes exploded, consumers felt wealthier and increased their spending accordingly — a phenomenon economists call the "wealth effect."

Lower interest rates and rising home values also caused homeowners to embark on a refinancing spree, and many increased the size of their mortgage in order to tap into their home's growing equity. Between 2001 and 2005, households cashed out a whopping $715 billion worth of home equity. They used the bulk of this money to repay other debts and make home improvements. But they also used it to increase spending on consumer goods and to pay for education and medical care.

At some point, however, growing debt becomes oppressive, and instead of fueling spending and economic growth it helps to dampen it. "You cannot keep consuming more than your income and accumulating these levels of debt forever," says Roubini. "Home values

are falling now, so the idea of using your home as a cash machine doesn't work anymore."

What the Federal Reserve gives, it can take away, and in the middle of 2004, it began to increase interest rates in order to tamp down inflation. As a result, mortgage rates rose, and the housing market eventually began to stall. Last year new home sales fell 17 percent, and sales of existing homes dropped 8 percent. [13] Home prices fell or flattened in many markets.

Mortgage-equity withdrawals fell in the third quarter of last year for the fourth time in a row. Homeowners are extracting less money from their homes, and, not surprisingly, growth in consumer spending slowed down as well. In the first quarter of 2006, consumer spending increased by 4.8 percent. In the second and third quarters, it increased by less than 3 percent.

But in the fourth quarter, economists were surprised. Consumers seemed more confident, and spending increased by 4.2 percent despite continued turmoil in the housing market. Economists reasoned that homeowners had more disposable income because gasoline prices fell.

Forecasts for economic growth this year depend in good measure on their outlook for the housing industry and the resulting impact on household wealth and debt burdens. "The housing market downturn will certainly be a restraint on consumer spending in the year ahead," says Sara Johnson, an economist at the forecasting firm Global Insight. But with disposable income on the rise — as inflation moderates and wages pick up steam — Johnson expects consumers to increase spending at about the same rate as last year.

She predicts 2007 economic growth of 2.7 percent, similar to what the Mortgage Bankers Association and the Federal Reserve Board forecast. All are predicting what economists call a "soft landing" for the recent overheated housing market.

But others are less optimistic and point out that the United States is in uncharted territory. Never has debt been so high compared to household income, and never have such a wide spectrum of Americans had access to debt. Thus, it is difficult to predict what will happen when that unwinds, as it has begun to do.

"The buildup phase, borrowing more and more, seems to have come to an end," says Weller of the Center for American Progress. "Borrowers do not trust that the housing boom will continue, and lenders are becoming nervous because they see the increase in defaults and foreclosures." Weller says Americans are now in the repayment phase, dedicating more money to service their debt and less money to consumption.

Roubini agrees and predicts what is called a "growth recession," with the economy growing only 1 percent for the rest of this year. If housing is as unhelpful on the way down as it was helpful on the way up, consumers may indeed retrench significantly.

BACKGROUND

Myth of Thrift

Critics of the explosion in consumer credit often bemoan the loss of America's capacity for thrift and a past when Americans were cash-and-carry customers. But according to historian Lendol Calder, that notion is a myth.

"Debt, in fact, was a 'heavy burthen' for the Pilgrims, a chronic headache for Colonial planters (including George Washington and Thomas Jefferson) and a common hardship for 19th-century farmers and workers," Calder wrote in *Financing the American Dream.* "A river of red ink runs through American history." [14]

In the early 1800s, nearly three-quarters of Americans lived on farms and borrowed, if necessary, from family members or merchants to buy essentials like seed and equipment. Storekeepers and farmers depended on one another for economic survival, assuming that loans would be repaid after harvest.

By the end of the 19th century, the Industrial Revolution had transformed the country. Less than half of the labor force still worked on farms, and working- and middle-class Americans were able to afford more than just the bare necessities. Factories were producing an array of consumer goods, from bicycles to kitchen appliances, but their prices were high, and consumers often needed to borrow money to pay for them.

By this time, borrowing options had expanded beyond relatives and shopkeepers to loan sharks and pawnbrokers, who became an increasingly common source of credit in the 1890s despite their exorbitant interest rates. "Because this kind of credit operated mostly in secret, it was easy for later generations to forget it existed," noted Calder. [15]

Installment Credit

The nature of credit dramatically changed in the early part of the 20th century. Once assembly-line techniques in the nation's factories had been perfected, prices began to decline for cars, refrigerators, washing machines and other consumer products, and the growing electrification of American homes made their widespread use possible.

"But the catalyst — the thing that helped to bring all these industrial and technological marvels within the reach of so many consumers — was the expanded use of installment credit," according to the Federal Reserve Bank of Boston. [16]

Back in the late 1880s, only Singer Sewing Machine allowed its customers to buy on credit, with a bit of money down and future payments in fixed, monthly installments. Thirty years later, Singer was no longer an anomaly. In 1919, the General Motors Acceptance Corp. became the first to extend installment credit to middle-class car buyers, and other manufacturers soon followed. Department stores and oil companies began to issue credit cards. These credit revolutionaries relied heavily on advertising in order to overcome the stigma of borrowing that clung from the days of loan sharks and pawnbrokers. "Buy Now, Pay Later" became a stock phrase by the end of the 1920s.

"Less and less a marker of improvidence and poverty, [consumer credit] became in time a badge of middle-class respectability," according to Calder. [17]

For the next 40 years, consumer credit consisted mostly of installment loans, until the credit card revolution took hold.

Credit Card Revolution

In 1951 Franklin National Bank introduced the first general-purpose bank card. Seven years later, Bank of America launched its card, mass mailing 60,000 of them to residents in Fresno, Calif.

"The bank hoped to attract customers with a new type of 'revolving credit' line, which could be used for purchases everywhere and paid off over time," according to the Web site "Secret History of the Credit Card," a companion to the "Frontline" documentary of the same name. "The idea was to tap into the pent-up consumer demands of World War II baby boomers." [18]

Soon, banks all over the country were mass mailing credit cards to anyone with an address, independent of their credit history. As card use rose so did mail fraud, as thieves stole the envelopes. "People were outraged by what some called usurious temptations, and bankers were flooded with massive defaults," said "Frontline."

Early 1900s *The nature of credit changes as manufacturers and stores extend installment credit to consumers. Federal government encourages homeownership.*

1911 Sears, Roebuck allows consumers to make installment payments.

April 19, 1916 Lenders from five states organize the American Association of Small Loan Brokers to standardize and police the small-loan business.

1919 General Motors becomes one of the first companies to extend installment credit to car buyers.

1932 Twenty-five states have passed laws requiring state licensing and supervision of small loan industry and capping interest rates on loans under $300.

1934 Congress creates the Federal Housing Administration (FHA) to insure mortgages and encourage homeownership.

1938 Government creates Fannie Mae to buy FHA-insured mortgages and pump liquidity into the mortgage markets.

1950s *Banks start issuing credit cards.*

1950 Diners Club Card becomes first general-purpose credit card.

1951 Franklin National Bank becomes the first bank to issue a general-purpose bank card.

1958 Bank of America launches credit card, mailing 60,000 to residents of Fresno, Calif.

1960s-1970s *Congress protects borrowers; Supreme Court loosens restrictions on credit card companies.*

1965 Higher Education Act creates the Guaranteed Student Loan Program.

1969 Truth in Lending Act establishes uniform methods for computing credit costs, disclosure of credit terms and resolving errors.

1974 Fair Credit Reporting Act mandates confidentiality for consumers' records.

1975 Equal Credit Opportunity Act prohibits discrimination against credit applicants on the basis of age, race, color, religion, national origin, sex or marital status.

1978 Fair Debt Collection Practices Act prohibits abusive, deceptive or unfair collection practices. . . . Supreme Court says banks can charge borrowers nationwide the interest rate in their home state, allowing credit card issuers to dramatically raise rates. . . . Bank of America issues first mortgage-backed security. . . . Middle Income Student Assistance Act extends student loan eligibility to middle- and upper-income students.

1980s-Present *Credit is extended to a wider array of Americans, who increase borrowing to record levels.*

1986 Tax Reform Act of 1987 phases out deductibility of consumer credit, except for mortgages.

1988 Fair Isaac Corp. introduces the FICO score; it becomes the standard measure of consumer credit risk.

1996 Supreme Court removes dollar limit on credit card penalties. Card issuers eventually triple penalties for late payments and exceeding credit limits.

2000 Ratio of household debt to personal disposable income reaches 100 percent for the first time since the government began collecting data.

2005 Bankruptcy Abuse Prevention and Consumer Protection Act of 2005 makes filing for bankruptcy more expensive, time consuming and restrictive. Filings reach record levels before bill takes effect, then plunge the following year. . . . Personal savings rate among Americans turns negative for first time since the Great Depression.

Sept. 29, 2006 Federal banking regulators issue lender guidelines designed to reduce the risk to borrowers of certain non-traditional mortgages.

Jan. 17, 2007 House cuts the interest rate on government-guaranteed student loans by half; Senate considers similar legislation.

Congress eventually stepped in and banned the mass mailing of active cards to consumers who had not requested them.

By the mid-1970s, fraud had subsided, and improved telecommunications and faster computers allowed banks and merchants to manage information and credit card debt more efficiently. The card business began to show a profit.

But that didn't last long. When the Federal Reserve raised interest rates in the early 1980s to fight inflation, credit card issuers found their profits squeezed. In the spring of 1981, the rate at which banks borrow money from the Federal Reserve Bank rose to 14 percent, but state usury laws limited the rate banks could charge on credit card balances to several points below that. As a result, credit card issuers were loaning money to credit card holders at lower interest rates than they themselves had to pay.

Citibank found a way around the problem, and, in the process, changed the nature of the business. A little-noticed 1978 Supreme Court ruling had allowed banks to charge borrowers nationwide whatever interest rate was allowed in the state where the credit cards were issued. So Citibank contacted officials in South Dakota, which was considering eliminating its usury laws. South Dakota, desperate for jobs, went ahead and repealed its usury laws and invited Citibank to move its credit card operations from New York. Soon Delaware too repealed its usury laws, attracting the credit card operations of Chase Manhattan, Manufacturer's Hanover and Chemical Bank. Banks located in those states raised their credit card rates, and kept them there.

"The inflationary spiral that pushed Citibank to the precipice of disaster propelled the credit card industry into a decade of enormous profits," said "Frontline." "Cardholders, it turned out, were willing to keep on paying 18 percent interest long after inflation subsided and the Federal Reserve lowered the interest rate it charged banks." [19]

But in the 1990s, competition increased in the credit card business, as non-bank companies, like AT&T, entered the market. Credit card issuers began lowering interest rates charged on card balances and eliminating annual fees. They started trolling for the most lucrative customers: those who incurred interest charges by running up card balances, and those who occasionally paid late, incurring penalty fees. Using sophisticated credit scoring that had been developed in the late 1980s, finan-

The number of payday loan offices, like this one in Philadelphia, has more than doubled in just four years, and the industry's annual loan volume has quadrupled — to $40 billion. The typical loan is for about $300 for two weeks at a cost of about $20 per $100 borrowed. Critics complain that payday loans are rarely short-term and that their fees translate into an annualized percentage rate of nearly 400 percent.

cial institutions tailored credit card programs to an individual consumer's risk of default. The higher the risk, the higher the interest rate.

Three major credit-reporting agencies (CRAs) — Equifax, Experian and TransUnion — monitor the credit habits of U.S. consumers. Creditors like banks, department stores and mortgage brokers register with the CRAs and supply them with information about their customers, including loan type, outstanding balances and payment history. In exchange, registered lenders have access to potential customers' credit records. CRAs also gather information from public records about bankruptcies, foreclosures and liens.

Payday Lending Comes Under Fire

Borrowers pay an annualized interest rate of nearly 400 percent

After her husband lost his job as a chef, Sandra Harris of Wilmington, N.C., faced a cash crunch. Unable to pay her car insurance, Harris took out a $200 payday loan, for a $50 fee. The tough times continued, and she borrowed more, incurring additional fees. When the lender demanded full payment, Harris turned to another payday lender. She eventually was paying $600 a month to cover fees on six different loans.

Harris' story, and dozens more, appear on the Web site for the Center for Responsible Lending, which accuses payday lenders of intentionally trapping consumers in a cycle of debt. Payday lenders, in turn, accuse the center of exaggerating the problems of payday lending and attacking an industry that provides consumers an essential service.

All agree, however, that payday lending is growing rapidly. The number of offices offering payday loans has more than doubled in just four years, and the industry's annual loan volume has quadrupled — to $40 billion. The industry has also consolidated, evolving from a mom-and-pop business to one dominated by about a dozen large lenders. [1] As traditional banks have reduced their short-term lending to high-risk borrowers, payday lenders have stepped in.

The low- and moderate-income workers who turn to payday loans usually do so during a temporary cash squeeze, looking for short-term credit to tide them over until their next paycheck. They give the lender a postdated check, and in exchange they get a loan. The typical loan is for about $300 for two weeks at a cost of $15 to $20 per $100 borrowed. [2]

Critics complain that payday loans are rarely short-term and that their fees translate into an annualized percentage rate (APR) of nearly 400 percent.

Payday lenders "don't really want you to pay off the loan," says Susan Lupton, a senior policy associate at the Center for Responsible Lending. "What they really want you to do is flip the loan every payday and pay more fees." Lupton says that because payment is due in full at the end of the two weeks, borrowers often find themselves forced to roll over the loan or take out a new loan to cover the old one. A typical borrower has nine loan transactions from a single payday loan store per year, according to the center. That means the typical borrower ends up paying more than $450 in fees on a $325 loan, says Lupton.

"That claim is ridiculous," says Lyndsey Medsker, a spokeswoman for the Community Financial Services

In 1989, credit reporting agencies began using this massive database to generate credit scores, which provide a snapshot of a borrower's ability to repay a loan. The most common credit score is a FICO score — developed by the Fair Isaac Corp., which provides software to the CRAs for calculating credit scores. FICO scores run between 300 and 850; the higher the score, the better terms a borrower will receive on a loan. Credit scoring has allowed lenders to better assess risk and charge accordingly, expanding the availability of credit to more marginal borrowers.

Rise of Mortgage Lending

Between 1890 and 1940, most American families were renters, and homeownership remained below 50 percent. That slowly changed after President Franklin D. Roosevelt began to promote homeownership as part of his New Deal. Roosevelt's administration created the Federal Housing Administration (FHA) to insure mortgages. By

shifting risk to the FHA, commercial banks were encouraged to join savings and loans in the mortgage market, increasing the pool of money available for lending.

The FHA also made mortgages more appealing to borrowers by refusing to insure variable-rate, high-down payment, short-maturity loans — the typical mortgage of that era. Instead, the FHA would insure only fixed-rate, self-amortizing mortgages, with down payments as low as 20 percent, and a long-term maturity of 20 years or more. [20]

By the 1950s, lenders found it profitable to make these loans without government insurance, and the market for "conventional" mortgages grew. By 1965, the homeownership rate had climbed to 63 percent.

But between the mid-1960s and the early '80s, the mortgage market faced a series of challenges that dampened the demand for housing: Inflation and interest rates spiked three times as Vietnam War spending ballooned the federal budget deficit, oil shocks caused energy prices

Association (CFSA), the industry trade organization. She says the center is misrepresenting the numbers by counting those nine transactions as rollovers of one loan. "Those are nine separate loans within a year," she says. Those fees, therefore, are for nearly $3,000 of borrowed funds. In fact, Medsker points out that many states limit to four the number of times a borrower can roll over a loan.

That's just semantics, Lupton says. "After four rollovers, the lender might give you a 24-hour waiting period," she says. "They'll say, 'pay us off today and then come back tomorrow, and we'll give you another loan.'" Whether you call it a rollover or a back-to-back transaction, Lupton says, it's often all the same line of credit.

The center recommends that borrowers consider other options before turning to a payday loan. It might be cheaper to take on more credit card debt, borrow from a credit union or from family or negotiate a payment schedule with creditors.

Payday lenders are regulated by the states, which usually have usury caps on interest rates of between 24 to 48 percent. Those rates would effectively prohibit payday lending and its triple-digit interest rates, but 37 states have exempted payday lending from the usury restrictions. Twelve states — including New York, New Jersey and Pennsylvania — have no exemptions, so payday lenders do not operate there.

Payday lenders would like to see those 12 states exempt their industry from the usury rules, while consumer advocates would like all the exemptions repealed. If they were repealed, says Medsker, "Payday lenders would not be able to pay employees and overhead costs, let alone make a profit."

The Federal Deposit Insurance Corporation, which insures bank deposits, confirms Medsker's view: "We find that fixed operating costs and high loan loss rates justify a large part of the high APR charged on payday advance loans."[3] Rolling back exemptions would put payday lenders out of business and remove what the industry calls an essential source of short-term loans.

Critics applauded last fall when Congress shut out payday lenders from one group of borrowers — Americans in uniform — by capping interest rates at 36 percent on loans to those in the military. The industry says military borrowers make up only 2 percent of its business.

In February, the industry took steps to address the growing criticism. The CFSA will now require its members to offer late customers the option of paying off a loan in four installments with no additional fees, but customers could use the option only once per year. It's a policy that some states, like Alabama and Florida, already require.

---

[1] Mark Flannery and Katherine Samolyk, "Payday Lending: Do the Costs Justify the Price?," FDIC Center for Financial Research, *Working Paper No. 2005-09*, June 2005, p. 1.

[2] *Ibid.*

[3] *Ibid.*, p. 2.

to jump and a new monetary policy led to less control over interest rates.

In the mid-1980s, the development of mortgage-backed securities expanded the amount of capital available for mortgage lending. During the Great Depression, the government had created Fannie Mae (the Federal National Mortgage Association) to buy FHA-insured mortgages from banks in order to increase the liquidity of the mortgage market. In 1968, the government privatized Fannie Mae and allowed it to purchase uninsured mortgages. The government created two more entities, Ginnie Mae (Government National Mortgage Association) and Freddie Mac (Federal Home Loan Mortgage Corp.), to buy mortgages from different segments of the market.

By the early '80s, these government-chartered corporations began to package the loans they bought into mortgage-backed securities that they sold to banks and pension funds. Soon large commercial banks also began buying mortgages from lenders, creating securities and selling them to investors — in direct competition with the government-created groups. As these securities became more sophisticated, with different grades of risk, the number of investors increased and began to include mutual funds, life insurance companies and foreigners.

By the 1990s, homeownership rates began to rise again, a trend accelerated by the advent of sophisticated computer programs using credit scoring to assess the risk of borrowers and loans. Since then, lenders have been able to develop mortgages tailored to individual home buyers. Just as in the credit card industry, the higher the risk the higher the rate.

While these changes have made mortgages available to more Americans than ever before, many consumer advocates say some home buyers have been placed in mortgages that they cannot afford, leading to the recent increase in default rates and foreclosures.

Debt Collectors' Tactics Questioned

Number of consumers' complaints skyrocketed

After Stephanie Clark and her husband fell behind on their car payments, the company that loaned them the money to buy the car hired a debt collector. According to a suit filed by the Clarks, the collector threatened them with arrest and impersonated a Verizon Wireless employee to obtain their cell phone records.

The finance company and the Clarks settled before the trial. [1]

Similar stories have abounded in recent years as so-called third-party debt collectors reportedly have adopted heavy-handed and sometimes even illegal practices to collect unpaid balances for credit card issuers, banks, retail stores, hospitals and government agencies.

As U.S. consumer debt ballooned in recent years, the ranks of the nation's professional debt collectors have more than doubled — from 70,000 employees in 1990 to 150,000 in 2005. The beefed up third-party collection agencies — which often buy uncollected debt for pennies on the dollar — succeeded in returning $39.3 billion in uncollected debt to creditors in 2005, according to the industry. [2]

As the nation's debt and number of debt collectors have risen, so have complaints about their collection tactics. According to the Federal Trade Commission (FTC), complaints against third-party debt collectors rose 560 percent between 1999 and 2005. In fact, consumers filed more complaints against third-party debt collectors in 2005 than against any other industry, according to the FTC's annual report. [3]

Most complaints involved allegations that the collectors:
- Demanded larger payments than are permitted by law;
- Harassed alleged debtors or others by calling repeatedly or continuously;
- Used false or misleading threats if consumers failed to pay alleged debts;
- Made impermissible calls to consumers' workplaces;
- Revealed alleged debts to third parties;
- Failed to send consumers written notices of the amount of debt owed, the name of the creditor, and the consumers' right to dispute the debt in writing within 30 days; and
- Failed to verify disputed debts.

"We were as shocked by the increase as the FTC and equally concerned as an industry," says Rozanne Anderson, general counsel for the Association of Credit and Collection Professionals — known as ACA International. Anderson says her organization filed a Freedom of Information Act request with the FTC so it could conduct a study of the complaints, which should be completed this spring. It wants to know whether consumers calling the FTC are

CURRENT SITUATION

Risk or Race?

Countrywide Financial Corp., the nation's largest mortgage lender, is reviewing loans to its 4,500 black and Hispanic borrowers in New York after the state's attorney general claimed the company was charging minorities higher mortgage rates than whites with similar credit histories. The company has denied any wrongdoing and said that once it completes its review it expects to find few such cases of discrimination.

In the past, racial discrimination in mortgage lending was easy to spot: When it occurred, minorities were simply denied access to mortgage credit. But with the proliferation of adjustable-rate mortgages, interest-only mortgages and other novel mortgage products and a better accounting for credit risk, mortgage lending to minorities has exploded in the last decade. Over a recent eight-year period, "home purchase lending to Hispanic borrowers increased by 159 percent and to African-American borrowers by 93 percent, while lending to whites grew by just 29 percent," according to the Joint Center for Housing Studies at Harvard University. [21]

Thus, the issue of discrimination has shifted from a question of access to a question of price.

As a Harvard study recently put it, "There is concern that some high-cost lenders actively seek out minority applicants who may be vulnerable to deceptive, high-pressure marketing tactics due to their limited product options and limited knowledge of the mortgage market." [22]

doing so to clarify what collection techniques are allowed or to actually lodge a complaint.

"That differentiation is extremely significant to the industry," says Anderson. "We intend to either do a better job of educating the general public and/or educating members of the industry about their duties under the law." The industry is regulated under the 1978 Fair Debt Collection Practices Act, which bans certain collection methods.

But the FTC says the calls are clearly complaints, not queries. "The numbers we report in our annual reports are all complaints, which is one category of inquiries," says Peggy Twohig, the agency's associate director for financial practices. "We are very concerned about the increase."

While the industry says it shares that concern, it points out in its literature that the 66,627 complaints filed in 2005 represent less than 1 percent of the total number of contacts between debt collectors and consumers. But the FTC says the problem may actually be worse than it appears. The FTC believes the complaints "represent just a small percentage of the total number of consumers who actually encounter problems with debt collectors," says the FTC report. Many consumers just don't call, possibly because they don't know what the agency does.

According to the Federal Trade Commission, complaints against so-called third-party debt collectors rose 560 percent between 1999 and 2005.

Some consumer advocates say the FTC is slow to investigate debt collectors, pointing out that the agency has initiated only about a dozen enforcement actions in the past six years. Twohig counters that there are several investigations going on right now. Besides, she adds, focusing only on the number of cases misses the point.

"You have to look at how we're enforcing the law," she says. "We've gone into federal court and asked for the immediate halting of the illegal practices and significant monetary remedies." For instance, in July 2005, a New Jersey federal court awarded the agency a record $10.2 million judgment against Check Investors, Inc., for, among other things, falsely threatening consumers with arrest to extract more money than was owed.

The FTC has also recommended several times that Congress close loopholes in the 1978 law and clarify the responsibilities of collection agencies. So far, there has been no legislative action.

---

[1] Sewall Chan, "An Outcry Rises as Debt Collectors Play Rough," *The New York Times*, July 5, 2006, p. A1.

[2] "Value of Third-Party Debt Collection to the U.S. Economy: Survey and Analysis," Price Waterhouse Coopers, June 27, 2006, p. ii.

[3] "Annual Report to Congress: Fair Debt Collection Practices Act," Federal Trade Commission, 2001-2006.

Numerous studies — from federal regulators, university researchers and consumer advocates — show that minorities are more likely to get a high-priced, subprime loan than whites with comparable incomes. One study even showed that the disparity is worse for well-off minorities. "While lower-income African-American borrowers were 2.4 times as likely to receive a loan from a sub-prime lender as lower-income white borrowers, upper-income African-American borrowers were 3.0 times more likely to receive such loans as upper-income white borrowers." [23]

But mortgage lenders say the studies are flawed because they don't take into account borrowers' credit risk, which is generally worse among minorities. Credit risk includes factors like late-payments history, bankruptcy filings and type of outstanding debt.

If those measures were taken into account, lenders say, there would be little evidence of discrimination. "This is a strictly risk-based thing going on here," says Dinham of the National Association of Mortgage Brokers and a broker himself in Texas. "As a rule, in my business, we don't discriminate on any basis."

Researchers, however, don't generally have access to that kind of credit-history data. Mortgage lenders say it's proprietary and usually won't release it. "There are periodically a group of lenders who will make an arrangement with a research organization to assess this kind of credit risk data," says William Apgar, a senior scholar at the Joint Center for Housing Studies. "But often those studies are not subject to any kind of peer review."

Major Sources of Federal Student Aid

Loan Providers

Federal Family Education Loan Program (FFELP) — private lenders make federally guaranteed student loans in partnership with school financial aid offices.

William D. Ford Federal Direct Loan Program — federal government directly makes federally guaranteed student loans to borrowers.

Perkins Loan Program — participating schools combine their own funds with a federal contribution to make loans to students with the greatest financial need.

Types of Loans Provided by FFELP & Direct Loan program

Subsidized Federal Stafford Loans — for students who pass a financial-needs test. Federal government pays all interest costs while borrowers are in school.

Unsubsidized Federal Stafford Loans — for students who do not meet a financial-needs test or need to supplement subsidized loans. Students are responsible for all interest costs, although interest payments may be deferred during school.

Federal PLUS Loans — for parents of dependent undergraduate students.

Federal Consolidation Loans — for borrowers who want to combine eligible loans into a single loan with longer repayment terms and lower monthly payments.

Federal Grants

Federal Pell Grant — provided to undergraduates and considered a foundation of federal financial aid. Unlike a loan, it does not have to be repaid. (Maximum award for 2006-07 and 2007-08: $4,050)

Federal Supplemental Educational Opportunity Grant — for undergraduates with exceptional financial need. (Maximum: $4,000)

Academic Competitiveness Grant — for students who successfully complete a rigorous high school program. (Maximum: $1,300).

National Science and Mathematics Access to Retain Talent Grant (Smart Grant) — for third- and fourth-year undergraduates who are eligible for the Pell Grant and who are majoring in physical, life or computer sciences, mathematics, technology or engineering, or in a foreign language determined critical to national security. Students must have a cumulative grade-point average of 3.0 in their major. (Maximum: $4,000)

Source: U.S. Department of Education

Student Debt Soars

In the last decade, there has been extraordinary growth in student loans. In 2004 nearly two-thirds of graduates from four-year schools carried student loan debt compared with fewer than one-half in 1993. Not only are more students borrowing to pay for college, they're borrowing larger amounts. Debt levels for graduating seniors increased by 58 percent during the past decade — averaging just over $19,000 after accounting for inflation. [24]

Tonya Walrond, a 21-year-old business administration major, was already approaching that figure after only two years at a private college in Florida. She owes $17,000 through federally guaranteed student loans. Grants and a part-time job also helped to cover college costs, but not completely, and last year Walrond came up short. She owes the school $3,000 in tuition, so she was not allowed to re-enroll this past fall. And the school won't release her transcripts to the less expensive public college she now attends in her home state of New York.

"That's the depressing part about it," says Walrond. "I went to school for two years, and it's like it didn't count. And I'm in debt for it."

Many factors account for the rise in student debt. College tuition is soaring, and not just at pricey private institutions. [25] The inflation-adjusted cost of attending a public university has climbed 35 percent in the past five years, one of the largest increases on record. [26] But federal Pell Grants — which low-come students like Walrond rely on and do not have to be repaid — have not kept up with college prices. Twenty years ago, the maximum Pell Grant would have covered 60 percent of tuition, fees, room and board at a public four-

Nevertheless, several of the studies have shown disparities. Apgar says the evidence is indisputable that there is some discrimination in mortgage lending. "But the question is a matter of extent."

Should Congress regulate credit card rates and fees?

YES
Tamara Draut
Director of Economic Opportunity, Demos

Written for *CQ Researcher*, February 2007

Stagnant wages and rising costs for essentials have forced many families to use credit cards to make ends meet. The deregulation of the credit card industry, which began in the late 1970s, has been a mixed blessing for Americans. It has expanded the availability of credit to include many individuals — but at a very high cost. Meanwhile, two Supreme Court rulings blocked states from protecting consumers from abusive credit card practices. And Congress has failed to step in and draw the line.

Today, unrestrained by meaningful guidelines like those that define fair-lending relationships in other financial services, the credit card industry is defined by capricious and unforgiving tactics. These include penalty fees of $39 or more for a tardy payment and interest rates of 29 percent and higher. Interest rate hikes are also applied retroactively to the existing balance, essentially raising the price of everything previously bought with the card. And, the clincher: Unlike in any other industry, a card company can change the terms of the agreement, including the annualized percentage rate (APR), at any time, for any reason.

This "gotcha" approach adds up to big profits for the issuing banks and empty pockets for consumers. Last year, the card companies collected more than $10 billion in fees alone, and overall the industry is one of the nation's most profitable, grossing in the range of $30 billion per year. This is due in no small part to the lack of any real parameters guiding the consumer/issuer relationship.

Rising debt has become a way of life for low- and middle-income households. Between 1990 and 2001, revolving consumer debt in America more than doubled, from $238 billion to $692 billion. Credit card debt continued to rise in the new century — increasing by 7.2 percent in 2004, totaling more than $820 billion by 2005. Meanwhile, the savings rate has steadily declined, and the number of people filing for bankruptcy since 1990 has more than doubled — to just over 2 million in 2005.

Families are overwhelmed by their debt and scared for their futures. After a decade of building up debt, they're worried that the next time a spouse gets laid off, the car breaks down or a child gets sick, their safety net will finally break. The statistics, and the personal stories of Americans everywhere, make it clear: There's a role for fair and reasonable parameters for the credit card industry.

NO
Kenneth J. Clayton
Managing Director of Card Policy, American Bankers Association

Written for *CQ Researcher*, February 2007

Price controls have never worked and never will. Economic performance depends upon a stable, efficient and secure means of exchanging value. Payment cards make this exchange possible 10,000 times every second. Nearly two-thirds of American families use payment cards routinely, taking for granted their convenience, reliability and security. Payment cards are not simply helping our economy along, they are driving it forward.

This is a direct result of strong competition within the industry and a wide range of consumer choices. The mere thought of imposing price controls can send a chill through the economy, just as it did in November 1991 when the Senate passed, after only a half-hour of debate, a cap on credit card interest rates. Recognizing that two-thirds of the economy is based on consumer spending, investors were not pleased, and the Dow Jones Industrial Average fell more than 120 points (nearly 4 percent) the next day. Fortunately, Congress quickly backed away from this disastrous policy.

Price controls do not make for sound economic policy. They hinder efficiency by creating room for other, less desirable forces to operate. These unintended consequences include long lines, shortages, paying in the black market or simply going without.

With more than 6,000 card issuers, the credit card market is among the most competitive in our economy. Industry competition, fueled in part by technological advancements, drove banks to adopt risk-based pricing methods, which in turn allows a broader spectrum of people to have access to credit. Whether young or old, high or low income, risk-based pricing allows individuals who manage their debt obligations well to get the best and lowest price for loans. Because their history suggests a greater potential for loss, individuals who have missed payments or pushed the boundaries of their credit limits naturally pay more.

In either case, customers have a wide range of choices if they are unhappy with their current card. Capping interest rates will only curtail credit access, meaning millions of card holders could lose their card privileges — a devastating body blow to the economy and to consumers. Capping fees makes no sense either. Most cardholders do not pay fees associated with being late or over their credit limit. This is because fees of this nature are completely avoidable and controlled by the individual.

AP Photo/Rich Pedroncelli

A student at California State University, San Marcos, parodies California Gov. Arnold Schwarzenegger during a protest in April 2005 against budget cuts and the rise in tuition and student fees at California's public colleges and universities. In the last decade, there has been extraordinary growth in student loans. In 2004 nearly two-thirds of graduates from four-year schools carried student loan debt compared with fewer than one-half in 1993.

the percentage a decade earlier. Twenty percent said student debt caused them to delay having children, up from 12 percent. [28]

President George W. Bush's proposed budget for fiscal year 2008 would raise to $4,600 the maximum Pell Grant, which has been frozen at $4,050 for the past four years. If approved, the increase would be the largest in 30 years. But the plan would partially finance that increase by diverting funds from other, smaller grant programs for low-income students, upsetting many college administrators. The president would also cut subsidies to private lenders who make federally guaranteed student loans.

"It's draconian," says Joe Belew, president of the Consumer Bankers Association. "They're looking at the private sector as a bottomless pit for cost savings." Belew says cuts in the subsidized interest rate to private lenders would drive many out of the student loan business.

The association doesn't much like ideas proposed by Congress either. Legislators are also looking to squeeze the profits of the private lending industry in order to finance relief for student borrowers. In January, the House easily passed legislation to cut in half the interest rate for federally subsidized loans to college students, to be phased in over five years. It would be funded by increased fees and smaller subsidies to private lenders. The Project on Student Debt, a nonprofit research and advocacy organization, estimates that the bill would save a student with $20,000 in debt roughly $4,000 over the life of a 10-year loan.

While the measure would not increase Pell Grants, Bob Shireham, the project's executive director, still calls it "a good first step." But he'd like to see Congress do more. "It's important for student loans to have enough borrower protections on the back end so that they aren't driving you into an impoverished situation post graduation."

A Senate bill sponsored by Massachusetts Democrat Edward M. Kennedy would also cut the interest rate on student loans and would create a Fair Payment Assurance program that would effectively cap loan payments at less than 10 percent of a borrower's income. It would also raise the maximum Pell Grant to $5,100.

The measure is being considered by the Senate Finance Committee, and Shireham expects the Senate to follow the House's lead and pass legislation that gives some relief to student borrowers.

year college. Now the maximum Pell Grant meets just 33 percent of those costs. [27] So students are turning increasingly to loans.

"Student debt is the coming catastrophe for the middle class," says Harvard Law School's Warren, who specializes in bankruptcy and consumer debt. "At the very moment that a young person wants to marry, start a family and buy a home, student debt acts as an anchor," Warren says, "keeping them financially vulnerable and often unable to make ends meet."

In a 2002 study, 14 percent of young adults reported that student loans caused them to delay marriage, double

Impact of Bankruptcy Law

Even as student, mortgage and credit card debt have increased — factors that can drive people into bankruptcy — bankruptcy filings have fallen dramatically, reaching their lowest levels since the 1980s in 2006.

That was no surprise. It followed a tremendous surge in filings the year before, as debtors rushed to their lawyers and the courthouse before a tough, new bankruptcy law went into effect in mid-October, 2005. The Bankruptcy Abuse Prevention and Consumer Protection Act raised filing fees, mandated credit counseling, increased paperwork and required those above a certain income level to enter a debt-repayment plan.

The extent of the drop-off in bankruptcies was surprising, however. More people filed for bankruptcy in the last quarter of 2005 than in all of 2006 combined.

Laura Fisher, a spokeswoman for the American Bankers Association, which lobbied for the new law, interpreted the decline as an indication that "some of the abuse has been wrung out of the system." [29]

But Lois Lupica, a scholar at the American Bankruptcy Institute, strongly disagrees. While she says it's too early to know exactly why bankruptcy filings dropped so sharply, abuse was never a problem. "I've never seen significant statistical evidence of abuse of the system," she says. "The vast majority of people who file are in a troubled financial place." Many are coping with job loss, illness or divorce, she said.

The higher cost of filing for bankruptcy might help to explain the dramatic decline, says Harvard's Warren. "That falls hardest on the poorest families in financial trouble, who might be shut out of the system," she adds. "This is a perversion of what the bill was designed to do, and that was to squeeze the richest families, not the poorest."

Warren is about to survey those in bankruptcy, which may shed some light on the trend in filings. But in the meantime, she is hearing reports that the new statute has emboldened debt collectors. Some debt collectors may be telling people that bankruptcy has been "repealed" and is no longer an option. "It doesn't matter if it's true," says Warren. "What matters is [whether] people believe it's true."

According to a survey of American Bankruptcy Institute members, most bankruptcy lawyers, judges and researchers believe bankruptcy filings will increase by at least 20 percent in 2007. "The economy is still fragile for many people," says Lupica. The usual factors of illness,

Workmen for a company that specializes in mortgage foreclosures clear out a house in June 2005 in Columbus, Ohio. Mortgages tailored to individual home buyers have enabled more Americans to buy homes, but many consumer advocates say some home buyers have been placed in mortgages that they cannot afford, leading to the recent increase in default rates and foreclosures.

divorce and job loss are not going away, and the rise in mortgage defaults and foreclosures may signal growing financial distress.

OUTLOOK

Contactless Credit

The average American has four credit cards, a number that is not expected to grow rapidly in the coming years, according to the Federal Reserve Bank of Kansas City. [30] So, credit card issuers are looking for ways to convince consumers to use those cards more, especially for small cash purchases.

According to Peppercoin, a payments-technology company, consumers spend $1.3 trillion a year on purchases of less than $5, and more than 99 percent of those are paid for with cash. [31] To credit card issuers, that's a huge untapped market.

One way to convince consumers to switch from cash to plastic is to increase convenience, and so card issuers are turning to cards that consumers wave, rather than swipe. "Just as the magnetic stripe expedited card payments as compared to impression machines and telephone authorization," says the Kansas City Fed, "contactless technology has the potential to do the same."

New technology allows cards or key fobs to be waved just above a scanner, and no signature is required. Drug stores like CVS, Duane Reade and Walgreens; fast-food outlets like Kentucky Fried Chicken and McDonald's; convenience stores like 7-Eleven and theater chains like AMC Theaters have begun to accept these new devices. Such "contactless" transactions take less than half the time of using cash, and some retailers say consumers spend more when using them.

The technology seems to be growing in popularity. Several financial institutions are offering the devices nationwide, including American Express, JPMorgan Chase, Bank of America, Citibank, KeyBank and WellsFargo. Already, 13 million contactless cards or key fobs are in the hands of consumers — a doubling since 2005 — and more than 30,000 U.S. merchants are now equipped to accept them, according to Celent, a research and advisory firm. Celent predicts consumers will use contactless payment for 15 percent of all purchases by 2011. [32] Some financial institutions are even teaming up with wireless phone companies to turn cell phones into waveable payment devices.

But convincing consumers to substitute waveable devices for cash might run into hurdles if financial institutions can't prove they're safe. Last October, a computer science professor at the University of Massachusetts, Kevin Fu, reported that he and his team of researchers were able to steal information from contactless cards. They had collected 20 of the cards, reversed engineered them, and made a scanner.

"We've demonstrated [that just by] walking by somebody in an elevator," said Fu, "you can skim all of their credit card information through their clothing, through their jeans, through their wallet." [33]

NOTES

1. Federal Reserve Board, "Flow of Funds Accounts of the United States," Tables D.1, D.2, Dec. 7, 2006.

2. Christian Weller and Derek Douglas, "One Nation Under Debt," *Challenge*, January/February 2007, p. 5.

3. Christian Weller, "Drowning in Debt," Center for American Progress, May 2006, p. 33.

4. "Recent Changes in U.S. Family Finances: Evidence from the 2001 and 2004 Survey of Consumer Finances," *Federal Reserve Board Bulletin*, February 2006, p. A1-A2.

5. "The New Rules Economy: A Policy Framework for the 21st Century," *Third Way*, February 2007, p. 7.

6. James Sherk, "Shared Prosperity," The Heritage Foundation, Oct. 16, 2006.

7. "National Delinquency Survey Results, Third Quarter 2006," The Mortgage Bankers Association, p. 2-3.

8. "The Plastic Safety Net: The Reality Behind Debt in America," Demos, October 2005, pp. 8, 10.

9. "Credit Cards: Increased Complexity in Rates and Fees Heightens Need for More Effective Disclosures to Consumers," Government Accountability Office, September 2006, p. 1.

10. Christian Weller, "Pushing the Limit: Credit Card Debt Burdens American Families," Center for American Progress, July 9, 2006, p. 11.

11. "Joint Recommendations of Consumer Groups on the Eve of the January 25, 2007 U.S. Senate Banking Committee Oversight Hearing on Unfair Credit Card Practices."

12. Bureau of Economic Analysis, U.S. Department of Commerce, "Gross Domestic Product: Fourth Quarter 2006," Table 7, Jan. 31, 2007.

13. National Association of Realtors, www.realtor.org/ research.nsf/pages/EcoIndicator?OpenDocument.

14. Lendol Calder, *Financing the American Dream: A Cultural History of Consumer Credit* (2001), p. 26.

15. *Ibid.*, p. 19.

16. "Credit History: The Evolution of Consumer Credit in America," Federal Reserve Bank of Boston, p. 8.

17. Calder, *op. cit.*, p. 20.

18. Robin Stein, "Secret History of the Credit Card," "Frontline," www.pbs.org/wgbh/pages/frontline/ shows/credit/more/rise.html.

19. *Ibid.*

20. "Evolution of the U.S. Housing Finance System," U.S. Department of Housing and Urban Development, April 2006, p. 6.

21. William C. Apgar and Allegra Calder, "The Dual Mortgage Market: The Persistence of Discrimination

in Mortgage Lending," Joint Center for Housing Studies, Harvard University, December 2005, p. 2.

22. *Ibid.*

23. Debbie Gruenstein Bocian, Keith S. Ernst and Wei Li, "Unfair Lending: The Effect of Race and Ethnicity on the Price of Subprime Mortgages," The Center for Responsible Lending, May 31, 2006, p. 7.

24. "Quick Facts About Student Debt," The Project on Student Debt, April 2006, p. 1.

25. For background, see Tom Price, "Rising College Costs," *CQ Researcher*, Dec. 5, 2003, pp. 1013-1044.

26. "2006 Trends in Higher Education Series: Executive Summary," p. 4, www.collegeboard.com/trends.

27. "2006 Trends in Higher Education Series: Pell Grants," p. 1, www.collegeboard.com/trends.

28. "Generation Debt: Student Loans, Credit Cards, and Their Consequences," Demos, Winter 2007, p. 2.

29. Helen Huntley, "Quiet in the Court," *St. Petersburg Times*, Oct. 8, 2006, p. 1D.

30. www.cardweb.com/cardtrak/news/2007/february/16a. html; "Contactless: The Next Payment Wave?" Terri Bradford, Federal Reserve Board of Kansas City, December 2005, p. 1.

31. Nancy Feig, "Contactless Cards Take a Bite Out of Small Cash Transactions," *Bank Systems & Technology*, Oct. 1, 2006, p. 12.

32. "Contactless and the Dawn of a New Payments Era," Celent press release, Sept. 5, 2006.

33. Eva Schuman, "Concerns About Contactless Card Security Could Slow Online Sales," *EWeek.com*, Nov. 3, 2006.

BIBLIOGRAPHY

Books

Calder, Lendol G., *Financing the American Dream: A Cultural History of Consumer Credit*, Princeton University Press, 1999.
A history professor at Augustana College examines the history of consumer credit from the age of the Pilgrims through the 20th century.

Manning, Robert D., *Credit Card Nation: The Consequences of America's Addiction to Credit*, Basic Books, 2000.
A sociology professor at the Rochester Institute of Technology explores Americans' attitude toward debt.

Warren, Elizabeth, and Amelia Warren Tyagi, *The Two-Income Trap: Why Middle-Class Mothers and Fathers Are Going Broke*, Basic Books, 2003.
A Harvard law professor and her daughter, a former McKinsey consultant, argue that the two-parent, middle-class family is on the brink of financial disaster.

Articles

Bajaj, Vikas, and Ron Nixon, "Subprime Loans Going from Boon to Housing Bane," *The New York Times*, Dec. 6, 2006, p. C1.
Minority buyers are especially hurt as interest rates rise.

Conkey, Christopher, "Credit-Card Issuers on the Spot," *The Wall Street Journal*, Jan. 25, 2007, p. A4.
The Senate Banking Committee holds hearings on credit card companies' disclosure, marketing and billing strategies.

Eckholm, Erik, "Seductively Easy, Payday Loans' Often Snowball," *The New York Times*, Dec. 23, 2006, p. A1.
Payday lending is a growing industry and may trap consumers in a cycle of debt.

"Panhandlers Beware," *The Economist*, Nov. 18, 2006, p. 81.
Credit card companies try to convince consumers to use "contactless" cards instead of cash for small purchases.

Prevost, Lisa, "The Homeowner's Day of Reckoning," *The Boston Globe Magazine*, Oct. 15, 2006, p. 27.
As property values soared, homeowners converted their home equity to cash, and now some may lose their homes as the real estate market softens.

Tedeschi, Bob, "A Move to Set 'Suitability' Rules," *The New York Times*, Nov. 17, 2006, p. 11.
Consumer advocates pressure the government to make mortgage originators legally responsible for placing home buyers in financially affordable loans.

Reports and Studies

"Annual Report 2006: Fair Debt Collection Practices Act," Federal Trade Commission, April 2006.
The government agency reports on the types of consumer complaints it has received about debt collectors and divides the complaints into categories.

"Consumer Counseling and Education Under BAPCPA: Year One Report," National Foundation for Credit Counseling, Oct. 16, 2006.
The report summarizes a survey of foundation members about the impact of the 2005 federal bankruptcy legislation on creditors seeking counseling and on the counseling firms themselves.

"Credit Cards: Increased Complexity in Rates and Fees Heightens Need for More Effective Disclosures to Consumers," Government Accountability Office, September 2006.
The investigative arm of Congress studies the credit card industry and determines that disclosures in credit card agreements are poorly written and confusing.

"The Dual Mortgage Market: The Persistence of Discrimination in Mortgage Lending," Joint Center for Housing Studies at Harvard University, December 2005.

The authors review past studies of housing discrimination and conclude that discrimination against minorities exists, although its extent is unclear.

"Losing Ground: Foreclosures in the Subprime Market and Their Cost to Homeowners," Center for Responsible Lending, December 2006.
Researchers at a consumer advocacy and research organization examine trends in the subprime market and determine that homeowners in this fast-growing segment of the market have experienced historically high foreclosure rates, despite low interest rates and economic growth.

"The Plastic Safety Net: The Reality Behind Debt in America," Center for Responsible Lending, October 2005.
The center reports on how consumers use credit cards.

"The Residential Mortgage Market and Its Economic Context in 2007," Mortgage Bankers Association, Jan. 30, 2007.
The association's senior economist describes how economic trends are affecting housing and mortgage markets.

"Trends in Higher Education Series," College Board, 2006.
The College Board, which administers college entrance exams, provides detailed statistics on college pricing and financing.

For More Information

American Bankers Association, 1120 Connecticut Ave., N.W., Washington, DC 20036; (800) 226-5377; www.aba.com. Represents banks on issues of national importance.

American Bankruptcy Institute, 44 Canal Center Plaza, Suite 404, Alexandria, VA 22314; (703) 739-0800; www.abiworld.org. Research and education organization dealing with insolvency matters.

Center for American Progress, 1333 H St., N.W., 10th Floor, Washington, DC 20005; (202) 682-1611; www.americanprogress.org. Liberal think tank headed by John D. Podesta, former chief of staff to President Bill Clinton and a law professor at Georgetown University.

Center for Responsible Lending, 302 W. Main St., Durham, NC 27701; (919) 313-8500; www.responsiblelending.org. Research and policy organization dedicated to protecting homeownership and family wealth by working to curb abusive financial practices.

Community Financial Services Association of America, 515 King St., Suite 300, Alexandria, VA 22314; (703) 684-1029; www.cfsa.net. The trade association of payday lenders that monitors state regulation of the industry.

Consumer Bankers Association, 1000 Wilson Blvd., Suite 2500, Arlington, VA 22209-3912; (703) 276-1750. The trade association for retail banks.

Consumer Federation of America, 1620 I St., N.W., Suite 200, Washington, DC 20006; (202) 387-6121; www.consumerfed.org. Advocates for pro-consumer policies.

Demos, 220 Fifth Ave., 5th Floor, New York, NY 10001; (212) 633-1405; www.demos.org. Think tank that promotes expanded economic opportunity for all.

Fannie Mae, 3900 Wisconsin Ave., N.W., Washington, DC 20016-2892; (800) 732-6643, (202) 752-7000; www.fanniemae.com. The Federal National Mortgage Corp. is a government created, publicly traded company that works with lenders to make sure they don't run out of mortgage funds, so more people can achieve their goal of homeownership.

Mortgage Bankers Association, 1919 Pennsylvania Ave., N.W., Washington, DC 20006; (202) 557-2700; www.mortgagebankers.org. National association for the mortgage industry.

National Association of Mortgage Brokers, 7900 Westpark Dr., Suite T-309, McLean, VA 22102; (703) 342-5900; www.namb.org. Trade association for mortgage brokers.

National Foundation for Credit Counseling, 801 Roeder Rd., Suite 900, Silver Spring, MD 20910; (301) 589-5600; www.nfcc.org. Promotes national agenda for financially responsible behavior.

Project on Student Debt, 2054 University Ave., Suite 500, Berkeley, CA 94704; (510) 559-9509; www.projectonstudentdebt.org. Promotes cost-effective solutions for making college affordable.

13

Controlling the Internet

Marcia Clemmitt

Waving "Orange Revolution" flags, Ukrainians gather in Kiev's Independence Square on Aug. 24, 2005, the 14th anniversary of Ukraine's break from the Soviet Union. During the Orange Revolution, which pressured the government to overturn 2004 election results as fraudulent, community Web sites posted information about where protesters needed assistance.

From *CQ Researcher*,
May 12, 2006.

Critics of a proposed, new America Online (AOL) policy discovered in April that AOL apparently was blocking e-mails mentioning DearAOL.com — a Web site set up by 600 organizations opposed to the policy.

"I tried to e-mail my brother-in-law about DearAOL.com, and AOL sent me a response as if he had disappeared," said Wes Boyd, co-founder of MoveOn.org, a liberal political group. "When I sent him an e-mail without the DearAOL.com link, it went right through." [1]

AOL blamed the blockage on a brief technical glitch. "A glitch is a glitch is a glitch," said AOL Communication Director Nicholas Graham. "As many as 65 other domains . . . were impacted," even though they had no connection to DearAOL. [2]

But many DearAOL activists note the timing of the blockage suspiciously coincided with their latest petition drive opposing AOL's plan to allow mass mailers to pay a fee to bypass AOL's spam filters.

Activists fear that under AOL's proposed rule change, messages from "poorer" users — such as nonprofit charities and political groups — would be blocked while commercial ads would sail through. They also worry that major portions of the Internet would be off-limits to citizens of certain countries.

The DearAOL activists note that it's not the first time a big Internet service provider (ISP) has blocked access to content it opposed, nor does the collateral blocking of unaffiliated sites necessarily prove it was an accident, given that last year Telus, a Canadian phone company and ISP, blocked access to a Web site run by its striking employees' union. In the process, access to more than 700 unrelated Web sites was blocked. [3]

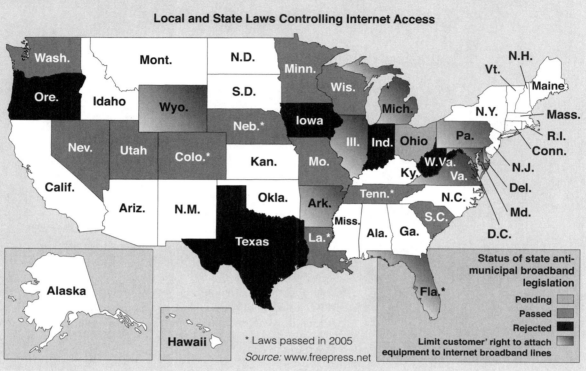

Internet Access Limited by 20 States

Twenty states have laws restricting municipally operated broadband lines and/or laws limiting consumers' right to attach equipment to their Internet lines. Five of the anti-municipal broadband laws were passed in 2005.

Local and State Laws Controlling Internet Access

Status of state anti-municipal broadband legislation

- Pending
- Passed
- Rejected
- Limit customer' right to attach equipment to Internet broadband lines

* Laws passed in 2005

Source: www.freepress.net

In the United States, the battle for Internet control is playing out over revision of the landmark 1996 Telecommunications Act, which deregulated the telecommunications industry to increase competition. [4] Much of the debate centers on so-called Net neutrality — or requiring ISPs to treat all Internet content equally.

Neutrality advocates say the policy has enabled the Internet to foster rapid innovation. With no gatekeeper regulating traffic, tiny start-up companies and college students have created a plethora of innovative products and services — from instant messaging and podcasting to e-Bay, search engines and Amazon.com. "The key to the Net's extraordinary innovation is that it doesn't allow a term like 'allow,'" wrote Lawrence Lessig, a professor of cyberlaw at Stanford University. [5]

But telephone and cable companies, which own the wires over which most Internet traffic travels, want to replace the Net's traditional "open-pipe" structure with a system of priority channels that "sniff" data to determine content and shift some traffic to high-priority lanes. Such a system is needed, the companies say, to ensure higher quality of service for customers downloading bandwidth-gobbling video, for example, and to raise funds to pay for extending fiber-optic cable and other infrastructure to carry today's much faster broadband Internet.

But media advocates say telephone and cable companies mostly want to protect their key businesses — video and voice transmissions — from new competitors offering the same services via broadband.

The big ISPs hope to remake the Internet in the "entertainment model," where big-money players control distribution channels, determining which content makes it onto the movie or television screen, says Jeffrey Chester, executive director of the Center for Digital Democracy. "Phone and cable companies know that if there's an open wire, their business is over," now that broadband connections are fast enough to carry video and voice telephony. "They have to make sure that their own content can receive premium treatment."

Such a model, Chester argues, is dangerous for democracy because the Internet is not just an entertainment medium but also a forum for discussion of public issues. And if some information moves faster, then other information necessarily moves more slowly, he notes. The slower information may never be seen, he adds, which spells death to Web sites where visibility is key. If ISPs can shunt some information to slower lanes while reserving the fast lanes for selected content, what happens to "content necessary for civic participation?" he asks.

David Isenberg, a fellow at Harvard Law School's Berkman Center for the Internet and Society, agrees on the link between Internet freedom and democracy. Freedom of Internet communication is "fundamental to freedom of speech," and "violating it should be anathema to democracy," he says.

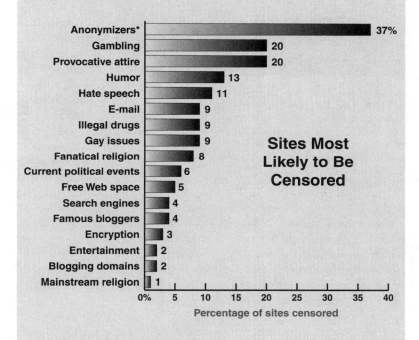

Off-Limits Web Sites

Sites that help Internet users in non-democratic countries avoid detection and those offering gambling are the most censored — after pornography and political dissent — among nations monitored by the OpenNet Initiative.

Sites Most Likely to Be Censored

Category	Percentage of sites censored
Anonymizers*	37%
Gambling	20
Provocative attire	20
Humor	13
Hate speech	11
E-mail	9
Illegal drugs	9
Gay issues	9
Fanatical religion	8
Current political events	6
Free Web space	5
Search engines	4
Famous bloggers	4
Encryption	3
Entertainment	2
Blogging domains	2
Mainstream religion	1

Percentage of sites censored

* Sites that help online users remain untraceable

Sources: Wired, OpenNet Initiative, Reporters Without Borders

Some members of Congress, mostly Democrats, are pushing so-called Net-neutrality legislation that would prohibit ISPs from prioritizing service by content. But after heavy lobbying by the cable and telephone industries, the House Energy and Commerce Committee on April 26 defeated a Net-neutrality amendment while finalizing its version of the telecom law overhaul. Chairman Joe L. Barton, R-Texas, said that while he supports the Federal Communications Commission (FCC) watching for potentially anti-competitive or censorial ISP treatment of Internet content, he doesn't believe "all the Draconian things" people predict will happen without a Net-neutrality amendment. [6]

A new group — the "Save the Internet" coalition — says it is rapidly gaining individual and institutional sup-

porters. By early May, the group claimed more than a half-million signatures on a petition demanding a Net-neutrality law. Backers range from the liberal MoveOn.org to conservative bloggers like "Instapundit" Glenn Reynolds and "Right Wing News." [7]

"Whenever you see people from the far left and the far right joining together about something that Congress is getting ready to do . . . what Congress is getting ready to do is basically un-American," said Craig Fields, director of Internet operations for Gun Owners of America. [8]

While some worry that powerful corporations want to stifle Internet freedom, others warn that various authoritarian governments in recent years have walled their citizens off from much of the Internet, even as they have promoted broadband use as an economy booster.

A worker helps install fiber-optic cable onto telephone lines in Louisville, Colo. President George W. Bush has called for "universal, affordable access for broadband technology by the year 2007," but critics say the goal can't be reached because of phone and cable company foot-dragging and the lack of a national broadband strategy.

Indeed, repressive governments have much to fear from an unfettered Internet. Modern telecommunications played a major role in Ukraine's "Orange Revolution," which "pressured the government to overturn its 2004 election results as fraudulent." [9] Demonstrators used cell phone messaging technology to gather "smart mobs" of protesters, while community Web sites posted information about where protesters needed assistance. [10]

China has promoted Internet use as a tool for economic growth while squelching certain content. With some 111 million Internet users, China is second only to the United States in total users but has strictly limited their access. China blocks Web sites, censors citizens' Web searches and tracks down people who publish critical opinions or information on blogs. The Chinese government — with the acquiescence of Google, Yahoo! and other search engines — not only censors Web sites that question government actions but also those dealing with teen pregnancy, homosexuality, dating, beer and even jokes. [11] (*See sidebar, p. 306.*)

Free-Internet advocates also complain that broadband rollout in the United States has stalled — particularly in rural areas. "This country needs a national goal . . . to have universal, affordable access for broadband technology by the year 2007," said President George W. Bush in March 2004. [12] But critics say that because of phone and cable company foot-dragging and the lack of a national broadband strategy, Bush's goal can't possibly be reached

and, in fact, the United States has fallen behind other industrialized countries in access to broadband. (*See graph, p. 304.*)

Installing fiber to carry broadband Internet to rural America is extremely expensive, says David Farber, distinguished career professor of computer science and public policy at Carnegie Mellon University. "I could run fiber to every ranch in Montana, but nobody would pay for it," he says. Nevertheless, private phone and cable companies are trying to block rural governments' efforts to offer residents broadband service on their own if the private market doesn't offer it or the service costs too much.

But low population density is not the obstacle to full broadband penetration so much as the lack of a national strategy to achieve that goal, says the advocacy group Free Press. It notes other low-density countries, such as Iceland and Canada, have more broadband coverage than the United States. [13]

As government, the telecom industry and Internet users debate control of the Net, here are some of the questions being discussed:

Is the global Internet in danger of being dismantled?

Enthusiasts say the Internet embodies the dream of a global medium allowing people on opposite sides of the planet to communicate as easily as if they were in the same room. Today, however, some say the global Internet is in danger of being fragmented into separate, unconnected networks.

For instance, authoritarian governments are building firewalls to block citizens' access to certain parts of the Net, especially the Web sites of opposition groups. In the past few years, China "has essentially shut its own Internet off from the world Internet," says Jean Camp, associate professor of informatics at Indiana University. "And they're just the first. Other countries could do it," too, increasing the likelihood of Internet fragmentation.

In late February, China set up a master list of new Chinese Internet addresses that will be maintained on Chinese-owned "root servers," according to Michael Geist, chairman of Internet and e-commerce law at University of Ottawa in Ontario, Canada. [14] Until now, worldwide coordination of Internet addresses has been handled by the U.S.-based Internet Corporation for Assigned Names and Numbers (ICANN). In addition, 13 so-called root-server computers scattered around the globe hold the master list that maps Web site names to the code numbers corresponding to their Internet addresses, or URLs.

China's action "doesn't mark the end of a global, interoperative Internet," but it demonstrates that countries may not always cooperate to keep the global Internet interoperable, said Geist. The global system would "break" if a parallel system duplicated existing addresses and diverted them to different computers, for example, or adopted different technical operating procedures.

The results of such an alternative Internet could be "creepy," says Lauren Weinstein, co-founder of People for Internet Responsibility. Different sites would pop up for the same Web address typed into computers in different countries. International e-mails might not get through, and variable or incompatible standards would stymie those trying to develop new business and communications applications, says Weinstein.

"The Internet . . . exists only if there is agreement about core functionality," he says. "For it to work, there has to be an awful lot of cooperation," and if enough countries become disgruntled with the current system, a split could develop.

But David Gross, coordinator for communications and information policy at the U.S. Department of State, says it's unlikely that a government would risk cutting itself off from the global community by launching an incompatible root system. "I have not heard any government official suggest that there would be benefits . . . in the creation of an independent root system" using existing Internet addresses. Gross said. "Any new network would . . . want to be interoperable with the current system."

Other pressures stem from simple growing pains. Organizations managing Internet technical standards are strained by rapid growth and the competing agendas of Web users and governments. [15]

As Internet users and uses proliferate, issues demanding collaborative solutions also proliferate, but today there is no specific structure to resolve them, says Weinstein. Despite its mind-boggling sophistication, the Internet is, in fact, in its "infancy," he says.

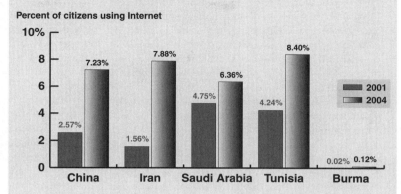

Internet Use Rose in Non-Democracies

Internet use has more than doubled in some of the world's most restrictive societies in recent years.

Percent of citizens using Internet

China: 2.57% (2001), 7.23% (2004)
Iran: 1.56% (2001), 7.88% (2004)
Saudi Arabia: 4.75% (2001), 6.36% (2004)
Tunisia: 4.24% (2001), 8.40% (2004)
Burma: 0.02% (2001), 0.12% (2004)

Legend: 2001, 2004

Sources: OpenNet Initiative; Reporters Without Borders

To keep the system interoperable, a new governance structure must develop that is embraced by an unusually diverse group of players, including governments, domestic and international businesses and individual users, says John Mathiason, an adjunct professor for international education and distance learning at Syracuse University. Today the world is just beginning to develop such a system, he says.

Dealing with copyright violations — such as the illegal downloading of music — is only one of many complications that must be worked out, he says. Currently, music copyright laws can be circumvented using servers located in countries that are not party to international copyright treaties, Mathiason says. If the Internet allows circumvention of national boundaries, he says, "You need to work out how conflicting schemes of copyright, commercial transactions and money are going to work."

Such protections don't yet exist, and more unresolved issues keep popping up, Mathiason says. "In a technical sense, the Internet is very robust," he says. "But, from a political point of view, it's very fragile. There is a great motivation by many people to keep it global and open. But when you have a conflict, then the issue is up in the air."

Today, ICANN is the closest thing to an Internet governing organization, although ostensibly it only manages certain technical parameters — mainly involving Internet addresses — and bases its decisions on input from businesses, governments and users around the world.

A World of Online Communities

Because the Internet developed free of corporate control, it's been a source of innovation, giving rise to new technologies and forums, including some that threaten traditional businesses and values. That's in stark contrast to the "entertainment model" phone and cable companies want to impose on the Internet, which critics say would limit such innovation.

A relative newcomer is **Meetup — www.meetup.com —** which helps people establish interest groups in their local communities. Founded in 2002, it claims 2 million members, including French-, Italian-, Japanese- and Spanish-speakers' groups, stay-at-home-moms' groups and book clubs.

Social-networking sites, where users post profiles and garner "friend" lists, are booming. **MySpace — www.myspace.com —** used by young people and celebrities alike, boasts 50 million members, and **Friendster — www.friendster.com —** 24 million. In South Korea, 15 million people — one-third of the population — belong to CyWorld. [1]

Partisan political networking and blogging sites have flourished over the past few years, but a recent entry, **Essembly — www.essembly.com —** hopes to exploit the social-networking phenomenon on a non-partisan basis. Essembly members post profiles, blog and list friends, as on MySpace, but they also participate in site-wide political dialogue.

Since Hurricane Katrina hit the Gulf Coast in 2005, a volunteer Internet service, the **Katrina People Finder Project — www.katrinalist.net —** has helped people locate missing loved ones. Along with a team of other computer experts, David Geilhufe developed a new computer tool, People Finder Information Formats, to aggregate data from various sources into one searchable, convenient source. [2]

New kinds of people-to-people links — often for the purpose of bypassing banks and other traditional institutions — pop up continually on the Internet. Several new sites feature people-to-people banking. **Kiva — www.kiva.org —** enables individuals in the United States to offer micro-financing help to entrepreneurs in developing countries by partnering with local organizations. Lenders can chip in capital in amounts as small as $25 to help people start bakeries, print shops and hair salons. Kiva reports 100 percent of its loans have been repaid or are being repaid.

Prosper — www.prosper.com — links up people who want to borrow money or are willing to lend it, for a return. Would-be borrowers seek cash to attend school, renovate a house, start a business or buy a big present for a 40th anniversary, and Prosper lenders name their own interest rates.

"The U.S. has been a very light-handed steward from the beginning," says Susan Crawford, an assistant professor of law at Cardozo Law School in New York City and ICANN board member. "ICANN becomes the issue of contention because the domain name system" — the Internet's system of coordinated address names and their corresponding code numbers — "is one of the very few choke points where you could censor content."

But even ICANN's "light-handed" approach to regulating the Internet has come under fire, in part because, while independent, it operates under the auspices of the U.S. Department of Commerce. For example, last summer, after long deliberation, ICANN announced that it would create a new "dot xxx" Internet domain where pornography Web sites could voluntarily register. The move was controversial worldwide but became more so when, shortly thereafter, ICANN reversed the decision at the behest of the Commerce Department, after heavy lobbying by conservative groups.

Commerce's intervention raised hackles and was seen as "very inappropriate," since it imposed a U.S. policy position on the Internet without consultation, says Crawford. In fact, Commerce's surprise intervention probably got more people worldwide to come down in favor of the xxx domain than would ever have done so otherwise, says Mathiason.

In another controversial move, ICANN in 2005 at the behest of the U.S. government, transferred ownership of the Internet domain for Kazakhstan — "dot kz" — from a group of Kazakhstan Internet users to an organization owned by the Kazakh government "without requiring consent from the existing owners," said Kieren McCarthy, a British technology writer. It also turned Iraq's domain over to a government-run group. [16]

"Previously, ICANN would take no action . . . unless both sides were in complete agreement," he said. "Now, ICANN had set itself up as the de facto world authority on who should run different parts of the Internet." [17]

In keeping with the Internet principle that the more people a network links the more value it has, Internet entrepreneurs and activists have long developed applications aimed at bringing more people online, sometimes for free.

For example, **FON software** — **http://en.fon.com/** — helps Wi-Fi (Wireless Fidelity) users worldwide get access to wireless Internet wherever they go, in return for registering to share their own wireless access with other FON members who pass by.

Internet services to help users get around government censorship also are under continual development by activists around the world.

Psiphon — developed by researchers at the University of Toronto — and the **Free Network Project**, or **Freenet**, developed by Scottish network technologist Ian Clarke, use computer networks in non-censoring countries to help people in information-censoring regimes communicate anonymously and freely.

To many Internet enthusiasts, the Net is first and foremost a publishing medium, and as faster broadband connections become the norm, the range of what's published continually expands. At photo-sharing site **Flickr** — **www.flickr.com** — members file, store and share their photos. And, true to the Internet's community-building tradition, Flickr members engage in plenty of two-way conversation about what they see. For example, in several popular ongoing games, Flickr mem-

bers snap and post mystery photos in a favorite city, like New York, Chicago or London, and fellow urban-enthusiasts try to guess where the photo was taken.

Among the newest wrinkles are sites where users can upload and share videos. The hot, new video site **YouTube** — **www.YouTube.com** — started up last year in the garage of two young techies looking to share home videos. Among the current offerings on the site created by Chad Hurley and Steve Chen — a sample guitar lesson posted by a group of music teachers advertising their pay services; a video art installation of a chair that disassembles then reassembles itself to music; performance clips of aspiring comics; and home and travel videos from around the world, from street dancing in Japan to scary driving behavior in India.

And of course, big advertisers also show up on YouTube, counting on the passing traffic — 30 million videos are viewed daily — to drum up interest in everything from new Nike sneakers to upcoming movies like "Superman Returns." [3]

[1] Micah L. Sifty, "Essembly.com: Finally, a Friendster for Politics," *Personal Democracy Forum*, March 13, 2006, www.personaldemocracy.com.

[2] Tin Zak, transcript, "Interview with Ethan Zuckerman," *Globeshakers*, Oct. 3, 2005, www.pghaccelerator.org.

[3] "YouTube: Way Beyond Home Videos," *Business Week Online*, April 10, 2006, www.businessweek.com.

Tension between the United States and other governments over non-Internet issues such as the Iraq war are exacerbating disgruntlement with ICANN, say some Internet scholars. "People just don't have the same good faith now that Washington will stay benevolent and not do anything to abuse its authority," said Lee McKnight, an associate professor of information economics and technology policy at Syracuse University's School of Information Studies. [18]

ICANN — and other organizations being considered to take over Internet management, such as the United Nations — are too likely to become enmeshed with the aims of big business and wealthy governments to make good long-term stewards, say many public-policy analysts. The only way to stave off a fragmented Net lies in civic groups stepping up to develop worldwide consensus on Internet issues, they argue.

"The world is on the path to more globalized governance" though the road is long, says Milton Mueller, a

professor of the political economy of communications at Syracuse University and co-founder of ICANN's Noncommercial Users Constituency.

Should telephone and cable companies be allowed to control the Internet?

As significantly faster broadband connections become the norm, telephone and cable companies that own the so-called last-mile wires connecting homes and businesses to the Internet say they need more control over how data travels and what kind of data users send in order to improve security, transmission quality and broadband access.

However, Internet-freedom advocates say the Internet only works when it's an "open pipe," with all data treated the same, and when users are free to place whatever software or hardware they want at the "pipe ends" without asking permission — just as electricity customers can plug in either a computer network or a toaster. Without these key qualities, the Internet cannot continue to foster business innovation and the open discussion crucial to democracy, say open-Net advocates.

Cable and telephone companies want permission to alter the open-pipe structure so they can "prioritize" and speed transmission of some data. Allowing companies to speed transmission of some content, such as video, would increase competition by allowing ISPs to specialize, says Chistopher Yoo, a professor of technology and entertainment law at Vanderbilt University Law School.

But others say allowing network owners to slow or speed data will mean that only wealthy individuals and companies would get higher-speed service, leaving poorer, non-commercial users and start-up businesses in slower-moving cyber obscurity. Such a system would also stifle innovation and allow cable and telephone companies to block, slow or charge exorbitant fees to companies like Vonage, which offers Voice Over Internet Protocol (VOIP), or telephone service via the Internet.

"Because the network is neutral, the creators of new Internet content and services need not seek permission . . . or pay special fees to be seen online," said Vinton Cerf, a key Internet software developer and Chief Internet Evangelist for Google. "As a result, we have seen an array of unpredictable new offerings" — from blogging to VOIP — "that might never have evolved had central control of the network been required." [19]

A neutral net is "critical" to America's competitiveness, he adds. "In places like Japan, Korea, Singapore and the United Kingdom, higher bandwidth and neutral broadband platforms are unleashing waves of innovation that threaten to leave the U.S. further and further behind," says Cerf.

In defending their proposal to charge customers more for priority transmission, some phone companies insist that some companies have already asked to be able to pay more for faster service.

"It's probably true that companies are . . . willing to pay for better treatment, but I think they're doing it out of fear," said Jeff Pulver, an Internet analyst. "It's legalized extortion." [20]

As for blocking telephone company competitors like Vonage, Ed Whitacre, CEO of SBC Communications, said he's not worried that his business will be eclipsed by online competitors, because he controls their transmission lines. "How do you think they're going to get to customers?" Whitacre asked. "Through a broadband pipe. Now what [Vonage and other Internet businesses]

would like to do is use my pipes free, but I ain't going to let them do that. . . . The Internet can't be free in that sense, because we and the cable companies have made an investment and for a Google or Yahoo or Vonage . . . to expect to use these pipes free is nuts!" [21]

But some technology scholars say Whitacre's plan could amount to double-charging. "This is a pretty dumb thing . . . to say," wrote Edward Felten, professor of computer science and public affairs at Princeton University. "If I were an SBC broadband customer, I'd be dying to ask Mr. Whitacre exactly what my monthly payment is buying if it isn't buying access to Google, Yahoo, Vonage and any other $%&^ Internet service I want to use." Many SBC customers sign up for the company's broadband services only to get access to Vonage or Google, so "why should Google pay SBC for this? Why shouldn't SBC pay Google instead?" [22]

Yoo acknowledges that there might be a "limited incentive" for cable Internet providers to discriminate against competing ISPs or for a telephone company to discriminate against VOIP providers. But "since different people want different things from the Internet," he says, encouraging "network diversity" would create a more vibrant marketplace where network providers can "compete on a basis other than price."

Moreover, allowing telecom companies to charge companies extra for priority online treatment would not put innovators at a disadvantage, as many fear, says James Gattuso, a senior fellow at the conservative Heritage Foundation. Instead, start-ups might be first in line to pay for priority transmission, because "if I were starting up a computing application, I would want to be able to say my new service is faster," he says. And start-ups "can get capital to pay for prioritized treatment," Gattuso says. "Money is easier to get than visibility." (*See "At Issue," p. 307.*)

Verizon's chief technology officer, Mark Wegleitner, says contrary to neutrality-advocates' fears, network owners have a strong incentive to help customers reach as many Web sites as possible. "We think the richest, broadest choice . . . makes for a happier consumer," he said. [23]

But others argue that if companies can "sniff" data packets and speed some information along faster than the rest it will hamper democratic discourse online. Web sites with controversial views might be relegated to the slow lanes, says the Center for Digital Democracy's Chester. And since nonprofits with "dot org" Internet addresses — where much of the civic discourse takes place online — often have little cash, their Internet communications will be shunted to the equivalent of a cyber "dirt road," he says. "This is being framed as a business story, but it's also a battle for the soul of our communications system."

In addition, start-up content providers could be strangled by red tape, he warns. "Today, anyone can open up a Web site and compete" for Internet users' attention. "Tomorrow, you'll have to show up at the office of the phone and cable companies" to get permission to attach your new application to the network, he says.

Advocates of a neutral Internet law say history indicates that phone and cable companies will not respect the Net's open nature on their own. According to Public Knowledge, a nonprofit that advocates for a free and open Internet, ISPs have tried to manipulate how broadband subscribers use the Net and have forbidden subscribers from using their broadband connections to provide content to the public — flying in the face of the Internet's tradition of offering publishing power to ordinary people. [24]

Other broadband contracts forbid home users from logging onto virtual private networks (VPNs), needed by telecommuters to access their workplace networks from home. And, until the FCC intervened last year, Madison River Telephone Co., which serves rural counties in Illinois and several Southern states, blocked subscribers from using Vonage's VOIP service. [25] The wireless company Clearwire, in Kirkland, Wash., blocks broadband services — such as streaming video or VOIP — that use a lot of bandwidth, and broadband providers have successfully lobbied for laws in nine states limiting how broadband consumers can use their own computers. [26]

Content blocking for ideological reasons also has occurred, according to Public Knowledge. Last year the Canadian ISP Telus blocked a Web site set up by a labor union representing Telus employees, who were in a dispute with the company. [27]

Should local governments be allowed to provide broadband Internet service?

Far fewer Americans have access to affordable broadband than citizens in other developed countries, and too few Americans have a choice of broadband Internet service providers — especially in rural areas. At the end of 2005, only 24 percent of rural households were using high-

speed Internet at home, compared to 39 percent of urban and suburban households. [28]

Running TV cables or upgrading phone lines to isolated homes in rural areas costs more and returns less profit than stringing cable or phone lines in high-density urban or suburban areas, so rural areas are usually the last to get new telecom services.

To overcome the problem, many local governments have begun installing or are considering installing their own networks, either on their own or in partnership with private companies. Local groups argue that such government-initiated efforts can spur more competitive broadband markets and widen access. But the cable and phone companies offering Internet services say government-provided broadband services siphon off subscription money that the companies could use to extend their broadband infrastructure.

In Sanborn, Iowa — population 1,300 — "we have lost nearly 50 percent of our subscribers" over the past four years to a municipal broadband service, not because of high prices or poor services but due to unfair competition, said Douglas Boone, CEO of the Premier Communications phone company, told the Senate Commerce Committee on Feb. 14. [29] Private ISPs cannot compete with local governments' broadband offerings, he said, because localities don't pay taxes, which eat up "more than 40 percent of our profits. It is difficult to compete when the local municipality starts . . . with a 40 percent discount." [30]

Furthermore, since most municipal broadband is in rural areas, the projects pose the biggest threat to the smallest ISPs, which generally serve rural areas neglected by the bigger cable and phone companies, according to Brett Glass, owner of a tiny wireless — Lariat.Net — in Laramie, Wyo. Subsidized local broadband networks also crowd out small wireless start-ups, which could mean less competition in the long run because wireless ISPs are potentially the biggest competitive threat to cable and telephone ISPs, he said. [31]

Opponents also argue that locally subsidized broadband is probably an unfair and inefficient use of public dollars. "It is unlikely that more than a small number of residents would benefit," wrote Joseph Bast, president of the Chicago-based free-market think tank Heartland Institute, making it hard to "justify the steep cost" that would be borne by all local taxpayers. The cost also can't be justified in the name of overall community improve-

CHRONOLOGY

1960s–1970s *Computer researchers develop non-centralized, user-controlled computer networks.*

1965 MIT researcher Lawrence Roberts creates first long-distance computer network, linking machines in Massachusetts and California.

1969 University of California at Los Angeles becomes the first node of ARPANET, the Internet's Pentagon-funded precursor.

1971 Michael Hart starts Project Gutenberg to put copyright-free works online.

1972 E-mail is invented and dubbed the first Internet "killer app."

1973 England and Norway become the Net's first international connections.

1974 AT&T declines invitation to run the Internet.

1975 First ARPANET mailing lists link people with shared interests.

1980s–1990s *Businesses join research institutions online. Internet viruses and spam invented.*

1982 Sending messages gets easier as a University of Wisconsin server automatically links computer numbers to names, in the prototype of the Domain Name System (DNS).

1984 Internet-wide DNS introduced. The Net has over 1,000 directly connected computers — called "hosts," or Internet service providers (ISPs).

1988 Cornell graduate student Robert Morris, son of a network-security expert, sends the first self-replicating virus.

1989 Internet has over 100,000 hosts.

1990 "The World" (world.std.com) is the first commercial ISP. The first remotely operable machine — the Internet Toaster — goes online.

1992 Internet has more than 1 million hosts.

1993 White House, U.N. go online.

1994 U.S. immigration lawyers Martha Siegel and Lawrence Cantor send out first spam, advertising their firm.

1996 Phone companies ask Congress to ban Internet telephones. Congress passes Telecommunications Act but doesn't ban the phones. . . . China requires Net users and ISPs to register with the police. . . . Saudi Arabia confines access to universities and hospitals.

1998 Private, nonprofit Internet Corporation for Assigned Numbers (ICANN) takes over DNS under a U.S. government contract.

1999 Somalia gets an ISP; Bangladesh and Palestinian Territories register domains.

2000s *Battles over Internet control heat up. Broadband allows voice and video to travel over the Internet. U.S. phone and cable industries consolidate and offer broadband.*

2000 Yahoo! bans auctions of Nazi memorabilia when it is unable to block French users from the product listings, as ordered by a French court.

2001 Internet2 — an ultra-fast broadband network for U.S. research institutions — carries a live musical, "The Technophobe and the Madman."

2002 FCC rules that cable broadband operators don't need to give competing ISPs access to their lines.

2003 First World Summit on the Information Society discusses global governance and access for developing nations.

2005 FCC rules phone companies don't need to give competing ISPs free access to broadband connections. India's domain, "dot in," swells from 7,000 sites in 2004 to more than 100,000 in 2005. . . . China jails dissident based on Net writings handed over by Yahoo!

2006 Google launches controversial Chinese search engine that censors information. . . . Congress considers "Net neutrality" legislation. . . . ICANN contract expires in September, and governments and citizens' groups mull global governance for the Internet.

ment, he argued, because "it is fanciful to imagine that municipal broadband is a cost-effective way to promote economic development." [32]

But advocates of municipal broadband point out that many of the projects are not competing against private business. "The overwhelming majority of current projects are the result of a public-private partnership," wrote city officials from four small Texas towns in a Feb. 13 letter to Sen. Kay Bailey Hutchison, R-Texas. They called the claim that the public-sector broadband threatens the private sector "a red herring." [33]

Supporters of municipal broadband also argue that the usual ban against the public sector competing with the private sector does not apply to broadband infrastructure because broadband is a public, not a private, good.

If high-speed Internet services "were a purely private good . . . like, say, golf clubs, I could buy an argument against government provision," said Thomas Rowley, a fellow at the University of Missouri-based Rural Policy Research Institute. But "its benefits go far beyond the individual user to improve an entire community's economy, schools, health care and public safety. As with all these services, if the private sector cannot or will not . . . provide it to all at affordable prices, the public sector must." [34]

BACKGROUND

Born in the USA

In the early 1960s, a nuclear clash between the Cold War superpowers, the United States and the Soviet Union, seemed imminent. U.S. researchers wondered: Could they build a communications network that could survive nuclear combat? [35] Their efforts spurred creation of the Internet, whose technological and social ramifications we are only today beginning to understand.

Traditional networks — like the phone system and Post Office — route messages through central switching points and are vulnerable to complete breakdown if vital nodes are knocked out. Paul Baran, an electrical engineer at the RAND Corporation, a think tank focusing on military issues, proposed a network with many nodes, each able to route data on to another network point until the data reached its destination. He also proposed chopping messages into smaller "packets" of digitized information. Each packet is separately addressed and travels on its own to the designated addressee computer.

The network plan — which several other researchers envisioned at the same time — seemed inefficient, but was in truth "extremely rugged," designed with doomsday in mind, explained technology and science fiction writer Bruce Sterling. Each digital packet "would be tossed like a hot potato from node to node to node, more or less in the direction of its destination, until it ended up in the proper place. If big pieces of the network had been blown away, that simply wouldn't matter; the packets would still stay airborne, lateralled wildly across the field by whatever nodes happened to survive." [36]

In 1969, the concept was made operational for the first time, when seven large computers at U.S. research institutions were linked into a non-centralized packet-switching communications network. Funded by the Defense Department's Advanced Research Projects Agency (DARPA), ARPANET allowed researchers to transmit data — and even program each other's computers — via dedicated high-speed lines.

Scientists were enthusiastic about ARPANET, which gave them access to hard-to-come-by user time on remote fast computers. By 1972, the network had 37 nodes. Through the 1970s, other computer networks in the United States and abroad were linked to the so-called ARPANET, and the Internet — the network of networks — was born.

From its earliest days the Internet's radically decentralized structure gave it an unprecedented ability to develop in ways that its inventors never anticipated, a characteristic at the heart of today's battles over the Net.

ARPANET was built to facilitate high-tech computing and government communications. But, to the surprise of many, high-tech users quickly adapted the system to a down-to-earth pursuit — sending mail electronically for free. By 1973 e-mail made up 75 percent of network traffic.

By 1975, users had developed another new application — mailing lists to broadcast individual messages to large numbers of subscribers. These discussion lists gave birth to the first Internet communities — groups around the world connected by networked computers and common interests. While some lists were work-related, many were not. The most popular of the early unofficial lists was SF-Lovers, a list for discussing science fiction.

As the Internet quietly fostered new ways of communicating, the traditional communications industry remained aloof. Internet users paid for the use of phone lines to transmit their data, but otherwise phone companies paid little attention to the Net. "We were fortunate

Rights Group Names 15 Internet "Enemies"

Reporters Without Borders, an international organization working to restore the press' right to inform citizens, recently listed the following 15 countries as "enemies of the Internet" because of their restrictive Internet policies:

Belarus: President Alexander Lukashenko often blocks access to opposition parties' Web sites, especially at election time. In August 2005, he harassed youths posting satirical cartoons online.

Burma: Home Internet connections are prohibited; access to opposition sites is systematically blocked, and Internet café computers record what customers are searching every five minutes for government-spying purposes.

China: Censorship technology and spying block all government criticism on the Internet. Intimidation, including the world's largest prison for cyber-dissidents, forces self-censorship by users. Some blogs and discussion groups post real-time news about events in China, but censors remove the postings later. China is exporting its cyber-surveillance expertise to other repressive countries, including Zimbabwe, Cuba and Belarus.

Cuba: Citizens may not buy computers or access the Internet without Communist Party authorization. Some Cubans get connected illegally but can only access a highly censored, government-controlled version of the Internet.

Iran: Ministry of Information blocks access to hundreds of thousands of Web sites, especially those dealing with sex and providing independent news. Several bloggers were imprisoned recently, including Mojtaba Saminejad, who got a two-year sentence for insulting Ayatollah Ali Khamenei.

Libya: There is no independent media, and the government controls the Internet, blocking access to dissident exile sites and targeting cyber-dissidents.

Maldives: Several opposition Web sites are filtered by President Maumoon Abdul Gayoom's regime. One of four people arrested in 2002 is still in prison for helping to produce an e-mailed newsletter criticizing government policies.

Nepal: King Gyanendra Bir Bikram Shah Dev's regime controls Internet access of citizens. Most online opposition publications, especially those seen as close to Maoist rebels, have been blocked inside the country. Bloggers discussing politics or human rights are under constant pressure from the authorities.

North Korea: The government only recently allowed a few thousand privileged citizens access to a highly censored version of the Internet, including about 30 pro-regime sites.

Saudi Arabia: The government blocks access to 400,000 sites to protect citizens from content — mainly sex, politics or religion — that violates Islamic principles and social standards.

Syria: The government restricts Internet access to a small number of privileged people, filters the Web and closely monitors online activity.

Tunisia: President Zine el-Abidine Ben Ali blocks opposition publications and other news sites, discourages e-mail because it is difficult to monitor and jails cyber-dissidents.

Turkmenistan: Internet use is essentially prohibited; there are no Internet cafés, and a censored version of the Web is only accessible through certain companies and international organizations.

---

in that there was absolutely no commercial Internet industry out there," said Robert Kahn, a former DARPA network developer who later founded the nonprofit Corporation for National Research Initiatives to promote information-infrastructure development. "There were no . . . Internet service providers; there was no commercial anything. So nobody . . . saw the original Internet initiative as a threat to their business." In fact, AT&T made a conscious decision to stay out of computer networking, he pointed out. "They thought they could make more money by selling . . . the underlying circuits." [37]

AT&T — at the time a telephone monopoly — was kept informed of ARPANET's progress but wasn't impressed. AT&T executive Jack Osterman said of one DARPA proposal, "First, it can't possibly work, and if it did, damned if we are going to allow the creation of a competitor to ourselves." [38]

In 1974, AT&T turned down an offer to run ARPANET. [39]

Battle of the Band

During the 1980s the decentralized Internet mushroomed from less than 1,000 host computers, mostly in

Uzbekistan: The state security service often asks Internet service providers (ISPs) to temporarily block access to opposition sites. Some Internet cafés warn users will be fined for viewing pornographic or banned political sites.

Vietnam: Filters "subversive" Internet content, spies on cyber-café users and jails cyber-dissidents.

Countries to Watch

Bahrain: Has begun to regulate the Internet; requires all online publications, including forums and blogs, to be officially registered.

Egypt: Censorship is minor, but the government has taken steps since 2001 to control online material; some criticism of the government is unwelcome.

European Union (EU): Holds ISPs responsible for content of Web sites they host, requiring them to block any page considered illegal; EU is studying a proposal to oblige ISPs to retain records of customers' online activity.

Kazakhstan: Online publications are under scrutiny because many government scandals have been revealed on Web sites. President Nursultan Nazarbayev's regime blocked two opposition party sites in October 2005.

Malaysia: Government intimidation of online journalists and bloggers has increased, notably at the country's only independent Internet daily, whose journalists have

Controlling Net Traffic

Here are the five most common ways that governments, primarily non-democratic states, control access to the Internet.

Filter Web content at national level
Arrest and prosecute cyber-dissidents
Monitor cyber-cafés
Require registration of Web sites
Use Web-filtering software

Sources: OpenNet Initiative; Reporters Without Borders

been threatened and its premises searched.

Singapore: The government intimidates Internet users, bloggers and Web site editors.

South Korea: Filters the Internet, blocking pornographic sites and publications that "disturb public order," including pro-North Korea sites; users who go too far in expressing anti-government opinions are punished.

Thailand: Filters the Internet to fight pornography, but has extended censorship well beyond this.

United States: Laws to prevent intercepting online traffic do not guarantee enough privacy; U.S. Internet firms, including Google, Yahoo!, Cisco Systems and Microsoft, are working with China to censor their material in China.

Zimbabwe: The government reportedly is getting Chinese equipment to monitor citizens' Internet usage; state telecom monopoly TelOne asked ISPs in June 2004 to sign contracts allowing it to monitor e-mail traffic and requiring them to block material the government deems illegal.

Source: Reporters Without Borders, 2005.

---

the United States, to millions worldwide, but the telephone and cable companies largely continued to ignore it. The Internet expanded from the research sector to the commercial sector in the mid- to late-'90s and began spawning e-commerce businesses and new ways to communicate, like the now ubiquitous Web sites. Nervous about potential competition, phone companies asked Congress in the mid-1990s to ban Internet telephony, but legislators refused.

A new world emerged in the late 1990s when broadband technology, using cable and optical fiber to transmit data at high speeds, allowed Internet users to send not just text but video and voice messages. While top speeds get faster all the time, the International Telecommunications Union defines broadband as transmissions of 256 kilobytes per second (Kbps) or faster — for both uploading and downloading — while the U.S. FCC deems broadband as transmissions of 200 Kbps or faster.

As communications digitized and speeded up, the telecommunications landscape changed for its dominant industries — telephone and cable-TV companies.

First, cable operators began offering Internet connections over their lines. Phone companies responded by adding so-called digital subscriber lines (DSL), which are

U.S. Lags in Broadband Penetration

Nearly 75 percent of the households in Hong Kong have broadband Internet connections compared to only one-third in the United States.

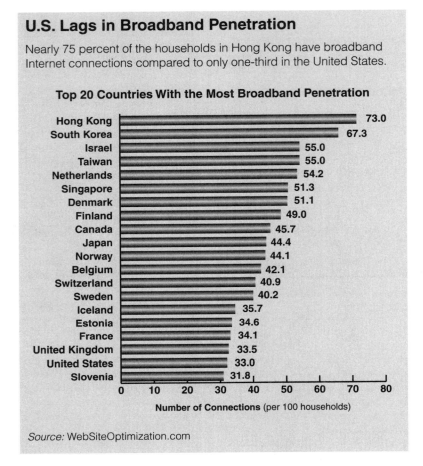

Top 20 Countries With the Most Broadband Penetration

Country	Connections
Hong Kong	73.0
South Korea	67.3
Israel	55.0
Taiwan	55.0
Netherlands	54.2
Singapore	51.3
Denmark	51.1
Finland	49.0
Canada	45.7
Japan	44.4
Norway	44.1
Belgium	42.1
Switzerland	40.9
Sweden	40.2
Iceland	35.7
Estonia	34.6
France	34.1
United Kingdom	33.5
United States	33.0
Slovenia	31.8

Number of Connections (per 100 households)

Source: WebSiteOptimization.com

The 1996 act was "oblivious to the power of the Internet and technology to revolutionize everything," said Michael Powell, who was appointed by President George W. Bush and chaired the FCC from 2001 to 2005. [41]

In the past few years, with Congress not yet willing to wade into telecom law again, the FCC, courts and state legislatures have been left to sort out increasingly bitter battles over broadband.

Phone companies have long been regulated as "common carriers' — open channels required to accept all traffic without discrimination, in return for being free of legal liability for communications they carry. Cable companies were not deemed common carriers; however, prior to 2002, the FCC required them to lease their broadband-Internet lines to competing ISPs on reasonable terms.

But the key principle of the 1996 act — and a guiding principle for the Bush administration — was that the telecom industry would do best if it were freed from government regulation. And, beginning in 2000, cable companies insisted they were unable to expand broadband access because regulation was crippling them. Cable operators' top complaint — the "open access" requirement to lease lines to competing ISPs.

In 2002 the FCC granted their request, saying that when consumers purchase cable-modem service, they are buying only an "information" service, not a traditional two-way communications service like telephone service. The decision exempted cable-modem providers from opening their lines to competing ISPs and from other rules.

Not all FCC commissioners were happy. Commissioner Michael Copps wrote that without open access "the Internet — which grew up on openness — may become the province of dominant carriers, able to limit access . . . to all but their own ISPs," a consequence he called "ironic." [42]

Independent ISPs continued to insist that the Internet is a two-way communications system and fought in court

broadband-capable wires with a range of speeds at around 128 Mbps — much slower than cable broadband.

Furthermore, the freewheeling, innovative Internet could now provide the telecommunication industries' two big-money products — video and voice communications.

In 1996, when Congress overhauled federal telecom law for the first time in several years, legislators believed they had created a framework for a competitive telecom marketplace that would last well into the future. [40] However, few foresaw that within a few years Internet companies like Google Video or Vonage would offer video and telephone service that would directly compete with the cable and phone companies — who own the transmission lines over which those competing products would travel.

for access to cable lines. But in June 2005, in *National Cable and Telecommunications Association v. Brand X Internet Services*, the Supreme Court sided with cable, overturning a lower court's ruling. [43]

The *Brand X* ruling opened the door for telephone companies to make the same argument — that broadband Internet services carried on phone lines shouldn't be subject to the century-old common-carrier rules. In August 2005, the FCC agreed. Beginning in August 2006, phone companies will no longer have to offer competing ISPs, such as AOL, free access to DSL connections. Phone companies will be able to sell or lease access to their DSL lines for whatever they deem fair value, although they will still be required to offer competitors free access to their slower dial-up connections.

As a result, most non-cable and non-telephone company ISPs "will disappear," says Crawford of Cardozo Law School. "The phone companies will just swallow them up, and there'll be much less choice of Internet providers." Phone and cable companies themselves will begin selling "bundles of services" — such as local and long-distance phone service along with DSL Internet service — that consumers will have no choice but to purchase.

Nevertheless, the FCC's decision will encourage "greater investment in . . . broadband networks," argued James C. Smith, senior vice president of SBC Communications, in defending their decision. [44]

But Internet advocates and some regulators are skeptical. Having one big phone company and one big cable company as the sole broadband providers in an area doesn't foster innovation and low price, says Copps. "I thought the '96 act was pretty clear in saying, 'Let's have competing providers, then deregulate.' But we kind of got it in reverse, deregulating before the competition had materialized."

Indeed, although the '96 law was intended to promote competition, the opposite has happened: The telephone and cable industries have been consolidating ever since — a worrisome fact because the Internet is a key communications channel for democracy, says Copps. In 2005, for example, the FCC approved a merger between SBC Communications and AT&T but bound the company to an enforceable Net-neutrality provision — barring the broadband giant from discriminating among Internet content — for two years. "This allows time for Congress to address the issue and for the American people to become involved," Copps says.

A university student in Manila logs onto the new Yahoo! Philippines site. Atypically, more than half the country's Internet users are women. Internet use is growing rapidly in Southeast Asia and the rest of the world, including societies that closely monitor, and censor, citizens' access.

As in many other countries, U.S. phone companies pledged in the 1990s to upgrade infrastructure for high-speed access. In the United States, Congress and the FCC loosened some regulations on the telephone industry, in part because companies argued they would use the extra profits to modernize transmission lines.

Many other governments, such as Japan and South Korea, aggressively monitored infrastructure improvements in their countries to be sure they were made. In many countries, phone companies remained heavily regulated monopolies, which could be compelled to build infrastructure. But the U.S. government relied on what it believed would be market incentives for the private sector to wire the country for broadband, without establishing a clear policy for getting it done or fully debating the economics of doing so.

Meanwhile, in the United States, rural regions, especially, have been fighting back against the big telecom companies' reluctance to extend broadband. With little or no broadband available in some markets or prices too high for lower-income families, local governments have set up their own fiber or wireless "pipes."

The governments often use fiber line already laid by a municipally owned power company or cooperate with private companies. The ISP Earthlink, for instance, is deploying wireless transmitters on light poles in

Googling in China Has Its Limits

As governments around the world bring more of their citizens online, they also are censoring information and opinion on the Internet and using networking technology to track down and punish political dissidents, according to Reporters Without Borders, a free-media advocacy group based in France.

Google has drawn press and congressional criticism recently for setting up a Chinese version of its Google.com search engine — Google.cn — which censors search results in line with government information-suppression guidelines. For example, a search for Tiananmen Square on Google.com turns up many images of tanks confronting unarmed demonstrators in 1989. But the same search on Google.cn produces smiling tourists posing for snapshots but few demonstrators.

"In countries such as China, where the mainstream media is subject to censorship, the Internet seemed to be the only way for dissidents to freely express their opinions," Reporters Without Borders Washington representative Lucie Morillon told the House Committee on International Relations on Feb. 15. "But, thanks to some U.S. corporations, Chinese authorities have managed to gradually shut down this 'open window' to the world." [1]

For example, both Google's and Yahoo's China sites have blocked some access to the U.S. government's Voice of America Web site and Radio Free Asia, as well as various other media sites around the world, Morillon said.

Meanwhile, Internet companies take varying approaches to dealing with Chinese-government repression, said Rebecca MacKinnon, a former Beijing bureau chief for CNN and now a fellow at Harvard Law School's Berkman Center for Internet and Society.

The anti-virus capability of Cisco Systems' "router" computers is, in effect, a built-in censorship device, said MacKinnon. By selling routers to China, the company is helping the Chinese government keep its citizens under surveillance and crack down on their political activity, she said, although it's not clear whether Cisco provides Chinese authorities with much training on the machines' capabilities. [2]

Microsoft provides instant messaging and Hotmail e-mail service to China but operates the programs on servers located outside of China to avoid having to hand over data to Chinese authorities. However, Microsoft also runs a Chinese version of its blog site, MSN Spaces, and censors the site according to Chinese requirements. It was widely criticized late last year when it deleted the work of blogger Zhao Jing, not just for Chinese viewers but worldwide. The company has since refined its processes so that global viewers can still read blogs blocked to Chinese Internet users, according to MacKinnon.

Unlike Microsoft and Google, Yahoo! runs its Chinese-language products on servers inside China and thus must comply with Chinese police requests to hand over information, noted MacKinnon. That compliance has led to the jailing of at least three dissidents, MacKinnon writes. "If I were one of those people or their loved ones, I would never forgive Yahoo!," she said. Recently, Reporters Without Borders reported that Yahoo cooperation also led Chinese officials to a fourth cyber-dissident, Wang Xiaoning, who received a 10-year prison sentence in 2003. [3]

To avoid such dilemmas, Google won't offer some products, such as Gmail or Blogger, on Google.cn "until we're comfortable that we can do so in a manner that respects our users' interest in the privacy of their personal communications," Andrew McLaughlin, Google's senior policy counsel, wrote on the company's blog [4]

"Filtering our search results" on Google.cn in accord with China's censorship requirements "clearly compromises our mission," but "failing to offer Google search at all to a fifth of the world's population . . . does so far more severely," McLaughlin argued.

Google's argument is that Google.cn users actually will get more information if Google itself does the filtering, because Google's filtering tools are more finely developed than the "very broad sweeps" of government censors, says Lauren Weinstein, co-founder of People for Internet Responsibility. While the claim is "not inaccurate technically," Weinstein says, it opens the company up "to a damaging side effect" — charges of hypocrisy. The perception has been created that the company may not be as committed to principles of privacy as it has always claimed, he says.

"And perceptions alone can do a lot of damage," he adds. For example, Google recently fought a U.S. Department of Justice request to turn over millions of search results in the name of protecting users' privacy. But, in the future, skeptics will remember that, in China, "you caved," and they'll ask, in light of that, " 'What happens next time?' " Weinstein says.

---

[1] Testimony before House Committee on International Relations, Feb. 15, 2006, www.rsf.org.

[2] Rebecca MacKinnon, "America's Online Censors," *The Nation*, Feb. 24, 2006.

[3] "Still No Reaction from Yahoo! After Fourth Case of Collaboration With Chinese Police Uncovered," Reporters Without Borders, April 28, 2006, www.rsf.org.

[4] Andrew McLaughlin, "Google in China," Official Google Blog, Jan. 2, 2006, http://googleblog.blogspot.com/2006/01/google-in-china.html.

Should Congress require Internet service providers to treat all content the same?

YES
Rep. Edward J. Markey, D-Mass.
Ranking Member, House Subcommittee on Telecommunications and the Internet

Written for *CQ Researcher*, May 2006

Ever since the Internet was first opened to commercial use in the early 1990s, it has been defined by its open exchange of ideas — an exchange that has fostered tremendous innovation and economic growth.

The Internet's traditional open architecture was protected by rules enforced by the Federal Communications Commission (FCC) that prohibited telecommunications carriers from engaging in discriminatory practices. However, those legal protections, which embodied the notion of "network neutrality," were removed by the FCC in August 2005. The telecommunications legislation now moving through Congress places the very nature of the Internet under attack by failing to provide strong, effective network-neutrality rules.

In essence, network neutrality means that broadband network owners such as AT&T or Verizon cannot discriminate against unaffiliated content providers on the Net but rather have to stay neutral with regard to the content flowing through their networks. Moreover, the phone companies cannot charge access fees to certain companies in exchange for faster content distribution to high-bandwidth customers, or to provide enhanced quality-of-service assurances.

Finally, the principle of network neutrality also protects consumers' freedom to use their choice of gadgets with their broadband connection, from computer modems and VOIP [voice over Internet protocol] phones, to Wi-Fi routers and other whiz-bang gizmos just over the horizon.

Without these protections, the open, free-market nature of the Internet — perhaps the purest example of a level playing field that we have ever seen — would be hijacked by large broadband-network owners and discarded in favor of a tiered superhighway of bandwidth haves and have-nots.

The current debate over network neutrality presents us with a choice: Should we favor the vision for the Internet's future as warped by a small handful of very large companies or should we safeguard the dreams of thousands of inventors, entrepreneurs, small businesses and other independent voices?

Already, we have begun to see the grass roots rise up in opposition to Rep. Joe Barton's telecom bill, with over 250,000 backers of an open and unrestricted Internet signing a petition to Congress. Lawmakers should listen to these voices and ensure that broadband network owners treat all forms of content the same so that we do not lose the open architecture that has allowed the Internet to become such a success.

NO
James L. Gattuso
Senior Fellow in Regulatory Policy, Heritage Foundation

Written for *CQ Researcher*, May 2006

Should Internet network owners, such as telephone and cable TV companies, be required to treat all Internet content equally? The idea — known as network neutrality — seems at first glance unobjectionable. What could be wrong with requiring neutrality? A lot, actually.

The key issue is whether network owners should be allowed to offer priority service, for a fee, to content providers who want it. Under a "network-neutral" system, all data is treated the same, with bits being transported to their destinations on a first-come, first-served, basis.

But what if a content provider wants higher-quality service? A firm providing Internet phone calls, for instance, may want to ensure that voice conversations have no delay. Why should it be banned from paying more to the network owner for priority transmission? Such differentiation is hardly a new concept. In the non-Internet world, priority service is offered for everything from package delivery to passenger trains.

Differentiation could also help provide much-needed Internet investment. A content provider, for instance, might contract with a network owner to provide capital for capacity expansion. But the incentive to do so is eliminated if it is required to allocate that new capacity on a first-come, first-served basis.

Regulation proponents argue, nevertheless, that network owners could abuse their power — perhaps blocking specific Web sites to further their own interests. But this is extremely unlikely. No major U.S. network operator has ever blocked a Web site, and if one does, consumers would switch to another operator in a nanosecond.

Rhetoric to the contrary, today's broadband market is a competitive one, with cable and telephone companies fighting each other for customers, and other technologies — such as wireless and satellite — also on offer. Moreover, if a network owner somehow does abuse its power, existing competition law is more than sufficient to address the problem.

Imposing new rules on the Internet would also invite endless litigation. Regulators would be drawn into years-long, lobbyist-driven policy quagmires as to whether this or that action is allowed or banned, and even what prices could be charged. This would be a bonanza for lobbyists and lawyers but would hurt innovation, investment and Internet users.

Proponents of neutrality regulation say the future of the Internet is at stake. They are right. These harmful and unnecessary new rules should be rejected.

U.S. Lags in Internet Speed

Downloading a typical DVD movie in the United States takes 18 times longer than in Japan.

Country	Internet Connection	Time
Japan	(26Mbit/s)	20 minutes
S. Korea	(20Mbit/s)	26 minutes
Belgium	(3Mbit/s)	44 minutes
Denmark	(2Mbit/s)	4.5 hours
USA	Cable Modem (1.5Mbit/s)	6 hours

Note: 1 megabit per second (Mbit/s) = 1 million bits per second
Source: International Telecommunication Union, Sept. 26, 2003

Philadelphia to offer a lower-cost connection, which the city will subsidize for some low-income residents.

But cable and phone companies have been fighting such efforts, lobbying state legislators to stave off what they see as publicly subsidized competition. Fourteen states now have laws restricting localities' ability to offer communications services to residents.

CURRENT SITUATION

Fighting for the Net

Congress is overhauling the 1996 telecom law just 10 years after it was enacted. This time, a top priority will be extending the nation's broadband capabilities — barely a blip on the radar screen a decade ago. "Net neutrality" will also be a major new buzzword in the debate.

Over the past year, a growing chorus of advocacy and consumer groups and Internet companies have argued that Congress should require Internet carriers to treat Net content neutrally, rather than shunting chosen data to high-priority — and presumably more expensive — lines. But cable and telephone companies say that preventing them from developing such higher-priced traffic amounts to excessive regulation and that offering priority services is the only way they can afford to roll out broadband to the entire country.

On April 27, the cable and telephone industries won round one of the battle when the House Energy and Commerce Committee approved its telecom bill, after rejecting, 22-34, a Net-neutrality provision sponsored by Rep. Edward J. Markey, D-Mass.

"There is a fundamental choice," said Markey. "It's the choice between the bottleneck designs of a . . . small handful of very large companies and the dreams and innovations of thousands of online companies and innovators." [45]

The final measure, drafted by Texas Republican Barton, instead authorized the FCC to investigate allegations that carriers are treating Internet content unfairly and to fine companies up to $500,000 for blocking or degrading access to Web sites.

The Senate also is expected to debate telecom overhaul legislation this year, although no schedule has been announced. Sen. Ron Wyden, D-Ore., has introduced a bill mandating that ISPs treat all Internet content equally, and Sens. Olympia Snowe, R-Maine, and Byron Dorgan, D-N.D., have drafted a similar bipartisan measure.

Senate Commerce Committee Chairman Ted Stevens, R-Alaska, said he supports neutrality in principle but isn't sure yet what will be in the bill. "We're going to have an enormous number of items that people want to put in," he said. [46]

Not surprisingly in a congressional election year, lobbying has intensified, as have political donations — just as they did in 1996, also an election year.

On April 26, the big computer-chip maker Intel joined a long list of computer and Internet companies — including Microsoft, Google, eBay and Amazon — and advocacy groups from across the political spectrum to push for a neutrality law. The retirees group AARP, the liberal political group MoveOn.org, the American Library Association and the libertarian Gun Owners of America all favor neutrality.

Meanwhile, critics of the telecom industry say phone and cable companies may be paying their way into the hearts of cash-strapped legislators running for re-election. As of March 31, for example, cable giant Comcast was Barton's top 2006 campaign contributor and AT&T was his fourth-biggest donor, according to the political funding Web site OpenSecrets.org. In Barton's 2003-2004 campaign, Comcast was his third-biggest donor and SBC was in second place.

Some Democrats who opposed Markey's Net-neutrality amendment also have financial ties to telecom. Rep. Bobby Rush, D-Ill., cosponsored Barton's telecom bill and is the founder of the Rebirth of Englewood Community Development Corp., a group in his home district that recently received a $1 million grant from the SBC Foundation. [47]

As Congress discusses telecom overhaul, other broadband-related bills are also up for consideration. In the House, Texas GOP Rep. Pete Sessions has introduced legislation to prevent municipalities from setting up broadband networks in localities where private broadband service is available. In the Senate, John McCain, R-Ariz., and Frank R. Lautenberg, D-N.J., are sponsoring a bill to allow local governments to offer broadband service.

However, few expect a comprehensive bill to pass in 2006. The '96 telecom law was several years in the making, and "I don't see why this would be any easier," said Carol Mattey, a former deputy chief of the FCC now with Deloitte & Touche's regulatory consulting practice. [48]

Google CEO Eric Schmidt unveils the firm's Chinese name in Beijing on April 12, 2006. With 111 million Internet users, China is second only to the United States in total number of users. The Chinese government — assisted by Google, Yahoo! and other computer companies — censors Web sites that question government actions or deal with teen pregnancy, homosexuality, dating, beer and even jokes.

Getty Images/Peter Parks

Whither ICANN?

This year also marks a significant milestone in the quest for global Internet governance. ICANN's current contract with the U.S. government to run the Internet's domain-name addressing system expires in September, and international groups have been discussing a possible new governance structure for several years.

Until the late 1990s, individual U.S. researchers and some small organizations ran the Internet's technical functions on behalf of the U.S. government. That structure was in keeping with the Net's history as a U.S.-developed technology. But as the 21st century neared, the Internet's swelling size and increasing global importance led President Bill Clinton to turn over control of Internet addresses to ICANN, a private, nonprofit group that manages technical aspects of the Net with input from private and public groups worldwide.

The U.S. government's intention, expressed in a series of contracts between ICANN and the Commerce Department, has been to eventually move toward more global control. Last year, however, the Bush administration announced that the international search for an alternate governing body had focused too much on government controls and that the United States would not turn over Net functions to international government bureaucrats — such as the United Nations — who

might stifle innovation or be too strongly influenced by repressive governments. [49]

The U.S. government is currently considering all options for the close of the current ICANN contract in September, says a spokesman for the Commerce Department's National Telecommunications and Information Administration, which oversees the agreement. At an international summit in November, participants agreed to create an Internet Governance Forum consisting of government, business and civil-society groups to discuss global Internet governance.

The goal is to create a forum with multiple stakeholders that will meet sometime in mid-2006 in Athens. The group will try to come to global consensus on the top issues involving the Internet, such as spam, cyber-crime, the intersection of national law and Internet principles on censorship.

OUTLOOK

Wireless Is "Happening"

If the Internet survives as an open medium, it may be because users — from software engineers to teenagers with pages on MySpace.com — demand security mechanisms that allow innovation while preventing domestic and international threats to Internet freedom, say technology experts.

Today, "the fact that tens of millions of machines in consumer hands are hooked up to networks that can convey reprogramming in a matter of seconds means that those computers stand exposed to near-instantaneous change" by malicious viruses and crippling loads of network-drowning spam, according to Jonathan Zittrain, professor of Internet governance at Oxford University.

The very real threat of Internet meltdown in a world of non-techie users will inevitably lead to a Net "locked down" by governments and ISPs in ways that eliminate user choice and innovation, Zittrain said, unless open-Internet supporters demand or develop improved network security and reliability while retaining users' ability to be creative. [50]

For example, personal computers could be sold with keyboard switches. In "red" mode, a PC would run whatever software it encountered, like PCs today; in "green" mode, it would run only software certified by its ISP. Users would pay more for an Internet connection that allowed them to run "red." [51]

"Corporate mass-market software" that dominates today's Net was developed with little thought to security, says Peter Neumann, principal scientist at the SRI Computer Science Laboratory in Menlo Park, Calif., and co-founder of People for Internet Responsibility. In a universally online world that could lead to a disastrous shutdown of vital Net-based systems, such as power, air-traffic control or electronic voting, he notes.

"The government has typically said the market will solve" security problems, but Microsoft and others "are making scads of money while all but ignoring security," he continues. Meanwhile, the industry has its "head in the sand" and won't change unless "we have enough people who understand the big picture" and take responsibility for it, Neumann says.

For U.S. consumers to make market choices on Internet service, a real market must develop, with three or more competing services available everywhere, not just the phone and cable companies that dominate today, said former FCC Chairman Powell. "We believe magical things happen at three," he said. [52]

Currently, wireless ISPs remain the best hope, although whether wireless technology is up to the job remains an open question. Some say wireless is poised to emerge strong in urban and rural areas. Nine years ago, "it was a technological curiosity," but today "it's happening," says Steve Stroh, a writer and an analyst for the broadband wireless Internet industry. He cites Trump Tower in Manhattan, which recently installed a wireless network for the entire building, and hundreds of rural wireless ISPs — called WISPs — that increasingly can extend broadband connections over long distances. An operator in eastern Washington state, for example, can reach customers 30-to-40 miles from its transmission point via large antennas, Stroh says.

To flourish, wireless needs access to dedicated bands on the electromagnetic spectrum, says Stroh, which could be a special problem in the United States, where — unlike in some other countries — much prime spectrum is already allocated to users like the Department of Defense. The spectrum issue is on Congress' agenda, with some legislators proposing to dedicate empty spaces in local broadcast TV spectra to wireless ISPs, for example.

The Internet's continued ability to allow unfettered communication and innovation rides on the outcome of all these debates, say longtime Net users like Karl Auerbach, a San-Francisco-based computer-network developer and former ICANN board member.

"These Internet governance debates are the visible aspects of the most significant change in the conception of nation-states, national sovereignty and the relationship of the individual to his/her government since at least the end of the Napoleonic wars," he says.

NOTES

1. Quoted in "AOL Censors E-Mail Tax Opponents," Electronic Frontier Foundation media release, April 13, 2006.

2. John Byrne, "Update: AOL Says Emails Protesting Its Own Service Blocked By Accident," *The Raw Story blog*, April 14, 2006.

3. Tom Barrett, "To Censor Pro-Union Web Site, Telus Blocked 766 Others," *The Tyee*, Aug. 4, 2005, http://thetyee.ca.

4. For background, see David Masci, "The Future of Telecommunications," *CQ Researcher*, April 23, 1999, pp. 329-352.

5. Lawrence Lessig, "Architecting Innovation," *The Industry Standard*, Sept. 8, 2001.

6. Quoted in Declan McCullagh, "Democrats Lose House Vote on Net Neutrality," *ZDNet.com*, http://news.zdnet.com.

7. *Save The Internet blog*, www.savetheinternet.com.

8. Quoted in *ibid.*

9. For background, see Kenneth Jost, "Russia and the Former Soviet Republics," *CQ Researcher*, June 17, 2005, pp. 541-564.

10. Daniel Henninger, "Here's One Use of U.S. Power Jacques Can't Stop," *The Wall Street Journal*, Dec. 17. 2004.

11. Declan McCullagh, "No Booze or Jokes for Googlers in China," CnetNews.com, http://news.com, Jan. 27, 2006.

12. "Promoting Innovation and Competitiveness," President Bush's Technology Agenda, March 26, 2004, www.whitehouse.gov.

13. S. Derek Turner, "Why Does the U.S. Lag Behind?" *Free Press*, February 2006.

14. Michael Geist, "The Credible Threat," *Circle ID*, Feb. 28, 2006, www.circleid.com.

15. Quoted in Declan McCullagh, "Internet Showdown in Tunis," CNET News.com, Nov. 11, 2005; http://news.com.com. For background, see Charles S. Clark, "Regulating the Internet," *CQ Researcher*, June 30, 1995, pp. 561-584.

16. Kieren McCarthy, "2005: The Year the U.S. Government Undermined the Internet," *The Register*, Dec. 29, 2005, www.theregister.co.uk.

17. *Ibid.*

18. Amol Sharma, "World Seeks a Wider Web Role," *CQ Weekly*, Nov. 14, 2005, p. 3042.

19. Testimony before Senate Committee on Commerce, Science and Transportation, Feb. 7, 2006.

20. Quoted in Marguerite Reardon, 'Qwest CEO Supports Tiered Internet," ZDNet.com, http://news.zdnet.com.

21. Quoted in "At SBC, All's Well About Scale and Scope," *Business Week Online*, Nov. 7, 2005.

22. Edward Felten, "Net Neutrality and Competition," *Freedom to Tinker blog*, www.freedom-to-tinker.com.

23. Quoted in Marguerite Reardon, "Verizon Says Net Neutrality Overhyped," CNET News.com, March 31, 2006, http://news.com.com.

24. John Windhausen, Jr., "Good Fences Make Bad Broadband," *A Public Knowledge White Paper*, Public Knowledge, Feb. 6, 2006.

25. *Ibid.*

26. *Ibid.* The nine states are Arkansas, Delaware, Florida, Illinois, Maryland, Michigan, Pennsylvania, Virginia and Wyoming.

27. *Ibid.*

28. John Horrigan, "Rural Broadband Internet Use," Pew Internet and American Life Project, February 2006.

29. Quoted in "Senate Commerce, Science, and Transportation Committee Holds Hearing on Communications Issues," Congressional Transcripts, Feb. 14, 2006, www.cq.com.

30. *Ibid.*

31. Quoted in Dana Blankenhorn, "You Get Muni Broadband by Demanding It," ZDNet blog, April 5, 2006.

32. Joseph L. Bast, "Municipally Owned Broadband Networks: A Critical Evaluation (Revised Edition)," www.heartland.org, October 2004.

33. www.baller.com/pdfs/Texas_2-14-06.pdf.

34. Thomas D. Rowley, "Where No Broadband Has Gone Before," Rural Policy Research Institute, Aug. 19, 2005.

35. For background, see *The Internet's Coming of Age*, Committee on the Internet in the Evolving Information Infrastructure (2001); and Barry M. Leiner, *et al.*, "A Brief History of the Internet," Internet Society, www.isoc.org.

36. Bruce Sterling, "A Short History of the Internet," *The Magazine of Fantasy and Science Fiction*, February 1993.

37. "Putting It All Together With Robert Kahn," *Ubiquity: An ACM IT Magazine and Forum*, www.acm.org.

38. Quoted in Lawrence Lessig, "It's the Architecture, Mr. Chairman," http://cyber.law.harvard.edu/works/lessig/cable/Cable.html.

39. Scott Bradner, "Blocking the Power of the Internet," *Networkworld*, Jan. 6, 2006, www.networkworld.com.

40. For background, see Masci, *op. cit.*; and Kathy Koch, "The Digital Divide," *CQ Researcher*, Jan. 28, 2000, p. 41-64.

41. Quoted in Elizabeth Wasserman, "The New Telecom Wars: Looking to Update a Landmark Law," *CQ Weekly*, Nov. 14, 2005, p. 3049.

42. Michael Copps, Dissenting Statement, GN. No. 00-185, www.fcc.gov.

43. *National Cable and Telecommunications Association v. Brand X Internet Services*, 543 U.S., 2005.

44. Quoted in "FCC Reclassifies DSL as Data Service," Analyst Views, IT Analyst Information on Demand, Northern Light, Sept. 20, 2005, www.centerformarketintelligence.com.

45. Quoted in Declan McCullagh, "Republicans Defeat Net Neutrality Proposal," CNet News.com, April 6, 2006, http://news.com.com.

46. Quoted in Declan McCullagh, "Senator: Net Neutrality May Not Happen," ZDNet News, March 22, 2006, http://news.zdnet.com.

47. "Donation Explanation Has Phony Ring," *Chicago Sun-Times*, April 26, 2006.

48. Quoted in Kelly M. Teal, "1996 Telecom Act Turns 10," *New Telephony*, Feb. 8, 2006, www.newtelephony.com.

49. Tim Receveur, "United States Says No UN Body Should Control Internet," *Washington File*, USInfo, U.S. State Department, Oct. 24, 2005, http://usinfostate.gov.

50. Jonathan Zittrain, "The Generative Internet," 2005; www.oiprc.ox.ac.uk/EJWP0306.pdf.

51. *Ibid.*

52. Quoted in "Michael Powell: We Need That Third Pipe," *IP Democracy*, April 3, 2006, www.ipdemocracy.com.

BIBLIOGRAPHY

Books

Borgman, Christine, *From Gutenberg to the Global Information Infrastructure: Access to Information in the Networked World*, MIT Press, 2003.
A professor of information studies at the University of California, Los Angeles, describes the technical and policy tradeoffs that libraries, universities, readers and researchers face as they shift from a culture of books to a world of online information.

Goldsmith, Jack, and Timothy Wu, *Who Controls the Internet? Illusions of a Borderless World*, Oxford University Press, 2006.
Professors specializing in cyberlaw at Harvard and Columbia, respectively, describe threats the global Internet has posed to national regimes. They argue national government have and are exercising power to control the Internet.

Thierer, Adam, and Wayne Crews, eds., *Who Rules the Net?: A New Guide to Navigating the Proposed Rules of the Road for Cyberspace*, Cato Institute, 2003.
Two libertarian analysts assembled essays that discuss the challenges of regulating cyberspace, including how international cyber-disputes should be settled and whether a multinational treaty should govern the Internet.

Yassini, Rouzbeh, *et al.*, *Planet Broadband*, Cisco Press, 2003.
An electrical engineer and advocate of cable broadband explains how broadband works and describes how high-speed Internet connections may change how consumers, businesses and researchers use the Net.

Articles

Chester, Jeffrey, "The End of the Internet?" *The Nation online*, www.thenation.com, Feb. 1, 2006.
An advocate of an open-access Internet describes the conflict between traditional Internet values and the economic and policy agendas of the phone and cable industries.

Cukier, Kenneth Neil, "No Joke," *Foreign Affairs*, foreignaffairs.org, Dec. 28, 2005.
A journalist describes U.S. and international views of Internet control and how changes in the way the Internet works are altering those views.

Goldsmith, Jack, and Timothy Wu, "Digital Borders," *Legal Affairs*, January/February 2006, www.legalaffairs.org.
Law professors at Harvard and Columbia, respectively, describe incidents in which national laws collide with traditional Internet principles like freedom of expression.

Hu, Jim, and Marguerite Reardon, "Cities Brace for Broadband War," CNET News.com, May 2, 2005, http:/news.com.com.

Battles are heating up between cities and towns that want to develop government-sponsored broadband networks and regional phone and cable companies that accuse local governments of engaging in unfair competition.

MacKinnon, Rebecca, "America's Online Censors," *The Nation online*, **www.thenation.com, Feb. 24, 2006.**
A fellow at Harvard Law School's Berkman Center for Internet and Society explores the economics and ethics of U.S. computer companies' cooperation with Chinese-government Internet censorship.

Manjoo, Farhad, "One Cable Company to Rule Them All," *Salon*, **Salon.com, March 17, 2004.**
A journalist discusses potential threats to Internet access posed by consolidation of media ownership.

Reardon, Margaret, "Broadband for the Masses?" **CNET News.com, www.com,com, April 14, 2004.**
Jim Baller — a lawyer for local governments — describes court challenges to their attempts to build broadband networks and defends such initiatives.

"Seven Questions: Battling for Control of the Internet," *Foreign Policy*, **www.foreignpolicy.com, November 8. 2005.**

Stanford University law professor and Internet expert Lawrence Lessig discusses conflicts between the United States and European Union over who should control the granting of Internet domain names.

Zittrain, Jonathan, "Without a Net," *Legal Affairs*, **January/ February 2006, www.legalaffairs.org.**
An Oxford University professor of Internet governance describes why burgeoning Internet-security threats like computer viruses mean that Internet law and technology require overhaul.

Studies and Reports

The Internet's Coming of Age, **Committee on the Internet in the Evolving Information Infrastructure, National Research Council, 2001.**
An expert panel recommends policies to accommodate more widespread Internet usage and new technologies.

Signposts in Cyberspace: The Domain Name System and Internet Navigation, **Computer Science and Telecommunications Board, National Research Council, 2005.**
An expert panel explains the Internet's address system and recommends policy to stabilize its future governance.

For More Information

Berkman Center for Internet and Society, Harvard Law School, 23 Everett St., 2nd Floor, Cambridge, MA 02138; (617) 495-7547; http://cyber.law.harvard.edu. A research program investigating legal, technical and social developments in cyberspace, in the United States and worldwide.

Center for Democracy and Technology, 1634 I St., N.W., #1100, Washington, DC 20006; (202) 637-9800; www.cdt.org. Advocates preservation of constitutional freedoms and democratic values in the developing digital world.

Center for the Digital Future at the University of Southern California Annenberg School, 300 South Grand Ave., Suite 3950, Los Angeles, CA 90071; (213) 437-4433; www.digitalcenter.org. A research program investigating the Internet's effects on individuals and societies.

Electronic Frontier Foundation, 454 Shotwell St., San Francisco, CA 94110; (415) 436-9333; www.eff.org. A nonprofit organization that advocates for and litigates on technological issues involving privacy, free speech, freedom to innovate and consumer rights.

Free Press, 100 Main St., PO Box 28, Northampton, MA 01061; (877) 888-1533; www.freepress.net. A national, nonpartisan organization that promotes public participation in debate on media policy and development of more competitive and public-interest-oriented media.

ICANN Watch, www.icannwatch.org. Membership organization of technology experts who study and write about management and policy issues affecting the Internet's domain-name address system.

Internet Governance Project, School of Information Studies, Syracuse University, Syracuse, NY 13244; (315) 443-5616; www.internetgovernance.org. An interdisciplinary group of academic researchers analyzing issues of global governance for the Internet.

National Cable and Telecommunications Association, 25 Massachusetts Ave., N.W., Suite 100, Washington, DC 20001-1413; (202) 222-2300; www.ncta.com. Represents the cable industry, the largest single provider of broadband Internet services in the United States.

Pew Internet and American Life Project, 1615 L St., N.W., Suite 700, Washington, DC 20036; (202) 419-4500; www.pewinternet.org. Provides data and analysis on Internet usage and its effects on American society.

Progress and Freedom Foundation, 1444 I St., N.W., Suite 500, Washington, DC 20005; (202) 289-8928; www.pff.org. A free-market-oriented think tank that studies public policy related to the Internet.

14

Rethinking Foreign Policy

Kenneth Jost

A soldier's boots and a flag-draped coffin dramatize the anti-war message at a rally and march on the National Mall on Jan. 27, 2007. Thousands of demonstrators in Washington and other cities urged Congress to end the Iraq war, which has claimed more than 3,000 U.S. troops and tens of thousands of Iraqi civilians.

From *CQ Researcher*, February 2, 2007.

W ith U.S. casualties rising in Iraq and public approval of his policies falling at home, President Bush got a small bit of hopeful foreign policy news in January from an unexpected source. Iran's stridently anti-American president, Mahmoud Ahmadinejad, appeared to be losing the confidence of the country's supreme leader, Ayatollah Ali Khamenei, for courting confrontation with the United States over its nuclear weapons program.

The semi-authoritative daily *Jomhouri-Eslami* — owned by Khamenei — pointedly admonished Ahmadinejad to leave nuclear matters to Khamenei and tweaked him for minimizing the U.N. Security Council's decision in December to impose trade sanctions against Iran for continuing its uranium-enrichment program. "The resolution is certainly harmful for the country," the newspaper said. [1]

Far from treating the signs of dissent in Tehran as encouraging, however, the State Department's spokesman on Jan. 19 blandly repeated the United States' willingness to negotiate with Iran on the nuclear issue. Meanwhile, President Bush was stepping up pressure on Iran by dispatching additional ships off Iran's coast and lashing out at Iran in his State of the Union speech on Jan. 23 for supporting Shiite death squads in Iraq.

The tough talk on Iran pleases administration supporters. "It seems to me the U.S. will be taking a tougher line with Iran, one way or another," Lawrence Kudlow, the conservative CNBC talk show host, wrote on his blog "MoneyPolitic$." [2] On Capitol Hill, however, Democrats were openly critical and even some Republicans voiced concern. "This whole concept of moving against Iran is bizarre," Senate Intelligence Committee Chairman Jay Rockefeller, D-W.Va., remarked. [3]

Disapproval of U.S. Policies Is Widespread

Two-thirds of the more than 26,000 people surveyed in 25 countries — including the United States — think the U.S. presence in the Middle East provokes more violence than it prevents (top graph). Nearly three-quarters disapprove of U.S. policies toward Iraq (bottom).

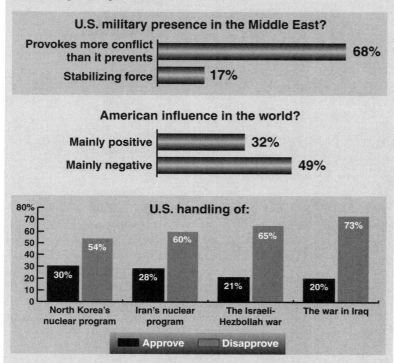

What is your opinion on:

U.S. military presence in the Middle East?

- Provokes more conflict than it prevents: **68%**
- Stabilizing force: **17%**

American influence in the world?

- Mainly positive: **32%**
- Mainly negative: **49%**

U.S. handling of:

	Approve	Disapprove
North Korea's nuclear program	30%	54%
Iran's nuclear program	28%	60%
The Israeli-Hezbollah war	21%	65%
The war in Iraq	20%	73%

Source: The poll was conducted for BBC World Service by the international polling firm GlobeScan; 26,381 people in Asia, Africa, Europe, South America, the Middle East and the United States were interviewed between Nov. 3, 2006, and Jan. 9, 2007

The emerging debate over Iran — and the full-blown debate over Iraq — are part of an even broader debate going on in foreign-policy circles over the past year. A growing number of experts representing diverse political and ideological backgrounds are saying U.S. foreign policy has gone fundamentally wrong under Bush and that a thoroughgoing change in approach is needed to regain support for U.S. foreign policy both at home and abroad.

Iraq necessarily forms part of the critique. "The focus on Iraq has diverted attention from a wide variety of domestic and global problems that have grown worse in the absence of U.S. attention and leadership," says Steven Hook, an associate professor at Ohio's Kent State University and lead author of a survey of U.S. foreign policy since World War II. [4]

More broadly, critics charge Bush with repeatedly displaying an arrogant and unrealistic belief in U.S. power and a disdain for multilateral institutions and international traditions. They cite as examples Bush's rejection of some international treaties negotiated during the 1990s, his endorsement of "preventive war" as a national security strategy and his self-proclaimed policy to export democracy to countries in the Middle East and elsewhere.

The result, these critics say, is a backlash of anti-Americanism around the world, even in countries closely allied with the United States. "U.S. policy in recent years has simply become too ambitious," says Anatol Lieven, a senior research fellow at the New America Foundation, a self-styled "radical centrist" think tank. "It's tried to do too much in too many directions simultaneously, and it's led to a very dangerous degree of overstretching."

A self-described progressive, Lieven joined with conservative foreign-policy expert John Hulsman to advocate what they call "ethical realism." As they wrote in a book-length manifesto in late 2006, ethical realism avoids the pitfalls of either "hard-line realism" or "utopian morality" by recognizing the limits of U.S. power while supporting the moral purpose of U.S. foreign policy to spread freedom and democracy. [5]

Lieven and Hulsman, now a fellow at the German Council on Foreign Relations in Berlin, criticize in particular the so-called neoconservative school of foreign policy, which advocates the assertive use of American power — including military might — to promote peace, democracy and economic freedom. (*See sidebar, p. 326.*) "The neoconservatives are impatient with history," says Hulsman, formerly of the Heritage Foundation. "The idea that we can rush that along is arrogant and wrong."

A similar criticism of Bush-administration policy appears in the final report of a mammoth review of U.S. foreign policy completed in September 2006 under the auspices of Princeton University's prestigious Woodrow Wilson School of Public and International Affairs. U.S. efforts to "unilaterally transform the domestic politics of other states" have increased anti-Americanism abroad, discouraged cooperation with U.S. policies and weakened the United States' global authority, write Professor John Ikenberry and Dean Anne-Marie Slaughter, co-directors of the review. [6]

Administration supporters and sympathetic observers reject the critique in its broad sweep and its particulars. "That's a cartoon version of either the president's policy or neo-conservatives," says Gary Schmitt, a senior fellow at the American Enterprise Institute (AEI) who served as executive director of the neoconservative Project for the New American Century from 1997 to 2005. "Neoconservatives aren't and the president isn't unaware of the difficulties" of implementing foreign-policy strategies.

"The problem is not the American penchant for unilateralism," says Michael Mandelbaum, a professor at the Johns Hopkins School for Advanced and International Studies in Washington and author of the 2005 book *The Case for Goliath.* "It's the limited possibilities for multilateralism because other countries don't contribute anything. The problem is not that the Americans don't do too much, but other countries don't do enough."

Even though Bush has not abandoned any of his policies, some observers say they see signs of a shift — in tone and substance — in the president's second term in office. "The administration began to pull back and move

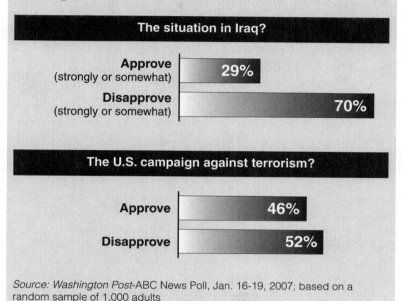

Most Americans Oppose Bush Iraq Policy

While 70 percent of Americans disapprove of the situation in Iraq, attitudes about the Bush administration's war on terrorism are more evenly divided.

Do you approve or disapprove of the way President Bush is handling:

The situation in Iraq?

Approve (strongly or somewhat)   29%
Disapprove (strongly or somewhat)   70%

The U.S. campaign against terrorism?

Approve   46%
Disapprove   52%

Source: Washington Post-ABC News Poll, Jan. 16-19, 2007; based on a random sample of 1,000 adults

toward a previous pattern with greater cooperation, a pullback from the use of force, and a pullback from 'regime change,' " says Jeffrey W. Legro, an associate professor at the University of Virginia and author of a new book on international strategy. [7]

"The White House has learned some bitter lessons about taking impulsive actions when it comes to military interventions and nation-building overseas," says Hook. "There is a more pragmatic sense now that the consequences of such interventions are profound, uncertain and of long-term duration."

As these debates continue, here are some of the questions being considered:

Should the United States emphasize multilateral over unilateral initiatives in foreign policy?

President Bush entered office in 2001 with a marked shift away from the emphasis on multilateralism in U.S.

Secretary of State Condoleezza Rice meets with Egyptian President Hosni Mubarak in Cairo in October 2006. During a subsequent meeting in January 2007, Rice did not repeat past criticisms of Mubarak's regime, instead praising Egypt as part of the Middle East's "moderate mainstream."

foreign policy under his predecessors, Presidents Bill Clinton and George H. W. Bush, his father. Critics said the change was substantive as well, citing as examples Bush's early decisions to renounce the newly created International Criminal Court as well as the Kyoto Protocol on global climate change. [8]

Bush followed a multilateral strategy in putting together the United Nations-authorized coalition to invade Afghanistan after the 9/11 terrorist attacks. But two years later, he spurned the U.N. Security Council and two important European allies, Germany and France, with his decision to invade Iraq and oust Saddam Hussein.

With the Iraq war now nearing its fourth anniversary, a wide range of foreign-policy experts fault the administration for what they describe as a penchant for going it alone in world affairs. "This administration has lost the respect of the international community because it has failed to understand that American power is magnified and made more authoritative when it is exercised through institutions," says Princeton's Ikenberry.

Up until the 9/11 attacks, Bush was "the most isolationist president" since World War II, according to Charles Kupchan, a senior fellow at the Council on Foreign Relations and a professor of international relations at Georgetown University. Now, after having shifted to a more internationalist stance during the invasion of Afghanistan, Kupchan says, unilateralism

appears to be re-emerging in administration rhetoric and policies.

Administration supporters say the argument is overstated. "The notion that somehow the United States was going to act unilaterally in world affairs is a straw man," says James Carafano, a defense expert at the Heritage Foundation. "That was never the administration's strategy."

Instead, Carafano says, the Bush administration has tried to put together so-called "coalitions of the willing" — countries willing to join with the United States on a case-by-case basis. But he says the experience in Iraq shows the limitations of that approach and emphasizes instead the importance of more durable bilateral alliances.

"It's ridiculous to call Iraq a unilateral action," Carafano explains. "We've got allies there." The important question, he continues, is "Who sticks with us?" — pointing as examples to Britain, Canada and newer allies such as Poland. "The Poles want to have a long and enduring relationship with the United States, and they're stepping up to the plate."

Frederick W. Kagan, a military historian and resident scholar at AEI, says the critique essentially focuses on the administration's willingness to take action — as in Iraq — without U.N. approval. "The United States is not obliged to seek U.N. authorization before taking any action in the world at all," says Kagan. "We are not at the stage where any nation has ceded its sovereignty to that point."

For their part, "ethical realism" manifesto authors Lieven and Hulsman both emphasize the practical value of multilateral action in world affairs while acknowledging instances when the United States may have to act on its own. "There will be cases when America has to act alone, but the contrasting examples of Kosovo and Afghanistan on one hand and Iraq on the other show how infinitely preferable it is to act whenever you can with local allies," Lieven says.

"You start at the multilateral level and — unlike the Bush administration — make good-faith efforts to get multilateral support," says Hulsman. "It's always good to start with that and see if you can get a good deal." Unilateral action is indicated, he says, only if the United States cannot get support from within or outside the affected region — "which will be, in practice, never."

Hulsman credits the administration with putting together an effective coalition in Afghanistan. And Lieven notes that the administration has pursued a multilateral approach in trying to get North Korea to renounce plans for a nuclear-weapons program.

Other experts also say the multilateralist critique of the administration has been overstated. "There's less difference than meets the eye" with the Clinton administration, according to Richard Betts, a professor and director of the Institute of War and Peace Studies at Columbia University in New York City. "It's more a distinction of style than of substance."

But Ikenberry rejects those arguments. "They're deeply wrong," he says. "They don't appreciate the way in which America has signaled to the world that it does not respect institutions and rules that the rest of the world looks to as forms of governance."

However the past policies are characterized, a wide range of experts agree that the United States needs to pursue multilateral strategies more strenuously in the future. "It makes sense to have like-minded allies with us on board," says Karin von Hippel, co-director of the Post-Conflict Reconstruction Project at the Center for Strategic and International Studies in Washington. "When the United States works unilaterally, other countries see it as being arrogant."

"There clearly needs to be more of a multilateral role as the limitations of U.S. power and leadership become apparent," says the University of Virginia's Legro.

Should the United States discard President Bush's doctrine of preventive war?

One year after the Sept. 11 terrorist attacks, in September 2002, President Bush formally set out a new "national security strategy" that explicitly declared the United States' intention to act "preemptively" when necessary "to prevent or forestall hostile acts by our adversaries." With the rise of private terrorist groups, the White House document explained, the United States would sometimes need to take "anticipatory action to defend ourselves, even if uncertainty remains as to the time and place of the enemy's attack." [9]

Bush depicted the idea of "preemptive action" as having a long historical pedigree. And the AEI's Schmitt likens the doctrine to President John F. Kennedy's decision to institute a naval blockade of Cuba during the 1962 missile crisis and President Clinton's unacted-on plans in the early 1990s for a possible strike against North Korean nuclear sites. "It's something that one has to keep in one's toolbox of statecraft, but it's not something that one does easily or often," says Schmitt.

American soldiers patrol outside Kabul, Afghanistan, in December 2006. Following the Sept. 11, 2001, attacks, President George W. Bush rallied international support for a U.S.-led invasion of Afghanistan to root out al Qaeda and the Taliban. More recently, however, Secretary of State Rice found little support among U.S. allies for sending more troops back to Afghanistan to put down a Taliban insurgency.

Most foreign-policy experts, however, read the document then — and still today — as setting out a new "preventive war" doctrine that goes beyond an accepted doctrine of preemptive action against an imminent threat. And with that understanding a wide range of foreign-policy experts view the doctrine as ill-advised, contrary to international law and — if followed by other countries — inimical to U.S. foreign-policy interests.

"The United States has strayed from the international community only to find out that the real problems facing the United States, including global terrorism, cannot be solved in isolation and that the United States — even with all of its strength — cannot go it alone," says Kent State's Hook.

Johns Hopkins Professor Mandelbaum calls the administration's argument "serious" though "not compelling."

"The logic is that since terrorists cannot be deterred, you have to strike them whenever you can," Mandelbaum explains. "Second, nuclear weapons change the calculus of international law in that the mere possession of nuclear weapons can be a great strategic setback. Therefore, if you wait for a rogue state to get nuclear weapons, it may be too late.

World Faces Many Cross-Border Challenges

Five years after the Sept. 11, 2001, terrorist attacks on the United States, the world "seems a more menacing place than ever," according to the Princeton Project on National Security. Here are some of the challenges confronting U.S. foreign policy:

- Americans and Iraqis are dying daily in an Iraqi conflict that some say is moving toward all-out civil war.

- Iran is seeking nuclear weapons, threatening to plunge the Middle East into chaos.

- Al Qaeda and its associated terrorist networks remain a potent threat while other terrorist sponsors, such as Hezbollah, are growing.

- Russia, riding high on rising oil prices, is seeking to reclaim its sphere of influence.

- North Korea is producing nuclear weapons and flexing its military muscle, as South Korea grows increasingly anti-American.

- Sino-Japanese relations are extremely tense; China is building relations with the rest of Asia and Africa in ways that exclude the United States.

- Populist Venezuelan President Hugo Chavez is fomenting a continent-wide anti-U.S. coalition in Latin America.

- Africa remains riven by conflict, poverty and disease.

- Global pandemics, such as avian flu, could threaten millions across continents.

- Climate change could trigger security consequences ranging from natural disasters to a fierce scramble for territory.

- U.S. budget deficits could undermine American global leadership and increase the risks of international financial crises.

Source: G. John Ikenberry and Anne-Marie Slaughter, "Forging a World of Liberty Under Law: U.S. National Security in the 21st Century," Princeton Project on National Security, September 2006

ical realism," says Hulsman. "You might need those troops somewhere else."

"In general, the international tradition [of deterrence] works well enough," says Lieven. "This notion that Iran or North Korea will suddenly fire a nuclear missile at Israel or the United States is absolutely crazy," because Iran and North Korea know they "would simply cease to exist the next day."

In their report, Princeton Professors Ikenberry and Slaughter call for updating the deterrence doctrine by announcing in advance that in the event of nuclear terrorism, the United States would hold the source of the nuclear weapons or material responsible. They also call preventive strikes "a necessary tool in fighting terror networks" but caution that any such actions should be "proportionate and based on intelligence that adheres to strict standards."

A preventive strike against a country should be "very rare," used "only as a last resort," and authorized by a multilateral institution like the United Nations Security Council or a broadly representative body such as NATO, Ikenberry and Slaughter argue. "If we can't convince even our most trusted allies that our course and policy is wise, then we are going to fail in the longer-term endeavor," Ikenberry explains.

Iraq casts a cloud over the preventive-war doctrine, but the

"There's something to be said for that argument, but I don't think it has any chance of establishing itself," Mandelbaum continues. "Partly because it violates international law too sharply. Partly because the other potential cases — North Korea and Iran — don't lend themselves to it. And partly because Iraq has gone badly."

Hulsman and Lieven are firmer in rejecting the Bush doctrine. "Fighting wars of choice is antithetical to eth-

Heritage Foundation's Carafano maintains that the conflict is being waged on a different ground: enforcement of the terms of the peace treaty that ended the first Gulf War in 1991. "We agreed to stop combat if Saddam Hussein agreed to do certain things," Carafano says. "He never did those things." Under those circumstances, he says, resuming combat operations is "traditional international law."

Other foreign-policy experts view the administration's rationale differently. "The emphasis on preventive war in Iraq was a departure," says Betts at Columbia. "We've done that before, but it was never in the mainstream of U.S. foreign policy."

Whatever the rationale for the war, experts across the ideological spectrum agree that the Iraq experience makes a future "preventive war" less likely but not out of the question. The doctrine "is down but not out," says Kupchan at the Council on Foreign Relations. "There will be much greater reluctance to implement that policy after Iraq."

"It's probable that the outcome in Iraq will have a cushioning effect on U.S. action the way that failure in Vietnam did for a while," Betts says. But, he adds, "I don't think the outcome in Iraq will turn people off to the idea that we should use preventive action when warranted."

Should the United States scale back efforts to export democracy to the Middle East and elsewhere?

Since the eve of the Iraq war, President Bush has repeatedly advocated promoting democracy not only in Iraq but also throughout the Middle East. With Iraq's fledgling democracy beset by sectarian violence, however, U.S. policy appears to be de-emphasizing the goal in the rest of the region. Secretary of State Condoleezza Rice visited Egypt in January 2007 without repeating her past criticisms of President Hosni Mubarak's autocratic regime. Instead, she praised Egypt as part of the "moderate mainstream" in the Middle East. [10]

Foreign-policy experts across the ideological spectrum agree the Bush administration's rhetoric raised unrealistic and unachievable expectations about exporting democracy to the Middle East and by analogy to the rest of the world. "History shows that promoting democracy is a long-term process and one that cannot be easily exported from one country to another," says Hook at Kent State.

"Democracy can be imported, but it can't be exported," says Mandelbaum, who is working on a book about democratization due out in fall 2007. "Democracy is more than just elections," he continues. "It's a whole set of institutions and practices. You can't just install them. It has to be homegrown over time." [11]

"Exporting democracy is really the wrong term," says Carafano at the Heritage Foundation. "There is no such thing as nation-building. Democracy really only takes root when it comes from below."

Going Nuclear?

Iran's stridently anti-American president, Mahmoud Ahmadinejad (top), may be losing the confidence of the country's supreme leader, Ayatollah Ali Khamenei, for confronting the United States over Iran's nuclear-weapons program. North Korean Leader Kim Jong II (bottom) may permit the resumption of six-power talks with the U.S., China, Japan, Russia and South Korea. Pyongyang has pressed for bilateral talks with Washington aimed at normalizing relations between the two countries. In early January, both the U.S. and Japan warned of unspecified tougher measures if North Korea conducted a second nuclear test following its first nuclear detonation on Oct. 9, 2006.

Advocates of democracy promotion cite the post-World War II reconstruction of Germany and Japan as evidence that U.S. assistance can be instrumental in fostering the establishment of stable democracies. Neoconservatives also point to the U.S. invasions of Grenada and Panama during the 1980s as successful efforts to install governments with democratic forms.

In more recent history, however, Hulsman and Lieven cite less auspicious examples of trying to establish democratic governments as well as uncertain consequences of democratization in terms of support for U.S. policies.

"Haiti, Somalia, Bosnia, Kosovo, Afghanistan and now Iraq," Hulsman says, listing countries where the United States has intervened since the 1990s. "What have we done in these examples? I keep wondering how many more times we're going to invade Haiti in my lifetime."

"Show me a success," echoes Lieven. He also points to recent examples in the Middle East — such as the Hamas victory in Palestinian elections in 2006 — to caution against expecting fledgling democracies to adopt pro-American policies. "In many countries, the early growth of democracy is intimately tied up with nationalism."

"There are times when you promote democracy, and it turns out to be problematic," the AEI's Schmitt concedes. "But on the whole the general trend is one of optimism and of strategic value."

Liberal advocates of democracy promotion also view overall U.S. efforts positively. "There are many places around the world where U.S. support for democracy has been beneficial," says Thomas Carothers, director of the Democracy and Rule of Law Project at the Carnegie Endowment for International Peace. He lists Eastern Europe and South Africa among other examples.

"Iraq has given democracy promotion a bad name in the United States and around the world," Carothers acknowledges. Within the United States, he notes, a recent poll by the German Marshall Fund found that a plurality of Americans — 48 percent to 45 percent — reject the goal of helping to establish democracy in other countries. [12] Meanwhile, the administration's expansive rhetoric has increased the perception around the world of hypocrisy in U.S. foreign policy, he adds. "Their deeds do not match their words."

Critics of the administration's policies question what they see as an after-the-fact adoption of democracy promotion as a goal of the Iraq war. "The war was in the first instance about security, about weapons of mass destruction

and about a belief that toppling Saddam Hussein could pacify the Middle East," says Kupchan of the Council on Foreign Relations. "It turned into a war for democracy once the original justifications for the war had evaporated."

Whatever the original goals, many experts say the Iraq experience makes similar U.S. adventures unlikely for the foreseeable future. "It sets back exporting democracy at the point of a gun, which is not a bad thing," says Columbia's Betts. "We're going to be a lot more careful of reforming nasty regimes by marching in and tossing them out."

Other experts, however, expect public support for democratization initiatives to return. "It may be that the United States reverts to a more evolutionary approach to democratization, which focuses on economic assistance and political support for civil society and domestic groups that would enable them to create their own solutions to problems," says Hook.

"There's a robust consensus that encouraging the development of democracy is a very good thing," says the University of Virginia's Legro. "Using force to encourage democracy is where things fall apart."

BACKGROUND

America Ascendant

The United States began asserting itself on the world stage early in its history and moved toward global pre-eminence in the two world wars of the 20th century. After World War II, the United States helped establish an array of multilateral and international institutions aimed at preventing future wars and promoting economic stability. It also adopted a policy of "containment" aimed at using diplomatic, economic and military means short of war to counter the challenge of global communism from the Soviet Union and "Red China." The Vietnam War, the long and ultimately unsuccessful conflict in Southeast Asia, however, prompted a rethinking of U.S. goals and strategies abroad. [13]

President George Washington ended his presidency with a farewell address warning against foreign entanglements, but — as neoconservative foreign-affairs analyst Kagan argues in his book *Dangerous Nation* — the United States was far from isolationist in the 19th century. The young republic invited the War of 1812 by confronting Great Britain over the blockade of U.S. shipping. A decade later, President James Monroe laid down his eponymous doctrine telling European powers to stay out of hemispheric affairs. Kagan depicts westward expansion as a policy of conquest — sometimes peaceful, sometimes not — and the Spanish-American War as a humanitarian intervention of choice that turned the United States into an imperial power.

The United States fought in and won the two world wars in the 20th century despite isolationist public opinion and pronouncements by leaders as both conflicts developed. President Woodrow Wilson campaigned in 1916 on keeping the United States out of the European conflict but asked Congress for a declaration of war barely six months later after German submarines continued to attack U.S. shipping. After the war, isolationist sentiment helped keep the United States out of the League of Nations and on the sidelines as war clouds formed again in Europe.

Like Wilson, President Franklin D. Roosevelt campaigned for re-election in 1940 on the strength of having kept the United States out of the European war. But he had already taken sides in 1939 by allowing Britain and France to buy arms from the United States and collaborating with Britain on the Lend-Lease program early in 1941. After the Japanese attack on Pearl Harbor on Dec. 7, Roosevelt asked for a declaration of war and then led the country in an unprecedented military and economic mobilization. The war ended with Germany and Japan defeated, Europe and the Soviet Union ravaged and the United States left standing as the strongest world power.

Before the war's end, the United States was already adopting a new, explicitly internationalist role in world affairs. It hosted the July 1944 conference at Bretton Woods, N.H., that led to the creation of two largely U.S.-financed international lending institutions: the World Bank to help countries rebuild and the International Monetary Fund to help countries out of short-term currency crises. The United States again took the lead role in the international conference in San Francisco in 1945 that established the United Nations — with a charter giving the United States a permanent and powerful role in its enforcement arm, the Security Council.

Postwar hopes for international peace faded quickly with official and popular concern about an emerging conflict with the Soviet Union. George Kennan, then the U.S. ambassador to Moscow, presciently analyzed Soviet policies in a now-famous anonymously written memo in 1946 that called for the United States to counter the ideologically charged challenge with a policy of "long-term, patient, but firm and vigilant containment." [14]

President Harry S Truman adopted that approach with such steps as aid to Greece and Turkey to defeat communist insurgencies, the Marshall Plan to rebuild Western Europe and the Berlin airlift to counter the Soviets' blockade of the city's western sectors. Truman also led the United States into the Korean War, which his successor, Dwight D. Eisenhower, ended in 1953 with an uneasy cease-fire and a heavily fortified "demilitarized zone" between the communist North and the pro-Western South Korea.

Through the 1950s, the United States avoided direct military confrontations with either the Soviet Union or China, communist-ruled after the defeat of the U.S.-backed Nationalist government in 1949. In the 1960s, however, Presidents John F. Kennedy and Lyndon B. Johnson came to view the war between the communist North and the pro-Western South Vietnam as a critical test of the containment policy.

The United States committed itself to South Vietnam's defense, but the U.S. troop buildup — eventually exceeding 500,000 soldiers — failed to repel a Vietcong invasion from the north. After four more years of war and with the pro-Western government still in power in Saigon, President Richard M. Nixon approved the 1973 treaty that ended the war with a cease-fire. Just two years later, however, a new invasion from the north toppled the Saigon government and unified Vietnam under a government communist in ideology and nationalist in sentiment.

America Conflicted

The United States conducted foreign policy from the 1970s on conflicted over the lessons to be drawn from the end of the Vietnam War. The "Vietnam War syndrome" introduced an explicit aversion to intervention abroad into many foreign policy debates but did not prevent Presidents Ronald Reagan or George H. W. Bush from sending U.S. troops into Grenada (1983), Panama (1989) and — most significantly — Kuwait (1991). In the 1990s President Clinton adopted "assertive multilateralism" as the watchword for U.S. foreign policy, but critics faulted the administration's actions in such trouble spots as Somalia, Rwanda, Haiti and the former Yugoslavia as either ill-advised or ineffective or both.

CHRONOLOGY

Post-World War II *The Allies' victory is followed by Cold War with Soviet Union.*

1947-50 Truman administration lays foundation of "containment" policy to limit Soviet expansion with aid to Greece and Turkey, Marshall Plan to rebuild Europe and North Atlantic Treaty Organization (NATO) to guarantee security of Western Europe.

1950-53 Korean War ends with cease-fire, North and South Korea divided.

1961-73 U.S. support for South Vietnam against communist North Vietnam leads to major escalation after 1965; protracted war ends in 1973 with North and South divided.

1970s-1980s *End of Vietnam War brings recriminations at home, calls for retrenchment abroad.*

1975 Saigon falls to North Vietnam. . . . Helsinki Accords concede communist control of Eastern Europe in return for Soviets' recognition of human rights.

1978 President Jimmy Carter makes human rights a major objective of U.S. foreign policy.

1979-81 Iranian hostage crisis: U.S. Embassy personnel in Tehran held for 15 months, released as President Carter leaves White House.

1982 President Ronald Reagan labels Soviet Union "evil empire," vows to support democracy in communist countries.

1983 U.S. invasion of Grenada. . . . Bombing of Marine barracks in Lebanon kills 241 servicemen.

1989 President George H.W. Bush approves invasion of Panama to oust dictator Manuel Noriega.

1990s *Cold War ends; U.S. is sole superpower.*

1990-91 First Gulf War: First President Bush forges U.N.-sanctioned coalition to oust Iraq from Kuwait.

1993 President Bill Clinton withdraws U.S. troops from Somalia.

1995-96 U.S. helps broker Dayton Accords to end Bosnian war.

1998 U.S. embassies in Kenya, Tanzania bombed; attacks later linked to al Qaeda.

1999 Serbia halts war in Kosovo after NATO bombing campaign, approved by Clinton.

2000-Present *President George W. Bush declares "war on terror"; launches wars in Afghanistan, Iraq.*

2001 President Bush renounces International Criminal Court, Kyoto Protocol on climate change. . . . Sept. 11 terrorist attacks leave nearly 3,000 Americans dead; Bush declares "war on terror," launches U.S.-led invasion of Afghanistan with U.N. backing. . . . Taliban ousted by November; pro-U.S. interim government installed in December.

2002 Bush labels Iran, Iraq, North Korea "axis of evil." . . . "National Security Strategy" says U.S. will act to "prevent or forestall" attacks by terrorists, other adversaries. . . . Congress grants Bush authority to use force in Iraq.

2003 Bush launches invasion of Iraq with U.S.-led coalition after failing to win U.N. backing; Saddam Hussein ousted, U.S. occupation under "provisional authority."

2004-05 U.S. transfers sovereignty to interim Iraqi government (June 2004); Iraqi national elections (January 2005); insurgency grows.

2006 Iran announces it has enriched small amount of uranium, adds to fears that it seeks nuclear weapons . . . North Korea announces it has carried out first nuclear test. . . . Democrats regain control of Congress; growing opposition to war in Iraq seen as major factor. . . . Bipartisan commission calls for redeployment of U.S. troops in Iraq, diplomatic efforts to end conflict.

2007 Bush says he will send 21,500 more troops to Iraq to quell sectarian violence; Democrats oppose plan, many Republicans voice doubts.

In his brief presidency, Gerald R. Ford made a signal contribution to U.S. foreign policy by helping negotiate the Helsinki Accords, the 1975 pact that effectively accepted communist domination of Eastern Europe in return for the Soviet Union's agreement to recognize human rights in the region. President Jimmy Carter went further in stressing human rights as a keystone of U.S. foreign policy and helped negotiate an historic peace treaty between Egypt and Israel that represented the first recognition of the Jewish state by an Arab nation.

But Carter's foreign policy accomplishments were lastingly overshadowed by the seizure of 52 U.S. embassy workers by Iranian militants in November 1979, a humiliating crisis that ended with their release the day Carter left office in January 1981. After seeking to defuse Cold War tensions, Carter also ended his presidency with a more bellicose atmosphere after the Soviet invasion of Afghanistan in 1980.

Reagan came to office as an outspoken anti-communist and an unapologetic former hawk on the Vietnam War. He quickly moved to increase U.S. military spending and sharpen rhetorical attacks on the Soviet Union. On the pretext of protecting U.S. citizens, Reagan sent U.S. troops to oust a Marxist regime in the tiny Caribbean island of Grenada. He also defied congressional opposition to help fund the anti-communist rebels known as contras fighting the leftist government in Nicaragua. Reagan told a succession of Soviet leaders that the Vietnam War syndrome was a thing of the past. When a suicide bomber attacked the U.S. Marine barracks in Beirut in 1983, killing 283 servicemembers, however, U.S. peacekeeping troops were withdrawn from Lebanon, and military intervention abroad was denounced except when America's "vital interests" were at stake.

As Reagan maintained rhetorical pressure on the Soviet Union, the communist government was itself collapsing. Reagan's admirers say the U.S. defense buildup forced the Soviet Union into an unaffordable arms race that contributed to economic stagnation and the country's eventual dissolution. In posthumously published interviews, Ford was quoted as saying the recognition of human rights in the Helsinki Accords played a more important role. [15]

Still others say reforms like the economic and political restructuring instituted by Mikhail S. Gorbachev beginning in the mid-1980s would have been adopted eventually without regard to U.S. policy. Whatever the causes, the combination of economic woes and pro-democracy protests in the satellite countries by 1991 brought down the communist empire and reduced the Soviet Union to the present-day Russian Federation.

In December 1989, during his first year in office, the first President Bush sent U.S. troops to Panama to assist a military coup in ousting President Manuel Noriega, who was facing indictment in the United States for drug trafficking. A year later, Bush responded to Saddam Hussein's August 1990 invasion of Kuwait by working in the United Nations to form a U.S.-led coalition to oust the Iraqi invaders. After a month-long bombing campaign, coalition ground forces moved in on Feb. 24, 1991, and succeeded within 100 hours in liberating Kuwait with only 149 allied servicemembers killed. Bush made the controversial decision not to pursue the retreating enemy soldiers further into Iraq or try to remove Hussein from power.

Clinton inherited an Iraq policy that included U.S. and British enforcement of "no-fly zones" preventing Hussein's government from conducting air attacks on Kurdish areas in the north or on the predominantly Shiite southern region. Despite the United States' enhanced primacy in the post-Cold War era, Clinton also faced an array of vexing foreign policy challenges in trouble spots where U.S. interests were less than evidently vital and U.S. public opinion less than engaged. [16] Public reaction to the sight of a slain U.S. soldier being dragged through the streets of Mogadishu in 1993 led Clinton to pull U.S. troops out of a U.N. nation-building effort in Somalia. With public support lacking, Clinton stayed out of the humanitarian intervention during the Rwanda genocide. And he wavered on U.S. military intervention in the former Yugoslavia in the face of European and domestic inertia even though he had called for the United States to intervene during his 1992 campaign.

Meanwhile, al Qaeda had formed as a multinational, anti-American terrorist organization and carried out attacks on U.S. embassies in Kenya and Tanzania in 1998 and the *USS Cole* in October 2000. Clinton approved a missile strike aimed at bin Laden in 1999, but it was called off. He left office with plans written — but not acted upon — to retaliate for the *Cole* attack, which killed 17 U.S. sailors and wounded 39 others. [17]

Is the Neoconservative Movement Dead?

That's not the point, say Robert and Frederick Kagan

Critics of the neoconservative movement are declaring it dead — a friendly-fire casualty of the Bush administration's failures in Iraq and elsewhere.

But two of the people most closely identified with the movement say its views have been misrepresented and its influence on Bush's policies overstated.

"I've always found it odd that people talk about a neoconservative vision of anything," says Frederick Kagan, a military historian and research fellow at the conservative American Enterprise Institute (AEI). "There is no cohesive neoconservative movement that gets together with regular congresses and decides what's the neoconservative line."

Like his younger brother, author and think-tank fellow Robert Kagan says he does not even call himself a neoconservative. And he scoffs at what he calls "the absurd conspiracy theory" that a small group of "neocons" outside the government effectively hijacked U.S. foreign policy under Bush.

The picture of a well-organized movement dating from the 1960s and unified around a vision of a muscular U.S. foreign policy pursuing peace, democracy and free markets may be overdrawn, experts and journalists sometimes concede.

"Neoconservatives do not make up an organized bloc — much less a 'cabal,' as is sometimes alleged," *Vanity Fair* Contributing Editor David Rose writes. [1] But the view of Bush's foreign policy as shaped by neoconservatives in and out of government is widespread.

G. John Ikenberry, a professor at Princeton University's Woodrow Wilson School of International Affairs, accuses the neoconservative movement of a "radical" reorientation of U.S. foreign policy after the Sept. 11, 2001, terrorist attacks that he says "squandered" the United States' moral authority in the world. In their ideology-spanning book *Ethical Realism*, Anatol Lieven and John Hulsman credit neoconservatives with "tremendous success" in making democracy-promotion a central element of U.S. strategy in the Muslim world — but they call the policy a failure in Iraq and Mideast politics in general. [2]

Neoconservatives reflect a long American tradition, say Robert (left) and Frederick Kagan.

As Robert Kagan explains, the original neoconservatives — literally, "new" conservatives — were one-time liberals and left-wingers who held on to hawkish anti-communist views during and immediately after the Vietnam War. Decades later, he says, the term has lost its original meaning. "I've never been on the left, and I don't consider myself a conservative," he says in a telephone interview from Brussels, where he writes a monthly column for *The Washington Post.*

In Robert Kagan's view, the post-Cold War neoconservatives are successors to a continuous tradition — detailed in his history of 19th-century U.S. foreign policy — of seeking global influence in pursuit of liberal goals. "Neoconservatives did not come along and change American tradition," he says. [3]

In a "statement of principles" in 1997, the neoconservative Project for a New American Century (PNAC) argued that the United States should increase defense spending, "challenge regimes hostile to our values" and accept "America's unique role in preserving and extending an international order friendly to our security, our prosperity and our principles." Signers included such future Bush administration officials as Vice President Dick Cheney, Defense Secretary Donald Rumsfeld and Undersecretary of Defense Paul Wolfowitz. [4]

"We did a pretty good job of putting that strategic vision on the table," says Gary Schmitt, who served as executive director of PNAC from 1997 to 2005. Schmitt is now a fellow with AEI; PNAC — housed in the same building — is somewhat dormant.

Robert Kagan says neoconservatives supported President Bill Clinton's military interventions in Haiti, Somalia, Bosnia and Kosovo against foreign-policy "realists" and Republican lawmakers who saw no vital U.S. interests at stake. "At the time we had more in tune with Clinton than with Republicans and conservatives," he says.

Today, neoconservatives such as the Kagans and PNAC Founding Chairman William Kristol, editor of the *Weekly Standard*, are among the lonely voices supporting Bush's plan to send additional troops to Iraq. Many others are bailing out, however — as Rose devastatingly detailed in his *Vanity Fair* cover story in January. "The biggest industry" in Washington, Robert Kagan says, are people trying to explain away their previous support for the Iraq war.

Ikenberry, writing with the Iraq war

Neoconservatives' policy fails in Iraq and the Mideast, say Anatol Lieven and John Hulsman (right).

(c) Claudio Vazquez

still in its first year, saw the invasion as "the neoconservatives'" "crowning achievement" until it "turned into a costly misadventure." The policies, he wrote, were "unsustainable" at home and unacceptable abroad. Today he sees only further vindication: "The failure of the Bush administration is a ratification of the intellectual bankruptcy of the neoconservatives."

Lieven, a self-described progressive, and the conservative Hulsman give neoconservatives credit for seeking to balance realism and morality and recognizing the role of "failed states" in fomenting Islamist extremism and anti-U.S. terrorism. But they say neoconservatives are too willing for the United States to go it alone in world affairs. "The neoconservative idea that we can act alone becomes a self-fulfilling prophecy," Hulsman says.

Kagan calls it "absurd" to equate neoconservatism with unilateralism. Neoconservativism, he says, "is all about having allies and having democratic allies."

Other foreign-policy experts see the neoconservatives' influence waning. "The neoconservatives' heyday is past," says Steven Hook, an associate professor at Kent State University in Ohio. But Charles Kupchan, a senior fellow with the Council on Foreign Relations and professor at Georgetown University, says they cannot be ignored as long as Bush remains in office.

"There is no question that what was a unified and quite coherent movement has suffered a loss of influence and internal fragmentation," Kupchan says. "But they're still out there. They're still influential. As long as Bush is president, the neoconservatives' view of the world will remain influential within the administration."

For his part, Kagan goes further and says neoconservative views will be influential in the next administration — even if a Democrat wins the White House. "When the next administration is in office, we're going to have the same debate," he says, "but people will change sides."

"Whoever is in the White House tends to favor the use of power" abroad, Kagan continues. "You can't tell me that Hillary Clinton won't get into the White House and want to meddle" in world affairs.

[1] David Rose, "Neo Culpa," *Vanity Fair*, January 2007, p. 82.

[2] G. John Ikenberry, "The End of the Neo-Conservative Movement," *Survival*, Vol. 46, No. 1 (spring 2004), pp. 7-22; Anatol Lieven and John Hulsman, *Ethical Realism: A Vision for America's Role in the World* (2006), pp. xiv-xv.

[3] Robert Kagan, *Dangerous Nation: America's Place in the World From Its Earliest Days to the Dawn of the Twentieth Century* (2007).

[4] Project for a New American Century (www.newamericancentury. org/statementofprinciples.htm).

Early in his presidency, Bush concentrated on domestic issues while bucking world opinion by refusing to join the International Criminal Court, renouncing the Kyoto Protocol and threatening to withdraw from the 1972 antiballistic missile treaty. In early August 2001, he claimed he had put U.S. foreign policy "on sound footing," in part by "strengthening our relationships with our allies." Poll results two weeks later, however, showed that at least 73 percent of those surveyed in four European countries — Britain, France, Germany and Italy — believed Bush made decisions "entirely on U.S. interests" without considering Europeans' views. [18]

The Sept. 11 attacks brought a wave of pro-American sentiment throughout much of the world, including in many Arab and predominantly Muslim countries. While pushing broad anti-terrorism legislation through Congress, Bush also rallied international support in the U.N. Security Council for a U.S.-led invasion of Afghanistan to root out al Qaeda and oust its Taliban hosts. A U.S. and British bombing campaign in October set the stage for ground troops and opposition Northern Alliance forces to topple the Taliban by mid-November. An international conference in Bonn laid the framework for an interim government to take over in December, headed by the pro-American Hamid Karzai. He continues to lead the country after having won a presidential election in December 2004. [19]

With Afghanistan seemingly under control, Bush broadened the "war on terror" in his State of the Union message in January 2002 by linking terrorist groups with what he called an "axis of evil" — Iran, Iraq and North Korea — aimed at destroying the United States. In September, the administration formally unveiled Bush's new doctrine in the 33-page "National Security Strategy of the United States." [20] After promising to seek international support, the document declared, "we will not hesitate to act alone, if necessary, to exercise our right of self-defense by acting preemptively against such terrorists."

Many foreign-policy experts were critical. Harvard Professor Graham Allison, a leading expert on national-security strategy, said the doctrine amounted to "a devaluation of deterrence and containment, as if those were 20th-century ideas that are now outmoded." [21]

Meanwhile, Bush and his national security team had been not so quietly laying plans for a possible invasion of Iraq. [22] With midterm elections less than a month away, Bush won approval from Congress for a resolution authorizing the use of force against Iraq — with or with-

A military museum in Beijing displays wax models representing the Chinese Navy, Army and Air Force along with a Chinese missile and satellite model. The destruction of a Chinese weather satellite by a Chinese missile on Jan. 12 prompted the United States to reiterate its opposition to any militarization of space.

America Challenged

The second President Bush entered the White House in January 2001 after having criticized Clinton's emphasis on multilateralism, humanitarian intervention and nation-building. Bush successfully went through United Nations channels in the 2001 war against Afghanistan but invaded Iraq in 2003 without U.N. sanction. Over the next three years, popular support for Bush's policies on terrorism and Iraq fell as clear successes proved elusive. Meanwhile, U.S.-led efforts failed to deter Iran and North Korea from nuclear weapons programs — advanced in North Korea's case, less so in Iran.

U.S. National Strategy Landmarks

The United States' "national security strategy" evolved from the Cold War policies of "containment" and "nuclear deterrence" aimed against the former Soviet Union to President George W. Bush's "preventive war" doctrine designed to forestall possible attacks by terrorists or other "adversaries."

1947 *Truman Doctrine* *Aims to contain communism through economic, military aid to Greece, Turkey.*

NSC 4/A [National Security Council] Launches peacetime covert actions to counter Soviets' "psychological warfare."

1950 *NSC-68 Calls for military buildup, shift to active containment to counter Soviets.*

1953 *NSC 162/2 Establishes "New Look" national security policy envisioning "massive retaliation" and optional use of nuclear weapons.*

1961 *NSAM 2 [National Security Action Memorandum] Authorizes counterinsurgency "for use in situations short of limited war."*

1963 *"Assured Destruction" DPM [Draft Presidential Memorandum] Calls for capacity to inflict "assured destruction" of Soviet government, military controls, population centers in event of first strike against U.S. nuclear forces — giving up emphasis on blocking Soviet ability to strike the U.S.*

1969 *Nixon Doctrine Looks to treaty partners to assume primary responsibility for providing manpower for defense against aggression.*

1978 *PD-30 [Presidential Directive] Makes promotion of human rights a "major objective" of U.S. foreign policy.*

1980 *PD-59 Calls for flexible use of nuclear weapons in case of aggression against U.S. interests.*

1982 *Reagan Doctrine Uses overt and covert aid to anti-communist resistance to roll back Soviet-backed governments in Third World.*

1992 *Draft Defense Planning Guidance Broaches plan to prevent emergence of rival superpower; later revised.*

1994 *NSSUS, "Engagement and Enlargement" [National Security Strategy of the United States] Promises "engagement" throughout the world, efforts to promote "democratic enlargement."*

2002 *NSSUS, "Preemption" Declares intention to act "preemptively" against terrorist groups, other adversaries, when necessary to "prevent or forestall" attacks, even if time and place are uncertain.*

Adapted from Richard K. Betts, "U.S. National Security Strategy: Lenses and Landmarks," Princeton Project on National Security, November 2004.

---

out approval from the United Nations. At the United States' urging, the U.N. Security Council on Dec. 23 declared Iraq in "material breach" of past U.N. resolutions requiring, among other things, dismantling of any weapons of mass destruction. U.S. efforts to get a second Security Council resolution authorizing an invasion foundered in the face of a promised veto from France and reluctance from Russia and other council members. Thwarted at the U.N., Bush on March 20 went ahead and — with a coalition said to include 48 other countries — launched the invasion that overthrew Hussein's government by mid-April.

Over the next three years, the administration's swaggering reaction to the Iraq military campaign — exemplified in Bush's famous declaration on May 1 that major combat operations were over — proved to be premature at best. Meanwhile, U.S. efforts to deter Iran and North Korea from their apparent pursuit of nuclear weapons were proving unavailing. Iran announced in April 2006 that it had enriched a small amount of uranium — a critical step toward nuclear weapons. North Korea conducted a nuclear test in October. The administration enlisted support from European countries and Russia on Iran and the East Asian powers of China, Japan and

South Korea on the North Korea issue. By the end of 2006, however, diplomatic efforts had not borne fruit.

By fall 2006, the administration's confident claims to be making progress in Iraq were failing to stem the growing discontent in Iraq, in Congress, in foreign policy circles and among the general public. Two broad reviews were underway: one by a bipartisan commission headed by former Secretary of State James A. Baker III and former Rep. Lee H. Hamilton, D-Ind., the other by the administration itself. Both were held back until after the midterm election. Opposition to U.S. policies in Iraq was widely seen as the primary factor in the Democrats' recapturing control of both houses of Congress for the first time in Bush's presidency.

Despite the changed political situation, Bush turned aside the Baker-Hamilton call for a redeployment of U.S. troops and diplomatic engagement with Iran and Syria. Instead, Bush used a nationwide address on Jan. 10 to announce that he would send an additional 21,500 troops to Iraq to try to quell the sectarian violence in Baghdad and elsewhere.

CURRENT SITUATION

World of Troubles

Despite Washington's preoccupation with Iraq, China is suddenly bidding for renewed attention after a quiet but dramatic demonstration that it may have the capacity to destroy American spy satellites in space.

A Chinese missile, launched in the early morning hours of Jan. 12 Beijing time, destroyed a Chinese weather satellite scheduled to be retired. China gave no advance notice of the action and withheld any information about it for a week afterward.

Coming more than two decades after the United States and the former Soviet Union had stopped testing anti-satellite weapons, the Chinese move prompted a State Department spokesman to reiterate U.S. opposition to any militarization of space. Foreign-policy experts differed over China's possible motives, but Council on Foreign Relations analysts observed that the test showed China "can play with the big boys in space." [23]

The Chinese test was a reminder as well that the United States faces a world of troubles beyond Iraq. China's surging economy and growing military give Beijing greater influence in East Asia than either the United States or Japan, while Russia is seeking to regain influence lost after the collapse of the Soviet Union. Columbia's Betts sees signs of "a re-emergence of great power conflict." Meanwhile, the Israeli-Palestinian conflict shows no signs of abating despite the U.S. efforts to restart a peace process. U.S. policies are unpopular in much of Europe. Venezuela's populist leader Hugo Chavez is rallying an anti-U.S. coalition in South America. And Africa's daunting problems of poverty and disease dwarf any U.S. initiatives to combat them.

In many ways, the array of problems makes the 21st century more difficult if not more dangerous than the Cold War's era of so-called mutually assured nuclear destruction. "In the 21st century, the game of American grand strategy is not a game of chess, but a Rubik's cube puzzle, where a lot of different pieces have to be put together," says Princeton's Ikenberry.

U.S. efforts to back North Korea and Iran away from a nuclear-weapons path reflect the administration's efforts to adapt strategies and tactics in differing geopolitical environments. In North Korea, the administration has sought to channel negotiations into six-power talks that include China, Japan, Russia and South Korea while Pyongyang has pressed for bilateral talks with Washington aimed at normalizing relations between the two countries. In Iran, the administration deferred to diplomatic efforts by European allies but more recently stepped up U.S. pressure on Tehran — in part because of Iran's apparent support for Shiite forces in the sectarian fighting inside Iraq.

The administration appears optimistic about the prospects for resumed six-power talks with North Korea following meetings in Berlin on Jan. 17 and 18 between the State Department's Asia chief and North Korean diplomats. Christopher Hill, assistant secretary of State for East Asia and Pacific affairs, said the meetings provided a "basis for making progress" in the aftermath of stalemated talks in December. In early January, both the United States and Japan had warned of unspecified tougher measures if North Korea conducted a second test following its first nuclear detonation on Oct. 9. [24]

The negotiating track appears to be on hold in Iran as the United States combines economic pressure and gunboat diplomacy to gain Tehran's attention on both the nuclear and Iraq issues. Dissatisfied with the relatively weak economic sanctions voted by the U.N. Security Council in December, U.S. officials are trying to pressure foreign governments and financial institutions to sever or cut back financial ties with Iran. The United

Should Congress try to block President Bush's ability to send additional troops to Iraq?

YES
Sen. Edward M. Kennedy, D-Mass.
Member, Senate Armed Services Committee

Written for *CQ Researcher*, January 2007

For four long years, President Bush's assertion of unprecedented power has gone unchecked by Congress. For too long, the administration was allowed to operate in secrecy. Not just in Iraq, but also here at home — detentions in defiance of the Geneva Conventions, eavesdropping on people's telephone calls, reading their mail and reviewing their financial records, all without judicial authorization.

The president has made clear that he intends to move ahead with his misguided plan to escalate the war. That's the hallmark of his presidency — to go it alone and ignore contrary opinions. The American people spoke out against the war at the ballot box in November. Our generals opposed the escalation. They do not believe adding more American troops can end a civil war or encourage the transfer of responsibility to the Iraqis, but their warnings have gone unheeded. Now Congress is about to consider a non-binding resolution of no confidence in the president's reckless, last-ditch effort to salvage his strategy.

Passage of the non-binding resolution will send an important message about the need for a different course in Iraq, but it's only a first step. The president has made clear that he intends to ignore non-binding resolutions. If we disagree with the president's failed course, it will take stronger action to stop him. We cannot stand by as the president sends more of our sons and daughters into a civil war.

I've introduced legislation to prohibit the president from raising troop levels in Iraq unless he obtains specific new authorization from Congress. The initial authorization bears no relevance to the current hostilities in Iraq. There were no weapons of mass destruction and no alliance with al Qaeda, and Saddam Hussein is no more. The president should not be permitted to escalate our involvement unless Congress grants its approval.

For too long Congress has given President Bush a blank check to pursue his disastrous policy. He should not be permitted to take the desperate step of sending even more troops to die in the quagmire of civil war without convincing Congress why this escalation can succeed. As the constitutional scholars concluded in their recent letter to leaders of Congress: "Far from an invasion of presidential power, it would be an abdication of its own constitutional role if Congress were to fail to inquire, debate and legislate, as it sees fit, regarding the best way forward in Iraq."

We must not abdicate that responsibility any longer.

NO
Sen. Johnny Isakson, R-Ga.
Member, Senate Foreign Relations Committee

Written for *CQ Researcher*, January 2007

President Bush has proposed increasing the number of American troops to serve with Iraqi security forces in securing, holding and building in those areas of Baghdad engulfed in sectarian violence.

The president has laid out a clear and precise plan that absolutely requires the cooperation and support of the Iraqi people and the Iraqi military. I believe that the president's plan is the best opportunity — and quite frankly the last opportunity — for the Iraqi government to create a foundation for political reconciliation.

As the president said in his State of the Union address, "This is not the fight we entered in Iraq, but it is the fight we're in." The president also told Congress that, regardless of what mistakes may have been made, "Whatever you voted for, you did not vote for failure."

While the ultimate success of the president's plan depends on the Iraqis and their government living up to their responsibilities, the opportunity for them to do so depends on our help in securing Baghdad.

Our enemies and the enemies of the Iraqi people watch our actions and listen to our words. Our commander in chief has committed our armed forces to a plan, and the Iraqi government has committed to be a full partner. At such a critical time, when our country is committed to this major battle in the overall global war on terror, the words of Congress should not send a mixed message to our troops, the Iraqi people or our enemies.

While the situation in Iraq is grave, it would turn dire if we prematurely withdraw our forces and withdraw funding necessary to move Iraq forward. During two weeks of hearings, every expert witness — without exception — testified that if the United States retreats or redeploys its troops, there would be catastrophic loss of life, and the potential for a regional conflict in the Middle East would increase exponentially.

As I see it, we have two options: We can choose an opportunity for success or we can choose a recipe for disaster. Our brave men and women in uniform and the people of Iraq deserve to see a successful outcome, and our national security depends on it.

I remain committed to ensuring that the future holds this promise.

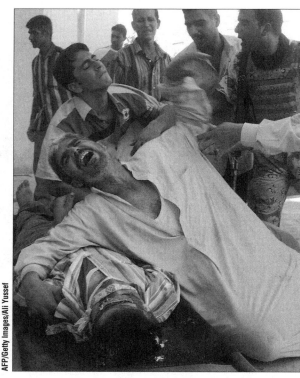

AFP/Getty Images/Ali Yussef

An Iraqi man mourns a dead relative in Baquba on July 12, 2006. At least 44,000 civilians have died since the U.S.-led invasion of Iraq in 2003, according to the Brookings Institution, and more than 3,000 American troops. The rising death toll has helped to turn U.S. public opinion against the war.

Clash of Views

As the casualty count for U.S. and Iraqi troops and Iraqi civilians continues to rise, sectarian violence in Baghdad and elsewhere shows few signs of abating. The continuing bloodshed fuels growing domestic opposition to the U.S. role in Iraq, but President Bush is moving ahead with his plan to raise U.S. troop levels there despite looming congressional action to go on record against the plan.

Bush presented the plan in his Jan. 10 address as part of a coordinated strategy with the government of Iraqi Prime Minister Nouri al-Maliki to restore order in Baghdad. In fact, Maliki had actually urged a different plan on Bush in November. Maliki wanted U.S. forces to form a protective cordon around Baghdad while Shiite-led Iraqi security forces tried to quell the Sunni-Shiite conflict.

Even in his address, however, Bush hinted at the tensions between the two governments by stressing Maliki's promise that his government would not allow "sectarian or political interference" with the efforts to end violence in Baghdad. "If the Iraqi government does not follow through on its promises," Bush said, "it will lose the support of the American people."

Bush passed over any mention of the recommendations to engage Iran and Syria in diplomatic efforts to restore order in Iraq. Instead, he blamed both countries for "allowing terrorists and insurgents to use their territory to move in and out of Iraq" and accused Iran of "providing material support for attacks on American troops." He promised to "seek out and destroy" networks providing weapons or training to "our enemies in Iraq."

Bush's plan drew virtually unanimous opposition from congressional Democrats, which was unabated after the president stood by his proposal in his State of the Union message on Jan. 23. A few Republicans also expressed outright opposition, while several others voiced doubts.

Opponents focused on two main themes: They doubted that the plan would succeed militarily or that Maliki would follow through with his political commitments. But the authors of the leading Senate resolution to oppose the plan also disagreed with Bush's decision to spurn diplomatic overtures.

Sponsored by Sens. Joseph R. Biden Jr., D-Del., Carl Levin, D-Mich., and Chuck Hagel, R-Neb., the resolution declared: "The United States should engage nations in the Middle East to develop a regional, internationally

States in January also dispatched a second aircraft-carrier strike group to the Persian Gulf and beefed up anti-missile defenses in two U.S. allies in the Gulf: Kuwait and Qatar. At the same time, officials confirmed that Bush had previously authorized U.S. troops inside Iraq to kill or capture Iranian operatives suspected of taking part in the sectarian violence. [25]

The tough moves against Iran appeared to recognize that — in contrast to economically strapped and diplomatically isolated North Korea — the United States was playing with a weak hand in dealing with Tehran. "Iran is riding a wave of Shiite resurgence, it has oil income, and it continues to have trade ties with European countries, China, and Russia," says Council on Foreign Relations fellow Kupchan. "Iran is holding a pretty good deck of cards."

sponsored peace and reconciliation process for Iraq." The Senate Foreign Relations Committee approved the resolution on Jan. 24 by a 12-9 vote — with Hagel joining the committee's 11 Democrats in voting for it.

Meanwhile, Republican senators are divided. A resolution drafted by Virginia's John W. Warner with bipartisan support "disagrees" with Bush's decision, while another — being prepared by Arizona's John McCain — would set "benchmarks" for progress in Iraq. The full Senate was expected to vote on the issue during the week of Feb. 5, with the House to follow later.

In Baghdad, meanwhile, Maliki is contending with his own problems in a divided government. Maliki presented the security plan to the Iraqi Parliament on Jan. 25 with his strongest pledge to date to crack down on sectarian militias, only to be met by a call from a leading Sunni lawmaker for oversight to make sure that Sunnis were not unfairly singled out. Despite the sharp exchange, the televised session ended with the Parliament voting to back the plan. [26]

To Princeton's Lieven and Hulsman, Iraq provides a case study of the ethical-realism critique that U.S. foreign policy goes astray when it pursues overly ambitious goals with too little regard for obstacles and too little attention to the need for support from other countries.

Iraq shows "the extreme difficulty of bringing about democracy in a deeply divided society and the difficulty of bringing about short-term economic development in a country with a weak government," says Lieven. "It also shows that even when an election is successful, it can be irrelevant to the purpose of nation-building."

Now, Hulsman says, the United States must look to other countries in the region, including Iran and Syria, to achieve any acceptable outcome. "The only way to leave this very fragile state, the only way it stays unitary, is to get the consent of the regional players," he says. "Any construct we leave will fall apart unless they agree."

OUTLOOK

"Rebalancing" U.S. Policy?

From its earliest days, the United States has been a nation with big ambitions. The founding generations saw the American Revolution as an example for other subjugated peoples to follow. Later generations envisioned — and fulfilled — the nation's "manifest destiny"

to reach from the Atlantic to the Pacific and beyond. Twentieth-century Americans saw a mission to "make the world safe for democracy."

Ambitions sometimes exceeded the reach. The United States did not annex Cuba or Nicaragua in the 19th century. The Senate turned away from the League of Nations and President Woodrow Wilson's internationalist vision after World War I. U.S. leaders talked about liberating the "enslaved peoples" of Eastern Europe during the Cold War but sent no help to Hungarians in 1956 or Czechoslovaks in 1968. The first President Bush left the Kurds and other Iraqi opponents of Saddam Hussein in the lurch after the first Gulf War.

Critics see a lesson that they say the current President Bush has failed to grasp: The United States can do only so much in world affairs. "There are opportunity costs in foreign policy," says Kent State Professor Hook. "The time, energy and resources devoted to one regional trouble spot divert time, energy and resources from other parts of the world."

Many critics of Bush's decision to raise troop levels in Iraq are using an analogy from the card game of blackjack to make their point — accusing him of a reckless decision to "double down," or double his bet in hopes of recouping his losses. Richard N. Haass, president of the Council on Foreign Relations and the State Department's director of policy planning in Bush's first two years in the White House, makes the same point with an analogy from the world of business.

By investing more in Iraq, Haass writes in an op-ed piece in *Financial Times*, Bush has failed to do what a prudent investor should do — "assess and rebalance" the U.S. foreign-policy portfolio. Beyond the likelihood that the troop increase will not bring success in Iraq, Haass says, the decision "limits the ability of the U.S. to focus on other matters, be they threats or opportunities. There are only so many troops, dollars and hours in the day to go round." [27]

Bush and other administration officials continue to profess optimism about Iraq. But Lt. Gen. David Petraeus, Bush's new choice to be U.S. commander in Iraq, was temperate in predicting success when he appeared before the Senate Armed Services Committee on Jan. 23. "There are no guarantees," he said. [28]

Administration supporters believe the plan has a chance for success. "Victory in Iraq is still possible at an acceptable level of effort," the AEI's Kagan writes in a 47-page report. [29]

Critics, however, say the U.S. military is simply ill-equipped to bring order to Iraq. "The shock-and-awe approach to nation-building has proved to be fatally flawed," says Hook, referring to the administration's description of the initial military campaign.

Meanwhile, America's remaining 25 coalition partners, including Britain, are pulling troops out of Iraq. And Secretary of State Rice, meeting with NATO diplomats in Brussels on Jan. 26, found little support among U.S. allies for sending more troops to Afghanistan, where a Taliban insurgency continues to fester. "The good will that has greased the machine that is the transatlantic partnership is just not there," says conservative foreign-policy expert Hulsman.

Some experts expect a post-Iraq retreat from international ventures. "The appetite of the American public for the broad-ranging internationalism of Bush's first term is clearly drying up," says Kupchan, at the Council on Foreign Relations. Others are less certain about the impact. "I don't think it's likely that the United States is going to retreat into isolationism," says Betts, of Columbia's Institute of War and Peace Studies. "But if there's real failure in Iraq, there will be a marginal tilt toward greater caution."

Whatever the outcome in Iraq, says the New America Foundation's Lieven, American policymakers must recognize the need to be realistic in defining U.S. national interests abroad and more cautious in committing U.S. resources. "If your resources aren't unlimited, you've got to choose," he says, adding: "You should be cautious and prudent when it comes to the lives of your soldiers and the international prestige of your country."

In the end, Schmitt, the AEI neoconservative, agrees. "Foreign policy is just made up of principles that have to be prudently applied," he says. "Sometimes you get it right, and sometimes you get it wrong."

NOTES

1. See Nazila Fathi and Michael Slackman, "Rebuke in Iran to Its President on Nuclear Role," *The New York Times*, Jan. 19, 2007, p. A1.

2. http://Kudlowsmoneypolitics.blogspot.com (Jan. 10, 2007).

3. Quoted in Mark Mazzetti, "Leading Senator Assails President on Iran Stance," *The New York Times*, Jan. 20, 2007, p. A1. See also John M. Donnelly,

"Democrats Warn Bush on Iran, Syria," *CQ Today*, Jan. 12, 2007.

4. Steven W. Hook and John Spanier, *American Foreign Policy Since World War II* (17th ed.), 2007.

5. Anatol Lieven and John Hulsman, *Ethical Realism: A Vision for America's Role in the World* (2006).

6. G. John Ikenberry and Anne-Marie Slaughter, "Forging a World of Liberty Under Law: U.S. National Security in the 21st Century," Princeton Project on National Security, September 2006; www.wws.princeton.edu/ppns/.

7. Jeffrey W. Legro, *Rethinking the World: Great Power Strategies and International Order* (2005).

8. For background, see the following *CQ Researcher* reports: Kenneth Jost, "International Law," Dec. 17, 2004, pp. 1049-1072; Mary H. Cooper, "Global Warming Treaty," Jan. 26, 2001, pp. 41-64; and Marcia Clemmitt, "Climate Change," Jan. 27, 2006, pp. 73-96.

9. White House, "The National Security Strategy of the United States," September 2002; www.whitehouse.gov/nsc/nss.html; cited in Hook and Spanier, *op. cit.*, pp. 325-328. For background, see Mary H. Cooper, "New Defense Priorities," *CQ Researcher*, Sept. 13, 2002, pp. 721-744; and Adriel Bettelheim, "Presidential Power," *CQ Researcher*, Nov. 15, 2002, pp. 945-968.

10. See Jackson Diehl, "Rice's Rhetoric, in Full Retreat," *The Washington Post*, Jan. 22, 2007, p. A18. For background, see Kenneth Jost and Benton Ives-Halperin, "Democracy in the Arab World," *CQ Researcher*, Jan. 30, 2004, pp. 73-100, and Peter Katel, "Middle East Tensions," *CQ Researcher*, Oct. 27, 2006, pp. 889-912.

11. Michael Mandelbaum, *Democracy's Good Name: The Rise and the Risks of the World's Most Popular Form of Government* (2007).

12. German Marshall Fund, "Transatlantic Trends 2006," p. 50; www.gmf.org.

13. Background drawn from Robert Kagan, *Dangerous Nation: America's Place in the World from Its Earliest Days to the Dawn of the Twentieth Century* (2006); Charles A. Kupchan, *The End of the American Era: U.S. Foreign Politics and the Geopolitics of the Twenty-First Century* (2002); and Hook and Spanier, *op. cit.*

14. For excerpts, see Hook and Spanier, *ibid.*, pp. 39-40. The full text is reproduced in George F. Kennan, *American Diplomacy: 1900-1950* (1951), pp. 107-128.

15. The Associated Press, "Ford Once Called Carter a 'Disaster'; Ex-President Also Said Reagan Got Too Much Cold War Credit," Jan. 13, 2007.

16. For background, see Kenneth Jost, "Foreign Policy and Public Opinion," *CQ Researcher*, July 15, 1994, pp. 601-624.

17. For background, see Kenneth Jost, "Re-examining 9/11," *CQ Researcher*, June 4, 2004, pp. 493-516.

18. Bush quoted in Frank M. Bruni, "At 6 Months, Bush Says, He's Doing Pretty Well," *The New York Times*, Aug. 4, 2001, p. A12; survey by the *International Herald Tribune*, Pew Research Center and Council on Foreign Relations reported in Adam Clymer, "Surveys Find European Publics Critical of Bush Policies," *The New York Times*, Aug. 16, 2001, p. A12.

19. For background, see Kenneth Jost, "Rebuilding Afghanistan," *CQ Researcher*, Dec. 21, 2001, pp. 1041-1064.

20. Available at www.whitehouse.gov/nsc/nss.pdf.

21. Quoted in Sonni Effron and Carol J. Williams, "Plan Likely to Further Isolate U.S.," *Los Angeles Times*, Sept. 21, 2002, p. 1A.

22. For a compact overview through early 2006, see Hook and Spanier, *op. cit.*, pp. 339-357. See also these *CQ Researcher* reports: David Masci, "Confronting Iraq," Oct. 4, 2002, pp. 793-816; David Masci, "Rebuilding Iraq," July 25, 2003, pp. 625-648; Pamela M. Prah, "War in Iraq," Oct. 21, 2005, pp. 881-908; and Peter Katel, "New Strategy in Iraq," Feb. 23, 2007.

23. Joanna Klonsky and Michael Moran, "China Ups Ante in Space," Council on Foreign Relations Daily Analysis, Jan. 19, 2007; www.cfr.org/publication/12454/china_ups_ante_in_space.html. The backgrounder provides links to news coverage and other resources. See also David E. Sanger and Joseph Kahn, "U.S. Officials Try to Interpret China's Silence Over Satellite," *The New York Times*, Jan. 22, 2007, p. A3.

24. See "U.S. Envoy Upbeat About North Korea Talks," *The New York Times*, Jan. 22, 2007, p. A10, and earlier coverage Jan. 5 and Jan. 19.

25. See Lionel Behner, "New Squeeze on Iran," Council on Foreign Relations Daily Analysis, Jan. 25, 2007; www.cfr.org/publication/12495/new_squeeze_on_iran.html?breadcrumb=%2F); Dafna Linzer, "Troops Authorized to Kill Iranian Operatives in Iraq," *The Washington Post*, Jan. 26, 2007, p. A1.

26. Account drawn from Marc Santora, "Iraq Leader and Sunni Officials in Sectarian Clash on Security," *The New York Times*, Jan. 26, 2007, p. A1.

27. Richard N. Haass, "America Needs to Rethink Its Portfolio," *Financial Times*, Jan. 17, 2007, p. 15.

28. See Peter Baker, "Defending Iraq War, Defiant Cheney Sees 'Enormous Successes,'" *The Washington Post*, Jan. 25, 2007, p. A1; Michael R. Gordon, "General Says New Strategy in Iraq Can Work Over Time," *The New York Times*, Jan. 24, 2007, p. A1.

29. Frederick W. Kagan, "Choosing Victory: A Plan for Success in Iraq," American Enterprise Institute, January 2007 (www.aei.org).

BIBLIOGRAPHY

Books

Harvey, Robert, *Global Disorder: America and the Threat of World Conflict*, Carroll & Graf, 2003.
A British journalist-author combines a comprehensive overview of post-9/11 world threats with a call for the United States to act as the "cornerstone" of world order while avoiding the risks of "unilateralism." Harvey is a columnist for the [London] *Daily Telegraph* and author of five other books on international relations. The book was published in paper as *Global Disorder: How to Avoid a Fourth World War* (2004).

Kagan, Robert, *Dangerous Nation: America's Place in the World from Its Earliest Days to the Dawn of the Twentieth Century*, Knopf, 2006.
A neoconservative foreign-policy expert and *Washington Post* columnist argues that the United States has played an assertive role in world affairs throughout its history. A planned second volume will cover 20th-century foreign policy. Includes detailed notes, 26-page bibliography.

Kupchan, Charles A., *The End of the American Era: U.S. Foreign Policy and the Geopolitics of the Twenty-first Century*, **Knopf, 2002.**
A senior fellow at the Council on Foreign Relations and a professor at Georgetown University synthesizes history and current events to argue that as the era of American primacy ends, the United States must work harder to cultivate a sense of "common interest" with emerging centers of power. Includes detailed notes, nine-page bibliography.

Lieven, Anatol, and John Hulsman, *Ethical Realism: A Vision for America's Role in the World*, **Random House, 2006.**
Coming from different political backgrounds, the authors argue that U.S. foreign policy must combine genuine morality with tough, practical common sense. Lieven is a senior fellow at the centrist New America Foundation; Hulsman, formerly with the conservative Heritage Foundation, is at the German Council on Foreign Relations.

Mandelbaum, Michael, *The Case for Goliath: How America Acts as the World's Government in the Twenty-First Century*, **Pantheon, 2005.**
A professor at the Johns Hopkins University's School of Advanced International Studies depicts the United States' role in world affairs not as an empire or a superpower but as the "world's government." Includes detailed notes.

Reports and Studies

Ikenberry, G. John, and Anne-Marie Slaughter (co-directors), *Forging a World of Liberty Under Law: U.S. National Security in the 21st Century: Final Report of the Princeton Project on National Security*, **Woodrow Wilson School of Public and International Affairs, 2006; www.wws.princeton.edu/ppns/.**
The report advances a series of proposals, including the creation of a global "Concert of Democracies," to strengthen security cooperation and promote creation of liberal democracy. Slaughter is dean and Ikenberry a professor at the Wilson School.

Books on Foreign Policy From CQ Press

CQ Press publishes a number of reference works on foreign policy, including:

American Foreign Policy Since World War II, 17th ed., by Steven W. Hook and John Spanier, provides a concise review of the conduct of American foreign policy. *U.S. Foreign Policy: The Paradox of World Power*, by Steven W. Hook is a foundational book covering the process of foreign-policy formulation. *Contemporary Cases in U.S. Foreign Policy: From Terrorism to Trade*, 2nd ed., edited by Ralph G. Carter, is a collection of 15 case studies with chapters on Iraq, North Korea and detainees' rights, among others.

In print and online, *Political Handbook of the World 2007* (2006) is a staple resource for in-depth political profiles on countries, territories and intergovernmental organizations. CQ Press also offers four regional political guides: *Political Handbook of Asia 2007* (2007); *Political Handbook of Africa 2007* (2006); *Political Handbook of Europe 2007* (2006); and *Political Handbook of the Middle East 2006* (2006).

For further in-depth analysis of the Middle East, *The Middle East*, 10th ed., (11th ed. available July 2007) is considered a classic text among students, professors and researchers. Jacob Bercovitch and Judith Fretter's *Regional Guide to International Conflict and Management from 1945 to 2003* (2004) provides information on 340 conflicts since World War II. Bert Chapman's *Researching National Security and Intelligence Policy* (2004) is a useful guide for researchers seeking resources on national security policy. Bruce Maxwell's *Terrorism: A Documentary History* (2002) is a ready-reference featuring 100 entries from 1972 through 2002. *World at Risk: A Global Issues Sourcebook* (2002) arranges global issues in a convenient A-to-Z format, covering 30 topics from arms control to war crimes.

For More Information

American Enterprise Institute, 1150 17th St., N.W., Washington, DC 20036; (202) 862-5800; www.aei.org. Conservative public-policy organization dedicated to research and education.

Carnegie Endowment for International Peace, 1779 Massachusetts Ave., N.W., Washington, DC 20036; (202) 483-7600; www.ceip.org. Think tank advancing international cooperation and U.S. international engagement.

Center for Strategic and International Studies, 1800 K St., N.W., Washington, DC 20006; (202) 887-0200; www.csis.org. Promotes global security by providing insight and policy solutions to decision-makers.

Council on Foreign Relations, 58 East 68th St., New York, NY 10021; (212) 434-9400; www.cfr.org. Nonpartisan foreign-policy think tank.

Heritage Foundation, 214 Massachusetts Ave., N.E., Washington DC 20002; (202) 546-4400; www.heritage.org. Conservative policy-research institute.

New America Foundation, 1630 Connecticut Ave., N.W., 7th Floor, Washington, DC 20009; (202) 986-2700; www.newamerica.net. Dedicated to bringing new voices and ideas into foreign-policy discourse.

Princeton Project on National Security, Woodrow Wilson School of Public and International Affairs, Princeton University, 423G Robertson Hall, Princeton, NJ 08544-1013; (609) 258-2228; www.wws.princeton.edu/ppns/. Academic initiative for developing a long-term U.S. national security strategy.

Project for the New American Century, 1150 17th St., N.W., Suite 510, Washington, DC 20036; (202) 293-4983; www.newamericancentury.org. Neoconservative think tank promoting U.S. global leadership.

15

Illegal Immigration

Peter Katel, Patrick Marshall and Alan Greenblatt

Mexican immigrants in Homestead, Fla., negotiate with a man seeking four workers on May 7, 2004. Illegal immigrants make up only about 5 percent of the U.S. work force, but critics say they are taking many Americans' jobs by offering to work for low wages and no benefits. Immigration advocates counter that immigrants do the jobs Americans don't want and bolster the economy.

From *CQ Researcher*,
May 6, 2005. (Updated May 21, 2007).

The only future awaiting María and Juan Gomez in their tiny village in Mexico was working the fields from sunup to sundown, living mostly on tortillas and beans. So a dozen years ago, when they were both 17, they crossed into the United States illegally, near San Diego. Now ensconced in the large Latino community outside Washington, D.C., they are working hard at building a life for themselves and their young son.

Juan and María (not their real names) follow a simple strategy — staying out of trouble and undercutting competitors. Juan does landscaping, charging about $600 for major yard work — about $400 less than the typical legal contractor. María cleans houses for $70 — house-cleaning services normally charge $85 or more.

They aren't complaining, but María and Juan know they offer bargain-basement prices. "You walk down the street, and every house being built, Hispanics are building it," María says in Spanish. "This country is getting more work for less money."

Indeed, some sectors of the economy might have a hard time functioning without illegal workers. Brendan Flanagan, director of legislative affairs for the National Restaurant Association, insists, "Restaurants, hotels, nursing homes, agriculture — a very broad group of industries — are looking for a supply of workers to remain productive," he says, because in many parts of the country, native workers aren't available at any price. Moreover, lobbyists for employers insist that their members can't tell false papers from the real ones that employees present to prove they're here legally.

But Harvard economist George Borjas counters that when an American employer claims he cannot find a legal or native-born worker willing to do a certain job, "[h]e is leaving out a very key part

Most Illegal Immigrants Live in Four States

More than half of the nation's more than 10 million illegal immigrants live in four states — California, Texas, Florida and New York.

Estimated Distribution of Illegal Immigrants
(average of data from 2002-2004)

■	300,000-2.4 Million
▨	200,000-250,000
▦	100,000-150,000
▩	55,000-85,000
□	20,000-35,000
□	Under 10,000

Source: Jeffrey S. Passel, "Estimates of the Size and Characteristics of the Undocumented Population," Pew Hispanic Center, March 21, 2005, based on data from the March 2004 "Current Population Survey" by the Census Bureau and Department of Labor

of that phrase. He should add 'at the wage I'm going to pay.' " [1]

Many Americans blame illegal immigrants like María and Juan not only for depressing wages but also for a host of other problems, including undermining U.S. security.

But the U.S. government refuses to tighten up the border, they say.

"The reason we do not have secure borders is because of an insatiable demand for cheap labor," says Rep. Tom Tancredo, R-Colo., a leading immigration-control advocate in Congress whose presidential campaign centers on the issue. "We have the ability to secure the border; we choose not to. The Democratic Party sees massive immigration — legal and illegal — as a massive source of voters. The Republican Party looks at the issue and says, 'Wow,

that's a lot of cheap labor coming across that border.' "

Some other politicians are following Tancredo's lead. In April 2005, California governor Arnold Schwarzenegger ratcheted up his anti-illegal immigration rhetoric. Praising anti-immigration activists monitoring the Mexican border in Arizona, he said, "Our federal government is not doing their job. It's a shame that the private citizen has to go in there and start patrolling our borders."

There are more than 10 million immigrants living illegally in the United States, compared with 3.5 million only fifteen years ago, according to the non-profit Pew Hispanic Center. [2] And since 2000 the illegal population has been growing by a half-million illegal immigrants a year — nearly 1,400 people a day, according to the Census Bureau and other sources. [3]

While illegal immigrants make up only about 5 percent of the U.S. work force, they are rapidly making their presence known in non-traditional areas for immigrants to settle such as the Midwest and South. Willing to work for low wages, undocumented workers are creating a political backlash among some residents in the new states, which have seen a nearly tenfold increase in illegal immigration since 1990.

"Immigration is now a national phenomenon in a way that was less true a decade ago," Mark Krikorian, executive director of the nonpartisan Center for Immigration Studies said. "In places like Georgia and Alabama, which had little experience with immigration before, people are experiencing it firsthand. Immigrants are working in chicken plants, carpet mills and construction. It's right in front of people's faces now." [4]

The debate has taken on populist undertones, says Dan Stein, president of the Federation for American Immigration Reform (FAIR), because some activists perceive a wide gap between policymakers' positions and popular sentiment in affected regions. "The issue is about elites, major financial interests and global economic forces arrayed against the average American voter," said Stein, whose group favors strict immigration policies. "The depth of anger should not be underestimated." [5]

Grass-roots organizations have formed in seven states to push for laws denying public services for illegal immigrants and Rep. Tancredo has decided to run for president in 2008 to "build a fire" around the need for immigration reform. [6]

But reform means different things to different people.

To Rep. F. James Sensenbrenner Jr., R-Wis., former chairman of the House Judiciary Committee, reform means imposing new restrictions on asylum seekers, blocking states from issuing driver's licenses to illegal immigrants and finishing a border fence near San Diego.

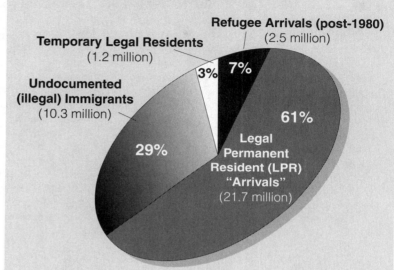

Majority of Immigrants in U.S. Are Legal

More than 21 million legal "permanent" immigrants live in the United States — more than twice the number of illegal immigrants.

Status of Immigrants in U.S.

Refugee Arrivals (post-1980) (2.5 million)

Temporary Legal Residents (1.2 million)

Undocumented (illegal) Immigrants (10.3 million)

3%   7%

29%   61%

Legal Permanent Resident (LPR) "Arrivals" (21.7 million)

Sources: Jeffrey S. Passel, "Estimates of the Size and Characteristics of the Undocumented Population," Pew Hispanic Center, March 21, 2005, based on data from the March 2004 "Current Population Survey" by the Census Bureau and Department of Labor

"We will never have homeland security if we don't have border security," Sensenbrenner said in March 2005. [7] Sensenbrenner's tough, new Real ID bill, which requires proof of citizenship or legal status in the United States in order to get a driver's license, was signed into law in May 2005 and will take effect in May 2008.

To Sen. John McCain, R-Ariz., reform means enabling illegal immigrants to stay here legally because, he contends, the nation's economy depends on them. "As long as there are jobs to be had . . . that won't be done by Americans [illegal immigrants] are going to come and fill those jobs," he said in April 2005. [8]

Echoing McCain, President Bush has endorsed the creation of a "guest worker" program that would grant temporary legal status to illegal workers. "If there is a job opening which an American won't do . . . and there's a willing worker and a willing employer, that job ought to

Immigration Debate Moves Behind the Wheel

The tension was high in suburban Atlanta in October 2005 when protesters confronted hundreds of illegal immigrants who were marching to demand the right to obtain driver's licenses.

The peaceful, sign-waving march soon turned ugly, as angry epithets were hurled back and forth across busy Buford Highway. "This is my country! You are criminals! You cannot have my country!" shouted D.A. King, a former insurance salesman and self-styled anti-immigrant vigilante. Boos and hisses erupted from the mostly Hispanic immigrants across the street. [1]

The heated exchange, caught by a CNN television crew, captured the intensifying debate over driver's licenses for illegal immigrants. Eleven states now issue such licenses, and several others are considering permitting similar laws, but a growing grass-roots movement opposes the licenses, including groups like the American Resistance Foundation, founded by King.

The immigrants' supporters say illegal workers are the backbone of the nation's economic success and that being able to drive legally would allow them to open bank accounts and do other tasks requiring an official identification card. It would also make America's roads safer, the proponents say, by holding immigrants to the same driving and insurance requirements as U.S. citizens. Unlicensed drivers are nearly five times more likely to be in a fatal crash than licensed drivers, and uninsured drivers cause 14 percent of all accidents, according to the AAA Foundation for Traffic Safety. [2] But King and others say uncontrolled immigration depresses wages, increases crime and causes neighborhood blight, and that granting undocumented workers driver's licenses would only legalize illegal behavior.

Until now the debate over immigrant driver's licenses has been restricted to a few traditional border states, like California, where a new law permitting undocumented workers to get licenses helped defeat Democratic Gov. Gray Davis during the 2003 gubernatorial recall election. Lawmakers repealed the law shortly after Arnold Schwarzenegger was inaugurated as governor, and Schwarzenegger has since vetoed related bills. He wants the licenses of undocumented workers to bear a unique mark.

Now the debate has moved to states throughout the country. In Utah and Tennessee, state laws now give illegal workers so-called "driving privilege cards," which warn in bold, red letters they cannot be used as legal identification. [3] New York State's motor-vehicles commissioner in April 2005 denied license renewals and suspended the licenses of illegal immigrants without a Social Security card or acceptable visa. [4] The state's Supreme Court, which made a preliminary ruling rejecting the commissioner's action, is currently hearing the issue.

Now some in Congress want to jump into the fray — even though issuing driver's licenses has long been the domain of the states. In January 2005, Wisconsin Republican Rep. F. James Sensenbrenner Jr. proposed the Real ID Act, which would establish national driver's license standards, toughen asylum requirements and speedy completion of a fence on the U.S.-Mexico border near San Diego. But the driver's license provision has caused the most debate.

"My bill's goal is straightforward: It seeks to prevent another 9/11-type attack by disrupting terrorist travel," Sensenbrenner said. The bill would require states to verify that driver's-license applicants reside legally in the United States before issuing a license that could be used for federal identification purposes, such as boarding an airplane. [5] The bill, which Sensenbrenner attached to a "must-pass" emergency military-spending bill, was approved by Congress and signed into law on May 11, 2005, and is scheduled to go into effect in May 2008. [6]

The bill's supporters say providing secure driver's licenses to illegal immigrants will improve national security, because licenses are now the de facto form of identification in the United States. The 9/11 Commission, which investigated the September 11, 2001, terrorist attacks, found that the attackers used driver's licenses rather than passports to avoid creating suspicion. [7] "At many entry points to vulnerable facilities, including gates for boarding aircraft," the commission's 2004 report noted, "sources of identification are the last opportunity to ensure that people are who they say they are and to check whether they are terrorists." [8]

be filled on a legal basis, no matter where the person comes from," Bush said after a meeting at his Texas ranch on March 23, 2005, with Mexican President Vicente Fox and Canadian Prime Minister Paul Martin. [9]

The issue of immigration has, in fact, divided the Republican Party, with the more conservative elements arguing for strict enforcement of the borders and expulsion of illegal aliens. The Republican-controlled House

During House debate, Sensenbrenner said that the Real ID bill might have prevented the Sept. 11 attacks because it requires that any license or ID card issued to visitors expire on the same date the person's visa expires.

"Mohammed Atta, ringleader of the 9/11 murderers, entered the United States on a six-month visa [which] expired on July 9, 2001. He got a [six-month] driver's license from the state of Florida on May 5, 2001," Sensenbrenner said. "Had this bill been in effect at the time, that driver's license would have expired on July 9, and he would not have been able to use that driver's license to get on a plane." [9]

Immigrants and community leaders in New York City protest on April 13, 2004, against a state policy that denies driver's licenses to hundreds of thousands of immigrants. The protest followed a crackdown on individuals without Social Security numbers.

Jack Martin, special projects director for the Federation for American Immigration Reform (FAIR), which seeks to halt illegal immigration, says the difficulty of distinguishing between "illegal aliens merely looking for jobs and potential terrorists looking to carry out attacks" argues against granting licenses to non-citizens. "People who have entered the country illegally — regardless of their motives — should not be able to receive a driver's license," he says.

But critics of the law say denying driver's licenses to illegal immigrants would pose a greater threat to U.S. safety. "Allowing a driver the possibility to apply for a license to drive to work means that person's photograph, address and proof of insurance will be on file at the local DMV," a recent *Los Angeles Times* editorial argued. "And that is something to make us all feel safer." [10] The Real ID Act "threatens to handcuff state officials with impossible, untested mandates, such as requiring instant verification

of birth certificates, without providing the time or resources needed," says the National Conference of State Legislatures. [11] Moreover, says Joan Friedland, a policy attorney with the National Immigration Law Center, the law is just "smoke and mirrors" because it is "an inadequate and meaningless substitute for real, comprehensive reform and doesn't resolve the problem of national security." But Martin says a national law that coordinates driver's-license policies across the nation is vital to security. "Right now, there is virtually a different approach in every state," he says. "People who wish to take advantage of the system can easily target whichever state has the most lax requirements."

— **Kate Templin**

[1] Quoted from "CNN Presents: Immigrant Nation: Divided Country," Oct. 17, 2004.

[2] www.aaafoundation.org/pdf/UnlicensedToKill2.pdf.

[3] T. R. Reid and Darryl Fears, "Driver's License Curtailed as Identification," *The Washington Post*, April 17, 2003, A3.

[4] Nina Bernstein, "Fight Over Immigrants' Driving Licenses Is Back in Court," *New York Times*, April 7, 2005, B6.

[5] www.house.gov/sensenbrenner/newsletterapril2005.pdf.

[6] Anne Plummer, "Immigration Provisions Likely to Remain in Supplemental Spending Bill, Reid Says," *CQ Today*, April 25, 2005.

[7] For background, see Kenneth Jost, "Re-examining 9/11," *CQ Researcher*, June 4, 2004, 493-516.

[8] National Commission on Terrorist Attacks Upon the United States, 390.

[9] Frank James, "Immigrant ID Rules Debated," *Chicago Tribune*, March 12, 2005, News Section, 1.

[10] "Real ID, Unreal Expectations," *Los Angeles Times*, April 6, 2005.

[11] National Conference of State Legislatures, www.ncsl.org.

passed H.R. 4437 in December 2005, a measure that contained procedures for securing the borders, harsher penalties for those assisting illegal entry into the country and provisions for deporting illegal aliens. The proposed

legislation does not provide for a guest worker program or any type of amnesty for illegal aliens.

The Senate has remained more liberal than the House on immigration matters, reaching agreement with the

Illegal Migrants Leaving Traditional States

Eighty-eight percent of the nation's illegal immigrants lived in the six traditional settlement states for immigrants in 1990, but the same states had only 61 percent of the total in 2004. In other words, an estimated 3.9 million undocumented migrants lived in other states — nearly a tenfold increase.

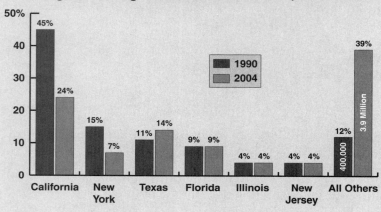

Changes in Immigrant Settlement Patterns, 1990-2004

Source: Jeffrey S. Passel, "Estimates of the Size and Characteristics of the Undocumented Population," Pew Hispanic Center, March 21, 2005, based on data from the March 2004 "Current Population Survey" by the Census Bureau and Department of Labor

White House on an immigration package in May 2007. The question going forward is whether the House, now controlled by Democrats, will accept the deal, or continue to hold a hard line.

President Bush himself leans more toward the moderate position, as opposed to the hard line exemplified by the old Republican House bill. "Massive deportation of the people here is unrealistic," Bush said in a speech on April 24, 2006. "It's just not going to work." [10]

At the state level, controversy over illegal immigration has helped build and destroy political careers. In California, for example, Schwarzenegger's promise to repeal legislation allowing illegal immigrants to obtain driver's licenses helped him topple Democrat Gray Davis in the 2003 recall election for governor. Tensions are still running high outside the political arena.

Some activists go so far as to call immigration a product of organized crime. "The same people responsible for drug shipments from the south are also dealing in sex

slaves and illegal labor and weapons," claims William Gheen, president of Americans for Legal Immigration, in Raleigh, N.C. "Our businesses should not be working with these people or encouraging these people. Some companies want more Third World labor on the territory of 'we the people' of the USA."

But Juan Hernandez, former director of the Center for U.S.-Mexico Studies at the University of Texas at Dallas, says immigration opponents are simply appealing to primitive fears. "There are many jobs that would not be performed if undocumented people were not here. Why can't we come up with ways in which individuals who want to come from Mexico to the United States can get a quick permit, come up, do a job and go back?"

Immigration control has long been a hot-button issue, but the concern in previous years was largely about jobs and wages. In post-9/11 America, many observers now also view illegal immigration as a national security matter.

"The borders are out of control," says T.J. Bonner, president of the National Border Patrol Council, the union representing some 10,000 border officers. He claims the patrol catches no more than a third of illegal border crossers. "We have a situation where business is controlling our immigration policy rather than sound decisions that take into account all the factors, including homeland security.

While some may dismiss Bonner's concerns as overly alarmist, others point out that stepped-up border-security spending is not stopping the growing illegal immigration.

Over the past thirteen years, billions of dollars have been spent on border-control measures, including walls and fences in urban areas, electronic sensors, and more personnel. In 2007, Bush requested $13 billion in border patrol and internal enforcement spending, up $3 billion from the previous year's total. From 1993 to 2004, the federal government tripled the Border Patrol to more than 11,000 officers, according to Wayne Cornelius, director of the Center for Comparative Immigration Studies at the University of California, San Diego. [11]

Former Customs and Border Protection commissioner Robert Bonner (no relation to T.J. Bonner mentioned previously) told lawmakers in 2005 that a reorganization that combined the Border Patrol, Immigration and Naturalization Service and the Customs Service into one agency under the Department of Homeland Security had improved deterrence. "This consolidation has significantly increased our ability to execute our anti-terrorism and traditional missions at our nation's borders more effectively than ever before," he said. [12]

Then why have illegal border crossings been increasing? For one thing, the government has nearly stopped enforcing sanctions approved in 1986 on employers who hire illegal immigrants. According to Mary Dougherty, an immigration statistician at the Department of Homeland Security, in 2003 the agency levied only $9,300 in fines against employers. Dougherty cautioned that her data might be incomplete, but *Time* reported in 2004 that the number of fines imposed on employers dropped 99 percent during the 1990s from 1,063 in 1992 to 13 in 2002. [13]

Demetrios Papademetriou, director of the Migration Policy Institute, a Washington think tank, says that illegal immigration "maintains a standard of living for everyone in America that is, in a sense, beyond what we can really afford. When you continue to have low-wage workers streaming in, all products and services become cheaper. It has actually become a subsidy to every person in America. We have all become hooked."

For instance, at least 50 percent of the nation's farm workers are poorly paid illegal immigrants. Americans spend less on food than the citizens of any other industrialized country, the Department of Agriculture's Economic Research Service found. [14]

In the final analysis, the lack of enforcement benefits employers and hurts workers, says Ana Avendaño Denier, director of the AFL-CIO Immigrant Worker Program. "Employers have a very vulnerable population to whom they can pay lower wages, and because of business control over public policy, it is OK to have this class of workers that is fully exploitable."

But problems here are unlikely to force illegal immigrants like Juan and María to return home.

"If it were just about us, yes," she says. "But for the sake of our son, no. Here he has a chance to go to college. In Mexico, no matter how hard we work we don't

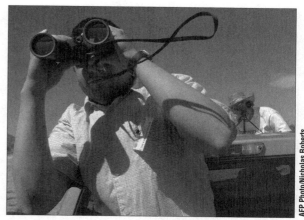

Members of the Minutemen activist group search for illegal immigrants crossing into the United States along a stretch of the Mexican border near Douglas, Ariz., on April 4, 2005. Members of the controversial group said they wanted to aid the understaffed U.S. Border Patrol.

have the possibility of paying for him to go to college. What we want is that he not suffer the humiliations we have had to suffer."

As Congress, the states, and citizens' groups debate the effects of illegal immigration, here are some of the key questions being asked:

Does illegal immigration hurt American workers?

Virtually every immigrant comes to the United States for one reason: to work.

About 96 percent of the 4.5 million illegal immigrant men now in the country are working, concludes Jeffrey Passel, a former U.S. Census Bureau demographer who is now senior research associate at the Pew Hispanic Center. All told, some 6 million immigrants — about 5 percent of the labor force — are in the country illegally.

Is the illegal work force large enough to hurt the job security of U.S. citizens?

Quite the contrary, argues John Gay, co-chair of the Essential Worker Immigration Coalition, a lobbying group of thirty-four employers — including hotels, restaurants, and building firms — that depend on immigrants. "I think back to the 1990s, a decade of economic growth," he says. "We ended with thirty-year lows in unemployment and a decade of record-setting immigration, legal and illegal. That tells me immigrants didn't displace millions of Americans; they helped employ Americans."

A group of 130 Mexicans who entered the United States illegally board a charter flight in Tucson, Ariz., to Mexico City on July 12, 2004. The flight is part of a "voluntary repatriation" program run jointly by the U.S. and Mexican governments.

Gay says low-paid workers help businesses thrive, allowing them to hire the native-born and legal immigrants for higher-paying jobs. In addition, immigrants are consumers themselves, so they boost the national economy.

But what helps businesses doesn't necessarily help Americans who share the lowest rungs of the socioeconomic ladder with illegal immigrants, according to Jared Bernstein, director of the Economic Policy Institute's Living Standards Program, which has strong ties to organized labor. "There is solid evidence that a large presence of low-wage immigrants lowers wages of domestic workers in low-wage sectors," Bernstein says. "Most economists should bristle at the notion that immigrants are filling jobs that native workers won't take. Maybe they won't take them because of low compensation and poor working conditions. In the absence of immigrants, the quality of some of those jobs probably would improve, and American workers probably would take them."

Bernstein favors controlling the flow of immigrant workers, rather than trying to bar them altogether.

But Michael McGarry, a maintenance worker in Aspen, Colo., and spokesman for the controversial Minuteman Project, says illegal immigrants hurt the economy and that they all should be kept out. The group deployed more than 100 volunteers — some of them armed — to spot and report illegal immigrants along a stretch of the Mexican border in April 2005. "People keep forgetting there is something called the law of supply and demand," says McGarry, who represented the group in April 2005 when it recruited citizens to report illegal immigrants along the Mexican border in Arizona. "If you flood the country with workers, that is going to compete down wages and benefits and conditions."

Harvard economist Borjas, whom many consider the leading expert on the economic effects of immigration, calculated that in the late 1990s immigration added a modest $10 billion to the economy — not a lot in a country with a national income in 1998 of about $8 trillion. [15]

The key, Borjas argues, is not the overall gain but who won and who lost because of illegal immigration. [16] "Some businesses gain quite a bit and are not willing to give up the privilege — agriculture, the service industry and upper-middle-class Californians who hire nannies and gardeners. People who gain, gain an incredible amount."

Borjas calculated that immigrants' work in 1998 helped those businesses gain roughly $160 billion, including the savings from the lower wages they were paying, plus their overall economic growth. [17] The figures don't distinguish between illegal and legal immigrants, but illegal immigrants are the majority of low-skilled entrants to the United States.

there was a note that footnote number 17 needs to be superscripted

Economist Philip Martin, an expert on U.S.-Mexico relations at the University of California, Davis, generally agrees with Borjas on the supply and demand side of the situation. "The economy would not come screeching to a halt" without illegal immigrants Martin says. At the same time, he acknowledges, they are "important to particular industries."

A detailed 2002 study of illegal Latino immigrants in Chicago — where they made up 5 percent of the work force — supports Martin's analysis. Two-thirds of the workers held low-wage jobs, including cleaning, packaging, child care, restaurant labor, grounds keeping, and maintenance. Wages were depressed by an average of 22 percent for men and 36 percent for women. (Wages of undocumented Eastern European men and women were depressed by 20 percent.) "Attaining additional levels of education, having English proficiency, and accumulating additional years of U.S. residency *do not neutralize the negative wage effect of working without legal status*," the report stressed (emphasis in original). [18]

The AFL-CIO's Avendaño acknowledges that undocumented workers push wages down. "Mexican workers are walking into a situation where an employer, with a wink and a nod, will say, 'I'll pay you less than the minimum wage.' It is very important for the AFL-CIO to not be put in a position where we're choosing domestic workers over foreign workers. To us, the answer is a reasonable immigration system."

Stein, of the Federation for American Immigration Reform (FAIR) argues that "earned legalization" proposals that include guest worker provisions, such as the legislation currently being debated in the Senate, amount to schemes to provide employers with a ready supply of low-wage workers. Once immigrants get legal permanent residence, they can't be exploited as readily as illegal immigrants, Stein says, so the lengthy legalization process keeps employers supplied with cheap labor.

"These are replacement workers for a very large swath of the American work force," he says. "I say, stop trying to shift the costs for cheap labor onto the backs of hardworking families. They try to sell us all on the idea that low-cost, illegal labor cuts consumer costs, but there are enormous, incalculable costs imposed on society at large [by illegal immigrants] — public education, emergency medical care, housing assistance, housing itself and criminal justice costs."

Are tougher immigration controls needed to protect national security?

"We have some people who are coming in to kill you and your children and your grandchildren," says Representative Tancredo, who has made immigration control his political mission. "Anyone seeking to come into this country without getting a lot of attention drawn to him would naturally choose the borders and come in under the radar screen along with thousands and thousands and thousands of others."

Tancredo worries about men like Mohammed and Mahmud Abouhalima, who were convicted for their roles in the 1993 bombing of the World Trade Center. The two Middle Eastern terrorists illegally took advantage of one of two immigration-reform programs to acquire "green cards" (which signify legal permanent resident status) under the 1986 Special Agricultural Workers Program for farm workers.

The brothers obtained the green cards through flaws in the Immigration and Naturalization Service (INS) inspection system, according to the National Commission on Terrorist Attacks Upon the United States (the 9/11 Commission). The agency's "inability to adjudicate applications quickly or with adequate security checks made it easier for terrorists to wrongfully enter and remain in the United States throughout the 1990s." [19]

In a sense, that failure followed logically from Justice Department policy. The report continues, "Attorney General [Janet] Reno and her deputies, along with Congress, made their highest priorities shoring up the Southwest border to prevent the migration of illegal aliens and selectively upgrading technology systems," the 9/11 Commission staff concluded. [20] (The INS was at that time part of the Justice Department.)

Unlike immigrants trekking across the desert, the nineteen September 11, 2001, terrorist attackers, including fifteen Saudis and a citizen of the United Arab Emirates (UAE), flew into the United States on airliners, their passports stamped with legally obtained student or tourist visas. [21]

To be sure, one airport immigration inspector stopped a member of the Sept. 11, 2001, attack team from entering the United States. Mohammed al Kahtani of Saudi Arabia was turned around at Orlando International Airport because he had a one-way ticket, little money, couldn't speak much English, and couldn't explain the reason he was visiting. "The inspector relied on intuitive experience . . . more than he relied on any objective factor that could be detected by 'scores' or a machine," the commission observed.

As a result, the commission said: "We advocate a system for screening, not categorical profiling. A screening system looks for particular, identifiable suspects or indicators of risk." [22]

CHRONOLOGY

1800s *After waves of European immigrants are welcomed, anti-immigrant resentment builds.*

1882 Chinese Exclusion Act specifically bars additional Chinese immigrants.

1920s *Public concern about the nation's changing ethnic makeup and hard economic times prompt Congress to limit immigration and set quotas intended to preserve the nation's ethnic makeup.*

1921–1929 Congress establishes a national-origins quota system, effectively excluding Asians and Southern Europeans.

1924 U.S. Border Patrol is created to stem the flow of illegal immigrants, primarily across the Mexican border.

1940s–1950s *Labor shortages and expansion of U.S. economy during World War II attract Mexican laborers. The United States. accepts war survivors, welcomes refugees from communist countries, and overhauls immigration laws.*

1942 U.S. creates Bracero guest worker program, allowing immigrant Mexican farm workers to work temporarily on American farms.

1948 Congress authorizes extra 200,000 visas for concentration camp survivors, later raising the number of visas to more than 400,000.

1952 Congress passes landmark Immigration and Nationality Act, codifying existing quota system favoring immigrants from northern Europe but exempting Mexican farm workers in Texas.

1953 United States exempts refugees fleeing communist countries from quota system.

1960s–1970s *Amid the growing civil rights movement, the United States scraps the biased quota system and admits more Asians and Latin Americans.*

1965 Major overhaul of immigration law scraps national quotas, giving preference to relatives of immigrants.

1966 Congress orders those fleeing Fidel Castro's Cuba to be admitted automatically if they reach U.S. shores.

1980s *Tide of illegal immigrants rises dramatically, prompting policymakers to act.*

1986 Number of illegal immigrants apprehended on U.S.-Mexican border reaches a peak of 1.7 million. Congress again overhauls immigration law, legalizing undocumented workers and, for the first time, imposing sanctions on employers of illegal immigrants.

1990s–2000s *Immigration laws fail to deter illegal immigrants, creating backlash that prompts another overhaul of immigration laws; national-security concerns cloud immigration debate after two terrorist attacks on U.S. soil by Middle Eastern visitors.*

1993 World Trade Center is bombed by Middle Eastern terrorists, two of whom had green cards; the mastermind had applied for political asylum.

1996 Number of illegal immigrants in the United States reaches 5 million; Congress passes major immigration-reform law beefing up border security and restricting political asylum.

1997 Most of California's anti-illegal immigrant statute is declared unconstitutional.

Sept. 11, 2001 Terrorists with visas attack World Trade Center and Pentagon; anti-immigrant backlash ensues.

2004 The 9/11 Commission points to "systemic weaknesses" in border-control and immigration systems.

Jan. 2005 President Bush calls for a "temporary worker" program that would not include "amnesty" for illegal immigrants.

May 2005 Rep. F. James Sensenbrenner's Real ID bill, which would block states from issuing driver's licenses to illegal immigrants, is signed into law.

April 2006 *April 9:* Hundreds of thousands of demonstrators march in the streets of cities across the United States, calling for legal status for illegal immigrants. *April 20:* Homeland Security Secretary Michael Chertoff announces a federal crackdown on employers who hire illegal aliens.

May 1, 2006 Hundreds of thousands of immigrants again took to the streets in cities across the country to call for legal status. Many left work and schools in an effort to demonstrate the economic importance of illegal immigrants.

Nov. 7, 2006 Hispanic voters, who had been trending more toward Republicans, give 69 percent of their support to Democrats in congressional races, according to exit polls.

May 2007 *May 1:* About 35,000 people turn out at two pro-immigrant rallies in Los Angeles, fewer than organizers had predicted and far fewer than the 650,000 who showed up at local rallies a year earlier. *May 9:* Church groups in major coastal cities announce that they are opening their churches as "sanctuaries" for undocumented families, the first faith-based sanctuary movement in twenty-five years. *May 17:* President Bush and a bipartisan group of senators announce agreement on a comprehensive bill to strengthen border protection and allow illegal immigrants eventual access to citizenship.

Sensenbrenner says the driver's-license prohibition in his Real ID bill will complicate life for terrorists who do manage to slip in. "If you read the 9/11 Report, they highlight how al Qaeda studied document fraud and other vulnerabilities in the system," said Jeff Lungren, a spokesman for Sensenbrenner. "They undertook the risk and effort to get valid U.S. driver's licenses and state I.D. cards . . . because they allow you to fit in." [23]

Immigrant-rights advocates argue, however, that Sensenbrenner's driver's-license provisions will complicate the lives of citizens and legal residents without damaging terrorists' capabilities.

Timothy Sparapani, legislative counsel for the American Civil Liberties Union (ACLU), says the law "is not going to do anything to deter people coming to this country." Instead, he argues, "the provisions . . . will make it much more complicated and burdensome for every American to get their first driver's licenses or renewals. They will not only have to prove they are citizens of a particular state, they will have to provide certified birth certificates; you'll have to go to a state birth certification agency. Some states don't have them."

Although terrorists have a track record for finding holes in the border-control system, border enforcement isn't actually targeting terrorists, says Jennifer Allen, director of the Border Action Network, a Tucson-based immigrant-defense organization. "A border wall is not going to deter terrorists," she argues. What stepped-up enforcement is achieving, she says, is "ongoing harassment" of people on the U.S. side of the border — particularly those whose Latin features identify them as possible foreigners.

Border Patrol union president Bonner acknowledges that most illegal immigrants are only looking for jobs. But he suggests that concentrating patrol forces on the 2,000-mile Southwest border is leaving the 3,145-mile Canadian border relatively unprotected. Some 9,000 officers are assigned to the Mexican border, he says, compared with only about 1,000 on the Canadian line. "We'll get a call from the Royal Canadian Mounted Police, and they'll say, 'Sixty Koreans landed here, and they're heading your way.' Sometimes we see them and sometimes we don't."

The Mexican and Canadian borders are indeed vulnerable, Papademetriou of the Migration Policy Institute acknowledges. But a 2003 institute report concludes that immigration policy is not an effective antiterrorism tool. A report he coauthored concluded: "The government's major successes in apprehending terrorists have not come from post-Sept. 11 immigration initiatives but from other efforts, such as international intelligence activities, law enforcement cooperation, and information provided by arrests made abroad." [24]

Should illegal immigrants in the United States be allowed to acquire legal status?

Legalization is one of the major dividing lines between illegal-immigration-control activists and employers and other immigrants'-rights advocates.

The guest worker proposal currently being considered in the Senate would allow foreigners to take jobs in the United States for a specified period, perhaps two years, and the time period would be twice renewable if the worker spends a year outside the United States. Foreigners already here illegally also would be able to join the program upon payment of a fine and then apply for permanent residence after eight years. Since they would go at the back of the immigration backlog, it would take at least thirteen years for a former illegal immigrant to become a citizen. Although President Bush generally supports the temporary worker portion of the proposal, he has not said whether he favors legalization.

Backers of the plan reject the term "amnesty," which implies a mass pardon for those covered by the proposal. "For security reasons, for human-rights reasons, and for labor reasons, there is a vested interest in legalizing or regularizing the status of individuals," says a member of Sen. John McCain's staff. "Senator McCain doesn't believe it's possible to round up everyone and send them home. [But] it can't be an amnesty. With high fines, background checks [for criminal violations] and through the temporary-worker program, people will be proving their reliability."

Critics of the Senate legislation argue that guest worker programs amount to amnesty, even if the term itself is not used. "The whole supposed guest-worker program is really an amnesty," says McGarry, of the Minuteman Project. "This would be a disaster. An amnesty, by definition, is something the government forgives. Breaking into the country is a crime."

Supporters of legalization claim that the main argument in favor of their position is that it is the only effective way to deal with the fact that undocumented immigrants are already here. And having illegal immigrants in the work force allows employers to pay them far less than they'd be able to earn as legal residents. Such

Mexico's Call for Reform Still Unheard

To some Americans, undocumented Mexicans are job-stealing, non-English-speaking threats to American culture, economic well-being, and national security. "I'm afraid that America could become a Third World country," Atlanta-area realtor Jimmy Herchek told CNN. "We're importing poverty by millions every year." [1]

To other observers, Mexicans and other illegal workers are crucial to the economy. "There are major benefits to both employers and consumers — in other words, all of us. [T]his supply of labor makes it possible to produce your goods and services more cheaply," said Wayne Cornelius, director of the Center for Comparative Immigration Studies at the University of California at San Diego. "So there are literally hundreds of thousands of employers in this country that have a major stake in continued access to this kind of labor."

And in Mexico, the 6 million illegal *migrantes* in the United States are viewed as heroes, often braving death in desert crossings to take tough construction and service jobs in the United States to support families back home. More than 3,000 Mexicans died trying to cross the border between 1996 and 2004, but those who arrive safely and find work in the United States sent home $16 billion last year — Mexico's third-largest source of revenue. [2]

However, the immigrants' courage and dedication to their families — not to mention the benefit to the U.S. economy from their low-wage labor — haven't earned them the right to work legally in the United States. Far from it, says Mexico's ambassador to the United States, Carlos de Icaza, who supports a program to allow *migrantes* to live and work legally in the United States. "Migrants are very vulnerable," he says in an interview at his office near the White House. "The difficult situation of these hard-working people makes them subject to abuse." Many are mistreated once they arrive in the United States — either by anti-immigrant activists, abusive border guards, or unscrupulous employers, who know illegal workers are reluctant to report salary and other abuses to authorities. Indeed, stories about U.S. mistreatment of migrants are daily fare in Mexico. *El*

Universal, one of Mexico City's most influential newspapers, reported in April that 4,400 Mexicans were injured or mistreated by anti-immigrant civilians or Border Patrol agents in 2004. [3]

Icaza says that setting up a legal way for Mexicans to work in the United States would direct them to communities where their labor is needed and wanted, helping to dissipate the tensions that arise now when lots of Mexicans arrive suddenly in communities offering seasonal jobs. Illegal immigrants have traditionally settled in California, Florida, New York and a few other states, but in recent years enclaves have sprung up in North Carolina, Georgia, Tennessee, and other states unaccustomed to the phenomenon. [4]

Often, local residents complain the new immigrants cost taxpayers money for health care, schools and social services and bring gang-related crime. "What I saw happen in California over thirty years is happening here in just a few years," James Burke, 57, a retired ironworker from Cullman, Ala., said as he signed up volunteers to push for immigration control. [5] Burke is part of a grass-roots movement seeking tougher immigration rules and border patrols. "Our goal is to stop illegal immigration and get rid of the illegal immigrants who are here," he said. [6]

Those goals are clearly at odds with the Mexican government's campaign to forge an immigration accord with the United States that would allow Mexicans to work here legally. Drawing on his apparent friendship with George W. Bush, Mexican President Vicente Fox began his presidency five years ago promising to strike an immigration deal with the United States. Shortly after taking office, Fox invited his newly elected American counterpart to his ranch. The two presidents assigned top officials to start negotiating a deal. "Geography has made us neighbors," Bush said, standing next to Fox, both men in cowboy boots. "Cooperation and respect will make us partners." [7]

In fact, the pre-9/11 climate was so immigration-friendly that Mexico's foreign minister confidently bragged that Mexico wouldn't settle for anything less

exploitation makes legalization "so crucial," says the AFL-CIO's Avendaño.

She says a December 2004 decision by the Appellate Division of the New York State Supreme Court proves

that an unfair, two-tiered labor system is acquiring legal status. The court ruled an illegal immigrant who was injured while working on a construction site was entitled to lost wages — but valued only at what he would have

than a deal legalizing Mexicans already in the United States. "It's the whole enchilada or nothing," Jorge G. Castañeda said. [8] So far, it's been *nada*. Nothing. For Fox the politician, the lack of action is especially bad news for his legacy. Mexico's constitution allows only one six-year term, and Fox's term ended in July 2006. Yet, comprehensive immigration reform in the United States seems as distant as ever.

"Fox staked his presidency on getting a bilateral [immigration] agreement

President Bush and Mexican President Vicente Fox discussed immigration at Bush's Texas ranch in March 2004. Bush supports a guest worker program for illegal immigrants in the U.S. but opposes legalization.

Getty Images/Rod Aydelotte

"Folks here could always go out and get a construction job for a decent wage," said Lee Bevang, in Covington, Ga. "But the contractors have totally taken advantage of illegal aliens, paying them wages no American can live on. My husband has been laid off. The concern about this is just huge." [10]

with the United States," says Manuel García y Griego, a specialist on U.S-Mexico relations at the University of Texas, Arlington. On the other hand, "Mr. Bush has spent his political capital very selectively, only on things that are close to his heart — making tax cuts permanent, Iraq. I don't see immigration in that category."

But Icaza insists the United States needs an accord as urgently as Mexico. For security reasons alone, he says, the United States must know who is living in the country illegally — and a legalization program would allow illegal residents to step forward with impunity.

Moreover, Icaza says, citing almost word-for-word the Council of Economic Advisers' latest annual report to the president: "The benefits to the U.S. economy are larger than the costs associated with Social Security, health, and education." [9]

But the amnesty proposal may not go very far if Bush perceives the issue as alienating his political base in the Southern and Midwestern "red states" that are now attracting many *migrantes*.

[1] Quoted in "CNN Presents: Immigrant Nation: Divided Country," Oct. 17, 2004.

[2] The desert death figure comes from Wayne Cornelius, "Controlling 'Unwanted' Immigration: Lessons from the United States, 1993-2004," Center for Comparative Immigration Studies, University of California-San Diego, Working Paper No. 92, December, 2004, 14, www.ccis-ucsd.org/PUBLICATIONS/wrkg92. pdf. The remittances figure comes from "Las Remesas Familiares en Mexico," Banco de Mexico, noviembre, 2004,http://portal.sre.gob.mx/ ime/pdf/Remesas_Familiares.pdf. In English, a study by the Inter-American Development Bank has slightly older statistics: "Sending Money Home: Remittance to Latin America and the Caribbean," May 2004, www.iadb. org/mif/v2/files/StudyPE2004eng.pdf.

[3] Jorge Herrera, *Impulsa Senado protección a connacionales*, 17, www.eluniversal.com.mx/pls/impreso/version_himprimir?p_id=124353&p_sec cion=2.

[4] Jeffrey S. Passel, "Estimates of the Size and Characteristics of the Undocumented Population," Pew Hispanic Center, March 21, 2005, www.pewhispanic.org.

[5] David Kelly, "Illegal Immigration Fears Have Spread; Populist Calls for Tougher Enforcement are Being Heard beyond the Border States," *Los Angeles Times*, April 25, 2005.

[6] *Ibid.*

[7] Mike Allen and Kevin Sullivan, "Meeting in Mexico, Presidents Agree to Form Immigration Panel," *The Washington Post*, Feb. 16, p. A1.

[8] Patrick J. O'Donnell, "Amnesty by Any Name is Hot Topic," *Los Angeles Times*, July 22, 2001, A1.

[9] "Economic Report of the President," February 2005, 115, www.ewic.org/documents/ERP2005-Immigration.pdf.

[10] Quoted in Kelly, "Illegal Immigration Fears Have Spread."

earned in his home country. "It is our view that plaintiff, as an admitted undocumented alien, is not entitled to recover lost earnings damages based on the wages he might have earned illegally in the United States. . . .

[W]e limited plaintiff's recovery for lost earnings to the wages he would have been able to earn in his home country." [25] In effect, Avendaño says, the ruling "legitimizes Third World labor conditions" in the United States.

Illegal Immigrants Mostly From Latin America

More than 80 percent of the more than 10 million undocumented immigrants in the United States in March 2004 were from Latin America, including 57 percent from Mexico.

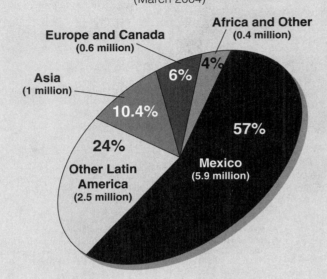

Illegal Immigrants in the U. S.
(March 2004)

Africa and Other
(0.4 million)

Europe and Canada
(0.6 million)

Asia
(1 million)

4%

6%

10.4%

24%

57%

Other Latin
America
(2.5 million)

Mexico
(5.9 million)

Note: Percentages do not add to 100 due to rounding.

Source: Jeffrey S. Passel, "Estimates of the Size and Characteristics of the Undocumented Population," Pew Hispanic Center, March 21, 2005, based on data from the March 2004 "Current Population Survey" by the Census Bureau and Department of Labor

BACKGROUND

Earlier Waves

The United States was created as a nation of immigrants who left Europe for political, religious, and economic reasons. After independence, the new nation maintained an open-door immigration policy for 100 years. Two great waves of immigrants — in the mid-1800s and the late nineteenth and early twentieth centuries — drove the nation's westward expansion and built its cities and its industrial base. [26]

But while the Statue of Liberty says America accepts the world's "tired . . . poor . . . huddled masses," Americans themselves vacillate between welcoming immigrants and resenting them — even those who arrive legally. For both legal and illegal immigrants, America's actions have been inconsistent and often racist.

In the nineteenth century, thousands of Chinese laborers were brought here to build the railroads and then were excluded — via the Chinese Exclusion Act of 1882 — in a wave of anti-Chinese hysteria. Other Asian groups were restricted when legislation in 1917 created "barred zones" for Asian immigrants. [27]

The racist undertones of U.S. immigration policy were by no means reserved for Asians. Describing Italian and Irish immigrants as "wretched beings," *The New York Times* on May 15, 1880, editorialized: "There is a limit to our powers of assimilation, and when it is exceeded the country suffers from something very like indigestion."

Nevertheless, from 1880 to 1920, the country admitted more than 23 million immigrants — first from Northern and then from Southern and Eastern Europe. In 1890, Census Bureau Director Francis Walker said the country was being overrun by "less desirable" newcomers from Southern and Eastern Europe, whom he called "beaten men from beaten races."

Immigration-control advocates say the solution lies in keeping out the bulk of illegal immigrants trying to enter while cracking down on businesses that employ illegal workers. "If you enforce the law against employers," Tancredo says, "people who cannot get employment will return" to their home countries. "They will return by the millions." That way, Tancredo says, a mass roundup would not be required.

Bernstein of the Economic Policy Institute favors a variant of the Tancredo approach that avoids its punitive aspects. Illegal immigrants "ought to have labor protection," he says. "That's not contradictory to the notion that illegals shouldn't be here. Employers should be held accountable for labor standards for all employees. The beauty part of erasing employer advantage is that it dampens the incentive for illegal flows."

In the 1920s, public concern about the nation's changing ethnic makeup prompted Congress to establish a national-origins quota system. Laws in 1921, 1924 and 1929 capped overall immigration and limited influxes from certain areas based on the share of the U.S. population with similar ancestry, effectively excluding Asians and Southern Europeans.

But the quotas only swelled the ranks of illegal immigrants — particularly Mexicans, who only needed to wade across the Rio Grande. To stem the flow, the United States in 1924 created the U.S. Border Patrol, the enforcement arm of the INS, to guard the 6,000 miles of U.S. land bordering Canada and Mexico.

During the early 1940s the United States relaxed its immigration policies, largely for economic and political reasons. The Chinese exclusion laws were repealed in 1943, after China became a wartime ally against Japan in 1941. And in 1942 — partly to relieve wartime labor shortages and partly to legalize and control the flow of Mexican agricultural workers into the country — the United States began the Bracero (Spanish for "laborer") guest worker program, which allowed temporary workers from Mexico and the Caribbean to harvest crops in Western states.

After the war, Congress decided to codify the scores of immigration laws that had evolved over the years. The landmark Immigration and Nationality Act of 1952, retained a basic quota system that favored immigrants from Northern Europe — especially the skilled workers and relatives of U.S. citizens among them. At the same time, it exempted immigrants from the Western Hemisphere from the quota system — except for the black residents of European colonies in the Caribbean.

Mass Deportation

The 1952 law also attempted to address the newly acknowledged reality of Mexican workers who crossed the border illegally. Border Patrol agents were given more power to search for illegal immigrants and a bigger territory in which to operate. "Before 1944, the illegal traffic on the Mexican border . . . was never overwhelming," the President's Commission on Migratory Labor noted in 1951, but in the past seven years, "the wetback traffic has reached entirely new levels. . . . [I]t is virtually an invasion." [28]

In a desperate attempt to reverse the tide, the Border Patrol in 1954 launched "Operation Wetback," transferring nearly 500 INS officers from the Canadian perimeter and U.S. cities to join the 250 agents policing the

An immigrant works on new homes being built in Homestead, Fla., on May 7, 2004. An estimated 337,000 undocumented immigrants live in Florida, according to the Department of Homeland Security.

U.S.-Mexican border and factories and farms. More than 1 million undocumented Mexican migrants were deported. Although the action enjoyed popular support and bolstered the prestige — and budget — of the INS, it exposed an inherent contradiction in U.S. immigration policy. The 1952 law contained a gaping loophole — the Texas Proviso — a blatant concession to Texas agricultural interests that relied on cheap labor from Mexico. "The Texas Proviso said companies or farms could knowingly hire illegal immigrants, but they couldn't harbor them," said Lawrence Fuchs, former executive director of the U.S. Select Commission on Immigration and Refugee Policy. "It was a duplicitous policy. We never really intended to prevent illegals from coming."

Immigration Reform

The foundation of today's immigration system dates back to 1965, when Congress overhauled the immigration rules. From the 1920s to the 1960s, immigration had been markedly reduced, thanks largely to the effects of the Great Depression, World War II, and the quota system established in the 1920s.

From 1930 to 1950, for instance, fewer than 4 million newcomers arrived — more than a 50 percent drop from the high immigration rates of the early twentieth century. The heated debates that had accompanied the earlier waves of immigration faded. "Immigration didn't even really exist as a big issue until 1965 because we just weren't letting that many people in," said Peter Brimelow, author of the 1995 bestseller *Alien Nation.*

That all changed in 1965, when Congress scrapped the national-origin quotas in favor of immigration limits for major regions of the world and gave preference to immigrants with close relatives living in the United States. The 1965 amendments to the 1952 Immigration and Nationality Act capped annual immigration at 290,000 — 170,000 from the Eastern Hemisphere and 120,000 from the Western Hemisphere. By giving priority to family reunification as a basis for admission, the amendments repaired "a deep and painful flaw in the fabric of American justice," President Lyndon B. Johnson declared at the time.

However, the law also dramatically changed the immigration landscape. Most newcomers now hailed from the developing world — about half from Latin America. While nearly 70 percent of immigrants had come from Europe or Canada in the 1950s, by the 1980s that figure had dropped to about 14 percent. Meanwhile, the percentage coming from Asia, Central America and the Caribbean jumped from about 30 percent in the 1950s to 75 percent during the '70s.

The government had terminated the Bracero program in December 1964, bowing to pressure from unions and exposés of the appalling conditions under which the *braceros* were living and working. But after having allowed millions of temporary Mexican laborers into the country legally for years, the government found that it was now impossible to turn off the spigot. Despite beefed-up Border Patrol efforts, the number of illegal migrants apprehended at the border jumped from fewer than 100,000 in 1965 to more than 1.2 million by 1985.

In 1978 the Select Commission on Immigration and Refugee Policy concluded that illegal immigration was the most pressing problem facing immigration authorities, a perception shared by the general public. [29] The number of border apprehensions peaked in 1986 at 1.7 million, driven in part by a deepening economic crisis in Mexico. Some officials felt the decade-long increase in illegal immigration was particularly unfair to the tens of thousands of legal petitioners waiting for years to obtain entry visas. "The simple truth is that we've lost control of our own borders," declared President Ronald Reagan, "and no nation can do that and survive." [30]

In the mid-1980s, a movement emerged to fix the illegal immigration problem. Interestingly, the debate

on Capitol Hill was marked by bipartisan alliances described by Sen. Alan K. Simpson, R-Wyo., as "the goofiest ideological-bedfellow activity I've ever seen." [31] Conservative anti-immigration think tanks teamed up with liberal labor unions and environmentalists favoring tighter restrictions on immigration. Pro-growth and business groups joined forces with longtime adversaries in the Hispanic and civil rights communities to oppose the legislation.

After several false starts, Congress passed the Immigration Reform and Control Act (IRCA) in October 1986 — the most sweeping revision of U.S. immigration policy in more than two decades. Using a carrot-and-stick approach, IRCA granted a general amnesty to all undocumented aliens who were in the United States before 1982 and imposed monetary sanctions — or even prison — against employers who knowingly hired undocumented workers for the first time. The law also included a commitment to beef up enforcement along the Mexican border.

IRCA allowed 3.1 million undocumented aliens to obtain legal status. Within two years, the number of would-be immigrants detained at the border each year fell from a peak of more than 1.7 million in 1986 to fewer than 900,000 in 1989.

"Once word spreads along the border that there are no jobs for illegals in the U.S., the magnet no longer exists," INS Commissioner Alan Nelson said in 1985. But that assessment was premature.

Political Asylum

Nowadays, illegal migrants come not only from neighboring countries but also from the world's far corners. Homeland Security Department officials have seized ships off the East and West coasts of the United States loaded with would-be illegal Chinese immigrants. Hundreds of others arrive on airplanes with temporary visas and simply stay past their visa-expiration dates.

As it is policing the borders, the department must also determine whether those immigrants seeking political asylum are truly escaping persecution or are merely seeking greener economic pastures. Historically, U.S. immigration law has been more receptive to political refugees if they come from communist countries.

"It used to be clear," said Doris Meissner, former INS commissioner. "Mexicans were economic, Cubans and Vietnamese were political. That changed when the

AT ISSUE

Are today's immigrants assimilating into U.S. society?

YES

Tamar Jacoby
Senior Fellow, Manhattan Institute; editor,
Reinventing the Melting Pot: The New
Immigrants and What it Means to be
American *(2004)*

From "Think Tank," Public Broadcasting Service, June 24, 2004

It's always been true that Americans have loved the immigrants of a generation or two ago and been frightened by the immigrants of their era. They think the past worked perfectly, and they look around and exaggerate how difficult it is in the present.

Your average American says, "Well, I hear all this Spanish spoken." But in the second generation, if you grow up here you may not learn [Spanish] in school; you may learn it on the street, but you become proficient in English. By the third generation, about two-thirds of Hispanics speak only English. You can be in Mexican-American neighborhoods in California and hear all the adults speaking to each other in Spanish, and the little siblings speak to each other in English.

The bulk of immigrants who are coming now are people who understand cultural fluidity, understand intermarriage [and] find that a natural, easy thing. They understand the mixing of cultures and find the binary nature of our views of race and our views of out and in very alien. And that bodes well for assimilation.

One statistic tells the story. In 1960, half of American men hadn't finished high school. Today, only 10 percent of American men have not finished high school. The people who used to drop out of high school in 1960 did a kind of job that Americans don't want to do anymore. Immigrants don't tend to displace American workers. They have some effect on wages — a small, temporary effect. But it's not a zero-sum game. They help grow the economy.

The key is [for immigrants to] buy into our political values and play by the rules. It's a balance between that sense of shared values and shared political ideals — and then [doing] whatever you want to do at home.

After 9/11, Americans were very frightened. Polls showed huge numbers — two-thirds or higher — thought that the borders should be closed or that we should have much lower [immigration] numbers. Some of those surface fears are ebbing, but I think people [remain] uneasy. [Yet] there's a kind of optimism and a faith in America and in America's power to absorb people that you could tap into. If you said we have control but we are absorbing them, I think you could get people to go for higher [immigration] numbers. And when you look at the big picture — are today's immigrants assimilating? The evidence is: Yes.

NO

Victor Davis Hanson
Senior Fellow, Hoover Institution; author,
Mexifornia: A State of Becoming *(2003)*

From *World Magazine*, April 2, 2005

With perhaps as many as 20 million illegal aliens from Mexico, and the immigration laws in shreds, we are reaching a state of crisis. Criminals abound to prey on illegal aliens because they assume their victims are afraid to call the police, carry mostly cash, don't speak English, live as transients among mostly young males and are not legal participants in their communities.

If there were not a perennial supply of cheap labor, wages would rise and would draw back workers to now despised seasonal jobs; something is terribly wrong when central California counties experience 15 percent unemployment and yet insist that without thousands of illegal aliens from Oaxaca crops won't be picked and houses not built. At some point, some genius is going to make the connection that illegal immigration may actually explain high unemployment by ensuring employers cheap labor that will not organize, can be paid in cash and often requires little government deductions and expense.

Attitudes about legality need to revert back to the pre-1960s and 1970s, when immigration was synonymous with integration and assimilation. We need to dispense with the flawed idea of multiculturalism and return to the ideal of multiracialism under the aegis of a unifying Western civilization.

First-generation meritocratic Asians at places like University of California at Berkeley and the University of California at Los Angeles provide an example. What is the Asian community doing that its Mexican counterpart is not? Is it family emphasis on education, a sense of separation from the motherland, a tendency to stress achievement rather than victimization, preference for private enterprise rather than government entitlement? We need to discuss these taboo and politically incorrect paradoxes if we really wish to end something like four of 10 California Hispanic high-school students not graduating. Too many are profiteering and finding careers out of perpetuating the failure of others — others who will be the dominant population of the American Southwest in another decade.

In all public discourse and debate, when the racial chauvinist screams "racist" in lieu of logic, we all need to quit recoiling or apologizing, and instead rejoin with "Shame on you, shame, shame, shame for polluting legitimate discussion with race."

We need to return to what is known to work: measured and legal immigration, strict enforcement of our existing laws, stiff employer sanctions, an end to bilingual documents and interpreters — in other words, an end to the disastrous salad bowl and a return to the successful melting pot.

Haitian boat people started coming in the 1970s. Their reasons for leaving were both political and economic." [32]

Unlike Cuban refugees arriving on boats — who are automatically admitted under the 1966 "Cuban Adjustment Act" — Haitian "boat people" in the 1970s were routinely imprisoned while their applications were being processed. In 1981, the U.S. government began intercepting Haitians' boats on the high seas and towing them back to Haiti. That practice continues. As for Cubans, the Clinton administration established a "wet foot/dry foot" policy — still in effect — that sends fleeing Cubans who don't actually touch U.S. soil back to Cuba; those who make a case for a "credible fear of persecution" in Cuba are sent on to third countries. Complicating the asylum picture, in the 1980s growing numbers of Central Americans began fleeing non-communist regimes in war-torn countries like El Salvador and Guatemala. But their chances of obtaining political asylum were slim, so many came in illegally.

Human rights advocates argued that the inconsistencies in the treatment of Central American and Haitian refugees amounted to racial and political discrimination. From 1981 through 1986, the federal government deported nearly 18,000 Salvadorans while granting permanent-resident status to 598. [33] During the same period, half of the immigrants from Poland — then under communist rule — were granted asylum.

"Cubans and Poles were accepted without significant questioning," said Ernesto Rodriguez, an immigration expert at the University of Houston, "Central Americans were grilled and usually not accepted, despite the fact that lives were endangered. [Polish President] Lech Walesa would never have survived in Guatemala."

Responding to the unequal treatment, churches and some U.S. communities — Berkeley, Los Angeles, Chicago and others — began offering sanctuary to Central American refugees. By 1985, the sanctuary movement had spread to more than 200 parishes of all denominations. In 1985 several leaders of the movement were tried for being part of an "alien-smuggling conspiracy."

Four years later, the sanctuary movement was vindicated when the U.S. government (in settling a lawsuit filed by a coalition of religious and refugee organizations) agreed to reconsider the cases of tens of thousands of Central Americans previously rejected for political asylum. A 1990 immigration law created a new "temporary protected status" shielding from immediate deportation people whose countries were torn by war or environmental disaster. The provision was written with Central Americans in mind. Eventually, so many cases clogged the system that in 1997 Congress passed the Nicaraguan Adjustment and Central American Relief Act, which allowed thousands of Central Americans to bypass the backlogged asylum system and apply directly for permanent legal residence.

But the 1990 law also made broader changes. It increased the number of foreigners allowed to enter the United States each year from 500,000 to 700,000 (dropping to 675,000 in 1995). More important, it nearly tripled the annual quota for skilled professionals from 55,000 to 144,000. To alter the 1965 law's preference for Latin American and Asian immigrants, it set new quotas for countries seen as having been unfairly treated by the earlier law, with newcomers from Europe and skilled workers receiving a greater share of entry visas.

Changes in 1996

In the 1990s nearly 10 million newcomers arrived on U.S. shores, the largest influx ever — with most still coming from Latin America and Asia.

President Bill Clinton realized early in his presidency that the so-called amnesty program enacted in 1986 had not solved the illegal-immigration problem. And in the border states, concern was growing that undocumented immigrants were costing U.S. taxpayers too much in social, health and educational services. On November 8, 1994, California voters approved Proposition 187, denying illegal immigrants public education or non-essential public-health services. Immigrants'-rights organizations immediately challenged the law, which a court later ruled was mostly unconstitutional. But the proposition's passage had alerted politicians to the intensity of anti-illegal immigrant sentiment. [34]

House Republicans immediately included a proposal to bar welfare benefits for legal immigrants in its "Contract with America," and in 1995, after the GOP had won control of the House, Congress took another stab at reforming the rules for both legal and illegal immigration. But business groups blocked efforts to reduce legal immigration, so the new law primarily focused on curbing illegal immigration.

The final legislation, which cleared Congress on September 30, 1995, nearly doubled the size of the Border Patrol and provided 600 new INS investigators.

It appropriated $12 million for new border-control devices, including motion sensors, set tougher standards for applying for political asylum and made it easier to expel foreigners with fake documents or no documents at all. [35] The law also severely limited — and in many cases completely eliminated — non-citizens' ability to challenge INS decisions in court. [36]

But the new law did not force authorities to crack down on businesses that employed illegal immigrants even though there was wide agreement that such a crackdown was vital. As the Commission on Immigration Reform had said in 1994, the centerpiece of any effort to stop illegal entrants should be to "turn off the jobs magnet that attracts them." By 1999, however, the INS had stopped raiding work sites to round up illegal immigrant workers and was focusing on foreign criminals, immigrant-smugglers, and document fraud. As for cracking down on employers, an agency district director told the *Washington Post*, "We're out of that business." The idea that employers could be persuaded not to hire illegal workers "is a fairy tale." [37]

Terrorism and Immigrants

The debate over immigration heated up dramatically after the September 11, 2001, terrorist attacks. Although none of the terrorists were immigrants, all were foreigners. And some had received help in obtaining housing and driver's licenses from members of Middle Eastern immigrant communities. [38]

There were no indications that Middle Eastern immigrants in general had anything to do with the attacks or with terrorism. But in the days and weeks following the attacks, federal agents rounded up more than 1,200 Middle Easterners on suspicion of breaking immigration laws, being material witnesses to terrorism, or supporting the enemy. By August 2002, most had been released or deported. [39]

Nevertheless, a senior Justice Department official said the jailings had "incapacitated and disrupted some ongoing terrorist plans." [40]

Whatever the effects on terrorism, there is no question that Sept. 11 attacks and the government response to the attacks put a dent in legal immigration. In fiscal 2002-2003, the number of people granted legal permanent residence (green cards) fell by 34 percent; 28,000 people were granted political asylum, 59 percent fewer than were granted asylum in fiscal 2000-2001. [41]

But the growth of illegal immigration under way before the attacks continued afterward, with 57 percent of the illegal immigrants coming from Mexico. [42] Due to the family-reunification provision in immigration law, Mexico is also the leading country of origin for legal immigrants — with 116,000 of the 705,827 legal immigrants in fiscal 2002-2003 coming from Mexico. [43] No Middle Eastern or predominantly Muslim countries have high numbers of legal immigrants, although Pakistan was thirteenth among the top fifteen countries of origin for legal immigrants in 1998. [44]

CURRENT SITUATION

A Difficult Fix

Amidst much fanfare, President Bush and a bipartisan group of ten senators announced an agreement on May 17, 2007, on a comprehensive, compromise plan to tighten border security and address the fate of the nation's 12 million illegal immigrants. "The agreement reached today is one that will help enforce our borders," Bush said. "But equally importantly, it will treat people with respect. This is a bill where people who live here in our country will be treated without amnesty, but without animosity."

The 380-page plan was worked out just in time to meet a deadline for the beginning of Senate debate on the issue. "The plan isn't perfect, but only a bipartisan bill will become law," said Sen. Edward M. Kennedy, D-Mass. The package was highly complex and contained provisions that either anger liberals such as Kennedy or conservatives such as his negotiating partner, Sen. Jon Kyl, R-Ariz., however, the backing of such a disparate coalition made Senate passage, in some form, appear likely.

The agreement would grant temporary legal status to virtually all illegal immigrants, allowing them to apply for residence visas and citizenship through a lengthy process. They would have to wait for eight years before applying for permanent resident status, pay fines of up to $5,000 and, heads of households would be forced to leave the country and reenter legally.

But this process could not begin for any illegal aliens — and a new guest worker program would also be put on hold — until after a tough border crackdown goes into effect. The deal calls for the deployment of 18,000 new Border Patrol agents and extensive new physical barriers, including 200 miles of vehicle barriers, 370 miles of fencing, and 70 ground-based camera and radar towers. In addition, funding would be provided for the detention of 27,500 illegal immigrants and new identification tools would be developed to help screen out illegal job applicants.

Prospects for anything resembling this deal remained murky. The House had been much more punitive in its approach during failed attempts prior to the 2006 election to address immigration. Despite the recent change in partisan control, there was still less sentiment in the House for any bill that was perceived as giving a break to illegal aliens. "Unless the White House produces 60 or 70 Republican votes in the House, it will be difficult to pass an immigration bill similar to the Senate proposal," said Rahm Emanuel, D-Ill., chairman of the House Democratic Caucus. [45]

Those votes are likely to be tough to get. Some staunch critics of immigration policy had been defeated in the 2006 elections, but for the most part they had been replaced by newcomers who also took a hard line against illegal immigration. "This proposal would do lasting damage to the country, American workers, and the rule of law," said Lamar Smith of Texas, ranking Republican on the House Judiciary Committee, in response to the deal between senators and the White House. "Just because somebody is in the country illegally doesn't mean we have to give them citizenship." [46]

Liberals and immigration advocacy groups also questioned the terms of the Senate proposal, particularly a change in visa applications. In contrast to the current system, which stresses family ties, a new, complex point system would favor skilled, educated workers. About 50 percent of the points would be based on employment criteria, with just 10 percent based on family connections."

While the battle over pending legislation heats up in Congress, the prospect of implementing the Real ID law, signed into law in 2005, is generating increasing controversy among the states. The law, which requires states to verify the citizenship of those applying for or renewing driver's licenses, is scheduled to go into effect in May 2008. But many state officials are warning that they do not have enough time and the task is far too expensive — an estimated $11 billion over five years — for the states to shoulder the verification burden alone. Indeed, at the end of April 2006, the National Governors Association and the National Conference of State Legislators issued a report saying that the states had been given neither enough time nor enough money to comply with the law and that implementation would take at least eight years.

"It's absolutely absurd," Mike Huckabee of Arkansas, then-chairman of the National Governors Association, told reporters. "The time frame is unrealistic; the lack of funding is inexcusable." [47] Since that time, several states including Maine, Montana, and Washington have decided to opt out of the Real ID program. This action will create major inconveniences for their residents who will not be able to use their driver's licenses to board planes or enter secure federal facilities. It could also shatter the federal government's plans for how Real ID will work. Patrick J. Leahy, D-Vt., suggested in early 2007 that the Real ID might have to be repealed.

Public Opinion

In April and May 2006, demonstrations in cities across the country drew hundreds of thousands of marchers. On May 1, hundreds of thousands more people participated in what some billed as "the Great American Boycott of 2006." The idea was for immigrants, legal and illegal, to demonstrate their economic contribution to the country by staying away from their jobs on May Day.

In terms of numbers alone, the demonstrations of April and May were impressive. But they may also have spurred a backlash among some sectors of the public. "The size and magnitude of the demonstrations had some kind of backfire effect," John McLaughlin, a Republican pollster, told reporters after the first round of marches. "The Republicans that are tough on immigration are doing well right now." [48]

That turned out not to be the case when the voters actually came to the polls. Some prominent critics of immigration policy, such as Republican Rep. Jim Ryun of Kansas, went down to defeat in November 2006. Republicans in general paid a clear price among Hispanics for their tough stand. Exit polling in 2006 suggested that 30 percent of Hispanics voted for Republicans in congressional races that year, while Democrats garnered 69 percent of the Hispanic vote. President Bush had taken 40 percent of the Hispanic vote in his reelection race two years earlier. [49] "I don't think we did ourselves any favors when we engaged the public in a major topic and didn't pass the legislation to deal with it," said Sen. Sam Brownback, R-Kan., a 2008 presidential contender. [50]

Perhaps partly in response, Republicans just after the election selected as their new national chairman Florida Sen. Mel Martinez, a prominent Cuban-American who had served in the Bush Cabinet. Ken Mehlman, the out-going chairman, told reporters that he was concerned about where the party stood with Hispanics. "Hispanics are not single-issue voters, but GOP officials said the tone of the immigration debate hurt the party's standing with the fastest-growing minority group," the *Washington Post* reported. [51]

State Debate

With Congress having failed as yet to act, officials at other levels of government have attempted to address the issue in a multitude of ways. Some cities have passed "zero-tolerance" policies toward illegal immigrants, dep-utizing local police to act as immigration enforcement officers. Hazelton, Pennsylvania, for example, passed an Illegal Immigration Relief Act that denies licenses to businesses that employ illegal aliens, fines landlords $1,000 for each illegal renter, and requires that city doc-uments be printed in English only. [52] Other cities, how-ever, have offered themselves up as "sanctuaries," refusing to cooperate with federal calls for tougher enforcement policies. Indeed, the sanctuary movement of the 1980s was revived in 2007 when congregants in Los Angeles, San Diego, and New York began offering their churches as homes for undocumented families. [53]

Hundreds of pieces of legislation have been intro-duced at the state level, including more than 1,100 bills during the first four months of 2007 alone. Georgia took perhaps the most comprehensive approach in a restrictive omnibus bill approved in 2006. The law requires that anyone receiving most public services provide verifica-tion of their legal status and prevents employers from taking a tax deduction for wages paid to illegal workers.

Voters in November 2006 approved a half-dozen restrictive initiatives at the ballot in Colorado and Arizona. Arizona voters two years earlier had approved Proposition 200, which requires proof of citizenship before voting. The new law also requires the state and local governments to check the immigration status of anyone applying for unspecified "public benefits" and to report any illegal immigrants who apply. [54]

Proponents said the law's "benefits" provision was designed to plug a loophole that enabled illegal immi-grants to obtain welfare because of holes in the system. "Such benefits are an incentive for illegal aliens to settle in Arizona and hide from federal authorities," state Rep. Russell Pearce, R-Mesa, said. [55]

But the law didn't actually prohibit anything that wasn't already forbidden, opponents said. Ray Ybarra, who was observing the Minuteman Project for the American Civil Liberties Union, told a reporter that it simply restated existing prohibitions on illegal immi-grants voting or getting welfare. He called the new law an outgrowth of "fear and misunderstanding." [56]

The law has led immigration-control forces to propose legislation that would bar illegal immigrants from state col-leges, adult-education classes, and utility and child-care assis-tance. The proposed legislation, which was under consideration in early May 2005, set off a new round of debate. Arizonans shouldn't have to subsidize services for peo-ple in the country illegally, argued state Rep. Tom Boone, R-Glendale, the bill's sponsor. Opponents countered that Hispanic citizens would have to suffer extra scrutiny simply because of their appearance. [57] A Democratic opponent tried to add sanctions against employers who hire illegal immi-grants. Republicans voted that down on the first attempt.

Perhaps because Arizona is on the border and its Proposition 200 passed by referendum, the legislation received more national attention than a similar measure enacted in Virginia in 2005. As in Arizona, the Virginia law requires anyone applying for non-emergency public benefits — such as Medicaid and welfare — to be a legal U.S. resident. The Democratic governor Mark Warner, downplayed the measure's effects, even as he signed it into law, saying it restated federal prohibitions against illegal immigrants receiving some public benefits. [58]

Arizona's law has become a model for immigration-control forces in other states, including Colorado and North Carolina.

Assimilation Debate

In small communities experiencing unprecedented waves of new immigrants, many residents feel that the over-whelming numbers of Latinos showing up in their towns are changing American culture. They say that Mexican immigrants — perhaps because they need only walk across the border to return home — stick to themselves and refuse to learn English or to assimilate as readily as previous waves of immigrants.

"They didn't want to socialize with anybody," said D.A. King, describing the Mexicans who moved into a house across the street from his Marietta, Georgia, home. "They filled their house full of people. At one time, there were 18 people living in this home." [59]

Harvard historian Samuel Huntington, in his controversial new book *Who Are We: The Challenges to America's National Identity*, worries that the sheer number of Latino immigrants has created a minority with little incentive to assimilate, potentially creating an America with a split identity. "Continuation of this large immigration [without improved assimilation] could divide the United States into a country of two languages and two cultures," writes Huntington, who heads the Harvard Academy for International and Area Studies. "Demographically, socially and culturally, the *reconquista* (reconquest) of the Southwestern United States by Mexican immigrants is well under way. Hispanic leaders are actively seeking to transform the United States into a bilingual society." [60]

But many reject Huntington's argument. "The same thing was said about African-Americans . . . about the Irish," a Georgia restaurant owner, who asked not to be identified, told CNN. "It's the same old song and over time it's proved to be a bunch of bologna. I believe these people are just like any other newcomers to this country. They can immigrate in and they're doing a great job here. And why should they be any different?" [61]

Those like Huntington and King say they are not against legal immigrants but oppose unchecked illegal immigration. King, in particular, is so furious with the government's refusal to enforce immigration laws against what he sees as the "invasion and the colonization of my country and my state and my city" that he founded the Marietta, Georgia-based American Resistance Foundation, which pushes for stricter enforcement of immigration laws. Whenever he calls the INS to report seeing dozens of undocumented workers milling on local street corners waiting for employers seeking day laborers, he says, "I have never gotten through to a person, and I've never gotten a return phone call." [62] "To whom does an American citizen turn when his government will not protect him from the Third World?" King asks. "What do we do now?"

Asa Hutchinson, former undersecretary of the Department of Homeland Security, which oversees the INS, offered a mixed message in addressing King's frustration.

"I would certainly agree with him that we have to enforce our law, and it's an important part of my responsibilities," Hutchinson told CNN in 2004. "But whenever you look at the family that is being very productive and has a great family life contributing to American society, but in fact they came here illegally, I don't think you could excuse the illegal behavior. But you also recognize

they're not terrorists. They're contributing to our society. We understand the humanitarian reasons that brought them here." [63] Hutchinson said the dilemma for U.S. officials is particularly difficult when those illegal immigrants have had children born here, who are now U.S. citizens. "Do you jerk the parents up and send them back to their home country and leave the two children here that are U.S. citizens? "Those are the problems that we're dealing with every day. Yes, we certainly want to enforce the law, but we have to recognize we also are a compassionate country that deals with a real human side as well."

Asylum

Political asylum accounts for few immigrants but plays an outsized role in the immigration debate. Most legal immigrants settle in the United States because the government decides to allow them in, and illegal immigrants come because they can. But asylum-seekers are granted refuge because the law requires it — not just federal law but international humanitarian law as well. The Convention Relating to the Status of Refugees of 1951, which was updated in 1967, says that no one fleeing political, racial or religious persecution can be returned involuntarily to a country where he or she is in danger. [64]

However, the United States and all other countries that grant asylum can determine who qualifies for that protection and who doesn't. "Irresponsible judges have made asylum laws vulnerable to fraud and abuse," Rep. Sensenbrenner said in promoting his Real ID bill, which would limit the right to asylum by raising the standard for granting asylum and allowing judges to take an applicant's demeanor into account. "We will ensure that terrorists like Ramzi Yousef, the mastermind of the first World Trade Center attack in 1993, no longer receive a free pass to move around America's communities when they show up at our gates claiming asylum," Sensenbrenner said. [65]

Civil liberties advocates say terrorists today could not breeze through an immigration inspection by demanding asylum because the 1996 immigration overhaul tightened after Yousef and others abused it. Above all, the 1996 immigration act authorized immigration inspectors to refuse entry to foreigners without passports or with illegally obtained travel documents. [66]

In addition, says Erin Corcoran, a Washington-based lawyer in the asylum-rights program of Human Rights First (formerly, the Lawyers Committee for Human Rights), asylum seekers now get their fingerprints and photos checked at each stage in the process. "Real ID just heightens the burden of proof that a genuine applicant must meet," Corcoran says, arguing that terrorists are more than capable of adjusting to the new security environment. "A terrorist would have everything in order."

The 1996 law tightened up the process in other ways as well. If a foreigner asks for asylum when trying to enter the United States, he must get a so-called "credible fear interview." If an asylum officer concludes that a "significant possibility" exists for the foreigner to win asylum, a judge might rule that the foreigner shouldn't be deported. If the asylum officer decides that foreigners haven't met the "credible fear" standard, they are held and then deported. But those who do meet the standard may be released while they await hearings on their asylum claims. [67]

And even getting to the first step of the asylum process is difficult. In fiscal 1999 through 2003, asylum was requested by 812,324 foreigners, but only 35,566 were granted credible fear interviews. [68] Of the 36,799 asylum applicants whose cases were decided during the same period, 5,891 were granted asylum or allowed to remain in the United States under the international Convention Against Torture; 19,722 applicants were ordered deported, and 1,950 withdrew their applications. Another 2,528 were allowed to become legal permanent residents. [69]

OUTLOOK

Focus on Mexico

Immigration predictions have a way of turning out wrong. The 1986 Immigration Reform and Control Act didn't control illegal immigration. The 1994 North American Free Trade Agreement didn't create enough jobs in Mexico to keep Mexicans from migrating. The 1996 Immigration Enforcement Improvement Act didn't lessen the flow of illegal immigrants. Cracking down on illegal crossings in big cities like San Diego and El Paso only funneled migrants into the deadly desert of northern Mexico. And announced measures to step up border enforcement didn't stop illegals from coming in — both before or after the Sept. 11, 2001, attacks — although legal immigration did drop.

Faced with such a track record, many immigration experts say legislation and law enforcement may not be the best ways to change immigration patterns, especially where illegal immigration is concerned. The May 2007 deal between senators and the White House was immediately

hailed by *Washington Post* editorial writers as a "breakthrough." Still, the newspaper worried that its provisions for allowing 400,000 low-skilled guest workers to enter the country each year for stays lasting no longer than two years — and totaling no more than six years — was "a system that invites rule-breaking by workers and employers and raises the specter of a future class of illegal immigrants. That is precisely the problem this bill was intended to solve. [70]

"The absence of consensus on alternatives locks in the current policy mix, under which unauthorized immigrants bear most of the costs and risks of 'control' while benefits flow impressively to employers and consumers," Cornelius of the University of California has concluded. "Promised future experiments with guest worker programs, highly secure ID cards for verifying employment eligibility and new technologies for electronic border control are unlikely to change this basic dynamic. [71] "The back door to undocumented immigration to the United States is essentially wide open," he said. "And it is likely to remain wide open unless something systematic and serious is done to reduce the demand for the labor." [72]

Steven Camarota, research director of the Washington-based Center for Immigration Studies, which advocates tougher immigration controls, agrees. "There is a fundamental political stalemate," he says. "You have a divide in the country between public opinion and elite opinion. Elite opinion is strong enough to make sure that the law doesn't get enforced but is not strong enough to repeal the law. Public opinion is strong enough to ensure that the law doesn't get repealed but not strong enough to get the law enforced. For most politicians a continuation of the status quo doesn't have a huge political downside."

Nevertheless, Stein of FAIR argues that Beltway insiders are only slowly catching on to what's happening in the country at large. "The issue is building very rapidly in terms of public frustration," he says. "You talk to [congressional] representatives, they'll tell you that you go to a town meeting and talk about the budget or one of the issues that the party wants to talk about, and the discussion will last five minutes. Mention immigration and two hours later you're still on it. It's on fire out there."

That's the reason every state and dozens of cities have pursued ad hoc solutions to the problems posed by the massive influx of new immigrants, both legal and illegal. Local officials and voters are hoping that lawmakers in Washington will be able to address this issue in a thorough way. Immigration is one of the few issues on which Bush has been willing to break with fellow conservative Republicans in attempting to find a compromise with Democrats. And congressional Democrats, who are enjoying their newfound majority status, have been unable to come to terms with the White House on other central issues of the day — notably Iraq. A comprehensive immigration law — something that eluded their GOP predecessors — would be a great coup. Nonetheless, like Republicans before them, Democrats are clearly split by the issue, with many of their members favoring a tougher approach than liberal lions such as Ted Kennedy.

Balancing the demands of the various constituencies involved in the immigration issue — employers, labor unions, communities that feel strapped by the demands immigrants put on their services and infrastructure, those who are angered by the presence of millions of illegal immigrant, and the fact that those millions are already present in this country — remains an incredibly difficult feat for Congress and the president o pull off.

NOTES

1. Quoted in "CNN Presents: Immigrant Nation: Divided Country," Oct. 17, 2004.

2. Jeffrey S. Passel, "Estimates of the Size and Characteristics of the Undocumented Population," March 21, 2005, Pew Hispanic Center, www.pewhispanic.org.

3. Census Bureau, *Statistical Abstract of the United States, 2004-2005*, p. 8; www.census.gov/prod/2004pubs/04statab/pop.pdf; Office of Policy and Planning, U.S. Immigration and Naturalization Service, "Estimates of the Unauthorized Immigration Population Residing in The United States: 1990 to 2000," http://uscis.gov/graphics/shared/statistics/publications/Ill_Report_1211.pdf; Steven A. Camarota, "Economy Slowed, But Immigration Didn't: The Foreign-Born Population 2000-2004," Center for Immigration Studies, November 2004, www.cis.org/articles/2004/back 1204.pdf.

4. Quoted in David Kelly, "Illegal Immigration Fears Have Spread; Populist Calls for Tougher Enforcement are Being Heard Beyond the Border States," *Los Angeles Times*, April 25, 2005.

5. *Ibid.*

6. *Ibid.*

7. Seth Hettena, "Congressmen Call on Senate to Pass Bill to Fortify Border Fence," Associated Press, March 29, 2005.

8. PR Newswire, "Senator John McCain Surprises U.S. Constitutional Development Class at Annapolis . . . ," April 21, 2005.

9. "President Meets with President Fox and Prime Minister Martin," White House, March 23, 2005, www.whitehouse.gov/news/releases/2005/03/print/20050323-5.html.

10. Elisabeth Bumiller, "In Immigration Remarks, Bush Hints He Favors Senate Plan," *The New York Times*, April 25, 2006, p. 22.

11. Wayne Cornelius, "Controlling 'Unwanted' Immigration: Lessons from the United States, 1993-2004," Center for Comparative Immigration Studies, University of California, San Diego, December 2004, 5, www.ccis-ucsd.org/PUBLICATIONS/wrkg92.pdf.

12. Statement, March 15, 2005; www.cbp.gov/xp/cgov/newsroom/commissioner/speeches_statements/mar17_05.xml.

13. Donald L. Bartlett and James B. Steele, "Who Left the Door Open," *Time*, Sept. 20, 2004, p. 51.

14. Birgit Meade, unpublished analysis, Economic Research Service, U.S. Department of Agriculture.

15. George J. Borjas, *Heaven's Door: Immigration Policy and the American Economy* (1999), pp. 87-104.

16. *Ibid.*, pp. 103-104.

17. *Ibid.*, pp. 90-91.

18. Chirag Mehta, *et al.*, "Chicago's Undocumented Immigrants: An Analysis of Wages, Working Conditions, and Economic Contributions," February 2002, www.uic.edu/cuppa/uicued/npublications/recent/undocimmigrants.htm.

19. "Immigration and Border Security Evolve, 1993 to 2001," Chapter 4 in "Staff Monograph on 9/11 and Terrorist Travel," National Commission on Terrorist Attacks Upon the United States, 2004, www.9-11commission.gov/staff_statements/911_TerrTrav_Ch4.pdf.

20. *Ibid.*

21. *Ibid.*

22. *The 9/11 Commission Report* (2004), pp. 248, 387.

23. T. R. Reid and Darryl Fears, "Driver's License Curtailed as Identification," *The Washington Post*, April 17, 2005, p. A3.

24. Muzaffar A. Chishti, *et al.*, "America's Challenge: Domestic Security, Civil Liberties, and National Unity After September 11," Migration Policy Institute, 2003, p. 7.

25. *Gorgonio Balbuena, et al., v. IDR Realty LLC, et al.*; 2004 N.Y. App. Div.

26. Unless otherwise noted, material in the background section comes from Rodman D. Griffin, "Illegal Immigration," *CQ Researcher*, April 24, 1992, pp. 361-384; Kenneth Jost, "Cracking Down on Immigration," *CQ Researcher*, Feb. 3, 1995, pp. 97-120; and David Masci, "Debate Over Immigration," *CQ Researcher*, July 14, 2000, pp. 569-592.

27. For background, see Richard L. Worsnop, "Asian Americans," *CQ Researcher*, Dec. 13, 1991, pp. 945-968.

28. Quoted in Ellis Cose, *A Nation of Strangers: Prejudice, Politics and the Populating of America* (1992), p. 191.

29. Cited in Michael Fix, ed., *The Paper Curtain: Employer Sanctions' Implementation, Impact, and Reform* (1991), p. 2.

30. Quoted in Tom Morganthau, *et al.*, "Closing the Door," *Newsweek*, June 25, 1984.

31. Quoted in Dick Kirschten, "Come In! Keep Out!," *National Journal*, May 19, 1990, p. 1206.

32. For background, see Peter Katel, "Haiti's Dilemma," *CQ Researcher*, Feb. 18, 2005, pp. 149-172.

33. Cose, *A Nation of Strangers*, p. 192.

34. Ann Chih Lin, ed. *Immigration*, CQ Press (2002), pp. 60-61.

35. William Branigin, "Congress Finishes Major Legislation; Immigration; Focus is Borders, Not Benefits," *The Washington Post*, Oct. 1, 1996, p. A1.

36. David Johnston, "Government is Quickly Using Power of New Immigration Law," *The New York Times*, Oct. 22, 1996, p. A20.

37. William Branigin, "INS Shifts 'Interior' Strategy to Target Criminal Aliens," *The Washington Post*, March 15, 1999, p. A3.

38. *The 9/11 Commission Report*, p. 215-223.

39. Adam Liptak, Neil A. Lewis, and Benjamin Weiser, "After Sept. 11, a Legal Battle On the Limits of Civil Liberty," *The New York Times*, August 4, 2002, p. A1. For background, see Patrick Marshall, "Policing the Borders," *CQ Researcher*, Feb. 22, 2002, pp. 145-168.

40. *Ibid.*

41. Deborah Meyers and Jennifer Yau, *U.S. Immigration Statistics in 2003*, Migration Policy Institute, Nov. 1, 2004, www.migrationinformation.org/USfocus/display.cfm?id=263; and Homeland Security Department, *2003 Yearbook of Immigration Statistics*, http://uscis.gov/graphics/shared/statistics/yearbook/index.htm.

42. Passel, "Estimates," p. 8.

43. Meyers and Yau, *U.S. Immigration Statistics in 2003*.

44. Lin, *Immigration*, p. 20.

45. Robert Pear and Jim Rutenberg, "Senators in Bipartisan Deal on Broad Immigration Bill," *The New York Times*, May 18, 2007, p. A1.

46. Karoun Demirjian, "Bipartisan Immigration Deal Reached," *Chicago Tribune*, May 18, 2007.

47. Pam Belluck, "Mandate for ID Meets Resistance From States," *The New York Times*, May 6, 2006.

48. David D. Kirkpatrick, "Demonstrations on Immigration are Hardening a Divide," *The New York Times*, April 17, 2006, p. 16.

49. Arian Campo-Flores, "A Latino 'Spanking,' " *Newsweek*, Dec. 4, 2006, p. 40.

50. Rick Montgomery and Scott Cannon, "Party Shift Won't End Immigration Debate," *The Washington Post*, Dec. 17, 2006, p. A11.

51. Jim VandeHei, "Florida Senator Will Be a Top RNC Officer," *The Washington Post*, Nov. 14, 2006, p. A4.

52. Anthony Faiola, "Looking the Other Way on Immigrants," *The Washington Post*, April 10, 2007, p. A1.

53. Louis Sahagun, "Giving Shelter From the Storm of Deportation," *Los Angeles Times*, May 9, 2007, p. B2.

54. "Proposition 200," Arizona Secretary of State, www.azsos.gov/election/2004/info/PubPamphlet/english/prop200.htm.

55. *Ibid.*

56. Jacques Billeaud, "Congressman: Prop 200's Passage was Key Moment in Effort to Limit Immigration," Associated Press, April 2, 2005.

57. Jacques Billeaud, "Arizona Lawmakers Try to Add Restrictions for Illegal Immigrants," Associated Press, March 24, 2005.

58. Chris L. Jenkins, "Warner Signs Limits on Immigrant Benefits," *The Washington Post*, March 30, 2005, p. B5.

59. Quoted in "CNN Presents: Immigrant Nation: Divided Country," Oct. 17, 2004.

60. Samuel Huntington, "The Hispanic Challenge," *Foreign Policy*, March/April 2004.

61. "CNN Presents."

62. King's quotes are from *ibid.*

63. Hutchinson's quotes are from *ibid.*

64. "The Wall Behind Which Refugees Can Shelter," U.N. High Commissioner for Refugees, 2001; www.unhcr.org.

65. Dan Robinson, "Congress — Immigration," Voice of America, Dec. 8, 2004, www.globalsecurity.org/security/library/news/2004/12/sec-041208-3c7be91f.htm.

66. "Asylum Seekers in Expedited Removal," United States Commission on International Religious Freedom, Executive Summary, 1-2, Feb. 8, 2005, www.uscirf.gov/countries/global/asylum_refugees/2005/february/index.html.

67. *Ibid.*

68. *Ibid.*, p. 295.

69. *Ibid.*

70. "Breakthrough on Immigration," *The Washington Post*, May 18, 2007, p. A22.

71. Cornelius, "Controlling 'Unwanted' Immigration," p. 24.

72. "CNN Presents."

BIBLIOGRAPHY

Books

Borjas, George J., *Heaven's Door: Immigration Policy and the American Economy*, **Princeton University Press, 2000.**
A Harvard economist who is a leading figure in the debate over immigration and the economy argues for encouraging immigration by the highly skilled while discouraging the entry of low-skilled workers.

Dow, Mark, *American Gulag: Inside U.S. Immigration Prisons*, **University of California Press, 2004.**
A freelance journalist penetrates the secretive world of immigrant detention and finds widespread abuse of prisoners who are granted few, if any, legal rights.

Huntington, Samuel P., *Who Are We?: The Challenges to America's National Identity*, **Simon & Schuster, 2004.**
A Harvard professor argues that mass immigration, especially from Latin America, is flooding the United States with people who are not assimilating into mainstream society.

Jacoby, Tamar, ed., *Reinventing the Melting Pot: The New Immigrants and What It Means To Be An American*, **Basic Books, 2004.**
Authors representing strongly differing views and experiences on immigration contribute essays on how the present wave of immigrants is changing — and being changed by — the United States. Edited by a pro-immigration scholar at the moderately libertarian Manhattan Institute.

Lin, Ann Chih, ed., and Nicole W. Green, *Immigration*, **CQ Press, Vital Issues Series, 2002.**
This useful collection of information on recent immigration policy and law changes also includes steps that other countries have taken to deal with issues similar to those under debate in the United States.

Articles

Cooper, Marc, "Last Exit to Tombstone," *L.A. Weekly*, **March 25, 2005, p. 24.**
A reporter visits the Mexican desert border towns where immigrants prepare to cross illegally into the United States and finds them undaunted by the dangers ahead.

Jordan, Miriam, "As Border Tightens, Growers See Threat to 'Winter Salad Bowl,' " *The Wall Street Journal*, **March 11, 2005, p. A1.**
Lettuce farmers plead with immigration officials not to crack down on illegal immigration at the height of the harvest season in Arizona.

Kammer, Jerry, "Immigration plan's assumption on unskilled workers contested," *San Diego Union-Tribune*, **March 31, 2005, p. A1.**

Even immigrants who once lacked legal status themselves are worried about the continued influx of illegal immigrants, because they drive down wages.

Porter, Eduardo, "Illegal Immigrants are Bolstering Social Security With Billions," *The New York Times*, April 5, 2005, p. A1.
Government figures indicate that illegal immigrants are subsidizing Social Security by about $7 billion a year by paying taxes from which they will never benefit.

Seper, Jerry, "Rounding Up All Illegals 'Not Realistic,' " *The Washington Times*, Sept. 10, 2004, p. A1.
The undersecretary of homeland security acknowledges that law enforcement officials are not hunting for all illegal immigrants, something he said would be neither possible nor desirable.

Reports and Studies

Lee, Joy, Jack Martin and Stan Fogel, *Immigrant Stock's Share of U.S. Population Growth, 1970-2004*, Federation for American Immigration Reform, 2005.
The authors conclude that more than half of the country's population growth since 1970 stems from increased immigration, raising the danger of overpopulation and related ills.

Orozco, Manuel, *The Remittance Marketplace: Prices, Policy and Financial Institutions*, Pew Hispanic Center, June 2004.
A leading scholar of remittances — money sent back home by immigrants — analyzes the growth of the trend and the regulatory environment in which it operates.

***Refugees, Asylum Seekers and the Department of Homeland Security: One Year Anniversary — No Time for Celebration*, Human Rights First, April 2004.**
Some rights of asylum-seekers are being eroded as the number of people granted asylum drops, the advocacy organization concludes, urging changes in procedures.

Stana, Richard M., "Immigration Enforcement: Challenges to Implementing the INS Interior Enforcement Strategy," General Accounting Office (now Government Accountability Office), testimony before House Judiciary Subcommittee on Immigration, June 19, 2002.
A top GAO official finds a multitude of reasons why immigration officials have not been able to deport criminal illegal immigrants, break up people-smuggling rings and crack down on employers of illegal immigrants.

For More Information

Center for Comparative Immigration Studies, University of California-San Diego, La Jolla, CA 92093-0548; (858) 822-4447; www.ccis-ucsd.org. This organization analyzes U.S. immigration trends and compares them with patterns in Europe and Asia.

Center for Immigration Studies, 1522 K St., N.W., Suite 820, Washington, DC 20005-1202; (202) 466-8185; www.cis.org. A think tank that advocates reduced immigration.

Civil Homeland Defense, P. O. Box 1579, Tombstone, AZ 85638; (520) 457-3008; www.civilhomelanddefense.us. This group is an offshoot of the Minuteman Project that encourages citizens to patrol the Mexican border in Arizona against illegal immigrants.

Federation for American Immigration Reform, 1666 Connecticut Ave., N.W., Suite 400, Washington, DC 20009; (202) 328-7004; http://fairus.org. This organiza-

tion is a leading advocate for cracking down on illegal immigration and reducing legal immigration.

Migration Dialogue, University of California, Davis, 1 Shields Ave., Davis, CA 95616; (530) 752-1011; http://migration.ucdavis.edu/index.php. An academic research center that focuses on immigration from rural Mexico and publishes two quarterly Web bulletins.

Migration Policy Institute, 1400 16th St., N.W., Suite 300, Washington, DC 20036; (202) 266-1940; www.migrationpolicy.org. This think tank analyzes global immigration trends and advocates fairer, more humane conditions for immigrants.

National Immigration Law Center, 3435 Wilshire Blvd., Suite 2850, Los Angeles, CA 90010; (213) 639.3900; http://nilc.org. Advocacy organization seeks to defend the legal rights of low-income immigrants.

16

Treatment of Detainees

Peter Katel and Kenneth Jost

Protesters call for changes in U.S. policies on the treatment of suspected terrorists during a Senate Armed Services Committee hearing on July 13, 2006.

From *CQ Researcher,*
August 25, 2006.

K illers," President George W. Bush has called the prisoners being held by the United States at Guantánamo Bay — murderers of civilians who don't deserve to be treated under the international laws of war. "These are terrorists," Bush declared in 2002. "They know no countries." [1]

But the top lawyers from the Army, Navy, Air Force and Marines disagree with their commander in chief. When the Senate Armed Services Committee asked them on July 16 if Congress should endorse the controversial trial and detention system created by Bush for enemy combatants, they answered no — emphatically.

"Clearly, we need a change," declared Major Gen. Jack Rives judge advocate general of the Air Force. His colleagues agreed.

In fact, military attorneys have argued for the past several years against the administration's refusal to apply the Geneva Conventions to the war on terrorism. The conventions are the set of treaties governing military conduct in wartime, including the treatment of prisoners and civilians.

Until the Supreme Court ruled in late June, the Bush administration had maintained that the conventions did not apply to prisoners captured in Afghanistan and other battlefields in the war on terrorists. That led to the use of interrogation methods, such as threatening prisoners with guard dogs, near-drowning by "waterboarding," sleep deprivation and forcing prisoners into painful "stress positions."

For the past two years, the abuse of detainees held at Bagram Air Base, in Afghanistan, Abu Ghraib prison in Iraq and the U.S. Naval Station at Guantánamo Bay, Cuba, have generated international outrage. Yet military lawyers, politicians and other critics of U.S.

Many Detainees Not Linked to Hostile Acts

More than half of the detainees at Guantánamo Bay have no history of hostile acts against the United States or its allies, according to an analysis of government data by lawyers for detainees (left). Nearly three-quarters of the detainees whom the U.S. government has characterized as "associated with" the al Qaeda terrorist network have not committed hostile acts against the United States or its allies.

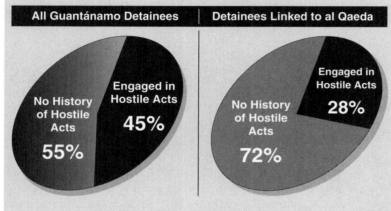

All Guantánamo Detainees	Detainees Linked to al Qaeda
Engaged in Hostile Acts **45%** / No History of Hostile Acts **55%**	Engaged in Hostile Acts **28%** / No History of Hostile Acts **72%**

Source: "Report on Guantánamo Detainees, A Profile of 517 Detainees Through Analysis of Department of Defense Data," Seton Hall University School of Law

policies had largely failed to get Bush and his top legal-affairs and military appointees to change policies on treatment of these prisoners, whom Bush defined as "unlawful combatants." [2]

In behind-the-scenes battles within the administration, military lawyers argued that the United States was violating the laws of warfare in seeming to condone abuse and torture of detainees. The lawyers also opposed the system of military courts proposed by Bush for war-on-terrorism prisoners at Guantánamo that denied many rights that the conventions grant even to irregular fighters who don't wear any country's uniform. [3]

"I'd only say I wish they'd taken our advice," says William H. Taft, IV, chief legal adviser to Secretary of State Colin Powell during President Bush's first term. [4]

Critics could be ignored or overruled — but not the U.S. Supreme Court.

In its landmark June 29 decision, the justices ruled, 5-3, that prisoners being held in the fight against the al Qaeda terrorist organization are entitled to the protections afforded by the Geneva Conventions. The suit challeng-ing the administration was brought on behalf of Salim Ahmed Hamdan, a Yemeni prisoner at Guantánamo who was Osama bin Laden's driver. [5]

"We fought very hard to get him a fair trial," Hamdan's military-appointed lawyer, Navy Lt. Cmdr. Charles Swift, told the Senate Judiciary Committee. He argued that the military's existing court-martial system — rather than tribunals known as military commissions — would suit that aim perfectly. *

Military lawyers and their congressional supporters argue that American lives may depend on whether the United States upholds Geneva standards for all detainees. "We will have more wars, and there will be Americans who will be taken captive," Arizona Republican Sen. John McCain, who was tortured during his five-and-a-half years as a prisoner of war in North Vietnam, told the Senate Armed Services Committee. "If we somehow carve out exceptions to treaties . . . then it will make it very easy for our enemies to do the same in the case of American prisoners."

Sen. Saxby Chambliss, R-Ga., responded, "It certainly irritates me to no end to think that we have to continue to do what's right at all times when the enemy that we're fighting is going to be cruel and inhuman to American men and women who wear our uniform [if] they might fall into their hands."

While the Supreme Court did not address the government's right to hold war-on-terror prisoners "for the duration of active hostilities," it ruled that Bush had exceeded his authority in establishing the commissions. Only Congress has the power to decide that the standard military justice system couldn't be used, the court majority wrote. The decision leaves lawmakers with two basic options: require detainees to be tried under the existing

---

* The lawsuit, *Hamdan v. Rumsfeld*, has delayed trials of other alleged terrorists.

court-martial system, or bow to the administration's wishes and create a new, legal version of the commissions. [6]

Retaining the commissions would, in effect, undercut the high court's ruling that Common Article 3 of the Geneva Conventions covers Guantánamo detainees. The provision requires that a prisoner on trial — even someone not fighting for a specific nation — be judged by a "regularly constituted court" that provides "all judicial guarantees which are recognized as indispensable by civilized peoples." And it prohibits "humiliating and degrading treatment" and well as "cruel treatment and torture." [7]

The high court's reasoning didn't sit well with some lawmakers.

"Where I'm from in South Dakota," Republican Sen. John Thune told his Armed Services colleagues, "when you talk about humiliating or degrading or those types of terms, in applying them to terrorists . . . people in my state would [not] be real concerned that we might be infringing on [the terrorists'] sense of inferiority."

But Sen. Lindsey Graham, R-S.C., resisted any implication that critics of the commission system want to coddle terrorists. "All the people who are out there ranting and raving [that] having . . . some basic due process cripples us in the war effort, you're flat wrong," said Graham, a colonel in the Air Force Reserve and a judge on the Air Force Court of Criminal Appeals. [8]

The debate over whether the rules of traditional warfare apply in the war on terrorists began in the months following the 9/11 terrorist attacks on the World Trade Center and the Pentagon. Then-White House Counsel Alberto Gonzales summed up the administration's mind-set in a Jan. 25, 2002, memo to Bush: "The war against terrorism is a new kind of war," wrote Gonzales, now the nation's attorney general. "The nature of the new war places a high premium on . . . the ability to quickly obtain information from captured terrorists and their sponsors in order to avoid further atrocities against

Where Are the Detainees?

About 14,000 detainees are being held by the United States, but the number fluctuates, especially following major offensives. Many prisoners captured in battle initially are held at bases in combat zones and are not included in the detainee figures below.

Locations of Detention Facilities	No. of Detainees
Afghanistan	
Bagram Air Force Base	500
Kandahar	100 to 200
Cuba	
Guantánamo Bay	**450**
Since the detention camp was opened, about 310 prisoners have been freed or transferred to their home countries or to other nations.	
Iraq	**12,800**
The majority of the prisoners captured in Iraq and Afghanistan are held at Abu Ghraib prison, Camp Bucca and various facilities around Baghdad airport.	
Other Locations	**30**
Human Rights Watch says more than two-dozen high-value detainees, sometimes called "ghost prisoners," are in CIA custody in undisclosed locations outside the United States.	

Sources: Department of Defense, Human Rights Watch

American civilians, and the need to try terrorists for war crimes." [9]

Taft and then-Secretary of State Powell were among a handful of officials who rejected Gonzales' approach. [10]

But Gonzales and other officials carried the day. At about the time he wrote his memo, the first prisoners were being shipped to Guantánamo. By mid-2006, the camp held about 450 detainees, according to the Department of Defense (DOD). The military itself conceded that some of the Guantánamo prisoners didn't belong there. The DOD says about 80 men have been released and another 230 transferred to their countries of origin, in most cases after Combatant Status Review Tribunals determined they hadn't fought the United States and had no other connections to terrorism, or did not pose a significant threat. [11]

The tribunals were set up after the Supreme Court ruled in 2004 that the Guantánamo prisoners could use habeas corpus petitions to challenge their detentions. [12]

That ruling landed the first major legal blow against the administration's detention policies. Only a month before, the scandal over prisoner abuses at Abu Ghraib had exploded, followed by leaked memos in which officials discussed how to avoid defining some interrogation methods as torture. By the end of 2004, the administration was forced to back down from a narrow definition of "torture" fashioned by a top Justice Department lawyer — that the term applied only to methods so extreme that they caused "organ failure" or the equivalent. [13]

Following that administration retreat, Congress at the end of 2005 passed the Detainee Treatment Act, sponsored by McCain, which prohibits "cruel, inhuman or degrading" treatment of any captive in American hands. A provision limiting court enforcement complicated the law's practical effect. [14]

The Supreme Court's *Hamdan* ruling further undermined the administration's detention and trial system for enemy fighters and terrorists. Captured in Afghanistan in 2001, Hamdan had acknowledged serving as a driver for al Qaeda leader Osama bin Laden. But the government charged him with participating in al Qaeda's conspiracy to kill Americans, which he denies. [15]

To the administration, Hamdan was exactly the kind of prisoner the new rules were designed to deal with — both an intelligence source and an alleged war criminal.

But military lawyers say Gonzales and other civilians blur the lines between intelligence gathering and war-crimes prosecution.

"That confusion has created all kinds of problems," says former Navy Judge Advocate General John D. Hutson, dean of Franklin Pierce Law Center in Manchester, N.H. For one thing, he argues, the administration hasn't distinguished among prisoners who clearly have valuable intelligence, those who had terrorist links but didn't possess any secrets and those who had neither.

But even an established connection to al Qaeda may mean less than the government alleges, according to Hutson. "Hamdan — we can pretend he was something else, but the reality is, he was a driver," Hutson says. "He is no more and no less a war criminal than Hitler's driver. To prosecute him for conspiracy is a very problematic proposition."

The charges against Hamdan have been described only in general terms, but an Air Force lawyer who works with the commission told *The New York Times* that the evidence, including photographs and Hamdan's statements to interrogators, added up to a "solid" case. [16]

As for other detainees, the Defense Department says they include former terrorist trainers, operatives and bomb makers who have provided "valuable insights" into al Qaeda methods and personnel. [17]

Meanwhile, the conflict over detention and trial has put military lawyers at odds with their civilian leaders. Swift, for example, told the Armed Services Committee the commissions' rules made a mockery of judicial fairness by allowing defendants to be kept out of the courtroom and barred from seeing at least some of the evidence against them.

To those who argue that following Geneva Convention rules would compromise America's defenses, Swift said: "Given the handcuffs put on its counsel, the accused is really the only one that can dispute the evidence against him. Without knowing what that evidence is, the accused is left undefended."

As the political, legal and military communities ponder how to treat prisoners, these are some of the major issues being debated:

Should Congress require wartime detainees to be treated according to the Geneva Conventions?

The *Hamdan* decision brought Congress face-to-face with a fundamental choice: Whether to create a system for imprisoning and trying detainees based on the Geneva Conventions.

The Supreme Court seemingly decided the issue when it rejected the administration's assertion that Common Article 3 of the conventions does not apply to Guantánamo detainees. "That reasoning is erroneous," the majority opinion said. "Common Article 3 . . . is applicable here." [18]

Moreover, military lawyers have testified that Common Article 3 has served as the minimum standard for decades on how troops must treat all prisoners. In fact, U.S. military personnel are required to meet an even higher threshold, treating all prisoners as uniformed prisoners of war representing a nation, Thomas J. Romig, a former Army judge advocate general, told the Senate Armed Services Committee. "And at that standard, you're never going to violate Common Article 3," he said.

Under the Geneva Conventions POWs must be allowed to keep their personal property, exercise and receive regular medical care. Common Article 3, on the other hand, imposes what military lawyers consider the bare essentials of how to treat an enemy, even a terrorist. [19]

But defining those bare essentials has become the biggest point of dispute between the administration and its critics.

"Common Article 3 is written in such generalities, it's almost like taking a blank piece of paper," says Andrew C. McCarthy, a former federal prosecutor who helped mount the case against the terrorists who tried to blow up the World Trade Center in 1993. " 'Judicial guarantees,' which are recognized as indispensable by civilized peoples — what does that mean? What does Common Article 3 tell you about whether you need to give terrorist defendants access to national-security secrets during trial? Is that indispensable to civilized peoples? Who knows?"

Variations on that theme have become a major feature of debates on detainee treatment. Daniel Dell'Orto, principal deputy general counsel at the Pentagon, told the House Armed Services Committee: "I don't want a soldier when he kicks down a door in a hut in Afghanistan searching for Osama bin Laden to have to worry about whether — when he does so and questions the individuals he finds inside, who may or may not be bin Laden's bodyguards, or even that individual himself — he's got to advise them of some rights before he takes a statement."

Former Navy Judge Advocate General Hutson says: "Yes, Common Article 3 is vague in some sense, I suppose, but life, and particularly law, are replete with vague terms: obscenity, probable cause, torture. If we need to explain what we believe those terms mean, then we should do it. We're just using vagueness as an excuse to avoid Common Article 3 and the Geneva Conventions."

But Hutson noted during an appearance before the Senate Armed Services Committee on July 13, "nobody — certainly not me" had argued that troops on a search mission should be required to give Miranda warnings.

As for how to define various terms in Common Article 3, Air Force Maj. Gen. Rives added that the provision has been incorporated into military law for more than 50 years with no objections raised.

Washington lawyer David B. Rivkin Jr., a former lawyer in the Reagan and George H.W. Bush administrations, zeroes in on Common Article 3's opening sentence, which specifies that it applies to conflicts occurring only in the countries that signed the convention. "Not every country has signed," Rivkin says, arguing that the restriction would make enforcement unmanageable. "So if you capture al Qaeda personnel in Afghanistan, which is a party to the Geneva Conventions, you have one set of rules, and if you make a capture in Somalia — I don't know if Somalia

Top military lawyers, or judge advocate generals (JAGs), testify before a Senate Armed Services Committee hearing on military tribunals for Guantánamo Bay detainees, on July 13, 2006. From left: Maj. Gen. Scott C. Black (Army), Rear Adm. James E. McPherson (Navy), Maj. Gen. Jack L. Rives (Air Force), Brig. Gen. Kevin M. Sandkulher (Marine Corps) and former JAGs Thomas J. Romig (Army) and John D. Hutson (Navy).

signed — then Common Article 3 doesn't apply. Does that make any sense?"

But Katherine Newell Bierman, a former Air Force captain who is now counterterrorism counsel for Human Rights Watch (HRW), says no such geographic limitation would exist if Congress simply adopted the protections of Common Article 3 in a statute.

Bierman notes that nothing in the provision requires every prisoner to be granted a trial. "But if you're going to sentence them, there has to be a fair trial," she says. What that means, she says, amounts to nothing more extravagant than giving the defendant a chance to defend himself, not forcing him to incriminate himself and ensuring he's not tortured — the elements of what an ordinary citizen would consider a fair trial.

Administration supporters insist that such seemingly simple notions of justice conflict with the plain reality that definitions of elementary matters vary widely from country to country. For instance, says Kris Kobach, a former Justice Department lawyer who now teaches at the University of Missouri School of Law, " 'Cruel and unusual punishment' can mean one thing in the United States, where we're trying to decide whether it's cruel to put someone to death by virtually pain-free lethal injection, whereas in another country the question is whether

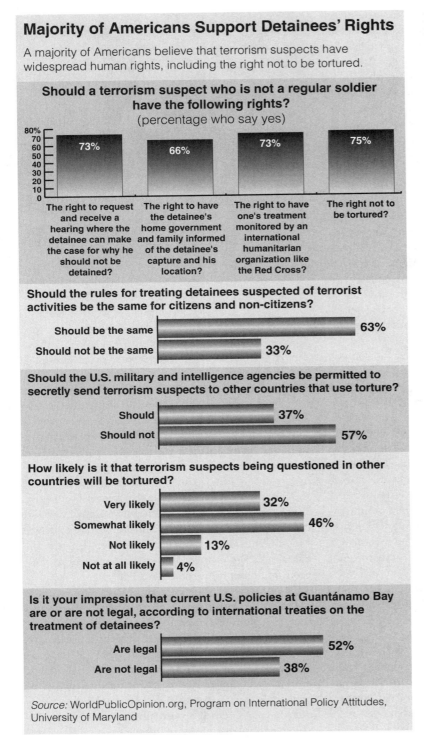

Majority of Americans Support Detainees' Rights

A majority of Americans believe that terrorism suspects have widespread human rights, including the right not to be tortured.

Should a terrorism suspect who is not a regular soldier have the following rights?
(percentage who say yes)

The right to request and receive a hearing where the detainee can make the case for why he should not be detained?	The right to have the detainee's home government and family informed of the detainee's capture and his location?	The right to have one's treatment monitored by an international humanitarian organization like the Red Cross?	The right not to be tortured?
73%	66%	73%	75%

Should the rules for treating detainees suspected of terrorist activities be the same for citizens and non-citizens?

- Should be the same: 63%
- Should not be the same: 33%

Should the U.S. military and intelligence agencies be permitted to secretly send terrorism suspects to other countries that use torture?

- Should: 37%
- Should not: 57%

How likely is it that terrorism suspects being questioned in other countries will be tortured?

- Very likely: 32%
- Somewhat likely: 46%
- Not likely: 13%
- Not at all likely: 4%

Is it your impression that current U.S. policies at Guantánamo Bay are or are not legal, according to international treaties on the treatment of detainees?

- Are legal: 52%
- Are not legal: 38%

Source: WorldPublicOpinion.org, Program on International Policy Attitudes, University of Maryland

---

public caning is cruel. This is a war in which very different cultures are involved."

Should Common Article 3 apply to CIA prisoners held in undisclosed locations in other countries?

Although attention has focused on detainees held by the military, there is also concern about prisoners being held in secret by the Central Intelligence Agency (CIA). Human Rights Watch (HRW) says media reports indicate that 30 such "ghost" detainees are being held, including high-ranking alleged terrorists. Government officials have confirmed some of the detentions. [20]

Administration critics say flatly that prisoners of the United States should not be held incommunicado but should be put on trial if they're believed to have committed crimes. "Secret detention is the gateway to torture," said Reed Brody, a special counsel for HRW, arguing that the Geneva Conventions on both POWs and detained civilians require International Red Cross access to all prisoners. [21]

But administration advocates argue that the relevance of the conventions to CIA prisoners detained as terrorists isn't clear.

"We're testing our definitions," the University of Missouri's Kobach says. "We have two categories that we know: traditional soldiers who become POWs when we capture them and garden-variety criminals who become defendants in civilian courts when we capture them. Terrorists fit somewhere in between. They're committing offenses against laws of war and terrorist acts that transcend normal criminal acts."

Kobach acknowledges that he could make the argument that even

CIA prisoners are entitled to military trials, but he said that the *Hamdan* decision doesn't provide guidance on whether alleged terrorists who are not being held by the Defense Department should get the same treatment. One common factor with the Guantánamo prisoners is that they have all been apprehended by the U.S. military," he says. "If someone has been apprehended by a foreign government, it wouldn't necessarily flow that he should go to Guantánamo."

"Ghost" detainees took center stage in 2004 following the disclosure of photographs of detainees being abused at Abu Ghraib prison in Iraq. On Sept. 9 — some five months after the prison abuse came to light — an Army general told the Senate Armed Services Committee that "dozens, perhaps up to 100" CIA detainees had been imprisoned secretly. [22]

At least one CIA prisoner died in custody at Abu Ghraib, apparently from a rifle butt blow to the head while in custody. The injury went undiscovered because he didn't get a medical screening when brought to the prison, as did prisoners held by the military. [23]

"Water-boarding," a form of torture that simulates drowning, reportedly was used on Khalid Shaikh Muhammed, a Pakistani whom the government's "9/11 Commission" called the "principal architect" of the 9/11 attacks. [24] No trials have been reported scheduled for Shaikh Muhammed or for any other spy-agency prisoner.

"There's some interagency discussion about what you do with these people long term once their intelligence value has been fully exploited," a U.S. intelligence official told the *Los Angeles Times* in 2004. "The CIA is an intelligence collection and analysis organization. This isn't the bureau of prisons." [25]

Bierman of HRW says putting the alleged terrorists on trial would solve the problem. "Anybody subject to the laws of war — and all these people are subject — should be prosecuted in fair trials," she says. "Prosecuting these guys would be a step ahead of hiding them and torturing them. The whole idea of socking them away is that these are people the law doesn't even reach. That is so fundamentally abhorrent to our values."

Rivkin agrees the status of CIA detainees should be "regularized." But his reasoning differs sharply from that of human-rights advocates. Creating a standard detention-and-trial process would cut down on lawsuits aimed at forcing disclosures of prisoners' whereabouts, he says. "Who needs that crap?"

Former CIA contractor David A. Passaro (left) faces up to 11 years in prison after being convicted on Aug. 17, 2006, of beating Afghan farmer Abdul Wali (right) in June 2003 during questioning about rocket attacks at a remote base in Afghanistan; Wali died two days later.

That view flows out of Rivkin's analysis that even Common Article 3 doesn't require POW-style detention — with food parcels from the Red Cross, and notification to detainees' families of where they are being held, among other provisions. "No, you do not have to tell the world where they are," he says. "You don't have to give them rights to which they are not entitled. It's not bad to have people disoriented, and it's not useful to tell the bad guys who we've captured. Let them wonder if the guy is alive or dead."

But Eugene R. Fidell, president of the National Institute of Military Justice, argues that imposing the Common Article 3 standard even on intelligence agencies someday might protect captured CIA officers from extreme abuse.

Practicality aside, Fidell says that because Common Article 3 imposes a minimum set of standards, it must be the baseline for treatment of all detainees, regardless of who holds them. "You can't say, 'Anybody in uniform, fine,' but if the CIA is holding them, the sky's the limit" regarding abuse.

Should the U.S. outlaw "extraordinary rendition"?

Another variant of CIA detention — "extraordinary rendition" — came to light in 2004. The secret procedure involves the seizure of terrorism suspects, usually outside the United States, by U.S. intelligence agents, who ship them to countries reputed to use torture during interrogations. [26]

Ex-CIA officer Michael Scheuer told *The New Yorker's* Jane Mayer that extraordinary rendition began during the Clinton administration, when the threat from bin Laden and associated terrorists first arose. The program expanded after 9/11, when government lawyers created a loophole in a requirement that war-on-terrorism prisoners be treated humanely: Only the military had to comply, not intelligence agencies. [27]

On the CBS news program "60 Minutes II," Scheuer said that countries receiving the suspects were supposed to assure the United States that the prisoners wouldn't be tortured. But no one took the assurances seriously, he said. The bottom line, he said, was that "extraordinary rendition" had produced "very useful" information. Asked if he condoned the use of torture, he replied, "It's OK with me. I'm responsible for protecting Americans." [28]

Only a few "rendered" prisoners have emerged from foreign prisons. Khaled al-Masri, a German of Kuwaiti origin, and Maher Arar, a Canadian citizen from Syria, say they were released after managing to prove their innocence. Both sued the United States for allegedly violating their rights, but the suits were dismissed after government lawyers said the trials would expose official secrets. [29]

Rendition is a long-established procedure for turning wanted people over to governments asking for them, says former State Department adviser Taft. He says rendition can be carried out without violating any laws or policies against delivering people to torturers. If another country asks for a citizen to be sent back because he's wanted for questioning or trial, "Before we would transfer anybody in those circumstances, we ensure that we are confident that they will be treated properly," he says. He adds that he wasn't involved in any extraordinary rendition cases and knows nothing of them beyond media reports.

If the requesting country has a spotty human-rights record, the State Department can ask to see the prisoner routinely, Taft says. And some countries are off-limits. "I would think that for every person who is bundled off — there should be confidence they will not be treated improperly," he says. "I thought that was the process."

Advocates of the Bush administration approach to counterterrorism acknowledge that human-rights protections may not be assured for terrorism suspects — but they say imposing such a rule would be impractical. "This is one area where Congress is not particularly entitled to the right to oversight," Rivkin says. "It just gets too much into the regulation of foreign policy and intelligence operations."

The process by which American officials evaluate the trustworthiness of other countries' pledges not to mistreat suspects is "too delicate and imprecise to try to reduce to writing," Rivkin says.

But administration critics argue that the Supreme Court's *Hamdan* ruling left no wiggle room about standards for prisoner treatment. "The language of the decision guarantees minimum Geneva Convention Common Article 3 rights to all detainees," says Neal Katyal, Hamdan's co-counsel, a professor at Georgetown Law School. He argues, moreover, that military-justice standards demand humane treatment across the board.

Attorney General Gonzales told the House Judiciary Committee in April that the United States is committed by treaty to not sending people to countries where their human rights would be violated. The 1987 Convention Against Torture and Other Cruel, Inhuman or Degrading Treatment or Punishment, which the Senate ratified in 1990, commits the U.S. not to "expel, return or extradite a person to another State where there are substantial grounds for believing that he would be in danger of being subjected to torture."

But in practice U.S. observance of the treaty is a "farce," says Joseph Margulies, a professor at Northwestern University Law School who is among the lead lawyers for Guantánamo detainees challenging their confinement. He cites the U.S. reliance on declarations by other countries that they won't torture prisoners.

Even some hard-line administration supporters are troubled by the possibility that the United States might wink at the prohibition. If the government doesn't believe that the prohibition against torture should apply to accused terrorists sent to their home countries, ex-prosecutor McCarthy says, officials should say so publicly. "Or else, we should stop doing it."

A critic of the administration's overall detainee policy takes that reasoning even further. Former Navy JAG Hutson favors outlawing extraordinary rendition. But, he adds, "If you're going to torture, you ought to, at least, have the moral courage to do it yourself. Don't send them to Saudi Arabia. It's even worse to contract it out to have it done by someone else."

BACKGROUND

Laws of War

The Constitution designates the president as "commander in chief of the Army and Navy of the United States." But the power to "make rules concerning captures on land and water" is reserved for Congress. Throughout history, Congress has passed laws governing trials before military courts or tribunals, but presidents or military commanders have sometimes skirted the required procedures. [30]

A full year before the Declaration of Independence, the Continental Congress in 1775 passed 69 "Articles of War" to regulate Army conduct. As commander in chief during the Revolutionary War, Gen. George Washington used the powers provided to convene tribunals to try suspected spies. In the most notable instance, Washington convened a board of 14 officers to try a captured British spy, Major John Andre, Gen. Benedict Arnold's infamous co-conspirator. The board found Andre guilty and recommended a death sentence, which Washington approved.

As a general in the War of 1812 and again in the first Seminole War (1817-1818), Andrew Jackson drew criticism for his broad view of his powers as a military commander. (He was elected president in 1828.) In 1818, Jackson faced a censure motion in Congress for having two British subjects tried and sentenced to death for inciting the Creek Indians against the United States. Although the House of Representatives rejected the censure motion, House and Senate committees strongly criticized his actions.

During the Civil War and again during World War II, the Supreme Court was called on to resolve challenges to presidential orders for trials of enemy belligerents. The Civil War provoked intense conflicts over the use of military trials during wartime. To enable the military to summarily arrest Confederate spies and sympathizers, President Abraham Lincoln suspended habeas corpus shortly after the war broke out in April 1861. A month later, Chief Justice Roger B. Taney, in his role as a circuit justice, ruled the action unconstitutional, but Lincoln ignored the decision. Over the next two years, hundreds of people suspected of aiding the secessionists were arrested and tried by ad hoc military tribunals, which sometimes ignored judicial orders to release the prisoners.

Congress passed a law sanctioning the suspension of habeas corpus in 1863 and adopted various rules for military tribunals, but their authority outside war zones remained doubtful. The Supreme Court dodged the issue in 1864, but after the war had ended, however, it ruled that martial law could not be imposed outside war theaters if civil courts were "open and their process unobstructed." The 1866 decision in *Ex parte Milligan* ordered

the release of a prominent Southern sympathizer, Lambdin Milligan, who had been convicted of conspiracy by a military tribunal and sentenced to death. [31]

In the meantime, military tribunals had been used in two other high-profile cases: the May 1865 trial of the Lincoln assassination conspirators and the August 1865 trial of Capt. Henry Wirz, the Confederate commander of the notorious Andersonville prison camp in Americus, Ga., where nearly 13,000 prisoners died. Speedy convictions and executions resulted in both cases. Military tribunals continued to be used in the South during the early years of Reconstruction. [32]

Like Lincoln, President Franklin D. Roosevelt tested the limits of the president's powers during World War II. And, as in the Civil War, the Supreme Court erected no obstacle to Roosevelt's actions. In 1943 and 1944, the court upheld the curfew and then the internment of Japanese-Americans on the West Coast. [33] A more direct confrontation with the judiciary, however, came in 1942 with the trial of eight German saboteurs. They were speedily brought to trial before a military commission specially convened by Roosevelt that deviated from prescribed procedures in several respects.

The saboteurs, who had come ashore in June 1942 in Florida and New York from German submarines, were rounded up after one turned informant. Roosevelt's order creating a seven-member commission to try the men authorized the tribunal to admit any "probative" evidence and to recommend a death sentence by a two-thirds vote instead of the normal unanimous verdict.

Seven of the men filed habeas corpus petitions, but the Supreme Court — also departing from regular procedure — rejected their pleas in a summary order issued on July 31, only two days after hearing arguments in the case, known as *Ex parte Quirin*. The court issued a full opinion on Oct. 29 — after six of the men had been executed. The justices unanimously ruled that the offenses fell within the tribunal's jurisdiction. They also upheld the procedures used: Some justices said they complied with the Articles of War; others said the Articles did not apply. [34]

The court again blinked at departures from standard military procedures in its 1946 decision upholding the war-crimes conviction of Gen. Tomoyuki Yamashita, the Japanese commander in the Philippines. Rushed to trial in late October 1945 on charges of failing to prevent wartime atrocities, Yamashita was found guilty and sentenced on Dec. 7 to death by hanging.

CHRONOLOGY

1860s-1946 *Conflicts arise among the three branches of government over the treatment of captured enemy soldiers and spies and respect for civil liberties vs. national-security concerns.*

1861 President Abraham Lincoln suspends habeas corpus, defying the Supreme Court and setting the stage for military trials of hundreds of accused Confederate agents.

1866 U.S. Supreme Court orders release of a Confederate sympathizer who had been sentenced to death, on the grounds that martial law can't be applied outside theaters of war as long as civilian courts are functioning.

1942 Supreme Court upholds military tribunal convictions of eight German saboteurs; six are executed.

1946 Gen. Tomoyuki Yamashita is executed after a quick — and some say unfair — military commission trial finds him guilty of not stopping atrocities by Japanese troops in the Philippines.

1949-1971 *In the wake of World War II atrocities, greater protection is offered for prisoners and civilians.*

1949 Geneva Conventions are revised to apply prisoner of war (POW) standards to prisoners in conflicts that aren't wars between nation-states.

1950 Congress enacts the Uniform Code of Military Justice, which grants defendants rights equal to those enjoyed by defendants in civilian courts and adopts the standards of Geneva's Common Article 3. The provision requires prisoners on trial — even those not fighting for a specific nation — to be judged by a "regularly constituted court."

1966 U.S. military command in Vietnam grants POW status to captives from the Vietcong guerrilla army.

1971 The massacre of 400-500 Vietnamese civilians in the village of My Lai leads to courts-martial for two officers; one is convicted and one acquitted.

2000s *Attacks on the World Trade Center and the Pentagon on Sept. 11, 2001, prompt the Bush administration*

to set up controversial special courts to try accused terrorists and "unlawful combatants."

Nov. 13, 2001 President George W. Bush signs an executive order establishing military commissions to try accused members and supporters of the al Qaeda terrorist network.

2002 Two groups of Guantánamo detainees file habeas corpus petitions challenging their confinement.

July 2003 A military commission rules that Salim Ahmed Hamdan, a driver for Osama bin Laden captured in Afghanistan, is eligible for trial; he is later charged with conspiracy.

April 27, 2004 CBS News' "60 Minutes II" televises photographs of U.S. troops abusing prisoners at Abu Ghraib prison.

June 28, 2004 U.S. Supreme Court rules, in *Rasul v. Bush*, that Guantánamo prisoners can go to court to demand they be freed.

Oct. 21, 2004 The first in a stream of internal government documents concerning treatment of detainees are released to the American Civil Liberties Union by the government.

December 2005 Congress passes the Detainee Treatment Act, prohibiting torture and mistreatment of prisoners while limiting detainees' right to challenge their detentions.

June 29, 2006 Supreme Court rules in *Hamdan v. Rumsfeld* that the president exceeded his authority in establishing military commissions.

July 13, 2006 Top military legal officers tell congressional committees that lawmakers shouldn't endorse the administration's military commission system.

Aug. 2, 2006 Attorney General Alberto R. Gonzales argues that Congress shouldn't ban coerced testimony in military trials of accused terrorists.

Aug. 17, 2006 Former CIA contract interrogator David A. Passaro faces up to 11 years in prison after being convicted of beating Afghan farmer Abdul Wali, who died two days later.

Yamashita filed a habeas corpus petition, but the high court rejected his request on Feb. 2, 1946, upholding the military commission's jurisdiction and procedures. In stinging dissents, however, Justices Frank Murphy and Wiley Rutledge strongly attacked, among other things, the validity of the charges, the limited time for Yamashita to prepare a defense and the sufficiency of the evidence against him. [35] He was hanged on Feb. 23.

"Military Justice"

Two major legal reforms adopted after the war fundamentally changed the laws of war. The Geneva Conventions extended previous POW protections to combatants in conflicts other than those between nation-states. The Uniform Code of Military Justice (UCMJ), approved by Congress in 1950, brought civilian-like procedures and protections into a system previously focused on discipline and command authority.

The widespread atrocities committed during World War II against civilians, combatants and POWs led humanitarian groups to strengthen the protections for wartime captives initially established by the Geneva Convention of 1929. The resulting four accords — signed in Geneva in 1949 — outlined provisions for treating "the wounded and sick" on the battlefield or at sea, prisoners of war and civilians. Each accord also included Common Article 3, which extends basic protections against violence, humiliating or degrading treatment and summary punishment to non-traditional conflicts such as civil wars or conflicts in which at least one side is not a nation-state. The Senate ratified the four treaties in 1954.

One purpose of the UCMJ was to establish a uniform system of military justice for what were then three services: Army, Navy and Coast Guard. But it was also intended to respond to criticism of the Army and Navy justice systems as unfair to service members accused of offenses. Harvard law Professor Edmund Morgan, who headed the committee that drafted the proposed code, said it was designed to "provide full protection of the rights of persons subject to the code without undue interference with appropriate military discipline and the exercise of appropriate military functions." Morgan's draft was introduced in Congress in February 1949 and formed the principal basis for the final version approved by Congress in May 1950. [36]

Another development would become crucial to the present debate over detainees. U.S. law and the military

code of conduct embraced Common Article 3, as the Supreme Court majority noted in its *Hamdan* decision. [37]

However, the United States exceeded that minimum treatment threshold during the Vietnam War. In 1966, the U.S. Military Assistance Command in Vietnam ordered enemy captives to be granted prisoner of war status, even if they belonged to the guerrilla force known as the Vietcong (which fought alongside the regular North Vietnamese Army). Vietcong captured performing "terrorism, sabotage or spying" operations were classified as civilian defendants and were to be treated under the Geneva Conventions. [38]

Military justice also demands punishment for war crimes committed by one's own troops. In the Vietnamese hamlet of My Lai in 1968, U.S. soldiers massacred some 400-500 civilians. Lt. William Calley, the senior officer on scene, was convicted of murder and sentenced to life at hard labor, though the sentence was later reduced to 10 years, and Calley was freed on parole. Calley's commanding officer, Capt. Ernest Medina, was acquitted on charges of failing to control the troops under him because prosecutors couldn't prove that he knew what the soldiers were doing. Two other officers were acquitted of lesser charges. [39]

After Vietnam, new questions about detainees grew out of American support for U.N. "peacekeeping missions." In 1993, efforts by Special Operations troops to capture warlord Mohammed Farah Aidid in Mogadishu, Somalia, went terribly wrong. The U.S. action — depicted in the book and movie "Black Hawk Down" — led to the deaths of 18 Americans. One of the dead soldiers was dragged through the city.

The U.N.'s peacekeeper role in civil conflicts has turned the world organization into an enforcer of the international laws of war. U.N. tribunals have been established to try war-crimes cases arising from massacres during the 1990s and early 2000s in the former Yugoslavia, Rwanda and Sierra Leone. As the new century opened, military justice was coming to be seen as the leading source of law in regions torn by conflict involving irregular forces. [40]

"War on Terror"

Within weeks of the 9/11 terrorist attacks on the World Trade Center and the Pentagon, President Bush and other administration officials came to view the capture and detention of al Qaeda members and adherents as

Geneva Conventions Protect Prisoners

Warfare has changed radically since the first of four Geneva Conventions was adopted in 1864. Well-ordered lines of uniformed infantrymen with rifles at the ready have given way to vast, highly mobile armies and atomic weapons as well as terrorists and stateless paramilitary groups.

The changes have strained the international treaties governing the military's treatment of combatants and civilians.

The Bush administration says the Geneva Conventions don't cover prisoners captured during the wars in Afghanistan and Iraq. "In my judgment, this new paradigm [in warfare] renders obsolete Geneva's strict limitations on questioning of enemy prisoners," Attorney General Alberto Gonzales advised the president in 2002. [1]

Gary Solis, former director of the law of war program at the U.S. Military Academy at West Point, dismisses Gonzales' view. "The Geneva conventions do apply to today's warfare," says the retired Marine Corps lieutenant colonel. "You just have to have half a brain to apply them."

The U.S. Supreme Court also stepped into the debate, ruling on June 29, 2006, in *Hamdan v. Rumsfeld* that U.S. plans to prosecute Salim Ahmed Hamdan and other detainees being held at the U.S. Naval Station in Guantánamo Bay, Cuba, violated the conventions.

The conventions grew out of the horrors witnessed in 1859 by Henri Dunant, a Swiss merchant, after a battle between Austrian and French forces during the Austro-Sardinian War. After Dunant saw the more than 40,000 soldiers who had been left dead or dying on the battlefield near Solferino, Italy, he organized volunteers to help both sides. [2]

Dunant went on to found the International Committee for Relief to the Wounded, which later became the International Committee of the Red Cross (ICRC). In 1864, Dunant convinced the Swiss government to hold a diplomatic conference to lay down rules for the treatment of battlefield casualties. [3]

Ten European governments sent representatives to the conference and adopted the Geneva Convention for the Amelioration of the Condition of the Wounded in Armies in the Field, more commonly known as the first Geneva Convention. [4] It protects wounded soldiers on the battlefield and the medical personnel attending to them. [5]

The second convention, adopted in 1929, required prisoners of war to be humanely treated, properly fed and quartered in conditions comparable to those used by their captors.

And following the Holocaust and other atrocities committed against civilians in World War II, a third convention

critical to the president's "war on terror." A month after the 9/11 attacks, an executive order signed by Bush on Nov. 13, 2001, calling for "enemy combatants" to be detained outside the United States and tried outside regular civilian or military courts, provoked immediate criticism and legal challenges. But the administration vigorously defended its plans and resisted changes, even after adverse court rulings. [41]

Bush's order directed that al Qaeda members, other terrorists and any others who had "harbored" them were to be "placed in the custody of the secretary of Defense," tried by military commissions to be created under newly written rules and regulations and denied any right to "seek the aid of" any U.S. court or international tribunal. Administration officials said the national terrorism emergency required special procedures, but the order drew

immediate criticism from a variety of sources, including military lawyers, civil libertarians, constitutional scholars and members of Congress from both parties.

Late in December, Defense Secretary Donald H. Rumsfeld announced that detainees from Afghanistan would be transported to Guantánamo — "the least worst place," he called it — but that no trials would be held there. The Pentagon first issued procedures for the tribunals in March 2002 in so-called Order No. 1, with still no trial site specified. More detailed rules continued to come out through 2003, but the delays also reflected the administration's decision to give priority to interrogating detainees, not trying them.

With criticism of the procedures continuing, the administration in early 2002 also began facing court challenges. Two groups of Guantánamo detainees filed

was created in 1949, protecting non-combatants and their property from harm. Protections given to ground troops in the first convention were also extended to wounded and shipwrecked sailors.

"In 1949, we had a unity in the world that we hadn't seen before and we're not likely to see again," Solis says. "The world was united in its abhorrence of the actions of the Nazis and the Japanese."

In 1977, the conventions were amended with two additional protocols to cover the use of modern weapons and protect victims of internal conflicts. [6]

In 2005, another protocol was added permitting the use of a hollow, red diamond symbol in addition to the traditional cross and crescent emblems of the Red Cross. This protocol was instrumental in bringing Israel into the international humanitarian movement because Magen David Adom, Israel's rescue service, refused to work under the cross or crescent, the Red Cross symbol used in Muslim countries. [7]

The most controversial part of the conventions of late has been Common Article 3, which appears in each of the four conventions and was cited in the *Hamdan* case. It protects non-combatants from violence, cruel treatment, degradation and torture; prevents the taking of hostages; and ensures prisoners the right of a fair trial by a "regularly constituted court." [8]

The burden of enforcing the conventions falls on signatory nations and international organizations like the ICRC, which performs regular inspections of POW camps. The

conventions became federal law in the United States after they were signed and ratified by Congress.

Despite their role in dictating foreign policy today and their importance to domestic and international law, the Geneva Conventions (GC) are only as strong as the member nations want them to be.

"If you approach the GC's in such a way as to find loopholes, and to work around them, then you can do it," Solis says. "Geneva depends on the good will of those who adopt it. . . . No law is going to deter the lawless."

— *Nicholas Sohr*

[1] Gail Gibson, "Abuse scandal puts Gonzales in spotlight," *The Houston Chronicle*, May 23, 2004.

[2] Michael Tackett, "Abuses in Iraq highlight standards for treatment," *Chicago Tribune*, May 12, 2004.

[3] Maria Trombly, "A Brief History of the Laws of War," *Reference Guide to the Geneva Conventions*, July 31, 2006, www.genevaconventions.org.

[4] Tackett, *op. cit.*

[5] Office of the United Nations High Commissioner for Human Rights, www.ohchr.org/english/.

[6] For background, see Kenneth Jost, "International Law," *CQ Researcher*, Dec. 17, 2004, pp. 1049-1072, and David Masci, "Ethics of War," *CQ Researcher*, Dec. 13, 2002, pp. 1013-1032.

[7] Alexander G. Higgins, "Red Cross changes emblem," *The Seattle Times*, Dec. 8, 2005.

[8] For full text of Common Article 3, see "Protection of victims of non-international armed conflicts," International Committee of the Red Cross, Dec. 31, 1988. www.icrc.org/Web/Eng/siteeng0.nsf/iwpList104/6D73335C674B821DC1256B66005951D1.

habeas corpus petitions in federal court in Washington, D.C., in February and May, generally denying involvement with al Qaeda and challenging their detention without trial or even charges. The administration argued not only that federal courts had no authority over Guantánamo since it was outside the United States but also that the president's war powers justified his actions. Two more habeas petitions were filed in June by two U.S. citizens — José Padilla and Yaser Hamdi — who were being held as enemy combatants, also without charges, at a naval brig in Charleston, S.C.

After lower-court proceedings, the cases reached the Supreme Court, which handed the administration limited but unmistakable setbacks on June 28, 2004. In the consolidated Guantánamo cases, the court ruled, 6-3, that federal courts could exercise jurisdiction over Guantánamo

prisoners' challenges. The majority noted that unlike the situation that prompted a contrary ruling in 1950, the government had virtual control over the Guantánamo base. [42]

The ruling in *Rasul v. Bush* settled only the jurisdictional issue and left all other questions for further development in lower courts. In the *Hamdi* and *Padilla* cases, the court upheld the president's authority to detain a U.S. citizen as an enemy combatant but also required some form of hearing before "a neutral decision-maker." [43]

In the meantime, Hamdan had been designated as eligible for trial by a military commission in July 2003, and a single charge of "conspiracy" was filed a year later, in July 2004.

The charging document accused Hamdan of "willingly and knowingly" joining al Qaeda in order to commit terrorism; it specified as "overt acts" his serving as

Georgetown University Law Professor Neal Katyal, left, and Navy Lt. Commander Charles Swift, lawyers for Guantánamo Bay detainee Salim Ahmed Hamdan, address the media following the Supreme Court's ruling against the Bush administration's proposed military tribunals on June 29, 2006. The court ruled the tribunals violate both American military law and the Geneva Conventions.

bin Laden's driver, delivering weapons and receiving arms training. Hamdan's trial opened at Guantánamo on Aug. 28 — the first of the military commission proceedings — even as his lawyers were pressing his habeas corpus petition.

An initial ruling granting Hamdan's petition put the trial on hold while the government appealed. The federal appeals court in Washington reversed the ruling in July 2005. His lawyers then appealed to the Supreme Court, which heard his case in March 2006.

Congress then entered the picture by passing the Detainee Treatment Act, which Bush signed on Dec. 30, 2005. Although its anti-torture provision received most of the attention, the act also curtailed judicial review of the Guantánamo cases. In two sections, the law limited review of decisions by the Combatant Status Review Tribunals. The new law also barred federal courts from hearing habeas corpus petitions filed by the Guantánamo detainees, but it did not say whether that provision applied to pending cases such as Hamdan's.

In ruling in Hamdan's case on June 29, the court held that the Detainee Treatment Act did not eliminate the court's jurisdiction over the case and that the military commissions established by Bush violated both the Uniform Code of Military Justice and the Geneva Conventions. In separate opinions, Justices John Paul

Stevens and Anthony M. Kennedy faulted several departures in the tribunal rules from regular court-martial procedures, including provisions to exclude the accused from portions of a trial, to allow hearsay evidence and to use non-lawyer judges who would not be appointed by the judge advocate general. In a brief concurrence, Justice Stephen G. Breyer added, "Nothing prevents the president from returning to Congress to seek the authority he believes necessary."

CURRENT SITUATION

Allowing Coercion?

The Bush administration, Senate and House committees and military and civilian lawyers of all stripes are arguing over whether testimony obtained under duress should be allowed in military trials of alleged terrorists.

A series of congressional hearings in the weeks following the *Hamdan* decision have been marked by administration attempts to preserve military commissions as they were first established by presidential order. After bad reviews from lawmakers and military lawyers, administration officials have been proposing commissions modeled more closely on courts-martial — but with permissive evidence rules that would allow coercive interrogations. [44]

"As we talk about whether or not coerced testimony should come in," Gonzales told the Senate Armed Services Committee on Aug. 2, "our thinking is that if it's reliable and if it's probative, as determined by a certified military judge, that it should come in. If you say that coerced testimony cannot come in, everyone is going to claim evidence has been coerced. Then we'll get into a fight with respect to every prosecution as to what is, in fact, coerced or what is not coerced." [45]

Maj. Gen. Scott C. Black, the Army's judge advocate general, opposed the use of coercion. "I don't believe that a statement that is obtained under coercive — under torture, certainly, and under coercive measures — should be admissible," he told the Senate Judiciary Committee on Aug. 2, 2006. [46]

On the same day, Attorney General Gonzales was explaining the administration's position. At a Senate Armed Services Committee hearing, Sen. McCain asked Gonzales if statements obtained through "illegal, inhumane treatment should be admissible."

After a long pause, Gonzales haltingly replied: "The concern that I would have about such a prohibition is, What does it mean? . . . If we could all reach agreement about the definition of cruel, inhumane and degrading treatment, then perhaps I could give you an answer. . . . Depending on your definition of something as degrading, such as insults, I would say that information should still come in." [47]

McCain called the proposal to use coercion a "radical departure" from standards of military conduct. And, he said, "We must remain a nation that is different from, and above, our enemies."

The exchanges showed that the question of whether torture or rough treatment is permissible remains very much alive, despite the Supreme Court's *Hamdan* decision, which ruled that Common Article 3 should apply to Guantánamo detainees. Even lawyers who support the Common Article 3 standard agreed that Congress isn't bound to uphold it.

"Sure, Congress could effectively disavow Common Article 3 by passing an inconsistent law," says military law expert Fidell. Constitutional scholar Laurence H. Tribe of Harvard Law School writes, however, that doing so would effectively require the United States to jettison all the other Geneva Conventions as well.

"Unless Congress is prepared to step up to the plate and say it is knocking Geneva out of the park, Geneva should be deemed to remain in place and therefore binding," Tribe wrote to David Remes, a Washington lawyer representing Guantánamo detainees who are challenging their detention (*see below*). [48]

Even before details of the administration proposal began to filter into the press, officials had made clear their opposition to using military-justice standards in terrorism trials for non-citizens.

"Full application of court-martial rules would force the government either to drop prosecutions or to disclose intelligence information to our enemies in such a way as to compromise ongoing or future military operations, the identity of intelligence sources and the lives of many," Dell'Orto, the Pentagon deputy general counsel, told the House Judiciary Committee on July 12. "Military necessity demands a better way."

Administration critics argue that the practicalities of the matter run in the other direction. A congressionally approved version of the military commission would be held up by court challenges, they said. "If . . . after more litigation we find ourselves right back here in four or five more years after we've litigated, then what are we going to end up with?" Lt. Cmdr. Swift, Hamdan's lawyer, asked the Senate Judiciary Committee on July 11. "Neither side will ever get a fair trial, and both Mr. Hamdan and the United States deserve one."

Legally speaking, says Hamdan's co-counsel Katyal, objections that court-martial procedures are too protective of defendants' rights to function effectively in terrorism cases ring hollow. In fact, Katyal told Senate Armed Services members, courts-martial can be closed to keep national-security matters secret, witnesses' identities can be hidden and officers who act as juries can be required to possess security clearances.

Meanwhile, the administration is discussing the possibility of allowing detainees to face life imprisonment or death based on evidence that was never disclosed to the accused at trial. [49]

Beyond the arguments over commissions vs. courts-martial looms a debate over the extent of the president's power. For instance, last December when Bush signed the Detainee Treatment Act banning torture of prisoners in U.S. military custody, he included a "signing statement" that suggested he was not bound by it. Indeed, Gonzales recently suggested that Bush might be inclined to retain his unilateral approach to terrorist crimes regardless of what Congress does. [50]

A July 18 exchange between Gonzales and Sen. Russell Feingold, D-Wis., made clear the president's views on the limits of congressional power. Feingold asked if Gonzales saw the Supreme Court as having ruled that "the president has to obey the statutes we write."

Gonzales replied: "Of course, we have an obligation to enforce the laws passed by the Congress. But the president also takes an oath, senator, to preserve, protect and defend the Constitution. And if, in fact, there are constitutional rights given to the president of the United States, he has an obligation to enforce those rights."

Other Prisoner Suits

Hamdan is only one of dozens of Guantánamo detainees who have challenged the United States' power to try or to hold them. While Hamdan awaits a government decision on what to do following the Supreme Court's June 29 decision, the rest of the lawsuits are pending in federal appeals court in Washington.

Military Lawyers Endorse Geneva Rules

The sight of uniformed officers arguing that detainees deserve more legal rights may cause some observers to wonder if the military has gone soft. But retired Air Force Col. Katherine Newell Bierman is among those who argue that treating prisoners humanely — aside from being legally required — simply makes good sense militarily.

"It's common-sense war fighting," says Bierman, now counterterrorism counsel for the advocacy group Human Rights Watch. "If you don't have some control over how your people are behaving, you lose discipline."

For Bierman as well as many active-duty military lawyers, the Geneva Conventions provide that control.

"When we train Marines, and soldiers, sailors and airmen, when we talk about handling people that we grab or get on the battlefield, we're normally talking in context of the Geneva Conventions regarding prisoners of war," Brig. Gen. Kevin Sandkuhler, the Marine Corps' top legal officer, told the Senate Armed Services Committee in July.

Administration officials suggest the military attorneys are making the classic soldier's mistake of fighting today's war with yesterday's doctrines. Attorney General Alberto R. Gonzales, testifying at a later hearing, echoed Republican lawmakers' comments that Geneva language such as "humiliating and degrading treatment," aren't adequately defined. "I wonder, given the times that we currently live in

and given this new enemy and this new kind of conflict, whether all of the provisions continue to make sense," Gonzales said, adding that he wasn't "in any way suggesting a retreat from the basic principles of Geneva, in terms of the humanitarian treatment."

In early 2006, recently retired generals began leveling attacks at Defense Secretary Donald H. Rumsfeld and, in some cases, at the Iraq war itself. "It speaks volumes that guys like me are speaking out from retirement about the leadership climate in the Department of Defense," said retired Maj. Gen. John Batiste, who led an infantry division in Iraq in 2004-2005. "I think we need a fresh start," he said. [1]

Another Iraq war veteran, retired Army Maj. Gen., Charles H. Swannack Jr., said Rumsfeld had "culpability" for abuse and torture at Abu Ghraib prison in Iraq. [2]

The attacks on Rumsfeld by retired generals, combined with criticism of the administration's detainee policy from military lawyers, led a noted constitutional scholar to remark half-jokingly that military-civilian relations had undergone a drastic change.

"For the first time in our nation's history, a military takeover of the government would move the country slightly to the left," Walter Dellinger quipped at a July 26 discussion of the *Hamdan* decision sponsored by the liberal American Constitution Society for Law and

Lawyers for about 65 prisoners held as "unlawful combatants" — but not yet charged with a crime like Hamdan — have filed habeas corpus petitions seeking to have their detentions ruled illegal.

The prisoners argue that the government hasn't proved that any of them fought for al Qaeda or the Taliban. The government has cited decisions by Combatant Status Review Tribunals concluding that the prisoners involved had indeed been fighters. Shortly after the tribunals began, Army Maj. Gen. Geoffrey D. Miller, then in command at Guantánamo said, "I have found no innocent people" at the camp. [51]

During the tribunal hearings, which began in 2004, prisoners appearing before the panels of three military officers had neither lawyers — nor access to the evidence against

them. Defense lawyer Remes calls the panels "pseudo-tribunals" designed to give a false impression that evidence had been fully and fairly evaluated in each detainee's case.

At the district court level, the habeas suits have produced contradictory rulings by the two judges who considered the cases. In January 2005, U.S. District Judge Richard J. Leon ruled that courts had little room to challenge the president's right to hold enemy prisoners." Any [judicial] role must be limited when, as here, there is an ongoing armed conflict and the individuals challenging their detention are non-resident aliens." [52]

Less than a month later, Judge Joyce Hens Green reached the opposite conclusion. "Although this nation unquestionably must take strong action under the leadership of the commander in chief to protect itself," she

Policy. Dellinger, now a professor at Duke University law school, was acting solicitor general under President Bill Clinton.

A conservative fellow panelist, a former lawyer during the Reagan and George H.W. Bush administrations, David B. Rivkin Jr., challenged military lawyers' oft-stated insistence that humane detention policies help assure civilized treatment of American military prisoners. "It is rubbish to talk about how our POWs will be mistreated" if the U.S. does not abide by the Geneva Conventions, he said, citing a consistent pattern of abuse and torture of U.S. POWs since World War II, including Korea and Vietnam. "The notion that the head cutters and the torturers are going to be motivated to behave better if we accord them Geneva treatment is laughable."

Meanwhile, criticism of administration detainee policies has emerged among civilians as well as the military. William H. Taft IV, a former legal adviser to Secretary of State Colin Powell, was among the first internal critics of prisoner policy when it was developed in 2001-2002. Powell himself warned then-Counsel to the President Gonzales that not applying Geneva Conventions standards to the detainees would "reverse over a century of U.S. policy and practice in supporting the Geneva Conventions and undermine the protections of the law of war for our troops, both in this specific conflict and in general." [3]

Another civilian critic, former Navy general counsel Alberto J. Mora, urged the administration to stop the mistreatment of prisoners at Guantánamo. "I was appalled by the whole thing," Mora told Jane Mayer of *The New Yorker* after resigning. "It was clearly abusive, and it was clearly contrary to everything we were ever taught about American values." [4]

Military lawyers, for their part, also cite professional pride in advocating adherence to the Geneva rules. "When we get a conviction, we can say forthrightly that we won because we had the best evidence — as opposed to, 'The [defendant] wasn't in the courtroom and didn't get to see any of the evidence against him,' " says Hardy Vieux, a former Navy JAG lawyer who serves on the board of the non-profit National Institute of Military Justice.

Among institute members, virtually all of them former military lawyers, "We're unanimous" in supporting a return to Geneva Convention rules, says Vieux. "I don't know of a dissenting voice."

---

[1] Thomas E. Ricks, "Rumsfeld Rebuked by Retired Generals," *The Washington Post*, April 13, 2006, p. A1.

[2] Peter Spiegel, "Another Retired General Joins Battalion of Rumsfeld Critics," *Los Angeles Times*, April 14, 2006, p. A5.

[3] Quoted in Colin L. Powell, "Memorandum To: Counsel to the President; Assistant to the President for National Security Affairs," Jan. 26, 2002. See also, William H. Taft IV, "Memorandum, to: Counsel to the President," Feb. 2, 2002; The memos, along with other internal administration documents concerning U.S. policy toward detainees, are available at www.nytimes.com/ref/international/24MEMO-GUIDE.html.

[4] Jane Mayer, "The Memo; how an internal effort to ban the abuse and torture of detainees was thwarted," *The New Yorker*, Feb. 27, 2006, p. 32. Mora's 22-page memo to the Navy's inspector general is available at www.newyorker.com/images/pdfs/moramemo.pdf.

---

wrote, "that necessity cannot negate the existence of the most basic fundamental rights." [53]

The Guantánamo habeas suits began in 2004, two years after Hamdan's case began. Though *Hamdan* focused on the legality of the military commissions, the Supreme Court's June decision has become an issue in the habeas cases. The Court of Appeals for the District of Columbia Circuit has ordered lawyers on both sides to present written arguments on how the *Hamdan* decision affected the habeas cases.

Government lawyers argued that *Hamdan's* upholding of Common Article 3 wasn't relevant to the habeas prisoners. The Geneva Convention doesn't grant any rights that an individual can go to court to demand, the government said. [54]

Moreover, the prisoners' challenges now have to be started over in the appeals court, which has "exclusive jurisdiction" under the Detainee Treatment Act of 2005, the government lawyers argued.

The prisoners' lawyers maintained that the *Hamdan* decision makes clear that the prisoners can challenge their detentions on the grounds that they violate the Geneva Conventions. The Supreme Court ruled that the conventions can be enforced by American courts, the lawyers said. Remes says habeas litigation could drag on for years. If the appeals court does not rule soon, he warns, the U.S. Supreme Court may not be able to decide the cases until late 2007. "By that time," Remes says, "the men at Guantánamo will have been there for more than five-and-a-half years."

President George W. Bush answers questions on the treatment of detainees at Guantánamo Bay during a joint press conference with Japanese Prime Minister Junichiro Koizumi at the White House on June 29, 2006, following the Supreme Court's rejection of the administration's trial and detention system.

OUTLOOK

"Blistering Fight"

The uncertainty surrounding the future of the war on terrorists makes for hesitancy on all sides about predicting the fate of Guantánamo detainees, and of detainee policy in general.

"We're still in mid-chapter," says military-law expert Fidell. "Our national course in constitutional law is not yet finished."

Ex-prosecutor McCarthy says conflict could arise over whether Common Article 3 creates rights that people in U.S. custody can claim — as opposed to rights that a foreign government would demand for its detained citizens.

"Pro-international law people are arguing that the Supreme Court crossed the Rubicon and made provisions of a treaty judicially enforceable by individuals," McCarthy says. "People on my side of the fence say that the Supreme Court didn't address that issue." The dispute is likely to come to a head in a "blistering fight," he says.

Margulies, who represents some Guantánamo detainees, raises the question of whether Guantánamo prisoners taken in Afghanistan could be held even after combat ended there.

"Could Congress define the conflict in such a way that even if Afghanistan, a sovereign state, orders the United States to leave or the conflict moves to a different place, you can still hold a guy who's picked up in Afghanistan?" he asks. Margulies says the answer is no but acknowledges that others may differ.

Former Justice Department official Kobach agrees that the question of how to define the end of conflict is likely to wind up in court. "If 20 years from now we're still engaged in a worldwide battle against the same enemy organizations, a case might be brought arguing that the war itself is over and the detainees should be released," he says. "I don't think it will fly."

For all the cloudiness obscuring views of the future, advocates on all sides of the divide over how to fight terrorists speak unequivocally about the dangers of taking the wrong path.

Former Reagan and George H.W. Bush administration lawyer Rivkin argues that granting treatment decreed by the Geneva Conventions to terrorists and other "unlawful combatants" would be a major step down the wrong road. "We have a civilization that is besieged by a bunch of barbarians and bad people," he says. "We are dealing with a grave threat to everything, to civilized law and order, to democracy. Much of the rest of the world has abandoned the stigmatization and de-legitimization of unlawful combatants. For us to say, 'We're to treat everyone the same, everyone's going to get the gold standard, everyone's going to get courts-martial,' given where the rest of the world is, would just complete this transformation. It would be unimaginably bad."

Meanwhile, detainees' advocates worry about continued Republican dominance in Washington and its likely effect on Supreme Court makeup.

If 86-year-old Justice John Paul Stevens — a member of the *Hamdan* majority — stays on the bench through the end of the Bush presidency, and the next president is a Democrat, "The Supreme Court will probably not shift to the right," says detainee lawyer Remes."

But if Stevens retires soon and Bush gets to pick his successor, "The Guantánamo prisoners could be dead meat," Remes says. "You could have a Supreme Court majority that would uphold unlimited, unreviewable executive power. That would be a sad day for America."

Getty Images/Jim Watson

Should detainee trials before military commissions be based on courts-martial?

YES

Eugene R. Fidell
President, National Institute of Military Justice

From testimony before the Senate Armed Services Committee, July 19, 2006

The National Institute of Military Justice believes that the highest priority for military justice is the achievement of public confidence in the administration of justice. The institute's basic approach is to strongly tilt military commissions in the direction of general courts-martial, our felony-level military court.

[T]here's no question that Congress cannot legislate every jot and title of the system . . . there is always going to be some presidential rulemaking. The president [should have the] power to depart from the Uniform Code of Military Justice (UCMJ) model [by stating] with particularity those facts that render it impracticable to follow the general court-martial model on any particular point — not a blanket presidential determination that general court-martial rules are impracticable across-the-board.

The president will not have satisfied the requirement if his justification is filled with vague generalities. Our proposal requires that Congress be notified of any determination of impracticability. Congress should stand ready to review determinations and intervene with legislation. And the president's determination that some rule is impracticable [would be] subject to judicial review for abuse of discretion or on the ground that it is contrary to law.

Congress could take certain things off the table — for example, the right to select your own uniformed defense counsel. Congress could conclude that that is part of the deluxe version of military justice that need not be extended to enemy combatants in the context of a military commission.

Congress might also conclude that some provisions are so critical to public confidence in the administration of justice that they should be placed beyond the president's power to make exceptions. Congress has already said that we don't want coerced testimony in a court-martial. I can't imagine that Congress would take a different position in a military commission.

"Public confidence in the administration of justice" is not another way of saying we have 100 percent assurance that every person who is charged will be convicted. Rather it is a shorthand way of summarizing all of those deeply held values that reflect the commitment of the Founders to due process of law and fundamental fairness. This sounds like an obvious proposition, but it bears repeating because there are those who believe the military commission system rules must ensure convictions. I believe they must ensure fairness. If that means some who are guilty may not ultimately be convicted, that is the price we pay for having a legal system.

NO

James J. Carafano
Senior Research Fellow, The Heritage Foundation

From testimony before the Senate Armed Services Committee, July 19, 2006

President Bush was right to argue that the concerted effort to destroy the capacity of transnational groups who seek to turn terrorism into a global corporate enterprise ought to be viewed as a long war. The Uniform Code of Military Justice (UCMJ) is not at all appropriate for the long war [because it] puts the protection of the right of the individual foremost, and then adds in accommodations for national security and military necessity.

For example, the UCMJ requires informing servicemen suspected of a crime of their Miranda rights. The exercise of Miranda rights is impractical on the battlefield. Hearsay evidence is prohibited in a court-martial. On the battlefield, reliable hearsay may be the only kind of evidence that can be obtained about the specific activities of combatants. Likewise, overly lenient evidentiary rules make sense when trying a U.S. soldier for a theft committed on base, but not when someone is captured on the battlefield and is being tried for war crimes committed prior to capture, perhaps in another part of the world.

Rather than amend court-martial procedures to address security concerns, it would be preferable to draft military commissions that put the interests of national security first, and then amend them to ensure that equitable elements of due process are included in the procedures.

After Sept. 11, the Bush administration's critics framed a false debate that indicated citizens had a choice between being safe and being free, arguing that virtually every exercise of executive power is an infringement on liberties and human rights. The issue of the treatment of detainees at Guantánamo Bay has been framed in this manner. It is a false debate. Government has a dual responsibility to protect the individual and to protect the nation. The equitable exercise of both is guaranteed when the government exercises power in accordance with the rule of law.

In wartime it's the courts' job to interpret the war, it's the president's job to fight the war and essentially it's the Congress' job to provide the president the right kinds of instruments to do that.

If we respect the purposes of the Geneva Conventions and want to encourage rogue nations and terrorists to follow the laws of war, we must give humane treatment to unlawful combatants. However, we ought not to reward them with the exact same treatment we give our own honorable soldiers. Mimicking the UCMJ sends exactly the wrong signal.

NOTES

1. Quoted in Richard A. Serrano, "Officials Agree on Prisoners' Status," *Los Angeles Times*, Jan. 29, 2002, p. A9.

2. *Ibid.*; for Bush's definition of prisoners, see David E. Sanger, "President Defends Military Tribunals in Terrorist Cases," *The New York Times*, Nov. 30, 2001, p. A1.

3. A virtual library of books, reports and articles exists on treatment of detainees in the war on terrorists. Selected examples include, "Article 15-6 Investigation of the 800th Military Police Brigade," [Taguba Report on Abu Ghraib], 2004 [undated], www.fas.org/irp/agency/dod/taguba.pdf; Tim Golden, "In U.S. Reports, Brutal Details of 2 Afghan Inmates' Deaths," *The New York Times*, May 20, 2006, p. A1. For a response to critics of U.S. detention practices, see Kenneth Anderson, "An American Gulag? Human rights groups test the limits of moral equivalency," *The Weekly Standard*, Jan 13, 2005. A voluminous file of government documents involving interrogations was released to the American Civil Liberties Union and can be found at www.aclu.org/safefree/torture/torture-foia.html#.

4. William H. Taft, IV, "Memorandum To: Counsel to the President," Feb. 2, 2002; Colin L. Powell, "Memorandum To: Counsel to the President; Assistant to the President for National Security Affairs," Jan. 26, 2002. The memos, along with other internal administration documents concerning U.S. policy toward detainees, are available at www.nytimes.com/ref/international/24MEMO-GUIDE.html.

5. The case is *Hamdan v. Rumsfeld*, 05-184 (2006). For an analysis of the court decision, see Kenneth Jost, *Hamdan v. Rumsfeld*, CQ Electronic Library, *CQ Supreme Court Collection* (2006), at http://library.cqpress.com/scc/scyb05-421-18449-991165. Only eight justices participated in the decision; Chief Justice John Roberts recused himself.

6. *Ibid.*

7. "Geneva Convention relative to the treatment of prisoners of war," adopted Aug. 12, 1949, available at www.unhchr.ch/html/menu3/b/91.htm.

8. For background on Graham's career, see Maura Reynolds, "Senate Insider on Military Justice," *Los Angeles Times*, July 13, 2006, p. A20.

9. Alberto R. Gonzales, "Memorandum for the President," Jan. 25, 2002, p. 1. The memo is one of a series of internal Bush administration documents, some leaked and some officially released through a Freedom of Information Act lawsuit by the American Civil Liberties Union. The leaked documents are collected on Web sites of several research and news organizations, including *The New York Times*. See "A Guide to the Memos on Torture," [undated] www.nytimes.com/ref/international/24MEMO-GUIDE.html.

10. For detailed explanations of their opposition, see William H. Taft, IV, "Memorandum To: Counsel to the President," Feb. 2, 2002; Colin L. Powell, "Memorandum To: Counsel to the President; Assistant to the President for National Security Affairs," Jan. 26, 2002, www.nytimes.com/ref/international/24MEMO-GUIDE.html.

11. The Defense Department maintains updated statistics and other information at the "Detainee Affairs" section of the Pentagon Web site, www.defenselink.mil/home/features/Detainee_Affairs. For a critical analysis of the tribunal rulings, see Mark Denbeaux, Joshua Denbeaux, *et al.*, "Report on Guantánamo Detainees," Seton Hall University School of Law, Feb. 8, 2006, http://law.shu.edu/news/guantánamo_report_final_2_08_06.pdf.

12. The case was *Hamdi v. Rumsfeld*, 542 U.S. 547 (2004). The Pentagon announced formation of the tribunals about a week after the Supreme Court decision. See John Hendren, "Pentagon Sets Review of Detainees," *Los Angeles Times*, July 8, 2004, p. A13.

13. For the article that broke the Abu Ghraib story, see Seymour Hersh, "Torture at Abu Ghraib," *The New Yorker*, May 10, 2004, www.newyorker.com/fact/content/?040510fa_fact. For the "organ failure" definition, see "Memorandum for Alberto R. Gonzales, Counsel to the President," Aug. 1, 2002, http://fl1.findlaw.com/news.findlaw.com/nytimes/docs/doj/bybee80102mem.pdf. For the Supreme Court decision, see Charles Lane, "Justices Back Detainee Access to U.S. Courts," *The Washington*

Post, June 29, 2004, p. A1. For the torture policy revision, see R. Jeffrey Smith and Dan Eggen, "Justice Expands 'Torture' Definition," *The Washington Post*, Dec. 31, 2004, p. A1.

14. For background on McCain, see "John McCain, CQ Politics in America Profile," CQ.com, updated April 2005.

15. For background on Hamdan, see Jonathan Mahler, "The Bush Administration vs. Salim Hamdan," *The New York Times Magazine*, Jan. 8, 2006, p. 44.

16. *Ibid.* The charge against Hamdan, undated and unsigned is available at www.defenselink.mil/news/Jul2004/d20040714hcc.pdf.\

17. "Information from Guantánamo Detainees," JTF-GTMO (Joint Task Force-Guantánamo), March 4, 2005, www.defenselink.mil/news/Mar2005/d20050304info.pdf.

18. *Hamdan v. Rumsfeld*, Supreme Court, 548 U.S. __(2006), pp. 67, 69.

19. "Relative to the Treatment of Prisoners of War, Geneva, 12 August 1949," [Geneva Convention III], http://www.globalissuesgroup.com/geneva/convention3.html; "Text of Geneva Conventions Article 3," The Associated Press, http://seattlepi.nwsource.com/national/1151AP_Guantanamo_Geneva_Conventions.html.

20. For an earlier, shorter list of CIA detainees, see "The United States 'Disappeared': The CIA's Long-Term 'Ghost Detainees,'" Human Rights Watch, October 2004, www.hrw.org/backgrounder/usa/us1004. p. 37.

21. "U.S.: Investigate 'Ghost Detainees," Human Rights Watch, Sept. 10, 2004, press release, http://hrw.org/english/docs/2004/09/10/usint9338_txt.htm.

22. Gen. Paul J. Kern quoted in Eric Schmitt and Douglas Jehl, "Army Said C.I.A. Hid More Detainees Than It Claimed," *The New York Times*, Sept. 9, 2004, p. A1.

23. Douglas Jehl and David Johnston, "C.I.A. Expands Its Inquiry Into Interrogation Tactics," *The New York Times*, Aug. 28, 2004, p. A10.

24. For an account of "water-boarding" used on Shaikh Muhammed, see James Risen, David Johnston and Neil A. Lewis, "Harsh C.I.A. Methods Cited in Top Qaeda Interrogations," *The New York Times*, May 12, 2004, p. A1; for a characterization and account of Shaikh Muhammed's role in the 9/11 plot, see *The 9/11 Commission Report* (2004), pp. 145-180.

25. Quoted in Greg Miller, "It's a Tough Time to be the Intelligence Chief," *Los Angeles Times*, Feb. 20, 2004, p. A23.

26. For the first U.S. journalistic reports, see Jane Mayer, "Outsourcing Torture: the secret history of America's 'extraordinary rendition' program," *The New Yorker*, Feb. 14, 2005, p. 106; Craig Whitlock, "A Secret Deportation of Terror Suspects," *The Washington Post*, July 25, 2004, p. A1; Megan K. Stack and Bob Drogin, "Detainee Says U.S. Handed Him Over For Torture," *Los Angeles Times*, Jan. 13, 2004, p. A1.

27. *Ibid.*

28. "CIA Flying Suspects to Torture?" CBS' "60 Minutes II," March 6, 2005, partial transcript available at http://cbs5.com/minutes/sixtyminutes_story_065094819.html.

29. Scott Shane, "Invoking Secrets Privilege Becomes a More Popular Legal Tactic by the U.S.," *The New York Times*, June 4, 2006, p. A32.

30. Background drawn in part from Louis Fisher, *Military Tribunals and Presidential Power: American Revolution to the War on Terrorism* (2005). See also briefs by the following "friends of the court" in *Hamdan v. Rumsfeld:* Military Historians; Former Attorneys General; Citizens for Common Defense, posted at www.hamdanvrumsfeld.com/briefs (last visited July 2006).

31. The citation is 71 U.S. 2 (1866). The earlier decision is *Ex parte Vallandingham*, 68 U.S. 243 (1864).

32. Four of the eight Lincoln conspirators were sentenced to death and were hanged on July 7, 1865; Wirz was hanged on Nov. 10, 1865.

33. The ruling in the curfew case is *Hirabayashi v. United States*, 320 U.S. 81 (1943); the ruling in the internment case is *Korematsu v. United States*, 323 U.S. 214 (1944). For background, see David Masci, "Reparations Movement," *CQ Researcher*, June 22, 2001, pp. 529-552.

34. The citation is 317 U.S. 1 (1942). For a full account, see Louis Fisher, *Nazi Saboteurs on Trial: A Military Tribunal and American Law* (2003). For background, see C. E. Noyes, "Sabotage," *Editorial Research Reports, 1941* (Vol. I), available at *CQ Researcher Plus Archives*, CQ Electronic Library, http://library.cqpress.com.

35. The decision is *In re Yamashita*, 327 U.S. 1 (1946).

36. See Edmund M. Morgan, "The Background of the Uniform Code of Military Justice," *Military Law Review*, Vol. 28 (April 1965).

37. *Hamdan v. Rumsfeld, op. cit.*, p. 68, n. 3.

38. For a summary of the Vietnam policy, see Jennifer Elsea, "Treatment of 'Battlefield Detainees' in the War on Terrorism," Congressional Research Service, Sept. 17, 2003, pp. 31-32.

39. For a detailed account of the My Lai massacre and aftermath, see Maj. Tony Raimondo, "The My Lai Massacre: A Case Study," School of the Americas, Fort Benning, Ga. [undated]; http://carlisle-www.army.mil/usamhi/usarsa/HUMANRT/Human%20Rights%202000/my-lai.htm. For legal details of the *Medina* case, see Fisher, *op. cit.*, *Military Tribunals and Presidential Power*, pp. 153-153.

40. In establishing the tribunals, U.N. member states aimed explicitly to restore or create the rule of law by establishing accountability for war crimes and crimes against humanity. The sites for the Rwanda, Sierra Leone and former-Yugoslavia tribunals are: Rwanda, http://69.94.11.53/default.htm; Sierra Leone, www.sc-sl.org/; former Yugoslavia, www.un.org/icty/.

41. For an overview, see Fisher, *op. cit.*, pp. 168-252; for Fisher's critical assessment, see pp. 253-260.

42. The earlier case is *Johnson v. Eisentrager*, 339 U.S. 763 (1950).

43. The decisions are *Rasul v. Bush*, 542 U.S. 466 (2004), and *Hamdi v. Rumsfeld*, 542 U.S. 507 (2004). The other U.S. citizen case, *Rumsfeld v. Padilla*, 542 U.S. 426 (2004), was dismissed on the grounds it had been filed in the wrong federal court.

44. For reports on Senate hearings concerning the debate, see R. Jeffrey Smith, "Top Military Lawyers Oppose Plan for Special Courts," *The Washington Post*, Aug. 3, 2006, p. A11; and Kate Zernike, "White House Asks Congress to Define War Crimes," *The New York Times*, Aug. 3, 2006, p. A16.

45. Committee testimony, Aug. 2, 2006.

46. Smith, *op. cit.*

47. *Ibid.*

48. Tribe's July 11, 2006, letter, confirmed by his office, was made available by Remes.

49. Jeffrey R. Smith, "On Prosecuting Detainees; Draft Bill Waives Due Process for Enemy Combatants," *The Washington Post*, July 28, 2006, p. A23.

50. For background see Kenneth Jost, "Presidential Power," *CQ Researcher*, Feb. 24, 2006, pp. 169-192.

51. Quoted in John Mintz, "Most at Guantánamo to Be Freed or Sent Home, Officer Says," *The Washington Post*, Oct. 6, 2004, p. A16. For a detailed look at the tribunals' operation, see Neil A. Lewis, "Guantánamo Prisoners Getting Their Day, but Hardly in Court," *The New York Times*, Nov. 8, 2004, p. A1.

52. Quoted in Charles Lane and John Mintz, "Detainees Lose Bid For Release," *The Washington Post*, Jan. 20, 2005, p. A3.

53. Quoted in Neil A. Lewis, "Judge Extends Legal Rights For Guantánamo Detainees," *The New York Times*, Feb. 1, 2005, p. A12.

54. For an analysis of the government's claims, see Lyle Denniston, "Government: Detainee cases must start over," Scotusblog, Aug. 1, 2006 (includes a link to government brief), www.scotusblog.com/movable-type/archives/2006/08/government_deta_1.html.

BIBLIOGRAPHY

Books

Fisher, Louis, *Military Tribunals & Presidential Power: American Revolution to the War on Terrorism*, University of Kansas Press, 2005.
A specialist at the Library of Congress on the power relationships between the three branches of government closely examines the development of the president's wartime authority in legal matters.

Margulies, Joseph, *Guantánamo and the Abuse of Presidential Power*, Simon & Schuster, 2006.
A law professor at the MacArthur Justice Center at Northwestern University Law School provides a non-legalistic narrative of his experiences in representing Guantánamo detainees.

Saar, Erik, and Viveca Novack, *Inside the Wire: A Military Intelligence Soldier's Eyewitness Account of Life at Guantánamo*, Penguin Press, 2005.
Confusion, ignorance and bigotry plagued the ranks of the military personnel who supervised and interrogated Guantánamo detainees, according to Saar, a former translator and interrogator, and *Time* reporter Novack.

Yoo, John, *The Powers of War and Peace*, University of Chicago Press, 2005.
A former top Justice Department lawyer in 2001-2003 explains how the government's detention policy grew out of the government's belief that presidents have greater power during wartime. Now a law professor at the University of California at Berkeley, Yoo helped craft the policy.

Articles

Golden, Tim, "After Terror, a Secret Rewriting of Military Law," *The New York Times*, Oct. 24, 2004, p. A1.
An investigative reporter digs into the legal and political origins of the detention and trial system centered at Guantánamo Bay.

Mahler, Jonathan, "The Bush Administration vs. Salim Hamdan," *The New York Times Magazine*, Jan. 8, 2006, p. 44.
A New York-based journalist who is writing a book about Hamdan traveled to Yemen to speak to the family of the man at the center of the Supreme Court's latest ruling on detainees.

Mayer, Jane, "The Memo; How an internal effort to ban the abuse and torture of detainees was thwarted," *The New Yorker*, Feb. 27, 2006, p. 32.
A Washington-based staff writer for *The New Yorker* details how the Navy's top civilian lawyer — now resigned — tried and failed to have mistreatment of detainees prohibited.

Rivkin, David B., Jr., and Lee A. Casey, "The Gitmo Decision," "Targeting Illegal Combatants," "Misreading *Hamdan v. Rumsfeld*," "Bush hatred and constitutional reality," *The Washington Times*, July 11-July 14, 2006.
Conservative lawyers who served in the Reagan and George H.W. Bush administrations lay out legal and political arguments for the present administration's detainee policy.

Weisman, Jonathan, and Michael Abramowitz, "White House Shifts Tack on Tribunals," *The Washington Post*, July 20, 2006, p. A3.
Two reporters track the administration's re-embrace of a harder line concerning detainee treatment following the Supreme Court's *Hamdan* decision.

Reports and Studies

Elsea, Jennifer, "Treatment of 'Battlefield Detainees' in the War on Terrorism," Congressional Research Service, Sept. 17, 2003.
The CRS dispassionately examines the controversy surrounding detainee treatment in light of history, recent litigation and options facing Congress.

Gardner, Nile, and James J. Carafano, "The UN's Guantánamo Folly: Why the United Nations Report is Not Credible," The Heritage Foundation, Feb. 27, 2006.
Conservative commentators argue that the U.N. report on detainees (above) is politically biased.

"JTF-GTMO [Joint Task Force-Guantánamo] Information on Detainees — Information From Guantánamo Detainees," Department of Defense, March 4, 2005.
Detainees have provided valuable information on matters ranging from terrorist support structures to bomb-making techniques to the identities of al Qaeda operatives, according to the Pentagon.

"Report on Torture and Cruel, Inhuman and Degrading Treatment of Prisoners at Guantánamo Bay, Cuba," Center for Constitutional Rights, July 2006. The liberal group uses notes by lawyers for detainees, government documents, press accounts and other sources to depict what it views as a pattern of treatment that violates international treaties and U.S. law.

"Situation of detainees at Guantánamo Bay," Report of the Chairperson of the Working Group on Arbitrary Detention, United Nations, Feb. 15, 2006. Legal and physical treatment of detainees violate international treaties that the United States has signed, the U.N. panel concluded.

For More Information

American Civil Liberties Union, 125 Broad St., 18th Floor, New York, NY 10004; www.aclu.org. Obtains and disseminates government documents on detention and litigates on behalf of detainees.

Center for Constitutional Rights, 666 Broadway, 7th Floor, New York, NY 10012; (212) 614-6464; www.ccr-ny.org/v2/home. Played a key role in the filing of habeas corpus lawsuits by Guantánamo detainees.

Department of Defense, Public Affairs, 1400 Defense Pentagon, Washington, DC 20301; (703) 428-0711; www.defenselink.mil/home/features/Detainee_Affairs. Provides information on detainees and related matters.

The Heritage Foundation, 214 Massachusetts Ave., N.E., Washington, DC 20002; (202) 546-4400; www.heritage.org. Supports the administration's approach to the detention and trial of prisoners in the war on terror.

MacArthur Justice Center, Northwestern University School of Law, 375 E. Chicago Ave., Chicago, IL 60611; (312) 503-3100; www.law.northwestern.edu/macarthur. Has been active in representing Guantánamo detainees.

National Institute of Military Justice, 4801 Massachusetts Ave., N.W., Washington, DC 20016; (202) 274-4322; www.nimj.org/. An organization of retired military lawyers that is participating in the debate on detainee treatment.